THE NETWORK TROUBLESHOOTING LIBRARY

TROUBLESHOOTING
TCP/IP

Analyzing the Protocols of the Internet

Mark A. Miller, P.E.

D0002858

M&T Books
A Division of MIS:Press
A Subsidiary of Henry Holt and Company, Inc.
115 West 18th Street
New York, New York 10011

© 1993 by M&T Publishing

Printed in the United States of America

Library of Congress Cataloging-in-Publication Data (to be assigned)

Miller, Mark A., 1955-
    Troubleshooting TCP/IP: analyzing the protocols of the Internet/ by Mark A. Miller
        p. cm.
    Includes bibliographical references and index
    ISBN 1-55851-268-3
    1. TCP/IP (Computer network protocol)   I. Title
TK5105.5.M52   1992   92-19203
004.6'2--dc20   CIP

96 95 94   5

Project Editor: Sarah Wadsworth
Copy Editor: Cheryl Goldberg

Cover Design: Lauren Smith Design
Production: Charlene Carpentier

To Buster, for his faithfulness

Contents

Table of Illustrations

Foreword

Writing the *Foreword* is something that I always look *forward* to for several reasons. First, it signals the end of numerous long hours, revisions, and telephone calls. Secondly, it provides a mechanism for me to present a road map for the reader, so that your navigation duties will be minimized. Finally, it provides an opportunity to say a few personal words about an otherwise very impersonal subject.

Presenting the Roadmap

This is the fifth volume of *The Network Troubleshooting Library*, and concentrates on the TCP/IP and related protocols. This book was inspired by the research that I did for the fourth volume, *Troubleshooting Internetworks* (M&T Books, 1991). In doing the research for that book, I wrote to a number of users of the Network General Corp. *Sniffer* Analyzer and asked them to contribute any interesting trace files that they may have saved. These submittals became the case studies that were used in the book. As I was surveying the numerous disks that I received, a trend emerged: There were more TCP/IP-related submittals than any other protocol suite—even more than DECnet, SNA, or NetWare. A light came on, and the idea of devoting an entire volume to TCP/IP was born.

This book is structured like the other volumes in that it makes a somewhat orderly progression from the bottom to the top of the protocol architecture. In this case, however, that architecture is the Defense Advanced Research Projects Agency (DARPA) architecture—the architecture out of which these protocols were developed. In Chapter 1 we will look at the place these protocols occupy within the world of internetworking. In Chapter 2 we will survey the support for the protocols among mainframe, minicomputer, LAN, and analyzer manufacturers. In Chapters 3 through 6, we will study the Network Interface, Internet, Host-to-Host, and Application/Process Layers. Each of these chapters will present an overview of the protocols themselves, and then present a number of case studies that illustrate the protocols working (and not working!). Chapter 7 is devoted to the topic of internetwork management, and Chapter 8 concludes with a glimpse into transition strategies for TCP/IP internetworks that may migrate to OSI protocols. Appendices A through H could be described as "useful information"—protocol parameters and documentation that I have needed to look up and that you may find handy as well.

A Few Personal Notes

As always, a number of people behind the scenes contributed to the volume that you are about to read. My editors at M&T Books, Brenda McLaughlin, Sarah Wadsworth, Tom Woolf, and Cheryl Goldberg spent many long hours to assure that the project would be completed on schedule.

Nancy Wright and Krystal Valdez did the word processing on the manuscript. David Hertzke of Integrated Computer Graphics took my hand-drawn scratchings and turned them into very legible figures. Thanks to the three of you for all your hard work.

On several occasions, specific tests were required to see how the protocols (running on live networks) would perform under "what if" conditions. Eural Authement, Chris Dutchyn, Ross Dunthorne, and Paul Franchois lent their expertise and time for these experiments.

I am indebted to several individuals who added their expertise to individual sections: Jay Allard, John Case, Dan Callahan, Bill Cohn, Michael Howard, Brian Meek, Larry Thomas, Ursula Sinkewicz, plus a host of folks from Banyan Systems Inc. Eural Authement, Paul Franchois, and Carl Shinn read the entire manuscript, making numerous suggestions for improvements. David Menges of the Colorado SuperNet, Inc. assisted with Internet-related questions and support issues.

The real heros and heroines are the network managers throughout the world who shared their experiences via Network General *Sniffer* trace files that became the basis for the 29 case studies that you will read. It is one thing to discuss a protocol from an academic point of view, but something quite different to see those protocols in action. In alphabetical order, these individuals are: Rohit Aggarwal, Gerald Aster, Eural Authement, Joe Bardwell, Ross Dunthorne, Chris Dutchyn, Tony Farrow, Paul Franchois, Dave Heck, Dell Holmes, James Knights, Iwan Lie, Jeff Logullo, Dan Milligan, Tom Morocz, Mark Ryding, Bob Sherman, Mendy Valinsky, and Wayne Veilleux.

Ed Lucente and Bob Bessin of Network General Corporation provided me with a *Sniffer* Analyzer to study the various problems submitted for case studies. Juancho Forlanda located some unusual trace files when my normal sources failed. Their generosity is greatly appreciated.

I am grateful for three friends, Lloyd Boggs, Gordon England, and Marsh Riggs, who provided encouragement during the writing of the manuscript.

Most importantly, Holly, Nicholas, and Nathan provided the supportive environment that makes the undertaking of such a project possible. Boomer helped me get up for an early morning run, Brutus tried real hard not to bark when we did, and Buster was the ever-faithful sentry. Thanks to all of you for your love.

Mark A. Miller
June 1992

Why This Book Is For You

This book, the fifth volume in *The Network Troubleshooting Library*, discusses one of the most popular internetworking architectures: TCP/IP and the protocols of the Internet. These protocols were developed as a result of requirements defined by the U.S. Government in the mid-1970s. The rigor of these protocols, together with their widespread use among various research universities and defense contractors, brought them to the commercial forefront in the 1980s. The dominance of TCP/IP as an internetworking solution continues to this day.

With the popularity of TCP/IP, a key issue for the internetwork manager is: given that TCP/IP is in place (and may be there for some time), how do I analyze these protocols? The objective of this book is to answer that question. Major topics of discussion include:

- How various LAN, MAN, and WAN architectures, including token ring, FDDI, X.25, and SMDS, support TCP/IP.
- The various layers of internet addressing, including the hardware, internet, and port addresses, and how they work together to communicate the end-user's application data.
- A layer-by-layer study of the DARPA architectural model, showing how TCP/IP and the related protocols such as ARP, RARP, ICMP, RIP, OSPF, UDP, TELNET, FTP, TFTP, BOOTP, SMTP, SNMP, and CMOT fit into that architecture.
- Over 25 case studies, taken from live internetworks, that demonstrate TCP/IP and the related protocols in use, typical problems that may occur, plus solutions.
- Time-saving appendices that present protocol parameters and documentation to assist in troubleshooting.

If TCP/IP is part of your internetwork, this book should be part of your library.

1

Using TCP/IP and the Internet Protocols

On the surface, the Transmission Control Protocol/Internet Protocol (TCP/IP) is just another networking buzzword. But dig deeper and we find one of the most popular solutions for internetworking and interoperability ever devised. More than simply two protocols, TCP/IP is an architecture that enables dissimilar hosts, such as a minicomputer from Digital Equipment Corp. (Maynard, MA) and a workstation from Sun Microsystems Inc. (Mountain View, CA), to communicate. This communication could be via Local Area Network (LAN), Metropolitan Area Network (MAN), Wide Area Network (WAN), or some hybrid internetwork technology— TCP/IP supports them all. You might call TCP/IP "the great communicator" or "the interoperability solution."

TCP/IP was developed, refined, and nurtured to meet the needs of the Internet. The Internet provides a worldwide mechanism for user-to-user, computer-to-computer communication that crosses corporate and national boundaries. The same TCP/IP protocols can meet any LAN or WAN connectivity requirements. But that's getting ahead of the story. We'll come back to the TCP/IP protocols in a little while. First, let's take a brief tour of the Internet.

1.1 The Challenge of the Internet

The word *internet* means different things to different people. Some use it as a verb, as in "to internetwork an IBM SNA environment with a DEC DECnet environment." Others use it as a noun to mean a network comprised of two or more dissimilar networks, i.e., an internet (or internetwork) between two Packet Switched Public Data Networks (PSPDNs). It is also a proper noun, *the Internet,* that refers to a collection of networks located around the world that interconnect for the purposes of user and computer communication.

Just as the word has diverse meanings, the Internet has diverse challenges. Let's assume you're connected to the Internet. Like you rely on the public telephone network, you depend on the Internet for communicating with your friends and associates. But what happens when there's a system failure? If the telephone network has a problem, you simply contact the Local Exchange Carrier (LEC) or Inter Exchange Carrier (IEC) responsible for your service. But when there's trouble with the Internet, service restoration is not as straightforward for several reasons. First, the Internet protocols are more complex than the telephone serving your home or business. Second, you're dealing with computer communication, which is more abstract than voice and more difficult to diagnose. Finally, because the Internet is an interconnected matrix of computer networks, identifying the problem is a greater challenge. Moreover, no one entity or procedure (such as dialing "0" for the operator to connect you to telephone repair) is available to address problems. (Granted, end users can pass the problem to the local administrator, but then the local administrator is stuck with it.) Whoever ends up with the Internet problem will have to test and diagnose it himself (or herself).

That brings us to the purpose of this book. Since the mid 1970s, the TCP/IP suite has been the glue that holds the Internet together. Several ancillary protocols, such as the Address Resolution Protocol (ARP), Internet Control Message Protocol (ICMP), User Datagram Protocol (UDP), Routing Information Protocol (RIP), and many others have also been developed along the way. The resulting mixture can be a challenge to troubleshoot; in many cases, it requires the help of a protocol analyzer. The purpose of this book is to demystify the process of troubleshooting TCP/IP-based internetworks. To do so, we will learn about the topology of the Internet, study the protocols used within the Internet, and examine case studies of actual Internet problems. But before going on to the mechanics, let's begin with a history lesson.

1.2 A Brief History of the Internet

The Internet with a capital "I" is one of the world's most interesting achievements of computer science and networking technology. The Internet provides a worldwide mechanism for user-to-user, computer-to-computer communication that spans corporate and national boundaries. This achievement is even more amazing because the Internet is self-governing: It is run by committees comprised largely of volunteers. Government organizations, such as the U.S. Department of Defense and individual states, subsidize the basic expenses. Much of the research into the Internet protocols is conducted at major U.S. research universities, such as the University of California, the University of Colorado, the University of Illinois, and the University of Texas. Let's see how this unique system evolved.

Today's Internet was born in 1969 as the Advanced Research Projects Agency Network (ARPANET), and was sponsored by the U.S. Defense Advanced Research Projects Agency (DARPA). The purpose of the ARPANET was to test and determine the viability of a communication technology known as packet switching [1-1]. The contract to build the original ARPANET was awarded to a firm known as Bolt, Baranek, and Newman (now BBN Communications, Inc., Cambridge, MA). ARPANET went online in September, 1969 at four locations: Stanford Research Institute (SRI), the University of California at Santa Barbara (UCSB), the University of California at Los Angeles (UCLA), and the University of Utah. The original hosts were Honeywell 316 minicomputers, known as Interface Message Processors (IMPs).

The initial test was successful, and the ARPANET grew quickly. At the same time, it became apparent that non-military researchers could also benefit from access to a network of this type, so leaders in the university and industrial research communities made proposals to the National Science Foundation (NSF) for a cooperative network of computer science researchers [1-2]. The NSF approved funding for the Computer Science Network (CSNET) in 1981.

In 1984, the ARPANET was split into two different networks: MILNET (for unclassified military traffic) and ARPANET (for non-military traffic and research). In 1984, the NSF established the Office of Advanced Scientific Computing (OASC) to further the development of supercomputers and to make access to them more widely available. The OASC developed the NSFNET to connect six supercomputing centers across the United States via T-1 lines operating at 1.544 Mbps. Because of these advancing technologies, the U.S. Department of Defense declared the ARPANET obsolete and dismantled it in June of 1990.

Lessons learned from the ARPANET have had a significant effect on a number of data communication technologies, such as LANs and packet switching. Recently, the NSFNET backbone was converted to transmission at the T-3 rate of 44.736 Mbps (see References [1-3] through [1-5].) We will further discuss the family of networks that this research has spawned in Section 1.4. References [1-6] and [1-7] provide interesting historical information on these early networks. Now, let's open a different history book and study the development of the protocols used for inter-network communication.

1.3 The Protocols of the Internet

For its first decade, the ARPANET grew quickly, adding an average of one new host computer every 20 days [1-8]. The original protocol for internal network communications was known as the Network Control Program (NCP). The NCP provided the functions of the Open Systems Interconnect (OSI) Reference Model's Network and Transport Layers, managing the flow of messages between host computers and intermediate packet switches. NCP was designed with the assumption that the underlying communication subnetwork (i.e., OSI Physical, Data Link, and Network Layers) provided a perfect communication channel. Given ARPANET's mission to support government and military networks, which could include radio links under battlefield conditions, the assumption of a reliable communication channel needed reconsideration. In January 1973, DARPA made the Transmission Control Protocol (TCP) a standard for the Internet because of its proven performance. The DARPA internetwork architecture (Figure 1-1) consisted of networks connected by gateways [1-9]. (Note that in the OSI sense of the word, these devices were actually routers, operating at the OSI Network Layer. By current definition, gateways may operate at all seven layers of the familiar OSI Reference Model. In this chapter, we will refer to these connectivity devices as gateways, then switch to the more appropriate term, router, when we begin our technical study in Chapter 2.) The DARPA model assumed that each network used packet switching technology and could connect to a variety of transmission media (LAN, WAN, radio, and so on.)

The DARPA Internet architecture consisted of four layers (Figure 1-2). The lowest layer was called the Network Interface Layer (it is also referred to as the Local Network or Network Access Layer) and comprised the physical link (e.g., LAN) between devices. The Network Interface Layer existed in all devices, including hosts and gateways.

The Internet Layer insulated the hosts from network-specific details, such as addressing. The Internet Protocol (IP) was developed to provide end-to-end datagram service for this layer. (Datagram service is analogous to a telegram in which the information is sent as a package.) The Internet Layer (and, therefore, IP) existed only in hosts and gateways.

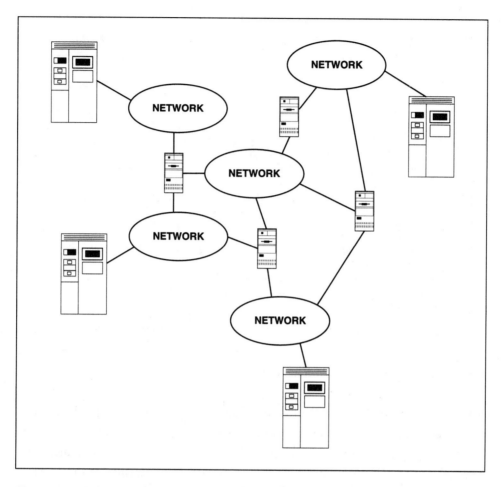

Figure 1-1. Networks connected with gateways (routers) to form an internetwork

While the Internet Layer provided end-to-end delivery of datagrams, it did not guarantee their delivery. Therefore, a third layer, known as the Service Layer (now called the Host-to-Host Layer), was provided within the hosts. As its name implies, the Service Layer defined the level of service the host applications required. Two protocols were created for the Service Layer: the Transmission Control Protocol (TCP) for applications needing reliable end-to-end service; and the User Datagram Protocol (UDP) for applications with less stringent reliability requirements. A third protocol, the Internet Control Message Protocol (ICMP) allowed hosts and gateways to exchange monitoring and control information.

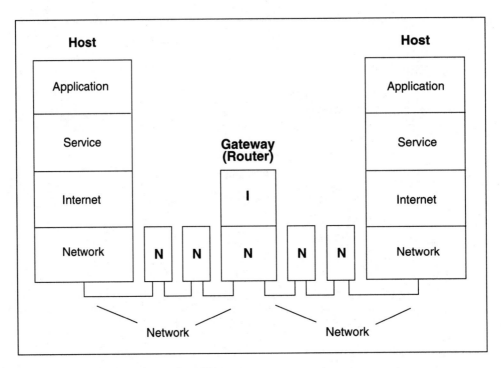

Figure 1-2. DARPA Layered Architecture

The highest DARPA layer, the Process/Application Layer, resided only in hosts and supported user-to-host and host-to-host processing or applications. A variety of standard applications were developed. These included the Telecommunications Network (TELNET) for remote terminal access, the File Transfer Protocol (FTP) for file transfer, and the Simple Mail Transfer Protocol (SMTP) for electronic mail.

Figure 1-3 compares the OSI and DARPA architectures. Observe that the OSI Physical and Data Link Layers represent the DARPA Network Interface (or Local Network) Layer; the OSI Network Layer corresponds to the Internet Layer; the OSI Transport Layer is functionally equivalent to the Host-to-Host (Service) Layer; and the OSI Session, Presentation, and Application Layers comprise the DARPA Process/Application Layer. References [1-10] through [1-13] describe the development of the ARPANET Reference Model and protocols. References [1-14] through [1-17] are examples of recent journal articles describing the history and applications of the TCP/IP protocols. Reference [1-18] is an excellent self-study guide for readers requiring further background into the protocols themselves.

OSI Layer	DARPA Architecture
Application	Process / Application Layer
Presentation	Process / Application Layer
Session	Process / Application Layer
Transport	Host-to-Host Layer
Network	Internet Layer
Data Link	Network Interface or Local Network Layer
Physical	Network Interface or Local Network Layer

Figure 1-3. Comparing OSI and DARPA Models

With this background into the development of the IP and TCP protocols, let's now turn to the history of the family of networks that use these protocols.

1.4 The Internet Family

A number of networks worldwide grew out of the ARPANET research to address non-military requirements. Collectively, they became known as the Internet. The common denominator among these networks was their use of the TCP/IP and related protocols to build the underlying communication infrastructure. Approximately 727,000 hosts are currently connected [1-19]. John Quarterman's excellent reference *The Matrix* [1-20] describes these worldwide networks in exacting detail.

The U.S. portion of the Internet (Figure 1-4) consists of a number of regional and mid-level networks connected into the NSFNET backbone. These include regional networks such as WESTNET; various supercomputer centers, such as the San Diego Supercomputer Center (SDSCNET) at the University of California at San Diego; the Space Physics Analysis Network (SPAN), used by NASA; the Computer Science Network (CSNET), funded by the NSF; the Because It's Time Network (BITNET), a worldwide network; and others.

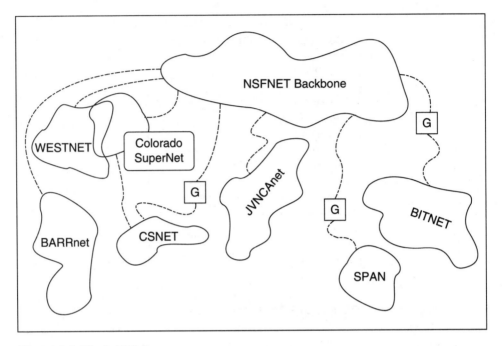

Figure 1-4. The Internet

(Courtesy Colorado SuperNet, Inc.)

Figure 1-5 shows a more detailed view of WESTNET, which connects the states of Idaho, Utah, Wyoming, Colorado, Arizona, and New Mexico. Within WEST-NET is the Colorado SuperNet or CSN (Figure 1-6). CSN connects a number of the universities, public libraries, and high technology companies such as Cray Computer Corp., Hewlett-Packard Co., McData Corp., and US West.

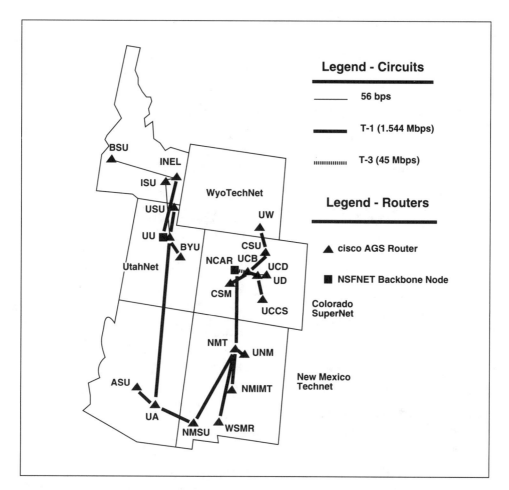

Figure 1-5. WESTNET Map. Summer 1992 (primary nodes only)

(Courtesy WESTNET)

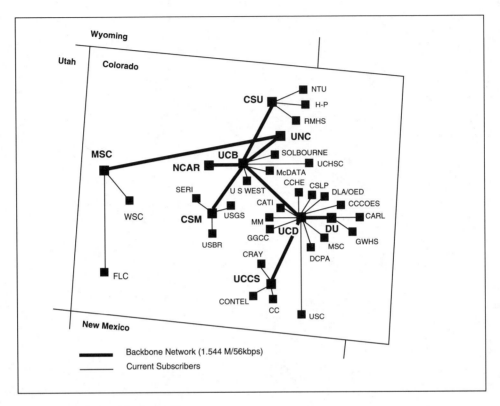

Figure 1-6. Colorado SuperNet

(Courtesy Colorado SuperNet, Inc.)

   In all, the NSFNET backbone (Figure 1-7) connects approximately 3,000 research organizations with 500,000 users. The transmission links comprising the backbone were recently converted from T-1 (1.544 Mbps) to T-3 (44.736 Mbps) rates to handle increasing traffic.

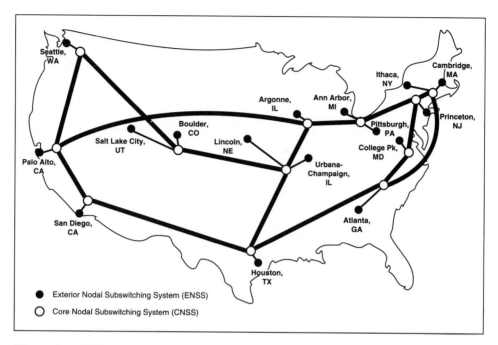

Figure 1-7. NSFNET Backbone Service (T3) 1992

(© Merit Network, Inc.)

Research continues into increasing the bandwidth to meet the needs of new generations of computers and emerging applications, such as imaging [1-21]. The NSF, with the help of Local Exchange Carriers (LECs), Inter Exchange Carriers (IXCs), computer manufacturers, and research universities, is currently sponsoring five test networks. The tests are being funded by the U.S. Government [1-22 and [1-23] and will form the basis of the National Research and Education Network (NREN). The technologies to be tested include Synchronous Optical Network (SONET) data links, operating at 622 Mbps; Asynchronous Transfer Mode (ATM) cell-relay switches; and the proposed ANSI High-Performance Parallel Interface (HPPI) for connection to host computers. The five test networks include Aurora (evaluating high-speed switching technologies); Blanca (testing SONET and HPPI); Casa (testing high-speed applications in a WAN environment); Nectar (testing operating systems to support high-speed networks); and Vistanet (studying traffic models and transport protocols). NREN is slated to begin operations in 1996.

13

The final issue in the history of the Internet is the current debate over commercialization. Until now, the Internet has been used for government communication and research; however, the Internet itself and the proven technologies it uses have broad commercial appeal [1-24]. Another application is dial-in service for users who do not have sufficient traffic to justify a dedicated Internet connection. Examples of this service include the California Education and Research Federation Network (CERFNET), (619)534-5087, Performance Systems International, Inc., (PSINET) (703)620-6651, and UUNET Technologies, (703)876-5050. Reference [1-25] discusses some of these user applications.

1.5 Documenting the Internet

An amazing characteristic of the largely volunteer Internet community is how well the protocols and procedures are documented. A second strength is the ease with which you can obtain these documents. Let's begin by looking at the Internet Activities Board (IAB) and the Internet Registry (IR) that govern the Internet.

The IAB is responsible for Internet design and future planning [1-26]. The board sets Internet standards; oversees Internet task forces; manages the publication of the Request for Comments (RFC) documents; performs strategic planning; acts as an international representative for the Internet community; and resolves technical issues.

Two task forces report to the IAB. The Internet Engineering Task Force (IETF) coordinates the technical aspects of the Internet and its protocols and assures that it functions effectively [1-27]. The Internet Research Task Force (IRTF) researches new technologies. Current plans call for the IAB to merge with the Internet Society, a non-profit organization of users and vendors with an interest in the ongoing success of the Internet [1-28].

The IAB produces numerous protocol standards and operational procedures that require dissemination and archiving. Most of these documents are known as Request for Comments documents (RFCs) and are reviewed by the appropriate IETF or IRTF members. Many of the Internet protocols have become U.S. Military standards and are assigned a MIL-STD number. For example, the Internet Protocol (IP) is described in both RFC 791 and MIL-STD-1777. You can obtain RFCs in hard copy from the Defense Data Network, Network Information Center (DDN NIC), or electronically via the Internet. RFC 1280, "IAB Official Protocol Standards" [1-29], describes the process of protocol standardization.

The Internet Registry (IR) serves as a central clearinghouse for all Internet addresses, documents, and so on. The IR is located at the DDN NIC at Government Systems, Inc. (Chantilly, VA). Two excellent documents to help new Internet users obtain RFCs, access remote hosts, use electronic mail, and so on are the "DDN New User Guide" [1-30] and RFC 1325, "FYI on Questions and Answers—Answers to Commonly Asked New Internet User Questions" [1-31]. Documents providing background on Internet documentation, protocols, and standards include RFC 1118, "A Hitchhiker's Guide to the Internet" [1-32] and RFC 1175, "FYI on Where to Start—A Bibliography of Internetworking Information" [1-33]. Several other bibliographies provide information on the Internet history, operation, and protocols; consult References [1-34] through [1-38] for further details. Readers who like suspense will enjoy Cliff Stoll's *The Cuckoo's Egg* [1-39], which describes the author's true experience tracking a hacker through the Internet.

1.6 Applying the Technologies of the Internet

In the previous sections of this chapter, we took a short trip down TCP/IP's memory lane. We studied how the U.S. Government sponsored the development of these protocols based on the research and development community's requirements. But what if you work for an organization that has nothing to do with research, the U.S. Government, or the Military? Can your organization benefit from TCP/IP and the Internet protocols? To find out, answer the following questions about your computing environment:

- Do you have a multivendor environment?

- Does your internetwork include LAN and WAN topologies?

- Do your users require file transfer, electronic mail, host terminal emulation, or network management?

The bottom line is that the requirements for most organizations' internetworks do not differ appreciably from those of the 1969-vintage ARPANET. Most of us require a multivendor, distributed architecture. We also need proven solutions and are eager to benefit from two decades of research and testing.

Even if you have no intention of connecting to the Internet, you can benefit from using TCP/IP. Those who implement these protocols will be in good company, as hundreds of vendors offer products to help configure, install, operate, and manage TCP/IP-based internetworks. (Appendix C lists a number of these vendors, although the list is growing so rapidly that it is impossible ever to be completely up to date.)

With this historical background, let's now return to the present and take a practical approach. Chapter 2 will discuss the Internet protocols and support for them among PC, Macintosh, DEC, IBM, and UNIX hosts. Chapters 3 through 7 will examine the Internet protocols and troubleshooting techniques. Our journey will coincide with the layers of the DARPA internetworking model, beginning with the Network Interface and ending with Process/Application Layers. In Chapter 8, we'll look at strategies for migrating from TCP/IP to OSI. So warm up that protocol analyzer, and let's begin!

1.7 References

[1-1] Rosner, Roy D. *Packet Switching: Tomorrow's Communications Today.* Wadsworth, Inc., 1982.

[1-2] CSNET CIC. "A CSNET Retrospective." CSNET News (Summer 1985):6-7.

[1-3] Braun, Hans-Werner. "The New NSFNET Backbone Network." *ConneXions* (December 1988): 6-9.

[1-4] Desmond, Paul. "NSFNET to Employ IBM T-3 Prototype Routers in Net." *Network World* (October 22, 1990):2,73-74.

[1-5] Messmer, Ellen. "Users' Fears Mount Over NSFNET Upgrade." *Network World* (December 9, 1991):9-10.

[1-6] Quarterman, John S. and Josiah C. Hoskins. "Notable Computer Networks." Communications of the ACM (October 1986):932-971.

[1-7] Schultz, Brad. "The Evolution of ARPANET." *Datamation* (August 1, 1988):71-74.

[1-8] Dern, Daniel P. "The ARPANET is Twenty: What We Have Learned and the Fun We Had." *ConneXions* (October 1989): 2-10.

[1-9] Leiner, B. M., et al. "The DARPA Internet Protocol Suite." RS-85-153, included in the DDN Protocol Handbook, Volume 2, pp. 2-27 to 2-49.

[1-10] Cerf, V.G. and R. E. Kahn, "A Protocol for Packet Network Intercommunication." IEEE Transactions on Communications (May 1974): 637-648.

[1-11] Padlipsky, M. A. "A Perspective on the ARPANET Reference Model." RFC 871, The Mitre Corp., September 1982.

[1-12] Cerf, Vinton G. and Edward Cain. "The DoD Internet Architecture Model." *Computer Networks* (October 1983):307-317.

[1-13] Cerf, Vint. "Requiem for the ARPANET." *ConneXions* (October 1991):27.

[1-14] Retz, David. "TCP/IP: DOD Suite Marches into the Business World." *Data Communications* (November 1987):209-225.

[1-15] Heiden, Heidi. "The Illustrious Career of TCP/IP." Government Data Systems (1988):30-32.

[1-16] The Wollongong Group, Inc. "Internetworking: An Introduction." June 1988.

[1-17] Forsberg, David. "The Interconnectivity Nightmare." Network World (August 27, 1990):42-61.

[1-18] 3Com Corporation. *Understanding TCP/IP*. Document number 92-0065-001, rev. B, June 1991.

[1-19] Mavine, April. "How Did We Get 727,000 Hosts?" *ConneXions* (May 1992): 49-51.

[1-20] Quarterman, John S. *The Matrix-Computer Networks and Conferencing Systems Worldwide*. Digital Equipment Corp., 1990.

[1-21] Kobielus, James. "Planned Super Networks Foreshadow 21st Century." *Network World* (August 26, 1991):1-52.

[1-22] Roberts, Mike. "NREN Bill Signed into Law." *ConneXions* (February 1992): 16-18.

[1-23] Kapor, M. "Building the Open Road: The NREN as Test-Bed for the National Public Network." Electronic Frontier Foundation, September 1991.

[1-24] Jackson, Kelly. "Commercialization of the Internet." *Communications Week* (October 2, 1989):25-27.

[1-25] Farrow, Rik. "E-Mail to the Outside World." *UnixWorld* (February 1991):1-4.

[1-26] Cerf, V. "The Internet Activities Board." RFC 1120, NRI, September 1989.

[1-27] Vandreuil, Gregory M. "A Brief History of the Internet Engineering Task Force and the Steering Group." *ConneXions* (April 1990): 22-24.

[1-28] Bob Brown. "Internet Society to Guide Research Network's Future." *Network World* (January 13, 1992): 9-10.

[1-29] Postel, J., Editor. "IAB Official Protocol Standards." RFC 1280, Internet Activities Board, March 1992.

[1-30] DDN Network Information Center. "DDN New User Guide." February 1991.

[1-31] Malkin, G., et. al. "FYI on Questions and Answers—Answers to Commonly Asked New Internet User Questions." RFC 1325, FTP Software, Inc., May 1992.

[1-32] Krol, E. "The Hitchhikers Guide to the Internet." RFC 1118, University of Illinois Urbana, September 1989.

[1-33] Bowers, K., T., et. al. "FYI on Where to Start: A Bibliography of Internetwork Information." RFC 1175, CNRI, August 1990.

[1-34] Jacobsen, Ole J. "Information about TCP/IP." *ConneXions*, The Interoperability Report (July 1988):14-15.

[1-35] Mogul, Jeffrey C. "The Experimental Literature of the Internet: An Annotated Bibliography." Digital Equipment Corp., August 1988.

[1-36] SRI International. "Bibliography About Network Protocols: A List for Background Reading." Network Information Systems Center, October 1989.

[1-37] Jacobsen, Ole J. "Information Sources." *ConneXions, The Interoperability Report* (December 1989):16-19.

[1-38] Spurgeon, Charles. "Network Reading List." The University of Texas at Austin Computation Center, 1990.

[1-39] Stoll, Cliff. *The Cuckoo's Egg.* Simon & Schuster (New York, NY), 1989.

CHAPTER 2

Supporting TCP/IP and the Internet Protocols

In Chapter 1, we discussed how TCP/IP and the Internet protocols were developed from requirements set forth by the U.S. Government. Various hardware and software vendors have shown a great deal of interest in these protocols for several reasons. First, the U.S. Government is a large customer and can generate a great deal of revenue with a single purchase order. Second, as the Internet and the number of connected hosts continues to grow, opportunities for products that support TCP/IP will abound. Finally, TCP/IP and the Internet protocols can serve any organization that needs to connect dissimilar hosts, such as an IBM mainframe to a DEC minicomputer or an Apple Macintosh. (Reference [2-1] provides insight into how the Internet protocols fit into the bigger picture of network architectures.)

Of course, anyone who sets up an internet using these protocols is bound to run into problems sooner or later. When you have a problem with your internet connection, you need to first understand the TCP/IP protocols, and then you need a protocol analyzer that supports these protocols.

In this chapter and the next, we'll provide the background you need to understand the TCP/IP protocols and to choose the proper analyzer for your internet. First, we'll provide a general overview of the protocols themselves. Second, we'll discuss how different computing platforms support these protocols. Third, we'll survey the tools available for troubleshooting. We'll defer a detailed discussion of the protocols until Chapter 3.

2.1 The Internet Protocols

TCP/IP and the Internet protocols support the Defense Advanced Research Projects Agency (DARPA) model of internetworking and its four defined layers: Network Interface, Internet, Host-to-Host, and Process/Application (see Figure 2-1).

Developed in the early 1970s, this model preceded the Open Systems Interconnection Reference Model (OSI-RM) by several years. Like DARPA, the OSI-RM was designed to internetwork dissimilar computer systems; however, the two models have different underlying assumptions. The DARPA model was designed to connect hosts serving the academic, research, government, and military populations, primarily in the United States. The OSI-RM was broader in scope. First, the OSI-RM was the product of an international standards body, the International Standards Organization (ISO). Thus, the OSI-RM received input from people in Europe and Asia, as well as from North America. Second, it had a much broader charter, the interconnection of Open Systems, and was not constrained by the type of system to be connected (e.g., academic, military, and so forth). To satisfy these two constraints, the ISO developed a seven-layer model, in contrast to DARPA's four-layer model. To summarize, the DARPA world was more specific, the OSI world more general. The result was two architectures that are almost, but not quite, parallel. We will study these differences in greater detail in the following chapters. In the meantime, let's take a brief look at the protocols we will be analyzing.

DARPA Layer	Protocol Implementation						OSI Layer
Process / Application	File Transfer	Electronic Mail	Terminal Emulation	File Transfer	Client / Server	Network Management	Application
	File Transfer Protocol (FTP)	Simple Mail Transfer Protocol (SMTP)	TELNET Protocol	Trivial File Transfer Protocol (TFTP)	Sun Microsystems Network File System Protocols (NFS)	Simple Network Management Protocol (SNMP)	Presentation
	MIL-STD-1780 RFC 959	MIL-STD-1781 RFC 821	MIL-STD-1782 RFC 854	RFC 783	RFCs 1014, 1057, and 1094	RFC 1157	Session
Host-to-Host	Transmission Control Protocol (TCP) MIL-STD-1778 RFC 793			User Datagram Protocol (UDP) RFC 768			Transport
Internet	Address Resolution ARP RFC 826 RARP RFC 903		Internet Protocol (IP) MIL-STD-1777 RFC 791		Internet Control Message Protocol (ICMP) RFC 792		Network
Network Interface	Network Interface Cards: Ethernet, StarLAN, Token Ring, ARCNET RFC 894, RFC 1042, RFC 1201						Data Link
	Transmission Media: Twisted Pair, Coax, Fiber Optics, Wireless Media, etc.						Physical

Figure 2-1. Comparing DARPA Protocols with OSI and DARPA Architectures

The first layer of the DARPA model is the Network Interface Layer, sometimes called the Network Access Layer or Local Network Layer, and it connects the local host to the local network hardware. As such, it comprises the functions of the OSI

Physical and Data Link Layers: It makes the physical connection to the cable system, it accesses the cable at the appropriate time (e.g., using a Carrier Sense Multiple Access with Collision Detection (CSMA/CD) or token passing algorithm), and it places the data into a frame. The frame is a package that envelopes the data with information, such as the hardware address of the local host and a check sequence to assure data integrity. The frame is defined by the hardware in use, such as an Ethernet LAN or an X.25 interface into a Packet Switched Public Data Network (PSPDN) WAN. The DARPA model shows particular strength in this area—it includes a standard for virtually all popular connections to LANs and WANs. These include Ethernet (RFC 894), IEEE 802 LANs (RFC 1042), ARCNET (RFC 1201), serial lines using the Serial Line Internet Protocol—SLIP (RFC 1055), and PSPDNs (RFC 877). As standards for Metropolitan Area Networks (MANs) emerge, there will undoubtedly be greater interest in the Fiber Distributed Data Interface-FDDI (RFC 1103) and the IEEE 802.6 standard, known as Switched Multimegabit Data Service-SMDS (RFC 1209.)

The Internet Layer transfers packets from host to host. Note that we said *packet* instead of frame. The packet differs from the frame in that it contains address information to facilitate its journey from one host to another *through the internetwork*; the address within the frame header gets the frame from host to host *on the same local network*. The protocol that operates the Internet Layer is known as the Internet Protocol (the IP in TCP/IP). Several other protocols are also required, however.

The Address Resolution Protocol (ARP) provides a way to translate between IP addresses and local network addresses, such as Ethernet, and is discussed in RFC 826. The Reverse Address Resolution Protocol (RARP), explained in RFC 903, provides the complementary function, translating from Ethernet addresses to IP addresses. (In some architectural drawings, ARP and RARP are shown slightly lower than IP to indicate their close relationship to the Network Interface Layer. In some respects, ARP/RARP overlap the Network Interface and Internet Layers.)

The Internet Control Message Protocol (ICMP) provides a way for the IP software on a host or gateway to communicate with its peers on other machines about any problems it might have in routing IP datagrams. ICMP, which is explained in RFC 792, is a required part of the IP implementation. One of the most frequently used ICMP messages is the Echo Request, commonly called the PING, which allows one device to test the communication path to another.

As the datagram traverses the Internet, it may pass through multiple gateways and their associated local network connections. Thus, there's a risk that packets may be lost or that a noisy communication circuit may corrupt data. The Host-to-Host Layer guards against these problems, however remote, and assures the reliable delivery of a datagram sent from the source host to the destination host. (Recall that one of the major objectives of the DARPA project was military communication, which, by definition, must be ultra-reliable.)

The Host-to-Host Layer defines two protocols: the User Datagram Protocol (UDP) and the Transmission Control Protocol (TCP). The minimum security UDP, described in RFC 768, provides minimal protocol overhead. UDP restricts its involvement to higher-layer port addresses, defining the length, and a checksum. TCP, detailed in RFC 793, defines a much more rigorous error control mechanism. TCP (of the TCP/IP nomenclature) provides much of the strength of the Internet protocol suite. TCP provides reliable datastream transport between two host applications by providing sequentiality for every octet (8-bit quantity of data) passed between the two applications.

End users interact with the host via the Process/Application Layer. Because of the user interface, a number of protocols have been developed for this layer. As its name implies, the File Transfer Protocol (FTP) transfers files between two host systems. FTP is described in RFC 959. To guarantee its reliability, FTP is implemented over TCP. When economy of transmission is desired, you may use a simpler program, the Trivial File Transfer Protocol (TFTP), described in RFC 783. TFTP runs on top of UDP to economize the Host-to-Host Layer as well.

Electronic mail and terminal emulation are two of the more frequently used Internet applications. The Simple Mail Transfer Protocol (SMTP), given in RFC 821, sends mail messages from one host to another. When accessing a remote host via the Internet, one must emulate the type of terminal the host wishes to see. For example, a DEC host may prefer a VT-100 terminal while an IBM host would rather see a 3278 or 3279 display station. The Telecommunications Network (TELNET) protocol provides remote host access and terminal emulation.

As internetworks become more complex, system management requirements increase as well. Two protocols meet these needs. The Simple Network Management Protocol (SNMP), given in RFC 1157, uses minimal overhead to communicate between the Manager (i.e., management console) and the Agent (i.e., the device, such as a router, being managed). A more complex alternative is the Common Management

Information Protocol (CMIP). When used with TCP/IP, the protocol is known as the Common Management Information Protocol over TCP/IP (CMOT for short). CMOT is based upon CMIP, but replaces the OSI Transport Layer with TCP. CMOT is described in RFC 1189, and will be discussed in detail in Chapter 7.

With that background into the Internet protocols, let's now turn our attention to the host systems that incorporate these protocols, starting with the large systems based upon UNIX, DEC's DECnet, or IBM's SNA.

2.2 Internet Support within UNIX Environments

In the early 1980s, DARPA provided a grant to the University of California at Berkeley to modify the already robust UNIX operating system. One of the changes was support for the Internet protocols. The Berkeley Software Distribution version 4.2 (BSD 4.2) included support for the TCP, IP, SMTP, and ARP protocols. That version proved satisfactory for use on LANs and smaller internetworks.

BSD 4.3 offered support for larger internetworks that included routers and WAN transmission facilities (e.g., 56 Kbps leased lines). The changes included routines for ICMP redirect messages, retransmission algorithms, packet time-to-live parameters, and so on. Reference [2-2] discusses these UNIX releases from a user's perspective and [2-3] considers the programming requirements.

It should come as no surprise that UNIX environments have strong support for the Internet protocols, since their primary clientele are academic, scientific, and research users. Interest among the business community increased in the mid-1980s, coinciding with the rapid growth in LANs. We'll look at the two key players in the commercial sector, DEC and IBM, next.

2.3 Internet Support within DECnet Environments

Digital Equipment Corp.'s (Maynard, MA) minicomputers have been extremely well-received among the scientific and engineering communities—the same users that have strong interest in the Internet protocols. DEC's Digital Network Architecture and VMS operating system have been widely accepted. DEC's version of UNIX, known as Ultrix, is also a popular choice. Several solutions are available from DEC and third-party vendors to integrate DEC VMS, DECnet, and the Internet protocols into one cohesive system. We'll begin by looking at solutions from DEC, then we'll consider offerings from third parties.

First, consider the differences between DECnet Phase IV and DEC's ADVAN-TAGE-NETWORKS (formerly called DECnet Phase V). Announced in 1982, DECnet Phase IV provided a proprietary architecture for LAN and WAN connectivity. It supported industry-standard protocols, such as Ethernet and CCITT X.25, at the lower OSI layers, but its upper layer protocols were proprietary. Announced in 1987, DECnet Phase V combined the protocols from DECnet Phase IV and OSI into a merged protocol stack. One stack supported the proprietary DECnet Phase IV, the other the emerging OSI protocols, such as the ISO 10589 (Intermediate Station-to-Intermediate Station, or IS-IS) used at the Network Layer, the OSI 8073 Transport Protocol, and so on. The ADVANTAGE-NETWORKS, announced in June of 1991, enhanced DECnet Phase V by adding a third protocol stack to the architecture—the Internet protocols. Thus, DEC gave users the best of all possible worlds, past, present, and future: DECnet proprietary protocols, TCP/IP, and OSI [2-4].

DECnet Phase IV users who wish to integrate VMS-based systems into a UNIX environment have several options [2-5]. One is to install a software gateway between the UNIX host and the DECnet host. DEC's TCP/IP Services for VMS is an example of such a gateway. A second option uses a common-denominator protocol to communicate between the two dissimilar operating systems. One example is the Kermit protocol, developed by Columbia University. (*Kermit, A File Transfer Protocol* [2-6] is an excellent reference on this subject.) Another common denominator is TCP/IP, which is supported by a number of vendors, including MultiNet from TGV, Inc. (Santa Cruz, CA) and WIN/TCP from the Wollongong Group, Inc. (Palo Alto, CA). Let's look at one of these in detail.

TGV's MultiNet supports TCP/IP and Xerox PUP among others. You install the software on any VAX/VMS system running version 4.5 or later, and it can communicate with a variety of hardware and protocols, including Ethernet, T-1, Digital Data Communications Message Protocol (DDCMP), and X.25. You use the VAX/VMS VMSINSTAL utility to install MultiNet on the VAX. Once in place, users have access to a variety of higher layer services. These include the TELNET, FTP, and SMTP protocols, plus Sun Microsystems Inc.'s (Mountain View, CA) Network File System (NFS). NFS is an interesting application of this software since it allows VAXes to serve as either NFS clients or NFS servers. Thus, NFS allows a VMS user to access files on a UNIX host as if they were local files. (We will discuss more specifics on NFS in Chapter 6.) References [2-7] through [2-9] illustrate the popularity of TCP/IP within DECnet environments.

Users of DEC ADVANTAGE-NETWORKS have several options for TCP/IP connectivity; the DEC architecture's inter-stack communication facilities and DEC's family of multiprotocol routers. The most straightforward solution is to take advantage of the communication channels between the three protocol stacks that the DEC architecture provides (see Figure 2-2). The inter-stack communication is designed for either DECnet-to-OSI or TCP/IP-to-OSI channels. From the DECnet side, an internal Data Access Protocol-to-File Transfer and Management (DAP-to-FTAM) gateway provides file transfer between DECnet Phase IV and OSI systems. An internal FTP-to-FTAM gateway facilitates file transfers from the TCP/IP-to-OSI side. Other gateways are planned between SMTP and X.400 (for electronic mail), and between TELNET and Virtual Terminal Protocol for remote host access. At the Transport Layer, the X/Open Transport Interface (XTI) permits applications to use either TCP or OSI-based transport protocols.

The ADVANTAGE-NETWORKS program also includes the WANRouter family of multiprotocol routers that provide WAN support for DECnet, TCP/IP, and OSI. At the high end is the DEC Network Integration Server, a hub device that combines bridging, routing, and CCITT X.25 packet switching. The server uses a Reduced Instruction Set Computer (RISC) platform to obtain the speed necessary to integrate LANs and WANs. Initial hardware support is for Ethernet, with future releases planned for token ring, FDDI, SMDS, and Frame Relay. Currently available protocols include DECnet, TCP/IP, and OSI; future plans include Novell's IPX and Apple's AppleTalk.

The WANRouter family includes the TCP/IP and OSI protocols. Supported data links include the DDCMP, High-level Data Link Control (HDLC), X.25, and Frame Relay.

A consistent theme of ADVANTAGE-NETWORKS is interoperability between DECnet, OSI, and the TCP/IP protocols. This theme runs from the VMS operating system level to the internetworking hardware. With DEC's strength in the UNIX world, we can safely predict widespread acceptance of the enhanced DECnet product line.

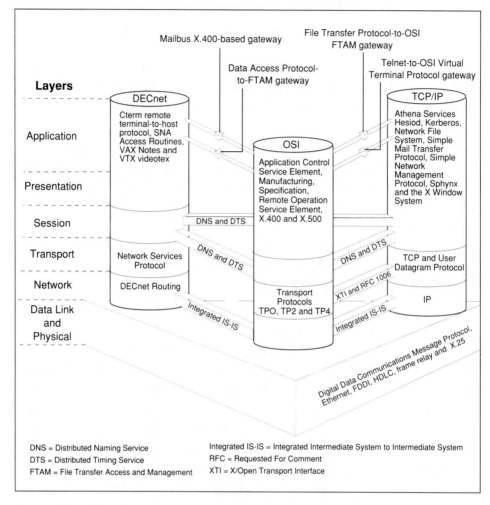

Figure 2-2. DEC's Rearchitected Network Strategy

(Copyright December 9, 1991 by Network World, Inc., Framingham, NH 01701.

Reprinted from Network World. *Source: Digital Equipment Corp., Maynard, MA)*

2.4 Internet Support within IBM SNA Environments

IBM's System Network Architecture (SNA) is one of the most popular inter-networking solutions for corporations of all sizes worldwide. IBM mainframes, communication controllers, workstations, and minicomputers all support Internet protocols, including TELNET, FTP, TFTP, NFS, and SMTP as well as lower-layer protocols, such as IP, ICMP, and TCP. (An excellent reference is IBM's *TCP/IP Tutorial and Technical Overview* [2-10].) We'll look at each IBM platform separately.

At the mainframe level, IBM offers products that add support for the Internet protocols within the VM and MVS operating systems. These products are known as TCP/IP for VM and TCP/IP for MVS, respectively. Both products support the client/server nature of the Internet protocols. For example, the TN3270 function allows an IBM PC workstation running TCP/IP to remotely access a VM or MVS host via a LAN. The PC would appear as a client, i.e., IBM 3270-series terminal. Both VM and MVS implement FTP for host-to-host file transfers. The FTP Type command translates data between the mainframe's EBCDIC format and the PC's ASCII format. Both operating systems support SMTP for electronic mail service. IBM also offers an interface to exchange messages between SMTP and the IBM PROFS system. Other higher-layer protocol functions available under VM and MVS include X-Windows and Sun Microsystem's NFS.

The IBM 3172 Interconnect Controller, shown in Figure 2-3, handles the hardware connection between the IBM host and the TCP/IP environment. The 3172 provides a hardware connection between the mainframe channel and token ring or Ethernet LANs, Manufacturing Automation Protocol (MAP) version 3.0 networks, IBM AIX/370 workstations, and DEC networks, although the DEC connection requires additional gateway software. Software that accompanies the 3172 controls the IBM channel, attached LAN hardware and the software interface to the TCP/IP functions on the host.

In addition to the mainframe environment, IBM supports TCP/IP on a number of other SNA platforms. IBM's version of UNIX, the Advanced Interactive Executive (AIX), runs on hardware, such as the PS/2, RT, RISC System/6000, and 9370. Support among these products for specific protocols varies, however, so consult IBM or Reference [2-10] for complete details. For DOS workstations, the TCP/IP for PC product supports protocols such as TELNET, FTP, and SMTP. OS/2 workstations use the OS/2 TCP/IP product, which adds capabilities such as server functions for TELNET, FTP, and SMTP. IBM provides TCP/IP support for midrange computers such as the AS/400 and System 88 and their operating systems (OS/400 and OS/88, respectively), though not as extensively as for DOS and OS/2 workstations.

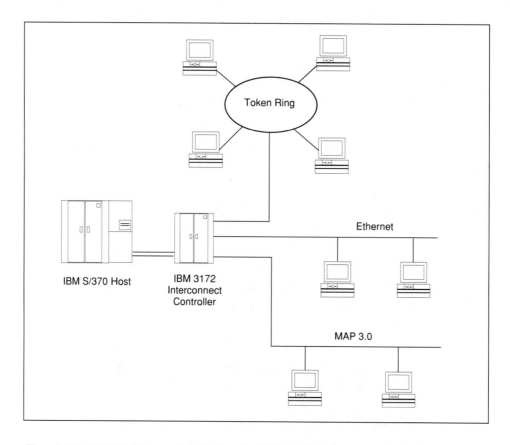

Figure 2-3. TCP/IP Connections using the IBM 3172 Interconnect Controller
(Reprinted by permission from TCP/IP Tutorial and Technical Overview GG24-3376-01
© by International Business Machines Corporation)

As a final example, consider the case in which a number of hosts are connected in a single internetwork (see Figure 2-4). This application is known as SNAlink, and it transfers TCP/IP-related information via an SNA backbone. In this example, four hosts running VM, MVS, DOS, and AIX are connected. The DOS machine is connected via an Ethernet and 3172 Interconnect Controller to the MVS host; the AIX and VM host are connected to a token ring. A number of applications are possible using IBM's family of TCP/IP software products. Any user can log in to any of the remote hosts using TN3270. Files may be transferred between hosts using FTP or TFTP. Electronic mail may be transferred between any of the users. Finally, a user on the AIX host may use NFS to access files on either the VM or MVS hosts. References [2-11] through [2-14] are examples of current articles describing other vendors that offer solutions for SNA and TCP/IP integration.

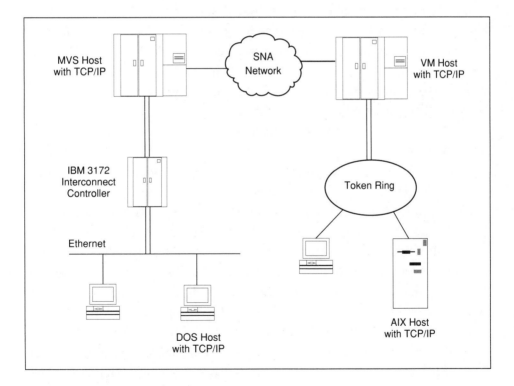

Figure 2-4. SNA link scenario
(Reprinted by permission from TCP/IP Tutorial and Technical Overview GG24-3376-01
© by International Business Machines Corporation)

2.5 Internet Support within DOS and OS/2 Environments

Recall from our history lesson in Chapter 1 that the TCP/IP protocols were developed in the early 1960s and the ARPANET came on-line in 1969. During the 1970s, ARPANET grew because of the addition of mainframe and minicomputer hosts. When the IBM PC was announced in 1981, a new market opened up for TCP/IP software developers—desktop PCs (as long as they were connected to LANs, which were in turn connected to the Internet). Considering the popularity of PCs and the LANs connecting them, it's no wonder that a number of companies have developed TCP/IP connectivity software to support DOS, OS/2, and Microsoft Windows-based workstations. DOS-based products are available from companies such as Beame and Whiteside Software Ltd. (Dundas, ON), FTP Software, Inc. (Wakefield, MA), IBM (White Plains, NY), Novell, Inc. (Provo, UT), Sun Microsystems, Inc. (Mountain View, CA), and The Wollongong Group (Palo Alto, CA). OS/2 workstations are supported by products from Essex Systems, Inc. (Peabody, MA), FTP Software, and IBM. Frontier Technologies Corp. (Mequon, WI) and Net-Manage, Inc. (Cupertino, CA) market a product supporting Microsoft Windows-based workstations. References [2-15], [2-16], and [2-17] review DOS, OS/2, and Windows-based products, respectively. With so many available products, first-time buyers are likely to be uncertain of the best choice for their application. We'll look at the architecture of some sample products and discuss the features to consider when shopping.

Novell's LAN WorkPlace for DOS [2-18] is designed for any DOS-compatible system connected to a TCP/IP-based network (see Figure 2-5a). The hardware connection to the LAN is made with an Ethernet, token ring, ARCNET, or other network interface via Novell's Link Support Layer (LSL) and Multiple-Link Interface Driver (MLID). LSL and MLID are components of Novell's Open Data Link Interface (ODI) which we will discuss in Section 2.7. The LSL and MLID provide Data Link Layer functions across a wide variety of Novell products, including the Net-Ware operating system. The TCP/IP Transport Driver supports the ARP/RARP, IP, ICMP, TCP, and UDP protocols, plus the NetBIOS interface (RFC 1001/1002). The TCP/IP Transport Driver provides a platform for communication services designed for the BSD 4.3 socket and NetBIOS Application Programming Interfaces (APIs). These higher-layer utilities include NetBIOS, third-party DOS socket, TELNET, and Windows 3.0 applications. Thus, the typical LAN user can access applications on remote hosts via IP routers in addition to the usual LAN-based utilities, such as file and print service, multi-user databases, and so forth.

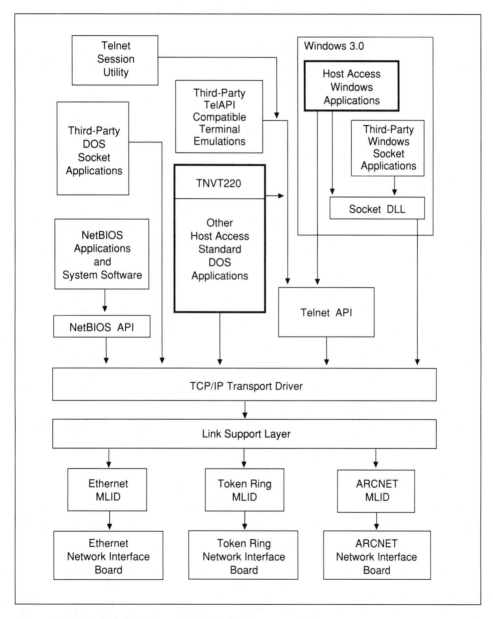

Figure 2-5a. LAN WorkPlace for DOS Architectural Overview
(Courtesy Novell, Inc.)

Another popular TCP/IP implementation for DOS is FTP Software, Inc.'s PC/TCP. An extremely flexible product, PC/TCP works with each of the four standard network card interfaces: Novell's ODI, 3Com/Microsoft's Network Driver Interface Specification (NDIS), IBM's Adapter Support Interface (ASI), and the Packet Driver. (There will be more on these LAN interfaces in Section 2.7). In fact, FTP Software wrote the Packet Driver Specification, which allowed the separation of the driver from the DOS protocol stack, and released it into the public domain in 1987. Using a Packet Driver, PC/TCP can concurrently support its TCP/IP protocol stack and a second stack, such as NetWare, VINES, LAN Manager, DECNet, and others.

PC/TCP contains components—such as a driver, a kernel, and programs—that span from the Data Link Layer to the Application Layer of the OSI Reference Model (see Figure 2-5b). The components vary, depending on the physical medium and the simultaneous use of other network applications. In its most common configuration, the PC/TCP applications sit above the generic PC/TCP kernel, which, in turn, sits either on top of a Packet Driver, an NDIS-to-Packet Driver, or an ODI-to-Packet Driver conversion module.

Third party developers can also use the PC/TCP kernel in their applications for network transport. Developers writing DOS applications can use a Native Mode API, a Berkeley Sockets emulation library, or they can access the TCP, UDP, and other application libraries. Developers writing Windows 3.x applications can use a Sockets Dynamic Link Library (DLL) and a Native Mode DLL. Other options include Remote Procedure Call (RPC) libraries.

Since each network application is different, you should do some hands-on comparison shopping before committing to one of these TCP/IP software products on a company-wide basis. In general, first consider the workstation software platform (e.g., DOS, OS/2, Windows), then support for your particular LAN hardware (e.g., IBM, 3Com, etc.). A closely-related issue is the workstation software and hardware driver's support for your LAN operating system (e.g., VINES or NetWare.) Next, look for specific features and the degree to which the product supports them. For file transfers using FTP, consider whether both FTP client and server functions are necessary and available. (Some products support the FTP client function, but not the FTP server.) For remote host access with terminal emulation requirements (TELNET), verify the type of terminal you need to emulate, such as DEC VT-100 or IBM 3278, then check the degree of support. For instance, does it offer a remappable keyboard, non-English characters, and so on. If electronic mail (SMTP) is necessary, look at the client/server capabilities. Most products offer client support, but few provide the host side. Other features that may be important include: developer's kits for writing custom applications, related products from the same manufacturer, such as an OS/2 or Windows version with a similar user interface, and ICMP network testing capabilities, such as the PING function. Table 2-1 provides a brief checklist to use when comparing different TCP/IP software packages.

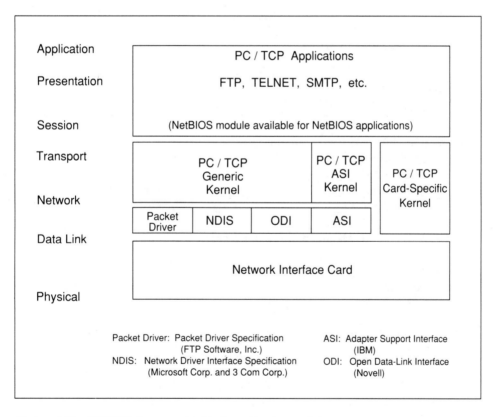

Figure 2-5b. PC/TCP Support for Various Hardware Drivers
(Courtesy FTP Software, Inc.)

Table 2-1. Workstation Internet Requirements

Workstation type _____

Workstation operating system _____ version _____

Network interface type _____

Network operating system _____ version _____

File Service Requirements

    FTP client _____

    FTP server _____

    NFS client _____

    NFS server _____

Electronic Mail Requirements

    SMTP client_____

    SMTP server_____

    POP2/POP3 _____

    Mail reader _____

Remote Host Access Requirements

    TELNET client_____

    TELNET server _____

    DEC emulation _____ Terminal type_____

    IBM emulation_____ Terminal type_____

Network Diagnostic/Management Requirements

    PING _____

    Finger _____

    SNMP agent _____

    SNMP manager _____

Network Interface Requirements

    NDIS _____

    ODI _____

    Packet Driver _____

    SLIP _____

    PPP_____

    X.25_____

2.6 Internet Support within Macintosh Workstations

A few years ago, because both the Macintosh and UNIX hosts existed in their own isolated worlds, it would be hard to imagine connecting them. TCP/IP has solved that problem, however.

As Vernon Keehan describes in "From Here to Connectivity" [2-19], there are several ways to connect Macs to UNIX hosts. The first is to install the AppleTalk protocol suite on a UNIX platform. One example of such a product is Pacer Software Inc.'s PacerLink, which is compatible with a variety of UNIX platforms from DEC, Hewlett-Packard, and Sun. A second connectivity solution is to use a Datagram Delivery Protocol (DDP)-to-IP router. Manufacturers such as Cayman Systems, Inc. (Cambridge, MA), Shiva Corp. (Cambridge, MA), and the Wollongong Group (Palo Alto, CA) provide this connectivity using either LocalTalk or Ethernet hardware.

The third solution involves a combination of several packages: MacTCP from Apple, one from various third-party developers, and the DDP-to-IP router.

MacTCP is a software driver written for the Macintosh operating system, and it is compatible with all versions including System 7.0 [2-20]. As shown in Figure 2-6, MacTCP provides functionality at the OSI Physical through Transport Layers and relies on third-party products for completion. MacTCP may also rely upon the support of a DDP-to-IP router to send/receive the appropriate DDP packets or IP datagrams. MacTCP implements the following protocols: IP, ICMP, UDP, ARP, RARP, RIP, Bootstrap Protocol (BOOTP), and TCP. These protocols provide the communication services that the higher-layer Session, Presentation, and Application functions require. The product contains interfaces for C and assembly language to facilitate the writing of application programs.

One vendor that uses MacTCP for a variety of Macintosh connectivity products is Intercon Systems Corp. (Herndon, VA). Intercon's Dispatcher/SMTP™ for Quick-Mail provides connectivity between the popular QuickMail software for the Macintosh (CE Software, West Des Moines, IA) and other networks that use SMTP, including UNIX, DEC, and IBM platforms. Dispatcher/SMTP runs on a Quick-Mail server (a Macintosh) that is also connected to the internet. A second software product from Intercon, WatchTower™, turns a Macintosh into an SNMP Network Management Station (NMS). WatchTower allows the Macintosh workstation to gather network performance statistics from SNMP Agents within the internetwork.

(Chapter 7 discusses SNMP in further detail.) A third product from Intercon, TCP/Connect II, supports the TELNET and FTP protocols. TCP/Connect II offers a number of DEC and IBM terminal emulations for TELNET. It supports both client and server capabilities for FTP. Electronic mail functions are also available, using the Post Office Protocol, version 2 (POP2) for message reception and SMTP for transmission.

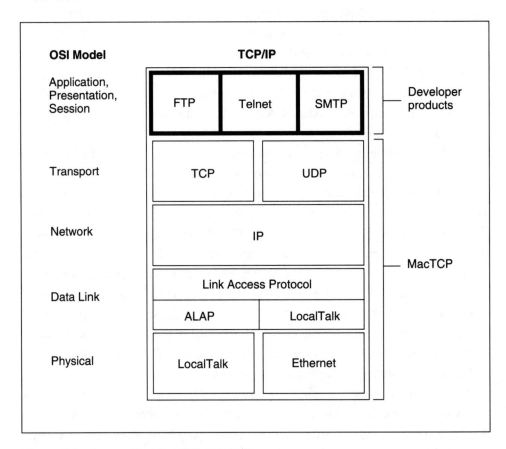

Figure 2-6. Comparing MacTCP with OSI
(Courtesy Apple Computer, Inc.)

Apple's MacTCP driver has opened up the world of the Internet to Macintosh users. Reference [2-21] details some of these possibilities from a user's perspective.

2.7 Internet Support within LAN Operating Systems

Traditionally, LANs have been used for print and file sharing and, occasionally, for remote access to another system. The internetworking capabilities of those systems have only become significant in the last few years, and the TCP/IP protocols have become the solution to many connectivity challenges [2-22]. Let's see the effect this has had on the software architecture of the LAN.

If we consider the architecture of a typical LAN, we could divide the OSI Reference Model's seven layers into several functional groups (see Figure 2-7). To begin, the typical LAN consists of hardware (Layers 1 and 2) and the operating system (Layers 5 through 7). The Network and Transport layers in between provide internetwork connectivity. These functions include routing the packet through the internetwork (the Network Layer function) and assuring that it gets there reliably (the Transport Layer function). If we only wanted a local network (not internetwork) function, we could design some mechanism to allow the operating system to communicate directly with the hardware. Developers of network operating systems, such as Banyan Systems Inc. (Westboro, MA), Novell Inc. (Provo, UT), and Microsoft Corp. (Redmond, WA), anticipated the need to internetwork LANs and built the required Network and Transport Layer functions into their operating systems. Banyan incorporates the VINES Internet Protocol (VIP) for the Network Layer and either the Sequenced Packet Protocol (SPP) or the VINES Interprocess Communications Protocol (VICP) at the Transport Layer of VINES version 5.0. Novell built the internetworking capabilities of NetWare version 3.1 on the Internetwork Packet Exchange (IPX) Protocol and either the Sequenced Packet Exchange (SPX) or the NetWare Core Protocol (NCP) for the Transport Layer. Microsoft's LAN Manager version 2.0 uses the NetBIOS Extended User Interface (NetBEUI) for the Network and Transport Layer functions.

To run TCP/IP over a LAN, you can either replace the existing Network/Transport Layer software with TCP/IP or send the TCP/IP information inside existing Network and Transport Layer protocols, a process known as *encapsulation*. If you replace the existing protocols, you must devise a mechanism to allow higher layer protocols to communicate with the LAN hardware, such as the Ethernet board. A software interface that resides at the upper portion of the Data Link Layer provides this link. It also eliminates the need for each higher-layer protocol stack to have its own hardware driver. In other words, the higher layers talk to the driver, and the driver talks to the hardware. Since the driver specifications are published, everyone's work is simpler.

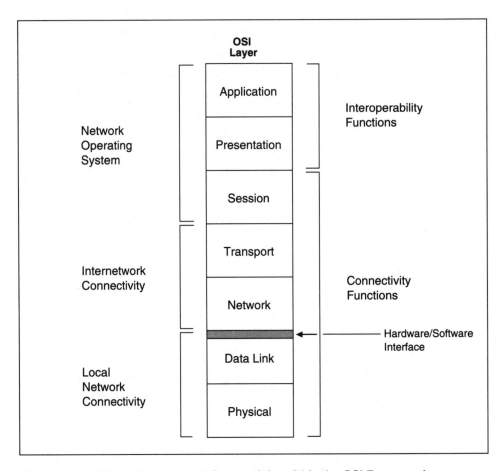

Figure 2-7. LAN and Internetwork Connectivity within the OSI Framework

Three such interfaces are widely used. The first is the Packet Drivers, which were originally specified by FTP Software and further developed at Brigham Young University (Provo, UT), Clarkson University (Potsdam, NY), and Columbia University (New York, NY) among others. (Reference [2-23] discusses these drivers in some detail. Some of these drivers are included in the Crynwr Packet Driver Collection—contact Russell Nelson <nelson@crynwr.com> for further information.)

The second Interface is the Network Driver Interface Specification (NDIS) developed by 3Com Corp. (Santa Clara, CA) and Microsoft and released as part of OS/2 LAN Manager [2-24]. The NDIS contains two components: a Medium Access Control (MAC) driver communicates with the LAN hardware and a protocol driver communicates with the higher layers. The NDIS insulates developers of higher-layer software from the need to write drivers for each type of hardware in use. The third interface, the Open Data Link Interface (ODI) comes from Novell [2-25]. Similar to both the Crynwr drivers and the NDIS, ODI provides a logical link between hardware and software.

Returning to Figure 2-7, note the drivers' function. They reside at the upper portion of the Data Link Layer, providing a way for the Internet protocol stack (i.e., TCP/IP plus applications) or the network operating system (e.g., NetWare) to access the hardware.

The second way to use TCP/IP over a LAN is to use both the native NOS protocols and TCP/IP at the Network and Transport Layers. The NOS protocols (e.g., VINES VIP and VSPP) remain in place and the Internet information (e.g., FTP/TCP/IP) is encapsulated within the VINES packet. This process is known as *tunneling* since the native protocols create a tunnel through which the data from the other protocol stack (i.e., TCP/IP) can pass. This tunnel is created by treating the Internet protocols as data within the packet created by the native network OS protocols. We'll see an example of encapsulation in the next section.

Now that we have a background in the ways in which LAN operating systems support the Internet protocols, let's study VINES, NetWare, and LAN Manager in more detail.

2.7.1 Banyan VINES

Banyan VINES was one of the first network operating systems to incorporate both LAN and WAN protocols (see Figure 2-8). VINES offers particularly strong support for these protocols at the OSI Physical and Data Link Layers. These layers offer the High-level Data Link Control (HDLC) protocol and CCITT X.25 for access to Packet Switched Public Data Networks (PSPDNs), plus asynchronous transmission. The VINES applications include file access, printing and electronic mail. A number of third-party products (shown on the left-hand side of the figure) are also available. VINES version 5.0 added the AppleTalk protocol stack (shown on the right-hand side of the figure). Another integral part of the VINES architecture is support for the Internet protocols, including ARP/RARP, IP, ICMP, TCP, and UDP. VINES also supports the usual applications, such as FTP, TELNET, and so on, using third-party packages.

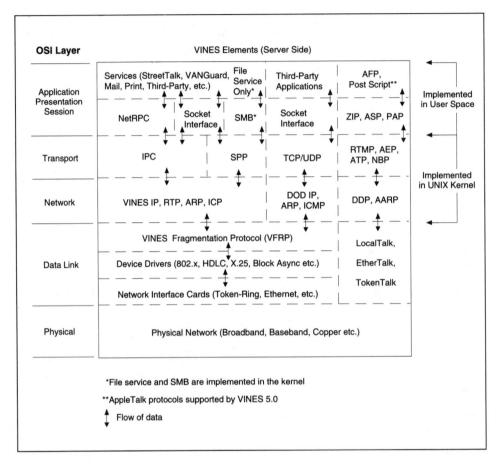

Figure 2-8. VINES Elements and the OSI Model (Server Side)
(Courtesy Banyan Systems, Inc.)

Banyan offers two alternatives for TCP/IP and VINES integration [2-26]. The first is the TCP/IP Routing Option, which allows the VINES server to route TCP/IP traffic between non-VINES (i.e., foreign) hosts (see Figure 2-9). In this case, the VINES server contains both the VINES and TCP/IP protocol stacks and participates in the TCP/IP internetwork. To illustrate how this works, we'll trace a message from Host 1 to Host 2. Host 1 generates the message (shown as User Data), adds the appropriate IP and TCP headers, accesses LAN 1, then builds a transmission frame with the appropriate Data Link Layer (DLL) header and trailer. When that frame arrives at VINES Server 1, the server encapsulates the IP datagram within a VINES IP packet by adding the VINES IP header information necessary to route the packet through the VINES network. When the distant server (VINES Server 2) receives the packet, it removes the VINES IP header, and the IP header routes the packet to its destination host.

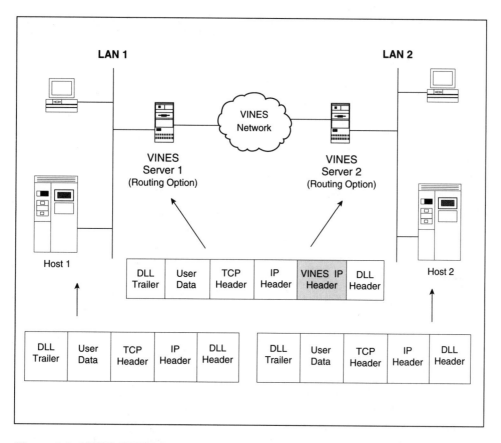

Figure 2-9. VINES TCP/IP Routing Option Encapsulation
(Courtesy Banyan Systems, Inc.)

The second alternative is the VINES Server-to-Server option, shown in Figure 2-10. This option allows VINES servers to route VINES traffic through a TCP/IP internetwork. In this case, the VINES server maps the VINES IP address of the desired destination host to an IP address that will allow for packet delivery. A message originating at Host 1 would be in the VINES-proprietary packet format. VINES Server 1 translates the VINES IP destination address to a DARPA IP destination address, adds the IP header, and sends the newly generated IP datagram to the TCP/IP internetwork. The destination VINES server (shown as Server 2) will remove the IP header and deliver the reconstructed VINES packet to its destination, VINES node Host 2.

With these two options, Banyan allows users to connect from a VINES to a TCP/IP-based internetwork.

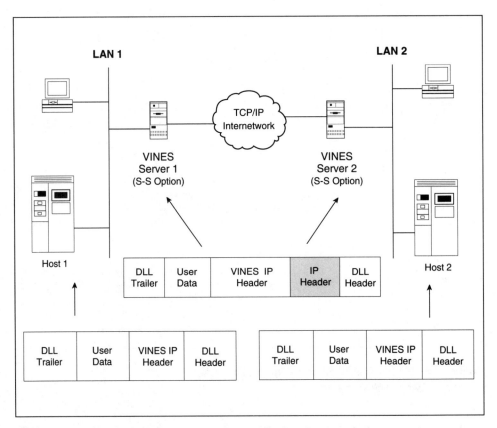

Figure 2-10. VINES TCP/IP Server-to-Server Option Encapsulation
(Courtesy Banyan Systems, Inc.)

2.7.2 Novell NetWare

Novell has greatly increased its support for the Internet protocols since it acquired Excelan in 1989. Excelan developed the Excelan Open System (EXOS) hardware, which dramatically improved the performance of TCP/IP-based workstations by incorporating an Intel 80186 communications processor and the Internet protocol drivers onto an Ethernet network card. Since much of the protocol processing was performed right on the board, it relieved the host's CPU of that task. However, for faster host CPUs (e.g., 80386 and 80486 platforms), you can achieve faster performance by incorporating the protocols directly into the operating system.

A natural extension to the EXOS line, therefore, was to incorporate the Internet protocols into the NetWare operating system. (See Figure 2-11. Note the similarity between the LAN WorkPlace for DOS—Figure 2-5a—and NetWare architectures at the lower layers.) The TCP/IP implementation built into NetWare version 3.11 is a NetWare Loadable Module (TCPIP/NLM) that acts as a transport subsystem using TCP/IP protocols to transport data. [2-27]. Applications may use one of three APIs to access this NLM. Third parties may write to Novell's Transport Layer Interface (TLI). The second API is NetWare NFS [2-28], which supports a Network File System (NFS) server. The third API is a BSD 4.3 socket library. Two applications are included with NetWare 3.11 as additional NLMs: a TCP/IP console (TCPCON) and an SNMP event logger (SNMPLOG). Another included software module, the SNMP NLM, is an SNMP agent for remote clients. Both SNMPLOG and TCPCON are clients of the SNMP agent NLM.

The IPX/IP Tunnel Module (known as IPTUNNEL.LAN) is of interest to protocol analysts. It allows one IPX-based (NetWare) network to communicate with another IPX network via an IP-based internetwork (see Figure 2-12). The NetWare server encapsulates the NetWare IPX packet within a UDP packet for transport across the IP internetwork. To the NetWare server, the IP internetwork looks like another LAN that requires another header (UDP/IP) to complete the communication path. Again referring to Figure 2-12, Server 1 would treat the IPX packet as data and add a UDP and IP header. At the destination, Server 2 would remove the UDP and IP headers, then send the remaining IPX packet into the NetWare network. It is also possible for a client node to use the IPTUNNEL.EXE driver (within the LAN WorkPlace for DOS package) to communicate with a remote NetWare server.

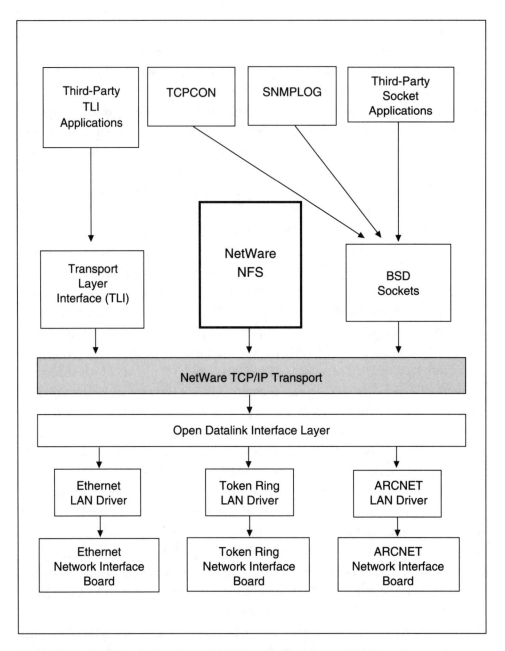

Figure 2-11. NetWare TCP/IP Transport Architectural Relationships
(Courtesy Novell, Inc.)

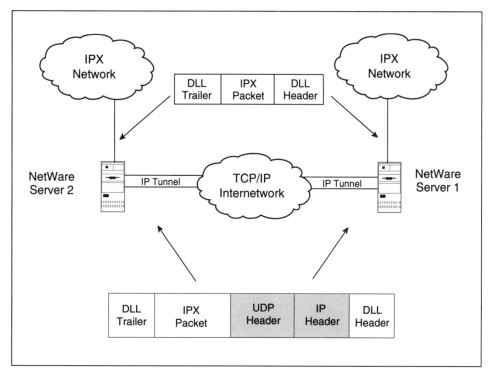

Figure 2-12. IP Tunnel Connecting Two IPX Networks
(Courtesy Novell, Inc.)

Because of NetWare's dominance in the industry, it is often necessary to integrate it into other systems, such as UNIX. References [2-29] and [2-30] explore several alternatives that use TCP/IP for these requirements.

2.7.3 Microsoft LAN Manager

Microsoft developed the LAN Manager operating system to run under OS/2 and take advantage of OS/2's multitasking operation. The LAN Manager architecture is designed for modularity at the hardware and software levels (see Figure 2-13 and Reference [2-31]). LAN Manager can be broken into three sections: hardware, protocol stacks, and the operating system. The modularity of the system becomes apparent in the protocol stacks. The protocol manager selects from the available stacks to determine which one is to be active. Each protocol stack communicates with the hardware driver using the NDIS that we discussed in Section 2.7.

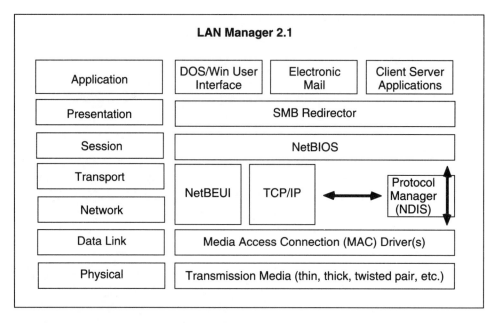

Figure 2-13. Microsoft LAN Manager 2.1 Architecture
(Courtesy Microsoft Corp.)

The protocol stack that is relevant to our discussion of TCP/IP is called the Microsoft TCP/IP and TCP/IP Utilities. The architecture of the TCP/IP utilities within LAN Manager version 2.1 is shown in Figure 2-14. Note that the figure represents two distinct products. The modules labeled LM 2.1, NetBIOS, TCP/IP, and Sockets come with LAN Manager 2.1. The TCP/IP Utilities include the FTP, rcp, and rsh utilities, Sockets, terminal emulators, BAPI, and TELNET modules. (The Bridge Application Program Interface (BAPI) is a specification written by 3Com Corp. that allows terminal emulators to communicate with TELNET. BAPI is required for the DOS version of the TCP/IP Utilities, but not for the OS/2 version.)

In designing the LAN Manager TCP/IP architecture, Microsoft has taken a different approach from Banyan and Novell. Banyan encapsulates VINES packets within IP datagrams or IP datagrams within VINES packets. Novell uses IP/IPX tunneling, which allows an IPX packet to fit within the IP datagram "tunnel." The LAN Manager TCP/IP transport performs no encapsulation or tunneling. Instead, the application process accesses the NetBIOS interface, which communicates with the TCP/IP protocol stack, then talks directly to the hardware.

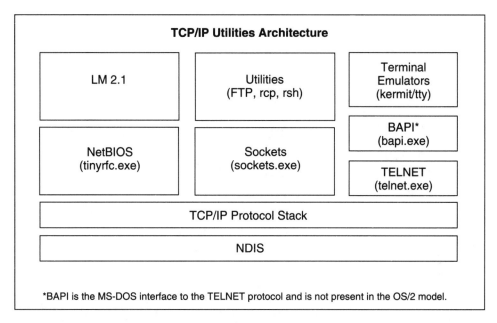

Figure 2-14. Microsoft LAN Manager TCP/IP Utilities Architecture
(Courtesy Microsoft Corp.)

2.8 Internetwork Analysis Tools

In the previous sections of this chapter, we examined the way networks, such as SNA and DECnet, or LAN operating systems, such as NetWare and VINES, support the Internet protocol suite. From such discussions, we can conclude that we're dealing with complex scenarios, such as encapsulating an IP datagram within a VINES packet and transmitting that packet over an X.25 link to another VINES network. When all goes well, the internetwork manager is a hero. But what happens when something fails?

Internetwork failures call for three things: well-trained analysts, the correct analysis tool, and a quick response. Chapter 2 of *Troubleshooting Internetworks* [2-33] discusses the "Ultimate Analyzer," looking at nine trends in current protocol analyzers. These include expert systems, PC-based analyzers, enhanced graphical user interfaces (GUIs), combination LAN/WAN analyzers, multiport/multiprocessing capabilities, support for emerging MAN/WAN protocols (e.g., Fiber Distributed Data Interface (FDDI) or Frame Relay), support for network management protocols (e.g., the Common Management Information Protocol (CMIP) or SNMP), remote data gathering and analysis, and integration with network simulation/modeling tools. Those needing further information on protocol analyzers may want to review that reference.

Readers already familiar with protocol analyzers may require additional information that deals specifically with analysis tools for TCP/IP-based internetworks. (RFC 1147 [2-34] discusses these requirements in further detail.) For example, readers will need to be aware that the term "network analyzer" means different things to different vendors. Some vendors may consider a network *monitor* to be a network *analyzer*. Monitors record traffic measurements, such as the number of frames transmitted per second or the number of frames that contain errors. These are not true analyzers since they are unable to decode the higher-layer protocol information contained within the transmitted frame. For the purposes of our comparison, we will only consider analyzers that can decode TCP and IP and at least one application protocol, such as FTP, TELNET, SMTP, and so on.

Readers wishing to solicit bids from various analyzer manufacturers can use Table 2-2 to survey vendors about their support for available LAN interfaces and Internet protocols. Table 2-3 gives the responses to a survey of 15 analyzer vendors. After studying that table, you may notice that several trends emerge. Not surprisingly, most vendors support UDP since its packet structure is so similar to TCP. ICMP is also a favorite since it is considered an integral part of IP. Of the routing protocols, RIP is favored over the emerging OSPF protocol. Almost all vendors decode applications, such as FTP and TELNET. For network management, SNMP is considerably more popular than CMOT. When you tailor your individual survey to your internetwork requirements, you may find slightly different results. Make sure you do your homework at this step; it is extremely troublesome (and frustrating) to make the wrong decision in such a critical area.

So far, we've surveyed the Internet protocols, studied how different vendors implement them, and looked at analysis tools. In subsequent chapters, we will study the protocols in more depth and look at case studies of the protocols in use taken from actual internetworks. For consistency, we've detailed all case studies using trace files from the Network General Corp. (Menlo Park, CA) *Sniffer* protocol analyzer. We will structure our discussion along the lines of the DARPA Internet model. Thus, Chapter 3 will consider the Network Interface Layer, Chapter 4 the Internet Layer, and so on. Now the real work begins.

Table 2-2. Evaluating TCP/IP Protocol Analyzers

Date _____

Vendor _____

Address_____

City, State, Zip _____

Phone _____

Fax _____

Contact Person _____

Model Number _____

Base Price_____

Price as Optioned _____

LAN Interfaces Supported

ARCNET _____	IEEE 802.3 _____
AppleTalk _____	IEEE 802.4 _____
Ethernet V1 _____	IEEE 802.5 _____
Ethernet V2_____	StarLAN_____
FDDI _____	Other _____
IBM PC Network _____	

Internet Protocols Supported

ARP/RARP _____	OSPF_____
BOOTP _____	RIP_____
CMIP/CMOT _____	SMTP_____
DNS _____	SNAP_____
FTP _____	SNMP _____
IP_____	TCP _____
ICMP_____	TELNET_____
NetBIOS _____	UDP_____
NFS_____	

Table 2-3. Vendor Support for Internet Protocols

Vendor: Protocol:	AG	Byt	Cab	CXR	FTP	HP	IDS	LEX	NGC	Nov	Pro	TTC	TEK	W&G
ARP/RARP:	S	S	S	S	S	S	S		S	S	S	S	S	S
BOOTP:					S							S		
CMIP/CMOT:									S					
DNS:	S			S	S				S	S		S	F	
FTP:	F			S	S	S	S	S	S	S	S	S	F	F
IP:	S	S	S	S	S	S	S	S	S	S	S	S	S	S
ICMP:	S		S	S	S	S	S	S	S	S	S	S	S	S
NetBIOS:	F			S	S	F	S	S	S	S	S	S	F	S
NFS:					S				S			S		
OSPF:					S					S				
RIP:	S				S	F	S		S	S	S	S	S	S
SMTP:			S	S	F	S	S	S				S	F	F
SNAP:	F			S	S	S	S		S	S	S	S	S	S
SNMP:	S			S	S	F	S	S	S	S	S	S	S	S
TCP:	F	S		S	S	S	S	S	S	S	S	S	S	S
TELN:	F			S	S	S	S	S	S	S		S	F	F
TFTP:	F			S	S			S	S	S	S	S	F	F
UDP:	S		S	S	S	S	S	S	S	S	S	S	S	S

Legend: S: Currently supports
              F: Committed future release

Protocol abbreviations:
ARP/RARP:	Address/Reverse Address Resolution Protocol
BOOTP:	Bootstrap Protocol
CMIP/CMOT:	Common Management Information Protocol, CMIP over TCP/IP TCP/IP
DNS:	Domain Name Service
FTP:	File Transfer Protocol
ICMP:	Internet Control Message Protocol
IP:	Internet Protocol
NetB:	NetBIOS
NSF:	Network File System (Sun Microsystems, Inc.)
OSPF:	Open Shortest Path First
RIP:	Routing Information Protocol

Protocol abbreviations, *continued*
SMTP: Simple Mail Transfer Protocol
SNAP: Sub-network Access Protocol
SNMP: Simple Network Management Protocol
TCP: Transmission Control Protocol
TELN: TELNET
TFTP: Trivial File Transfer Protocol
UDP: User Datagram Protocol

Vendor abbreviations:
AG: AG Group, Inc.
Byt: Bytex Corp.
Cab: Cabletron Systems, Inc.
CXR: CXR/Digilog, Inc.
FTP: FTP Software, Inc.
HP: Hewlett-Packard Company
IDS: International Data Sciences, Inc.
LEX: LEXCEL
NGC: Network General Corp.
Nov: Novell, Inc.
Pro: Protools, Inc.
TEK: Tekelec
TTC: Telecommunications Techniques Corp. (NetLens Group)
W&G: Wandel & Goltermann Technologies

2.9 References

[2-1]   Baker, M. Steven. "The Black Art." *UNIX Review* (January 1992): 37-43.

[2-2]   Krol, E. "The Hitchhikers Guide to the Internet." RFC 1118, University of Illinois Urbana, September 1989.

[2-3]   Frost, Lyle. "Bridging Networks." *UNIX Review* (May 1991):46-52.

[2-4]   Smalley, Eric. "DEC Crafts Three-Towered Vision of Open Systems." *Network World* (December 9, 1991):1-37.

[2-5]   Montgomery, John I. "Helping VMS Break the TCP/IP Barrier." *Digital Review* (December 10, 1990).

[2-6]   da Cruz, Frank. *Kermit: A File Transfer Protocol.* Digital Press, 1987.

[2-7]   Rooney, Paula. "TCP/IP Isn't Perfect, But It's Here and It Works." *Digital News Extra* (September 30, 1991): 25-26.

[2-8]   Snyder, Joel. "TCP/IP Software for VMS Adds Features, Applications." *Digital News* (September 2, 1991).

[2-9]   Bynon, David W. "Holding Hands." *DEC Professional* (March 1991).

[2-10] IBM. *TCP/IP Tutorial and Technical Overview.* Document number GG24-3376-02, September 1991.

[2-11] Dickens, Charles. "How to Integrate 3270 SNA, DEC, and TCP/IP Networks." *McData Link* (1991):1-26.

[2-12] Miller, David. "TCP/IP and the AS/400: Computer Matrimony." *LAN Computing* (September 1990):42-44.

[2-13] Birkhead, Evan. "SNA-Internet Strategies Emerge." *LAN Computing* (October 1991):6.

[2-14] O'Brien, Timothy. "Interlink Offers TCP/IP, NFS Wares for LAN Micros." *Network World* (November 25, 1991):17-18.

[2-15] Derfler, Frank J. Jr. "TCP/IP for Multiplatform Networking." *PC Magazine* (June 27, 1989):247-272.

[2-16] Grossman, Evan O. "Programs Link OS/2-Based PCs to TCP/IP." *PC Week/Reviews* (June 25, 1990):106-109.

[2-17] Bing, George. "The All-in-One Tool for TCP/IP Connectivity." *Network Computing* (December 1991): 24-26.

[2-18] Novell. *LAN WorkPlace for DOS Administrator's Guide.* Publication No. 100-000882-001, 1990.

[2-19] Keenan, Vernon. "From Here to Connectivity." *MacWeek* (September 24, 1991):20-22.

[2-20] Apple Computer, Inc. *Apple MacTCP Administrator's Guide*, 1989.

[2-21] Snyder, Joel. "TCP/IP for the Mac." *LAN* (May 1992): 93-100.

[2-22] Sharkey, Scott, Gregory Pruden, Gregory Boyd and Ira Hertzoff. "TCP/IP Provides Passage to Foreign LANs." *LAN Technology* (April 1989):23-28.

[2-23] Romkey, John and Sharon Fisher. "Under the Hood: Packet Drivers." *BYTE* (May 1991):297-303.

[2-24] Richer, Mark. "Who Needs Universal Network Interface Standards?" *Data Communications* (September 21, 1990): 71-72.

[2-25] Breidenbach, Susan. "Network Driver Wars: it's NDIS vs. ODI." *LAN Times* (January 21, 1991): 35.

[2-26] Banyan Systems Inc. *VINES TCP/IP Option Guide*. Document number 092050-000, February 1988.

[2-27] Novell. NetWare v3.11 *TCP/IP Transport Supervisor's Guide*. Publication No. 100-000945-001, 1991.

[2-28] Novell. *NetWare NFS Supervisor's Guide.* Publication No. 100-000955-002, 1991.

[2-29] Cohen, Dave. "How to Get NetWare and TCP/IP to Coexist." *LAN Technology* (February 1991):57-67.

[2-30] Cohen, Dave. "Alternatives for NetWare and TCP/IP Coexistence." *LAN Technology* (June 1991):71-80.

[2-31] Grieves, Michael. "LAN Manager: Stuck in Tomorrowland." *Data Communications* (February 1991): 97-100.

[2-32] Allard, Jay. *Personal Communication*, January 16, 1992.

[2-33] Miller, Mark A. *Troubleshooting Internetworks*. San Mateo, CA: M&T Books, Inc., 1991.

[2-34] Stine, R., Editor. "Tools for Monitoring and Debugging TCP/IP Internets and Interconnected Devices." RFC 1147, SPARTA, Inc., April 1990.

CHAPTER 3

Troubleshooting the Network Interface Connection

We will begin our study of TCP/IP analysis by examining problems that can occur at the DARPA architectural model's Network Interface Layer, which makes the connection to local or wide-area networks (recall our discussion in Section 2.1). The popularity of the Internet protocols has produced Request for Comments (RFC) documents, detailing implementations over virtually every type of LAN and WAN, including ARCNET, Ethernet, IEEE 802, and Packet Switched Public Data Networks (PSPDNs) using the CCITT's X.25 protocol.

To connect to LANs, the Network Interface Layer must exist in all hosts and routers, although its implementation may change across the internetwork (see Figure 3-1a). Thus Host A must have a consistent attachment to Router B, but the destination Host Z may be of a different type. In other words, you can start with an Ethernet and end with a token ring as long as you maintain pair-wise consistencies.

Figure 3-1b shows the options for the Network Interface Layer, and their supporting RFCs. Recall that the higher layer information (e.g., IP, TCP, and so on) is treated as data inside the transmitted frame (see Figure 3-1c). The headers and trailers are defined by the particular LAN or WAN in use, e.g., ARCNET, token ring, etc. Immediately following the Local Network header is the IP header, then the TCP header, and, finally, the higher layer Application data, which might be FTP, TELNET, and so forth.

In summary, the TCP segment comprises the TCP header plus the application data. The IP process treats the TCP segment as data, adds the IP header, and produces the IP datagram. The Local Network process adds the frame header and trailer and transmits that frame on the physical network, such as the Ethernet cable or the X.25 link.

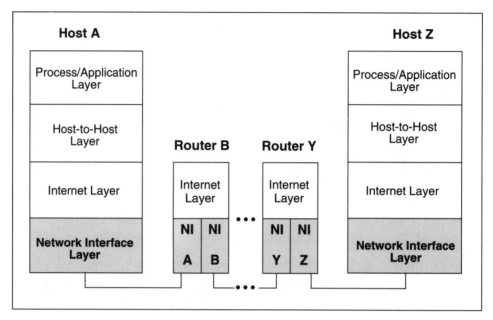

Figure 3-1a. The Network Interface Connection

DARPA Layer	Protocol Implementation						OSI Layer
Process / Application	File Transfer	Electronic Mail	Terminal Emulation	File Transfer	Client / Server	Network Management	Application
	File Transfer Protocol (FTP)	Simple Mail Transfer Protocol (SMTP)	TELNET Protocol	Trivial File Transfer Protocol (TFTP)	Sun Microsystems Network File System Protocols (NFS)	Simple Network Management Protocol (SNMP)	Presentation
	MIL-STD-1780 RFC 959	MIL-STD-1781 RFC 821	MIL-STD-1782 RFC 854	RFC 783	RFCs 1014, 1057, and 1094	RFC 1157	Session
Host-to-Host	Transmission Control Protocol (TCP) MIL-STD-1778 RFC 793			User Datagram Protocol (UDP) RFC 768			Transport
Internet	Address Resolution ARP RFC 826 RARP RFC 903		Internet Protocol (IP) MIL-STD-1777 RFC 791		Internet Control Message Protocol (ICMP) RFC 792		Network
Network Interface	Network Interface Cards: Ethernet, StarLAN, Token Ring, ARCNET RFC 894, RFC 1042, RFC 1201						Data Link
	Transmission Media: Twisted Pair, Coax, Fiber Optics, Wireless Media, etc.						Physical

Figure 3-1b. DARPA Network Interface Layer Protocols

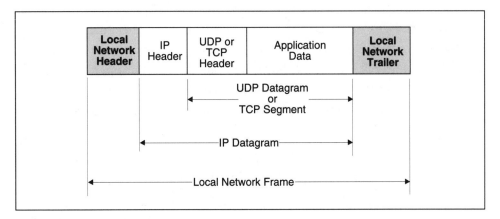

Figure 3-1c. The Internet Transmission Frame

In this chapter, we'll study how various Network Interface Layer options support TCP/IP and the constraints on those implementations when they transmit TCP/IP-related information. The case studies in Section 3.11 will illustrate these protocol interactions in detail. A good reference about support for the Network Interface Layer is RFC 1122, "Requirements for Internet Hosts: Communications Layers" [3-1]. We'll begin by examining how ARCNET networks support TCP/IP.

3.1 ARCNET

ARCNET, which stands for Attached Resource Computer Network, was developed by Datapoint Corp. in 1977. ARCNET is a token passing architecture that supports a number of Physical Layer alternatives, including a linear bus, a star, or a branching tree [3-2]. The original version supported a transmission rate of 2.5 Mbps and up to 255 workstations. It is standardized as ANSI 878.1. An estimated 4 million ARCNET nodes were installed at the end of 1991 [3-3], and a number of manufacturers, including Standard Microsystems Corp. (Hauppauge, NY) and NCR Microelectronics (Dayton, OH), provide ARCNET components.

The Internet standard for ARCNET, RFC 1201 [3-4], suggests methods for encapsulating both IP and ARP datagrams within the ARCNET frame. Three frame formats are available, as shown in Figure 3-2. (Note that this RFC supercedes the older version (RFC 1051) and makes a number of protocol enhancements that have improved TCP/IP support.) The short frame format (Figure 3-2a) limits transmitted client data to 249 octets (an octet represents 8 bits of information). The long

59

frame (Figure 3-2b) allows between 253 and 504 octets of client data. An exception frame (Figure 3-2c) is used with frames having between 250 and 252 octets of client data. (Note that Figure 3-2 shows the frame formats that appear in the software buffers; the hardware transmits formats that duplicate the Destination ID (DID), do not send the Unused and Protocol ID fields, and add some hardware framing.)

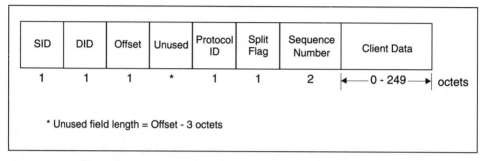

Figure 3-2a. ARCNET Short Frame Format

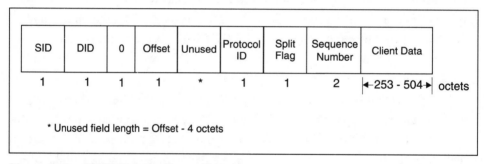

Figure 3-2b. ARCNET Long Frame Format

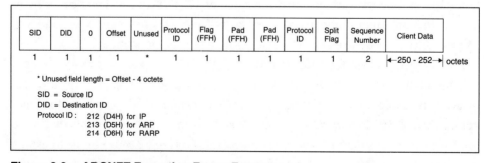

Figure 3-2c. ARCNET Exception Frame Format

The ARCNET frame may contain up to 512 octets, of which 504 octets may be client data. The sender fragments larger packets, using the Split Flag and Sequence Number fields for identification. The Split Flag takes on one of three values depending on the fragmentation required. Unfragmented packets use Split Flag = 0. The first fragment of a fragmented packet uses Split Flag = $((T-2)*2)+1$, where T is the total number of expected fragments. Subsequent fragments use Split Flag = $((N-1)*2)$, where N is the number of this fragment.

For example, assume that a packet requires eight fragments. The Split Flag values would be:

Fragment	Split Flag (decimal)
1	13
2	2
3	4
4	6
5	8
6	10
7	12
8	14

The ARCNET frame may contain up to 120 fragments, yielding a maximum value of 238 decimal (or EE in hexadecimal. Throughout this text, we will use an uppercase h (H) to represent hexadecimal numbers). This allows up to 60,480 octets per packet (120 * 504 = 60,480). All fragments belonging to the same packet use an identical 2-octet sequence number.

Another unique characteristic of ARCNET is the addressing structure it uses to define an 8-bit address field. This structure allows 255 unique hardware addresses, plus a broadcast designation (address = 0). (This address is implemented with an 8-position DIP switch that you set manually on each ARCNET card. An error in duplicating these switch settings can cause a complete network failure, so use caution when setting the address and other options on the ARCNET card.)

To correlate the 8-bit ARCNET address with the 32-bit IP address, RFC 1201 considers three scenarios: Unicast, Broadcast, and Multicast. (Section 4.1 will discuss the IP addresses in detail.) Unicast IP addresses may be mapped to an ARC-

NET address using the Address Resolution Protocol (ARP), which we will discuss in Section 4.3.1. Broadcast IP addresses are mapped to the ARCNET broadcast address of 0. Multicast IP addresses must also be mapped to the ARCNET broadcast address since ARCNET has no provision for multicasting.

RFC 1201 also discusses the transmission of ARP and Reverse Address Resolution Protocol (RARP) packets that may be required to support the more common IP datagrams. When ARP is used, the ARP packet will indicate ARCNET hardware by setting the ARP Hardware Type = 7. RARP packets are transmitted in a similar fashion.

3.2 Ethernet

Developed by DEC, Intel, and Xerox (known collectively as DIX) in 1973, Ethernet was the first LAN to achieve widespread acceptance. The first version, known as Experimental Ethernet, operated at 3 Mbps and used 8-bit addresses. It was later upgraded to Ethernet version 1 and finally to the Ethernet version 2 that we use today, which transmits at 10 Mbps and uses 48-bit addresses. Much of Ethernet's development coincided with research into the Internet protocols. As a result, many TCP/IP-based internetworks contain Ethernet segments.

A word of caution is in order, however. In the early 1980s, DIX turned over the Ethernet Standard [3-5] to the IEEE as a model for today's IEEE 802.3, Carrier Sense Multiple Access Bus with Collision Detection (CSMA/CD) network. The IEEE made improvements in the DIX version and published IEEE 802.3 in 1983 [3-6]. Thus, the Ethernet and IEEE 802.3 standards are not identical. Section 3.6.1 will discuss further examples of these differences. In this section, we will examine Ethernet and in Section 3.3, IEEE 802.3.

The Ethernet frame format (Figure 3-3) defines a length between 64 and 1,518 octets including the header, data, and trailer. The header consists of Destination and Source addresses that are 6 octets (48 bits) each and a 2-octet field known as the Type (or EtherType) field. ARP or RARP perform any address mapping between the 32-bit IP address and the 48-bit Ethernet address, which we will explore in Section 4.2. The Ethernet-designated Destination Address for Broadcast frames is all ONEs (FFFFFFFFFFFFH). The Type designates the higher-layer protocol in use within the Data field. Appendix E defines and gives a number of these Ethernet protocol types. Examples relevant to the Internet protocols include 0800H (IP), 0805H (X.25 Level 3), and 0806H (ARP).

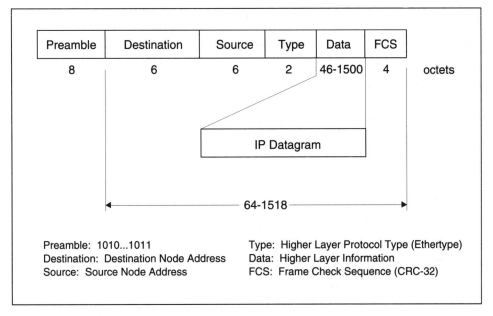

Figure 3-3. Ethernet Frame with IP Datagram
(Courtesy Digital Equipment Corp.)

The Data field itself must be between 46 and 1,500 octets in length. Should an extremely short IP datagram be transmitted (i.e., fewer than 46 octets), the IP process must pad the Data field with zeros to reach the minimum length. (This padding is not considered part of the IP datagram length and is not counted in the Total Length field within the IP header.) The maximum length of the Ethernet Data field is 1,500 octets, which also constrains the IP datagram length. Recall that the default IP datagram Maximum Transmission Unit (MTU) is 576 octets, which easily fits inside one Ethernet frame. The information within the IP datagram is transmitted as a series of octets in numerical order (i.e., first octet transmitted first, second octet transmitted second, and so on). The Internet Standard for Ethernet networks, RFC 894 [3-7] and Appendix B of the IP specification (RFC 791) provide further details on the specific data formats.

3.3 IEEE 802.3

The IEEE project 802 is concerned with internetworking between LANs and MANs. All of the IEEE 802 series of LANs (802.3, 802.4, and 802.5) are covered by the same Internet standard, RFC 1042 [3-8]. These LANs, therefore, exhibit similar characteristics, notably a common addressing format and the use of the IEEE 802.2 Logical Link Control mechanism, that facilitate their interconnection. The primary differences are in the Medium Access Control (MAC) header formats, which are unique to each transmission frame type as dictated by the requirements of the topology. We will point out these differences and similarities as we proceed through our discussion of the IEEE 802 LANs.

As we discussed in the last section, the IEEE 802.3 standard is similar but not identical to the DIX Ethernet. Figure 3-4 shows the IEEE 802.3 frame format. Several differences between the IEEE 802.3 and the Ethernet frame are readily apparent. First, the IEEE 802.3 Destination and Source address fields may have a length of 2 or 6 octets, although the 6-octet length (matching the Ethernet address lengths) is most common. ARP maps the IP address (32 bits) to the IEEE 802.3 address (48 bits). The ARP hardware code for IEEE 802 networks is 6. Broadcast addresses for both Ethernet and IEEE 802 networks are consistent, however, and use all ONEs.

Next, the IEEE 802.3 frame defines a Length field, which specifies the length of the Data unit. Recall that in the Ethernet frame this position was the Type, indicating the higher-layer protocol in use. These 2 octets (the Type or Length fields) distinguish the frame format—Ethernet or IEEE 802.3, respectively. If the Data Link Layer driver mixes these up, confusion results. For example, a destination host expecting an Ethernet frame with a Type field will be unable to respond to an IEEE 802.3 frame that contains the Length field. This is because the destination host's higher-layer software can recognize only a finite number of Types, such as IP (0800H), ARP (0806H), DECnet Phase IV (6003H), and DEC LAT (6004H). Suppose that the transmitting host had an IEEE 802.3 driver and the Data field was 1,500 octets (05DCH) long. The transmitting host would insert 05DCH in the Length field, which the destination host would be unable to recognize. We will look at an example of this confusion in Section 3.11.4.

The Data field contains the information from the higher layers, plus two IEEE-defined headers. The first header is the Logical Link Control (LLC) header, defined by IEEE 802.2 [3-9]. The LLC header includes Destination and Source Service Access Point addresses (DSAP and SSAP, respectively) plus a Control field. The second header is the Sub-Network Access Protocol (SNAP), described in Reference [3-10]. The SNAP header includes a Protocol ID or Organization Code field

(3 octets) plus an Ethernet Type field, or EtherType (2 octets). The combination of the LLC and SNAP headers allows the higher-layer protocol to be identified with both a SAP and an Type designation. The balance of the Data field contains the higher-layer information, such as an IP datagram.

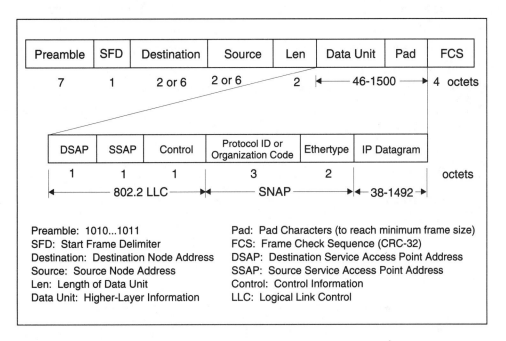

Figure 3-4. IEEE 802.3 Frame Including 802.2 LLC Header and IP Datagram
(Courtesy IEEE)

3.4 IEEE 802.5

Another IEEE 802 network of interest is the token ring, described in the IEEE Standard 802.5 [3-11]. The token ring's popularity is due partially to strong support from major networking companies, such as Apple, IBM, and Proteon. Its success is also due to its built-in internetworking. This provision is known as Source Routing [3-12] and uses the Routing Information (RI) field to connect rings via bridges. The RI field specifies the path the frame must take from its source to its destination. The mechanism for determining that path is called Route Discovery. (Chapter 6 of *Troubleshooting Internetworks* [3-13] discusses the Source Routing protocol and gives several internetwork examples.)

Figure 3-5 shows the token ring frame format. An IP datagram occupies the Information field of the token ring frame. Any necessary routing information precedes the Information field. The Information field contains the IEEE 802.2 LLC header (3 octets), SNAP header (5 octets), and the IP datagram. Given a minimum IP datagram header of 20 octets, the protocol overhead (LLC + SNAP + IP) is, thus, 28 octets per IP datagram. The maximum length of the Information field (and, thus, the encapsulated IP datagram) varies, depending on a parameter known as the Token Holding time. This parameter specifies the length of time any one node may hold the token before it must pass the token to its downstream neighbor. RFC 1042 gives an example for a Token Holding time of nine milliseconds that results in a maximum length of the IP header plus datagram of 4,464 octets.

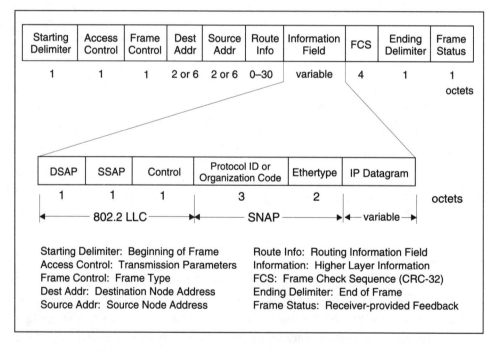

Figure 3-5. IEEE 802.5 Frame with IP Datagram
(Courtesy IEEE)

When bridges connect multiple rings, the Largest Frame (LF) parameter within the RI field controls the maximum frame size and, thus, the maximum IP datagram length. The LF parameter assures that a source station does not transmit a frame length that exceeds an intermediate bridge's processing or memory capabilities. If an intermediate bridge cannot handle a particular frame length, all devices along that transmission path must use a shorter frame. Currently defined LF lengths are between 516 and 62,543 octets.

As a final note, RFC 1042 clarifies the differences between the IEEE and Internet procedures for transmitting the data on the cable. The IEEE specifies numbers in bit-wise little-endian order, i.e., the way they are transmitted on the cable [3-10]. The Internet specifies numbers in byte-wise big-endian order. The following table shows examples of commonly-used numbers:

Usage	IEEE HEX	IEEE Binary	Internet Binary	Internet Decimal
LLC UI Op Code	C0	11000000	00000011	3
LLC SAP for SNAP	55	01010101	10101010	170
LLC XID	F5	11110101	10101111	175
LLC XID, P	FD	11111101	10111111	191
LLC TEST	C7	11000111	11100011	227
LLC TEST, P	CF	11001111	11110011	243
LLC XID Info	818000			129.1.0

3.5 Switched Multimegabit Data Service (SMDS)

The IEEE 802.6 standard describes a network topology known as a Distributed Queue Dual Bus (DQDB) [3-14]. The Switched Multimegabit Data Service (SMDS) is an emerging technology based on the IEEE 802.6 standard.

As its name implies, DQDB consists of two buses arranged in a loop topology and is intended for metropolitan or wide area use, such as a loop around metropolitan Denver, CO. (Strictly speaking, SMDS has no distance limitations.) When one organization needs to transmit data to another, it can use SMDS as the connection between the two LANs.

Bell Communication Research, Inc. (Bellcore), the jointly-owned research organization, developed SMDS as a data transport standard for use by the Regional
Bell Operating Companies (RBOCs). SMDS is a packet switched data transport
mechanism that provides connectionless service. Bellcore describes SMDS in
Technical Report TR-TSV-000772 [3-15], which defines the Subscriber Network
Interface (SNI) and the SMDS Interface Protocol (SIP). The SMDS SNI resembles other network interfaces, such as ISDN or X.25, in that it functions as a point
of data ingress and egress between the user and the transmission facility; by con-
forming to the interface specification, both the user and the network can communicate efficiently.

SIP is a three-layer protocol. SIP Level 1 provides physical data transport and
is usually implemented at the DS-1 (1.544 Mbps) or DS-3 (44.736 Mbps) rates.
SIP Level 2 defines the frame format, including the header and trailer, for data
transmission. Level 2 functions include detecting errors and segmenting and
reassembling the variable length SIP Level 3 Protocol Data Unit (PDU). The
length of the SIP Level 2 frame is fixed at 53 octets. The Level 3 PDU includes
the additional address and control information needed to transfer the user information from source to destination via the SMDS network reliably. The SIP Level
3 PDU may contain up to 9,188 octets of data.

As SMDS becomes more popular, it is reasonable to expect that SMDS networks
will need to carry TCP/IP traffic. The Bellcore specification [3-15] suggests a scenario for interconnecting TCP/IP end systems using SMDS (see Figure 3-6). End
System A includes the higher layers, TCP, IP, and the MAC layer specific to the
attached LAN. End System B also includes the higher TCP and IP layers, but the
lower layers connect to the SMDS network using SIP. A router ties together the
LAN and SMDS network, connecting to the LAN MAC layer on one side and the
SMDS SIP layers on the other.

The Internet community is also working on solutions for internetworking between
LANs and SMDS for the transmission of IP and ARP packets [3-16]. The resulting packet structure incorporates the SMDS SIP headers, the IEEE 802.2 header,
the SNAP header, and the IP/ARP information (see Figure 3-7). For efficient transmission on the SMDS network, the Level 3 PDU is segmented into many smaller
SIP Level 2 frames. The SIP L3 PDU may contain up to 9,188 octets of data, the
SIP L2 PDU only 44 octets. Thus, one L3 PDU may generate a number of L2

frames. The data structure in Figure 3-7 shows the order of the fields and the IP/ARP data as it would be assembled prior to the fragmentation process that occurs at SIP L2.

Within the SIP Level 3 header, the Higher Layer Protocol ID (HLPI) field must be set to a value of 1, indicating IEEE 802.2 LLC. The SMDS Information field then begins with the IEEE 802.2 LLC header, which includes the DSAP and SSAP fields (set to AAH) and the Control field, set to 3 (Type 1 Unnumbered Information). The next fields include the SNAP header, which contains the Organization code (set to zero) and an EtherType. The EtherType for IP packets is 0800H and 0806H for ARP. The total length of the SIP Level 3 PDU may not exceed 9,188 octets, thus allowing an IP datagram to have an MTU of up to 9,180 octets.

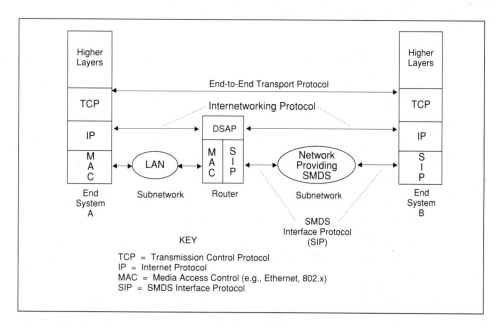

Figure 3-6. Using SMDS with the Internet Protocols
(Reprinted with permission from TR-TSV-000772, Copyright ©1991 Bellcore.)

69

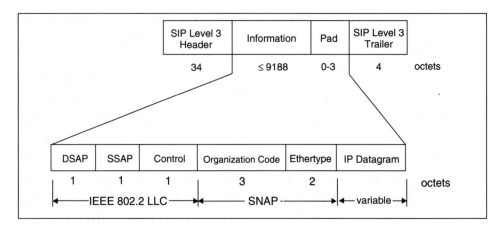

SIP Level 3 Header	Information	Pad	SIP Level 3 Trailer	
34	≤ 9188	0-3	4	octets

DSAP	SSAP	Control	Organization Code	Ethertype	IP Datagram	
1	1	1	3	2		octets

◄────── IEEE 802.2 LLC ──────► ◄────── SNAP ──────► ◄─ variable ─►

Figure 3-7. SMDS SIP Level 3 PDU with IP Datagram
(Reprinted with permission from TR-TSV-000772, Copyright © 1991 Bellcore)

SMDS promises to enhance the speed, reliability, and subscriber services for metropolitan area and wide area data transport services. These services come out of the addressing features (such as Source and Destination address screening) incorporated in the SMDS standard. One such subscriber benefit is the ability to use the SMDS 8-octet addressing scheme to create Logical IP Subnetworks (LISs), also known as closed user groups. (ARP translates Internet addresses to/from SMDS addresses. The ARP Hardware Address length is eight (HA=8) and the Hardware Type is 14.) Within an LIS, the hosts may communicate with each other directly via the SMDS. When communicating to a host outside of that LIS, an IP router performs the network address translation.

SMDS is slated for implementation in three phases [3-17]. Phase I (1992) will offer service to individual Local Access Transport Areas (LATAs) with a demand for SMDS service. Phase 2 (1992-1994) will extend the service nationally and internationally. Bellcore has written specifications for the interfaces between the Local Exchange Carriers (LECs) and Inter-Exchange Carriers (IXCs). Phase 3 (1995) will offer enhanced network management and high-speed network access using the Synchronous Optical Network (SONET). SMDS is an emerging technology that holds much promise for meeting tomorrow's requirements for high-speed data transport.

3.6 FDDI

The Fiber Distributed Data Interface (FDDI) is a standard for fiber optic data transmission developed by the American National Standards Institute (ANSI) and defined in Reference [3-18]. FDDI is a token passing ring architecture, operating at 100 Mbps. (The actual data rate for FDDI is 125 Mbps, but one out of five bits are used for overhead.) Because of its transmission rate, FDDI may emerge as an important alternative to Ethernet or token ring for local TCP/IP data transport.

The FDDI frame structure (Figure 3-8) is similar to that for IEEE 802.5. The maximum frame size is 4,500 octets (or 9,000 symbols, with 4 bits/symbol). When 6-octet addressing (the most common) is used, the MAC-Layer header (Preamble through Source address) uses 16 octets, and the MAC-Layer trailer uses 6 octets. Subtracting the headers from the maximum frame size leaves 4,478 octets for data. As we saw in the last section, the IEEE 802.2 LLC header requires 3 octets and the SNAP header requires 5 octets. Subtracting these yields the maximum IP datagram length of 4,470 octets.

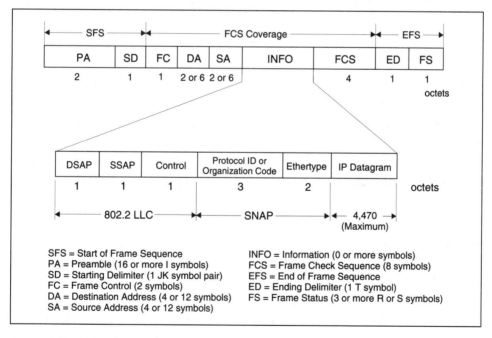

Figure 3-8. FDDI Frame with IP Datagram
(Courtesy American National Standards Institute)

Like IEEE 802 networks, FDDI networks use ARP to map the 32-bit Internet addresses to the 48-bit FDDI addresses [3-19]. An ARP Hardware Type = 1 designates the FDDI hardware used to provide interoperability with bridged Ethernet networks. Readers needing further information on FDDI should consult References [3-20] and [3-21]. Emerging FDDI standards that support twisted pair transmission media and interfaces to the Synchronous Optical Network (SONET) are discussed in Reference [3-22].

3.7 Serial Lines

For years, digital and analog leased lines have been the mainstay of host-to-host and LAN-to-LAN connections. As TCP/IP-based internets grew larger, leased lines became a natural solution for the WAN connection. Two protocols have been developed to support TCP/IP-based data transmission over those topologies: the Serial Line IP (SLIP) and the Point-to-Point Protocol (PPP).

SLIP, described in RFC 1055 [3-23], frames IP datagrams on a serial line. SLIP is not an Internet standard, but it is included in BSD 4.3 UNIX. As the RFC describes, SLIP performs no other protocol functions.

SLIP defines two characters: END (octal 300 or decimal 192) and ESC (octal 333 or decimal 219). To transmit, the SLIP host begins sending the IP datagram. It replaces any data octet equivalent to the END character with the 2-octet sequence of ESC plus octal 334 (decimal 220). It replaces any octet equal to the ESC character with the 2-octet sequence of ESC plus octal 335 (decimal 221). After completing the datagram transmission, it sends an END character. (Note that the ESC character used with SLIP is not the ASCII escape character.)

Because SLIP is non-standard, it has no maximum packet size. Many systems adhere to the maximum packet size used by the Berkeley UNIX SLIP of 1,006 octets (excluding the SLIP framing characters). Because of its non-standard status, any SLIP implementation must assure that the packet size is compatible at both ends of the link before transmitting data.

The Point-to-Point Protocol (PPP), described in RFC 1171 [3-24], is the second protocol used for serial line connections. Unlike SLIP, PPP is a standard protocol for use over asynchronous or synchronous serial lines. RFC 1171 describes three main components of PPP: HDLC encapsulation, a Link Control Protocol (LCP), and a family of Network Control Protocols (NCPs). LCP packets initialize the Data Link Layer of the communicating devices. NCP packets negotiate the Network Layer connection between the two endpoints. Once the LCP and NCP configuration is complete, datagrams may be transmitted over the link. Let's look at the PPP frame structure in detail.

The PPP frame is based upon the ISO High Level Data Link Control (HDLC) protocol (known as ISO 3309) which has been implemented by itself and also incorporated into many other protocol suites, including X.25, Frame Relay, and ISDN. (The 1979 HDLC standard addresses synchronous environments; the 1984 modification extends the usage to asynchronous environments. When asynchronous transmission is used, all octets are transmitted with 1 start bit, 8 data bits, and 1 stop bit.) The PPP frame (see Figure 3-9) includes fields for beginning and ending Flags (set to 07H); an Address (set to FFH, the all-stations address); Control (set to 03H, for Unnumbered Information); Protocol (a 2-octet field identifying the higher-layer protocol in use); Information (the higher-layer information, with a default maximum length of 1,500 octets), and a Frame Check Sequence (2 octets).

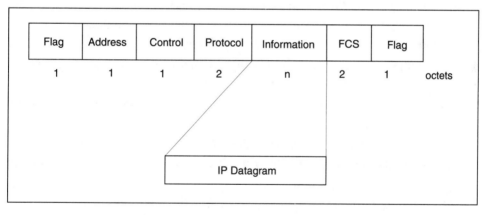

Figure 3-9. Point-to-Point Protocol Frame with IP Datagram

RFC 1171 specifies values for the Protocol field; examples include:

Value	Protocol
0021H	Internet Protocol
0023	ISO CLNP
0025	Xerox NS IDP
0027	DECnet Phase IV
0029	AppleTalk
002B	Novell IPX
8021	Internet Protocol Control Protocol (IPCP)
C021	Link Control Protocol (LCP)

PPP's second component is the Link Control Protocol (LCP), which deals with Data Link Layer issues. LCP defines four steps for link control. Phase 1, Link Establishment and Configuration Negotiation, sends Configuration packets to the remote end, negotiating issues such as the maximum receive unit, the link encryption method, and so on. Phase 2, Link Quality Determination, is an optional process that determines whether the link is of high enough quality to support the proposed Network Layer protocol. Phase 3, Network Layer Protocol Configuration Negotiation, allows the Network Control Protocols (NCP) to configure the Network Layer protocols. The final step, Phase 4, handles link termination. LCP also defines packet formats for establishing and terminating the link. These packets are encapsulated within the Information field of the PPP frame (Figure 3-9) and would be identified by Protocol = C021H.

PPP's third objective is to develop a family of NCPs to transmit Network Layer information. RFC 1171 describes the IP Control Protocol (IPCP) that initializes the IP protocol module at both end points. In other words, IPCP must initiate the Network Layer connection before the IP processes may exchange IP datagrams. RFC 1171 also defines a format for IPCP packets, which would be encapsulated within the PPP frame. The IPCP packet would be identified within the PPP frame with Protocol = 8021H.

To summarize the protocol interactions, the LCP initiates the Data Link Layer, IPCP initiates the IP Layer, and the IP processes send IP datagrams within the PPP frame. The Protocol field would be set to 0021H to indicate that the frame contained an IP datagram. Maximum length of the IP datagram would be identical to the negotiated length of the PPP Information field, with a default of 1,500 octets. The connection would terminate in the reverse order.

3.8 Public Data Networks Using X.25

Much of the early work that produced TCP/IP and the Internet protocols was also applicable to the development of packet switching technologies. Some of the most popular WANs are Packet Switched Public Data Networks (PSPDNs) that use the X.25 protocol. X.25 can, therefore, be considered a by-product of much of this research and is frequently used in conjunction with the TCP/IP protocols for the WAN element of an internetwork.

The X.25 standard encompasses three layers of protocols for the Physical Layer, the Frame Layer, and the Packet Layer. The Physical Layer defines the X.21 protocol, a digital interface that is primarily used in Europe. In North America, the X.21 bis (equivalent to EIA-232-D) is used. The Frame (or Data Link) Layer protocol is known as the Link Access Procedure Balanced (LAPB) protocol. The Packet (or Network) Layer protocol is simply called the Packet Layer Protocol (PLP).

In previous sections, we discussed the transmission of IP datagrams within the Data Link Layer *frames*, such as Ethernet or token ring. The X.25 protocols transmit the IP datagram within a PLP *packet*, which, in turn, carries the IP datagram. Figure 3-10 shows the LAPB frame structure, which is identical to the HDLC or Synchronous Data Link Control (SDLC) formats that are familiar to many readers. The LAPB frame begins and ends with a Flag character (01111110 binary or 7EH). It contains separate fields for address and control information and a Frame Check Sequence (FCS). The PLP packet is carried inside the frame's Information field.

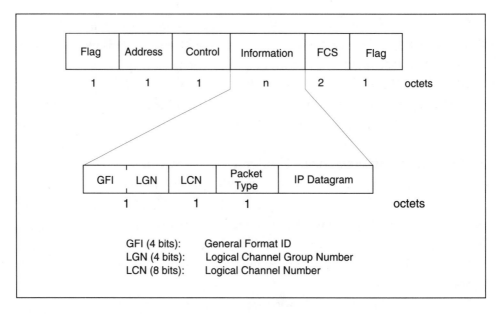

Figure 3-10. X.25 LAPB Frame with IP Datagram
(Courtesy CCITT X.25-1988)

When the virtual circuit (i.e., WAN connection) is first established, the Call Request packet specifies a value of CCH (binary 11001100 or decimal 204) to indicate that IP will be used within the packet. The IP datagram is then placed within a PLP data packet for transmission. A 4-octet PLP header precedes the IP datagram and specifies the General Format ID (GFI) used for control purposes; the Logical Channel Group Number (LGN) and Logical Channel Number (LCN) that identify the logical channel and a Packet Type field, containing packet sequence numbers and flags. The maximum size of the IP datagram transmitted over X.25 is 576 octets, unless both sender and receiver negotiate otherwise. RFC 877 [3-25] specifies additional details. *Inside X.25: A Manager's Guide* [3-26], is an excellent handbook for network administrators.

3.9 Frame Relay

The International Telegraph and Telephone Consultative Committee (CCITT) originally developed Frame Relay (FR) as a protocol for use on the Integrated Services Digital Network (ISDN) D-Channel. The original protocol was called the Link Access Protocol for the D-Channel (LAPD). FR is a packet switching technology, similar to X.25, that offers a reliable way to transport data over a WAN link. FR improves on its predecessor primarily through its faster processing speed.

FR has cranked up its processing speed by streamlining the way it deals with information. Most protocols, such as X.25, that operate within the communications subnetwork (i.e., the OSI Physical, Data Link and Network Layers) process information at all three layers: the Physical Layer decodes the bits, the Data Link Layer decodes the frame, and the Network Layer decodes the packet. Both frames and packets perform error checking to assure reliable communication. But while this method increases the reliability of the data transmission, it also increases overhead in the number of bits transmitted and the time required to process the bits. FR eliminates the Network Layer (i.e., packet) processing and performs only a few Data Link Layer functions. For example, FR checks the frame for errors, but it does not automatically request a retransmission if it discovers one. Should an error occur, the processes within the sender and receiver take responsibility for that function.

Note that FR operates under two assumptions. The first is that the underlying communications subnet is more reliable than the networks of ten years ago. With the trend within telephone networks of replacing copper circuits with fiber optic cable, this is a valid argument. If the communication subnetwork is reliable, Why bother with all the rigorous error control? Second, FR technology assumes that if an error does sneak by, the sending and receiving devices are usually computers with the intelligence to diagnose and cure the problem. For example, they can ask for a retransmission.

The FR frame structure is shown in Figure 3-11 and resembles the X.25 frame shown in Figure 3-10. You can see the differences in the formats in the first 2 octets following the Flag character. In the X.25 LAPB frame, these 2 octets are used for the Address and Control fields. The Information field would contain the X.25 packet. For FR, the first 2 octets comprise the FR header and are followed by the higher-layer information, such as an IP datagram.

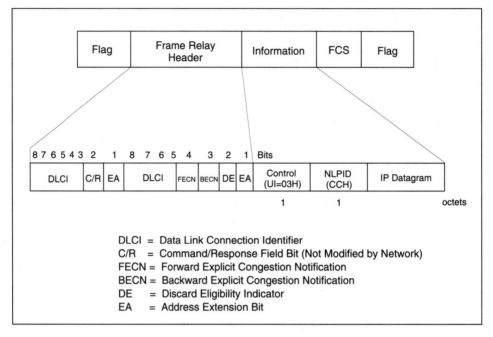

Figure 3-11. Frame Relay Frame with IP Datagram

The FR header contains a number of subfields. The longest of these is the Data Link Connection Identifier (DLCI), which identifies the virtual circuit used for any particular communication path. (A virtual circuit is a logical communication channel between the end-user equipment, or Data Terminal Equipment (DTE), and the FR network, or Data Circuit-Terminating Equipment (DCE). The FR network interface is defined at the physical communication line between DTE and DCE.) Multiple virtual circuits may exist at this interface. For example, if a router is the DTE, it may serve 50 workstations on a LAN, which could each conceivably have a virtual circuit (identified with the DLCI field) into the FR network. The DLCI field (10 bits in length) allows up to 1,024 virtual circuits, although some are reserved for network diagnostic purposes. These circuits are further defined as Permanent Virtual Circuits (PVCs) and are established when the DTE is attached to the FR network.

When a frame enters the FR network (via the DCE), the workstation checks the Frame Check Sequence (FCS) at the end of the frame checks for errors. If an error is present, the frame is discarded. If the FCS passes, the workstation examines the DLCI field and a table lookup determines the correct outgoing link. If a table entry does not exist for a particular frame, the frame is discarded. (By now, you should appreciate why FR is a streamlined protocol—if the frame contains any errors or if there is any confusion over how to process the frame, the frame is simply discarded. The higher-layer protocols within the machines at either end of the link must recover from the problem.)

The FR header contains 3 bits to indicate congestion on the FR network. The first 2 bits are known as Explicit Congestion Notification (ECN) bits. Any node within the FR network can send an ECN bit in two directions: downstream using the Forward ECN (or FECN) bit and upstream using the Backward ECN (or BECN) bit. The third bit used for congestion control is the Discard Eligibility (DE) bit. The DE bit indicates which frames should be discarded to relieve congestion. An addendum to ANSI T1.606 (ANSI T1S1.2/91-454) discusses these congestion management principles.

Returning to Figure 3-11, the Command/Response (C/R) and Extended Address (EA) complete the FR Header. The C/R bit was defined for LAPD, but is not used with FR networks. The EA bits allow the FR Header to extend to 3 or 4 octets in length to accommodate more DLCI addresses.

The Internet standard [3-27] provides specifics for implementing multiprotocol traffic over FR networks. The key word in RFC 1294's title is "multiprotocol" since the FR Information field has several variations. Consistent among all the variants, however, are the Control field and the Network Level Protocol ID (NLPID). The Control field may either specify Unnumbered Information (UI) with a field value of 03H or Exchange Identification (XID) with a field value of AF or BFH. ISO and CCITT administer the NLPID and identify the type of protocol used within the Information field. RFC 1294 gives the following examples:

NLPID	Usage
00H	Null Network Layer (not used with Frame Relay)
80	SNAP
81	ISO CLNP
82	ISO ESIS
83	ISO ISIS
CC	Internet IP
CE	EtherType (unofficial temporary use)

Of particular interest to Internet designers is NLPID = CCH, which indicates that the frame contains an IP datagram. If a protocol does not have an NLPID, the 1-octet NLPID field is replaced with a 6-octet field. That field includes NLPID = 80H (indicating the SNAP), followed by the 5-octet SNAP header. The Ether-Type within the SNAP header would then identify the higher- layer protocol in use. An ARP packet is an example of a SNAP-encoded frame. The first 6 octets of the Information field (i.e., NLPID plus SNAP) would contain 80-00-00-00-08-06H. The 80 identifies NLPID = SNAP, the 00-00-00 is the SNAP Organization ID and the 08-06 is the EtherType for ARP. Inverse ARP performs the conversion between DLCIs and protocol addresses, and it is described in RFC 1293 [3-28]. Other formats for routed and bridged frames have been defined as well, consult RFC 1294 for specific details.

A number of carrier and equipment vendors joined together in 1991 to establish the Frame Relay Forum. The purpose of the Forum was to promote FR technology from a standards and a user perspective [3-29]. On the standards side, ANSI T1.606 describes the service; standards such as T1.617, T1.618, and T1S1.2/91-454 deal with signaling, core aspects, and congestion management, respectively [3-30]. The Frame Relay Forum also publishes a newsletter [3-31] and provides information on upcoming conferences and the status of standards. Contact the Frame Relay Forum Secretariat at (415) 962-2579 for further details.

Both users [3-32] and carriers [3-33] have been expressing interest in FR services. Like other data transport services, especially those using new or emerging technologies, FR networks must be designed with careful consideration for the end-user application. Users need to understand where FR fits into their WAN strategies along with existing technologies, such as X.25 packet switching, and emerging technologies, such as SMDS. Reference [3-34] provides further details on design constraints to consider. A number of carriers, such as AT&T (Morristown, NJ), BT North America Inc. (San Jose, CA), CompuServe Inc. (Columbus, OH), MCI Communications Corp. (Washington, DC), and Williams Telecommunications Group (Tulsa, OK) are vying for a position in the new marketplace. An excellent overview on the various applications for FR is *The Buyer's Guide to Frame Relay Networking*, [3-35].

As a final note, readers interested in further details on MANs should investigate Kessler and Train's book entitled *Metropolitan Area Networks: Concepts, Standards, and Protocols* [3-36]. Hume and Seaman's "X.25 and Frame Relay: Packet

Switched Technologies for Wide Area Connectivity" [3-37] offers an interesting perspective on WAN connectivity. In Section 3.11, we will examine case studies showing problems that can occur with the various LAN, MAN, and WAN network interface connections.

3.10 Troubleshooting the Network Interface Connection

So far in this chapter, we have explored the hardware configurations upon which a TCP/IP-based internetwork may operate, including options for LANs (Ethernet or token ring), MANs (SMDS), and WANs (serial lines or PSPDNs). The large number of available and documented alternatives attest to the popularity of the protocols. Reviewing Figure 3-1b, notice that we are still discussing the physical, not the logical, communication path.

If you're like most TCP/IP administrators, you'll spend as much (if not more) time troubleshooting the hardware (i.e., the Network Interface Layer) as the higher-layer software. If a connector is bad or a network interface card is defective, you must troubleshoot and repair those elements before moving up the protocol stack to analyze the TCP/IP protocols. A companion volume to this book, the *LAN Troubleshooting Handbook*, [3-38] discusses LAN hardware troubleshooting in detail. Here are some key points to consider:

- First, check the basic communication path between devices. Broken cables, loose connectors, and so on can cause what appear to be more complex problems.

- Check for compliance with standards. For example, verify that all workstations on an Ethernet are transmitting Ethernet not IEEE 802.3 frames. Or verify that all segments have the correct cable type, such as the RG58A/U used with IEEE 802.3 10BASE2 networks, not the RG59A/U used with video systems such as VCRs.

- Systematically isolate the problem to a single LAN, MAN, or WAN segment. It is rare for two segments to fail simultaneously.

In our next section, we will examine case studies that demonstrate Network Interface Layer problems typical for TCP/IP-based internetworks.

3.11 Case Studies

In light of our previous discussion of the protocols used at the DARPA Network Interface Layer, let's look at some case studies of actual situations that illustrate the operation of the protocols. For consistency, we captured all data with the Network General *Sniffer* protocol analyzer.

3.11.1 Initializing a Token Ring Workstation

In our first case study, we'll look at how a workstation becomes an active member of a token ring network, prior to initiating any higher-layer service, such as a file transfer using FTP (see Figure 3-12). In general, the workstation must complete two steps before TCP/IP or any higher-layer protocols can be activated. First, the workstation must make the physical (electrical) connection to the token ring network. Second, it must make the logical connection into the token passing system, assuring its proper standing among its peers. Let's examine these processes in detail.

The token ring standard (IEEE 802.5) defines two types of transmission frames. A Logical Link Control (LLC) frame carries user data, such as an electronic mail message. A Medium Access Control (MAC) frame transmits network management information. (These frame types are distinguished by the first two bits of the Frame Control field: 00 = MAC and 01 = LLC.) The MAC frames are always transmitted first (because one of their functions is network initialization), then a combination of MAC and LLC frames may be transmitted. The IEEE 802.5 standard defines a total of 25 MAC frames, which perform a number of network management functions.

Two examples of MAC-related functions are the Active Monitor (AM) and the Standby Monitor (SM). All token ring controller chips (such as Texas Instruments' TMS380) can perform these functions. The AM function observes the overall health of the network, making sure that the token circulates properly, that transmitted frames circle the ring only once, and so on. The workstation with the highest address (the 48-bit address stored in a ROM on the network interface card) is selected to be the AM. All other workstations assume an SM function and assure the proper operation of the AM. (This is somewhat akin to parents leaving their children with a sitter. The sitter watches the children, but the children also report any unusual actions, such as excessive telephone use, of the sitter.) The AMs and SMs identify themselves by periodically transmitting the Active Monitor Present (AMP) and Standby Monitor Present (SMP) frames.

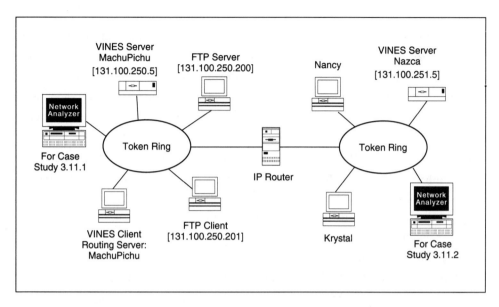

Figure 3-12. IEEE 802.5 Network with Banyan VINES and TCP/IP

In this example (see Trace 3.11.1 at the end of this section), a workstation (designated FTP Client) wishes to enter the token ring network on the left-hand side of the TCP/IP Router. The network analyzer is placed on the left-hand ring, network [131.100.250.x] to capture the data. Only the network analyzer and the server (designated FTP Server) are currently active. The server is the AM and transmits an AMP frame approximately every seven seconds. When the TR client is turned on, its NIC actuates the relay connected to its port within the token ring wiring hub, known as the Multistation Access Unit (MSAU). Because the relay actuation momentarily disrupts the signal transmission, the AM transmits a Ring Purge MAC frame to test the transmission path.

Next, the FTP client transmits a frame to itself (see Frame 6, the MAC Duplicate Address Test (DAT)), to determine whether another workstation with the same address is active on the ring. If two identical addresses existed, both stations might respond to a transmission and would confuse the recipient. Thus, if the new station received a response to the DAT frame, it would abort its login.

Each workstation maintains a register containing the address of its nearest upstream neighbor. When this address changes (or is entered for the first time) the workstation reports a change in the Stored Upstream Address (SUA) to the

83

Configuration Report Server (CRS). (The CRS is a functional address that maintains the logical topology of the ring for purposes of network management.) Notice that a second DAT frame is sent in Frame 8, followed by a Report SUA Change in Frame 9. In Frame 11, the server also reports an SUA change. As a passive device, the network analyzer does not participate in these logical ring transmissions.

In Frames 12 through 15 the client requests its parameters from another functional address, the Ring Parameter Server (RPS). The RPS is not active; therefore, the FTP Client uses its default parameters and continues. The AM station has been keeping track of the transmission interruptions caused by the new workstation's MSAU relay actuation and transmits an error report to another functional address, the Ring Error Monitor (REM), in Frame 16.

Finally, the new workstation participates in a Ring Poll, which verifies its status as an SM, since the AM (FTP Server) is already selected. Frames 17 and 18 (AMP then SMP) show this ring poll, which repeats every seven seconds (Frames 23-24 and 25-26). The Internet protocols become active in Frame 19, when the FTP Client uses ARP to determine a hardware address that matches internet address 131.100.250.200. ICMP and TCP information is also transmitted (Frames 21-22 and 27-29, respectively), before an FTP session begins in Frame 30. The TCP sequence is known as a three-way handshake, which we will look at in detail in Section 5.5.5.

To summarize, the FTP Client underwent the following MAC-Layer functions to make the physical and logical connection to the token ring network:

Event 1   The relay actuation triggers the transmission of a Ring Purge frame.

Event 2   The new node transmits one or two Duplicate Address Test frames.

Event 3   The new node and its downstream neighbor report a Stored Upstream Address change to the Configuration Report server.

Event 4   The new node requests Initialization parameters from Ring Parameter server (maximum 4 tries).

Event 5   The new node's downstream neighbor transmits a Report Error frame.

Event 6   The new node participates in a Ring Poll.

Sniffer Network Analyzer data 16-Jan-92 at 14:54:28,FTPXCHNG.TRC, Pg 1

SUMMARY		Delta T	Destination	Source	Summary
M	1		LAN Manager	NwkGnlE00E1A	IBMNM Trace Tool Present
	2	2.009	Broadcast	FTP Server	MAC Active Monitor Present
	3	6.998	Broadcast	FTP Server	MAC Active Monitor Present
	4	6.998	Broadcast	FTP Server	MAC Active Monitor Present
	5	2.900	Broadcast	FTP Server	MAC Ring Purge
	6	0.001	FTP Client	FTP Client	MAC Duplicate Address Test
	7	0.000	Broadcast	FTP Server	MAC Active Monitor Present
	8	0.001	FTP Client	FTP Client	MAC Duplicate Address Test
	9	0.001	Config Srv	FTP Client	MAC Report SUA Change
	10	0.017	Broadcast	FTP Client	MAC Standby Monitor Present
	11	0.000	Config Srv	FTP Server	MAC Report SUA Change
	12	0.000	Param Server	FTP Client	MAC Request Initialization
	13	0.000	Param Server	FTP Client	MAC Request Initialization
	14	0.000	Param Server	FTP Client	MAC Request Initialization
	15	0.000	Param Server	FTP Client	MAC Request Initialization
	16	2.166	Error Mon.	FTP Server	MAC Report Soft Error
	17	4.798	Broadcast	FTP Server	MAC Active Monitor Present
	18	0.017	Broadcast	FTP Client	MAC Standby Monitor Present
	19	4.032	Broadcast	FTP Client	ARP C PA=[131.100.250.200] PRO=IP
	20	0.003	FTP Client	FTP Server	ARP R PA=[131.100.250.200] HA=10005A2502CE PRO=IP
	21	0.003	FTP Server	FTP Client	ICMP Echo
	22	0.003	FTP Client	FTP Server	ICMP Echo reply
	23	2.937	Broadcast	FTP Server	MAC Active Monitor Present
	24	0.016	Broadcast	FTP Client	MAC Standby Monitor Present
	25	6.981	Broadcast	FTP Server	MAC Active Monitor Present
	26	0.016	Broadcast	FTP Client	MAC Standby Monitor Present
	27	0.903	FTP Server	FTP Client	TCP D=21 S=3592 SYN SEQ=82509567 LEN=0 WIN=1800
	28	0.005	FTP Client	FTP Server	TCP D=3592 S=21 SYN ACK=82509568 SEQ=48955135 LEN=0 WIN=1800
	29	0.003	FTP Server	FTP Client	TCP D=21 S=3592 ACK=48955136 WIN=1800

30	0.042	FTP Client	FTP Server	FTP R PORT=3592 220-hewey PC/TCP 2.0 FTP Server by FTP Software re...
31	0.150	FTP Server	FTP Client	TCP D=21 S=3592 ACK=48955253 WIN=1683
32	3.461	FTP Server	FTP Client	FTP C PORT=3592 USER anonymous<0D><0A>
33	0.003	FTP Client	FTP Server	TCP D=3592 S=21 ACK=82509584 WIN=1784
34	0.032	FTP Client	FTP Server	FTP R PORT=3592 230 User OK, no password<0D><0A>
35	0.125	FTP Server	FTP Client	TCP D=21 S=3592 ACK=48955279 WIN=1774
36	2.252	Broadcast	FTP Server	MAC Active Monitor Present
37	0.015	Broadcast	FTP Client	MAC Standby Monitor Present
38	3.428	FTP Server	FTP Client	FTP C PORT=3592 PWD<0D><0A>
39	0.004	FTP Client	FTP Server	TCP D=3592 S=21 509589 WIN=1795
40	0.009	FTP Client	FTP Server	FTP R PORT=3592 250 Current working directory is C:\MIKES\PCTCP<0D>...

Trace 3.11.1. Token Ring Station Initialization

In our next example, we'll see how information passes from one server to another within an IP tunnel.

3.11.2 Transmitting Banyan VINES Packets Through the Internet

In Section 2.7, we discussed the concept of tunneling or encapsulation. Recall that in this process, a LAN operating system, such as NetWare or VINES, uses the Internet protocols to transmit data over a WAN connection. The process is often referred to as an IP tunnel.

Figure 3-12 illustrates the tunneling process using a VINES internetwork. The VINES client is connected to network 131.100.250.X and must access a server (Nazca) on another network, 131.100.251.X. An IP-based internetwork connects the two rings. Several steps are necessary to complete the connection. First, the client must attach to its routing server (MachuPichu) on the local ring. Next, the local server encapsulates the VINES packets in an IP datagram for transmission on the internetwork. Finally, the distant server (Nazca) receives the token ring frame, strips off the token ring header, IP header, and token ring trailer and returns the VINES packet to the way it was before encapsulation in the IP datagram. Let's use the analyzer to examine this process.

The placement of the analyzer is vital to understanding the protocol interaction. In this example, we located the analyzer on the distant ring (review Figure 3-12). If the analyzer were on the local ring, it would only be able to see the traffic going into the router; by locating the analyzer on the distant ring you can verify the data coming out of the router and the communication line in between. The analyzer is capturing both VINES and IP packets. The VINES packets represent traffic between the client and the routing server, MachuPichu. The IP packets represent traffic (via the IP Router) between the routing server, MachuPichu, and the server on the client's ring, Nazca.

In Trace 3.11.2a, we observe several interactions, including a MAC AMP frame (sent from IP Router in Frame 4) and the MAC SMP frames sent from the other ring stations (Frames 5 and 6). In Frame 7, the router and server begin exchanging IP packets that come from node 131.100.250.5 (MachuPichu, the client's routing server) to the target server (Nazca), node 131.100.251.5. The IP packets contain the requests from, and responses to, the client for file service.

Trace 3.11.2b. shows the details of Frame 7, the client's request for a file search. (Frame 8 contains the server's reply, which is not shown in Trace 3.11.2b.) Note that the token ring header also contains the SNAP header (IEEE 802.2 LLC plus Ether-Type) shown in Figure 3-5. The SNAP header uses DSAP = AAH, SSAP = AAH, and Control = 03H (Unnumbered Information or UI). The Protocol ID = 000000H (not indicated in the trace file, but available in the hexadecimal decode), with an EtherType= 0800H (IP). The 20-octet IP header is transmitted next. It identifies source network address 131.100.250.5 (MachuPichu) and destination network address 131.100.251.5 (Nazca). These addresses confirm the communication between the two VINES servers. Note that IP datagrams in both directions are given an ID number (e.g., 20253 in Frame 7) from the originating node. The final portion of the IP datagram is the VINES packet itself.

We may derive two conclusions from this example. First, the placement of the analyzer has a dramatic effect on the data that is captured during encapsulation. (Move the analyzer to either side of an encapsulating server and observe the results for yourself.) Second, multiple protocols, such as IP and VINES, may exist on an internetwork simultaneously. This requires a number of protocol interpreters within the analyzer. Make sure that your analyzer can analyze all of your protocols.

Sniffer Network Analyzer data 15-Jan-92 at 19:40:38, file TCPTUNEL.TRC Pg 1

SUMMARY	Delta T	Destination	Source	Summary
M 1		Nazca	IP Router	VMATCH Call
				Port=00C0 (Unknown)
				ID=0 Procedure=100
				Arguments=<0006>
2	0.004	Nazca	IP Router	VMATCH Call
				Port=00C0 (Unknown)
				ID=0 Procedure=100
				Arguments=<0007>
3	0.009	Nazca	IP Router	VSTRTK C NewIncome
				IncomeType=Detail
4	2.701	Broadcast	IP Router	MAC Active Monitor Present
5	0.014	Broadcast	IBM 38235C	MAC Standby Monitor Present
6	0.019	Broadcast	Nazca	MAC Standby Monitor Present
7	1.214	Nazca	IP Router	SMB C Search
				\TEMP\????????.???
8	0.013	IP Router?	Nazca	SMB R 1 entry found
9	0.081	Nazca	IP Router	SMB C Search
				\TEMP\????????.???
10	0.037	IP Router	Nazca	SMB R 15 entries found
11	0.024	Nazca	IP Router	SMB C Check dir \TEMP
12	0.013	IP Router	Nazca	SMB R OK
13	0.359	Nazca	IP Router	VSPP Ack NS=854 NR=875
				Window=879
				RID=0027 LID=0011
14	0.086	Nazca	IP Router	SMB too short to decode
15	0.012	IP Router	Nazca	SMB R Got Disk Attributes
16	0.341	Nazca	IP Router	VSPP Ack NS=855 NR=876
				Window=880 RID=0027
				LID=0011
17	3.093	Nazca	IP Router	VSTRTK C NewIncome
				IncomeType=Detail

Trace 3.11.2a. VINES Packet Tunneling Summary

Sniffer Network Analyzer data 15-Jan-92 at 19:40:38, file TCPTUNEL.TRC Pg 1

- Frame 7 -

```
DLC:      - - - - - DLC Header- - - - -
DLC:
DLC:      Frame 7 arrived at  19:40:44.533; frame size is 140 (008C hex) bytes.
DLC:      AC: Frame priority 0,  Reservation priority 0,  Monitor count 0
DLC:      FC: LLC frame,  PCF attention code: None
DLC:      FS: Addr recognized indicators: 00, Frame copied indicators: 00
DLC:      Destination = Station IBM   11A83D, Nazca
DLC:      Source = Station IBM   39078A, IP Router
DLC:
LLC:      - - - - - LLC Header - - - - -
LLC:
LLC:      DSAP = AA, SSAP = AA, Command, Unnumbered frame: UI
LLC:
SNAP:     - - - - - SNAP Header - - - - -
SNAP:
SNAP:     Type = 0800 (IP)
SNAP:
IP:       - - - - - IP Header- - - - -
IP:
IP:       Version = 4, header length = 20 bytes
IP:       Type of service = 00
P:           0 0 0 .   . . . . = routine
IP:.         . . . 0   . . . . = normal delay
IP:          . . . .   0 . . . = normal throughput
IP:          . . . .   . 0. . = normal reliability
IP:       Total length = 118 bytes
IP:       Identification = 20253
IP:       Flags = 0X
IP:       . 0 . .    . . . . = may fragment
IP:       . . 0 .    . . . . = last fragment
IP:       Fragment offset = 0 bytes
IP:       Time to live = 254 seconds/hops
IP:       Protocol = 83 (VINES)
IP:       Header checksum = 7143 (correct)
IP:       Source address = [131.100.250.5]
IP:       Destination address = [131.100.251.5]
IP:       No options
IP:
VFRP:     - - - - - VINES FRP Header - - - - -
VFRP:
VFRP:     Fragmentation byte = 03
```

```
VFRP:          0 0 0 0   0 0 . .  = Unused
VFRP:          . . . .   . . 1 .  = End of packet
VFRP:          . . . .   . . . 1  = Beginning of packet
VFRP:
VFRP:          Sequence number = 186
VFRP:
VIP:           - - - - - VINES IP Header - - - - -

VIP:
VIP:           Checksum = A7D8
VIP:           Packet length = 96
VIP:
VIP:           Transport control = 5E
VIP:              0 . . .   . . . .  = Unused
VIP:              . 1 . .   . . . .  = Contains RTP redirect message
VIP:              . . 0 .   . . . .  = Do not return metric notification packet
VIP:              . . . 1   . . . .  = Return exception notification packet
VIP:              . . . .   1 1 1 0  = Hop count remaining (14)
VIP:
VIP:           Protocol type = 2 (Sequenced Packet Protocol - VSPP)
VIP:
VIP:           Destination network.subnetwork = 0000067A.0001
VIP:           Source network.subnetwork = 00000384.8001
VIP:
VSPP:          - - - - - VINES SPP Header - - - - -
VSPP:
VSPP:          Source port = 0203
VSPP:          Destination port = 0253
VSPP:
VSPP:          Packet type = 1 (Data)
VSPP:
VSPP:          Control = 60
VSPP:             0 . . .   . . . .  = Unused
VSPP:             . 1 . .   . . . .  = End of message
VSPP:             . . 1 .   . . . .  = Beginning of message
VSPP:             . . . 0   . . . .  = Do not abort current message
VSPP:             . . . .   0 0 0 0  = Unused
VSPP:
VSPP:          Local connection ID  = 0011
VSPP:          Remote connection ID = 0027
VSPP:
VSPP:          Sequence number  = 852
VSPP:          Acknowledgment number = 872
```

```
VSPP:       Window = 876
VSPP:
SMB:        - - - - - SMB Search Directory Command - - - - -
SMB:
SMB:        Function = 81 (Search Directory)
SMB:        Tree id (TID) = 002A
SMB:        Process id   (PID) = 0E67
SMB:        File pathname = "\TEMP\????????.???"
SMB:        Maximum number of search entries to return = 25
SMB:        Attribute flags = 0008
SMB:        . . . .   . . . .    . . 0 .   . . . .   = File(s) not changed since last archive
SMB:        . . . .   . . . .    . . . 0   . . . .   = No directory file(s)
SMB:        . . . .   . . . .    . . . .   1 . . .   = Volume label info
SMB:        . . . .   . . . .    . . . .   . 0 . .   = No system file(s)
SMB:        . . . .   . . . .    . . . .   . . 0 .   = No hidden file(s)
SMB:        . . . .   . . . .    . . . .   . . . 0   = No read only file(s)
SMB:
```

Trace 3.11.2b. VINES Packet Tunneling Details

3.11.3 Collisions on an Ethernet

Ethernet and IEEE 802.3 networks operate under a principle known as Carrier Sense, Multiple Access with Collision Detection (CSMA/CD). This means that any station wishing to transmit must first listen to the cable (i.e., carrier sense) to detect whether any other station is transmitting. If the station hears no other signals, it may proceed. Otherwise, it must repeat the carrier sense process later. During periods of heavy traffic, several stations may be waiting for the station to complete its transmission. If those stations make the carrier sense test simultaneously, different stations may conclude that the cable is not in use and that it's OK to proceed. When this happens, signals from the two stations collide, neither transmits data and precious bandwidth is wasted. In short, everyone loses. Collisions also become self-perpetuating; as more stations collide, more bandwidth is wasted, more stations need to transmit, and so on. These collisions may occur on any Ethernet or 802.3 network, regardless of the higher-layer protocol in use, because they are a hardware or electrical signal phenomenon.

In this case study, an Ethernet is running a mixture of DECnet and Internet protocols, such as TCP (see Trace 3.11.3a). We chose this protocol/hardware combination because when the TCP/IP protocols were developed in the 1970s, Ethernet networks were by far the most common LAN solution; therefore, TCP/IP and Ethernet are frequently associated. Thus, if you have TCP/IP you probably have some Ethernet networks (and vice versa), and you'll probably see collisions.

Let's see how such collisions would appear on a network analyzer. Without warning, frames appear with no identifiable Source or Destination address (see Frames 5, 9, 12, 14, 18, 19, etc.). The network analyzer places question marks (????????????) in place of the normal 12 hexadecimal characters since it cannot decode that information. The summary of the frame (on the right hand side of the trace) indicates that the highest layer within that frame is the Data Link Control (DLC) Layer. This means that the analyzer was also unable to decode any data from the frame's Information field. Note the BAD FRAME indication in the summary.

The details of Frames 18 and 19 (see Trace 3.11.3b) yield little additional information. Both frames are fragments (less than the required 64 octets in length) and have bad alignment, which indicates that the frame does not contain an integral number of octets. There are two clues, however. The first is in the hexadecimal decode of the Address fields. In Frame 18, the decoded data is all ONEs (FF FF FF. . .), indicating that it may have been a Broadcast frame with the Destination address intended to be FFFFFFFFFFFFH. In Frame 19, part of the Destination address is 01 04 80H. Unfortunately, neither of the fragments contains enough information to decode the Source address. If you know the Source address, you might be able to fix the problem by swapping in a new network interface card (assuming the collisions were caused by a faulty CSMA/CD controller chip on the card). The second clue is the time stamp at the top of the trace file (10:18:08). This indicates that the collisions occurred at 10:18 AM. On most networks, the heavy traffic periods are between 10:00 and 11:00 AM and between 2:00 and 3:00 PM. The network administrator could study the network for several days and determine whether the collisions were more prevalent during these peak periods. If so, the administrator could logically segment the network with a bridge to isolate the traffic between the bridged segments. Such bridging would improve overall network performance and reduce collisions.

Sniffer Network Analyzer data 26-Jan-89 at 10:18:08, file COLSN.ENC, Pg 1

SUMMARY	Delta T	Destination	Source	Summary
M 1		DECnet002130	DECnet001F30	Ethertype=6007 (DEC LAVC)
2	0.0334	01048003C04D	820D00008000	Ethertype=825E (Unknown)
3	0.0312	Sun 0A508D	3Com 02D383	TCP D=3184 S=6000
				ACK=191069101
				SEQ=1600831189
				LEN=32 WIN=11557
4	0.0001	01048003C04D	821100008000	Ethertype=825E (Unknown)
5	0.0318	????????????	????????????	DLC, BAD FRAME, size=8 bytes
6	0.0094	01048003C04D	820A00008000	Ethertype=825E (Unknown)
7	0.0116	3Com 02D383	Sun 0A508D	TCP D=6000 S=3184
				ACK=1600831221
				SEQ=191069101
				LEN=40 WIN=4096
8	0.0014	Sun 0A508D	3Com 02D383	TCP D=3184 S=6000
				ACK=191069141
				WIN=11517
9	0.0161	????????????	????????????	DLC, BAD FRAME, size=7 bytes
10	0.0087	DECnet000130	0000C9007311	LAT C Data D=9301 S=7E13
				NR=92 NS=62 Len=2
11	0.0654	3Com 05D2DB	0080D3004852	ATP C ID=2196 LEN=6
12	0.0201	????????????	????????????	DLC, BAD FRAME, size=2 bytes
13	0.0083	3Com 05D2DB	0080D3004852	ATP D ID=2196
14	0.0656	????????????	????????????	DLC, BAD FRAME, size=5 bytes
15	0.0051	0000C9007311	DECnet000130	LAT R Data D=7E13 S=9301
				NR=64 NS=95 Len=15
16	0.0758	KinetxA09827	3Com 4DE473	NBP C Request ID=31
17	0.0013	DECnet000130	0000C9007311	LAT C Data D=9301 S=7E13
				NR=95 NS=65 Len=3
18	0.0223	????????????	????????????	DLC, BAD FRAME, size=5 bytes
19	0.0292	????????????	????????????	DLC, BAD FRAME, size=3 bytes
20	0.0168	0000C9007311	Cisco 006A04	Telnet R PORT=5112 u
21	0.0051	01048003C04D	820A00008000	Ethertype=825E (Unknown)
22	0.0039	????????????	????????????	RI Invalid length
23	0.0191	A5B191A5B99D	80D0A195818C	Ethertype=BDC9 (Unknown)
24	0.0281	01048003C04D	820A00008000	Ethertype=825E (Unknown)
25	0.0190	Sun 0A508D	3Com 02D383	TCP D=3184 S=6000
				ACK=191069141
				SEQ=1600831221
				LEN=32 WIN=11557

26	0.0088	Sun	0A508D	3Com	02D383	TCP D=3184 S=6000
						ACK=191069181 WIN=11517
27	0.0054	DECnet000130		0000C9007311		LAT C Data D=9301 S=7E13
						NR=97 NS=67 Len=3
28	0.0244	???????????		???????????		DLC, BAD FRAME, size=11 bytes

Trace 3.11.3a. Ethernet Collision Summary

Sniffer Network Analyzer data 26-Jan-89 at 10:18:08, file COLSN.ENC, Pg 1

```
- - - - - - - - - - - - - - - Frame 18 - - - - - - - - - - - - - - - -
DLC:   —— DLC Header ——
DLC:
DLC:   Frame 18 arrived at  10:18:09.6937; frame size is 5 (0005 hex) bytes.
DLC:   FRAME ERROR= Fragment   Bad alignment
DLC:

ADDR  HEX                        ASCII
0000    FF FF FF FF FF              .....
- - - - - - - - - - - - - - - Frame 19 - - - - - - - - - - - - - - - -
DLC:   —— DLC Header ——
DLC:
DLC:   Frame 19 arrived at  10:18:09.7229; frame size is 3 (0003 hex) bytes.
DLC:   FRAME ERROR= Fragment   Bad alignment
DLC:

ADDR  HEX                        ASCII
0000    01 04 80                   ...
```

Trace 3.11.3b. Ethernet Collision Details

3.11.4 Incompatibilities Between Ethernet and IEEE 802.3 Frames

Technical standards assure that all parties involved with a project or procedure can communicate accurately. This "communication" could be a bolt communicating with a nut (adhering to the same number of threads per inch) or a terminal communicating with a host computer (adhering to the same character set, such as ASCII). Unfortunately, the Ethernet world has two separate standards that are both loosely termed "Ethernet." The original Ethernet, last published in 1982 by DEC, Intel, and Xerox, is called the "Blue Book." The second standard, IEEE 802.3, accommodates elements of the other IEEE LAN standards, such as the IEEE 802.2 Logical Link Control header.

In this case study, a user tries to access some higher-layer TCP/IP functions, TCP-CON, but he can't because the lower layer connection had failed due to the confusion of the two Ethernets on the internet. Let's see what happened.

In Section 2.7, we discussed Novell's NetWare operating system and its TCP/IP Transport facility. TCPCON, which is one of TCP/IP's functions, provides SNMP-based management functions through the server's console. To access TCPCON, the user logs into the server from his workstation, executes the remote console (RCON-SOLE) command, then loads TCPCON.

The internetwork topology consists of several Ethernet segments that connect a number of devices. The NetWare server doubles as an IP router and connects to both local and remote hosts (see Figure 3-13). The network administrator (David, shown in Trace 3.11.4a) wishes to access TCPCON to check some SNMP statistics at the remote host. He must first log in to his NetWare server. Looking for the nearest file server, he broadcasts a NetWare Core Protocol (NCP) packet in Frame 1, then repeats the request every 0.6 seconds. But he receives no response.

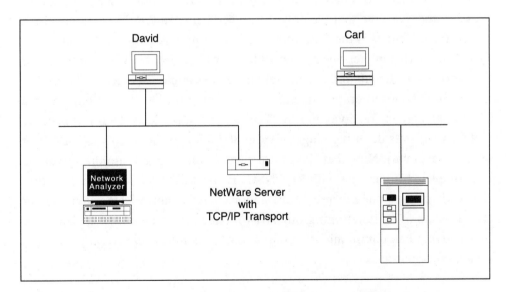

Figure 3-13. IEEE 802.3 Network with Novell NetWare and TCP/IP

Trace 3.11.4b shows the details of the NCP Nearest Service Query and indicates that David's workstation (address H-P 06CA73) was transmitting an Ethernet frame. We know this because the frame header contains an EtherType (8137H) instead of a Length field. David realizes that the server was configured for IEEE 802.3 framing and speculates that the problem might be a frame incompatibility. He reconfigures the workstation by editing the Protocol.ini file to include a driver (IPXDRV.DOS) that accepts the IEEE 802.3 frame type.

A second attempt (Trace 3.11.4c) proves successful. David's workstation requests the nearest server and receives a response from five: NW Svr 2, NW Svr 3, H-P 133A5B, NW Svr 1, and H-P 136A06 (Frames 2 through 6). The NCP algorithm then selects the first responding server (NW Svr 2, shown in Frame 2) and creates a connection to that server in Frame 9. The connection is confirmed and a buffer size accepted in Frames 10 through 12. David is now logged in to the server and can finish gathering the SNMP statistics. Trace 3.11.4d examines the NCP Nearest Service Query packet after the workstation reconfiguration. Note that the EtherType field has been replaced with the 802.3 length = 34 octets. All other aspects of the frame are identical. Reviewing Figures 3-3 and 3-4, note that the only difference between the Ethernet and IEEE 802.3 frame formats is the field following the Source Address: Ethernet specifies the Type (the higher-layer protocol type, in this case, NetWare) while IEEE 802.3 counts the length of the Data field (in this example, 34 octets). The receiving station cannot tolerate a mistake in the frame format. If it is expecting a length (0022H) and receives an EtherType (8137H), it rejects the frame because that frame is outside of the range of valid 802.3 length fields (0000-05DCH or 46-1500 decimal). Now that David has successfully logged into the server, he can complete his business with RCONSOLE and TCPCON. Moral of the story: If a newly configured "Ethernet" workstation cannot communicate with its server (but appears to be functioning otherwise), check the frame format. Until the lower layers can communicate, you cannot transmit or receive any TCP/IP-related information.

Sniffer Network Analyzer data 31-Jan-92 at 4:54:50, file ETHERNET.ENC, Pg 1

SUMMARY	Delta T	Destination	Source	Summary
M 1		Broadcast	David	NCP C Find nearest file server
2	0.5503	Broadcast	David	NCP C Find nearest file server
3	0.6042	Broadcast	David	NCP C Find nearest file server
4	0.6042	Broadcast	David	NCP C Find nearest file server
5	0.6042	Broadcast	David	NCP C Find nearest file server
6	0.6042	Broadcast	David	NCP C Find nearest file server
7	0.6042	Broadcast	David	NCP C Find nearest file server
8	0.6042	Broadcast	David	NCP C Find nearest file server
9	0.6042	Broadcast	David	NCP C Find nearest file server
10	0.6042	Broadcast	David	NCP C Find nearest file server
11	0.6042	Broadcast	David	NCP C Find nearest file server
12	0.6042	Broadcast	David	NCP C Find nearest file server

Trace 3.11.4a. Attempted TCPCON Login Summary

Sniffer Network Analyzer data 31-Jan-92 at 4:54:50 file ETHERNET.ENC, Pg 1

- - - - - - - - - - - - - - - Frame 1 - - - - - - - - - - - - - - - -
```
DLC:  ------ DLC Header ------
DLC:
DLC:  Frame 1 arrived at  14:54:52.9662; frame size is 60 (003C hex) bytes.
DLC:  Destination = BROADCAST FFFFFFFFFFFF, Broadcast
DLC:  Source    = Station H-P  06CA73, David
DLC:  Ethertype = 8137 (Novell)
DLC:
XNS:  ------ XNS Header ------
XNS:
XNS:  Checksum = FFFF
XNS:  Length = 34
XNS:  Transport control = 00
XNS:        00C0 .... = Reserved
XNS:        .... 0000 = Hop count
XNS:  Packet type = 17 (Novell NetWare)
XNS:
XNS:  Dest  net = 00000000, host = FFFFFFFFFFFF,
      socket = 1106 (NetWare Service Advertising)
```

XNS: Source net = 00000000, host = 08000906CA73, socket = 16390 (4006)
XNS:
NCP: ——— NetWare Nearest Service Query ———
NCP:
NCP: Server type = 0004 (file server)

Trace 3.11.4b. Attempted NetWare Server/TCPCON Login Details

Sniffer Network Analyzer data 31-Jan-92 at 4:47:46, file IEEE802.ENC, Pg 1

SUMMARY	Delta T	Destination	Source	Summary
M 1		Broadcast	David	NCP C Find nearest file server
2	0.0008	David	NW Svr 2	NCP R ISD
3	0.0003	David	NW Svr 3	NCP R HR
4	0.0004	David	H-P 133A5B	NCP R GL
5	0.0002	David	NW Svr 1	NCP R IC2
6	0.0001	David	H-P 136A06	NCP R ICTEMP
7	0.0018	Broadcast	David	XNS RIP request:
				find 1 network, 00133ADE
8	0.0005	David	NW Svr 2	XNS RIP response:
				1 network, 00133ADE at 1 hop
9	0.0012	NW Svr 2	David	NCP C Create Connection
10	0.0034	David	NW Svr 2	NCP R OK
11	0.0013	NW Svr 2	David	NCP C Propose buffer size
				of 1024
12	0.0004	David	NW Svr 2	NCP R OK Accept buffer
				size of 1024
13	0.0300	David	H-P 11D4BD	NCP R H2O
14	0.0016	David	H-P 133A76	NCP R BOOKS
15	0.0272	NW Svr 2	David	NCP C Logout
16	0.0023	David	H-P 138AAA	NCP R OLD
17	0.0008	David	NW Svr 2	NCP R OK
18	0.0012	NW Svr 2	David	NCP C Get server's clock
19	0.0004	David	NW Svr 2	NCP R OK

Trace 3.11.4c. Successful NetWare Server Login Summary

Sniffer Network Analyzer data 31-Jan-92 at 4:47:46, file IEEE802.ENC, Pg 1

- - - - - - - - - - - - - - - Frame 1 - - - - - - - - - - - - - - - -
DLC: ——- DLC Header ——-
DLC:
DLC: Frame 1 arrived at 14:48:13.7824; frame size is 60 (003C hex) bytes.
DLC: Destination = BROADCAST FFFFFFFFFFFF, Broadcast
DLC: Source   = Station H-P   06CA73, David
DLC: 802.3 length = 34
DLC:
XNS: ——- XNS Header ——-
XNS:
XNS: Checksum = FFFF
XNS: Length = 34
XNS: Transport control = 00
XNS: 0000 . . . . = Reserved
XNS: . . . . 0000 = Hop count
XNS: Packet type = 17 (Novell NetWare)
XNS:
XNS: Dest   net = 00000000, host = FFFFFFFFFFFF,
         socket = 1106 (NetWare Service Advertising)
XNS: Source net = 00000000, host = 08000906CA73, socket = 16390 (4006)
XNS:
NCP: ——- NetWare Nearest Service Query ——-
NCP:
NCP: Server type = 0004 (file server)

Trace 3.11.4d. Successful NetWare Server Login Details

3.11.5 Transmitting IP Datagrams Over a PSPDN

In Section 3.8, we discussed the principles behind sending IP datagrams over a
Packet Switched Public Data Network (PSPDN) using the X.25 protocol. In this
case study (see Figure 3-14), we will examine the interactions between TCP/IP and
the Internet protocols with the X.25 protocol.

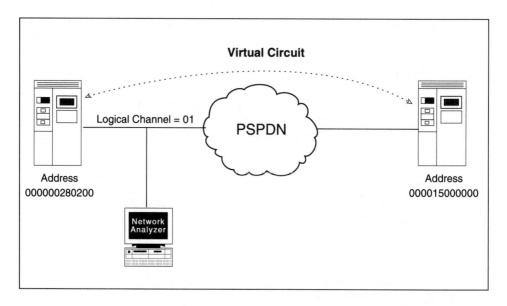

Figure 3-14. Internet Protocols over a PSPDN

To begin, recall that X.25 defines an interface between a packet mode DTE (the user) and a DCE (the network). To capture the internetwork transmission, you must place the analyzer at the DTE/DCE interface. Before any higher-layer (e.g., IP) data can be transmitted, an X.25 Virtual Call must be established end to end between the two hosts via the network. Trace 3.11.5a reveals that this occurs in Frame 79; it is an X.25 Call Request packet, transmitted on Logical Channel 001 and destined for remote host 000015000000. The X.25 packet, shown in Trace 3.11.5b, contains a Protocol Identification field within the Call User Data field that identifies the higher-layer protocol in use. The value of CCH in the Protocol Identification field tells the destination address (000015000000) that the sender (000000280200) will be using IP. Frame 80 contains a Data Link Layer response (from LAPB, but shown as HDLC in the trace. LAPB is a derivative of HDLC so the *Sniffer* has given it the generic name). The destination node's Packet Level response is received in Frame 81 (Call Accepted). The DCE Link Level sends an acknowledgement in Frame 83, and data transfer begins in Frame 84. The data is transmitted on Logical Channel 01 as a single packet (More data bit = 0). Note that the total length of the IP datagram is 46 octets, so it fits completely within the X.25 default packet length of 128 octets. The IP header identifies the protocol within that datagram as the Interior Gateway Protocol (IGP). The internet source address (XXX.YYY.165.2) is broadcasting the IGP information to all hosts on this network (destination address 255.255.255.255). Frame 85 contains a Packet Level acknowledgement (Receive Ready), indicating receipt of the packet at the local X.25 interface. We know that this acknowledgement did not come from the distant host because the Delivery Confirmation bit within the Packet Level header = 0. The value (0) indicates local acknowledgements, a positive value (1) indicates remote (i.e., distant host) acknowledgements.

Returning to the data summary (Trace 3.11.5a), we can observe a communication problem between the Source and Destination hosts. In Frame 87, the local host requests a file using the Trivial File Transfer Protocol (TFTP) described in Chapter 6. (Read Request File = network-conf). Three seconds later, it repeats the request (Frame 89). The DTE process appears to be functioning properly since the packet sequence counter is incrementing correctly (PS = 2 in Frame 87, PS = 3 in Frame 89). The local DCE's Packet Level process acknowledges the request with PR = 4 in Frame 90, but never responds with the requested file. The DTE makes a fourth attempt for the file in Frame 94, with equally disappointing results (Frame 95). Undaunted, the DTE requests a different file (cyg-x1-confg) in Frame 97. Three tries later (Frame 104) this file has yet to be received.

The local DTE makes a second Call Request, this time using Logical Channel 002 (Frame 107). By now the local DCE is completely confused and responds with a Clear Request (Frame 109), which is confirmed by the DTE in Frame 111.

The trace file does not identify the exact source of the problem, but it appears to be at the local DTE/DCE interface. The DTE is not the likely culprit since its processes appear to know what they want and have demonstrated patience in their repeated requests. At this point, the network administrator should enlist the aid of the PSPDN analysis center to isolate the problem with the DCE side of the X.25 interface.

Sniffer Network Analyzer data 19-Oct-89 at 15:09:24, file CISX251.SYC Pg 1

SUMMARY	Delta T	From DCE	From DTE
79	6.7309		HDLC R I NR=1 NS=1 P/F=0
			X.25 001 Call Req
			Dst:000015000000

						Src:000000280200 TCP_IP
80	0.0085	HDLC C RR	NR=2		P/F=0	
81	0.0099	HDLC R I	NR=2 NS=1 P/F=0			
		X.25 001 Call Acc				
82	0.0583					HDLC R I NR=2 NS=2 P/F=0
						X.25 001 Data PR=0 PS=0
						IP D=[255.255.255.255]
						S=[131.100.165.2]
						LEN=26 ID=0
83	0.0086	HDLC C RR	NR=3		P/F=0	
84	1.3943					HDLC R I NR=2 NS=3 P/F=0
						X.25 001 Data PR=0 PS=1
						IP D=[255.255.255.255]
						S=[131.100.165.2]
						LEN=26 ID=0
85	0.0112	HDLC R I	NR=4 NS=2 P/F=0			
		X.25 001 RR	PR=2			
86	0.0087					HDLC C RR NR=3 P/F=0
87	36.4935					HDLC R I NR=3 NS=4 P/F=0
						X.25 001 Data PR=0 PS=2
						IP D=[255.255.255.255]
						S=[131.100.165.2]
						LEN=33 ID=0
						UDP D=69 S=28624 LEN=33
						TFTP Read request
						File=network-confg
88	0.0092		HDLC C RR	NR=5 P/F=0		
89	3.0128					HDLC R I NR=3 NS=5 P/F=0
						X.25 001 Data PR=0 PS=3
						IP D=[255.255.255.255]
						S=[131.100.165.2]
						LEN=33 ID=1
						UDP D=69 S=28624 LEN=33
						TFTP Read request
						File=network-confg
90	0.0122		HDLC R I NR=6 NS=3 P/F=0			
			X.25 001 RR PR=4			

Trace 3.11.5a. X.25 Call Request and IP Data Transfer

Sniffer Network Analyzer data 19-Oct-89 at 15:09:24 file CISX251.SYC Pg 1

- - - - - - - - - - - - - - - Frame 79 - - - - - - - - - - - - - - - -
DLC: ——- DLC Header ——-
DLC:
DLC: Frame 79 arrived at 15:21:44.3950; frame size is 23 (0017 hex) bytes.
DLC: Destination = DCE
DLC: Source   = DTE
DLC:
HDLC: ——- High Level Data Link Control (HDLC) ——-
HDLC:
HDLC: Address = 03 (Response)
HDLC: Control field = 22
HDLC: 001. .... = N(R) = 1
HDLC: ...0 .... = Poll/Final bit
HDLC: .... 001. = N(S) = 1
HDLC: ....0 = I (Information transfer)
HDLC:
X.25: ——- X.25 Packet Level ——-
X.25:
X.25: General format id = 10
X.25:   .0.. .... = Delivery confirmation bit
X.25:   ..01 .... = Sequence numbering modulo 8
X.25:   .... 0000 = Logical channel group number = 0
X.25: Logical channel number = 01
X.25: Packet type identifier = 0B (Call request)
X.25: Address length field = CC
X.25:   1100 .... = Source length = 12 digits
X.25:   .... 1100 = Destination length = 12 digits
X.25: Destination address = 000015000000
X.25: Source address = 000000280200
X.25: Facility length = 0
X.25: Protocol identification = CC (TCP_IP)
X.25:
X.25: [4 bytes of user data = CC000000]
X.25:

- - - - - - - - - - - - - - - Frame 80 - - - - - - - - - - - - - - - -
DLC: ——- DLC Header ——-
DLC:
DLC: Frame 80 arrived at 15:21:44.4036; frame size is 2 (0002 hex) bytes.
DLC: Destination = DTE
DLC: Source   = DCE

DLC:
HDLC: ———— High Level Data Link Control (HDLC) ————
HDLC:
HDLC: Address = 03 (Command)
HDLC: Control field = 41
HDLC: 010. .... = N(R) = 2
HDLC: ...0 .... = Poll/Final bit
HDLC: .... 0001 = RR (Receive ready)
HDLC:

- - - - - - - - - - - - - - - - Frame 81 - - - - - - - - - - - - - - - - -
DLC: ———— DLC Header ————
DLC:
DLC: Frame 81 arrived at 15:21:44.4135; frame size is 5 (0005 hex) bytes.
DLC: Destination = DTE
DLC: Source   = DCE
DLC:
HDLC: ———— High Level Data Link Control (HDLC) ————
HDLC:
HDLC: Address = 01 (Response)
HDLC: Control field = 42
HDLC: 010. .... = N(R) = 2
HDLC: ...0 .... = Poll/Final bit
HDLC: .... 001. = N(S) = 1
HDLC: ....0 = I (Information transfer)
HDLC:
X.25: ———— X.25 Packet Level ————
X.25:
X.25:   General format id = 10
X.25:   .0.. .... = Delivery confirmation bit
X.25:   ..01 .... = Sequence numbering modulo 8
X.25:   .... 0000 = Logical channel group number = 0
X.25:   Logical channel number = 01
X.25:   Packet type identifier = 0F (Call accepted)
X.25:

- - - - - - - - - - - - - - - - Frame 82 - - - - - - - - - - - - - - - - -
DLC: ———— DLC Header ————
DLC:
DLC: Frame 82 arrived at 15:21:44.4719; frame size is 51 (0033 hex) bytes.
DLC: Destination = DCE
DLC: Source   = DTE
DLC:

```
HDLC: ——— High Level Data Link Control (HDLC) ———
HDLC:
HDLC: Address = 03 (Response)
HDLC: Control field = 44
HDLC:        010. .... = N(R) = 2
HDLC:        ...0 .... = Poll/Final bit
HDLC:        .... 010. = N(S) = 2
HDLC:        .... ...0 = I (Information transfer)
HDLC:
X.25: ——— X.25 Packet Level ———
X.25:
X.25: General format id = 10
X.25:        0....... = Qualifier bit
X.25:        .0...... = Delivery confirmation bit
X.25:        ..01.... = Sequence numbering modulo 8
X.25:        .... 0000 = Logical channel group number = 0
X.25: Logical channel number = 01
X.25: Data packet info = 00
X.25:        000. .... = P(R) = 0
X.25:        ...0 .... = More bit
X.25:        .... 000. = P(S) = 0
X.25:        .... ...0 = Packet type identifier (Data)
X.25:
IP:   ——— IP Header ———
IP:
IP:   Version = 4, header length = 20 bytes
IP:   Type of service = 00
IP:        000. .... = routine
IP:        ...0 .... = normal delay
IP:        .... 0... = normal throughput
IP:        .... .0.. = normal reliability
IP:   Total length = 46 bytes
IP:   Identification = 0
IP:   Flags = 0X
IP:   .0. .... = may fragment
IP:   ..0. .... = last fragment
IP:   Fragment offset = 0 bytes
IP:   Time to live = 2 seconds/hops
IP:   Protocol = 9 (IGP)
IP:   Header checksum = 9059 (correct)
IP:   Source address = [131.100.165.2]
IP:   Destination address = [255.255.255.255]
IP:   No options
```

IP: [26 byte(s) of data]

```
- - - - - - - - - - - - - - - Frame 83 - - - - - - - - - - - - - - - -
DLC:  —— DLC Header ——
DLC:
DLC:  Frame 83 arrived at  15:21:44.4805; frame size is 2 (0002 hex) bytes.
DLC:  Destination = DTE
DLC:  Source    = DCE
DLC:
HDLC: —— High Level Data Link Control (HDLC) ——
HDLC:
HDLC: Address = 03 (Command)
HDLC: Control field = 61
HDLC:   011. . . . . = N(R) = 3
HDLC:   . . . 0 . . . . = Poll/Final bit
HDLC:   . . . . 0001 = RR  (Receive ready)
HDLC:


- - - - - - - - - - - - - - - Frame 84 - - - - - - - - - - - - - - - -
DLC:  —— DLC Header ——
DLC:
DLC:  Frame 84 arrived at  15:21:45.8748; frame size is 51 (0033 hex) bytes.
DLC:  Destination = DCE
DLC:  Source    = DTE
DLC:
HDLC: —— High Level Data Link Control (HDLC) ——
HDLC:
HDLC: Address = 03 (Response)
HDLC: Control field = 46
HDLC:     010. . . . . = N(R) = 2
HDLC:     . . . 0 . . . . = Poll/Final bit
HDLC:     . . . . 011. = N(S) = 3
HDLC:     . . . . . . . 0 = I (Information transfer)
HDLC:
X.25:  —— X.25 Packet Level ——
X.25:
X.25:  General format id = 10
X.25:         0. . . . . . . = Qualifier bit
X.25:         .0. . . . . . = Delivery confirmation bit
X.25:         . .01 . . . . = Sequence numbering modulo 8
X.25:         . . . . 0000 = Logical channel group number = 0
X.25:  Logical channel number = 01
X.25:  Data packet info = 02
```

106

X.25:   000. . . . . = P(R) = 0
X.25:   . . .0 . . . . = More bit
X.25:   . . . . 001. = P(S) = 1
X.25:   . . . . . . .0 = Packet type identifier (Data)
X.25:
IP: —— IP Header ——
IP:
IP: Version = 4, header length = 20 bytes
IP: Type of service = 00
IP: 000. . . . . = routine
IP: . . .0 . . . . = normal delay
IP: . . . . 0. . . = normal throughput
IP: . . . . .0. . = normal reliability
IP: Total length = 46 bytes
IP: Identification = 0
IP: Flags = 0X
IP: .0. . . . . . = may fragment
IP: . .0. . . . . = last fragment
IP: Fragment offset = 0 bytes
IP: Time to live = 2 seconds/hops
IP: Protocol = 9 (IGP)
IP: Header checksum = 9059 (correct)
IP: Source address = [131.100.165.2]
IP: Destination address = [255.255.255.255]
IP: No options
IP: [26 byte(s) of data]

- - - - - - - - - - - - - - - Frame 85 - - - - - - - - - - - - - - - -
DLC: —— DLC Header ——
DLC:
DLC: Frame 85 arrived at 15:21:45.8861; frame size is 5 (0005 hex) bytes.
DLC: Destination = DTE
DLC: Source   = DCE
DLC:
HDLC: —— High Level Data Link Control (HDLC) ——
HDLC:
HDLC: Address = 01 (Response)
HDLC: Control field = 84
HDLC: 100. . . . . = N(R) = 4
HDLC: . . .0 . . . . = Poll/Final bit
HDLC: . . . . 010. = N(S) = 2
HDLC: . . . . . . .0 = I (Information transfer)
HDLC:

```
X.25:    ——- X.25 Packet Level ——-
X.25:
X.25:    General format id = 10
X.25:           . . 01 . . . . = Sequence numbering modulo 8
X.25:           . . . . 0000 = Logical channel group number = 0
X.25:    Logical channel number = 01
X.25:    Flow control info = 41
X.25:    010 . . . . . = P(R) = 2
X.25:    . . . 0 0001 = Packet type identifier (Receive ready)
X.25:
```

Trace 3.11.5b. X.25 Call Request Details

3.11.6 Encapsulating IP Packets Inside AppleTalk Packets

In our final example, we will discuss another alternative for multiprotocol Internet connectivity: an AppleTalk gateway. As we discussed in Section 2.6, Apple developed the AppleTalk protocol suite, which is described in *Inside AppleTalk*, [3-39]. Apple supports the Internet protocols via a product called MacTCP which supports the Network and Transport Layers over LocalTalk (the 230 Kbps twisted pair network), Ethernet/IEEE 802.3, or token ring. In the internetwork shown in Figure 3-15, a FastPath DDP-to-IP gateway from Shiva Corp. (Cambridge, MA) connects a LocalTalk and an Ethernet network. The FastPath supports AppleTalk, TCP/IP, and DECnet protocols, plus SNMP network management.

In this example, a user (Jeff) is using an Apple PowerBook computer on the LocalTalk network, Apple's MacTCP software, and Intercon's TCP/Connect II application package. Jeff wishes to access a UNIX host on the Ethernet network. The process for the protocols is for Jeff's workstation to communicate with the FastPath using the AppleTalk protocols, the FastPath converts the AppleTalk to Internet protocols, then communicates to the UNIX host via the Ethernet network. If we were to place the network analyzer on the LocalTalk side, we would observe LocalTalk frames containing AppleTalk data; with the analyzer on the Ethernet side, we observe Ethernet frames containing TCP/IP data. Let's look and see.

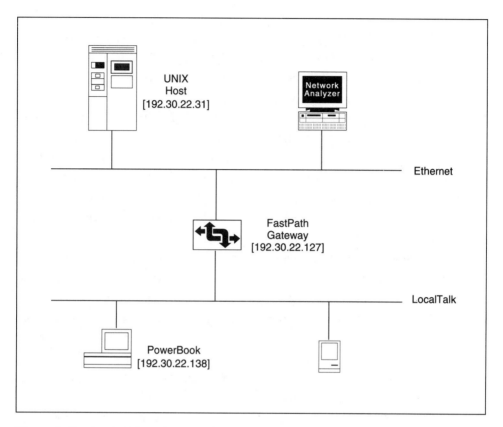

Figure 3-15. AppleTalk to Internet Gateway

With the analyzer on the Ethernet side, we can capture the communication between the Ethernet network card inside the FastPath and the Ethernet network card inside the UNIX host. Trace 3.11.6a shows a summary of these frames; extraneous traffic on the Ethernet network was filtered out for clarity. Beginning in Frame 9, Jeff initializes a TCP connection to the TELNET port on the remote host. The initialization is a three-way handshake, with Jeff asking for a connection (Frame 9), the host responding (Frame 10), and Jeff confirming the arrangement (Frame 11). Looking at the details of those frames (Trace 3.11.6b), the IP header contains the source of the data (Internet address 192.30.22.138, the Power-Book) and the designated destination, 192.30.22.31, the UNIX host. The TCP header addresses the destination process (Destination Port = 23 [TELNET]). The only clue that another protocol suite is in use is in the TCP options contained in

Frame 9. Note that the originating station (Jeff) requires a maximum TCP segment size of 536 octets, a constraint imposed by MacTCP. When the TCP segment size is added to the TCP header (20 octets) and the IP header (also 20 octets), a maximum IP datagram size of 576 octets results.

Returning to Trace 3.11.6a, we see the host begin the TELNET options negotiation process, first asking for Jeff's terminal type (Frame 12). Jeff's workstation requests a suppress go-ahead (Frame 15) and responds to the terminal type (Frame 18), plus other parameters (Frames 19 through 26). Jeff then signals the host to log in by hitting the carriage return and linefeed in succession <CR><LF>, which is represented in hexadecimal by <0D><0A> in Frame 29. The Host responds by asking for Jeff's login (Frame 30) and Jeff's workstation responds by sending the login (Guest) one character at a time (Frames 41 through 55). Note that the Host echoes each character (e.g., Frame 42) and that the workstation sends a TCP acknowledgement between each successive character (e.g., Frame 43). Jeff's workstation sends another <CR><LF> in Frame 57, prompting the host to request his password. The password (apple) is transferred one character at a time in Frames 71 through 87, but this time the host does not echo the password characters to the workstation. We only see a TCP acknowledgement from the host to Jeff between password characters. Now that the login and password are validated, Jeff may go about his business on the UNIX host.

In this chapter, we have laid the foundation for internetworking by looking into the many ways that the DARPA Network Interface Layer may be implemented on LANs, MANs, and WANs. In the next chapter, we will study the layer responsible for routing and addressing, the Internet Layer.

Sniffer Network Analyzer data 5-Feb-92 at 16:54:54, file DDPIP.ENC, Pg 1

SUMMARY	Delta T	Destination	Source	Summary
9		UNIX Host	FastPath	TCP D=23 S=28529
				SYN SEQ=3613179760
				LEN=0 WIN=10843
10	0.0012	FastPath	UNIX Host	TCP D=28529 S=23
				SYN ACK=3613179761
				SEQ=724864001
				LEN=0 WIN=4096

11	0.0170	UNIX Host	FastPath	TCP D=23 S=28529
				ACK=724864002 WIN=10843
12	0.0508	FastPath	UNIX Host	Telnet R PORT=28529
				IAC Do Terminal type
13	0.0166	UNIX Host	FastPath	TCP D=23 S=28529
				ACK=724864005 WIN=10840
15	0.2170	UNIX Host	FastPath	Telnet C PORT=28529
				IAC Do Suppress go-ahead
16	0.0013	FastPath	UNIX Host	Telnet R PORT=28529
				IAC Will Suppress go-ahead
17	0.0178	UNIX Host	FastPath	TCP D=23 S=28529
				ACK=724864008 WIN=10837
18	0.0143	UNIX Host	FastPath	Telnet C PORT=28529
				IAC Will Terminal type
19	0.0012	FastPath	UNIX Host	Telnet R PORT=28529
				IAC SB ...
20	0.0165	UNIX Host	FastPath	TCP D=23 S=28529
				ACK=724864014 WIN=10831
21	0.0809	UNIX Host	FastPath	Telnet C PORT=28529
				IAC SB ...
22	0.1126	FastPath	UNIX Host	TCP D=28529 S=23
				ACK=3613179782 WIN=4096
23	0.0018	FastPath	UNIX Host	Telnet R PORT=28529
				IAC Will Echo
24	0.0233	UNIX Host	FastPath	TCP D=23 S=28529
				ACK=724864059 WIN=10798
25	0.0232	UNIX Host	FastPath	Telnet C PORT=28529
				IAC Do Echo
26	0.1514	FastPath	UNIX Host	TCP D=28529 S=23
				ACK=3613179785 WIN=4096
29	0.6094	UNIX Host	FastPath	Telnet C PORT=28529 <0D><0A>
30	0.0036	FastPath	UNIX Host	Telnet R PORT=28529
				<0D><0A>login:
32	0.0193	UNIX Host	FastPath	TCP D=23 S=28529
				ACK=724864068 WIN=10834
41	0.5279	UNIX Host	FastPath	Telnet C PORT=28529 G
42	0.0026	FastPath	UNIX Host	Telnet R PORT=28529 G
43	0.0169	UNIX Host	FastPath	TCP D=23 S=28529
				ACK=724864069 WIN=10842
44	0.2052	UNIX Host	FastPath	Telnet C PORT=28529 u
45	0.0025	FastPath	UNIX Host	Telnet R PORT=28529 u
46	0.0171	UNIX Host	FastPath	TCP D=23 S=28529
				ACK=724864070 WIN=10842

47	0.0831	UNIX Host	FastPath	Telnet C PORT=28529 e
48	0.0025	FastPath	UNIX Host	Telnet R PORT=28529 e
49	0.0171	UNIX Host	FastPath	TCP D=23 S=28529
				ACK=724864071 WIN=10841
51	0.1882	UNIX Host	FastPath	Telnet C PORT=28529 s
52	0.0026	FastPath	UNIX Host	Telnet R PORT=28529 s
53	0.0170	UNIX Host	FastPath	TCP D=23 S=28529
				ACK=724864072 WIN=10842
54	0.2058	UNIX Host	FastPath	Telnet C PORT=28529 t
55	0.0026	FastPath	UNIX Host	Telnet R PORT=28529 t
56	0.0163	UNIX Host	FastPath	TCP D=23 S=28529
				ACK=724864073 WIN=10842
57	0.3692	UNIX Host	FastPath	Telnet C PORT=28529 <0D><0A>
58	0.0077	FastPath	UNIX Host	Telnet R PORT=28529 <0D><0A>
59	0.0166	UNIX Host	FastPath	TCP D=23 S=28529
				ACK=724864075 WIN=10841
64	0.2520	FastPath	UNIX Host	Telnet R PORT=28529 Password:
65	0.0170	UNIX Host	FastPath	TCP D=23 S=28529
				ACK=724864084 WIN=10834
71	0.3686	UNIX Host	FastPath	Telnet C PORT=28529 a
72	0.0282	FastPath	UNIX Host	TCP D=28529 S=23
				ACK=3613179795 WIN=4096
73	0.1660	UNIX Host	FastPath	Telnet C PORT=28529 p
74	0.0339	FastPath	UNIX Host	TCP D=28529 S=23
				ACK=3613179796 WIN=4096
75	0.1594	UNIX Host	FastPath	Telnet C PORT=28529 p
76	0.0405	FastPath	UNIX Host	TCP D=28529 S=23
				ACK=3613179797 WIN=4096
85	0.1536	UNIX Host	FastPath	Telnet C PORT=28529 l
86	0.0463	FastPath	UNIX Host	TCP D=28529 S=23
				ACK=3613179798 WIN=4096
87	0.1245	UNIX Host	FastPath	Telnet C PORT=28529 e
91	0.0754	FastPath	UNIX Host	TCP D=28529 S=23
				ACK=3613179799 WIN=4096
92	0.0850	UNIX Host	FastPath	Telnet C PORT=28529 <0D><0A>
93	0.0048	FastPath	UNIX Host	Telnet R PORT=28529 <0D><0A>
94	0.0164	UNIX Host	FastPath	TCP D=23 S=28529
				ACK=724864086 WIN=10841
95	0.5532	FastPath	UNIX Host	Telnet R PORT=28529
				<0D><0A>**********
96	0.0309	UNIX Host	FastPath	TCP D=23 S=28529
				ACK=724864495 WIN=10434

97	0.7618	FastPath	UNIX Host	Telnet R PORT=28529
				TERM = (vt100)
98	0.0172	UNIX Host	FastPath	TCP D=23 S=28529
				ACK=724864510 WIN=10828

Trace 3.11.6a. AppleTalk to Internet Gateway Summary

Sniffer Network Analyzer data 5-Feb-92 at 16:54:54, file DDPIP.ENC, Pg 1

- - - - - - - - - - - - - - - - Frame 9 - - - - - - - - - - - - - - - - -
DLC: ——- DLC Header ——-
DLC:
DLC: Frame 9 arrived at 16:54:58.1627; frame size is 60 (003C hex) bytes.
DLC: Destination = Station 1000E0019B07, UNIX Host
DLC: Source   = Station KinetxA13296, FastPath
DLC: Ethertype = 0800 (IP)
DLC:
IP: ——- IP Header ——-
IP:
IP: Version = 4, header length = 20 bytes
IP: Type of service = 00
IP: 000. . . . . = routine
IP: . . .0 . . . . = normal delay
IP: . . . . 0. . . = normal throughput
IP: . . . . .0. . = normal reliability
IP: Total length = 44 bytes
IP: Identification = 352
IP: Flags = 0X
IP: .0. . . . . . = may fragment
IP: . .0. . . . . = last fragment
IP: Fragment offset = 0 bytes
IP: Time to live = 59 seconds/hops
IP: Protocol = 6 (TCP)
IP: Header checksum = D186 (correct)
IP: Source address = [192.30.22.138]
IP: Destination address = [192.30.22.31]
IP: No options
IP:
TCP: ——- TCP header ——-
TCP:
TCP: Source port = 28529
TCP: Destination port = 23 (Telnet)

113

```
TCP:    Initial sequence number = 3613179760
TCP:    Data offset = 24 bytes
TCP:    Flags = 02
TCP:    ..0. .... = (No urgent pointer)
TCP:    ...0 .... = (No acknowledgment)
TCP:    .... 0... = (No push)
TCP:    .... .0.. = (No reset)
TCP:    .... ..1. = SYN
TCP:    .... ...0 = (No FIN)
TCP:    Window = 10843
TCP:    Checksum = BE2B (correct)
TCP:
TCP:    Options follow
TCP:    Maximum segment size = 536
TCP:


- - - - - - - - - - - - - - - - Frame 10 - - - - - - - - - - - - - - - -
DLC:    ------ DLC Header ------
DLC:
DLC:    Frame 10 arrived at  16:54:58.1640; frame size is 60 (003C hex) bytes.
DLC:    Destination = Station KinetxA13296, FastPath
DLC:    Source     = Station 1000E0019B07, UNIX Host
DLC:    Ethertype  = 0800 (IP)
DLC:
IP:     ------ IP Header ------
IP:
IP:     Version = 4, header length = 20 bytes
IP:     Type of service = 00
IP:           000. .... = routine
IP:           ...0 .... = normal delay
IP:           .... 0... = normal throughput
IP:           .... .0.. = normal reliability
IP:     Total length = 44 bytes
IP:     Identification = 2082
IP:     Flags = 0X
IP:     .0.. .... = may fragment
IP:     ..0. .... = last fragment
IP:     Fragment offset = 0 bytes
IP:     Time to live = 30 seconds/hops
IP:     Protocol = 6 (TCP)
IP:     Header checksum = E7C4 (correct)
IP:     Source address = [192.30.22.31]
IP:     Destination address = [192.30.22.138]
```

```
IP:      No options
IP:
TCP:     ——- TCP header ——-
TCP:
TCP:     Source port = 23 (Telnet)
TCP:     Destination port = 28529
TCP:     Initial sequence number = 724864001
TCP:     Acknowledgment number = 3613179761
TCP:     Data offset = 24 bytes
TCP:     Flags = 12
TCP:     ..0. .... = (No urgent pointer)
TCP:     ...1 .... = Acknowledgment
TCP:     .... 0... = (No push)
TCP:     .... .0.. = (No reset)
TCP:     .... ..1. = SYN
TCP:     .... ...0 = (No FIN)
TCP:     Window = 4096
TCP:     Checksum = 1F58 (correct)
TCP:
TCP:     Options follow
TCP:     Maximum segment size = 1024
TCP:


- - - - - - - - - - - - - - - - Frame 11 - - - - - - - - - - - - - - - - -
DLC:     ——- DLC Header ——-
DLC:
DLC:     Frame 11 arrived at  16:54:58.1810; frame size is 60 (003C hex) bytes.
DLC:     Destination = Station 1000E0019B07, UNIX Host
DLC:     Source     = Station KinetxA13296, FastPath
DLC:     Ethertype  = 0800 (IP)
DLC:
IP:      ——- IP Header ——-
IP:
IP:      Version = 4, header length = 20 bytes
IP:      Type of service = 00
IP:          000. .... = routine
IP:          ...0 .... = normal delay
IP:          .... 0... = normal throughput
IP:          .... .0.. = normal reliability
IP:      Total length = 40 bytes
IP:      Identification = 353
IP:      Flags = 0X
IP:      .0. .... = may fragment
```

IP: . . 0 . . . . . = last fragment
IP: Fragment offset = 0 bytes
IP: Time to live = 59 seconds/hops
IP: Protocol = 6 (TCP)
IP: Header checksum = D189 (correct)
IP: Source address = [192.30.22.138]
IP: Destination address = [192.30.22.31]
IP: No options
IP:
TCP: ——- TCP header ——-
TCP:
TCP: Source port = 28529
TCP: Destination port = 23 (Telnet)
TCP: Sequence number = 3613179761
TCP: Acknowledgment number = 724864002
TCP: Data offset = 20 bytes
TCP: Flags = 10
TCP: . . 0 . . . . . = (No urgent pointer)
TCP: . . . 1 . . . . = Acknowledgment
TCP: . . . . 0 . . . = (No push)
TCP: . . . . . 0 . . = (No reset)
TCP: . . . . . . 0 . = (No SYN)
TCP: . . . . 0 = (No FIN)
TCP: Window = 10843
TCP: Checksum = 1B06 (correct)
TCP: No TCP options
TCP:

Trace 3.11.6b. AppleTalk to Internet Gateway Details

3.12 References

[3-1]   Braden, R. "Requirements for Internet Hosts: Communication Layers."
          RFC 1122, Internet Engineering Task Force, October 1989.

[3-2]   *ARCNET Designer's Handbook*, Document 61610, Datapoint Corp., 2nd
          edition, 1988.

[3-3]   Dryden, Patrick. "ARCNET Heads for Official Sanction." *LAN Times*
          (November 4, 1991):1-89.

[3-4]   Provan, D. "Transmitting IP Traffic over ARCNET Networks." RFC 1201,
          Novell, Inc., February 1991.

[3-5]   *The Ethernet, A Local Area Network-Data Link Layer and Physical Layer
          Specification*, version 2.0, November 1982. Published by DEC, INTEL and
          XEROX, DEC document number AA-K759B-TK.

[3-6]   Institute of Electrical and Electronics Engineers. "Carrier Sense Multiple
          Access with Collision Detection (CSMA/CD) Access Method and Physi-
          cal Layer Specifications." ISO 8802-3, ANSI/IEEE Std 802.3, 1990.

[3-7]   Horning, Charles. "A Standard for the Transmission of IP Datagrams over
          Ethernet Networks." RFC 894, Symbolics Cambridge Research Center,
          April 1984.

[3-8]   Postel, J. and J. Reynolds. "A Standard for the Transmission of IP Data-
          grams over IEEE 802 Networks." RFC 1042, ISI, February 1988.

[3-9]   Institute of Electrical and Electronics Engineers. "Logical Link Control."
          ISO 8802-2, IEEE Standard 802.2, 1989.

[3-10]   Institute of Electrical and Electronics Engineers. "Overview and Architec-
          ture." IEEE Standard 802-1990, December 1990.

[3-11]   Institute of Electrical and Electronics Engineers. "Token Ring Access Method and Physical Layer Specification." IEEE Standard 802.5, 1989.

[3-12]   Institute of Electrical and Electronic Engineers. "Source Routing Supplement to IEEE 802.1d (MAC Bridges)." IEEE Standard P802.5M/D5, August 15, 1991.

[3-13]   Miller, Mark A. *Troubleshooting Internetworks.* San Mateo, CA: M&T Books, Inc., 1992.

[3-14]   Institute of Electrical and Electronics Engineers. "Distributed Queue Dual Bus (DQDB) Subnetwork of a Metropolitan Area Network (MAN)." ANSI/IEEE 802.6-1990, ISO DIS 8802-6, 1991.

[3-15]   Bell Communications Research, Inc. "Generic System Requirements in Support of Switched Multi-megabit Data Service." TR-TSV-000772, May 1991.

[3-16]   Piscitello, D. and J. Lawrence. "The Transmission of IP Datagrams over the SMDS Service." RFC 1209, Bell Communications Research, March 1991.

[3-17]   Cox, Tracy, et. al. "SMDS: The Beginning of WAN Superhighways." *Data Communications* (April 1991): 105-110.

[3-18]   American National Standards Institute. "Fiber Distributed Data Interface (FDDI)—Token Ring Media Access Control (MAC)." ANSI X3.139-1987.

[3-19]   Katz, D. "A Proposed Standard for the Transmission of IP Datagrams over FDDI Networks." RFC 1188, Merit/NSFNET, October 1990.

[3-20]   Ross, Floyd E., James R. Hamstra, Robert L. Fink. "FDDI: A LAN Among MANs." *Computer Communication Review* (July 1990): 16-31.

[3-21] Sherman, Doug. "Understanding FDDI: Standards, Features, and Applications." *3TECH, the 3Com Technical Journal* (Winter 1992): 18-31.

[3-22] Wolter, Mark S. "ANSI X3T9.5 Update: Future FDDI Standards." *ConneXions* (October 1991): 21-23.

[3-23] Romkey, J. "A Nonstandard for Transmission of IP Datagrams Over Serial Lines: SLIP." RFC 1055, June 1988.

[3-24] Perkins, D. "The Point-to-Point Protocol for the Transmission of Multi-Protocol Datagrams over Point-to-Point Links." RFC 1171, CMU, July 1990.

[3-25] Korb, J. T. "A Standard for the Transmission of IP Datagrams Over Public Data Networks." RFC 877, Purdue University, September 1983.

[3-26] Schlar, Sherman K. *Inside X.25: A Manager's Guide*. New York, NY: McGraw Hill, 1990.

[3-27] Bradley, T., et. al. "Multiprotocol Interconnect over Frame Relay." RFC 1294, Wellfleet Communications, Inc., January 1992.

[3-28] Bradley, T., et. al. "Inverse Address Resolution Protocol". RFC 1293, Wellfleet Communications, Inc., January 1992.

[3-29] Merritt, John. "The Future of Frame Relay." TE&M, (January 1, 1992): 33-35.

[3-30] American National Standards Institute. "Integrated Services Digital Network (ISDN)—Architectural Framework and Service Description for Frame-Relaying Bearer Service." T1.606, 1990.

[3-31] *Frame Relay Forum News*, published quarterly by The Frame Relay Forum, telephone (415) 962-2579.

[3-32] Taylor, Steven A. "Plain Talk About Frame Relay." *Networking Management* (January 1992): 1-60.

[3-33] Layland, Robin. "Public Frame Relay: The Price is Right." *Data Communications* (January 1992): 50-58.

[3-34] Johnson, Johna T. "Coping With Public Frame Relay: A Delicate Balance." *Data Communications* (January 21, 1992): 31-38.

[3-35] Jones, T., Rehbehn, K., Jennings, E. "The Buyer's Guide to Frame Relay Networking." Netrix Systems Corporation, 1991.

[3-36] Kessler, Gary C. and David A. Train. *Metropolitan Area Networks Concepts, Standards and Services*. New York, NY: McGraw-Hill, Inc., 1992.

[3-37] Hume, Sharon and Alison Seaman. "X.25 and Frame Relay: Packet Switched Technologies for Wide Area Connectivity." *3Tech, the 3Com Technical Journal* (Winter 1992): 33-45.

[3-38] Miller, Mark A. *LAN Troubleshooting Handbook*. San Mateo, CA: M&T Books, Inc., 1989.

[3-39] Sidhu, Gursharan, et. al. *Inside AppleTalk*. Second Edition. New York, NY: Addison-Wesley Publishing Company, Inc., 1990.

CHAPTER 4

Troubleshooting the Internetwork Connection

In the previous chapter, we discussed the options for the DARPA Network Interface (or Local Network) Layer, ranging from ARCNET to SMDS. In this chapter, we move up one layer in the DARPA architectural model and explore the Internet Layer. This layer is analogous to the OSI Network Layer and is responsible for delivering a package of data (known as a datagram) from its source to its destination via the internetwork. Note that this internetwork may include the Internet, a corporate internet or any of the LAN and WAN transmission channels that we studied in Chapter 3.

One of the principal functions of the Network Interface Layer is routing. Routing gets a data packet from one host to another via the internetwork. Several steps occur during the routing process. First, each device must have a logical address that uniquely identifies it within the internetwork. This internet address is independent of any Hardware or Physical address, such as the 48-bit Data Link Layer address of an Ethernet or token ring workstation. A mechanism is also necessary to associate the Logical address within the datagram with the Physical address within the LAN, MAN or WAN frame. The Address Resolution Protocol (ARP) and the Reverse Address Resolution Protocol (RARP) handle this translation.

Second, you may set up the Logical address to identify individual hosts and/or subnetworks (such as LANs) within a network. Third, you must distribute intelligent devices, known as routers, throughout the internetwork to guide the packets to their destination. Routers decide on the appropriate path for the packets to take by comparing address information from within the packet with information they have accumulated about the internetwork topology. The Routing Information Protocol (RIP) and the Open Shortest Path First (OSPF) protocol are two of the interior gateway protocols (IGP) that routers use to communicate among themselves. Reference [4-1] is an excellent overview of internetworking hardware; [4-2] discusses routing principles in general, and [4-3] studies IP routing in particular.

Finally, the Internet Control Message Protocol (ICMP) establishes a mechanism for performance feedback and communication within the internetwork. ICMP permits tests, diagnostic procedures, and flow control among various devices. Barry Shein's "The Internet Protocols: A Functional Overview" [4-4] is an excellent article that puts all of these protocols in perspective. We'll begin our study of the Internet Layer with the Internet Protocol.

4.1 Internet Protocol (IP)

The Internet Protocol (IP) was developed to "provide the functions necessary to deliver a package of bits (an internet datagram) from a source to a destination over an interconnected system of networks" [4-5]. IP is primarily concerned with delivery of the datagram. Equally important, however, are the issues that IP does not address, such as the end-to-end reliable delivery of data or the sequential delivery of data. IP leaves those issues for the Host-to-Host Layer and the implementations of TCP and UDP that reside there.

The term *datagram* refers to a package of data transmitted over a connectionless network. Connectionless means that no connection between source and destination is established prior to data transmission. Datagram transmission is analogous to mailing a letter. With both a letter and a datagram, you write a Source and Destination address on the envelope, place the information inside and drop the package into a mailbox for pickup. But while the post office uses blue or red mailboxes, the Internet uses your network node as the pickup point.

Another type of data transmission is a virtual circuit connection, which uses a connection-oriented network. A virtual circuit is analogous to a telephone call, where the Destination address is contacted and a path defined through the network prior to transmitting data. IP is an example of a datagram-based protocol, TCP of a virtual circuit-based protocol.

In the process of delivering datagrams, IP must deal with addressing and fragmentation. The address assures that the datagram arrives at the correct destination, whether it's across town or across the world. Notice from Figure 4-1a that unlike the Network Interface Layer, the Internet Layer must be implemented with a consistent protocol, such as the Internet Protocol, on an end-to-end basis for addressing consistency. Figure 4-1b illustrates the protocols implemented at the Internet Layer.

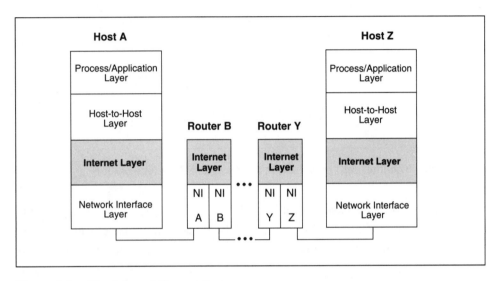

Figure 4-1a. The Internet Connection

DARPA Layer	Protocol Implementation						OSI Layer
Process / Application	File Transfer	Electronic Mail	Terminal Emulation	File Transfer	Client / Server	Network Management	Application
	File Transfer Protocol (FTP)	Simple Mail Transfer Protocol (SMTP)	TELNET Protocol	Trivial File Transfer Protocol (TFTP)	Sun Microsystems Network File System Protocols (NFS)	Simple Network Management Protocol (SNMP)	Presentation
	MIL-STD-1780 RFC 959	MIL-STD-1781 RFC 821	MIL-STD-1782 RFC 854	RFC 783	RFCs 1014, 1057, and 1094	RFC 1157	Session
Host-to-Host	Transmission Control Protocol (TCP) MIL-STD-1778 RFC 793			User Datagram Protocol (UDP) RFC 768			Transport
Internet	Address Resolution ARP RFC 826 RARP RFC 903		Internet Protocol (IP) MIL-STD-1777 RFC 791		Internet Control Message Protocol (ICMP) RFC 792		Network
Network Interface	Network Interface Cards: Ethernet, StarLAN, Token Ring, ARCNET RFC 894, RFC 1042, RFC 1201						Data Link
	Transmission Media: Twisted Pair, Coax, Fiber Optics, Wireless Media, etc.						Physical

Figure 4-1b. DARPA Internet Layer Protocols

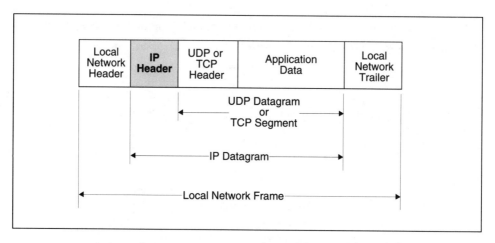

Figure 4-1c. The Internet Transmission Frame and IP Header Position

Fragmentation is necessary because the LANs and WANs that any datagram may traverse can have differing frame sizes, and the IP datagram must always fit within the frame, as shown in Figure 4-1c. (We saw this explicitly in the frame structures shown in Figures 3-2 through 3-11. For example, an ARCNET frame can accommodate only up to 504 octets of data, while FDDI carries up to 4,470 octets.) Specific fields within the IP header handle the addressing and fragmentation functions (see Figure 4-2). Note from the figure that each horizontal group of bits (called a word) is 32 bits wide.

```
                        1 1 1 1 1 1 1 1 1 1 2 2 2 2 2 2 2 2 2 2 3 3
    0 1 2 3 4 5 6 7 8 9 0 1 2 3 4 5 6 7 8 9 0 1 2 3 4 5 6 7 8 9 0 1   Bits
```

Ver	IHL	Type of Service	Total Length
Identifier		Flags	Fragment Offset
Time to Live	Protocol	Header Checksum	
Source Address			
Destination Address			
Options + Padding			

Figure 4-2. Internet Protocol (IP) Header Format

The IP header contains a minimum of 20 octets of control information. Version (4 bits) defines the current version of the IP protocol and should equal 4. Internet Header Length (IHL - 4 bits) measures the length of the IP header in 32-bit words. (The minimum value would be five 32-bit words, or 20 octets). The IHL also provides a measurement (or offset) where the higher-layer information, such as the TCP header, begins within that datagram. The Type of Service (8 bits) indicates the quality of service requested for the datagram. Values include:

Bits 0-2:	**Precedence (or relative importance of this datagram)**
	111 - Network Control
	110 - Internetwork Control
	101 - CRITIC/ECP
	100 - Flash Override
	011 - Flash
	010 - Immediate
	001 - Priority
	000 - Routine
Bit 3:	Delay, 0=Normal Delay, 1=Low Delay
Bit 4:	Throughput, 0=Normal Throughput, 1=High Throughput
Bit 5:	Reliability, 0=Normal Reliability, 1=High Reliability
Bits 6-7:	Reserved for future use (set to 0)

The Total Length field (16 bits) measures the length, in octets, of the IP datagram (IP header plus higher-layer information). The 16-bit field allows for a datagram of up to 65,535 octets, although all hosts must be able to handle datagrams of at least 576 octets.

The next 32-bit word contains three fields that deal with datagram fragmentation/reassembly. Recall that the IP datagram may be up to 65,535 octets long. What happens if the endpoint of a WAN that handles such a datagram is attached to an IEEE 802.3 LAN with a maximum data field size of 1,500 octets? IP fragments the large IP datagram into smaller pieces (i.e., fragments) that *will* fit. The Destination node reassembles all the fragments (sort of the antithesis of Humpty Dumpty). The sender assigns the Identification field (16 bits) to help reassemble the fragments into the datagram. Three flags indicate how the fragmentation process will be handled:

Bit 0:	Reserved (set to 0)
Bit 1:	(DF) 0=May fragment, 1-Don't fragment
Bit 2:	(MF) 0=Last fragment, 1-More fragments

The last field in this word is a 13-bit fragment offset, which indicates where a fragment belongs in the complete message. This offset is measured in 64-bit units. The case study in Section 4.8.2 will illustrate the fragmentation process.

The next word in the IP header contains a Time-to-Live (TTL) measurement, which is the maximum amount of time the datagram can live within the internet. When TTL=0, the datagram is destroyed. This field is a failsafe measure, preventing misaddressed datagrams from wandering the internet forever. TTL may be measured in either router hops or seconds. If the measurement is in seconds, the maximum is 255 seconds, or 4.25 minutes (a long time to be lost in today's high-speed internetworks).

The Protocol field (8 bits) following the IP header identifies the higher-layer protocol in use. Examples include:

Decimal	Keyword	Description
1	ICMP	Internet Control Message Protocol
6	TCP	Transmission Control Protocol
17	UDP	User Datagram Protocol

RFC 1340, "Assigned Numbers" [4-6] and Appendix G provide a more detailed listing of the protocols defined. A 16-bit header checksum completes the third 32-bit word.

The fourth and fifth words of the IP header contain the Source and Destination addresses, respectively. Recall that we discussed hardware addresses for the DARPA Network Interface Layer (or OSI Data Link Layer) in Chapter 3. The addresses within the IP header are the Internet Layer (or OSI Network Layer) addresses. The Internet address is a Logical address that gets the IP datagram through the Internet to the correct host and network (LAN, MAN, or WAN). Reference [4-7] is an excellent analysis of addressing schemes used within different LAN and WAN topologies, including X.25, IEEE 802, and IP. In the next section we will study IP addressing in detail.

4.2 Internetwork Addressing

Each 32-bit IP address is divided into Host ID and Network ID sections and may take one of five formats ranging from Class A to Class E, as shown in Figure 4-3. The formats differ in the number of bits they allocate to the Host IDs and Network IDs and are identified by the first 3 bits.

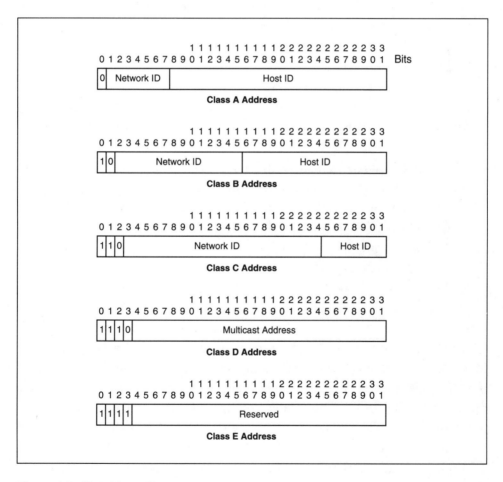

Figure 4-3. IP Address Formats

Class A addresses are designed for very large networks with many hosts. They are identified by Bit 0 = 0. Bits 1 through 7 identify the network, and Bits 8 through 31 identify the host. With a 7-bit Network ID, only 128 Class A addresses are available. Of these, addresses 0 and 127 are reserved [4-8].

The majority of organizations that have distributed processing systems that include LANs and hosts use Class B addresses. Class B addresses are identified with the first 2 bits having a value of 10 (binary). The next 14 bits identify the network. The remaining 16 bits identify the host. A total of 16,384 Class B addresses are possible, however addresses 0 and 16,383 are reserved.

Class C addresses are generally used for smaller networks, such as LANs. They begin with a binary 110. The next 21 bits identify the network. The remaining 8 bits identify the host. A total of 2,097,152 Class C addresses are possible, with addresses 0 and 2,097,151 reserved.

Class D addresses begin with a binary 1110 and are intended for multicasting. Class E addresses begin with a binary 1111 and are reserved for future use.

All IP addresses are written in dotted decimal notation, in which each octet is assigned a decimal number from 0 to 255. For example, network [10.55.31.84] is represented in binary as 00001010 00110111 00011111 1010100. The first bit (0) indicates a Class A address, the next 7 bits (0001010) represent the Network ID (decimal 10) and the last 24 bits (00110111 00011111 1010100) represent the Host ID.

Class A addresses begin with 1-127, Class B with 128-191, Class C with 192-223, and Class D with 224-254. Thus, an address of [150.100.200.5] is easily identified as a Class B address.

As discussed above, the IP addresses are divided into two fields that identify a network and a host. A central authority assigns the Network ID and the local network administrator assigns the Host ID. Routers send packets to a particular network using the Network ID, and that network completes the delivery to the host. If an organization has two networks, it could request two Network ID assignments from the central authority. But this would cause the routing tables within hosts and routers to expand considerably. The popularity of LANs in the mid-1980s, therefore, inspired the Internet community to revise the IP address structure. The new structure allows for an additional field to identify a subnetwork within an assigned Network ID. Thus the [Network, Host] address format is replaced with [Network, Subnetwork, Host] format. The space for the Subnetwork field comes from reduc-

128

ing the Host field. The central authority assigns the Network ID, and the individual organization assigns the Subnetwork IDs and the Host IDs on each subnetwork.

The Address Mask differentiates between various subnetworks. A Subnet Mask is a 32-bit number that has ONEs in the Network ID and Subnetwork ID field and ZEROs in the Host ID field. The router or the host implement a mathematical function that performs a logical AND function between the Subnet Mask and a particular IP address to determine whether a datagram can be delivered on the same subnet, or whether it must go through an IP router to another subnet.

A host or router that needs to make a routing decision uses the Subnet Mask for assistance and the logical AND function to arrive at its conclusion. For example, suppose the Destination address is D and My address is M. Further suppose that the Subnet Mask is [255.255.255.0]. Two calculations are made: Subnet Mask AND Address D, plus Subnet Mask AND Address M. The result of the AND function strips off the host portion of the address, leaving only the network and subnet portions. (Recall that the Host ID field is filled with ZEROs and that any number AND ZERO is still ZERO.) From the calculations, we have two results, each representing a Network ID and a Subnet ID. The two results are then compared and used to make a routing decision. When the two results are identical, Addresses M and D are on the same subnetwork. If Addresses M and D are not equal, the two addresses are on different subnetworks, and the datagram must go to a router for delivery.

If the host doesn't know which Subnet Mask to use, it uses ICMP to discover the right one. The host broadcasts an ICMP Address Mask Request message and waits for an ICMP Address Mask Reply from a neighboring router. If an Address Mask is used improperly and a datagram is sent to a router erroneously, the router that identifies the misdirected packet returns an ICMP Redirect message. We will look at this scenario in section 4.8.5.

RFC 950 "Internet Standard Subnetting Procedure", [4-9] was written to cover subnet-related issues. Jeffrey Mogul's "Subnetting: A Brief Guide" [4-10] and Mike Stone's "Guide to TCP/IP Network Addressing" [4-11] discuss the topic from an implementation perspective. RFC 1118 "The Hitchhiker's Guide to the Internet," [4-12] discusses UNIX-related subnetting issues.

Several addresses are reserved to identify special purposes [4-6, page 4], [4-13, page 14]:

Address	Interpretation
[Net = 0, Host = 0]	This host on this network
[Net = 0, Host = H]	Specific Host H on this network (Source address only)
[Net = all ONEs, Host = all ONEs]	Limited broadcast (within the source's subnetwork)
[Net = N, Host = all ONEs]	Directed broadcast to network (Destination address only)
[Net = N, Sub = all ONEs, Host = all ONEs]	Directed broadcast to all subnets on Network N
[Net = N, Sub = S, Host = all ONEs]	Directed broadcast to all hosts on Subnet S, Network N
[Net = 127, Host = any]	Internal host loopback address

The following two numbers are used for network numbers, but not IP addresses:

[Net = N, Host = 0]	Network N, No Host
[Net = N, Sub = S, Host = 0]:	Subnet S, No Host

Abbreviations: Net = Network ID
Sub = Subnet ID
Host = Host ID

RFC 1118 [4-12] issues two cautions about IP addresses. First, it notes that BSD 4.2 UNIX systems require additional software for subnetting; BSD 4.3 systems do not. Second, some machines use an IP address of all ZEROs to specify a broadcast, instead of the more common all ONEs. BSD 4.3 requires the system administrator to choose the broadcast address. Use caution, since many problems, such as broadcast storms, can result when the broadcast address is not implemented consistently over the network. RFC 1009 [4-13] also discusses cautions in this area.

4.3 Address Translation

In the last two sections, we looked at the differences between the Internet address, used by IP, and the Local address, used by the LAN or WAN hardware. We observed that the IP address was a 32-bit Logical address, but that the Physical address depends on the hardware. For example, ARCNET has an 8-bit and Ethernet a 48-bit Hardware address. Since we may know one of these addresses but not the other, protocols are provided to map the Logical and Physical addresses to each other. Since two translations may be necessary (Logical to Physical and Physical to Logical), two protocols have been developed. The Address Resolution Protocol (ARP) described in RFC 826 [4-14] translates from an IP address to a Hardware address. The Reverse Address Resolution Protocol (RARP), detailed in RFC 903 [4-15] as its name implies, does the opposite. Let's look at these protocols separately.

4.3.1 Address Resolution Protocol (ARP)

Let's assume that a device, Host X, on an Ethernet wishes to deliver a datagram to another device on the same Ethernet, Host Y. Host X knows Host Y's Destination Protocol (IP) address, but does not know its Hardware (Ethernet) address. It would, therefore, broadcast an ARP packet within an Ethernet frame to determine Host Y's hardware address. The ARP packet is shown in Figure 4-4. The packet consists of 28 octets, primarily addresses, which are contained within the Data field of a LAN frame. The sender broadcasts an ARP packet within a LAN frame requesting the information that it lacks. The device that recognizes its own protocol address responds with the sought-for hardware address. The individual fields of the ARP message show how the protocol operates.

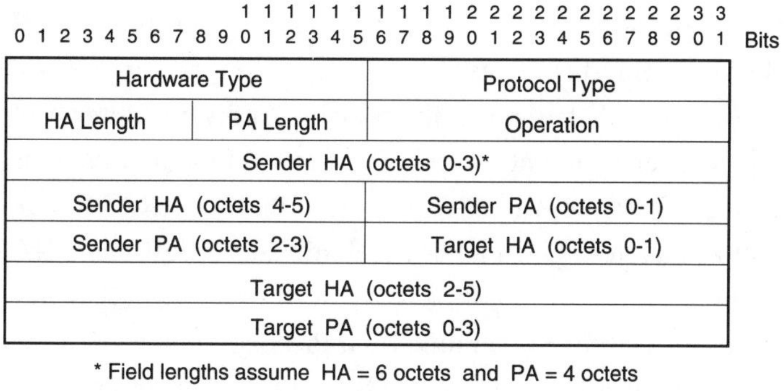

```
                                1 1 1 1 1 1 1 1 1 1 2 2 2 2 2 2 2 2 2 2 3 3
            0 1 2 3 4 5 6 7 8 9 0 1 2 3 4 5 6 7 8 9 0 1 2 3 4 5 6 7 8 9 0 1   Bits
```

Hardware Type		Protocol Type	
HA Length	PA Length	Operation	
Sender HA (octets 0-3)*			
Sender HA (octets 4-5)		Sender PA (octets 0-1)	
Sender PA (octets 2-3)		Target HA (octets 0-1)	
Target HA (octets 2-5)			
Target PA (octets 0-3)			

* Field lengths assume HA = 6 octets and PA = 4 octets

Figure 4-4. Address Resolution Protocol (ARP) and Reverse Address Resolution Protocol (RARP) Packet Formats

The first field, Hardware, (2 octets) defines the type of hardware in use. Current values are listed in RFC 1340. Examples include Hardware = 1 (Ethernet), 6 (IEEE 802 Networks), 7 (ARCNET), and 11 (LocalTalk). The second field, Protocol (2 octets), identifies the protocol address in use. For example, protocol = 0800H would identify IP addresses.

The second word allows the ARP packet to be used with a variety of address structures rather than restricting its use to only two, such as IP (32 bits) and IEEE 802 (48 bits). This makes the protocol more adaptive. The Hardware Length (HLEN), 1 octet, and Protocol Length (PLEN), 1 octet, specify the lengths, in octets, of the addresses to be used. Figure 4-4 represents the most common scenario. The Hardware Address (HA) requires 6 octets or 48 bits (HLEN=6); the Protocol Address (PA) needs 4 octets or 32 bits (PLEN=4). The Operation field (2 octets) defines an ARP Request =1 and ARP Reply=2.

The next fields contain the addresses themselves. With an ARP Request message, the target Hardware address field is unknown and is sent filled with ZEROs. The ARP Reply packet from the target host will insert the requested address in that field. When it receives the ARP Reply, the originating station records that information in a table, called the ARP cache. The ARP cache reduces internetwork traffic asking to resolve the same address on multiple occasions. Routers' ARP caches have a finite lifetime, which prevents the table from growing too large.

4.3.2 Reverse Address Resolution Protocol (RARP)

Most hosts on networks are smart enough to remember their own Hardware and Protocol addresses. But diskless workstations rely on the server for much of their intelligence. Such a workstation would know its Hardware address, which is coded into ROM, but the server might assign a Protocol address of which the workstation was unaware. The Reverse Address Resolution Protocol (RARP) can discover an unknown Protocol address given a known Hardware address and a RARP server to supply the answer.

The process of determining an unknown Protocol address is similar to that of finding an unknown Hardware address. The same packet structure is used (review Figure 4-4), with only minor modifications to the field values. The Operation field adds two new values: 3 (RARP Request) and 4 (RARP Reply). When the RARP Request is made, the Sender Hardware address, Sender Protocol address, and Target Hardware address are transmitted. The RARP Reply contains the sought-after Target Protocol address.

Douglas Comer's articles, "Mapping Internet Addresses" [4-16] and "Determining an Internet Address at Startup" [4-17] provide additional insight into the basis and operation of these protocols.

4.3.3 Proxy ARP

RFC 925 [4-18] defines a variation on the ARP process, known as Proxy ARP or promiscuous ARP. Suppose that two networks use the same IP network address, designated A and B. Router R, running ARP, connects the two networks. Now, suppose that a host on Network A wishes to communicate with another host on Network B, but doesn't know its Hardware address. The host on Network A would broadcast as ARP Request, seeking the Hardware address of the remote host. Router R would intercept the request and reply with HA=R, which would be stored in the host's ARP cache. Subsequent communication between the two hosts would go via R, which would use its own lookup table to forward the packet to Network B. Black [4-19] and Comer [4-20] discuss the advantages and disadvantages of Proxy ARP.

4.3.4 Bootstrap Protocol (BOOTP)

The Bootstrap Protocol, described in RFC 951 [4-21], is an alternative to ARP/RARP. The protocol gets it name from the fact that it is meant to be contained within a bootstrap ROM. BOOTP is designed for diskless clients that need information from a server, such as their own IP address, the server's IP address or the name of a file (i.e., the boot file) to be loaded into memory and then executed. The client broadcasts a Boot Request packet, which is answered by a Boot Reply packet from the server.

One of the significant differences between ARP/RARP and BOOTP is the layer of protocol they address. ARP/RARP packets are contained within local network frames and transmitted on the local network. BOOTP packets are contained within IP datagrams, contain a UDP header, and are transmitted on the internetwork. The designated server can, therefore, be several router hops away from the client. Two reserved port numbers are used for BOOTP Server (port 67) and BOOTP Client (port 68).

The individual fields of the BOOTP packet are shown in Figure 4-5. The OpCode (OP, 1 octet) specifies a BOOTREQUEST (OP=1) or BOOTREPLY (OP=2). Hardware address Type (HTYPE, 1 octet) and Hardware address Length (HLEN, 1 octet) are similar to those fields in the ARP/RARP packet. The HOPS field (1 octet) is optional for use in cross-router booting. The Transaction ID (4 octets) correlates the boot requests and responses. The Seconds field (2 octets) allows the client to count the elapsed time since it started the bootup sequence. Two unused octets complete the third word of the BOOTP packet.

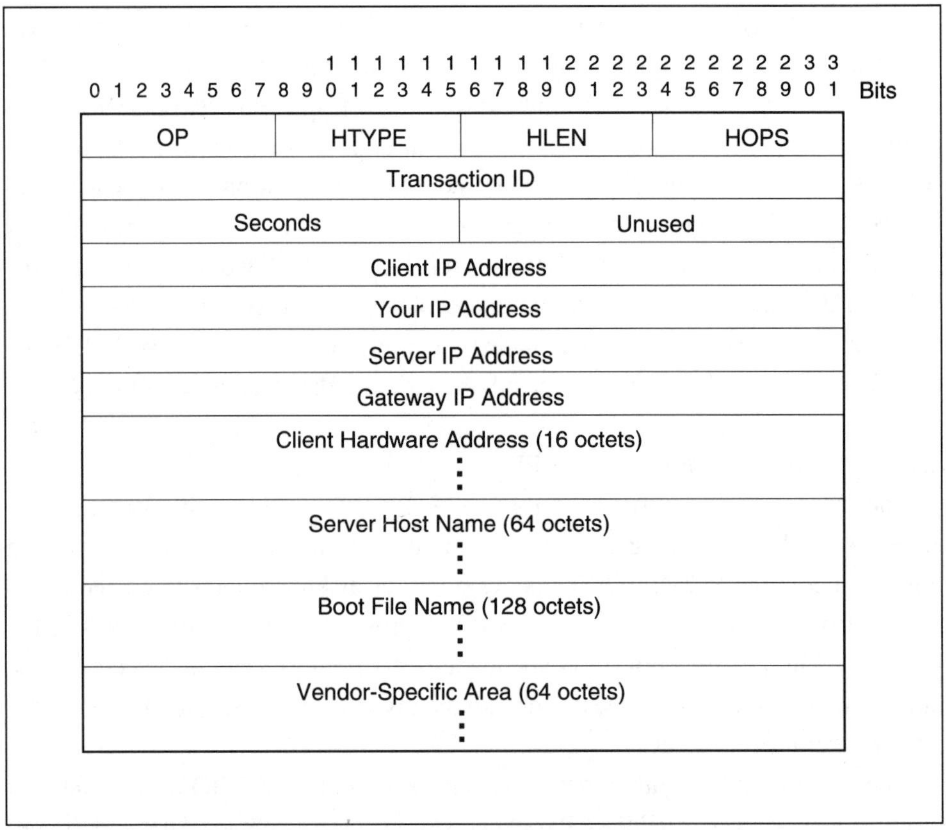

Figure 4-5. Bootstrap Protocol (BOOTP) Packet Format

The next four words designate the various IP addresses. The client states the addresses it knows and the server fills in the rest. These include the Client IP address (filled in by Client), Your IP address (filled in by the server if the Client does not know its own address), Server IP address, and Gateway router IP address. The Client

HA (16 octets), Boot File Name (128 octets), and a Vendor-Specific Area (64 octets), containing information to be sent from the server to the client, complete the packet.

In summary, BOOTP improves on the ARP concept by allowing the address resolution process to occur across routers. Although it uses IP/UDP, it is small enough to fit within a bootstrap ROM on the client workstation. Mogul's "Booting Diskless Hosts: The BOOTP Protocol" [4-22] describes the client/server interaction in further detail.

4.4 Datagram Routing

So far, we've learned that hosts transmit datagrams and use a 32-bit address to identify the source and destination of the datagram. The host drops the datagram into the internetwork, and the datagram somehow finds its way to its destination. That "somehow" is the work of routers, which examine the Destination address, compare that address with their internal routing tables, and send the datagram on the correct outgoing communication circuit.

Router operation involves several processes [4-2, page 5]. First, the router creates a routing table to gather information from other routers about the optimum path to each packet. This table may be static (i.e., manually built) and fixed for all network conditions, or dynamic (i.e., constructed by the router according to the current topology and conditions). Dynamic routing is considered the better technique because it adapts to changing network conditions. The router uses a metric, or measurement, of the shortest distance between two endpoints to help determine the optimum path. It determines the metric using a number of factors, including the shortest distance, or least cost path, to the destination. The router plugs the metric into one of two algorithms to make a final decision on the correct path. A Distance Vector algorithm makes its choice based upon the distance to a remote node. A Link State algorithm also includes information about the status of the various links connecting the nodes and the topology of the network.

The various routers within the network use the Distance Vector or Link State algorithms to inform each other of their current status. Because routers use them for intra-network communication, the protocols that make use of these algorithms are referred to as Interior Gateway Protocols (IGPs). The Routing Information Protocol (RIP) is an IGP based upon a Distance Vector algorithm. The Open Shortest Path First (OSPF) protocol is an IGP based on a Link State algorithm. We'll look at these two algorithms separately in the following sections. If one network wishes to communicate routing to another network, it uses an Exterior Gateway Protocol (EGP). An EGP is described in RFC 904 [4-23]. An example of an EGP is the Border Gateway Protocol (BGP), described in RFC 1105, that is used within NSFNET. An excellent article on routing is Callon's "Routing in an Internetwork Environment" [4-24].

4.4.1 Routing Information Protocol (RIP)

The Routing Information Protocol described in RFC 1058 [4-25] is used for intra-router (or intra-gateway) communications. RIP is based on a Distance Vector algorithm, sometimes referred to as a Ford-Fulkerson algorithm after its developers L. R. Ford, Jr. and D. R. Fulkerson. A Distance Vector algorithm is one in which the routers periodically exchange information from their routing tables. The routing decision is based on the best path between two devices, which is often the path with the fewest hops or router transversals. The Internet standard warns that many LAN operating systems have their own RIP implementations. Therefore, it is important to adhere to the Internet standard to alleviate interoperability problems.

RFC 1058 acknowledges several limitations to RIP. RIP allows a path length of 15 hops, which may be insufficient for large internetworks. Routing loops are possible for internetworks containing hundreds of networks, because of the time required to transmit updated routing table information. Finally, the metrics used to choose the routing path are fixed and do not allow for dynamic conditions, such as a measured delay or a variable traffic load.

RIP assumes that all devices (hosts and routers) contain a routing table. This table contains several entries: the IP address of the destination; the metric, or cost, to get a datagram from the host to the destination; the address of the next router in the path to the destination; a flag indicating whether the routing information has been recently updated; and timers.

Routing information is exchanged via RIP packets, shown in Figure 4-6, which are transmitted to/from UDP port number 520. The packet begins with a 32-bit header and may contain as many as 25 messages, giving details on specific networks. The first field of the header is 1 octet long and specifies a unique command. Values include:

Command	Meaning
1	Request for routing table information
2	Response containing routing table information
3	Traceon (obsolete)
4	Traceoff (obsolete)
5	Reserved for Sun Microsystems

The second octet contains a RIP Version Number (currently Version = 1). Octets 3 and 4 are set equal to ZERO. The next 2 octets identify the Address Family being transmitted within that RIP packet; RFC 1058 only defines a value for IP with Address Family ID = 2.

The balance of the RIP packet contains entries for routing information. Each entry includes the destination IP address and the metric to reach that destination. Metric values must be between 1 and 15, inclusive. A metric of 16 indicates that the desired destination is unreachable. Up to 25 of these entries (from the Address Family Identifier through the Metric) may be contained within the datagram. We will see an example of RIP in Section 4.8.8.

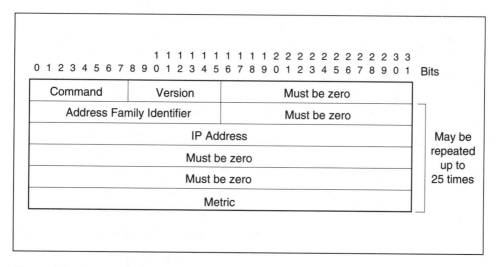

Figure 4-6. Routing Information Protocol (RIP) Packet

4.4.2 Open Shortest Path First Protocol (OSPF)

The Open Shortest Path First Protocol is a Link State algorithm that offers several advantages over RIP's Distance Vector algorithm. These advantages include the ability to configure hierarchical (instead of flat) topologies; to quickly adapt to changes within the internet; to allow for large internetworks; to calculate multiple minimum-cost routes that allow traffic load to be balanced over several paths; and to authenticate the exchange of routing table information. The protocol uses the IP address and Type of Service field of each datagram (review Figure 4-2) for its operation. An optimum path can be calculated for each Type of Service.

The Internet standard for OSPF is RFC 1247 [4-26]. OSPF Protocol analysis and experience are discussed in RFC 1245 and RFC 1246, respectively. Recently, there has been a great deal of interest in this protocol; references [4-27] through [4-30] are examples of articles on the subject.

OSPF packets are carried within IP datagrams and designated as IP protocol = 89. If the datagram requires fragmentation, the IP process handles that function. The five OSPF packet types have a common 24-octet header as shown in Figure 4-7. The first 32-bit word includes a Version Number (1 octet), an OSPF Packet Type (1 octet), and a Packet Length field (2 octets), which measures the length of the OSPF packet including the header. Five packet types are defined:

Type	Meaning
1	Hello
2	Database Description
3	Link State Request
4	Link State Update
5	Link State Ack

The next two fields define the Router ID of the source of that packet (4 octets) and the Area ID (4 octets) that the packet came from. (OSPF's hierarchical structure defines autonomous groups of networks, hosts, and routers as an Area. Areas may be connected to form a backbone.)

The balance of the OSPF packet header contains a Checksum (2 octets), an Authentication Type (Autype, 2 octets), and an Authentication field (8 octets), used to validate the packet.

Following the OSPF packet header is another header specific to the routing information being conveyed. Hello packets (OSPF Packet Type = 1) are periodic transmissions that convey information about neighboring routers. Database Description packets (OSPF Packet Type = 2) convey information needed to initialize the topological databases of adjacent devices. Link State Request packets (OSPF Packet Type = 3) obtain current database information from a neighboring router. Link State Update packets (OSPF Packet Type = 4) advertise the status of various links within the internet. Finally, Link State Acknowledgement packets (OSPF Type = 5) verify the receipt of database information.

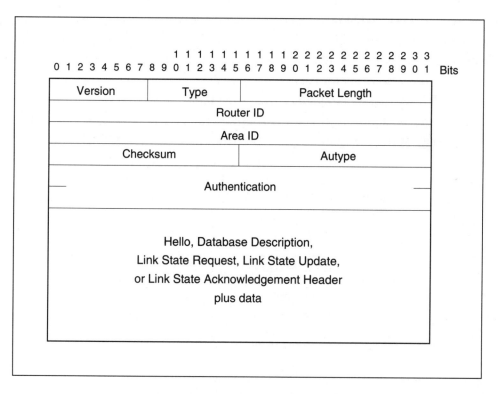

Figure 4-7. Open Shortest Path First (OSPF) Packet Header Format

4.5 Intra-Network Communications (ICMP)

If the Internet were flawless, it would always route datagrams to their intended destination without errors, excessive delays, or retransmissions. Unfortunately, this is not the case. (If it were, you wouldn't be reading a book on troubleshooting!) As we studied in Section 4.1, IP provides a connectionless service to the attached hosts but requires an additional module, known as the Internet Control Message Protocol (ICMP), to report errors that may have occurred in processing those datagrams. Examples of errors include undeliverable datagrams or incorrect routes. Other uses for the protocol include testing the path to a distant host (known as a PING) or requesting an Address Mask for a particular subnet. ICMP is considered an integral part of IP and must be implemented in IP modules contained in both hosts and routers. The standard for ICMP is RFC 792 [4-31].

ICMP messages are contained within IP datagrams. In other words, ICMP is a user (client) of IP, and the IP header precedes the ICMP message. Thus, the datagram would include the IP header, the ICMP header, and ICMP data. Protocol=1 identifies ICMP within the IP header. A Type field within the ICMP header further identifies the purpose and format of the ICMP message. Any data required to complete the ICMP message would then follow the ICMP header.

The standard defines thirteen ICMP message formats, each with a specific ICMP header format. Two of these formats (Information Request/Reply) are considered obsolete and several others share a common message structure. The result is six unique message formats, shown in Figure 4-8. The first three fields are common to all headers. The Type field (1 octet) identifies one of the thirteen unique ICMP messages. These include:

Type Code	ICMP Messages
0	Echo Reply
3	Destination Unreachable
4	Source Quench
5	Redirect
8	Echo

Type Code	ICMP Messages
11	Time Exceeded
12	Parameter Problem
13	Timestamp
14	Timestamp Reply
15	Information Request (obsolete)
16	Information Reply (obsolete)
17	Address Mask Request
18	Address Mask Reply

The second field is labeled Code (1 octet), and it elaborates on specific message types. For example, the Code field for the Destination Unreachable message indicates whether the network, host, protocol, or port was the unreachable entity. The third field is the Checksum (2 octets) on the ICMP message. Because ICMP messages are of great value in internetwork troubleshooting, we will look at all of the ICMP messages in detail. Internet standards describing ICMP formats and usage include the original standard, RFC 792 [4-31]; implementing congestion control, RFC 896 [4-32]; use of source quench messages, RFC 1016 [4-33]; and Subnet Mask Messages, RFC 950 [4-9].

The Echo message (ICMP Type=8) tests the communication path from a sender to receiver via the internet. On many hosts, this function is called PING. The sender transmits an Echo message, which may also contain an Identifier (2 octets) and a Sequence Number (2 octets). Data may be sent with the message. When the destination receives the message, it reverses the Source and Destination addresses, recomputes the Checksum and returns an Echo Reply (ICMP Type=0). The contents of the Data field (if any) would also be returned to the sender.

The Destination Unreachable message (ICMP Type=3) is used when the router or host is unable to deliver the datagram. This message is returned to the Source host of the datagram in question and describes the reason for the delivery problem in the Code field:

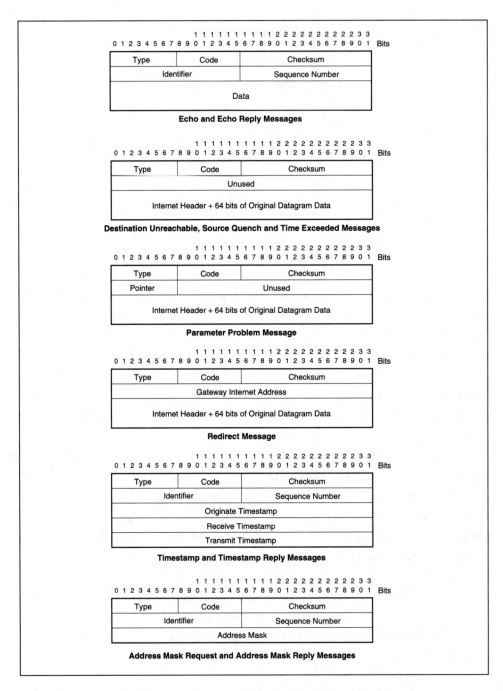

Figure 4-8. Internet Control Message Protocol (ICMP) Message Formats

Code	Meaning
0	Net Unreachable
1	Host Unreachable
2	Protocol Unreachable
3	Port Unreachable
4	Fragmentation Needed and DF Set
5	Source Route Failed

Routers may use codes 0, 1, 4, or 5. Hosts may use codes 2 or 3. For example, when a datagram arrives at a router, it will do a table lookup to determine the outgoing path to use. If the router determines that the Destination network cannot be reached (i.e., a distance of infinite hops away), a Net Unreachable message will be returned. Similarly, if a host cannot process a datagram because the requested protocol or port is inactive, a Protocol Unreachable or Port Unreachable message, respectively, would be returned. Included in the Destination Unreachable message is the IP header plus the first 64 bits (8 octets) of the datagram in question. This returned data should help the host diagnose the failure in the transmission process.

The advantage of connectionless datagram transmission is its simplicity. The disadvantage is its inability to regulate the traffic on the network. (For an analogy, consider the problem that your local post office faces. To handle the maximum number of letters, it should install enough boxes to handle the holiday rush. However, this might be considered wasteful because many of the boxes are only partially used during the summer.) If a router or host gets congested, it may send a Source Quench message (ICMP Type=4) to the source of the datagrams asking it to reduce its output. This mechanism is similar to traffic signals that regulate the flow of cars into a freeway. The Source Quench message does not use the second 32-bit word of the ICMP header, but fills it with ZEROs. The rest of the message contains the IP header and first 8 octets of the datagram that triggered the request.

Hosts do not always choose the correct Destination address for a particular datagram and occasionally send one to the wrong router. This is most likely to occur when the host is initialized and its routing tables are incomplete. When such a routing mistake occurs, the router receiving the datagram improperly will return a Redirect message to the host identifying a better route. The Code field would contain the following information:

Code	Message
0	Redirect datagrams for the network
1	Redirect datagrams for the host
2	Redirect datagrams for the type of service and network
3	Redirect datagrams for the type of service and host

The Redirect message (ICMP Type=5) contains the correct router (gateway) address to reach the desired destination. In addition, the IP header plus the first 8 octets of the datagram in question are returned to the source host to aid in the diagnostic process.

Another potential problem of connectionless networks is that datagrams can get lost within the network and wander for an excessive amount of time. Alternatively, congestion could prevent all fragments of a datagram from being reassembled within the host's required time. Either of these situations can trigger an ICMP Time Exceeded message (ICMP Type=11). The message defines two codes: Time-to-Live Exceeded in Transmit (code=0) and Fragment Reassembly Time Exceeded (code=1). The balance of the message has the same format as the Source Quench message: the second word contains all ZEROs, and the rest of the message contains the IP header and first 8 octets of the offending datagram.

Higher-layer processes, such as TCP, recognize datagrams that cannot be processed because of errors and discards them, relying upon a higher layer process to recognize the problem and take corrective action. Parameter problems within an IP datagram header (such an incorrect Type of Service field) may send an ICMP Parameter Problem message (ICMP Type=12) to the source of the datagram, identifying the location of the problem. The message contains a pointer that identifies the octet with the error. The rest of the message contains the IP datagram header plus the first 8 octets of data, as before.

The Timestamp Message (ICMP Type=13) and Timestamp Reply (ICMP Type=14) measure the round-trip transit time between two machines and synchronize their clocks. The first two words of the Timestamp and Timestamp Reply messages are similar to the Echo and Echo Reply messages. The next three fields contain timestamps, measured in milliseconds since midnight, Universal Time (UT). The Timestamp Requester fills in the Originate field upon transmission;

the recipient fills in the Receive Timestamp when it receives the request. The recipient fills in the Transmit Timestamp when it sends the Timestamp Reply message. The Requester may now estimate the remote processing and round-trip transit times. (Note that these are only estimates because network delay is a highly dynamic and variable measurement.) The remote processing time is the Received Timestamp minus the Transmit Timestamp. The round-trip transit time will be the Timestamp Reply message arrival time minus the Originate Timestamp. With these two calculations, the two clocks can be synchronized.

Finally, Address Mask Request (ICMP Type=17) and Address Mask Reply (ICMP Type=18) were added to the ICMP message in response to subnetting requirements (RFC 950). It is assumed that the requesting host knows its own Internet address. (If it doesn't, it uses RARP to discover the Internet address). It then broadcasts the Address Mask Request message to the Destination address [255.255.255.255]. The Address Mask field of the ICMP message would be filled with all ZEROs. The IP router that knows the correct address mask would respond. For example, the response for a Class B network (without subnetting) would be [255.255.0.0]. A Class B network using an 8-bit subnet field would be [255.255.255.0]. Barry Gerber's article "IP Routing: Learn to Follow the Yellow Brick Road" [4-34] contains additional examples of Subnet Mask usage. Section 4.8.5 will show how an incorrect Subnet Mask can hinder network communication.

4.6 Domain Name System (DNS)

The 32-bit IP addresses and the various classes defined for these addresses provide an extremely efficient way to identify devices on an internetwork. Unfortunately, remembering all of those addresses can be overwhelming. To solve that problem, a system of hierarchical naming, known as the Domain Name System, was developed. DNS is described in RFCs 1034 and 1035 [4-35].

DNS is based upon several premises. First, it arranges the names hierarchically, like the numbering plan devised for the telephone network. Just as a telephone number is divided into a country code, an area code, an exchange code, and finally a line number, the DNS root is divided into a number of top-level domains, defined in RFC 920. These are:

Domain	Purpose
MIL	U.S. Military
GOV	Other U.S. Government
EDU	Educational
COM	Commercial
NET	NICs and NOCs
ORG	Non-profit Organizations
CON	Two-letter country code, e.g. US represents the United States, CA represents Canada, and so on.

Specific sites would be under each top-level domain. For example, the University of Ferncliff could use the edu domain designation (using the traditional lower-case letters), and it would be shown as ferncliff.edu. The University could then designate names for its departments, such as cs.ferncliff.edu (Computer Science) or ee.ferncliff.edu (Electrical Engineering). A particular host in the Electrical Engineering department could be named voltage.ee.ferncliff.edu. A user with a login on that host could be identified as jones @ voltage.ee.ferncliff.edu. Note that the @ sign separates the user from the remainder of the Host address.

The second DNS premise is that devices are not expected to remember the IP addresses of remote hosts. Rather, Name Servers throughout the internetwork provide this information. The requesting device thus assumes the role of a client, and the Name Server provides the necessary information, known as a resource record.

The format for client/server interaction is a DNS message, shown in Figure 4-9. The message header is 12 octets long, and describes the type of message. The next four sections provide the details of the query or response.

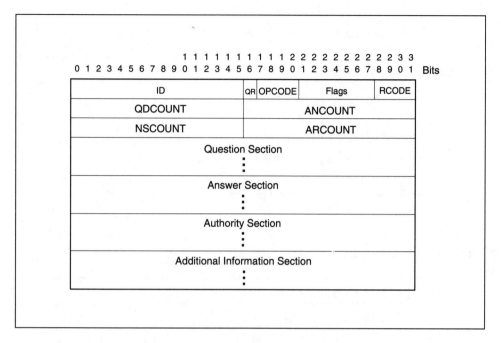

Figure 4-9. Domain Name System (DNS) Message Format

The first field within the header is an Identifier (16 bits) that correlates the queries and responses. The QR bit identifies the message type as a Query (QR = 0) or a Response (QR = 1). An OPCODE field (4 bits) further defines a Query:

OPCODE	Meaning
0	Standard Query (QUERY)
1	Inverse Query (IQUERY)
2	Server Status request (STATUS)
3-15	Reserved

Four Flags are then transmitted to further describe the message:

Bit Number	Meaning
5	Authoritative Answer (AA)
6	Truncation (TC)
7	Recursion Desired (RD)
8	Recursion Available (RA)
9-11	Reserved (set to 0)

A Response Code (RCODE) completes the first word:

Field	Meaning
0	No error
1	Format error
2	Server error
3	Name error
4	Not implemented
5	Refused
6-15	Reserved for future use

The balance of the header contains fields that define the lengths of the remaining four sections:

Field	Meaning
QDCOUNT	Number of Question entries
ANCOUNT	Number of resource records in the Answer section
NSCOUNT	Number of name server resource records in the Authority section
ARCOUNT	Number of resource records in the Additional Records section.

Following the header is the Question section, plus the Answer sections (Answer, Authority, or Additional Information). We will look at an example of a DNS message in section 4.8.1.

4.7 Troubleshooting the Internetwork Connection

When planning a strategy to diagnose internetwork-related problems, it is important to reconsider the functions of the DARPA Internet Layer discussed in Section 4.1. Recall that its principle function is routing, with the desired result being connectivity between two hosts. Associated with routing are the issues of addressing, subnet assignments, and masks. Because addresses are not always known, protocols such as ARP/RARP and BOOTP may be used. The Domain Name System may also assist in this process.

Intelligent devices known as routers use the addresses to guide the datagram through the internet. Those routers communicate with each other using an IGP, such as RIP or OSPF. Because the routing mechanism doesn't always function properly, another protocol, ICMP, helps the hosts determine what went wrong.

One frequently used test is the ICMP Echo (PING) message used to verify connectivity between internet devices. The PING can be used in a sequential manner to isolate a problem. For example, first PING a host on your subnet, then PING a router, then PING a host on the other side of that router, and so on until the faulty connection is identified. Another maintenance utility known as *traceroute* is available with some host operating systems. *Traceroute* uses ICMP messages to verify each segment along a path to a distant host. *Traceroute* must be used with some caution, however, as it can generate large amounts of internetwork (and/or Internet) traffic.

To summarize, if a problem occurs in the internet and the Network Interface Layer looks healthy (review Section 3.10), look for the significant events at the Internet Layer. These relate to datagram delivery. The processes of address discovery, address assignment, communication between routers, and notification of router errors may offer clues about the reason for a problem with the delivery of your datagram. The following case studies will show examples of these clues.

4.8 Case Studies

We have studied a number of protocols in this chapter, including ARP, IP, ICMP, RIP, and OSPF. We have also looked at IP addressing schemes and Subnet Masks. Next, let's look at some case studies that illustrate these protocols in action.

4.8.1 Login to a Remote Host

In our first example, we'll look at the processes necessary to login to a remote host using the UNIX TELNET utility (See Trace 4.8.1a). The network administrator, Paul, resides on an Ethernet segment (Network 132) in one location, and the remote host that he needs to access resides on a different segment (Network 129) in another part of the country (see Figure 4-10).

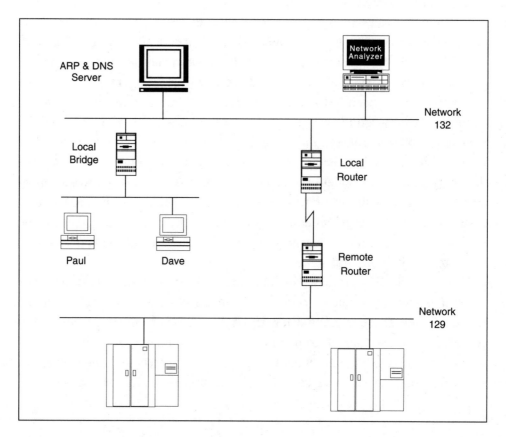

Figure 4-10. Login to Remote Host

First, Paul must find the Domain Name System (DNS) Server. To do so, he broadcasts an ARP Request packet within an Ethernet frame identifying the Protocol Address, PA=[132.163.128.1], for the Internet Protocol (IP), but with an unknown Hardware Address (HA=0) as shown in Frame 1 of Trace 4.8.1b. The Name Server responds in Frame 2, identifying its HA=08002006B501H. Paul now knows how to reach the Name Server.

He next locates the address for the remote host fs1.cam.nist.gov that he wishes to login to. The DNS request is transmitted in Frame 3, with a response given in Frame 4 of Trace 4.8.1c, indicating that fs1.cam.nist.gov is located at [129.6.80.33]. Recall that Paul is located on Network 132 and the Name Server says that his desired destination is located on another network (Network 129). A router must now spring into action. Paul broadcasts an ARP Request packet looking for the router (address [132.163.1.1] in Frame 5 of Trace 4.8.1a). The router responds with its hardware address in Frame 6 (HA=000093E0807BH).

Paul now has all the information he needs. In Frame 7 he initiates a TCP connection (via a three-way handshake, which we will study in Chapter 5) with the remote host.

The details of the Connection Establishment message verify that Paul knows where to find his desired host (see Trace 4.8.1d). In the Data Link Control (DLC, or frame) header, Paul addresses this message to the Proteon router (address ProteonE0807B). We know that this frame is transmitted on a DIX Ethernet (not an IEEE 802.3) LAN, because of the EtherType field identified IP=0800 H. (Had it been an IEEE 802.3 frame, a Length field would have been shown instead of the EtherType field.) The IP header identifies Paul's workstation as the source of the datagram [132.163.129.15], with the destination address of the remote host on a different network of [129.6.80.33]. The TCP header specifies the Destination Port=23 (TELNET). The TCP flags indicate that Paul wants to establish a connection, since the Synchronize flag is set (SYN=1). Paul also specifies that he can accept a maximum segment size of 512 octets.

In the subsequent frames (8 through 20 of Trace 4.8.1a), Paul's workstation and the remote host negotiate various TELNET parameters, such as the Terminal Type (Frames 10 through 12), Echo (Frames 15 and 16) and Login (Frames 17 through 20). Once Paul is logged in, he can complete his business with the remote host.

To summarize, Paul's workstation undertakes the following steps:

1.   Identify DNS Name Server (ARP)
2.   Identify remote host address (DNS)
3.   Identify required router (ARP)
4.   Establish connection with remote host (TCP)
5.   Negotiate parameters with remote host (TELNET)
6.   Initiate remote terminal session (TELNET).

In the next case study, we will examine how IP fragments long messages.

Sniffer Network Analyzer data 21-Jun-90 at 13:37:00, LOGIN.ENC, Pg 1

SUMMARY	Delta T	Destination	Source	Summary
M 1		Broadcast	Paul	ARP C PA=[132.163.128.1] PRO=IP
2	0.0006	Paul	Name Svr	ARP R PA=[132.163.128.1] HA=08002006B501 PRO=IP
3	0.0016	Name Svr	Paul	DNS C ID=3 OP=QUERY NAME=fs1.cam.nist.gov
4	0.0026	Paul	Name Svr	DNS R ID=3 STAT=OK NAME=fs1.cam.nist.gov
5	0.0088	Broadcast	Paul	ARP C PA=[132.163.1.1] PRO=IP
6	0.0010	Paul	Router	ARP R PA=[132.163.1.1] HA=000093E0807B PRO=IP
7	0.0016	Router	Paul	TCP D=23 S=3133 SYN SEQ=9947492 LEN=0 WIN=1024
8	0.1081	Paul	Router	TCP D=3133 S=23 SYN ACK=9947493 SEQ=80448000 LEN=0 WIN=4096
9	0.0032	Router	Paul	TCP D=23 S=3133 ACK=80448001 WIN=1024
10	2.1818	Paul	Router	Telnet R PORT=3133 IAC Do Terminal type
11	0.0029	Router	Paul	TCP D=23 S=3133 ACK=80448004 WIN=1021
12	0.0027	Router	Paul	Telnet C PORT=3133 IAC Will Terminal type
13	0.1134	Paul	Router	Telnet R PORT=3133 IAC SB ...

14	0.0070	Router	Paul	Telnet C PORT=3133 IAC SB ...
15	0.1912	Paul	Router	Telnet R PORT=3133 IAC
				Will Echo
16	0.0053	Router	Paul	Telnet C PORT=3133 IAC Do Echo
17	0.2566	Paul	Router	Telnet R PORT=3133 login:
18	0.0033	Router	Paul	Telnet C PORT=3133 IAC
				Do Suppress go-ahead
19	0.1113	Paul	Router	Telnet R PORT=3133 IAC
				Don't Echo
20	0.2591	Router	Paul	TCP D=23 S=3133
				ACK=80448057 WIN=968

Trace 4.8.1a. Login to Remote Host Summary

Sniffer Network Analyzer data 21-Jun-90 at 13:37:00, file LOGIN.ENC, Pg 1

- - - - - - - - - - - - - - - Frame 1 - - - - - - - - - - - - - - - -
DLC: ——- DLC Header ——-
DLC:
DLC: Frame 1 arrived at 13:37:06.3280; frame size is 60 (003C hex) bytes.
DLC: Destination = BROADCAST FFFFFFFFFFFF, Broadcast
DLC: Source   = Station 3Com 1AB9BE, Paul
DLC: Ethertype   = 0806 (ARP)
DLC:
ARP: ——- ARP/RARP frame ——-
ARP:
ARP: Hardware type = 1 (10Mb Ethernet)
ARP: Protocol type = 0800 (IP)
ARP: Length of hardware address = 6 bytes
ARP: Length of protocol address = 4 bytes
ARP: Opcode 1 (ARP request)
ARP: Sender's hardware address = 3Com 1AB9BE, Paul
ARP: Sender's protocol address = [132.163.129.15]
ARP: Target hardware address = 000000000000, 000000000000
ARP: Target protocol address = [132.163.128.1]
ARP:

- - - - - - - - - - - - - - - Frame 2 - - - - - - - - - - - - - - - -
DLC: ——- DLC Header ——-
DLC:
DLC: Frame 2 arrived at 13:37:06.3287; frame size is 60 (003C hex) bytes.
DLC: Destination = Station 3Com 1AB9BE, Paul
DLC: Source   = Station Sun 06B501, Name Svr

DLC: Ethertype = 0806 (ARP)
DLC:
ARP: ——- ARP/RARP frame ——-
ARP:
ARP: Hardware type = 1 (10Mb Ethernet)
ARP: Protocol type = 0800 (IP)
ARP: Length of hardware address = 6 bytes
ARP: Length of protocol address = 4 bytes
ARP: Opcode 2 (ARP reply)
ARP: Sender's hardware address = Sun   06B501, Name Svr
ARP: Sender's protocol address = [132.163.128.1]
ARP: Target hardware address = 3Com 1AB9BE, Paul
ARP: Target protocol address = [132.163.129.15]
ARP:

Trace 4.8.1b. Login to Remote Host ARP/RARP Details

Sniffer Network Analyzer data 21-Jun-90 at 13:37:00, LOGIN.ENC, Pg 1

- - - - - - - - - - - - - - - - Frame 3 - - - - - - - - - - - - - - - - -
DLC: —— DLC Header ——
DLC:
DLC: Frame 3 arrived at 13:37:06.3304; frame size is 76 (004C hex) bytes.
DLC: Destination = Station Sun   06B501, Name Svr
DLC: Source   = Station 3Com 1AB9BE, Paul
DLC: Ethertype = 0800 (IP)
DLC:
IP: —— IP Header ——
IP:
IP: Version = 4, header length = 20 bytes
IP: Type of service = 20
IP: 001 . . . . . = priority
IP: . . .0 . . . . = normal delay
IP: . . . . 0 . . . = normal throughput
IP: . . . . .0 . . = normal reliability
IP: Total length = 62 bytes
IP: Identification = 30
IP: Flags = 0X
IP: .0 . . . . . . = may fragment
IP: . .0 . . . . . = last fragment
IP: Fragment offset = 0 bytes
IP: Time to live = 64 seconds/hops

IP: Protocol = 17 (UDP)
IP: Header checksum = 701A (correct)
IP: Source address = [132.163.129.15]
IP: Destination address = [132.163.128.1]
IP: No options
IP:
UDP: ——— UDP Header ———-
UDP:
UDP: Source port = 1116 (Domain)
UDP: Destination port = 53
UDP: Length = 42
UDP: Checksum = 54EF (correct)
UDP:
DNS: ——— Internet Domain Name Service header ———-
DNS:
DNS: ID = 3
DNS: Flags = 01
DNS: 0... .... = Command
DNS: .000 0... = Query
DNS: .... ..0. = Not truncated
DNS: ....1 = Recursion desired
DNS: Flags = 0X
DNS: ...0 .... = Unicast packet
DNS: Question count = 1, Answer count = 0
DNS: Authority count = 0, Additional record count = 0
DNS:
DNS: Question section:
DNS: Name = fs1.cam.nist.gov
DNS: Type = Host address (A,1)
DNS: Class = Internet (IN,1)
DNS:
DNS: [Normal end of "Internet Domain Name Service header".]
DNS:

- - - - - - - - - - - - - - - - Frame 4 - - - - - - - - - - - - - - - - -
DLC: ——— DLC Header ———-
DLC:
DLC: Frame 4 arrived at 13:37:06.3330; frame size is 92 (005C hex) bytes.
DLC: Destination = Station 3Com 1AB9BE, Paul
DLC: Source   = Station Sun   06B501, Name Svr
DLC: Ethertype = 0800 (IP)
DLC:

```
IP: ——— IP Header ———
IP:
IP:  Version = 4, header length = 20 bytes
IP:  Type of service = 00
IP:       000. .... = routine
IP:       ...0 .... = normal delay
IP:       .... 0... = normal throughput
IP:       .... .0.. = normal reliability
IP:  Total length = 78 bytes
IP:  Identification = 60111
IP:  Flags = 0X
IP:  .0.. .... = may fragment
IP:  ..0. .... = last fragment
IP:  Fragment offset = 0 bytes
IP:  Time to live = 30 seconds/hops
IP:  Protocol = 17 (UDP)
IP:  Header checksum = A778 (correct)
IP:  Source address = [132.163.128.1]
IP:  Destination address = [132.163.129.15]
IP:  No options
IP:
UDP: ——— UDP Header ———
UDP:
UDP:  Source port = 53 (Domain)
UDP:  Destination port = 1116
UDP:  Length = 58
UDP:  No checksum
UDP:
DNS: ——— Internet Domain Name Service header ———
DNS:
DNS:  ID = 3
DNS:  Flags = 85
DNS:  1... .... = Response
DNS:  .... .1.. = Authoritative answer
DNS:  .000 0... = Query
DNS:  .... ..0. = Not truncated
DNS:  Flags = 8X
DNS:  ...0 .... = Unicast packet
DNS:  1... .... = Recursion available
DNS:  Response code = OK (0)
DNS:  Question count = 1, Answer count = 1
DNS:  Authority count = 0, Additional record count = 0
DNS:
```

DNS: Question section:
DNS: Name = fs1.cam.nist.gov
DNS: Type = Host address (A,1)
DNS: Class = Internet (IN,1)
DNS: Answer section:
DNS: Name = fs1.cam.nist.gov
DNS: Type = Host address (A,1)
DNS: Class = Internet (IN,1)
DNS: Time-to-live = 2589119 (seconds)
DNS: Address = [129.6.80.33]
DNS:
DNS: [Normal end of "Internet Domain Name Service header".]
DNS:

Trace 4.8.1c. Login to Remote Host DNS Details

Sniffer Network Analyzer data 21-Jun-90 at 13:37:00, LOGIN.ENC, Pg 1

- - - - - - - - - - - - - - - - Frame 7 - - - - - - - - - - - - - - - - -
DLC: ——- DLC Header ——-
DLC:
DLC: Frame 7 arrived at 13:37:06.3445; frame size is 60 (003C hex) bytes.
DLC: Destination = Station PrteonE0807B, Router
DLC: Source   = Station 3Com 1AB9BE, Paul
DLC: Ethertype = 0800 (IP)
DLC:
IP: ——- IP Header ——-
IP:
IP: Version = 4, header length = 20 bytes
IP: Type of service = 00
IP: 000. . . . . = routine
IP: . . .0 . . . . = normal delay
IP: . . . . 0. . . = normal throughput
IP: . . . . .0. . = normal reliability
IP: Total length = 44 bytes
IP: Identification = 31
IP: Flags = 0X
IP: .0. . . . . . = may fragment
IP: . .0. . . . . = last fragment
IP: Fragment offset = 0 bytes
IP: Time to live = 64 seconds/hops
IP: Protocol = 6 (TCP)

```
IP:   Header checksum = A3D3 (correct)
IP:   Source address = [132.163.129.15]
IP:   Destination address = [129.6.80.33]
IP:   No options
IP:
TCP: ―――― TCP header ――――
TCP:
TCP:  Source port = 3133
TCP:  Destination port = 23 (Telnet)
TCP:  Initial sequence number = 9947492
TCP:  Data offset = 24 bytes
TCP:  Flags = 02
TCP:   ..0. .... = (No urgent pointer)
TCP:   ...0 .... = (No acknowledgment)
TCP:   .... 0... = (No push)
TCP:   .... .0.. = (No reset)
TCP:   .... ..1. = SYN
TCP:   .... ...0 = (No FIN)
TCP:  Window = 1024
TCP:  Checksum = EAAF (correct)
TCP:
TCP:  Options follow
TCP:  Maximum segment size = 512
TCP:
```

Trace 4.8.1d. Login to Remote Host TCP Details

4.8.2 Fragmenting Long Messages

In this case study, we will investigate how a host fragments a long message into multiple IP datagrams for transmission on a TCP/IP-based internetwork. In this example, the source is a station (DEC 029487) that wishes to send a large SUN RPC file to another station (Intrln 00027C0) on the same LAN. Three frames are needed to transmit the message (see Trace 4.8.2 and Figure 4-11). The message requires a User Datagram Protocol (UDP) header to identify the source and destination ports at the communicating hosts.

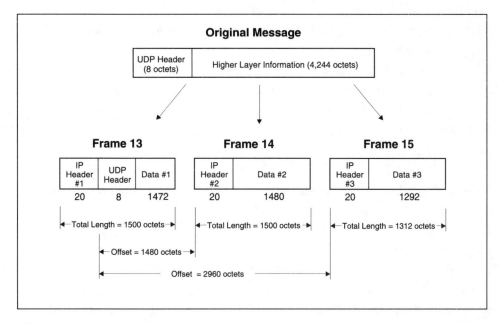

Figure 4-11. IP Fragments

   The message contains 4,244 octets of data, plus an 8-octet UDP header, for a total of 4,252 octets. The message is divided into three frames, with 1,472, 1,480, and 1,292 octets of data each (Frames 13, 14, and 15, respectively). Frame 13 has a total length of 1,500 octets (matching the maximum Ethernet frame size) and indicates that more fragments, associated with message ID=59738, are on the way. The next higher-layer protocol within the first fragment is UDP (Protocol=17, UDP). The Source and Destination addresses [XXX.YYY.0.33] and [XXX.YYY.0.10] identify the network. The UDP header indicates that the total message length is 4,252 octets. This includes the UDP header (8 octets) plus the data (4,244 octets). Thus, the 1,500 octets of Frame 13 consist of the IP header (20 octets), the UDP header (8 octets), and the first data fragment (1,472 octets).

   The second frame also contains 1,514 octets of information (14 octets of Ethernet frame header plus 1,500 octets of data). The IP header indicates that this fragment is 1,500 octets in length and that more fragments associated with message ID=59738 are coming. The fragment offset is 1,480, indicating that the data within Frame 14 starts 1,480 octets after the beginning of the original datagram. Note that the second IP header comprises 20 octets of Frame 14's data, but it does not count in the offset calculation because the IP header is not part of the original message.

The third fragment (Frame 15) contains 1,312 octets of information, consisting of a 20-octet IP header and 1,292 octets of data. This third IP header uses the same message ID=59738 but indicates that no more fragments are coming (the More Fragments bit=0). This fragment belongs 2,960 octets after the beginning of the original message.

Let's now see if the IP module in the Source host was working properly. The UDP header in Frame 13 says that the total length of this message is 4,252 octets. This is divided into the UDP header (8 octets), Data Fragment 1 (1,472 octets), Data Fragment 2 (1,480 octets), and Data Fragment 3 (1292 octets). Each fragment requires a 20-octet IP header, which does not count in the total. Each frame requires 14 octets of Ethernet header, which also does not count in the total. Reviewing Figure 4-11, we can see that the fragment offsets are also correct 1,480 (8 + 1,472) for Fragment 2, and 2,960 (8 + 1,472 + 1,480) for Fragment 3. We can, therefore, conclude that the IP module within station DEC 029487 was functioning properly.

Sniffer Network Analyzer data 10-Dec-86 at 11:20:38, file TCPIP.ENC, Pg 1

```
- - - - - - - - - - - - - - - Frame 13 - - - - - - - - - - - - - - - -
SUMMARY    Delta T    Destination        Source      Summary
   13      0.0152     Intrln0027C0 DEC   029487      DLC Ethertype=0800,
                                                         size=1514 bytes
                                                     IP   D=[XXX.YYY.0.10]
                                                          S=[XXX.YYY.0.33]
                                                          LEN=1480 ID=59738
                                                     UDP D=2049 S=1026 LEN=4252


DLC: ——— DLC Header ———
DLC:
DLC: Frame 13 arrived at  11:20:35.9514; frame size is 1514 (05EA hex) bytes.
DLC: Destination = Station Intrln0027C0
DLC: Source     = Station DEC   029487
DLC: Ethertype  = 0800 (IP)
DLC:
```

IP: ———- IP Header ———-
IP:
IP: Version = 4, header length = 20 bytes
IP: Type of service = 00
IP: 000. .... = routine
IP: ...0 .... = normal delay
IP: .... 0... = normal throughput
IP: .... .0.. = normal reliability
IP: Total length = 1500 bytes
IP: Identification = 59738
IP: Flags = 2X
IP: .0.. .... = may fragment
IP: ..1. .... = more fragments
IP: Fragment offset = 0 bytes
IP: Time to live = 255 seconds/hops
IP: Protocol = 17 (UDP)
IP: Header checksum = 6421 (correct)
IP: Source address = [XXX.YYY.0.33]
IP: Destination address = [XXX.YYY.0.10]
IP: No options
IP:
UDP: ——— UDP Header ———-
UDP:
UDP: Source port = 1026
UDP: Destination port = 2049 (Sun RPC)
UDP: Length = 4252 (not all data contained in this fragment)
UDP: No checksum
UDP:
UDP: [1472 byte(s) of data]
UDP:

- - - - - - - - - - - - - - - - Frame 14 - - - - - - - - - - - - - - - - - -

SUMMARY	Delta T	Destination	Source	Summary	
14	0.0022	Intrln0027C0 DEC	029487	DLC	Ethertype=0800, size=1514 bytes
				IP	D=[XXX.YYY.0.10] S=[XXX.YYY.0.33] LEN=1480 ID=59738
				UDP	continuation ID=59738

DLC: ——— DLC Header ———-
DLC:
DLC: Frame 14 arrived at 11:20:35.9536; frame size is 1514 (05EA hex) bytes.

```
DLC: Destination = Station Intrln0027C0
DLC: Source      = Station DEC   029487
DLC: Ethertype  = 0800 (IP)
DLC:
IP: ——— IP Header ———
IP:
IP:  Version = 4, header length = 20 bytes
IP:  Type of service = 00
IP:       000. .... = routine
IP:       ...0 .... = normal delay
IP:       .... 0... = normal throughput
IP:       .... .0.. = normal reliability
IP:  Total length = 1500 bytes
IP:  Identification = 59738
IP:  Flags = 2X
IP:  .0.. .... = may fragment
IP:  ..1. .... = more fragments
IP:  Fragment offset = 1480 bytes
IP:  Time to live = 255 seconds/hops
IP:  Protocol = 17 (UDP)
IP:  Header checksum = 6368 (correct)
IP:  Source address = [XXX.YYY.0.33]
IP:  Destination address = [XXX.YYY.0.10]
IP:  No options
IP:
UDP: [1480 byte(s) of data, continuation of IP ident=59738]
```

- - - - - - - - - - - - - - - - Frame 15 - - - - - - - - - - - - - - - - -

SUMMARY	Delta T	Destination	Source	Summary
15	0.0019	Intrln0027C0 DEC	029487	DLC Ethertype=0800,
				size=1326 bytes
				IP D=[XXX.YYY.0.10]
				S=[XXX.YYY.0.33]
				LEN=1292 ID=59738
				UDP continuation ID=59738

```
DLC: ——— DLC Header ———
DLC:
DLC: Frame 15 arrived at  11:20:35.9556; frame size is 1326 (052E hex) bytes.
DLC: Destination = Station Intrln0027C0
DLC: Source      = Station DEC   029487
DLC: Ethertype  = 0800 (IP)
DLC:
```

```
IP:  ——— IP Header ———
IP:
IP:  Version = 4, header length = 20 bytes
IP:  Type of service = 00
IP:      000. .... = routine
IP:      ...0 .... = normal delay
IP:      .... 0... = normal throughput
IP:      .... .0.. = normal reliability
IP:  Total length = 1312 bytes
IP:  Identification = 59738
IP:  Flags = 0X
IP:  .0.. .... = may fragment
IP:  ..0. .... = last fragment
IP:  Fragment offset = 2960 bytes
IP:  Time to live = 255 seconds/hops
IP:  Protocol = 17 (UDP)
IP:  Header checksum = 836B (correct)
IP:  Source address = [XXX.YYY.0.33]
IP:  Destination address = [XXX.YYY.0.10]
IP:  No options
IP:
UDP: [1292 byte(s) of data, continuation of IP ident=59738]
```

Trace 4.8.2. IP Fragments

4.8.3 Measuring the Aging of ARP Tables

One of the router parameters that network managers must determine is the time period for aging the ARP tables. If the tables age too quickly, the network devices must resend ARP messages to discover the correct Hardware address of an intended destination. Retransmitting ARPs needlessly consumes internetwork bandwidth. Conversely, if the tables age out too slowly (or not at all), the transmission might go to an obsolete (or incorrect) address. Router manufacturers allow the administrator to tailor the ARP table's aging period to respond to local traffic patterns. After you set the time period, it is useful to test the aging with a protocol analyzer to verify proper operation. Let's see how to do this.

First, we filter the data to show only the ARP messages (Trace 4.8.3a). From this, we see that several devices are active, including Wellfleet Link Node routers (shown as Router LN1 and Router LN2), a Cisco Systems IGS router (shown as

163

Router IGS), and a Sun SPARCstation (shown as Sparcstn). For a consistent test, all of the ARP Request messages ask for a device on the same subnet [192.92.168.X]. The Delta T column gives the time between transmissions in seconds and measures the delay between ARP Requests and Replies.

To determine whether the ARP table of a particular device is operating properly, the analyzer further filters the data to show only the transmission to and from that device. Trace 4.8.3b shows a Wellfleet Link Node router. Frame 4 is set as the baseline for all time measurements. By adding the Delta T measurements, we can determine the time between the transmission of any two frames. Router LN1 broadcasts an ARP message in Frame 4 looking for the Hardware address associated with [192.92.168.3]. Router LN2 responds almost immediately in Frame 6. The next time this Hardware address is requested is almost 158 seconds (about 2½ minutes) later in Frame 142 (we calculate this by adding the significant Delta T measurements: 11.0+1.9+14.1+130.7=157.7 seconds). Another Wellfleet router responds (Frame 144). The ARP cache timer within the Wellfleet routers was set to age out after two minutes. We note that the ARP Request is retransmitted after 2½ minutes, thus verifying the proper operation of the timer. From this we can also conclude that the ARP tables in both LN1 and LN2 are functioning properly, since the same values are used for ARP requests and replies on several occasions. Consider implementing a similar test any time you install a new router to verify its proper operation and eliminate the possibility of excessive traffic due to unnecessary ARP Requests.

Sniffer Network Analyzer data 17-Feb-92 at 13:25:20, ARPTST1.ENC, Pg 1

SUMMARY	Delta T	Destination	Source	Summary		
M 4		Broadcast	Router LN1	ARP	C PA=[192.92.168.3]	PRO=IP
5	0.0001	Broadcast	Router LN1	ARP	C PA=[192.92.168.3]	PRO=IP
6	0.0005	Router LN1	Router LN2	ARP	R PA=[192.92.168.3]	
					HA=0000A2009459 PRO=IP	
7	0.0010	Router LN1	Router LN2	ARP	R PA=[192.92.168.3]	
					HA=0000A2009459 PRO=IP	
17	11.0782	Broadcast	Router IGS	ARP	R PA=[192.92.168.1]	
					HA=00000C0079AF PRO=IP	
21	1.9512	Broadcast	Router LN2	ARP	C PA=[192.92.168.6]	PRO=IP
22	0.0002	Broadcast	Router LN2	ARP	C PA=[192.92.168.6]	PRO=IP

23	0.0001	Router LN2	SparcStn	ARP	R PA=[192.92.168.6]
					HA=080020103170 PRO=IP
36	14.1529	Broadcast	Router IGS	ARP	C PA=[192.92.168.3] PRO=IP
37	0.0006	Router IGS	Router LN2	ARP	R PA=[192.92.168.3]
					HA=0000A2009459 PRO=IP
142	130.7503	Broadcast	Router LN1	ARP	C PA=[192.92.168.3] PRO=IP
143	0.0001	Broadcast	Router LN1	ARP	C PA=[192.92.168.3] PRO=IP
144	0.0005	Router LN1	Router LN2	ARP	R PA=[192.92.168.3]
					HA=0000A2009459 PRO=IP
145	0.0010	Router LN1	Router LN2	ARP	R PA=[192.92.168.3]
					HA=0000A2009459 PRO=IP
154	6.2799	Broadcast	Router LN2	ARP	C PA=[192.92.168.6] PRO=IP
155	0.0002	Broadcast	Router LN2	ARP	C PA=[192.92.168.6] PRO=IP
156	0.0001	Router LN2	SparcStn	ARP	R PA=[192.92.168.6]
					HA=080020103170 PRO=IP
165	7.9092	Broadcast	Router LN2	ARP	C PA=[192.92.168.1] PRO=IP
166	0.0001	Broadcast	Router LN2	ARP	C PA=[192.92.168.1] PRO=IP
167	0.0015	Router LN2	Router IGS	ARP	R PA=[192.92.168.1]
					HA=00000C0079AF PRO=IP
168	0.0009	Router LN2	Router IGS	ARP	R PA=[192.92.168.1]
					HA=00000C0079AF PRO=IP

Trace 4.8.3a. ARP Messages from Various Routers

Sniffer Network Analyzer data 17-Feb-92 at 13:25:20, ARPTST1.ENC, Pg 1

SUMMARY	Delta T	Rel Time	Destination	Source	Summary	
M 4	0.0000		Broadcast		Router LN1	ARP C
						PA=[192.92.168.3]
						PRO=IP
5	0.0001	0.0001	Broadcast	Router LN1	ARP C	
						PA=[192.92.168.3]
						PRO=IP
6	0.0005	0.0007	Router LN1	Router LN2	ARP R	
						PA=[192.92.168.3]
						HA=0000A2009459
						PRO=IP
7	0.0010	0.0018	Router LN1	Router LN2	ARP R	
						PA=[192.92.168.3]
						HA=0000A2009459
						PRO=IP

142	157.9338	157.9357	Broadcast	Router LN1	ARP	C
						PA=[192.92.168.3]
						PRO=IP
143	0.0001	157.9359	Broadcast	Router LN1	ARP	C
						PA=[192.92.168.3]
						PRO=IP
144	0.0005	157.9365	Router LN1	Router LN2	ARP	R
						PA=[192.92.168.3]
						HA=0000A2009459
						PRO=IP
145	0.0010	157.9375	Router LN1	Router LN2	ARP	R
						PA=[192.92.168.3]
						HA=0000A2009459
						PRO=IP

Trace 4.8.3b. ARP Messages from a Wellfleet Link Node Router

4.8.4 Duplicate IP Addresses

In Section 4.1, we looked at the differences between the Physical (Hardware) address and the Logical (Internet Protocol) address on any internet node. Recall that a ROM on the network interface card (Ethernet, token ring, and so on) normally contains the Physical address, while the network administrator assigns the Logical address. Let's see what happens when human error affects address assignments.

In this scenario, two engineers, Wayne and Benoit, wish to establish TELNET sessions with a router. The router's TELNET capabilities allow administrators to access its configuration files for network management. Wayne establishes his session first (see Trace 4.8.4a). The TCP connection is established in Frames 1 through 3, and the TELNET session initiates beginning in Frame 5. Wayne's session appears to be proceeding normally until Benoit starts to transmit in Frame 43. Benoit sends an ARP broadcast looking for the same router (Frame 43), which responds in Frame 44. Benoit then establishes his TCP connection in Frames 45 through 48, and like Wayne, initiates a TELNET session beginning in Frame 49. Benoit doesn't realize, however, that his presence on the internetwork has caused Wayne's connection to fail. Let's see why.

Details of Wayne's TCP connection message (Frame 1) are shown in Trace 4.8.4b. Note that Wayne is communicating to the router using IP source address [131.195.116.250] on the same Class B network. Wayne is accessing the TELNET port on the router, and using Sequence Number=265153482. The router acknowledges the use of this sequence number in its response, shown in Frame 2.

In Trace 4.8.4c, Benoit's TCP connection message looks similar (Frame 45). Benoit claims that his Source Address=[131.195.116.250] (the same as Wayne's) and that the Destination Address=[131.195.116.42]. The TCP header also identifies the same Destination Port (23, for TELNET), but uses a different Sequence Number (73138176).

We can now see why Wayne's TELNET connection failed. When Benoit established a connection with the router using the same IP source address as Wayne's, confusion resulted. The router was examining the IP source address, not the Hardware (Data Link Layer) address. As a result, it was unable to differentiate between the duplicate IP addresses.

We traced the problem to a duplicate entry on the network manager's address database. Unknowingly, he had given both Wayne and Benoit the same IP address for their workstations. After discovering this mistake, Wayne changed his workstation configuration file to incorporate a unique IP address and no further problems occurred.

Sniffer Network Analyzer data 11-Oct-91 at 10:49:04, IPDUPLIC.ENC, Pg 1

SUMMARY	Delta T	Destination	Source	Summary
M 1		Router	Wayne	TCP D=23 S=2588 SYN
				SEQ=265153482
				LEN=0 WIN=1024
2	0.0014	Wayne	Router	TCP D=2588 S=23 SYN
				ACK=265153483
				SEQ=331344504 LEN=0 WIN=0
3	0.0016	Router	Wayne	TCP D=23 S=2588
				ACK=331344505 WIN=1024
4	0.0019	Wayne	Router	TCP D=2588 S=23
				ACK=265153483 WIN=2144
5	0.0048	Wayne	Router	Telnet R PORT=2588 IAC
				Will Echo
6	0.0304	Wayne	Router	Telnet R PORT=2588 <0D><0A>
7	0.0896	Router	Wayne	Telnet C PORT=2588 IAC Do Echo
8	0.3010	Wayne	Router	TCP D=2588 S=23
				ACK=265153486 WIN=2141

9	0.0312	Router	Wayne	Telnet C PORT=2588 IAC
				Do Suppress go-ahead
10	0.3005	Wayne	Router	TCP D=2588 S=23
				ACK=265153489 WIN=2138
11	0.4320	Router	Wayne	Telnet C PORT=2588 c
12	0.3000	Wayne	Router	TCP D=2588 S=23
				ACK=265153490 WIN=2137
13	0.0016	Router	Wayne	Telnet C PORT=2588 d
14	0.2984	Wayne	Router	TCP D=2588 S=23
				ACK=265153491 WIN=2136
15	0.0016	Router	Wayne	Telnet C PORT=2588 2
16	0.2985	Wayne	Router	TCP D=2588 S=23
				ACK=265153492 WIN=2135
17	0.0016	Router	Wayne	Telnet C PORT=2588 <0D><0A>
18	0.0024	Wayne	Router	Telnet R PORT=2588
				<0D><0A>CD_BAS1_2>
19	0.1206	Router	Wayne	TCP D=23 S=2588
				ACK=331344857 WIN=1012
20	0.7757	Router	Wayne	Telnet C PORT=2588 s
21	0.0025	Wayne	Router	Telnet R PORT=2588 s
22	0.1552	Router	Wayne	TCP D=23 S=2588
				ACK=331344858 WIN=1023
23	0.1939	Router	Wayne	Telnet C PORT=2588 h
24	0.0030	Wayne	Router	Telnet R PORT=2588 h
25	0.1326	Router	Wayne	TCP D=23 S=2588
				ACK=331344859 WIN=1023
26	0.0158	Router	Wayne	Telnet C PORT=2588
27	0.0030	Wayne	Router	Telnet R PORT=2588
28	0.1458	Router	Wayne	TCP D=23 S=2588
				ACK=331344860 WIN=1023
29	0.0410	Router	Wayne	Telnet C PORT=2588 i
30	0.0026	Wayne	Router	Telnet R PORT=2588 i
31	0.1212	Router	Wayne	TCP D=23 S=2588
				ACK=331344861 WIN=1023
32	0.1134	Router	Wayne	Telnet C PORT=2588 n
33	0.0034	Wayne	Router	Telnet R PORT=2588 n
34	0.1575	Router	Wayne	TCP D=23 S=2588
				ACK=331344862 WIN=1023
35	0.2039	Router	Wayne	Telnet C PORT=2588 t
36	0.0027	Wayne	Router	Telnet R PORT=2588 t
37	0.1229	Router	Wayne	TCP D=23 S=2588
				ACK=331344863 WIN=1023
38	0.1116	Router	Wayne	Telnet C PORT=2588 <0D><0A>

39	0.0332	Wayne	Router	Telnet R PORT=2588 <0D><0A><0D><0A>Ethernet 0 line protocol is...
40	0.0026	Router	Wayne	TCP D=23 S=2588 ACK=331345399 WIN=1024
41	0.0165	Wayne	Router	Telnet R PORT=2588 ute output rate 19325 bits/sec, 22 packets/sec<0D>...
42	0.2203	Router	Wayne	TCP D=23 S=2588 ACK=331345750 WIN=649
43	41.4005	Broadcast	Benoit	ARP C PA=[131.195.116.42] PRO=IP
44	0.0007	Benoit	Router	ARP R PA=[131.195.116.42] HA=00000C00A145 PRO=IP
45	0.0013	Router	Benoit	TCP D=23 S=15165 SYN SEQ=73138176 LEN=0 WIN=2048
46	0.0015	Benoit	Router	TCP D=15165 S=23 SYN ACK=73138177 SEQ=331390708 LEN=0 WIN=0
47	0.0031	Router	Benoit	TCP D=23 S=15165 ACK=331390709 WIN=2048
48	0.0018	Benoit	Router	TCP D=15165 S=23 ACK=73138177 WIN=2144
49	0.0068	Benoit	Router	Telnet R PORT=15165 IAC Will Echo
50	0.0297	Benoit	Router	Telnet R PORT=15165 <0D><0A>
51	0.2341	Router	Benoit	Telnet C PORT=15165 IAC DoEcho
52	0.2997	Benoit	Router	TCP D=15165 S=23 ACK=73138180 WIN=2141
53	0.0323	Router	Benoit	Telnet C PORT=15165 IAC Do Suppress go-ahead
54	0.2995	Benoit	Router	TCP D=15165 S=23 ACK=73138183 WIN=2138

Trace 4.8.4a. Duplicate IP Address Summary

TROUBLESHOOTING TCP/IP

Sniffer Network Analyzer data 11-Oct-91 at 10:49:04, IPDUPLIC.ENC, Pg 1

```
- - - - - - - - - - - - - - - - Frame 1 - - - - - - - - - - - - - - - -
DLC:  ——- DLC Header ——-
DLC:
DLC:  Frame 1 arrived at  10:49:08.4044; frame size is 60 (003C hex) bytes.
DLC:  Destination = Station Cisco 00A145, Router
DLC:  Source      = Station Intrln06C202, Wayne
DLC:  Ethertype  = 0800 (IP)
DLC:
IP:   ——- IP Header ——-
IP:
IP:   Version = 4, header length = 20 bytes
IP:   Type of service = 00
IP:        000. .... = routine
IP:        ...0 .... = normal delay
IP:        .... 0... = normal throughput
IP:        .... .0.. = normal reliability
IP:   Total length = 44 bytes
IP:   Identification = 13
IP:   Flags = 0X
IP:   .0.. .... = may fragment
IP:   ..0. .... = last fragment
IP:   Fragment offset = 0 bytes
IP:   Time to live = 64 seconds/hops
IP:   Protocol = 6 (TCP)
IP:   Header checksum = 8A14 (correct)
IP:   Source address = [131.195.116.250]
IP:   Destination address = [131.195.116.42]
IP:   No options
IP:
TCP:  ——- TCP header ——-
TCP:
TCP:  Source port = 2588
TCP:  Destination port = 23 (Telnet)
TCP:  Initial sequence number = 265153482
TCP:  Data offset = 24 bytes
TCP:  Flags = 02
TCP:  ..0. .... = (No urgent pointer)
TCP:  ...0 .... = (No acknowledgment)
TCP:  .... 0... = (No push)
TCP:  .... .0.. = (No reset)
TCP:  .... ..1. = SYN
```

TCP: ....0 = (No FIN)
TCP: Window = 1024
TCP: Checksum = 9DAF (correct)
TCP:
TCP: Options follow
TCP: Maximum segment size = 1460
TCP:

- - - - - - - - - - - - - - - Frame 2 - - - - - - - - - - - - - - - -
DLC: ——— DLC Header ———
DLC:
DLC: Frame 2 arrived at 10:49:08.4059; frame size is 60 (003C hex) bytes.
DLC: Destination = Station Intrln06C202, Wayne
DLC: Source   = Station Cisco 00A145, Router
DLC: Ethertype = 0800 (IP)
DLC:
IP: ——— IP Header ———
IP:
IP: Version = 4, header length = 20 bytes
IP: Type of service = 00
IP: 000. .... = routine
IP: ...0 .... = normal delay
IP: .... 0... = normal throughput
IP: .... .0.. = normal reliability
IP: Total length = 44 bytes
IP: Identification = 0
IP: Flags = 0X
IP: .0.. .... = may fragment
IP: ..0. .... = last fragment
IP: Fragment offset = 0 bytes
IP: Time to live = 255 seconds/hops
IP: Protocol = 6 (TCP)
IP: Header checksum = CB20 (correct)
IP: Source address = [131.195.116.42]
IP: Destination address = [131.195.116.250]
IP: No options
IP:
TCP: ——— TCP header ———
TCP:
TCP: Source port = 23 (Telnet)
TCP: Destination port = 2588
TCP: Initial sequence number = 331344504
TCP: Acknowledgment number = 265153483

TCP: Data offset = 24 bytes
TCP: Flags = 12
TCP: ..0. .... = (No urgent pointer)
TCP: ...1 .... = Acknowledgment
TCP: .... 0... = (No push)
TCP: .... .0.. = (No reset)
TCP: .... ..1. = SYN
TCP: ....0 = (No FIN)
TCP: Window = 0
TCP: Checksum = A367 (correct)
TCP:
TCP: Options follow
TCP: Maximum segment size = 1460
TCP:

Trace 4.8.4b. Duplicate IP Address Details (Original station)

Sniffer Network Analyzer data 11-Oct-91 at 10:49:04, IPDUPLIC.ENC, Pg 1

- - - - - - - - - - - - - - - Frame 45 - - - - - - - - - - - - - - - -
DLC: —— DLC Header ——
DLC:
DLC: Frame 45 arrived at 10:49:54.6082; frame size is 60 (003C hex) bytes.
DLC: Destination = Station Cisco 00A145, Router
DLC: Source   = Station Intrln05E253, Benoit
DLC: Ethertype = 0800 (IP)
DLC:
IP: —— IP Header ——
IP:
IP: Version = 4, header length = 20 bytes
IP: Type of service = 10
IP: 000. .... = routine
IP: ...1 .... = low delay
IP: .... 0... = normal throughput
IP: .... .0.. = normal reliability
IP: Total length = 44 bytes
IP: Identification = 1
IP: Flags = 0X
IP: .0.. .... = may fragment
IP: ..0. .... = last fragment
IP: Fragment offset = 0 bytes
IP: Time to live = 64 seconds/hops

IP: Protocol = 6 (TCP)
IP: Header checksum = 8A10 (correct)
IP: Source address = [131.195.116.250]
IP: Destination address = [131.195.116.42]
IP: No options
IP:
TCP: ——- TCP header ——-
TCP:
TCP: Source port = 15165
TCP: Destination port = 23 (Telnet)
TCP: Initial sequence number = 73138176
TCP: Data offset = 24 bytes
TCP: Flags = 02
TCP: ..0. .... = (No urgent pointer)
TCP: ...0 .... = (No acknowledgment)
TCP: .... 0... = (No push)
TCP: .... .0.. = (No reset)
TCP: .... ..1. = SYN
TCP: ....0 = (No FIN)
TCP: Window = 2048
TCP: Checksum = 5FCA (correct)
TCP:
TCP: Options follow
TCP: Maximum segment size = 1460
TCP:

- - - - - - - - - - - - - - - Frame 46 - - - - - - - - - - - - - - - - -
DLC: ——- DLC Header ——-
DLC:
DLC: Frame 46 arrived at 10:49:54.6097; frame size is 60 (003C hex) bytes.
DLC: Destination = Station Intrln05E253, Benoit
DLC: Source   = Station Cisco 00A145, Router
DLC: Ethertype = 0800 (IP)
DLC:
IP: ——- IP Header ——-
IP:
IP: Version = 4, header length = 20 bytes
IP: Type of service = 00
IP: 000. .... = routine
IP: ...0 .... = normal delay
IP: .... 0... = normal throughput
IP: .... .0.. = normal reliability
IP: Total length = 44 bytes

```
IP:   Identification = 0
IP:   Flags = 0X
IP:   .0.. .... = may fragment
IP:   ..0. .... = last fragment
IP:   Fragment offset = 0 bytes
IP:   Time to live = 255 seconds/hops
IP:   Protocol = 6 (TCP)
IP:   Header checksum = CB20 (correct)
IP:   Source address = [131.195.116.42]
IP:   Destination address = [131.195.116.250]
IP:   No options
IP:
TCP:  ──── TCP header ────
TCP:
TCP:  Source port = 23 (Telnet)
TCP:  Destination port = 15165
TCP:  Initial sequence number = 331390708
TCP:  Acknowledgment number = 73138177
TCP:  Data offset = 24 bytes
TCP:  Flags = 12
TCP:  ..0. .... = (No urgent pointer)
TCP:  ...1 .... = Acknowledgment
TCP:  .... 0... = (No push)
TCP:  .... .0.. = (No reset)
TCP:  .... ..1. = SYN
TCP:  .... ...0 = (No FIN)
TCP:  Window = 0
TCP:  Checksum = B505 (correct)
TCP:
TCP:  Options follow
TCP:  Maximum segment size = 1460
TCP:
```

Trace 4.8.4c. Duplicate IP Address Details (Duplicate station)

4.8.5 Incorrect Address Mask

As discussed in Section 4.2, system implementors can use subnetworks to form a hierarchical routing structure within an internetwork.

Subnet addressing works as follows: A 32-bit IP address is comprised of a Network ID plus a Host ID. For example, a Class B network uses 16 bits for the network portion and 16 bits for the host portion. If an internet has multiple physical networks (e.g., LANs), the 16-bit host portion of the address can be further divided into a subnetwork address (representing the particular physical network, such as an Ethernet) and a host address (representing a particular device on that Ethernet.) Class B addresses commonly use 8-bit subnetting. This would give a Network ID of 16 bits, a Subnetwork ID of 8 bits and a Host ID of 8 bits. Thus, it could uniquely identify up to 254 subnetworks (i.e., LANs) each having up to 254 hosts (i.e., workstations, servers and so on.) Recall that the all ZEROs and all ONEs addresses are not allowed, thus reducing the theoretical limit of 256 subnetworks and 256 hosts to 254 of each (256-2=254). The first 16 bits (the Network ID) would deliver the datagram to the access point for the network (the router). The router would then decide which of the 254 subnetworks this datagram was destined for. The router uses a Subnet Mask to make that decision. Subnet Masks are stored within the host and obtained using the ICMP Address Mask Request message. This case study will show what happens when the host uses an incorrect Subnet Mask.

In this example, a network manager, Paul, wishes to check the status of a host on a different segment but connected via a bridge (see Figure 4-10). Paul's workstation software stores a number of parameters, including the Subnet Mask. The network in question is a Class B network, without subnetting. The Subnet Mask should be set for [255.255.0.0], corresponding with a Network ID of 16 bits and a Host ID of 16 bits. Since subnetting is not used, all datagrams for the local network should be delivered directly, but datagrams destined for another network should go through the router. Paul uses the ICMP Echo (PING) command to check the status of his host (a Sun 4 Server), but there's a delay in the ICMP Echo Reply. Let's see what happened.

Paul's workstation first broadcasts an ARP message, looking for a router (Frames 1-2 in Trace 4.8.5a). This step is unexpected, since a router is not required for this transaction. Next, it attempts an ICMP Echo message (Frame 3). If all systems are functioning properly, an ICMP Echo Reply should follow the ICMP Echo immediately. In Paul's case, however, the ICMP Redirect message in Frame 4 follows the ICMP Echo. The Redirect message (see Trace 4.8.5b) indicates that it is redirecting datagrams for the host (ICMP Code=1), and that the correct router (gateway) for this operation is [132.163.132.12]. Paul's workstation then sends another ARP Request, looking for address [132.163.132.12] in Frame 5. The Sun 4 Server responds with HA=0800200C1DC3H (Frame 6). The ICMP Echo and Echo Reply then proceed as expected in Frames 7 and 8. The question remains: Why did Paul's workstation access the router, causing the ICMP Redirect Message?

The second ICMP Echo (Frame 7) sent from Paul's workstation [132.163.129.15] to the Sun 4 Server [132.163.132.12] provides a clue. Note that both devices are on the same network [132.163]. Since this is a Class B network without subnetting, the Subnet Mask should be [255.255.0.0]. When Paul examined the Subnet Mask in his workstation parameters, he found that it had been set for a Class B network with an 8-bit subnet address field, i.e., [255.255.255.0]. When his workstation calculated the Subnet Mask, it came up with:

```
Subnet Mask             11111111  11111111  11111111  00000000
      AND
Source Address          10000100  10100011  10000001  00001111
[132.163.129.15]
Result #1               10000100  10100011  10000001  00000000


Subnet Mask             11111111  11111111  11111111  00000000
      AND
Destination Address 1000100   10100011  10000100  00001100
[132.163.132.12]
Result #2               1000100   10100011  10000100  00000000
```

Because the workstation found that Result #1 and Result #2 were different, it incorrectly concluded that the two devices were on different subnetworks, requiring the assistance of the router. When Paul reconfigured his workstation's Subnet Mask to [255.255.0.0], the ICMP Echo and Echo Replies proceeded without router intervention.

Sniffer Network Analyzer data 13-Feb-92 at 14:50:26, SUBNETC.ENC, Pg 1

SUMMARY	Delta T	Destination	Source	Summary
M 1		Broadcast	Paul	ARP C PA=[132.163.1.1] PRO=IP
2	0.0011	Paul	Router	ARP R PA=[132.163.1.1]
				HA=000093E0A0BF PRO=IP
3	0.0022	Router	Paul	ICMP Echo
4	0.0021	Paul	Router	ICMP Redirect (Redirect
				datagrams for the host)
5	11.7626	Broadcast	Paul	ARP C PA=[132.163.132.12]
				PRO=IP
6	0.0008	Paul	Sun4Svr	ARP R PA=[132.163.132.12]
				HA=0800200C1DC3 PRO=IP
7	0.0023	Sun4Svr	Paul	ICMP Echo
8	0.0016	Paul	Sun4Svr	ICMP Echo reply

Trace 4.8.5a. Subnet Mask Misconfiguration Summary

Sniffer Network Analyzer data 13-Feb-92 at 14:50:26, SUBNETC.ENC, Pg 1

```
- - - - - - - - - - - - - - - Frame 3 - - - - - - - - - - - - - - - - -
ICMP: —— ICMP header ——
ICMP:
ICMP: Type = 8 (Echo)
ICMP: Code = 0
ICMP: Checksum = 719E (correct)
ICMP: Identifier = 1315
ICMP: Sequence number = 1
ICMP: [256 bytes of data]
ICMP:
ICMP: [Normal end of "ICMP header".]
ICMP:
- - - - - - - - - - - - - - - Frame 4 - - - - - - - - - - - - - - - - -
ICMP: —— ICMP header ——
ICMP:
ICMP: Type = 5 (Redirect)
ICMP: Code = 1 (Redirect datagrams for the host)
ICMP: Checksum = 738C (correct)
ICMP: Gateway internet address = [132.163.132.12]
ICMP: IP header of originating message (description follows)
ICMP:
```

```
IP:  ——- IP Header ——-
IP:
IP:  Version = 4, header length = 20 bytes
IP:  Type of service = 00
IP:       000. .... = routine
IP:       ...0 .... = normal delay
IP:       .... 0... = normal throughput
IP:       .... .0.. = normal reliability
IP:  Total length = 284 bytes
IP:  Identification = 2
IP:  Flags = 0X
IP:  .0.. .... = may fragment
IP:  ..0. .... = last fragment
IP:  Fragment offset = 0 bytes
IP:  Time to live = 63 seconds/hops
IP:  Protocol = 1 (ICMP)
IP:  Header checksum = 6C7D (correct)
IP:  Source address = [132.163.129.15]
IP:  Destination address = [132.163.132.12]
IP:  No options
ICMP:
ICMP: [First 8 byte(s) of data of originating message]
ICMP:
ICMP: [Normal end of "ICMP header".]
ICMP:


- - - - - - - - - - - - - - - - Frame 7 - - - - - - - - - - - - - - - - -
ICMP:  ——- ICMP header ——-
ICMP:
ICMP: Type = 8 (Echo)
ICMP: Code = 0
ICMP: Checksum = 4070 (correct)
ICMP: Identifier = 13905
ICMP: Sequence number = 1
ICMP: [256 bytes of data]
ICMP:
ICMP: [Normal end of "ICMP header".]
ICMP:


- - - - - - - - - - - - - - - - Frame 8 - - - - - - - - - - - - - - - - -
ICMP:  ——- ICMP header ——-
ICMP:
ICMP: Type = 0 (Echo reply)
```

ICMP: Code = 0
ICMP: Checksum = 4870 (correct)
ICMP: Identifier = 13905
ICMP: Sequence number = 1
ICMP: [256 bytes of data]
ICMP:
ICMP: [Normal end of "ICMP header".]
ICMP:

Trace 4.8.5b. Subnet Mask Misconfiguration ICMP Details

4.8.6 Using ICMP Echo Messages

ICMP messages can answer many questions about the health of the network. The ICMP Echo/Echo Reply messages, commonly known as the PING, are probably the most frequently used.

You invoke PING from your host operating system to test the path to a particular host. If all is well, a message will return, verifying the existence of the path to the host or network. One caution is in order, however: unpredictable results can occur if you PING an improper destination address. For example, PINGing address [255.255.255.255] (limited broadcast within this subnet) may cause excessive internetwork traffic. Let's look at an example.

One lonely weekend, a network administrator decides to test the paths to some of the hosts on his internet. He has two ways to accomplish this. He could send an ICMP Echo message to each host separately, or he could send a directed broadcast to all hosts on his network and subnetwork. He decides to enter the Destination address [129.99.23.255] that PINGs all of the hosts on Class B network 129.99, subnet 23. Trace 4.8.6a shows the result. Frame 683 is the ICMP Echo (PING); and he receives 27 frames containing ICMP Echo Reply messages. Note that all of the reply messages are directed to the originator of the ICMP Echo message, workstation SilGrf020C5D. Also note that the Wellfleet routers on this network did not respond to the PING because their design protects against such a transmission. Other hosts or routers may be designed in a similar manner.

Details of the ICMP Echo (Frame 683) and the first ICMP Echo Reply (Frame 684) are given in Trace 4.8.6b. The Echo's Destination address is set for broadcast, and it indicates that the Echo Replies come back to the originating station. As the trace shows, the message originator [129.99.23.146] has specified that all hosts on subnet 23 should respond by setting the Destination address to [129.99.23.255]. The first response (Frame 684) is from device [129.99.23.17], followed by responses from 26 other hosts (Frames 685 through 712). Also note that the ICMP header contains an Identifier (18501) that correlates Echo and Echo Reply messages, in case PINGs to/from different hosts occur simultaneously. The 56 octets of data transmitted with the Echo message are returned with the Echo Reply.

We can draw one clear conclusion from this exercise: The ICMP Echo message can be a very valuable troubleshooting tool, but make sure of your destination before you initiate the command. A PING to a broadcast address could have a great impact on the internetwork traffic.

Sniffer Network Analyzer data 17-Feb-92 at 15:31:08, PINGTST4.ENC, Pg 1

SUMMARY	Delta T	Destination	Source		Summary
683		Broadcast	SilGrf	020C5D	ICMP Echo
684	0.0004	SilGrf020C5D	SilGrf	060C44	ICMP Echo reply
685	0.0004	SilGrf020C5D	SilGrf	020FF9	ICMP Echo reply
686	0.0003	SilGrf020C5D	Sun	106604	ICMP Echo reply
687	0.0003	SilGrf020C5D	Sun	0F5DC2	ICMP Echo reply
688	0.0002	SilGrf020C5D	Sun	08FE6B	ICMP Echo reply
689	0.0003	SilGrf020C5D	SilGrf	021193	ICMP Echo reply
690	0.0001	SilGrf020C5D	SilGrf	02137B	ICMP Echo reply
691	0.0004	SilGrf020C5D	Sun	094668	ICMP Echo reply
692	0.0003	SilGrf020C5D	Prteon1064D6		ICMP Echo reply
693	0.0002	SilGrf020C5D	Sun	062A16	ICMP Echo reply
694	0.0002	SilGrf020C5D	Sun	00DAFF	ICMP Echo reply
695	0.0002	SilGrf020C5D	CMC	A00666	ICMP Echo reply
696	0.0002	SilGrf020C5D	Sun	00E849	ICMP Echo reply
697	0.0003	SilGrf020C5D	Sun	005513	ICMP Echo reply
698	0.0001	SilGrf020C5D	NSC	010212	ICMP Echo reply
699	0.0002	SilGrf020C5D	00802D0020F8		ICMP Echo reply
700	0.0001	SilGrf020C5D	Exceln 231835		ICMP Echo reply
701	0.0002	SilGrf020C5D	00802D002202		ICMP Echo reply
702	0.0001	SilGrf020C5D	DEC	0A136F	ICMP Echo reply
703	0.0001	SilGrf020C5D	DECnet00F760		ICMP Echo reply
704	0.0001	SilGrf020C5D	Sun	0045AD	ICMP Echo reply
705	0.0001	SilGrf020C5D	Intel	0361A8	ICMP Echo reply
706	0.0001	SilGrf020C5D	Sun	0A73A2	ICMP Echo reply

707	0.0001	SilGrf020C5D	DEC	0D0B05	ICMP Echo reply
708	0.0001	SilGrf020C5D	Sun	00F725	ICMP Echo reply
709	0.0001	SilGrf020C5D	SilGrf	020C38	ICMP Echo reply
712	0.0211	SilGrf020C5D	Intrln	008248	ICMP Echo reply

Trace 4.8.6a. ICMP Echo to IP Address [X.X.X.255] Summary

Sniffer Network Analyzer data 17-Feb-92 at 15:31:08, PINGTST4.ENC, Pg 1

- - - - - - - - - - - - - - - Frame 683 - - - - - - - - - - - - - - - - -
DLC: ——- DLC Header ——-
DLC:
DLC: Frame 683 arrived at 15:31:50.3581; frame size is 102 (0066 hex) bytes.
DLC: Destination = BROADCAST FFFFFFFFFFFF, Broadcast
DLC: Source   = Station SilGrf020C5D
DLC: Ethertype = 0800 (IP)
DLC:
IP: ——- IP Header ——-
IP:
IP: Version = 4, header length = 20 bytes
IP: Type of service = 00
IP: 000. .... = routine
IP: ...0 .... = normal delay
IP: .... 0... = normal throughput
IP: .... .0.. = normal reliability
IP: Total length = 84 bytes
IP: Identification = 16898
IP: Flags = 0X
IP: .0.. .... = may fragment
IP: ..0. .... = last fragment
IP: Fragment offset = 0 bytes
IP: Time to live = 255 seconds/hops
IP: Protocol = 1 (ICMP)
IP: Header checksum = 474F (correct)
IP: Source address = [129.99.23.146]
IP: Destination address = [129.99.23.255]
IP: No options
IP:
ICMP: ——- ICMP header ——-
ICMP:
ICMP: Type = 8 (Echo)
ICMP: Code = 0

ICMP: Checksum = 851E (correct)
ICMP: Identifier = 18501
ICMP: Sequence number = 0
ICMP: [56 bytes of data]
ICMP:
ICMP: [Normal end of "ICMP header".]
ICMP:

- - - - - - - - - - - - - - - - Frame 684 - - - - - - - - - - - - - - - - -
DLC: ——- DLC Header ——-
DLC:
DLC: Frame 684 arrived at 15:31:50.3585; frame size is 98 (0062 hex) bytes.
DLC: Destination = Station SilGrf020C5D
DLC: Source   = Station SilGrf060C44
DLC: Ethertype = 0800 (IP)
DLC:
IP: ——- IP Header ——-
IP:
IP: Version = 4, header length = 20 bytes
IP: Type of service = 00
IP: 000. .... = routine
IP: ...0 .... = normal delay
IP: .... 0... = normal throughput
IP: .... .0.. = normal reliability
IP: Total length = 84 bytes
IP: Identification = 985
IP: Flags = 0X
IP: .0.. .... = may fragment
IP: ..0. .... = last fragment
IP: Fragment offset = 0 bytes
IP: Time to live = 255 seconds/hops
IP: Protocol = 1 (ICMP)
IP: Header checksum = 8666 (correct)
IP: Source address = [129.99.23.17]
IP: Destination address = [129.99.23.146]
IP: No options
IP:
ICMP: ——- ICMP header ——-
ICMP:
ICMP: Type = 0 (Echo reply)
ICMP: Code = 0
ICMP: Checksum = 8D1E (correct)
ICMP: Identifier = 18501

ICMP: Sequence number = 0
ICMP: [56 bytes of data]
ICMP:
ICMP: [Normal end of "ICMP header".]
ICMP:

Trace 4.8.6b. ICMP Echo to IP Address [X.X.X.255] Details

4.8.7 Misdirected Datagrams

In section 4.5, we studied the operation of the Internet Control Message Protocol (ICMP) and saw how to the ICMP Redirect message (ICMP Type=5) corrects routing problems. A unique code within the ICMP message specifies the datagrams to be redirected (review Figure 4-8).

In this example, a workstation wishes to communicate with a remote host on another subnetwork (see Figure 4-12). Unfortunately, the workstation's configuration file is incorrect, and its initial attempt to communicate with the remote host fails (see Trace 4.8.7a). From out of the internet comes an intelligent router to the rescue! Router 234 (the workstation's default router) recognizes the error and issues an ICMP Redirect in Frame 4. The workstation obliges, switches its transmissions to the correct path (Router 235) in Frame 5, and successfully establishes a TELNET session with the remote host (Frames 6 through 20). Let's look inside the ICMP messages and see what happened (Trace 4.8.7b).

The workstation's initial transmission (Frame 3) is directed to Router 234, with the datagram destined for the remote Host address [XXX.YYY.0.154]. We know that a router will be involved in the communication because the Source address (the workstation)[XXX.YYY.0.152], and the Host address [XXX.YYY.0.154] are on different subnetworks. Router 234 responds to this initial transmission by issuing an ICMP Redirect in Frame 4. We can now identify the IP address of Router 234, (the Source address, [XXX.YYY.0.234], of the ICMP Redirect). The ICMP header indicates a Redirect for the host (ICMP Code=1) and the correct path, which is via Router 235, address [XXX.YYY.0.235].

The workstation sees the error of its ways and changes the Destination hardware address to be Router 235 (Frame 5). Note that the Source and Destination IP addresses did not change between Frame 3 and Frame 5. In other words, the workstation knew who it wanted to communicate with, it just didn't know how to get there. Frame 6 shows the confirmation of the redirected path; that datagram is a response from the remote host (IP Source address = [XXX.YYY.0.154]).

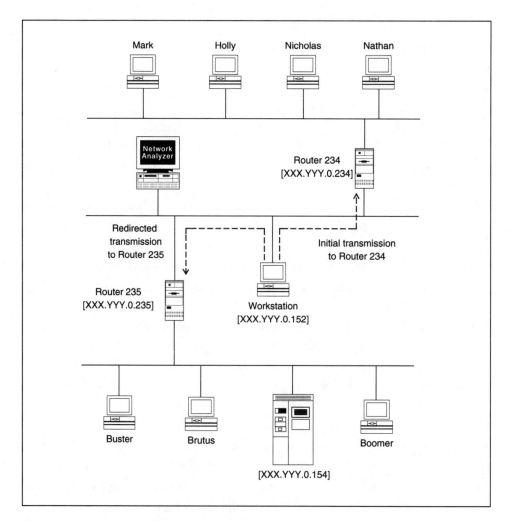

Figure 4-12. Misdirected Datagram Topology

Upon further study, the network manager discovered that the workstation's default gateway had been set incorrectly. When this parameter was changed to reflect Router 235 (instead of Router 234) the problem did not reoccur.

Sniffer Network Analyzer data 2-Mar-90 at 10:17:44, RICMP.ENC, Pg 1

SUMMARY	Delta T	Destination	Source	Summary
3	0.0162	Router 234	Workstation	Telnet R PORT=2909 <0D><0A>
4	0.0029	Workstation	Router 234	ICMP Redirect (Redirect datagrams for the host)
5	0.0118	Router 235	Workstation	Telnet R PORT=2909 $
6	0.0941	Workstation	Router 235	TCP D=23 S=2909 ACK=813932917 WIN=4096
7	3.7848	Workstation	Router 235	Telnet C PORT=2909 p
8	0.0088	Router 235	Workstation	Telnet R PORT=2909 p
9	0.0065	Workstation	Router 235	TCP D=23 S=2909 ACK=813932918 WIN=4096
10	0.3042	Workstation	Router 235	Telnet C PORT=2909 s
11	0.0082	Router 235	Workstation	Telnet R PORT=2909 s
12	0.0881	Workstation	Router 235	TCP D=23 S=2909 ACK=813932919 WIN=4096
13	0.0053	Workstation	Router 235	Telnet C PORT=2909
14	0.0080	Router 235	Workstation	Telnet R PORT=2909
15	0.1858	Workstation	Router 235	TCP D=23 S=2909 ACK=813932920 WIN=4096
16	0.5343	Workstation	Router 235	Telnet C PORT=2909 -
17	0.0078	Router 235	Workstation	Telnet R PORT=2909 -
18	0.0577	Workstation	Router 235	TCP D=23 S=2909 ACK=813932921 WIN=4096
19	0.1744	Workstation	Router 235	Telnet C PORT=2909 a
20	0.0078	Router 235	Workstation	Telnet R PORT=2909 a

Trace 4.8.7a. Misdirected Datagram Summary

Sniffer Network Analyzer data 2-Mar-90 at 10:17:44, RICMP.ENC, Pg 1

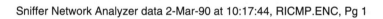

- - - - - - - - - - - - - - - - Frame 3 - - - - - - - - - - - - - - - - -
DLC: ——- DLC Header ——-
DLC:
DLC: Frame 3 arrived at 10:21:01.5697; frame size is 74 (004A hex) bytes.
DLC: Destination = Station XXXXXX 002461, Router 234
DLC: Source   = Station XXXXXX 01BB41, Workstation
DLC: Ethertype = 0800 (IP)
DLC:

```
IP:  ——- IP Header ——-
IP:
IP:  Version = 4, header length = 20 bytes
IP:  Type of service = 00
IP:        000. .... = routine
IP:        ...0 .... = normal delay
IP:        .... 0... = normal throughput
IP:        .... .0.. = normal reliability
IP:  Total length = 42 bytes
IP:  Identification = 2931
IP:  Flags = 0X
IP:  .0.. .... = may fragment
IP:  ..0. .... = last fragment
IP:  Fragment offset = 0 bytes
IP:  Time to live = 30 seconds/hops
IP:  Protocol = 6 (TCP)
IP:  Header checksum = 31A8 (correct)
IP:  Source address = [XXX.YYY.0.152]
IP:  Destination address = [XXX.YYY.0.154]
IP:  No options
IP:
TCP: ——- TCP header ——-
TCP:
TCP:  Source port = 23 (Telnet)
TCP:  Destination port = 2909
TCP:  Sequence number = 813932913
TCP:  Acknowledgment number = 63520058
TCP:  Data offset = 20 bytes
TCP:  Flags = 18
TCP:  ..0. .... = (No urgent pointer)
TCP:  ...1 .... = Acknowledgment
TCP:  .... 1... = Push
TCP:  .... .0.. = (No reset)
TCP:  .... ..0. = (No SYN)
TCP:  .... ...0 = (No FIN)
TCP:  Window = 9116
TCP:  Checksum = 0105 (correct)
TCP:  No TCP options
TCP:  [2 byte(s) of data]
TCP:
Telnet:——- Telnet data ——-
Telnet:
```

Telnet:<0D><0A>
Telnet:

- - - - - - - - - - - - - - - Frame 4 - - - - - - - - - - - - - - - - -
DLC: ——- DLC Header ——-
DLC:
DLC: Frame 4 arrived at 10:21:01.5726; frame size is 70 (0046 hex) bytes.
DLC: Destination = Station XXXXXX 01BB41, Workstation
DLC: Source   = Station XXXXXX 002461, Router 234
DLC: Ethertype = 0800 (IP)
DLC:
IP: ——- IP Header ——-
IP:
IP: Version = 4, header length = 20 bytes
IP: Type of service = 00
IP: 000. .... = routine
IP: ...0 .... = normal delay
IP: .... 0... = normal throughput
IP: .... .0.. = normal reliability
IP: Total length = 56 bytes
IP: Identification = 0
IP: Flags = 0X
IP: .0.. .... = may fragment
IP: ..0. .... = last fragment
IP: Fragment offset = 0 bytes
IP: Time to live = 255 seconds/hops
IP: Protocol = 1 (ICMP)
IP: Header checksum = 5CA3 (correct)
IP: Source address = [XXX.YYY.0.234]
IP: Destination address = [XXX.YYY.0.152]
IP: No options
IP:
ICMP: ——- ICMP header ——-
ICMP:
ICMP: Type = 5 (Redirect)
ICMP: Code = 1 (Redirect datagrams for the host)
ICMP: Checksum = EE0C (correct)
ICMP: Gateway internet address = [XXX.YYY.0.235]
ICMP: IP header of originating message (description follows)
ICMP:
IP: ——- IP Header ——-
IP:
IP: Version = 4, header length = 20 bytes

```
IP:   Type of service = 00
IP:       000. .... = routine
IP:       ...0 .... = normal delay
IP:       .... 0... = normal throughput
IP:       .... .0.. = normal reliability
IP:   Total length = 42 bytes
IP:   Identification = 2931
IP:   Flags = 0X
IP:   .0.. .... = may fragment
IP:   ..0. .... = last fragment
IP:   Fragment offset = 0 bytes
IP:   Time to live = 29 seconds/hops
IP:   Protocol = 6 (TCP)
IP:   Header checksum = 32A8 (correct)
IP:   Source address = [XXX.YYY.0.152]
IP:   Destination address = [XXX.YYY.0.154]
IP:   No options
ICMP:
ICMP: [First 8 byte(s) of data of originating message]
ICMP:
ICMP: [Normal end of "ICMP header".]
ICMP:


- - - - - - - - - - - - - - - Frame 5 - - - - - - - - - - - - - - - - -
DLC:  ——— DLC Header ———
DLC:
DLC:  Frame 5 arrived at  10:21:01.5845; frame size is 74 (004A hex) bytes.
DLC:  Destination = Station XXXXXX 00244F, Router 235
DLC:  Source     = Station XXXXXX 01BB41, Workstation
DLC:  Ethertype  = 0800 (IP)
DLC:
IP:   ——— IP Header ———
IP:
IP:   Version = 4, header length = 20 bytes
IP:   Type of service = 00
IP:       000. .... = routine
IP:       ...0 .... = normal delay
IP:       .... 0... = normal throughput
IP:       .... .0.. = normal reliability
IP:   Total length = 42 bytes
IP:   Identification = 2932
IP:   Flags = 0X
IP:   .0.. .... = may fragment
```

IP: ..0. .... = last fragment
IP: Fragment offset = 0 bytes
IP: Time to live = 30 seconds/hops
IP: Protocol = 6 (TCP)
IP: Header checksum = 31A7 (correct)
IP: Source address = [XXX.YYY.0.152]
IP: Destination address = [XXX.YYY.0.154]
IP: No options
IP:
TCP: ——- TCP header ——-
TCP:
TCP: Source port = 23 (Telnet)
TCP: Destination port = 2909
TCP: Sequence number = 813932915
TCP: Acknowledgment number = 63520058
TCP: Data offset = 20 bytes
TCP: Flags = 18
TCP: ..0. .... = (No urgent pointer)
TCP: ...1 .... = Acknowledgment
TCP: .... 1... = Push
TCP: .... .0.. = (No reset)
TCP: .... ..0. = (No SYN)
TCP: ....0 = (No FIN)
TCP: Window = 9116
TCP: Checksum = E9EC (correct)
TCP: No TCP options
TCP: [2 byte(s) of data]
TCP:
Telnet:——- Telnet data ——-
Telnet:
Telnet:$
Telnet:

- - - - - - - - - - - - - - - - Frame 6 - - - - - - - - - - - - - - - - -

DLC: ——- DLC Header ——-
DLC:
DLC: Frame 6 arrived at 10:21:01.6787; frame size is 60 (003C hex) bytes.
DLC: Destination = Station XXXXXX 01BB41, Workstation
DLC: Source   = Station XXXXXX 00244F, Router 235
DLC: Ethertype = 0800 (IP)
DLC:

```
IP:  —— IP Header ——
IP:
IP:  Version = 4, header length = 20 bytes
IP:  Type of service = 00
IP:       000. .... = routine
IP:       ...0 .... = normal delay
IP:       .... 0... = normal throughput
IP:       .... .0.. = normal reliability
IP:  Total length = 40 bytes
IP:  Identification = 37695
IP:  Flags = 0X
IP:  .0.. .... = may fragment
IP:  ..0. .... = last fragment
IP:  Fragment offset = 0 bytes
IP:  Time to live = 58 seconds/hops
IP:  Protocol = 6 (TCP)
IP:  Header checksum = 8DDD (correct)
IP:  Source address = [XXX.YYY.0.154]
IP:  Destination address = [XXX.YYY.0.152]
IP:  No options
IP:
TCP:  —— TCP header ——
TCP:
TCP:  Source port = 2909
TCP:  Destination port = 23 (Telnet)
TCP:  Sequence number = 63520058
TCP:  Acknowledgment number = 813932917
TCP:  Data offset = 20 bytes
TCP:  Flags = 10
TCP:  ..0. .... = (No urgent pointer)
TCP:  ...1 .... = Acknowledgment
TCP:  .... 0... = (No push)
TCP:  .... .0.. = (No reset)
TCP:  .... ..0. = (No SYN)
TCP:  .... ...0 = (No FIN)
TCP:  Window = 4096
TCP:  Checksum = 21B1 (correct)
TCP:  No TCP options
TCP:
```

Trace 4.8.7b. Misdirected Datagram Details

4.8.8 Confused Routers

For our final example, we'll consider a case of false advertising by a router (see Figure 4-13). This internetwork consists of a number of Ethernet segments and one Apollo token ring connected by routers. Workstations wishing to communicate with other hosts are getting confused because two routers want their datagrams. As a result, the two routers become locked in a battle, with the workstation coming out the loser. Let's see what happened.

In this scenario, a router (designated Router A in Figure 4-13) connected an Ethernet segment and an Apollo token ring. (The Apollo token ring is a proprietary network designed by Apollo Computer, now part of Hewlett-Packard, to connect Apollo workstations.) Confusion occurs between Router A and Router E, which is also connected to the Ethernet segment.

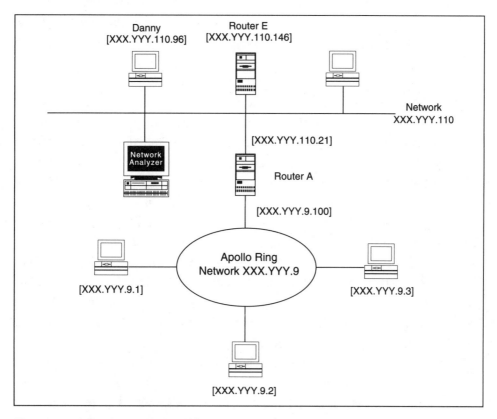

Figure 4-13. Confused Router Topology

The network manager, Danny, address [XXX.YYY.110.96], has a workstation on the Ethernet segment and wishes to communicate with Router E, address [XXX.YYY.110.146], shown in Trace 4.8.8a. Danny sends an ARP message in Frame 13, and Router E responds in Frame 14 with its Hardware address 90000A200226CH). Next, Danny initiates a TCP connection in Frame 15 via Router E, asking for a host on an Ethernet 3 hops away. Instead of the expected TCP handshake, Router E tells Danny to redirect his datagrams to Router A (Frame 16), and then passes Danny's TCP connect request to Router A (Frame 17).

Unfortunately, Router A does not agree, and tells Danny to redirect his datagrams back to Router E (Frame 18). Router A then passes the same TCP connect request back to Router E (Frame 19). Router E now disagrees, and sends a redirect to Router A, along with the same TCP connect request (Frames 20 and 21). Note the identical Sequence Number in Frames 15, 17, 19, and 21: SEQ=170068605. The routers are passing the same TCP message back and forth because neither knows what to do with it. The scenario repeats for some time (Frames 22 through 35). Danny's TCP connect request is stuck in a routing loop.

An examination of the RIP broadcasts from both Router A and Router E yielded a clue to the problem. Router E's (Trace 4.8.8b) RIPs include 17 routing messages. Danny scrutinized all of the network addresses, along with the number of router hops (the metric) required to reach those other networks. All of the information looked correct, except for the Routing data in Frame 16. The IP address of [P.P.9.0] (the Apollo token ring network) showed a metric of 16, or unreachable. This metric was clearly incorrect, since the Apollo network was only one hop away— via Router A. The desired network, however, did not appear in Router E's broadcast.

A similar analysis was then made of Router A's RIP broadcasts (Trace 4.8.8c). A total of 17 Routing data frames were included in the broadcast. Routing Data Frame 17 correctly identified the Ethernet segment [Q.Q.110.0] as being one hop away. Unfortunately, a number of other networks that could not be reached via Router A were being advertised as reachable. In addition, the target network was not listed in this RIP message, either.

The network manager concluded that both Router A and Router E had corrupted routing tables. To correct the problem, he took both routers out of service, reconfigured them, and brought them back up. No further problems were noted— the RIP routing loop had been corrected.

Sniffer Network Analyzer data 15-May-91 at 14:31:02, ATEST.ENC, Pg 1

SUMMARY	Delta T	Destination	Source	Summary
13	1.1843	Broadcast	Danny	ARP C PA=[XXX.YYY.110.146] PRO=IP
14	0.0009	Danny	Router E	ARP R PA=[XXX.YYY.110.146] HA=0000A200226C PRO=IP
15	0.0019	Router E	Danny	TCP D=23 S=14663 SYN SEQ=170068605 LEN=0 WIN=1024
16	0.0008	Danny	Router E	ICMP Redirect (Redirect datagrams for the host)
17	0.0002	Router A	Router E	TCP D=23 S=14663 SYN SEQ=170068605 LEN=0 WIN=1024
18	0.0120	Danny	Router A	ICMP Redirect (Redirect datagrams for the network)
19	0.0033	Router E	Router A	TCP D=23 S=14663 SYN SEQ=170068605 LEN=0 WIN=1024
20	0.0008	Router A	Router E	ICMP Redirect (Redirect datagrams for the host)
21	0.0001	Router A	Router E	TCP D=23 S=14663 SYN SEQ=170068605 LEN=0 WIN=1024
22	0.0098	Router E	Router A	ICMP Redirect (Redirect datagrams for the network)
23	0.0024	Danny	Router A	ICMP Redirect (Redirect datagrams for the host)
24	0.0098	Danny	Router A	ICMP Redirect (Redirect datagrams for the network)
25	0.0028	Router E	Router A	TCP D=23 S=14663 SYN SEQ=170068605 LEN=0 WIN=1024
26	0.0015	Router A	Router E	ICMP Redirect (Redirect datagrams for the host)
27	0.0001	Router A	Router E	TCP D=23 S=14663 SYN SEQ=170068605 LEN=0 WIN=1024
28	0.0108	Router E	Router A	ICMP Redirect (Redirect datagrams for the network)
29	0.0037	Danny	Router A	ICMP Redirect (Redirect datagrams for the host)

193

30	0.0084	Danny	Router A	ICMP Redirect (Redirect datagrams for the network)
31	0.0032	Router E	Router A	TCP D=23 S=14663 SYN SEQ=170068605 LEN=0 WIN=1024
32	0.0008	Router A	Router E	ICMP Redirect (Redirect datagrams for the host)
33	0.0001	Router A	Router E	TCP D=23 S=14663 SYN SEQ=170068605 LEN=0 WIN=1024
34	0.0089	Router E	Router A	ICMP Redirect (Redirect datagrams for the network)
35	0.0049	Danny	Router A	ICMP Redirect (Redirect datagrams for the host)

Trace 4.8.8a. Routing Loop Summary

Sniffer Network Analyzer data 15-May-91 at 14:31:02, ERIP.ENC, Pg 1

- - - - - - - - - - - - - - - Frame 1 - - - - - - - - - - - - - - - -
DLC: —— DLC Header ——
DLC:
DLC: Frame 1 arrived at 14:31:17.3235; frame size is 386 (0182 hex) bytes.
DLC: Destination = BROADCAST FFFFFFFFFFFF, Broadcast
DLC: Source   = Station 0000A200226C, Router E
DLC: Ethertype = 0800 (IP)
DLC:
IP: —— IP Header ——
IP:
IP: Version = 4, header length = 20 bytes
IP: Type of service = 00
IP: 000. .... = routine
IP: ...0 .... = normal delay
IP: .... 0... = normal throughput
IP: .... .0.. = normal reliability
IP: Total length = 372 bytes
IP: Identification = 35481
IP: Flags = 0X
IP: .0.. .... = may fragment
IP: ..0. .... = last fragment
IP: Fragment offset = 0 bytes
IP: Time to live = 30 seconds/hops
IP: Protocol = 17 (UDP)

194

```
IP:  Header checksum = B3E4 (correct)
IP:  Source address = [XXX.YYY.110.146]
IP:  Destination address = [XXX.YYY.110.0]
IP:  No options
IP:
UDP: ────── UDP Header ──────
UDP:
UDP: Source port = 520 (Route)
UDP: Destination port = 520
UDP: Length = 352
UDP: Checksum = 157F (correct)
UDP:
RIP: ────── RIP Header ──────
RIP:
RIP: Command = 2 (Response)
RIP: Version = 1
RIP: Unused  = 0
RIP:
RIP: Routing data frame 1
RIP:    Address family identifier = 2 (IP)
RIP:    IP Address = [A.A.0.0]
RIP:    Metric    = 2
RIP:
RIP: Routing data frame 2
RIP:    Address family identifier = 2 (IP)
RIP:    IP Address = [B.B.0.0]
RIP:    Metric    = 3
RIP:
RIP: Routing data frame 3
RIP:    Address family identifier = 2 (IP)
RIP:    IP Address = [C.C.0.0]
RIP:    Metric    = 2
RIP:
RIP: Routing data frame 4
RIP:    Address family identifier = 2 (IP)
RIP:    IP Address = [D.D.0.0]
RIP:    Metric    = 2
RIP:
RIP: Routing data frame 5
RIP:    Address family identifier = 2 (IP)
RIP:    IP Address = [E.E.0.0]
RIP:    Metric    = 1
RIP:
RIP: Routing data frame 6
```

195

```
RIP:    Address family identifier = 2 (IP)
RIP:    IP Address = [F.F.0.0]
RIP:    Metric    = 2
RIP:
RIP: Routing data frame 7
RIP:    Address family identifier = 2 (IP)
RIP:    IP Address = [G.G.0.0]
RIP:    Metric    = 2
RIP:
RIP: Routing data frame 8
RIP:    Address family identifier = 2 (IP)
RIP:    IP Address = [H.H.0.0]
RIP:    Metric    = 2
RIP:
RIP: Routing data frame 9
RIP:    Address family identifier = 2 (IP)
RIP:    IP Address = [I.I.0.0]
RIP:    Metric    = 2
RIP:
RIP: Routing data frame 10
RIP:    Address family identifier = 2 (IP)
RIP:    IP Address = [J.J.0.0]
RIP:    Metric    = 4
RIP:
RIP: Routing data frame 11
RIP:    Address family identifier = 2 (IP)
RIP:    IP Address = [K.K.0.0]
RIP:    Metric    = 3
RIP:
RIP: Routing data frame 12
RIP:    Address family identifier = 2 (IP)
RIP:    IP Address = [L.L.0.0]
RIP:    Metric    = 3
RIP:
RIP: Routing data frame 13
RIP:    Address family identifier = 2 (IP)
RIP:    IP Address = [M.M.0.0]
RIP:    Metric    = 1
RIP:
RIP: Routing data frame 14
RIP:    Address family identifier = 2 (IP)
RIP:    IP Address = [N.N.0.0]
RIP:    Metric    = 3
RIP:
```

RIP: Routing data frame 15
RIP: Address family identifier = 2 (IP)
RIP: IP Address = [O.O.0.0]
RIP: Metric   = 3
RIP:
RIP: Routing data frame 16
RIP: Address family identifier = 2 (IP)
RIP: IP Address = [P.P.9.0]
RIP: Metric   = 16 (Unreachable)
RIP:
RIP: Routing data frame 17
RIP: Address family identifier = 2 (IP)
RIP: IP Address = [Q.Q.0.0]
RIP: Metric   = 3
RIP:

Trace 4.8.8b. Router E RIP Broadcast Message

Sniffer Network Analyzer data 15-May-91 at 14:22:04, ARIP.ENC, Pg 1

- - - - - - - - - - - - - - - - Frame 1 - - - - - - - - - - - - - - - - -

DLC: ——- DLC Header ——-
DLC:
DLC: Frame 1 arrived at 14:22:30.9929; frame size is 386 (0182 hex) bytes.
DLC: Destination = BROADCAST FFFFFFFFFFFF, Broadcast
DLC: Source   = Station 0207010024FB, Router A
DLC: Ethertype = 0800 (IP)
DLC:
IP: ——- IP Header ——-
IP:
IP: Version = 4, header length = 20 bytes
IP: Type of service = 08
IP: 000. .... = routine
IP: ...0 .... = normal delay
IP: .... 1... = high throughput
IP: .... .0.. = normal reliability
IP: Total length = 372 bytes
IP: Identification = 47689
IP: Flags = 0X
IP: .0.. .... = may fragment
IP: ..0. .... = last fragment
IP: Fragment offset = 0 bytes

IP: Time to live = 10 seconds/hops
IP: Protocol = 17 (UDP)
IP: Header checksum = 98A9 (correct)
IP: Source address = [XXX.YYY.110.21]
IP: Destination address = [XXX.YYY.110.0]
IP: No options
IP:
UDP: —— UDP Header ——
UDP:
UDP: Source port = 520 (Route)
UDP: Destination port = 520
UDP: Length = 352
UDP: Checksum = 14FC (correct)
UDP:
RIP: ——- RIP Header ——
RIP:
RIP: Command = 2 (Response)
RIP: Version = 1
RIP: Unused = 0
RIP:
RIP: Routing data frame 1
RIP: Address family identifier = 2 (IP)
RIP: IP Address = [A.A.111.0]
RIP: Metric   = 4
RIP:
RIP: Routing data frame 2
RIP: Address family identifier = 2 (IP)
RIP: IP Address = [B.B.112.0]
RIP: Metric   = 4
RIP:
RIP: Routing data frame 3
RIP: Address family identifier = 2 (IP)
RIP: IP Address = [C.C.0.0]
RIP: Metric   = 3
RIP:
RIP: Routing data frame 4
RIP: Address family identifier = 2 (IP)
RIP: IP Address = [D.D.113.0]
RIP: Metric   = 4
RIP:
RIP: Routing data frame 5
RIP: Address family identifier = 2 (IP)
RIP: IP Address = [E.E.9.0]
RIP: Metric   = 1

```
RIP:
RIP:  Routing data frame 6
RIP:      Address family identifier = 2 (IP)
RIP:      IP Address = [F.F.0.0]
RIP:      Metric    = 2
RIP:
RIP:  Routing data frame 7
RIP:      Address family identifier = 2 (IP)
RIP:      IP Address = [G.G.90.0]
RIP:      Metric    = 4
RIP:
RIP:  Routing data frame 8
RIP:      Address family identifier = 2 (IP)
RIP:      IP Address = [H.H.0.0]
RIP:      Metric    = 3
RIP:
RIP:  Routing data frame 9
RIP:      Address family identifier = 2 (IP)
RIP:      IP Address = [I.I.0.0]
RIP:      Metric    = 5
RIP:
RIP:  Routing data frame 10
RIP:      Address family identifier = 2 (IP)
RIP:      IP Address = [J.J.0.0]
RIP:      Metric    = 4
RIP:
RIP:  Routing data frame 11
RIP:      Address family identifier = 2 (IP)
RIP:      IP Address = [K.K.0.0]
RIP:      Metric    = 3
RIP:
RIP:  Routing data frame 12
RIP:      Address family identifier = 2 (IP)
RIP:      IP Address = [L.L.0.0]
RIP:      Metric    = 3
RIP:
RIP:  Routing data frame 13
RIP:      Address family identifier = 2 (IP)
RIP:      IP Address = [M.M.0.0]
RIP:      Metric    = 3
RIP:
RIP:  Routing data frame 14
RIP:      Address family identifier = 2 (IP)
RIP:      IP Address = [N.N.0.0]
```

```
RIP:    Metric   = 3
RIP:
RIP: Routing data frame 15
RIP:    Address family identifier = 2 (IP)
RIP:    IP Address = [O.O.0.0]
RIP:    Metric   = 3
RIP:
RIP: Routing data frame 16
RIP:    Address family identifier = 2 (IP)
RIP:    IP Address = [P.P.0.0]
RIP:    Metric   = 4
RIP:
RIP: Routing data frame 17
RIP:    Address family identifier = 2 (IP)
RIP:    IP Address = [Q.Q.110.0]
RIP:    Metric   = 1
RIP:
```

Trace 4.8.8c. Router A RIP Broadcast Message

In this chapter we have covered a number of protocols that work together to deliver datagrams within the internet from one host to another. Since this transmission is based upon the Internet Protocol's connectionless service, guaranteed delivery of those datagrams must be assured by another process, the Host-to-Host Layer. We will study the two protocols that operate at the Host-to-Host Layer, UDP and TCP, in the next chapter.

4.9 References

[4-1]   Roman, Bob. "Making the Big Connection." 3TECH, *The 3Com Technical Journal* (Summer 1990): 14-25.

[4-2]   Roman, Bob. "How Routing Works: A Sequel to 'Making the Big Connection'." 3TECH, *The 3Com Technical Journal* (Fall 1991):5-9.

[4-3]   Ramsay, Clint. "The Fundamentals of IP Routing." 3TECH, *The 3Com Technical Journal* (Summer 1990):26-33.

[4-4]   Shein, Barry. "The Internet Protocols: A Functional Overview." *ConneX-ions* (July 1987): 2-9.

[4-5]   Postel, J. "Internet Protocol," RFC 791, ISI, September 1981.

[4-6]   Reynolds, J. and J. Postel, "Assigned Numbers," RFC 1340, ISI, July 1992.

[4-7]   White, Gene. *Internetworking and Addressing*. New York, NY: McGraw-Hill, Inc., 1992.

[4-8]   Kirkpatrick, S., et. al. "Internet Numbers", RFC 1166, July 1990.

[4-9]   Mogul, J., et. al. "Internet Standard Subnetting Procedure," RFC 950, Stanford, August 1985.

[4-10]   Mogul, Jeffrey. "Subnetting: A Brief Guide." *ConneXions* (January 1989): 2-9.

[4-11]   Stone, Mike. "Guide to TCP/IP Network Addressing." *LAN Technology* (April 1991): 41-46.

[4-12]   Krol, E., "The Hitchhikers Guide to the Internet," RFC 1118, University of Illinois Urbana, September 1989.

[4-13]   Braden, R., et. al. "Requirements for Internet Gateways," RFC 1009, ISI, June 1987.

[4-14]   Plummer, D. "An Ethernet Address Resolution Protocol, or Converting Network Protocol Addresses to 48-bit Ethernet Addresses for Transmission on Ethernet Hardware," RFC 826, Symbolics, Inc., November 1982.

[4-15]   Finlayson, R., et. al. "A Reverse Address Resolution Protocol," RFC 903, Stanford University, June 1984.

[4-16] Comer, Douglas. "Mapping Internet Addresses to Ethernet Addresses." *ConneXions* (December 1987): 2-7.

[4-17] Comer, Douglas. "Determining an Internet Address at Startup." *ConneXions* (January 1988): 10-14.

[4-18] Postel, J. "Multi-LAN Address Resolution", RFC 925, ISI, October 1984.

[4-19] Black, Uyless. *TCP/IP and Related Protocols.* New York, NY: McGraw-Hill, Inc., 1992.

[4-20] Comer, Douglas E. *Internetworking with TCP/IP.* 2nd ed. Englewood Cliffs, NJ: Prentice Hall, Inc., 1991.

[4-21] Gilmore, John. "Bootstrap Protocol (BOOTP)", RFC 951, Sun Microsystems, September 1985.

[4-22] Mogul, Jeffrey. "Booting Diskless Hosts: The BOOTP Protocol." *ConneXions* (October 1988): 14-18.

[4-23] Mills, Dave, "Exterior Gateway Protocol Formal Specification," RFC 904, April 1984.

[4-24] Callon, Ross, et. al. "Routing in an Internetwork Environment." *ConneXions* (August 1989): 2-7.

[4-25] Hedrick, C. "Routing Information Protocol." RFC 1058, Rutgers University, June 1988.

[4-26] Moy, John, "OSPF Version 2," RFC 1247, Proteon, Inc., July 1991.

[4-27] Moy, John. "OSPF: Next Generation Routing Comes to TCP/IP Networks." *LAN Technology* (April 1990): 71-79.

[4-28] Seifert, William M. "OSPF: The First Wave of Next-Generation Routing Protocols." Business Communications Review (July 1991): 31-34.

[4-29] Hume, Sharon. "A Technical Tour of OSPF." 3TECH, The 3Com Technical Journal (Summer 1991): 44-56.

[4-30] Medin, Milo S. "The Great IGP Debate — Part Two: The Open Shortest Path First (OSPF) Routing Protocol." *ConneXions* (October 1991): 53-61.

[4-31] Postel, J. "Internet Control Message Protocol," RFC 792, ISI, September 1981.

[4-32] Nagle, John. "Congestion Control in IP/TCP Internetworks," RFC 896, Ford Aerospace and Communications Corporation, January 1984.

[4-33] Prue, W., et. al. "Something a Host Could Do with Source Quench: The Source Quench Introduced Delay (SQuID)," RFC 1016, ISI, July 1987.

[4-34] Gerber, Barry. "IP Routing: Learn to Follow the Yellow Brick Road," *Network Computing* (April 1992) 98-106.

[4-35] Mockapetris, P. "Domain Names: Implementation and Specification", RFC 1035, ISI, November 1987.

CHAPTER 5

Troubleshooting the Host-to-Host Connection

Datagrams and virtual circuits both convey information on an end-to-end basis. But each is associated with different benefits and costs. The datagram provides low overhead at the expense of rigorous reliability; the virtual circuit offers high reliability at the cost of high overhead. The choice depends on the reliability necessary for the data being transferred. For example, because humans are involved in sending electronic mail, error detection is built into the transmission process. If a message is lost en route, the intended recipient can simply ask the sender to retransmit the message. An electronic mail message could, therefore, be sent as a datagram. File transfers, on the other hand, demand a high degree of reliability and should employ the connection-oriented virtual circuit.

In this chapter, we will study the two protocols that implement datagrams and virtual circuits: the User Datagram Protocol (UDP) and the Transmission Control Protocol (TCP). Other host-related issues are discussed in RFC 1123, "Requirements for Internet Hosts: Application and Support." The first issue to consider is how UDP and TCP fit into the DARPA architectural model.

5.1 The Host-to-Host Connection

In Chapter 3, we learned that the Network Interface Layer handles the physical connection for the LAN or WAN. In Chapter 4, we explored the Internet Layer, which routes IP datagrams from one device to another on the same network or on a different network via the internetwork. The Internet Layer also administers the 32-bit Internet addresses (used with IP) and takes care of intra-internetwork communication (with ICMP).

Figure 5-1a shows the DARPA architectural model; as you can see, the Host-to-Host Layer is the first layer that operates exclusively within the hosts, not in the routers. So assuming that the IP datagram has arrived at the Destination host, what issues must the host (and the architect designing the internetwork) deal with in order to establish and use the communication link between the two end points?

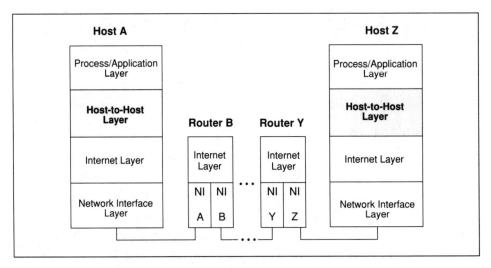

Figure 5-1a. The Host-to-Host Connection

First, we must assume that the host has more than one process at its disposal. Therefore, the datagram will require additional addressing to identify the host process to which it will apply. This additional address is carried within the UDP or TCP header and is known as a Port address (more on ports in Section 5.2). Another issue to consider is reliability of the datagram; the hosts will want assurance that the datagram arrived correctly. Both the UDP and TCP headers address this concern. A third consideration is the overhead associated with the host-to-host transmission. The overhead directly relates to the type of connection—TCP or UDP—employed. It is the requirements of the Process/Application Layer that determine the choice between TCP and UDP. As shown in Figure 5-1b, the File Transfer Protocol (FTP), Telecommunications Network (TELNET) protocol, and Simple Mail Transfer Protocol (SMTP) run over TCP transport. The Trivial File Transfer Protocol (TFTP), Simple Network Management Protocol (SNMP), and Sun Microsystems Inc.'s Network File System (NFS) protocols work with UDP. We will study these protocols in depth in Chapter 6.

Figure 5-1c shows where the overhead occurs. The Local Network header and trailer delimit the transmission frame and treat the higher-layer information as data inside the frame. The IP header is the first component of overhead, followed by the UDP or TCP headers. The UDP header requires 8 octets, the TCP header a minimum of 20 octets. As we will see in the following sections, the overhead relates directly to the rigor of the protocols.

As noted above, both UDP and TCP use Port addresses to identify the incoming data stream and multiplex it to the appropriate Host process. We'll look at the functions of the Port addresses next.

DARPA Layer	Protocol Implementation						OSI Layer
Process / Application	File Transfer	Electronic Mail	Terminal Emulation	File Transfer	Client / Server	Network Management	Application
	File Transfer Protocol (FTP)	Simple Mail Transfer Protocol (SMTP)	TELNET Protocol	Trivial File Transfer Protocol (TFTP)	Sun Microsystems Network File System Protocols (NFS)	Simple Network Management Protocol (SNMP)	Presentation
	MIL-STD-1780 RFC 959	MIL-STD-1781 RFC 821	MIL-STD-1782 RFC 854	RFC 783	RFCs 1014, 1057, and 1094	RFC 1157	Session
Host-to-Host	Transmission Control Protocol (TCP) MIL-STD-1778 RFC 793			User Datagram Protocol (UDP) RFC 768			Transport
Internet	Address Resolution ARP RFC 826 RARP RFC 903		Internet Protocol (IP) MIL-STD-1777 RFC 791		Internet Control Message Protocol (ICMP) RFC 792		Network
Network Interface	Network Interface Cards: Ethernet, StarLAN, Token Ring, ARCNET RFC 894, RFC 1042, RFC 1201						Data Link
	Transmission Media: Twisted Pair, Coax, Fiber Optics, Wireless Media, etc.						Physical

Figure 5-1b. DARPA Host-to-Host Layer Protocols

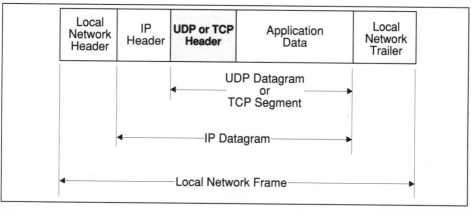

Figure 5-1c. The Internet Transmission Frame and UDP/TCP Header Position

5.2 Port Addresses

In our tour of the DARPA architectural model, we've encountered addresses for each layer. Let's review these briefly. The Network Interface (or OSI Physical and Data Link) Layer requires a Hardware address. The Hardware address is assigned to the network interface card and is typically a 48-bit number that resides in a ROM on the board itself. The Hardware address uniquely identifies each workstation on the LAN or WAN. Because that address resides in hardware, it remains constant as the device is moved from one network to another.

The Internet (or OSI Network) Layer requires a Logical address, which identifies the network to which a host is attached. As we discussed in Section 4.3, this Internet (or IP) address may be further subdivided into Subnetwork and Host IDs. This address is a 32-bit number that the network administrator assigns to the device. If the device were to be moved from one network to another, a different Internet address would be necessary. The ARP and RARP protocols that we studied in Section 4.4 correlate the Internet Layer and Network Interface Layer addresses.

The third layer of addressing is used at the Host-to-Host (or OSI Transport) Layer and completes the DARPA addressing scheme. This address is known as a Port address, and it identifies the user process or application within the host. Each host is presumed to have available multiple applications, such as electronic mail, databases, and so on. An identifier, known as a Port number, specifies the process the user wishes to access. These Port numbers are 16 bits long and are standardized according to their use. Internet administrators assign Port numbers 0-255; other numbers are available for local administration. A complete listing of the assigned ports is available in RFC 1060, "Assigned Numbers." Some examples are given in Table 5-1.

In summary, a message sent from one host to another requires three addresses at the source and the destination to complete the communication path. The Port address (16 bits) identifies the user process (or application) and is contained within the UDP or TCP header. The Internet address (32 bits) identifies the network and host that the process is running on and is located inside the IP header. On some hosts, the combination of the Port address and the IP address is referred to as a socket. The Hardware address (usually 48 bits) completes the Data address on the local network. The Hardware address, which is in the Data Link Layer header, is physically configured on the network interface card.

With that background, let's see how UDP and TCP use the Port address to complete the host-to-host connection.

Table 5-1. Port Assignments

Decimal	Keyword	Description
1	TCPMUX	TCP Port Service Multiplexer
5	RJE	Remote Job Entry
7	ECHO	Echo
11	USERS	Active Users
13	DAYTIME	Daytime
17	QUOTE	Quote of the Day
19	CHARGEN	Character Generator
20	FTP-DATA	File Transfer [Default Data]
21	FTP	File Transfer [Control]
23	TELNET	TELNET
25	SMTP	Simple Mail Transfer
37	TIME	Time
42	NAMESERVER	Host Name Server
43	NICNAME	Who Is
53	DOMAIN	Domain Name Server
67	BOOTPS	Bootstrap Protocol Server
68	BOOTPC	Bootstrap Protocol Client
69	TFTP	Trivial File Transfer
79	FINGER	Finger
102	ISO-TSAP	ISO-TSAP
103	X400	X.400
104	X400-SND	X.400-SND
109	POP2	Post Office Protocol — Version 2
110	POP3	Post Office Protocol — Version 3
137	NETBIOS-NS	NetBIOS Name Service
138	NETBIOS-DGM	NetBIOS Datagram Service
139	NETBIOS-SSN	NetBIOS Session Service
144	NEWS	News
146	ISO-TP0	ISO-TP0
147	ISO-IP	ISO-IP
161	SNMP	SNMP

Table 5-1. Port Assignments, *continued*

Decimal	Keyword	Description
162	SNMPTRAP	SNMPTRAP
163	CMIP-Manage	CMIP/TCP Manager
164	CMIP-Agent	CMIP/TCP Agent
165	XNS-Courier	Xerox
201	AT-RMTP	AppleTalk Routing Maintenance
202	AT-NBP	AppleTalk Name Binding
203	AT-3	AppleTalk Unused
204	AT-ECHO	AppleTalk Echo
206	AT-ZIS	AppleTalk Zone Information
246	DSP3270	Display Systems Protocol

5.3 User Datagram Protocol (UDP)

As its name implies, the User Datagram Protocol, described in RFC 768 [5-1], provides a connectionless host-to-host communication path. UDP assumes that IP, which is also connectionless, is the underlying (Internet Layer) protocol. Because this service has minimal overhead, UDP has a relatively small header, as shown in Figure 5-2. The resulting message, consisting of the IP header, UDP header and user data is called a UDP datagram.

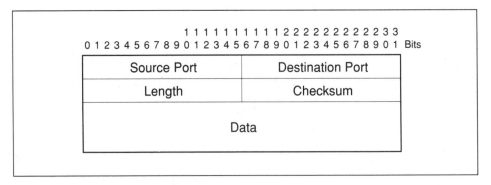

Figure 5-2. User Datagram Protocol (UDP) Header

The first two fields are the Source and Destination Port numbers (each 2 octets long), discussed in Section 5.2. The Source Port field is optional, and when not in use is filled with ZEROs. The Length field (2 octets) is the length of the UDP datagram, which has a minimum value of 8 octets. The Checksum field (2 octets) is also optional and may be filled with ZEROs if the Upper Layer Protocol (ULP) process does not require a checksum. When the checksum is used, it is calculated from the so-called Pseudo header, which includes the Source and Destination addresses, plus the Protocol field from the IP header (see Figure 5-3). By including the IP address in its calculations for the checksum, the Pseudo header assures that the UDP datagram is delivered to the correct Destination network and host. The IP Protocol field within the Pseudo header would equal 17 for UDP.

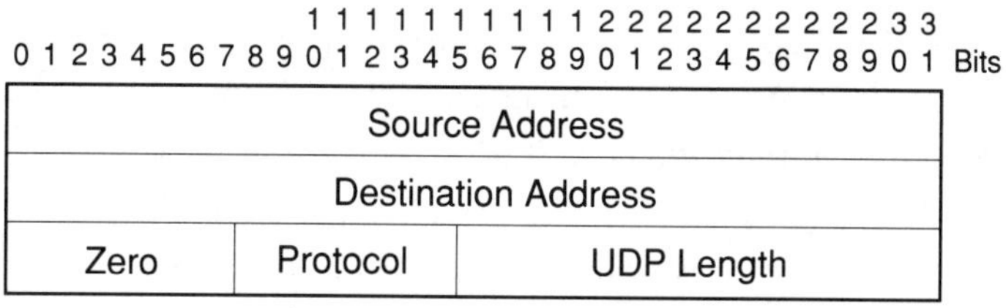

Figure 5-3. UDP Pseudo Header

In summary, the IP Destination address routes the datagram to the correct host on the specified network, then the UDP Port address routes the datagram to the correct host process. Thus, the UDP adds Port addressing capabilities to IP's datagram service. Examples of host processes that use UDP as the host-to-host protocol include the Time protocol, Port number 37; the Domain Name Server (DNS), Port number 53; the Bootstrap Protocol (BOOTP) server and client, Port numbers 67 and 68, respectively; the Trivial File Transfer Protocol (TFTP), Port number 69; and the Sun Microsystems Remote Procedure Call (SunRPC), Port number 111. All of these applications assume that if the host-to-host connection were to fail, a higher layer function, such as DNS, would recover. Applications that require more reliability in their end-to-end data transmissions use the more rigorous TCP, which we will discuss next.

5.4 Transmission Control Protocol (TCP)

In Chapter 1, we learned that the Internet protocols were designed to meet U.S. Government and Military requirements. These requirements dictated that the data communication system be able to endure battlefield conditions. The Internet protocol designed specifically to meet the rigors of the battlefield was the Transmission Control Protocol, described in RFC 793 [5-2]. Unlike UDP, TCP is a connection-oriented protocol that is responsible for reliable communication between two end processes. The unit of data transferred is called a stream, which is simply a sequence of octets. The stream originates at the ULP process and is subsequently divided into TCP segments, IP datagrams, and Local Network frames. RFC 1180, "A TCP/IP Tutorial" [5-3], offers a useful summary of the way the TCP information fits into the related protocols, such as IP, and the Local Network connection, such as Ethernet. RFC 869, "The TCP Maximum Segment Size and Related Topics" [5-4], describes the relationships between TCP segments and IP datagrams.

TCP handles six functions: basic data transfer, reliability, flow control, multiplexing, connections, and precedence/security. We will discuss these functions in detail in Section 5.5.

The TCP header (see Figure 5-4) has a minimum length of 20 octets. This header contains a number of fields, relating to connection management, data flow control, and reliability, which UDP did not require.

The TCP header starts with two Port addresses (2 octets each) to identify the logical host processes at each end of the connection.

The Sequence Number field (4 octets) is the sequence number given to the first octet of data (when the SYN flag bit is set, the sequence number indicates the Initial Sequence Number (ISN) selected. The first data octet sent uses the next sequence number [ISN+1]). The sequence number assures the sequentiality of the data stream, which is a fundamental component of reliability.

The Acknowledgement Number field (4 octets) verifies the receipt of data. This protocol process is called Positive Acknowledgement or Retransmission (PAR). The process requires that each unit of data (the octet, in the case of TCP) be explicitly acknowledged. If it is not, the sender will time-out and retransmit. The value in the acknowledgement is the next octet (i.e., the next sequence number) expected from the other end of the connection. When the Acknowledgement field is in use (i.e., during a connection), the ACK flag bit is set.

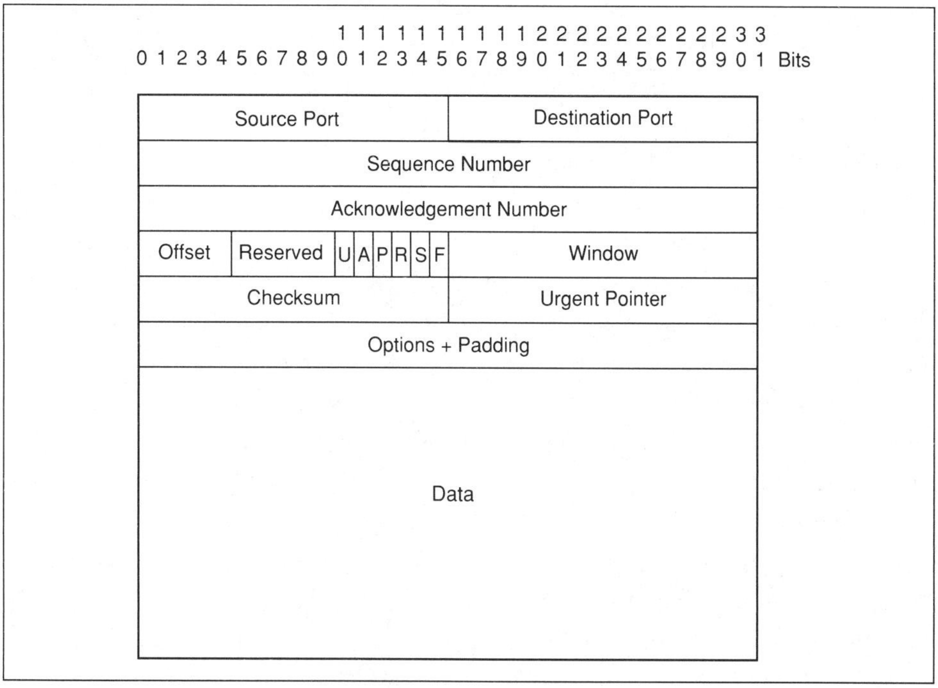

```
                          1 1 1 1 1 1 1 1 1 1 2 2 2 2 2 2 2 2 2 2 3 3
          0 1 2 3 4 5 6 7 8 9 0 1 2 3 4 5 6 7 8 9 0 1 2 3 4 5 6 7 8 9 0 1  Bits
```

Source Port	Destination Port
Sequence Number	
Acknowledgement Number	

Offset	Reserved	U	A	P	R	S	F	Window

Checksum	Urgent Pointer
Options + Padding	
Data	

Figure 5-4. Transmission Control Protocol (TCP) Header

The next 32-bit word (octets 13-16 in the header) contains a number of fields used for control purposes. The Data Offset field (4 bits) measures the number of 32-bit words in the TCP header. Its value indicates where the TCP header ends and the ULP data begins. The Offset field is necessary because the TCP header has a variable, not fixed, length; therefore, the position of the first octet of ULP data may vary. Since the minimum length of the TCP header is 20 octets, the minimum value of the Data Offset field would be five 32-bit words. The next 6 bits are reserved for future use and set equal to ZERO.

Six flags that control the connection and data transfer are transmitted next. Each flag has its own 1-bit field. These flags include:

URG: Urgent Pointer field significant
ACK: Acknowledgement field significant
PSH: Push function
RST: Reset the connection

SYN: Synchronize Sequence numbers

FIN: No more data from sender

We will study use of these flags in greater detail in Section 5.5.

The Window field (2 octets) provides end-to-end flow control. The number in the Window field indicates the quantity of octets, beginning with the one in the Acknowledgement field, that the sender of the segment can accept. Note that like the Acknowledgement field, the Window field is bi-directional. Since TCP provides a full-duplex communication path, both ends send control information to their peer process at the other end of the connection. In other words, my host provides both an acknowledgement and a window advertisement to your host, and your host does the same for mine. In this manner, both ends provide control information to their remote partner.

The Checksum field (2 octets) is used for error control. The checksum calculation includes a 12-octet Pseudo header, the TCP header and ULP data. The TCP Pseudo header (shown in Figure 5-5) is similar to the UDP Pseudo header shown in Figure 5-3. Its purpose is to provide error control on the IP header, the TCP header, and the data. The fields included in the TCP Pseudo header include the Source and Destination address, the protocol, and the TCP Length. The TCP Length field includes the TCP header and Upper-Layer Protocol (ULP) data, but not the 12-octet Pseudo header.

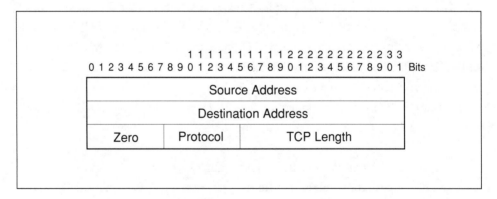

Figure 5-5. TCP Pseudo Header

The Urgent Pointer field (2 octets) allows the position of urgent data within the TCP segment to be identified. This field is used in conjunction with the Urgent (URG) control flag and points to the Sequence number of the octet that follows the urgent data. In other words, the Urgent pointer indicates the beginning of the routine (non-urgent) data.

Options and Padding fields (both variable in length) complete the TCP header. The Options field is an even multiple of octets in length and specifies options required by the TCP process within the host. One option is the maximum TCP segment size, which mandates the amount of data that the sender of the option is willing to accept. We saw this option used by the AppleTalk workstation in Trace 3.11.6. The Padding field contains a variable number of ZEROs that ensure that the TCP header ends on a 32-bit boundary.

Now that we've explored the fields within the TCP header, we'll see how they provide the six TCP functions: basic data transfer, reliability, flow control, multiplexing, connections, and precedence/security.

5.5 TCP Functions

TCP is a rigorous protocol, rich with the functionality demanded by its government-backed designers. In this section, we'll explore each of the six areas of TCP operation separately, and conclude with a summary of the TCP state diagram. References [5-5] and [5-6] discuss the concepts of the User/TCP interface in greater detail; however, for our troubleshooting purposes, we'll focus on understanding the protocol interactions, not the internal protocol operations.

5.5.1 Basic Data Transfer

A TCP module transfers a series of octets, known as a segment, from one host to another. Data flows in both directions, making for a full-duplex connection. The TCP modules at each end determine the length of the segment and indicate this length in the Options field of the TCP header.

Occasionally, a TCP module requires immediate data delivery and can't wait for the segment to fill completely. An upper-layer process would trigger the Push (PSH) flag within the TCP header, and tell the TCP module to immediately forward all of the queued data to the receiver.

5.5.2 Reliability

So far, we've assumed that Host B has received all the data sent from Host A. Unfortunately, there's no such network utopia in the real world. The transmitted data could be lost, inadvertently duplicated, delivered out of order, or damaged. If damage occurs, the checksum will fail, alerting the receiver to the problem. The other conditions are more complex, and TCP must have mechanisms to handle them.

The cornerstones of TCP's reliability are its Sequence and Acknowledgement numbers. The Sequence number is logically attached to each outgoing octet. The receiver uses the Sequence number to determine whether any octets are missing or have been received out of order. TCP is a Positive Acknowledgement with Retransmission (PAR) protocol. This means that if data is received correctly, the receiving TCP module generates an Acknowledgement (ACK) number. If the transmitting TCP module does not receive an acknowledgement within the specified time, it will retransmit. No Negative Acknowledgements (NAKs) are allowed.

Figure 5-6 illustrates the TCP reliability services. (For simplicity, we'll assume that a large data file is being sent from Host A to Host B.) The first segment (SEQ 128-143) is acknowledged without error. The second segment (SEQ 144-159) is not so fortunate and experiences a transmission error. Since that segment never arrives at Host B, no acknowledgement (ACK = 160) is issued. As a result, Host A times out and retransmits the second segment (SEQ 144-159). Internetworks, by definition, contain multiple communication paths. Each of these may have a different propagation delay. Given this variance, it may be difficult to determine the appropriate timeout period. The greater the number of possible paths, the more difficult it becomes to calculate an accurate TCP timer value. Comer [5-6] presents an excellent summary of the retransmission and timer issues. Partridge [5-7] discusses how TCP timers affect the protocol's performance, and Karn [5-8] discusses an algorithm known as Karn's Algorithm used to calculate the network Round Trip Time (RTT), which impacts the retransmission timers.

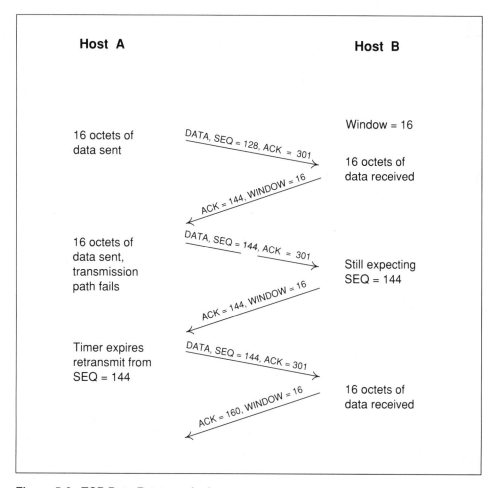

Figure 5-6. TCP Data Retransmissions

5.5.3 Flow Control

Let's begin by reviewing some terms and concepts, then we'll discuss how they relate to the Flow Control mechanism. Recall from the previous section that the Sequence number is attached by the sending device to the TCP segment and counts each octet transmitted. The Acknowledgement number indicates the next expected Sequence number; i.e., the next octet of data expected from the other end of the connection. A third metric, also included within the TCP header, is the Window number. The Window indicates how many more sequence numbers the sender of the Window is prepared to accept, and is described in RFC 813 [5-9]. In doing this, the Window controls the flow of data from sender to receiver. Thus, if Host A sends Window = 1024 to Host B, it has much more available buffer space than if Host A sends Window = 10. In the first case, Host A grants Host B permission to transmit 1,024 octets of data past the current Sequence number; in the second case, only 10.

Window = 0 and Window = 1 are two special cases of "sliding" window operations. If a host returns Window = 0, it has shut down communication and will accept no more octets from the other end of the connection. Window = 1 is sometimes known as "stop-and-wait" transmission. The top portion of Figure 5-7 illustrates what happens when Window = 1. (For simplicity, we'll assume that the data is transmitted from Host A to Host B and that acknowledgements go in the opposite direction. In reality, TCP allows full-duplex operation. Therefore, data could also flow from Host B to Host A, with corresponding acknowledgements from Host A to Host B.) Host A has a large, 523K-octet file to send. Host B has set Window = 1, thereby limiting data transmissions to one octet before each acknowledgement. Thus, Host A must wait for Host B's acknowledgement before it can transmit each octet of data. Not very efficient, you might say, and few analysts would disagree.

Now suppose that Host B obtains additional buffer space and increases the value to Window = 8. Host A can now send 8 octets of data (SEQ 103-110, inclusive) before requiring an acknowledgement. When the acknowledgement arrives, it indicates the next expected Sequence number (e.g., ACK = 111 would indicate that octets numbered 103-110 arrived correctly and it is permissible to send eight more, beginning with SEQ = 111.) Similarly, an increase to Window = 16 would allow a corresponding increase in the quantity of data transmitted. We use the term *flow control* to describe the effect of the sliding window operation because you can control the flow of data by adjusting the window value.

The window size is a parameter that requires some optimization. Too many small segments generate needless ACKs, but large segments utilize more buffers. The case study given in Section 5.7.8 provides an example of a window-related problem.

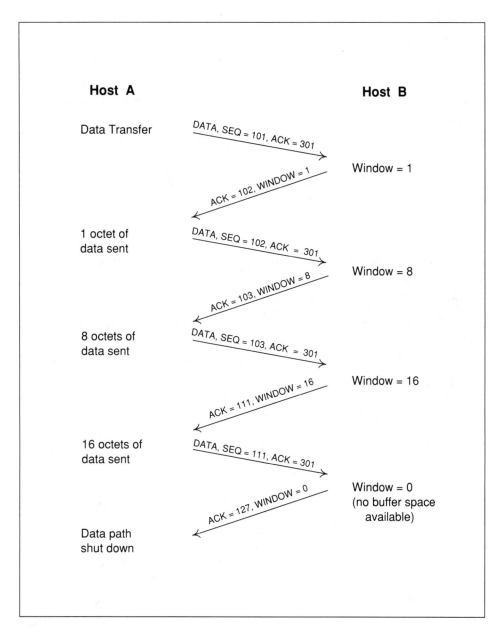

Figure 5-7. TCP Data Transfer (Window size varying)

5.5.4 Multiplexing

The TCP module assumes that its associated host may be a multi-function system. Indeed, the host may offer the user an entire menu of applications, and the user may want to use several of them simultaneously. TCP provides a multiplexing function to accommodate these diverse needs. In Section 5.2, we learned that the Port address (16 bits) uniquely identifies an end-user process. The host binds, or associates, a particular port with a process. Some processes, such as the major application protocols FTP, TELNET, and SMTP, have assigned port numbers. Others may be dynamically assigned as the need arises.

A Socket is the concatenation of the Internet address and the Port address. A Connection is the association of a pair of Sockets, although a Socket is not restricted to one connection. For example, if a host has a port assigned to the TELNET protocol—say, Port 23—there's nothing to preclude connections from multiple terminals (i.e., remote sockets) to that port. The host can also have other processes, such as the File Transfer Protocol, operating on another port, such as Port 21. Thus, we can say that TCP provides true *multiplexing* (the term stems from the Greek noun meaning "many paths") of the data connections into and out of a particular host.

5.5.5 Connections

Because TCP is a connection-oriented protocol, a logical connection (known as a virtual circuit) must be established between the two end users before any ULP data can be transmitted. The logical connection is a concatenation of many physical connections, such as Host A to LAN A, connecting to Router 1, connecting via a WAN link to Router 2, and so on. Managing this end-to-end system is much easier if you use a single identifier—the logical connection.

The logical connection is established when the ULP process recognizes the need to communicate with a distant peer and passes an OPEN command across the user/TCP interface to the TCP module in the host. The OPEN command is one of a number of primitives described in the TCP standard, RFC 793. A primitive is an event that requests or responds to an action from the other side of the user/TCP interface. The primary TCP primitives include OPEN, SEND, RECEIVE, CLOSE, STATUS, and ABORT. Many parameters traverse the user/TCP interface with the primitive, and therefore more descriptive names such as PASSIVE OPEN or ACTIVE OPEN are often used. Each host operating system may modify these primitives for its particular use.

The OPEN command triggers what is referred to as a three-way handshake, shown in Figure 5-8. The three-way handshake ensures that both ends are prepared to transfer data, reducing the likelihood of data being sent before the distant host can accept it. (If either host becomes confused from an attempted three-way handshake, the confused host sets the Reset (RST) flag, indicating that the segment that arrived was not intended for this connection.) In most cases, one TCP module initiates the connection and another responds. However, it is possible for two TCP modules to request a connection simultaneously; RFC 793 elaborates on this condition. In Figure 5-8, the initiating module (Host A) generates a TCP segment with the Synchronize (SYN) flag set (SYN=1) and an initial Sequence number chosen by the module (e.g., sequence=100). The number selected is called the Initial Sequence Number (ISN); the first data octet would contain Sequence=101 (ISN+1). If the connection request was acceptable, the remote TCP module (Host B) would return a TCP segment containing both an acknowledgement for Host A's ISN (ACK=101), plus its ISN (SEQ=300). Both the Synchronize and Acknowledgement (ACK) flag bits would be set (SYN=1, ACK=1). Note that the two TCP modules are not required to have the same ISN since these numbers are administered locally. An acknowledgement from the initiating module, Host A, is the third step of the three-way handshake. This TCP segment includes the Sequence number (SEQ=101), plus an acknowledgement for Host B's desired ISN (ACK=301). With the connection established, data transfer may commence, beginning with SEQ=101.

To manage connection-related issues, the TCP module maintains a record known as a Transmission Control Block (TCB). The TCB stores a number of variables, including the Local and Remote Socket numbers, the security/precedence of the connection, and pointers to identify incoming and outgoing data streams. Two other TCP functions already discussed, reliability and flow control, manage the data transfer process. The Sequence numbers, acknowledgements, and Window numbers are the mechanisms that the reliability, flow control, and data transfer functions use to ensure their proper operation.

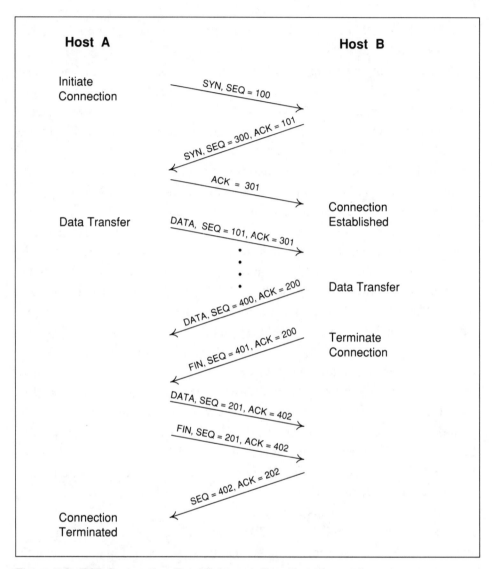

Figure 5-8. TCP Connection Establishment, Data Transfer, and Termination Events

Let's assume the data transfer is complete and the connection is no longer required. Because TCP provides a full-duplex connection, either side may initiate the disconnect. The other end, however, must continue to receive data until the remote module has finished sending it. The TCP connection can be terminated in one of three ways: The local host can initiate the termination, the remote host can initiate it, or both can close the connection simultaneously. The shut-down procedure is the same in all three cases. For example, if the local host has completed its business, it can generate a TCP segment with the Finish (FIN) flag set (FIN=1). The local host will continue to receive data from the remote end until it receives a TCP segment with FIN=1 from the remote end. When the second Finish segment is acknowledged, the connection is closed.

The bottom of Figure 5-8 illustrates this scenario. Host B has finished transferring its last data segment (SEQ=400) and terminates the connection by sending [FIN, SEQ=401, ACK=200]. Host A needs to complete its business first and sends [DATA, SEQ=201, ACK=402], which acknowledges Host B's FIN.

With no more data to send, Host A may then transmit [FIN, SEQ=201, ACK=402], which indicates its own desire to close the connection, and acknowledges Host B's FIN. Host B acknowledges Host A's FIN with [SEQ=402, ACK=202], and the connection is closed.

5.5.6 Precedence/Security

As a military application, TCP required precedence and security. Therefore, these two attributes may be assigned for each connection. The IP Type of Service field and security option may be used to define the requirements associated with that connection. Higher-layer protocols, such as TELNET, may specify the attribute required, and the TCP module will then comply on behalf of that ULP.

5.5.7 The TCP Connection State Diagram

Like many computer processes, TCP operation is best summarized with a state diagram, shown in Figure 5-9a and discussed in detail in "TCP Connection Initiation: An Inside Look" [5-10]. TCP operation progresses from one state to another in response to events, including user calls, incoming TCP segments, and timeouts. The user calls are commands that cross the User/TCP interface; i.e., the functions that support the communication between user processes. These include OPEN, SEND, RECEIVE, CLOSE, ABORT, and STATUS. When a TCP segment arrives, it must be examined to determine if any of the flags are set, particularly the SYN, ACK, RST, or FIN. The timeouts include the USER TIMEOUT, RETRANSMISSION TIMEOUT, and the TIME-WAIT TIMEOUT.

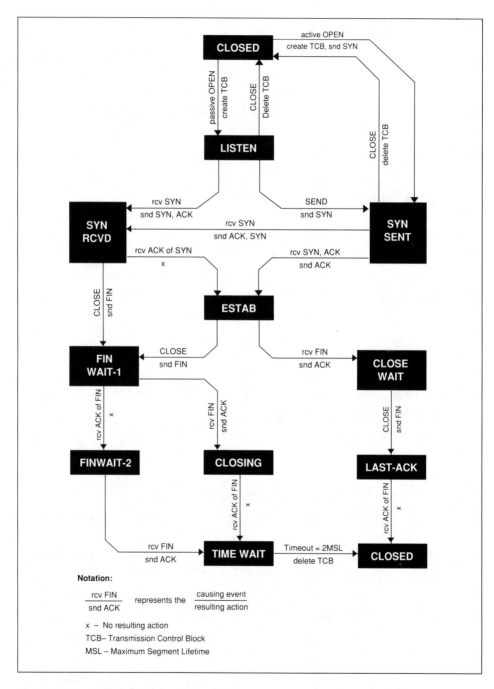

Figure 5-9a. TCP Connection State Diagram

The first state entered by the TCP process is CLOSED, indicating no connection state at all. A passive OPEN creates a Transmission Control Block (TCB), which moves the process to the LISTEN state. It then waits for a connection from a remote TCP and port. If a SYN is received, a SYN, ACK is sent in response. Should another ACK be received, the connection reaches the ESTABLISHED state. When the data transfer is complete at the near end, a CLOSE is issued and a FIN sent, moving to the state to FIN-WAIT-1 and subsequently FIN-WAIT-2 or CLOSING. After waiting to confirm that the remote TCP has received the ACK of its FIN, the TCB is deleted and the connection reaches the CLOSED state. In a similar manner, a FIN received from the other end of the connection moves the process to state CLOSE-WAIT, pending the completion of the local user's requirements for that connection. When the ACK of the FIN has been received, the connection once again reaches the CLOSED state. Further explanations of the various states are given in Figure 5-9b.

The meanings of the states are:

LISTEN – represents waiting for a connection request from any remote TCP and port.

SYN-SENT – represents waiting for a matching connection request after having sent a connection request.

SYN-RECEIVED – represents waiting for a confirming connection request acknowledgment after having both received and sent a connection request.

ESTABLISHED – represents an open connection, data received can be delivered to the user. The normal state for the data transfer phase of the connection.

FIN-WAIT-1 – represents waiting for a connection termination request from the remote TCP, or an acknowledgement of the connection termination request previously sent.

FIN-WAIT-2 – represents waiting for a connection termination request from the remote TCP.

CLOSE-WAIT – represents waiting for a connection termination request from the local user.

CLOSING – represents waiting for a connection termination request acknowledgment from the remote TCP.

LAST-ACK – represents waiting for an acknowledgment of the connection termination request previously sent to the remote TCP (which includes an acknowledgment of its connection termination request).

TIME-WAIT – represents waiting for enough time to pass to be sure the remote TCP received the acknowledgment of its connection termination request.

CLOSED – represents no connection state at all.

Figure 5-9b. TCP Connection States

5.6 Troubleshooting the Host-to-Host Connection

In this chapter, we've studied the two protocols that provide end-to-end (or host-to-host) connectivity. We've seen that UDP provides connectionless service and is typically used for applications that need Port identification (or multiplexing) and basic error control. TCP offers connection-oriented service and rigorously maintains Sequence and Acknowledgement numbers to guarantee data delivery. The price for TCP's extensive error control is its additional header overhead (20 vs. 8 octets).

What should you do when the host-to-host connection fails? First, you need to determine the underlying transport protocol—UDP or TCP. If the protocol is UDP, verify that connectionless service is adequate for the application. If it is, then a problem such as multiple retransmissions may result from the upper-layer protocol's assumptions regarding the transport mechanism. For instance, because it has experienced overhead savings all along, the ULP may tolerate an occasional overhead-producing glitch in communications.

TCP is much more complex. In addition to verifying the Port number, look for significant events in the TCP connection. These include the three-way handshake (using the SYN and ACK flags) and the connection termination (using the RST and FIN flags). During the data transfer phase, verify that the Sequence numbers, Acknowledgements, and Window sizes are appropriate for the application, and remember that Window=0 will close the communication path in the opposite direction.

In short, determine whether the transmitted data is reaching its destination. If it's not, study the Internet Layer for problems, as discussed in Chapter 4. If it is, examine the UDP and TCP headers to determine the source of the delivery problem. RFC 816, "Fault Isolation and Recovery" [5-11], contains some interesting thoughts on internet vs. host analysis.

Now that we're steeped in the theory behind UDP and TCP operation, let's examine some case studies that demonstrate how these protocols operate (and where they might fail).

5.7 Case Studies

The case studies in this section concentrate on issues that demonstrate the host-to-host connection. We'll start with examples that use the datagram-based

UDP, then we'll move to more complex examples that require the connection-oriented TCP.

5.7.1 Using BOOTP with UDP Transport

The Bootstrap Protocol (BOOTP), described in RFC 951 [5-12] and RFC 1084 [5-13], allows a client device to obtain its bootup parameters from a server. BOOTP runs over the UDP transport and uses two defined ports: Port 67 (BOOTP Server) and Port 68 (BOOTP Client). Because it uses the connectionless UDP as the transport, the connection depends on the end-user processes for reliability. The BOOTP message has a standard format (review Figure 4-5) for both client requests and server replies, which adds to the protocol's simplicity.

Once the client locates its server and boot file, it uses the Trivial File Transfer Protocol (TFTP) to obtain the actual file, as described in References [5-14] and [5-15]. Let's look at what happens when the client can't find its server.

In this example, a Retix bridge is configured to obtain its SNMP parameters from a Sun workstation located on another segment (see Figure 5-10). Upon power-up, the bridge broadcasts a BOOTP request, looking for the BOOTP server (see Trace 5.7.1a). Unfortunately, the administrator of the Sun workstation has not loaded the BOOTP daemon on the Sun workstation, so the BOOTP requests go unanswered. Note that the BOOTP request packets are staggered in time and transmitted at relatively long intervals (2 to 17 seconds apart).

When the bridge administrator realizes that his device is not operating properly, he studies the repeated BOOTP requests, theorizing that the BOOTP server is not listening and therefore not responding. His assumption is correct. After the BOOTP daemon is loaded on the Sun workstation, the bridge receives a response (Frame 4 of Trace 5.7.1b). The bridge then requests its bootfile from the Sun workstation and receives its information in Frame 6. An acknowledgement from the bridge (Frame 7) completes the transaction.

Details of the scenario (Trace 5.7.1c) show how the BOOTP and TFTP protocols work together. The BOOTP request (Frame 3) contains the boot file name (90034CF1) that the bridge requires. The BOOTP reply (Frame 4) contains a server-assigned IP address for the client [132.163.1.10], and the address of the BOOTP server [132.163.160.2]. The location of the Boot file name (/tftp/90034CF1) is also included. Next, the bridge sends a TFTP Read request in Frame 5. The BOOTP server responds with a data packet containing the configuration parameters the bridge requires. A TFTP ACK from the bridge completes the transaction. With the BOOTP daemon properly installed on the Sun workstation, the bridge can receive its configuration parameters and begin initialization.

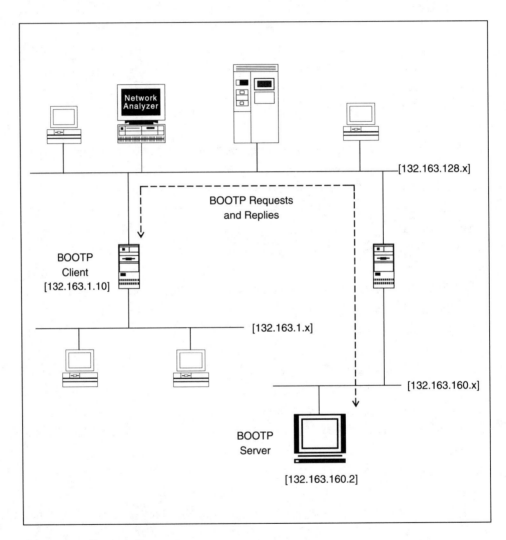

Figure 5-10. Booting Remote Bridge Using BOOTP

Sniffer Network Analyzer data 5-Sep-91 at 14:02:52, RETXBOOT.ENC, Pg 1

SUMMARY	Delta T	Destination	Source	Summary
M 1		090077000001	Retix 034CF1	DSAP=80, I frame
2	10.8868	Broadcast	Retix 034CF1	BOOTP Request
3	2.2928	Broadcast	Retix 034CF1	BOOTP Request
4	9.8320	Broadcast	Retix 034CF1	BOOTP Request
5	2.0745	Broadcast	Retix 034CF1	BOOTP Request
6	11.0334	Broadcast	Retix 034CF1	BOOTP Request
7	2.1841	Broadcast	Retix 034CF1	BOOTP Request
8	6.1166	CMC 614107	Retix 034CF1	ARP R PA=[0.0.0.0] HA=080090034CF1 PRO=IP
9	7.2104	Broadcast	Retix 034CF1	BOOTP Request
10	2.0746	Broadcast	Retix 034CF1	BOOTP Request
11	8.1893	090077000001	Retix 034CF1	DSAP=80, I frame
12	7.2135	Broadcast	Retix 034CF1	BOOTP Request
13	2.2931	Broadcast	Retix 034CF1	BOOTP Request
14	15.4028	Broadcast	Retix 034CF1	BOOTP Request
15	2.0747	Broadcast	Retix 034CF1	BOOTP Request
16	13.2180	Broadcast	Retix 034CF1	BOOTP Request
17	2.2931	Broadcast	Retix 034CF1	BOOTP Request
18	8.7395	Broadcast	Retix 034CF1	BOOTP Request
19	2.0746	Broadcast	Retix 034CF1	BOOTP Request
20	17.6970	Broadcast	Retix 034CF1	BOOTP Request
21	2.1838	Broadcast	Retix 034CF1	BOOTP Request
22	7.7562	Broadcast	Retix 034CF1	BOOTP Request
23	2.0747	Broadcast	Retix 034CF1	BOOTP Request
24	12.1260	Broadcast	Retix 034CF1	BOOTP Request
25	2.1836	Broadcast	Retix 034CF1	BOOTP Request
26	5.4624	Broadcast	Retix 034CF1	BOOTP Request
27	2.0746	Broadcast	Retix 034CF1	BOOTP Request
28	5.4625	Broadcast	Retix 034CF1	BOOTP Request
29	2.2931	Broadcast	Retix 034CF1	BOOTP Request
30	16.4951	Broadcast	Retix 034CF1	BOOTP Request
31	2.0746	Broadcast	Retix 034CF1	BOOTP Request

Trace 5.7.1a. Bridge BOOTP Unanswered Request Summary

Sniffer Network Analyzer data 16-Mar-92 at 09:48:26, BOOTP.ENC, Pg 1

SUMMARY	Delta T	Destination	Source	Summary
M 1		090077000001	Retix 034CF1	DSAP=80, I frame
2	6.6956	090077000001	Retix 034CF1	DSAP=80, I frame
3	4.1908	Broadcast	Retix 034CF1	BOOTP Request
4	0.5307	Retix 034CF1	Sun 0AB646	BOOTP Reply
5	0.0053	Sun 0AB646	Retix 034CF1	TFTP Read request
				File=/tftpboot/90034CF1
6	0.2037	Retix 034CF1	Sun 0AB646	TFTP Data packet NS=1 (Last)
7	0.0033	Sun 0AB646	Retix 034CF1	TFTP Ack NR=1
8	50.2652	090077000001	Retix 034CF1	DSAP=80, I frame

Trace 5.7.1b. Bridge BOOTP Request/Reply Summary

Sniffer Network Analyzer data 16-Mar-92 at 09:48:26, BOOTP.ENC, Pg 1

- - - - - - - - - - - - - - - Frame 3 - - - - - - - - - - - - - - - - -

BOOTP: ——- BOOTP Header ——-
BOOTP:
BOOTP: Boot record type   = 1 (Request)
BOOTP: Hardware address type = 1 10Mb Ethernet
BOOTP: Hardware address length = 6 bytes
BOOTP:
BOOTP: Hops = 0
BOOTP: Transaction id = 0000063F
BOOTP: Elapsed boot time = 0 seconds
BOOTP:
BOOTP: Client self-assigned IP address   = [0.0.0.0] (Unknown)
BOOTP: Client hardware address   = Retix 034CF1
BOOTP:
BOOTP: Host name   = ""
BOOTP: Boot file name = "90034CF1"
BOOTP:
BOOTP: [Vendor specific information]
BOOTP:

```
- - - - - - - - - - - - - - - Frame 4 - - - - - - - - - - - - - - - -
BOOTP: ——- BOOTP Header ——-
BOOTP:
BOOTP: Boot record type      = 2 (Reply)
BOOTP: Hardware address type  = 1 10Mb Ethernet
BOOTP: Hardware address length = 6 bytes
BOOTP:
BOOTP: Hops = 0
BOOTP: Transaction id = 0000063F
BOOTP: Elapsed boot time = 0 seconds
BOOTP:
BOOTP: Client self-assigned IP address   = [0.0.0.0] (Unknown)
BOOTP: Client server-assigned IP address = [132.163.1.10]
BOOTP: Server IP address          = [132.163.160.2]
BOOTP: Gateway IP address         = [132.163.160.2]
BOOTP: Client hardware address       = Retix 034CF1
BOOTP:
BOOTP: Host name     = ""
BOOTP: Boot file name = "/tftpboot/90034CF1"
BOOTP:
BOOTP: [Vendor specific information]
BOOTP:


- - - - - - - - - - - - - - Frame 5 - - - - - - - - - - - - - - - -
TFTP: ——- Trivial file transfer ——-
TFTP:
TFTP: Opcode = 1 (Read request)
TFTP: File name = "/tftpboot/90034CF1"
TFTP: Mode = "octet"
TFTP:
TFTP: [Normal end of "Trivial file transfer".]
TFTP:


- - - - - - - - - - - - - - - Frame 6 - - - - - - - - - - - - - - - -
TFTP: ——- Trivial file transfer ——-
TFTP:
TFTP: Opcode = 3 (Data packet)
TFTP: Block number = 1
TFTP: [160 bytes of data] (Last frame)
TFTP:
TFTP: [Normal end of "Trivial file transfer".]
TFTP:
```

```
- - - - - - - - - - - - - - - Frame 7 - - - - - - - - - - - - - - - -
TFTP: ——- Trivial file transfer ——-
TFTP:
TFTP: Opcode = 4 (Ack)
TFTP: Block number = 1
TFTP:
TFTP: [Normal end of "Trivial file transfer".]
TFTP:
```

Trace 5.7.1c. Bridge BOOTP Request/Reply Details

5.7.2 Clock Synchronization with UDP

As we've discussed, applications for UDP are not mission critical; that is, the internetwork manager won't get fired if the datagram gets lost and must be retransmitted. One example of such an application is the synchronization of the clocks on all the hosts on the internetwork. The synchronization information is included in a single datagram. Should one of the synchronization datagrams get lost, a retransmission can easily be requested. Besides, it makes little sense to establish a connection using a TCP three-way handshake (which uses three TCP segments), send one segment of data, then use several more segments to close the connection. UDP seems ideal for this application. Let's see how it works.

The protocol selected is the Time protocol, described in RFC 868 [5-16]. Time is a relatively simple protocol that can be used with either UDP or TCP. It uses Port 37 and operates as shown in Figure 5-11. The Time server listens on Port 37 for a Time Request datagram. The user transmits an empty datagram to Port 37, which prompts the server to return a 32-bit number representing the current time. The user receives the Time datagram and uses that information to synchronize its clock with that of the server. The timestamp itself (the 32-bit number) counts the number of seconds that have expired since midnight on January 1, 1900, Greenwich Mean Time (GMT). RFC 868 states that this measurement will be useable until the year 2036. (The network engineer figures he'll be enjoying his retirement in Hawaii by 2036, so he decides to use the Time protocol for his internetwork.)

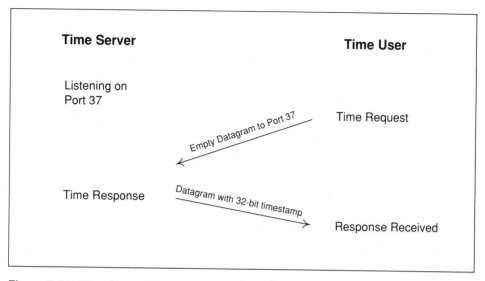

Figure 5-11. Time Protocol Implemented with UDP Transport

The internetwork in question is a series of bridged token ring networks, shown in Figure 5-12. The Time server is a Sun SPARCstation 2 running BSD UNIX 4.3 and attached to network [142.56.20.0]. The user in question is a Sun SPARCstation IPX, also running BSD UNIX 4.3 but attached to network [142.56.17.0].

Although the Time protocol is extremely simple, some confusion occur. As the network manager discovers, the programmer who wrote the code for the user system (the Sun IPX) used an incorrect Destination Port number. We see the problem in Trace 5.7.2a. In Frame 175, the user sends an empty UDP packet to Port 2057. We know that this packet is empty because its length is only 8 octets, the length of the UDP header (review Figure 5-2). In Frame 176, the Time server (via Bridge 17.3) returns an ICMP Destination Unreachable message, specifying that the selected port is unreachable. A check of the originating message shows a total length of 28 octets, which comprise the IP header (20 octets) and the UDP header (8 octets). Both the Source and Destination addresses are correct and the checksum passes. Clearly, the Destination port (2057) causes the problem; the Time server is listening at Port 37 and does not hear the request for a timestamp.

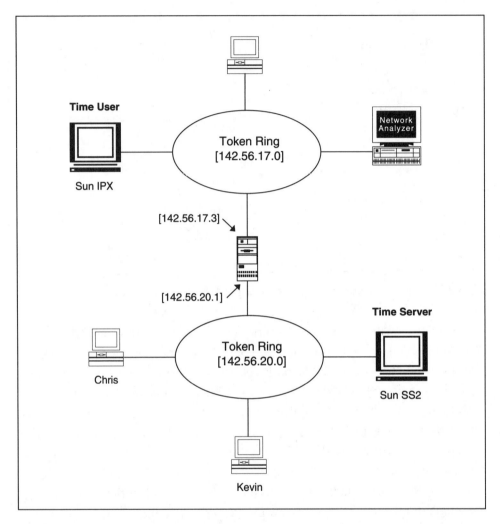

Figure 5-12. Time Service

Once the systems programmer rewrote his code, the time service request succeeds (see Trace 5.7.2b). The Sun IPX transmits an empty UDP packet in Frame 157, and the Sun SPARCstation 2 Time server [142.56.20.16] sends a correct response via the bridge. Both the request and the response are correctly addressed to and from Port 37. In the Time response (Frame 158), note that the message returned is four octets. This data is shown as the last eight hexadecimal characters in the printout: AD 67 8E FD, which corresponded to the appropriate time from the Time server.

This example illustrates two important points: UDP is clearly adequate for many host-to-host applications, but the correct addressing of the host port is vital to the success of the transmission.

Sniffer Network Analyzer data 10-Mar-92 at 12:52:50, TIME_BAD.TRC, Pg 1

```
- - - - - - - - - - - - - - - - Frame 175 - - - - - - - - - - - - - - - - -
UDP: ——- UDP Header ——-
UDP:
UDP: Source port = 1157
UDP: Destination port = 2057
UDP: Length = 8
UDP: No checksum
UDP:

- - - - - - - - - - - - - - - Frame 176 - - - - - - - - - - - - - - - -
ICMP: ——- ICMP header ——-
ICMP:
ICMP: Type = 3 (Destination unreachable)
ICMP: Code = 3 (Port unreachable)
ICMP: Checksum = F066 (correct)
ICMP: IP header of originating message (description follows)
ICMP:
IP: ——- IP Header ——-
IP:
IP: Version = 4, header length = 20 bytes
IP: Type of service = 00
IP:        000. .... = routine
IP:        ...0 .... = normal delay
IP:        .... 0... = normal throughput
IP:        .... .0.. = normal reliability
IP: Total length = 28 bytes
IP: Identification = 60919
IP: Flags = 0X
IP: .0.. .... = may fragment
IP: ..0. .... = last fragment
IP: Fragment offset = 0 bytes
IP: Time to live = 59 seconds/hops
IP: Protocol = 17 (UDP)
IP: Header checksum = 5055 (correct)
```

IP: Source address = [142.56.17.4]
IP: Destination address = [142.56.20.16]
IP: No options
ICMP:
ICMP: [First 8 byte(s) of data of originating message]
ICMP:
ICMP: [Normal end of "ICMP header".]
ICMP:

Trace 5.7.2a. Time Request to Incorrect Port Number

Sniffer Network Analyzer data 10-Mar-92 at 12:40:00, TIME_WRK.TRC, Pg 1

- - - - - - - - - - - - - - - Frame 157 - - - - - - - - - - - - - - - - -
IP: ——- IP Header ——-
IP:
IP: Version = 4, header length = 20 bytes
IP: Type of service = 00
IP: 000. .... = routine
IP: ...0 .... = normal delay
IP: .... 0... = normal throughput
IP: .... .0.. = normal reliability
IP: Total length = 28 bytes
IP: Identification = 49402
IP: Flags = 0X
IP: .0.. .... = may fragment
IP: ..0. .... = last fragment
IP: Fragment offset = 0 bytes
IP: Time to live = 60 seconds/hops
IP: Protocol = 17 (UDP)
IP: Header checksum = 7C52 (correct)
IP: Source address = [142.56.17.4]
IP: Destination address = [142.56.20.16]
IP: No options
IP:
UDP: ——- UDP Header ——-
UDP:
UDP: Source port = 1141 (Time)
UDP: Destination port = 37
UDP: Length = 8
UDP: No checksum
UDP:

ADDR	HEX		ASCII
0000	10 40 00 00 C9 09 23 4C	08 00 20 0B 8A A7 AA AA	.@....#L.. .....
0010	03 00 00 00 08 00 45 00	00 1C C0 FA 00 00 3C 11	......E.......<.
0020	7C 52 8E 38 11 04 8E 38	14 10 04 75 00 25 00 08	|R.8...8...u.%..
0030	00 00		..

- - - - - - - - - - - - - - - - Frame 158 - - - - - - - - - - - - - - - - -

```
IP:  ------- IP Header -------
IP:
IP:  Version = 4, header length = 20 bytes
IP:  Type of service = 00
IP:        000. .... = routine
IP:        ...0 .... = normal delay
IP:        .... 0... = normal throughput
IP:        .... .0.. = normal reliability
IP:  Total length = 32 bytes
IP:  Identification = 27066
IP:  Flags = 0X
IP:  .0.. .... = may fragment
IP:  ..0. .... = last fragment
IP:  Fragment offset = 0 bytes
IP:  Time to live = 59 seconds/hops
IP:  Protocol = 17 (UDP)
IP:  Header checksum = D48E (correct)
IP:  Source address = [142.56.20.16]
IP:  Destination address = [142.56.17.4]
IP:  No options
IP:
UDP: ------- UDP Header -------
UDP:
UDP: Source port = 37 (Time)
UDP: Destination port = 1141
UDP: Length = 12
UDP: No checksum
UDP:
UDP: [4 byte(s) of data]
UDP:
```

ADDR	HEX		ASCII
0000	18 40 08 00 20 0B 8A A7	00 00 C9 09 23 4C AA AA	.@.. ....#L..
0010	03 00 00 00 08 00 45 00	00 20 69 BA 00 00 3B 11	......E.. i...;.
0020	D4 8E 8E 38 14 10 8E 38	11 04 00 25 04 75 00 0C	...8...8...%.u..
0030	00 00 AD 67 8E FD		...g..

Trace 5.7.2b. UDP Time Service Details

237

5.7.3 Establishing and Terminating TCP Connections

In Section 5.5.5, we learned that the TCP connection must be established with a three-way handshake prior to any transmission of data. Once the data has been transferred, a modified three-way handshake terminates the connection. Let's study how these operations function, using a PC and its server as examples.

In this case study, a PC wishes to establish several logical connections to a Sun server via a single Ethernet physical connection. Different Port numbers identify the different logical connections (created using TCP's multiplexing capabilities). Let's follow the steps of one of these logical connections from establishment to data transfer to termination (see Trace 5.7.3a).

A TCP segment identifies the connection establishment with the Synchronize bit set (SYN = 1) and no data in the segment (LEN = 0). We can see this in Frame 706, along with an initial Sequence number, ISN = 1988352000. Also note that the Sun server is initiating this connection and that it is advertising a rather large window size (WIN = 24576). The Source port (S = 20) identifies the File Transfer Protocol (FTP), and the Destination port (D = 1227) is assigned by the Sun server. The PC responds with a similar synchronize segment in Frame 707; the receipt of the server's segment is acknowledged (ACK = 1988352001), the PC's ISN is sent (SEQ = 201331252), but a smaller window size is allowed (WIN = 1024). Note that the Source and Destination port numbers are now reversed, since the original source (the Sun server) has now become the PC's destination. Frame 708 completes the connection establishment, with the server acknowledging the PC's ISN (ACK = 201331253).

The details of the connection establishment are shown in Trace 5.7.3b. Note that one TCP option (the maximum segment size) is used. Maximum segment size = 1460 indicates transmission over an Ethernet/IEEE 802.3 LAN. The Ethernet/IEEE 802.3 can accommodate 1,500 octets of data within the frame. Of these, 20 octets are used for the TCP header and another 20 octets for the IP header, leaving 1,460 octets for the TCP segment. Data transfer may now proceed.

Data transfer begins in Frame 710 with a TCP segment of 1,024 octets (LEN = 1024). (Note that Frame 709 belongs to a previously established FTP connection destined for another port (D = 1219) on the same PC. While Frame 709 illustrates TCP's port multiplexing capabilities, it has nothing to do with the current discussion since it belongs to another logical connection.) The PC acknowledges receipt of the data in Frame 713 by sending ACK = 1988353025 (1988352001 + 1024 = 1988353025).

The PC will not permit any more data at this time, and it indicates this by shutting its window (WIN = 0). In Frame 715, the PC's processor has caught up with its back-log (note that it was servicing port 1219 in Frame 714) and restores data flow by send-ing WIN = 1024. The server responds with another 1,024 octets in frame 716. This process proceeds normally until the server completes its business.

In Frame 779, the server finished its business and sends the Finish flag (FIN = 1) along with its last 114 octets of data. The PC responds with an acknowledge-ment in Frame 780 (ACK = 1988384884), then sends a second segment (Frame 781) containing both an ACK and a FIN. Note that the details in Trace 5.7.3c indi-cate that the PC does not shut down the connection, but permits up to 910 more octets of data from the other end (Window = 910). The server has said its piece, however; it acknowledges the FIN and closes its end of the connection in Frame 782. Both ends of the logical connection are now closed.

In the following example, we'll see what happens when both ends are unable to maintain the connection and the Reset (RST) flag is required.

Sniffer Network Analyzer data 27-Mar-91 at 09:04:54, TCPMEDLY.ENC, Pg 1

SUMMARY	Delta T	Destination	Source	Summary
706	0.0027	PC	Sun Server	TCP D=1227 S=20 SYN SEQ=1988352000 LEN=0 WIN=24576
707	0.0139	Sun Server	PC	TCP D=20 S=1227 SYN ACK=1988352001 SEQ=201331252 LEN=0 WIN=1024
708	0.0006	PC	Sun Server	TCP D=1227 S=20 ACK=201331253 WIN=24576
709	0.0007	PC	Sun Server	FTP R PORT=1219 150 ASCII data connection
710	0.0993	PC	Sun Server	TCP D=1227 S=20 ACK=201331253 SEQ=1988352001 LEN=1024 WIN=24576
711	0.0733	Sun Server	PC	TCP D=21 S=1219 ACK=1972865105 WIN=951
712	0.0008	PC	Sun Server	FTP R PORT=1219 226 ASCII Transfer complete <0D><0A>

713	0.0529	Sun Server	PC	TCP D=20 S=1227 ACK=1988353025 WIN=0
714	0.0535	Sun Server	PC	TCP D=21 S=1219 ACK=1972865135 WIN=956
715	0.0790	Sun Server	PC	TCP D=20 S=1227 ACK=1988353025 WIN=1024
716	0.0015	PC	Sun Server	TCP D=1227 S=20 ACK=201331253 SEQ=1988353025 LEN=1024 WIN=24576
717	0.1379	Sun Server	PC	TCP D=20 S=1227 ACK=1988354049 WIN=0
718	0.0644	Sun Server	PC	TCP D=20 S=1227 ACK=1988354049 WIN=1024
719	0.0015	PC	Sun Server	TCP D=1227 S=20 ACK=201331253 SEQ=1988354049 LEN=1024 WIN=24576
720	0.0553	Sun Server	PC	TCP D=20 S=1227 ACK=1988355073 WIN=1024
721	0.0015	PC	Sun Server	TCP D=1227 S=20 ACK=201331253 SEQ=1988355073 LEN=1024 WIN=24576
722	0.0575	Sun Server	PC	TCP D=20 S=1227 ACK=1988356097 WIN=1024
.				
.				
.				
779	0.0008	PC	Sun Server	TCP D=1227 S=20 FIN ACK=201331253 SEQ=1988384769 LEN=114 WIN=24576
780	0.0204	Sun Server	PC	TCP D=20 S=1227 ACK=1988384884 WIN=910
781	0.0616	Sun Server	PC	TCP D=20 S=1227 FIN ACK=1988384884 SEQ=201331253 LEN=0 WIN=910
782	0.0006	PC	Sun Server	TCP D=1227 S=20 ACK=201331254 WIN=24576

Trace 5.7.3a. TCP Connection Establishment and Termination Summary

Sniffer Network Analyzer data 27-Mar-91 at 09:04:54, TCPMEDLY.ENC, Pg 1

- - - - - - - - - - - - - - - Frame 706 - - - - - - - - - - - - - - - - -
TCP: ——- TCP header ——-
TCP:
TCP: Source port = 20 (FTP data)
TCP: Destination port = 1227
TCP: Initial sequence number = 1988352000
TCP: Data offset = 24 bytes
TCP: Flags = 02
TCP: ..0. .... = (No urgent pointer)
TCP: ...0 .... = (No acknowledgment)
TCP: .... 0... = (No push)
TCP: .... .0.. = (No reset)
TCP: .... ..1. = SYN
TCP: ....0 = (No FIN)
TCP: Window = 24576
TCP: Checksum = D02F (correct)
TCP:
TCP: Options follow
TCP: Maximum segment size = 1460
TCP:

- - - - - - - - - - - - - - - Frame 707 - - - - - - - - - - - - - - - - -
TCP: ——- TCP header ——-
TCP:
TCP: Source port = 1227
TCP: Destination port = 20 (FTP data)
TCP: Initial sequence number = 201331252
TCP: Acknowledgment number = 1988352001
TCP: Data offset = 24 bytes
TCP: Flags = 12
TCP: ..0. .... = (No urgent pointer)
TCP: ...1 .... = Acknowledgment
TCP: .... 0... = (No push)
TCP: .... .0.. = (No reset)
TCP: .... ..1. = SYN
TCP: ....0 = (No FIN)
TCP: Window = 1024
TCP: Checksum = 0DEB (correct)
TCP:
TCP: Options follow
TCP: Maximum segment size = 1460

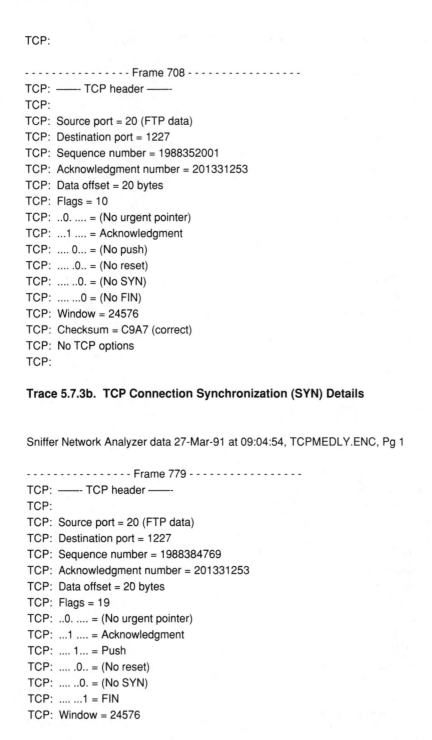

TCP:

- - - - - - - - - - - - - - - Frame 708 - - - - - - - - - - - - - - - -
TCP: ——- TCP header ——-
TCP:
TCP: Source port = 20 (FTP data)
TCP: Destination port = 1227
TCP: Sequence number = 1988352001
TCP: Acknowledgment number = 201331253
TCP: Data offset = 20 bytes
TCP: Flags = 10
TCP: ..0. .... = (No urgent pointer)
TCP: ...1 .... = Acknowledgment
TCP: .... 0... = (No push)
TCP: .... .0.. = (No reset)
TCP: .... ..0. = (No SYN)
TCP: ....0 = (No FIN)
TCP: Window = 24576
TCP: Checksum = C9A7 (correct)
TCP: No TCP options
TCP:

Trace 5.7.3b. TCP Connection Synchronization (SYN) Details

Sniffer Network Analyzer data 27-Mar-91 at 09:04:54, TCPMEDLY.ENC, Pg 1

- - - - - - - - - - - - - - - Frame 779 - - - - - - - - - - - - - - - -
TCP: ——- TCP header ——-
TCP:
TCP: Source port = 20 (FTP data)
TCP: Destination port = 1227
TCP: Sequence number = 1988384769
TCP: Acknowledgment number = 201331253
TCP: Data offset = 20 bytes
TCP: Flags = 19
TCP: ..0. .... = (No urgent pointer)
TCP: ...1 .... = Acknowledgment
TCP: .... 1... = Push
TCP: .... .0.. = (No reset)
TCP: .... ..0. = (No SYN)
TCP: ....1 = FIN
TCP: Window = 24576

```
TCP:  Checksum = 492C (correct)
TCP:  No TCP options
TCP:  [114 byte(s) of data]
TCP:


- - - - - - - - - - - - - - - - Frame 780 - - - - - - - - - - - - - - - -
TCP:  ———- TCP header ———-
TCP:
TCP:  Source port = 1227
TCP:  Destination port = 20 (FTP data)
TCP:  Sequence number = 201331253
TCP:  Acknowledgment number = 1988384884
TCP:  Data offset = 20 bytes
TCP:  Flags = 10
TCP:  ..0. .... = (No urgent pointer)
TCP:  ...1 .... = Acknowledgment
TCP:  .... 0... = (No push)
TCP:  .... .0.. = (No reset)
TCP:  .... ..0. = (No SYN)
TCP:  .... ...0 = (No FIN)
TCP:  Window = 910
TCP:  Checksum = A5A6 (correct)
TCP:  No TCP options
TCP:


- - - - - - - - - - - - - - - - Frame 781 - - - - - - - - - - - - - - - -
TCP:  ———- TCP header ———-
TCP:
TCP:  Source port = 1227
TCP:  Destination port = 20 (FTP data)
TCP:  Sequence number = 201331253
TCP:  Acknowledgment number = 1988384884
TCP:  Data offset = 20 bytes
TCP:  Flags = 11
TCP:  ..0. .... = (No urgent pointer)
TCP:  ...1 .... = Acknowledgment
TCP:  .... 0... = (No push)
TCP:  .... .0.. = (No reset)
TCP:  .... ..0. = (No SYN)
TCP:  .... ...1 = FIN
TCP:  Window = 910
TCP:  Checksum = A5A5 (correct)
TCP:  No TCP options
```

TCP:

```
- - - - - - - - - - - - - - - - Frame 782 - - - - - - - - - - - - - - - -
TCP:  ——- TCP header ——-
TCP:
TCP:  Source port = 20 (FTP data)
TCP:  Destination port = 1227
TCP:  Sequence number = 1988384884
TCP:  Acknowledgment number = 201331254
TCP:  Data offset = 20 bytes
TCP:  Flags = 10
TCP:  ..0. .... = (No urgent pointer)
TCP:  ...1 .... = Acknowledgment
TCP:  .... 0... = (No push)
TCP:  .... .0.. = (No reset)
TCP:  .... ..0. = (No SYN)
TCP:  .... ...0 = (No FIN)
TCP:  Window = 24576
TCP:  Checksum = 4933 (correct)
TCP:  No TCP options
TCP:
```

Trace 5.7.3c. TCP Connection Termination (FIN) Details

5.7.4 Reset TCP Connection

The TCP header contains six flags that manage the virtual circuit. In Section 5.7.3, we saw how the Acknowledgement (ACK), Synchronize (SYN), and Finish (FIN) flags are used for connection management and data transfer under normal conditions. One of the remaining flags, known as the Reset (RST) flag, is used when a TCP segment arrives that is not intended for the current connection. The RST flag is also used if a TCP module detects a fatal error or if the application process unilaterally decides to close the connection. One possible scenario is when one TCP module crashes during a session. The term used to describe this condition is a "half-open connection" because one end is maintaining its Sequence numbers and other transmission-related parameters, while the other is not. When the crashed host returns to life, its Sequence numbers are unlikely to be the same as those it was using prior to the crash. As a result, it sends unexpected (and thus unacknowledged) Sequence numbers to the host at the other end of the link.

244

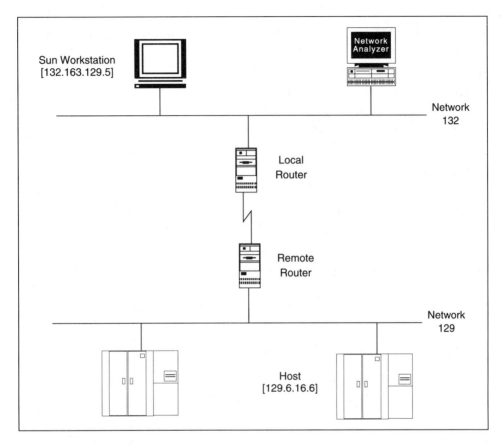

Figure 5-13. TCP Connection Reset

When the crashed host realizes that it has caused this confusion, it sends a Reset to its distant partner, which triggers a three-way handshake to re-establish the connection. Let's see how the Reset flag is used in a failure scenario.

In this case, a Sun workstation is communicating with a remote host located in another part of the country. A TELNET session is in progress over the internet, with the workstation emulating a host terminal. Two routers connect the local and remote Ethernet networks (see Figure 5-13). Without warning, the user loses his response from the host, and starts hitting the RETURN key, hoping for a miracle (sound familiar?). We can see his frustration in Trace 5.7.4a. In Frame 3, all appears to be fine, but after almost two minutes of waiting (119.8658 seconds) the Sun sends a carriage return. (Note the <0D> <00> output pattern, indicating that an ASCII Carriage Return <0D> has been transmitted.) The Sun sends these characters (<0D> <00> <0D> <00>...) at increments of 2 seconds apart, then 4 seconds, 8, 16, and so on, attempting to wake up the remote host.

Unfortunately, the efforts are in vain. The remote host gets confused, sends a TCP Reset (RST=1) in Frame 13 and disables future receptions by setting Window = 0. The Sun resets the connection, but also acknowledges the last data octet that it received in Frame 3 (ACK = 20881447). Clearly, the Sun does not want to end the conversation since it keeps Window = 4096.

The problem is traced to a bad Ethernet card connecting the remote host to its local network. The card's operation is intermittent, working part of the time — such as when the TELNET session was initialized — then failing for no apparent reason. When the failure occurred, it caused a half-open TCP connection, and ultimately the mysterious TCP Reset. When the faulty Ethernet card was replaced, no further problems occurred.

Sniffer Network Analyzer data 14-Sep-90 at 11:43:30, TCPRST.ENC, Pg 1

SUMMARY	Delta T	Destination	Source	Summary
M 1		Router	Sun 01DF5E	TCP D=23 S=1169
				ACK=20881319 WIN=4096
2	5.0808	Sun 01DF5E	Router	Telnet R PORT=1169
				FILE: ROUT (NO CHANGES)
3	0.1189	Router	Sun 01DF5E	TCP D=23 S=1169
				ACK=20881447 WIN=4096
4	119.8658	Router	Sun 01DF5E	Telnet C PORT=1169 <0D><00>...
5	0.8820	Router	Sun 01DF5E	Telnet C PORT=1169 <0D><00>...
6	2.0002	Router	Sun 01DF5E	Telnet C PORT=1169 <0D><00>...
7	4.0001	Router	Sun 01DF5E	Telnet C PORT=1169 <0D><00>...
8	8.0006	Router	Sun 01DF5E	Telnet C PORT=1169 <0D><00>...
9	16.0010	Router	Sun 01DF5E	Telnet C PORT=1169 <0D><00>...
10	32.0020	Router	Sun 01DF5E	Telnet C PORT=1169 <0D><00>...
11	64.0039	Router	Sun 01DF5E	Telnet C PORT=1169 <0D><00>...
12	64.0040	Router	Sun 01DF5E	Telnet C PORT=1169 <0D><00>...
13	0.2722	Sun 01DF5E	Router	TCP D=1169 S=23 RST WIN=0
14	0.0021	Router	Sun 01DF5E	TCP D=23 S=1169 RST
				ACK=20881447 WIN=4096

Trace 5.7.4a. TCP Connection Reset (RST) Summary

Sniffer Network Analyzer data 14-Sep-90 at 11:43:30, TCPRST.ENC, Pg 1

- - - - - - - - - - - - - - - - Frame 13 - - - - - - - - - - - - - - - -
DLC: —— DLC Header ——
DLC:
DLC: Frame 13 arrived at 12:24:26.1927; frame size is 60 (003C hex) bytes.
DLC: Destination = Station Sun   01DF5E
DLC: Source   = Station PrteonE0807B, Router
DLC: Ethertype = 0800 (IP)
DLC:
IP: —— IP Header ——
IP:
IP: Version = 4, header length = 20 bytes
IP: Type of service = 00
IP: 000. .... = routine
IP: ...0 .... = normal delay
IP: .... 0... = normal throughput
IP: .... .0.. = normal reliability
IP: Total length = 40 bytes
IP: Identification = 25254
IP: Flags = 0X
IP: .0.. .... = may fragment
IP: ..0. .... = last fragment
IP: Fragment offset = 0 bytes
IP: Time to live = 19 seconds/hops
IP: Protocol = 6 (TCP)
IP: Header checksum = AE75 (correct)
IP: Source address = [129.6.16.6]
IP: Destination address = [132.163.129.5]
IP: No options
IP:
TCP: —— TCP header ——
TCP:
TCP: Source port = 23 (Telnet)
TCP: Destination port = 1169
TCP: Sequence number = 20881447
TCP: Data offset = 20 bytes
TCP: Flags = 04
TCP: ..0. .... = (No urgent pointer)
TCP: ...0 .... = (No acknowledgment)
TCP: .... 0... = (No push)
TCP: .... .1.. = Reset
TCP: .... ..0. = (No SYN)

TCP: ....0 = (No FIN)
TCP: Window = 0
TCP: Checksum = 25EE (correct)
TCP: No TCP options
TCP:

- - - - - - - - - - - - - - - Frame 14 - - - - - - - - - - - - - - - -
DLC: ——- DLC Header ——-
DLC:
DLC: Frame 14 arrived at 12:24:26.1948; frame size is 60 (003C hex) bytes.
DLC: Destination = Station PrteonE0807B, Router
DLC: Source   = Station Sun 01DF5E
DLC: Ethertype = 0800 (IP)
DLC:
IP: ——- IP Header ——-
IP:
IP: Version = 4, header length = 20 bytes
IP: Type of service = 00
IP: 000. .... = routine
IP: ...0 .... = normal delay
IP: .... 0... = normal throughput
IP: .... .0.. = normal reliability
IP: Total length = 40 bytes
IP: Identification = 25255
IP: Flags = 0X
IP: .0.. .... = may fragment
IP: ..0. .... = last fragment
IP: Fragment offset = 0 bytes
IP: Time to live = 30 seconds/hops
IP: Protocol = 6 (TCP)
IP: Header checksum = A374 (correct)
IP: Source address = [132.163.129.5]
IP: Destination address = [129.6.16.6]
IP: No options
IP:
TCP: ——- TCP header ——-
TCP:
TCP: Source port = 1169
TCP: Destination port = 23 (Telnet)
TCP: Sequence number = 398210404
TCP: Acknowledgment number = 20881447
TCP: Data offset = 20 bytes
TCP: Flags = 14

TCP: ..0. .... = (No urgent pointer)
TCP: ...1 .... = Acknowledgment
TCP: .... 0... = (No push)
TCP: .... .1.. = Reset
TCP: .... ..0. = (No SYN)
TCP: ....0 = (No FIN)
TCP: Window = 4096
TCP: Checksum = 15EE (correct)
TCP: No TCP options
TCP:

Trace 5.7.4b. TCP Reset Connection (RST) Details

5.7.5 Repeated Host Acknowledgements

TCP is one of a class of PAR protocols that requires a positive acknowledgement within a specified time period, or it will retransmit the data. The acknowledgement mechanism uses the 32-bit Acknowledgement number and sets the Acknowledgement (ACK) flag. The ACK flag tells the recipient TCP module to process the Acknowledgement field. The Acknowledgement field counts each octet of information received and indicates which octet is expected next. What happens when the receiver does not properly acknowledge incoming data?

In this case, an X-Windows terminal is communicating with a minicomputer. The terminal sends some information, but then seemingly locks up. At first, the administrator suspects the terminal. But closer analysis reveals a defect in the host. Let's find out why.

Both the terminal and the host are attached to the same Ethernet, and the protocol analyzer is set to capture all traffic between the two devices. The initial trace reveals a TCP connection between Port 3319 and Port 6000 (the X-Windows port), as seen in Trace 5.7.5a. It is unusual, however, that all communication between host and terminal consists of TCP acknowledgements and that they all flow in one direction—host to terminal. These acknowledgements repeat roughly every millisecond (0.0008 seconds).

A detailed study of one of the frames reveals the problem (see Trace 5.7.5b). The host's TCP module is stuck in a loop in which it was unable to increment the Acknowledgement number, so each TCP segment contains the same information. The IP datagram contains a total of 40 octets: 20 for the IP header and 20 for the

TCP header. No higher-layer data is ever transmitted. The window size is large (WIN = 4096), but the Acknowledgement number never changes (ACK = 28122874). When the terminal receives this segment, it is unable to transmit additional information because the host always asks for the same segment: 4,096 octets beginning at Sequence number 28122874. Since the host prevented the terminal from proceeding, the terminal appears to lock up.

To find the solution, the network administrator contacts the developer of the host software. The developer finds a bug in the TCP module that prevents the Acknowledgement number from incrementing. When the administrator installs a software patch, the terminal-to-host communication works as expected.

Sniffer Network Analyzer data 1-Oct-91 at 11:14:40, HOSTACK.ENC, Pg 1

SUMMARY	Delta T	Destination	Source	Summary
M 1		Terminal	Host	TCP D=6000 S=3319
				ACK=28122874 WIN=4096
2	0.0008	Terminal	Host	TCP D=6000 S=3319
				ACK=28122874 WIN=4096
3	0.0008	Terminal	Host	TCP D=6000 S=3319
				ACK=28122874 WIN=4096
4	0.0008	Terminal	Host	TCP D=6000 S=3319
				ACK=28122874 WIN=4096
5	0.0008	Terminal	Host	TCP D=6000 S=3319
				ACK=28122874 WIN=4096
6	0.0008	Terminal	Host	TCP D=6000 S=3319
				ACK=28122874 WIN=4096
7	0.0008	Terminal	Host	TCP D=6000 S=3319
				ACK=28122874 WIN=4096
8	0.0008	Terminal	Host	TCP D=6000 S=3319
				ACK=28122874 WIN=4096
9	0.0008	Terminal	Host	TCP D=6000 S=3319
				ACK=28122874 WIN=4096
10	0.0008	Terminal	Host	TCP D=6000 S=3319
				ACK=28122874 WIN=4096
11	0.0008	Terminal	Host	TCP D=6000 S=3319
				ACK=28122874 WIN=4096
12	0.0008	Terminal	Host	TCP D=6000 S=3319
				ACK=28122874 WIN=4096

13	0.0008	Terminal	Host	TCP D=6000 S=3319
				ACK=28122874 WIN=4096
14	0.0008	Terminal	Host	TCP D=6000 S=3319
				ACK=28122874 WIN=4096
15	0.0008	Terminal	Host	TCP D=6000 S=3319
				ACK=28122874 WIN=4096
16	0.0008	Terminal	Host	TCP D=6000 S=3319
				ACK=28122874 WIN=4096
17	0.0008	Terminal	Host	TCP D=6000 S=3319
				ACK=28122874 WIN=4096
18	0.0008	Terminal	Host	TCP D=6000 S=3319
				ACK=28122874 WIN=4096
19	0.0008	Terminal	Host	TCP D=6000 S=3319
				ACK=28122874 WIN=4096
20	0.0008	Terminal	Host	TCP D=6000 S=3319
				ACK=28122874 WIN=4096

Trace 5.7.5a. Repeated Host TCP Acknowledgements (Summary)

Sniffer Network Analyzer data 1-Oct-91 at 11:14:40, HOSTACK.ENC, Pg 1

DLC: ——- DLC Header ——-
DLC:
DLC: Frame 1 arrived at 11:14:41.7541; frame size is 60 (003C hex) bytes.
DLC: Destination = Station XXXXXX 101C43, Terminal
DLC: Source   = Station XXXXXX 032608, Host
DLC: Ethertype = 0800 (IP)
DLC:
IP: ——- IP Header ——-
IP:
IP: Version = 4, header length = 20 bytes
IP: Type of service = 00
IP: 000. .... = routine
IP: ...0 .... = normal delay
IP: .... 0... = normal throughput
IP: .... .0.. = normal reliability
IP: Total length = 40 bytes
IP: Identification = 17411
IP: Flags = 0X
IP: .0.. .... = may fragment
IP: ..0. .... = last fragment
IP: Fragment offset = 0 bytes

```
IP:   Time to live = 30 seconds/hops
IP:   Protocol = 6 (TCP)
IP:   Header checksum = F380 (correct)
IP:   Source address = [XXX.YYY.1.235]
IP:   Destination address = [XXX.YYY.4.98]
IP:   No options
IP:
TCP: ——- TCP header ——-
TCP:
TCP:  Source port = 3319
TCP:  Destination port = 6000 (X Windows)
TCP:  Sequence number = 3524369
TCP:  Acknowledgment number = 28122874
TCP:  Data offset = 20 bytes
TCP:  Flags = 10
TCP:  ..0. .... = (No urgent pointer)
TCP:  ...1 .... = Acknowledgment
TCP:  .... 0... = (No push)
TCP:  .... .0.. = (No reset)
TCP:  .... ..0. = (No SYN)
TCP:  .... ...0 = (No FIN)
TCP:  Window = 4096
TCP:  Checksum = 2E33 (correct)
TCP:  No TCP options
TCP:
```

Trace 5.7.5b. Repeated Host TCP Acknowledgements (Details)

5.7.6 Using the Finger User Information Protocol

In Chapter 4, we discovered that the ICMP Echo (Ping) command can test the transmission path between two devices on an internetwork. Another utility, known as the Finger User Information Protocol (Finger) and described in RFC 1288 [5-17], also provides some end-to-end testing. Finger provides an interface to a database of users attached to a particular host, called the Remote User Information Program (RUIP).

Finger consists of a query/response interaction based on TCP transport. To initiate Finger, a TCP connection is established with Port 79 (the Finger port) on the remote host. Then the local host's Finger utility sends a query to RUIP at the remote host. The remote host responds with the information requested.

When used in an internet environment, the Finger utility not only checks the end-to-end communication path (like the ICMP Echo), but it also verifies that the remote host knows of the remote user's existence. Let's see how to use the Finger protocol.

The network manager wishes to check on one of his users, Kevin Anderson. From his PC, he establishes a TCP connection with the Sun server to which Kevin is attached (see Trace 5.7.6a). Note that the Destination port requested in the initial TCP connection segment, Frame 801, is the Finger port, 79. The three-way handshake is completed in Frame 803, and the network manager's RUIP sends a query to the server, requesting information for the user. The details of the query are shown in Trace 5.7.6b, indicating that the user name or user id (kpa) are sent with the query. Note that the Push (PSH) flag is used to send data on its way immediately.

The Sun server responds with an acknowledgement (Frame 805), followed by the RUIP response (Frame 806). The response contains 174 octets of data that pertain to user kpa. We learn the following about the user:

Login name: kpa   In real life: Kevin P. Anderson
Directory: /home/h0 008/kpa   Shell: /bin/csh
Last login Wed Mar 27 09:22 on ttyp0 from h0009z
No unread mail
No plan

With the answer transmitted, the server's RUIP closes the connection in Frame 807 by setting the Finish (FIN) flag. The PC acknowledges the server's FIN (Frame 808) and sends a FIN of its own (Frame 809). The server acknowledges the final transaction in Frame 810.

In all, it took only 10 frames to learn about user kpa, his directory, shell, last login, and so on. Some of this information may be considered sensitive for security reasons, and network administrators are advised to read the security issues detailed in the Finger standard, RFC 1288. However, if you can surmount these concerns, the Finger protocol can be a valuable addition to your bag of troubleshooting techniques.

Sniffer Network Analyzer data 27-Mar-91 at 09:04:54, TCPMEDLY.ENC, Pg 1

SUMMARY	Delta T	Destination	Source	Summary
801	57.9373	Sun Server	PC	TCP D=79 S=1228 SYN SEQ=134222388 LEN=0 WIN=1024
802	0.0009	PC	Sun Server	TCP D=1228 S=79 SYN ACK=134222389 SEQ=2009792000 LEN=0 WIN=4096
803	0.0130	Sun Server	PC	TCP D=79 S=1228 ACK=2009792001 WIN=1024
804	0.0441	Sun Server	PC	TCP D=79 S=1228 ACK=2009792001 SEQ=134222389 LEN=5 WIN=1024
805	0.1348	PC	Sun Server	TCP D=1228 S=79 ACK=134222394 WIN=4096
806	0.0433	PC	Sun Server	TCP D=1228 S=79 ACK=134222394 SEQ=2009792001 LEN=174 WIN=4096
807	0.0002	PC	Sun Server	TCP D=1228 S=79 FIN ACK=134222394 SEQ=2009792175 LEN=0 WIN=4096
808	0.0225	Sun Server	PC	TCP D=79 S=1228 ACK=2009792176 WIN=850
809	0.4897	Sun Server	PC	TCP D=79 S=1228 FIN ACK=2009792176 SEQ=134222394 LEN=0 WIN=850
810	0.0006	PC	Sun Server	TCP D=1228 S=79 ACK=134222395 WIN=4096

Trace 5.7.6a. Finger User Information Summary

Sniffer Network Analyzer data 27-Mar-91 at 09:04:54, TCPMEDLY.ENC, Pg 1

- - - - - - - - - - - - - - - - Frame 804 - - - - - - - - - - - - - - - -
TCP: ——- TCP header ——-
TCP:
TCP: Source port = 1228
TCP: Destination port = 79 (Finger)
TCP: Sequence number = 134222389
TCP: Acknowledgment number = 2009792001
TCP: Data offset = 20 bytes
TCP: Flags = 18
TCP: ..0. .... = (No urgent pointer)
TCP: ...1 .... = Acknowledgment
TCP: .... 1... = Push
TCP: .... .0.. = (No reset)
TCP: .... ..0. = (No SYN)
TCP: ....0 = (No FIN)
TCP: Window = 1024
TCP: Checksum = 2B9A (correct)
TCP: No TCP options
TCP: [5 byte(s) of data]
TCP:

```
ADDR  HEX                                                      ASCII
0000  08 00 20 09 42 A4 00 00  C0 3C 55 17 08 00 45 00       .. .B....<U...E.
0010  00 2D 02 C3 00 00 40 06  63 75 8B B1 FE 5F 8B B1       .-....@.cu..._..
0020  FE D0 04 CC 00 4F 08 00  12 35 77 CA FE 01 50 18       .....O...5w...P.
0030  04 00 2B 9A 00 00 6B 70  61 0D 0A 00                   ..+...kpa...
```

- - - - - - - - - - - - - - - - Frame 805 - - - - - - - - - - - - - - - -
TCP: ——- TCP header ——-
TCP:
TCP: Source port = 79 (Finger)
TCP: Destination port = 1228
TCP: Sequence number = 2009792001
TCP: Acknowledgment number = 134222394
TCP: Data offset = 20 bytes
TCP: Flags = 10
TCP: ..0. .... = (No urgent pointer)
TCP: ...1 .... = Acknowledgment
TCP: .... 0... = (No push)
TCP: .... .0.. = (No reset)
TCP: .... ..0. = (No SYN)

TCP: ....0 = (No FIN)
TCP: Window = 4096
TCP: Checksum = F61F (correct)
TCP: No TCP options
TCP:
```
ADDR  HEX                                                      ASCII
0000  00 00 C0 3C 55 17 08 00   20 09 42 A4 08 00 45 00    ...<U... .B...E.
0010  00 28 D6 EE 00 00 3C 06   93 4E 8B B1 FE D0 8B B1    .(....<..N......
0020  FE 5F 00 4F 04 CC 77 CA   FE 01 08 00 12 3A 50 10    ._.O..w......:P.
0030  10 00 F6 1F 00 00 64 2E   62 79 6E 61               ......d.byna
```

- - - - - - - - - - - - - - - - Frame 806 - - - - - - - - - - - - - - - - -

TCP: —— TCP header ——
TCP:
TCP: Source port = 79 (Finger)
TCP: Destination port = 1228
TCP: Sequence number = 2009792001
TCP: Acknowledgment number = 134222394
TCP: Data offset = 20 bytes
TCP: Flags = 18
TCP: ..0. .... = (No urgent pointer)
TCP: ...1 .... = Acknowledgment
TCP: .... 1... = Push
TCP: .... .0.. = (No reset)
TCP: .... ..0. = (No SYN)
TCP: ....0 = (No FIN)
TCP: Window = 4096
TCP: Checksum = CAA6 (correct)
TCP: No TCP options
TCP: [174 byte(s) of data]
TCP:
```
ADDR  HEX                                                      ASCII
0000  00 00 C0 3C 55 17 08 00   20 09 42 A4 08 00 45 00    ...<U... .B...E.
0010  00 D6 D6 F3 00 00 3C 06   92 9B 8B B1 FE D0 8B B1    ......<.........
0020  FE 5F 00 4F 04 CC 77 CA   FE 01 08 00 12 3A 50 18    ._.O..w......:P.
0030  10 00 CA A6 00 00 4C 6F   67 69 6E 20 6E 61 6D 65    ......Login name
0040  3A 20 6B 70 61 20 20 20   20 20 20 20 09 09 09 49    : kpa         ...I
0050  6E 20 72 65 61 6C 20 6C   69 66 65 3A 20 48 42 4F    n real life:....
0060  0D 0A 44 69 72 65 63 74   6F 72 79 3A 20 2F 68 6F    ..Directory: /ho
0070  6D 65 2F 68 30 30 30 38   2F 6B 70 61 20 20 20 20    me/h0008/kpa
0080  20 20 20 20 20 20 09 53   68 65 6C 6C 3A 20 2F 62    .Shell: /b
0090  69 6E 2F 63 73 68 0D 0A   4C 61 73 74 20 6C 6F 67    in/csh..Last log
00A0  69 6E 20 57 65 64 20 4D   61 72 20 32 37 20 30 39    in Wed Mar 27 09
00B0  3A 32 32 20 6F 6E 20 74   74 79 70 30 20 66 72 6F    :22 on ttyp0 fro
```

00C0	6D 20 68 30 30 30 39 7A	0D 0A 4E 6F 20 75 6E 72	m h0009z..No unr
00D0	65 61 64 20 6D 61 69 6C	0D 0A 4E 6F 20 50 6C 61	ead mail..No Pla
00E0	6E 2E 0D 0A		n...

Trace 5.7.6b. Finger User Information Details

5.7.7 Tape Backups Via an Internetwork

In the last few years, the price of hard disk storage on PCs has dropped to the point where it's not uncommon to have 80-100 MB of storage per workstation. But with this increasing storage comes increasing risk: the failure of a large hard disk can have disastrous consequences. To minimize this risk, many users routinely back up their hard disk onto either floppies or a tape drive.

In this case, the network engineer wants to back up his hard disk to a Sun SPARC-station server with an attached tape drive. Software in both the PC and server use TCP as the transport mechanism for the backup via an internetwork (see Figure 5-14). But when the engineer begins the backup procedure on the PC side, the process suddenly fails. Initially, he suspects a faulty tape drive. But further analysis reveals another problem.

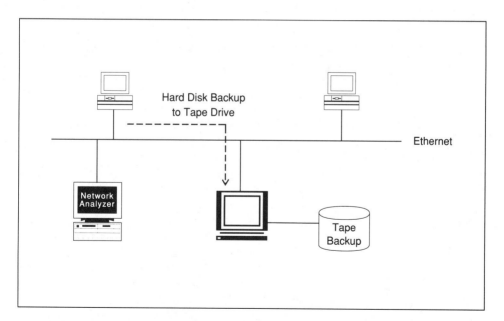

Figure 5-14. PC-to-Server Backup via Ethernet

The analysis begins with the server (shown as SPARCstn in Trace 5.7.7) sending a Window=4096 in Frame 32 to the PC, then waiting for the data to transfer. The PC begins downloading the backup in Frame 33 and gives the server a Window=905. The server acknowledges this data with a TCP segment of 35 octets in length (Frame 34). In response, the PC reduced its window size to 870 octets (905-35=870). Clearly, the PC's window size is more limiting than that of the server. The server, however, abruptly sends a Window=0 in Frame 37. This segment is repeated in Frames 39 and 41. The server shuts down the communication link from the PC to the tape drive. The engineer theorizes that the server does this so it can process the incoming TCP segment and transfer the data to the tape drive. Unfortunately, the PC software does not know that this delay is necessary. The PC interprets the Window=0 as a termination command and issues a TCP Reset (RST) command in Frame 42. This is followed by a Finish (FIN) command in Frame 44. The tape backup is aborted, but the hard disk has not been backed up completely.

The solution is to insert some delay into the PC's TCP module. When the tape drive is busy, the Sun workstation instructs its TCP module (on the server) to send Window=0, preventing the transfer of additional data. As long as the tape drive is busy, it continues to send Window=0. The TCP module in the PC is rewritten to accept the TCP segment with Window=0 and then wait 10 seconds for the tape drive to catch up. If it receives two more segments with Window=0, then the PC resets the connection. Now the backups proceed without a hitch via the internetwork.

Sniffer Network Analyzer data 27-Mar-91 at 09:04:54, TAPEBACK.ENC, Pg 1

SUMMARY	Destination	Source	Summary
32	PC 386	SPARCstn	TCP D=1022 S=1023
			ACK=694630 SEQ=1839168103
			LEN=17 WIN=4096
33	SPARCstn	PC 386	TCP D=1023 S=1022
			ACK=1839168120 WIN=905
34	PC 386	SPARCstn	TCP D=1022 S=1023
			ACK=694630 SEQ=1839168120
			LEN=35 WIN=4096
35	SPARCstn	PC 386	TCP D=1023 S=1022
			ACK=1839168155 WIN=870
36	SPARCstn	PC 386	RSHELL C PORT=1023 <00>

37	PC 386	SPARCstn	TCP D=1023 S=514
			ACK=698772 WIN=0
38	SPARCstn	PC 386	RSHELL C PORT=1023 <00>
39	PC 386	SPARCstn	TCP D=1023 S=514
			ACK=698772 WIN=0
40	SPARCstn	PC 386	RSHELL C PORT=1023 <00>
41	PC 386	SPARCstn	TCP D=1023 S=514
			ACK=698772 WIN=0
42	SPARCstn	PC 386	TCP D=514 S=1023 RST
			ACK=1839040002 WIN=1024
43	SPARCstn	PC 386	TCP D=1023 S=1022
			ACK=1839168155 WIN=1024
44	SPARCstn	PC 386	TCP D=1023 S=1022 FIN
			ACK=1839168155 SEQ=694630
			LEN=0 WIN=1024
45	PC 386	SPARCstn	TCP D=1022 S=1023
			ACK=694631 WIN=4096
46	PC 386	SPARCstn	TCP D=1023 S=514
			ACK=698772 WIN=1536
47	PC 386	SPARCstn	TCP D=1023 S=514
			ACK=698772 WIN=3072
48	SPARCstn	PC 386	TCPD=1023 S=1022 RST
			ACK=1839168155 WIN=1024

Trace 5.7.7. Tape Backup with Window = 0

5.7.8 Optimizing the TCP Window Size

The previous case study showed what the receiver's window can do. We saw that when the distant host sends a value of Window=0, the transmission path to the host effectively shuts down. If you receive a large window (say, Window=8192), you can transmit a reasonable amount of data. Depending upon the application, there should be an optimum window size that won't cause the transmitter to wait for unnecessary acknowledgements (i.e., the window is too small), yet won't overwhelm the receiver with more data than it can handle (i.e., the window is too large). As in Goldilocks and the Three Bears, you need to find the window size that is "just right."

Two documents provide useful information about optimizing the window size: RFC 879, "The TCP Maximum Segment Size and Related Topics" [5-4], and RFC 813, "Window and Acknowledgement Strategy in TCP" [5-9]. Let's study an inter-network that needs some help in this area.

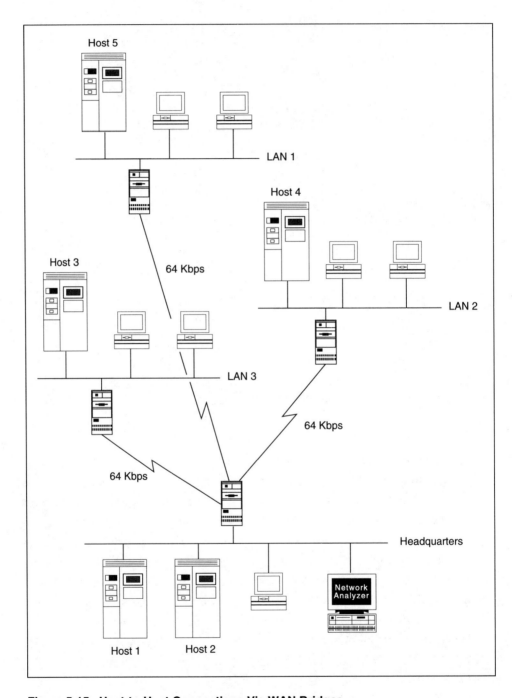

Figure 5-15. Host-to-Host Connections Via WAN Bridges

In the following case study, the internetwork consists of a headquarters location connected to three remote Ethernet segments (see Figure 5-15). Each remote segment contains a UNIX host plus a number of workstations. The remote segments are connected via bridges and 64-Kbps leased lines. The remote hosts contact these peers on a periodic basis to transfer files using a File Transfer Protocol (FTP) facility. In addition, the PC users use TELNET for remote host access. The problem is that while two hosts on the same segment can communicate without a problem, the hosts can't contact other hosts at a remote location without excessive delays and interrupts of the FTP session. Let's see why these problems occur.

To study the problem, the network engineer captures the data between one host on the headquarters segment (Hdqr Host) and another host on a remote segment. He places the analyzer on the headquarters segment to capture the information coming to and from the remote host via the bridge (see Trace 5.7.8a). The initial analysis does not reveal any frames with errors. The remote host initiates a TCP connection in Frames 2 through 4, then starts an FTP session. The user identifies himself (Buster, in Frame 9), a password is transmitted (Frame 11), and an account sent (Frame 15). The login completes in Frame 17, and the user can proceed. The only indication that a problem exists is the delays between frames, shown in Frames 9, 15, 17, and 19. These delays range from 6 to 18 seconds and indicate a transmission problem between the two communicating hosts.

The headquarters host initiates a second TCP data connection beginning in Frame 26. Note that the Destination ports are different—the first connection (Frames 2 through 4) uses Destination port=21 (FTP Control) and Source Port=4979. The second connection uses Source port=20 (FTP data) and Destination Port=4980. By all appearances, the two hosts should have established a full-duplex connection. Note also that both hosts return Window=0 in Frames 26 and 27, but subsequently revise that number in Frames 28, 29, and 30.

Data transfer begins in Frame 31, with 512 octets of information. Successive frames convey 512 and 256 octets of data, respectively. An unexpected association of Sequence and Acknowledgement numbers occurs, however, in Trace 5.7.8b:

Frame	Data (octets)	Beginning Sequence	Ending Sequence	Acknowledgement
31	512	55278459	55278970	53214721
32	512	55278971	55279482	53214721
33	256	55279483	55279738	53214721
34	0	53214721	53214721	55278971

Frames 31 through 33 contain data from the headquarters host to the remote host. During this time, no data is received in the other direction, since the Acknowledgement number remains constant (ACK=53214721). Frame 34 contains an acknowledgement from the remote host, but note that it is the acknowledgement for the third previous segment (Frame 31). In other words, Frames 32 and 33 are still en route to the remote host, somewhere in the link between the two bridges.

The data transfer continues for a number of segments, until the headquarters host abruptly terminates the connection in Frame 149 via the RST flag (see Trace 5.7.8a). The FTP connection is then closed, and no additional data can be transferred. The immediately preceding frames provide the answer:

Frame	Sequence	Acknowledgement	Outstanding Data (octets)
144	55310931		
145		55306995	3,936
146	55311373		
147		55306995	4,378

The headquarters host transmits 442 octets of data in Frame 144, the remote host acknowledges a lesser amount (ACK=55306995), leaving 3,936 octets of data unacknowledged (55310931 - 55306995 = 3,936). The problem worsens in Frames 146 and 147, with 4,378 unacknowledged octets (55311373 - 55306995 = 4,378).

Somewhere between the processing of Frames 144 and 146 a threshold within the host that counts the maximum allowable outstanding octets is crossed, causing the headquarters host to reset the connection. This threshold is half the allowable window size. The host has Window=8,192, half of which is 4,096. In Frame 145,

3,936 octets are outstanding; in Frame 146 that number increases to 4,378, exceeding the threshold of 4,096.

The reason for the large amount of outstanding data is traced to inadequate I/O buffers on the WAN side of the bridges. Adding I/O buffers improves transmission. A second parameter, the discard threshold, is also increased inside the bridges. The discard threshold determines the maximum number of MAC-level frames that can be queued within the bridge. Setting this parameter to a higher value also improves the internetwork response. With these two bridge parameters adjusted, no further problems occur.

Sniffer Network Analyzer data 23-Jan-91 at 03:10:38, TRACE.ENC, Pg 1

SUMMARY	Delta T	Destination	Source	Summary
M 1		Bridge	Hdqtr Host	ARP R PA=[143.130.1.5]
				HA=08000B001180 PRO=IP
2	0.0248	Hdqtr Host	Bridge	TCP D=21 S=4979 SYN
				SEQ=44830720 LEN=0 WIN=4096
3	0.5002	Bridge	Hdqtr Host	TCP D=4979 S=21 SYN
				ACK=44830721 SEQ=55214045
				LEN=0 WIN=8192
4	0.0258	Hdqtr Host	Bridge	TCP D=21 S=4979
				ACK=55214046 WIN=4096
5	0.2294	Bridge	Hdqtr Host	TCP D=4979 S=21
				ACK=44830721 WIN=8192
6	1.1449	Bridge	Hdqtr Host	TCP D=4979 S=21
				ACK=44830721 WIN=8192
7	2.7069	Bridge	Hdqtr Host	FTP R PORT=4979
				220 1100JD1100
				Service ready for new user
				<0D><0A>
8	0.0635	Hdqtr Host	Bridge	TCP D=21 S=4979
				ACK=55214090 WIN=4096
9	14.7769	Hdqtr Host	Bridge	FTP C PORT=4979
				USER Buster<0D><0A>
10	0.1605	Bridge	Hdqtr Host	FTP R PORT=4979
				331 User name okay,
				need password.<0D><0A>
11	0.0465	Hdqtr Host	Bridge	FTP C PORT=4979 PASS
				pass<0D><0A>

12	0.2198	Bridge	Hdqtr Host	TCP	D=4979 S=21
					ACK=44830745 WIN=8192
13	0.7356	Bridge	Hdqtr Host	FTP	R PORT=4979
					332 Need account for login.
					<0D><0A>
14	0.0597	Hdqtr Host	Bridge	TCP	D=21 S=4979
					ACK=55214155 WIN=4096
15	6.7912	Hdqtr Host	Bridge	FTP	C PORT=4979
					ACCT Rufus<0D><0A>
16	0.2171	Bridge	Hdqtr Host	TCP	D=4979 S=21
					ACK=44830761 WIN=8192
17	14.4493	Bridge	Hdqtr Host	FTP	R PORT=4979
					230 User logged in, proceed
					<0D><0A>
18	0.1431	Hdqtr Host	Bridge	TCP	D=21 S=4979
					ACK=55214186 WIN=4096
19	18.7942	Hdqtr Host	Bridge	FTP	C PORT=4979
					PORT 143,130,2,1,19,116
					<0D><0A>
20	0.2157	Bridge	Hdqtr Host	TCP	D=4979 S=21
					ACK=44830786 WIN=8192
21	0.2449	Bridge	Hdqtr Host	FTP	R PORT=4979
					200 Command okay.<0D><0A>
22	0.0551	Hdqtr Host	Bridge	FTP	C PORT=4979
					RETR faithful.jog
					<0D><0A>
23	0.2195	Bridge	Hdqtr Host	TCP	D=4979 S=21
					ACK=44830809 WIN=8192
24	2.0346	Bridge	Hdqtr Host	FTP	R PORT=4979
					150 File status okay;
					about to open data conn...
25	0.0371	Hdqtr Host	Bridge	TCP	D=21 S=4979
					ACK=55214259 WIN=4096
26	1.0401	Bridge	Hdqtr Host	TCP	D=4980 S=20 SYN
					SEQ=55278458 LEN=0 WIN=0
27	0.0275	Hdqtr Host	Bridge	TCP	D=20 S=4980 SYN
					ACK=55278459 SEQ=53214720
					LEN=0 WIN=0
28	0.2321	Bridge	Hdqtr Host	TCP	D=4980 S=20
					ACK=53214721 WIN=8192
29	0.0279	Hdqtr Host	Bridge	TCP	D=20 S=4980
					ACK=55278459 WIN=4096

30	0.0099	Hdqtr Host	Bridge	TCP	D=20 S=4980
					ACK=55278459 WIN=8192
31	0.9281	Bridge	Hdqtr Host	TCP	D=4980 S=20
					ACK=53214721 SEQ=55278459
					LEN=512 WIN=8192
32	0.0070	Bridge	Hdqtr Host	TCP	D=4980 S=20
					ACK=53214721 SEQ=55278971
					LEN=512 WIN=8192
33	0.0025	Bridge	Hdqtr Host	TCP	D=4980 S=20
					ACK=53214721 SEQ=55279483
					LEN=256 WIN=8192
34	0.3243	Hdqtr Host	Bridge	TCP	D=20 S=4980
					ACK=55278971 WIN=8192
35	0.0792	Bridge	Hdqtr Host	TCP	D=4980 S=20
					ACK=53214721 SEQ=55279739
					LEN=512 WIN=8192
36	0.0033	Bridge	Hdqtr Host	TCP	D=4980 S=20
					ACK=53214721 SEQ=55280251
					LEN=204 WIN=8192
37	0.0873	Hdqtr Host	Bridge	TCP	D=20 S=4980
					ACK=55280251 WIN=8192
38	0.0514	Bridge	Hdqtr Host	TCP	D=4980 S=20
					ACK=53214721 SEQ=55280455
					LEN=512 WIN=8192
39	0.0040	Bridge	Hdqtr Host	TCP	D=4980 S=20
					ACK=53214721 SEQ=55280967
					LEN=512 WIN=8192
40	0.0042	Bridge	Hdqtr Host	TCP	D=4980 S=20
					ACK=53214721 SEQ=55281479
					LEN=432 WIN=8192
41	0.1563	Hdqtr Host	Bridge	TCP	D=20 S=4980
					ACK=55281479 WIN=8192
42	0.0448	Bridge	Hdqtr Host	TCP	D=4980 S=20
					ACK=53214721 SEQ=55281911
					LEN=512 WIN=8192
43	0.0042	Bridge	Hdqtr Host	TCP	D=4980 S=20
					ACK=53214721 SEQ=55282423
					LEN=512 WIN=8192
44	0.0045	Bridge	Hdqtr Host	TCP	D=4980 S=20
					ACK=53214721 SEQ=55282935
					LEN=361 WIN=8192
45	0.1611	Hdqtr Host	Bridge	TCP	D=20 S=4980
					ACK=55281911 WIN=8192

.
.
.

128	0.0018	Bridge	Hdqtr Host	TCP	D=4980 S=20 ACK=53214721 SEQ=55306733 LEN=37 WIN=8192
129	0.2577	Hdqtr Host	Bridge	TCP	D=20 S=4980 ACK=55303791 WIN=8192
130	0.0573	Bridge	Hdqtr Host	TCP	D=4980 S=20 ACK=53214721 SEQ=55306770 LEN=225 WIN=8192
131	0.0051	Bridge	Hdqtr Host	TCP	D=4980 S=20 ACK=53214721 SEQ=55306995 LEN=512 WIN=8192
132	0.0037	Bridge	Hdqtr Host	TCP	D=4980 S=20 ACK=53214721 SEQ=55307507 LEN=352 WIN=8192
133	0.0416	Hdqtr Host	Bridge	TCP	D=20 S=4980 ACK=55304243 WIN=8192
134	0.0378	Bridge	Hdqtr Host	TCP	D=4980 S=20 ACK=53214721 SEQ=55307859 LEN=512 WIN=8192
135	0.0628	Hdqtr Host	Bridge	TCP	D=20 S=4980 ACK=55305267 WIN=8192
136	0.0429	Bridge	Hdqtr Host	TCP	D=4980 S=20 ACK=53214721 SEQ=55308371 LEN=512 WIN=8192
137	0.0044	Bridge	Hdqtr Host	TCP	D=4980 S=20 ACK=53214721 SEQ=55308883 LEN=512 WIN=8192
138	0.0521	Hdqtr Host	Bridge	TCP	D=20 S=4980 ACK=55305709 WIN=8192
139	0.0285	Bridge	Hdqtr Host	TCP	D=4980 S=20 ACK=53214721 SEQ=55309395 LEN=512 WIN=8192
140	0.1706	Hdqtr Host	Bridge	TCP	D=20 S=4980 ACK=55306221 WIN=8192
141	0.0368	Bridge	Hdqtr Host	TCP	D=4980 S=20 ACK=53214721 SEQ=55309907 LEN=512 WIN=8192
142	0.1640	Hdqtr Host	Bridge	TCP	D=20 S=4980 ACK=55306995 WIN=8192

143	0.0393	Bridge	Hdqtr Host	TCP	D=4980 S=20
					ACK=53214721 SEQ=55310419
					LEN=512 WIN=8192
144	0.0048	Bridge	Hdqtr Host	TCP	D=4980 S=20
					ACK=53214721 SEQ=55310931
					LEN=442 WIN=8192
145	0.1554	Hdqtr Host	Bridge	TCP	D=20 S=4980
					ACK=55306995 WIN=8192
146	0.0211	Bridge	Hdqtr Host	TCP	D=4980 S=20
					ACK=53214721 SEQ=55311373
					LEN=59 WIN=8192
147	0.1795	Hdqtr Host	Bridge	TCP	D=20 S=4980
					ACK=55306995 WIN=8192
148	0.1987	Hdqtr Host	Bridge	TCP	D=20 S=4980
					ACK=55306995 WIN=8192
149	1.4094	Bridge	Hdqtr Host	TCP	D=4980 S=20 RST WIN=0
150	0.5261	Bridge	Hdqtr Host	FTP	R PORT=4979
					426 Connection is closed:
					A DDP ABORT WAS EXECUTED...
151	0.0648	Hdqtr Host	Bridge	TCP	D=21 S=4979
					ACK=55214312 WIN=4096

Trace 5.7.8a.   TCP Window Management Summary

Sniffer Network Analyzer data 23-Jan-91 at 03:10:38, TRACE.ENC, Pg 1

```
- - - - - - - - - - - - - - - Frame 31 - - - - - - - - - - - - - - - - -
TCP: ——- TCP header ——-
TCP:
TCP: Source port = 20 (FTP data)
TCP: Destination port = 4980
TCP: Sequence number = 55278459
TCP: Acknowledgment number = 53214721
TCP: Data offset = 20 bytes
TCP: Flags = 10
TCP: ..0. .... = (No urgent pointer)
TCP: ...1 .... = Acknowledgment
TCP: .... 0... = (No push)
TCP: .... .0.. = (No reset)
TCP: .... ..0. = (No SYN)
TCP: .... ...0 = (No FIN)
TCP: Window = 8192
```

TCP: Checksum = 27AC (correct)
TCP: No TCP options
TCP: [512 byte(s) of data]
TCP:

- - - - - - - - - - - - - - - - Frame 32 - - - - - - - - - - - - - - - -
TCP: ——- TCP header ——-
TCP:
TCP: Source port = 20 (FTP data)
TCP: Destination port = 4980
TCP: Sequence number = 55278971
TCP: Acknowledgment number = 53214721
TCP: Data offset = 20 bytes
TCP: Flags = 10
TCP: ..0. .... = (No urgent pointer)
TCP: ...1 .... = Acknowledgment
TCP: .... 0... = (No push)
TCP: .... .0.. = (No reset)
TCP: .... ..0. = (No SYN)
TCP: ....0 = (No FIN)
TCP: Window = 8192
TCP: Checksum = 16E8 (correct)
TCP: No TCP options
TCP: [512 byte(s) of data]
TCP:

- - - - - - - - - - - - - - - - Frame 33 - - - - - - - - - - - - - - - -
TCP: ——- TCP header ——-
TCP:
TCP: Source port = 20 (FTP data)
TCP: Destination port = 4980
TCP: Sequence number = 55279483
TCP: Acknowledgment number = 53214721
TCP: Data offset = 20 bytes
TCP: Flags = 10
TCP: ..0. .... = (No urgent pointer)
TCP: ...1 .... = Acknowledgment
TCP: .... 0... = (No push)
TCP: .... .0.. = (No reset)
TCP: .... ..0. = (No SYN)
TCP: ....0 = (No FIN)
TCP: Window = 8192
TCP: Checksum = 0C2D (correct)

TCP: No TCP options
TCP: [256 byte(s) of data]
TCP:

- - - - - - - - - - - - - - - Frame 34 - - - - - - - - - - - - - - - -
TCP: ——- TCP header ——-
TCP:
TCP: Source port = 4980
TCP: Destination port = 20 (FTP data)
TCP: Sequence number = 53214721
TCP: Acknowledgment number = 55278971
TCP: Data offset = 20 bytes
TCP: Flags = 10
TCP: ..0. .... = (No urgent pointer)
TCP: ...1 .... = Acknowledgment
TCP: .... 0... = (No push)
TCP: .... .0.. = (No reset)
TCP: .... ..0. = (No SYN)
TCP: ....0 = (No FIN)
TCP: Window = 8192
TCP: Checksum = D84E (correct)
TCP: No TCP options
TCP:

Trace 5.7.8b. TCP Window Management Acknowledgements

Sniffer Network Analyzer data 23-Jan-91 at 03:10:38, TRACE.ENC, Pg 1

- - - - - - - - - - - - - - - Frame 144 - - - - - - - - - - - - - - - -
TCP: ——- TCP header ——-
TCP:
TCP: Source port = 20 (FTP data)
TCP: Destination port = 4980
TCP: Sequence number = 55310931
TCP: Acknowledgment number = 53214721
TCP: Data offset = 20 bytes
TCP: Flags = 10
TCP: ..0. .... = (No urgent pointer)
TCP: ...1 .... = Acknowledgment
TCP: .... 0... = (No push)
TCP: .... .0.. = (No reset)
TCP: .... ..0. = (No SYN)
TCP: ....0 = (No FIN)

TCP: Window = 8192
TCP: Checksum = 1AD5 (correct)
TCP: No TCP options
TCP: [442 byte(s) of data]
TCP:

- - - - - - - - - - - - - - - - Frame 145 - - - - - - - - - - - - - - - - -
TCP: ——- TCP header ——-
TCP:
TCP: Source port = 4980
TCP: Destination port = 20 (FTP data)
TCP: Sequence number = 53214721
TCP: Acknowledgment number = 55306995
TCP: Data offset = 20 bytes
TCP: Flags = 10
TCP: ..0. .... = (No urgent pointer)
TCP: ...1 .... = Acknowledgment
TCP: .... 0... = (No push)
TCP: .... .0.. = (No reset)
TCP: .... ..0. = (No SYN)
TCP: ....0 = (No FIN)
TCP: Window = 8192
TCP: Checksum = 6AD6 (correct)
TCP: No TCP options
TCP:

- - - - - - - - - - - - - - - - Frame 146 - - - - - - - - - - - - - - - - -
TCP: ——- TCP header ——-
TCP:
TCP: Source port = 20 (FTP data)
TCP: Destination port = 4980
TCP: Sequence number = 55311373
TCP: Acknowledgment number = 53214721
TCP: Data offset = 20 bytes
TCP: Flags = 10
TCP: ..0. .... = (No urgent pointer)
TCP: ...1 .... = Acknowledgment
TCP: .... 0... = (No push)
TCP: .... .0.. = (No reset)
TCP: .... ..0. = (No SYN)
TCP: ....0 = (No FIN)
TCP: Window = 8192
TCP: Checksum = E735 (correct)

TCP: No TCP options
TCP: [59 byte(s) of data]
TCP:

- - - - - - - - - - - - - - - Frame 147 - - - - - - - - - - - - - - - -
TCP: ——- TCP header ——-
TCP:
TCP: Source port = 4980
TCP: Destination port = 20 (FTP data)
TCP: Sequence number = 53214721
TCP: Acknowledgment number = 55306995
TCP: Data offset = 20 bytes
TCP: Flags = 10
TCP: ..0. .... = (No urgent pointer)
TCP: ...1 .... = Acknowledgment
TCP: .... 0... = (No push)
TCP: .... .0.. = (No reset)
TCP: .... ..0. = (No SYN)
TCP: ....0 = (No FIN)
TCP: Window = 8192
TCP: Checksum = 6AD6 (correct)
TCP: No TCP options
TCP:

- - - - - - - - - - - - - - - Frame 148 - - - - - - - - - - - - - - - -
TCP: ——- TCP header ——-
TCP:
TCP: Source port = 4980
TCP: Destination port = 20 (FTP data)
TCP: Sequence number = 53214721
TCP: Acknowledgment number = 55306995
TCP: Data offset = 20 bytes
TCP: Flags = 10
TCP: ..0. .... = (No urgent pointer)
TCP: ...1 .... = Acknowledgment
TCP: .... 0... = (No push)
TCP: .... .0.. = (No reset)
TCP: .... ..0. = (No SYN)
TCP: ....0 = (No FIN)
TCP: Window = 8192
TCP: Checksum = 6AD6 (correct)
TCP: No TCP options
TCP:

```
- - - - - - - - - - - - - - - - Frame 149 - - - - - - - - - - - - - - - -
TCP: ——- TCP header ——-
TCP:
TCP: Source port = 20 (FTP data)
TCP: Destination port = 4980
TCP: Sequence number = 55311432
TCP: Data offset = 20 bytes
TCP: Flags = 04
TCP: ..0. .... = (No urgent pointer)
TCP: ...0 .... = (No acknowledgment)
TCP: .... 0... = (No push)
TCP: .... .1.. = Reset
TCP: .... ..0. = (No SYN)
TCP: .... ...0 = (No FIN)
TCP: Window = 0
TCP: Checksum = 7ABA (correct)
TCP: No TCP options
TCP:


- - - - - - - - - - - - - - - - Frame 150 - - - - - - - - - - - - - - - -
FTP: ——- FTP data ——-
FTP:
FTP: 426 Connection is closed: A DDP ABORT WAS EXECUTED...
FTP:


- - - - - - - - - - - - - - - - Frame 151 - - - - - - - - - - - - - - - -
TCP: ——- TCP header ——-
TCP:
TCP: Source port = 4979
TCP: Destination port = 21 (FTP)
TCP: Sequence number = 44830809
TCP: Acknowledgment number = 55214312
TCP: Data offset = 20 bytes
TCP: Flags = 10
TCP: ..0. .... = (No urgent pointer)
TCP: ...1 .... = Acknowledgment
TCP: .... 0... = (No push)
TCP: .... .0.. = (No reset)
TCP: .... ..0. = (No SYN)
TCP: .... ...0 = (No FIN)
TCP: Window = 4096
TCP: Checksum = D30A (correct)
TCP: No TCP options
TCP:
```

Trace 5.7.8c. TCP Window Management Reset Condition

This chapter marks the three-quarter point in our journey from the bottom to the top of the DARPA protocol stack. We have now made the LAN, MAN, or WAN hardware connection at the Network Interface Layer, transmitted the datagrams at the Internet Layer, and assured the reliability of those datagrams at the Host-to-Host Layer. Now we need some application data to send! We'll discuss these applications in the next chapter by studying protocols for file transfer, electronic mail, and remote host access.

5.8 References

[5-1]   Postel, J. "User Datagram Protocol." RFC 768, ISI, August 1980.

[5-2]   Postel, J., editor. "Transmission Control Protocol." RFC 793, ISI, September 1981.

[5-3]   Socolofsky, T., et. al. "A TCP/IP Tutorial." RFC 1180, Spider Systems Ltd., January 1991.

[5-4]   Postel, J. "The TCP Maximum Segment Size and Related Topics." RFC 879, ISI, November 1983.

[5-5]   Black, Uyless. *TCP/IP and Related Protocols*. New York, NY: McGraw-Hill, Inc., 1992.

[5-6]   Comer, Douglas E. *Internetworking with TCP/IP*. 2nd ed. Englewood Cliffs, NJ: Prentice Hall, Inc., 1991.

[5-7]   Partridge, Craig. "Improving Your TCP: Look at the Timers." *ConneXions* (July 1987): 13-14.

[5-8]   Karn, Phil. "Improving Your TCP: Karn's Algorithm." *ConneXions* (October 1988): 23.

[5-9]   Clark, David D. "Window and Acknowledgement Strategy in TCP." RFC 813, MIT Laboratory for Computer Science, July 1982.

[5-10] Minshall, Greg. "TCP Connection Initiation: An Inside Look." *ConneXions* (July 1988): 2-11.

[5-11] Clark, David D. "Fault Isolation and Recovery." RFC 816, MIT Laboratory for Computer Science, July 1982.

[5-12] Croft, W. et. al. "Bootstrap Protocol (BOOTP)." RFC 951, Sun Microsystems, September 1985.

[5-13] Reynolds, J. "BOOTP Vendor Information Extensions." RFC 1084, ISI, December 1988.

[5-14] Finlayson, Ross. "Bootstrap Loading Using TFTP." RFC 906, Stanford University, June 1984.

[5-15] Mogul, Jeffrey. "Booting Diskless Hosts: the BOOTP Protocol." *ConneXions* (October 1988): 14-18.

[5-16] Postel, J., et. al. "Time Protocol." RFC 868, ISI, May 1983.

[5-17] Zimmerman, D. "The Finger User Information Protocol." RFC 1196, Center for Discrete Mathematics and Theoretical Computer Science, December 1991.

CHAPTER 6

Troubleshooting the Process/Application Connection

In this chapter, we'll study the Process/Application Layer functions. At this layer, the user interacts with the host to perform user functions. These functions may include file transfer using the Trivial File Transfer Protocol (TFTP) or the more complex File Transfer Protocol (FTP); client/server file operations via Sun Microsystems Inc.'s Network File System (NFS); remote host access with the Telecommunications Network (TELNET) protocol; or electronic mail using the Simple Mail Transfer Protocol (SMTP). All of these protocols exhibit their own characteristics and challenges. We'll begin by exploring how they fit into the DARPA architectural model.

6.1 The Process/Application Connection

The Process/Application Layer sits at the very top of the DARPA architectural model. Unlike the Host-to-Host, Internet, and Network Interface Layers, which are transparent to end users, the Process/Application Layer is accessed by users directly via the host's operating system. (Network analysts, of course, must be prepared to troubleshoot problems at any layer!) End users use this layer's functions to perform computer operations such as file transfer, electronic mail, and so on (see Figure 6-1a).

Figure 6-1b shows examples of the significant Process/Application protocols and the standards that describe them. Since these protocols provide functions that relate to the OSI Session, Presentation, and Application Layers, they are sometimes referred to as Upper-Layer Protocols (ULPs). Figure 6-1c shows the position of the

Application (ULP) data within the transmission frame. The lower-layer headers and trailers all serve to reliably transfer the ULP information from one host to another via the internetwork.

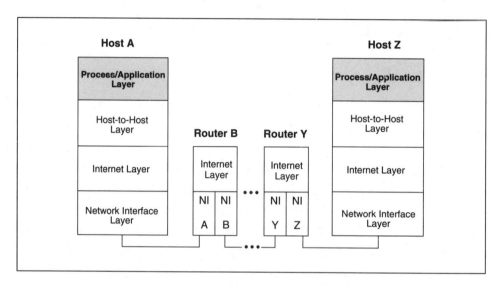

Figure 6-1a. The Process/Application Connection

DARPA Layer	Protocol Implementation						OSI Layer
	File Transfer	Electronic Mail	Terminal Emulation	File Transfer	Client / Server	Network Management	Application
Process / Application	File Transfer Protocol (FTP)	Simple Mail Transfer Protocol (SMTP)	TELNET Protocol	Trivial File Transfer Protocol (TFTP)	Sun Microsystems Network File System Protocols (NFS)	Simple Network Management Protocol (SNMP)	Presentation
	MIL-STD-1780 RFC 959	MIL-STD-1781 RFC 821	MIL-STD-1782 RFC 854	RFC 783	RFCs 1014, 1057, and 1094	RFC 1157	Session
Host-to-Host	Transmission Control Protocol (TCP) MIL-STD-1778 RFC 793			User Datagram Protocol (UDP) RFC 768			Transport
Internet	Address Resolution ARP RFC 826 RARP RFC 903		Internet Protocol (IP) MIL-STD-1777 RFC 791		Internet Control Message Protocol (ICMP) RFC 792		Network
Network Interface	Network Interface Cards: Ethernet, StarLAN, Token Ring, ARCNET RFC 894, RFC 1042, RFC 1201						Data Link
	Transmission Media: Twisted Pair, Coax, Fiber Optics, Wireless Media, etc.						Physical

Figure 6-1b. DARPA Process/Application Layer Protocols

276

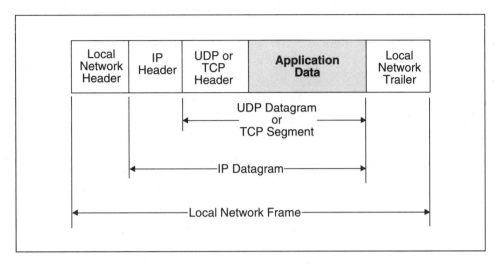

Figure 6-1c. The Internet Transmission Frame and Application Data Position

To complete our tour of the DARPA architectural model, we will study the significant Process/Application protocols, beginning with TFTP. Several references provide details on the protocols discussed in this chapter. Stallings' *Handbook of Computer Communications Standards, Volume 3, The TCP/IP Protocol Suite* [6-1], contains individual chapters on the common application protocols, such as FTP, TELNET, and SMTP. RFC 1123, "Requirements for Internet Hosts: Application and Support" [6-2] details requirements that hosts must provide to properly support file transfer, remote host access, and electronic mail. Specific details and parameters for these protocols are provided in RFC 1340, "Assigned Numbers", [6-3]. An excerpt of RFC 1340 is provided in Appendix G for reference.

6.2 Trivial File Transfer Protocol (TFTP)

The Trivial File Transfer Protocol, described in RFC 783 [6-4], reads and writes files or mail messages from one host to another. TFTP offers no other functions. TFTP's strength is its simplicity. It transfers 512-octet blocks of data without excessive overhead. Because it is implemented on UDP transport, TFTP is one of the easiest ULPs to implement, but it does not guarantee data reliability.

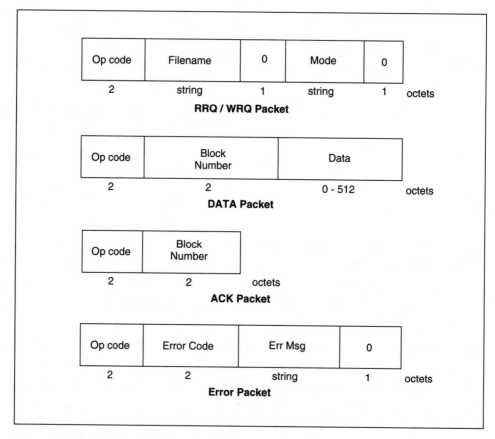

Figure 6-2. Trivial File Transfer Protocol (TFTP) Packet Formats

TFTP defines five packet types, which are distinguished by an Opcode (operation code) field (see Figure 6-2):

Opcode	Operation
1	Read Request (RRQ)
2	Write Request (WRQ)
3	Data (DATA)
4	Acknowledgement (ACK)
5	Error (ERROR)

The Read Request (RRQ, Opcode=1) and Write Request (WRQ, Opcode=2) packets have the same structure. Following the Opcode (2 octets), a string of netascii characters specifies the filename. (The netascii code is an 8-bit code defined by the ANSI standard X3.4-1968). An octet containing ZERO terminates the filename. The Mode field (also a string) specifies which of three data transfer modes are to be used. The choices are netascii, octet (raw 8-bit bytes), and mail. The mail mode is defined as netascii characters destined for a user instead of a host. The Mode field is terminated by an octet containing ZERO.

The Data packet (Opcode=3) transfers information. A Block number (2 octets) follows the Opcode and identifies the particular 512-octet block of data being sent. The Data field (0-512 octets in length) carries the actual information. Blocks less than 512 octets in length (i.e., 0-511 octets) indicate the end of an atomic unit of transmission.

The ACK packet (Opcode=4) is used for acknowledgement. It contains a Block Number field (2 octets) that corresponds to the similar number in the Data packet being acknowledged. For simplicity, TFTP incorporates the lock-step acknowledgement, which requires each data packet to be acknowledged prior to the transmission of another. In other words, because TFTP operates over UDP, not TCP, it has no provisions for a window mechanism, and all packets (except ERROR packets) must be acknowledged. ACK or ERROR packets acknowledge DATA and WRQ packets; DATA or ERROR packets acknowledge RRQ or ACK packets. ERROR packets require no acknowledgement.

The ERROR packet (Opcode=5) may be used to acknowledge any of the other four packet types. It contains a 2-octet error code that describes the problem:

Value	Meaning
0	Not defined, see error message (if any)
1	File not found
2	Access violation
3	Disk full or allocation exceeded
4	Illegal TFTP operation
5	Unknown transfer ID
6	File already exists
7	No such user

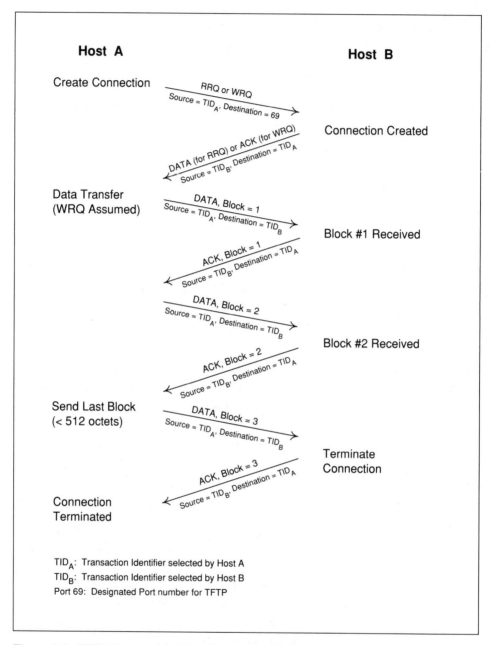

Figure 6-3. TFTP Connection, Data Transfer, and Termination

An error message (ErrMsg) consisting of a netascii string followed by a ZERO completes the packet. When errors occur, an ERROR packet is transmitted and the connection is terminated. Hosts generate ERROR packets for three types of events: when the host that cannot satisfy a request such as locating a file; when the host receives a delayed or duplicate packet; or when the host loses access to a resource such as a disk during the transfer.

Figure 6-3 shows TFTP's operation. Host A issues a RRQ or WRQ and receives a response of either DATA (for RRQ) or ACK (for WRQ). Each host initiating a connection chooses a random number between 0 and 65,535 for use as a Transfer Identifier (TID). The TID passes to UDP, which uses it as a Port address. When the RRQ or WRQ is initially transmitted from Host A, it selects a TID to identify its end of the connection and designates Destination=69, the TFTP port number. If the connection is accepted, the remote host, Host B, returns its TID B subscript as the source with the TID A subscript as the destination. If a WRQ was the initial transmission, an ACK with Block number=0 is returned. If the transmission was RRQ, a DATA packet with Block number=1 is returned. Data transfer then proceeds in 512-octet blocks, with each host identifying the appropriate Source and Destination TIDs with each DATA or ACK packet. The receipt of a DATA packet with less than 512 octets signals the termination of the connection. If errors occur during transmission, they generate an ERROR packet containing the appropriate Error Code. An example of this is provided in Section 6.8.1.

6.3 File Transfer Protocol (FTP)

One of the most popular Process/Application protocols is the File Transfer Protocol, described in RFC 959 [6-5]. As its name implies, FTP allows local or remote client and server machines to share files and data using TCP's reliable transport.

The complete FTP service includes a User-FTP and a Server-FTP, as shown in Figure 6-4. The User-FTP includes a User Interface (UI), a User Protocol Interpreter (PI), and a User Data Transfer Process (DTP). The Server-FTP includes a Server-PI and a Server-DTP, but excludes the user interface. The User-PI initiates the logical control connection, which uses the TELNET protocol. The user (or client) uses an internally-assigned Port number to connect to Server Port number 21, designated for FTP control. The data to be transferred passes from another self-assigned port on the User-DTP to Port number 20 (designated FTP data) on the Server-DTP. Thus, two Port numbers are used for the two logical communication paths: control and data.

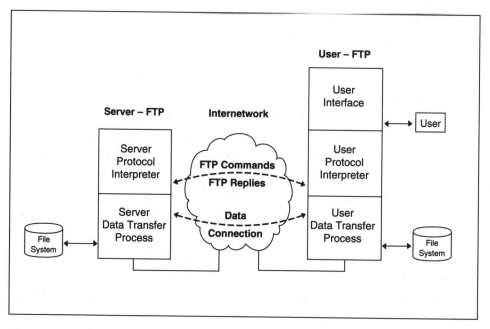

Figure 6-4. File Transfer Protocol (FTP) Model

6.3.1 Data Representation, Data Structures, and Transmission Modes

Three parameters are required to completely specify the data or file to be transferred: the Data Representation, the Data Structure, and the Transmission Modes. The data may be represented in one of four ways: ASCII (the default is 8-bit characters); EBCDIC (8-bit characters); Image (8-bit contiguous bytes), which transfers binary data; and Local, which uses a byte size defined by the local host. Similarly, there are three types of data structures: the File Structure (the default), which is a continuous sequence of data bytes; the Record Structure, which consists of continuous records; and the Page Structure, which is comprised of independent, indexed pages. Three transmission modes are available, including Stream

Mode (a transmitted stream of bytes), Block Mode (a header plus a series of data blocks) and Compressed Mode (used for maximizing bandwidth). The proper operation of the data transfer between the User and Server Data Transfer Processes depends on the control commands that go between the User and Server Protocol Interpreters. We'll look at these commands next.

6.3.2 FTP Commands

FTP commands and replies are communicated between the Server and User Protocol Interpreters (review Figure 6-4). These commands are defined in three categories: Access Control, Transfer Parameter, and Service.

6.3.2.1 Access Control Commands. The Access Control commands determine which users may access a particular file, and are invoked by the Server-FTP:

Command Code and Argument	Usage
USER <SP> <username> <CRLF>	Identifies the user
PASS <SP> <password> <CRLF>	User's password
ACCT <SP> <account-information> <CRLF>	User's account
CWD <SP> <pathname> <CRLF>	Change working directory
CDUP <CRLF>	Change to Parent directory
SMNT <SP> <pathname> <CRLF>	Structure Mount
REIN <CRLF>	Reinitialize, terminating the user
QUIT <CRLF>	Logout
<SP>	Represents a Space character
<CRLF>	Represents Carriage Return, Line Feed characters

6.3.2.2 Transfer Parameter Commands. The Transfer Parameter commands are used to alter the default parameters used to transfer data on a FTP connection:

Command Code and Argument	Usage
PORT <SP> <host-port> <CRLF>	Specifies the data port to be used
PASV <CRLF>	Requests the Server DTP to listen on a data port
TYPE <SP> <type-code> <CRLF>	Representation type: ASCII, EBCDIC, Image, or Local
STRU <SP> <structure-code> <CRLF>	File structure: File, Record, or Page
MODE <SP> <mode-code> <CRLF>	Transmission mode: Stream, Block, or Compressed

6.3.2.3 Service Commands. Service commands define the file operation requested by the user. The convention for the pathname argument is determined by the FTP Server's local conventions:

Command Code and Argument	Usage
RETR <SP> <pathname> <CRLF>	Retrieve a copy of the file from the other end
STOR <SP> <pathname> <CRLF>	Store data at the Server
STOU <CRLF>	Store Unique
APPE <SP> <pathname> <CRLF>	Append
ALLO <SP> <decimal-integer> [<SP> R <SP> <decimal-integer>] <CRLF>	Allocate storage
REST <SP> <marker> <CRLF>	Restart transfer at checkpoint
RNFR <SP> <pathname> <CRLF>	Rename from

Command Code and Argument	Usage
RNTO <SP> <pathname> <CRLF>	Rename to
ABOR <CRLF>	Abort previous service command
DELE <SP> <pathname> <CRLF>	Delete file at Server
RMD <SP> <pathname> <CRLF>	Remove directory
MKD <SP> <pathname> <CRLF>	Make directory
PWD <CRLF>	Print working directory
LIST [<SP> <pathname>] <CRLF>	List files or text
NLST [<SP> <pathname>] <CRLF>	Name list
SITE <SP> <string> <CRLF>	Site parameters
SYST <CRLF>	Determine operating system
STAT [<SP> <pathname>] <CRLF>	Status
HELP [<SP> <string>] <CRLF>	Help information
NOOP <CRLF>	No operation

6.3.3 FTP Replies

An FTP reply consists of a three-digit number and a space, and is followed by one line of text. Each digit of the reply is significant. The first digit (value 1-5) determines whether the response is good, bad, or incomplete. The second and third digits are encoded to provide additional details regarding the reply. The values for the first digit are:

    1yz ....Positive Preliminary reply
    2yz ....Positive Completion reply
    3yz ....Positive Intermediate reply
    4yz ....Transient Negative Completion reply
    5yz ....Permanent Negative Completion reply

The values for the second digit are:

x0z ....Syntax
x1z ....Information
x2z ....Connections
x3z ....Authentication and accounting
x4z ....Unspecified as yet
x5z ....File system

The third digit gives a finer definition for each function category specified by the second digit. An example would be:

211: System status
212: Directory status
213: File status
214: Help message

The FTP specification, RFC 959, elaborates in great detail on the states and conditions that trigger these reply messages. Another useful reference is Romkey's "FTP's Tireless Problems" [6-6], which describes some of the shortcomings of the protocol's implementation under different operating systems.

6.3.4 FTP Operation

A typical scenario in which FTP is used to retrieve a file from a remote host begins when the user initiates a connection to the remote host by entering "FTP [host address]". For example, to retrieve an RFC, the user would enter "FTP NIC.DDN.MIL" to access the Network Information Center of the Defense Data Network. The host responds by asking for the username and password. If the desired file is not in the root directory, the user must change to the proper subdirectory. For example, the user would type "CD RFC" to change to the subdirectory that contains the RFCs. (Note that some host systems abbreviate certain commands. For example, the CWD command to change the current directory becomes CD. Most systems support the HELP command, which lists the commands or abbreviations accepted by the system.) The third step is for the user to tell the host the action required, such as file transfer. For example, to retrieve an RFC, the command would be "GET RFCnnnn.TXT," where *nnnn* represents the number of the desired RFC. If the file transfer requires a different mode (such as binary), the user must specify that mode before invoking the GET command. The file transfer would then begin, and the user would terminate the FTP connection (using the FTP QUIT command) when all business was completed. Another example of an FTP session is given in the case study in Section 6.9.2.

6.4 Sun Microsystems Network File System (NFS)

No discussion about the Application/Process Layer would be complete without mentioning Sun Microsystems Inc.'s Network File System, commonly known as NFS. Sun released NFS in 1985 as part of the Sun Operating System (SunOS) included with Sun workstations. Since then, the NFS protocols have been adopted for a wide variety of computing platforms, including PCs, minicomputers, and large hosts.

NFS is based on a client/server paradigm where the *client* is the local computer that runs the application and the *server* is the computer that manages the file or application program. A LAN or WAN may run between the client and the server. In other words, NFS does not restrict the location of the client or server, and it provides transparent access to files regardless of their location. Any one machine can operate as both a client and a server.

Another advantage of NFS is that it allows the user to access files regardless of the operating system under which they are stored. Therefore, NFS allows directories and files to be shared between, say, an MS-DOS machine and other machines running UNIX, DEC's VMS, IBM's MVS, or Apple Computer's Macintosh operating system. Of course, if all machines are running NFS, NFS assures access to those files.

The foundation for the Sun protocols are the UDP and IP transport protocols, which may operate on a number of LAN/WAN interfaces. As we know, UDP provides a connectionless transport, which is not error-free. The NFS client/server paradigm therefore uses a stateless protocol in which one operation (or state) must complete before another initiates. Thus, after the client makes a request, it must wait for the server's response. If the server does not respond or delays its response, the client repeats its request. A server crash therefore will not impact the client. If the client has received the application file, then the client/server interaction is complete; if the client has not received the file, it will continue to resend the file request until the server is reinitialized. This aspect of the stateless protocol is particularly useful when you add the complexity of an internetwork between client and server.

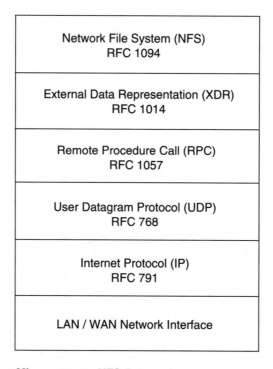

Network File System (NFS)
RFC 1094

External Data Representation (XDR)
RFC 1014

Remote Procedure Call (RPC)
RFC 1057

User Datagram Protocol (UDP)
RFC 768

Internet Protocol (IP)
RFC 791

LAN / WAN Network Interface

Figure 6-5. The Sun Microsystems NFS Protocols

The protocols that, in aggregate, make up the Sun suite are comprised of three separate modules: the Remote Procedure Call (RPC), the External Data Representation (XDR), and NFS. These three sit on top of UDP and IP (see Figure 6-5). Sun has developed RFCs for each module. The first layer of the Sun protocol stack is the RPC, defined in RFC 1057 [6-7]. The RPC establishes a logical connection between client and server. As with the establishment of a telephone call, the client sends a message to the server and waits for the server's reply. The server's reply includes the results of the requested procedure. The next layer is the XDR, specified in RFC 1014 [6-8]. XDR provides OSI Presentation Layer functions; it describes and encodes the data that is transferred to and from the client and server. The NFS protocol, described in RFC 1094 [6-9], sits at the top of the Sun protocol stack. The NFS protocol defines the file and directory structures and procedures for the client and server. References [6-10] and [6-11] provide excellent background on the Sun protocols and how they compare with other distributed file systems, such as AT&T's Remote File Sharing (RFS) protocols.

The importance of the Sun protocols lies in their strong ties to the UNIX environment, coupled with the historical tie between UNIX and the Internet protocols. In other words, if you use UNIX, you are likely to also use the TCP/IP and Sun protocols. An in-depth study of these protocols is beyond the scope of this text; refer to Malamud's *Analyzing Sun Networks* [6-12] for further information.

6.5 TELNET

TELNET, which stands for Telecommunications Network, is a protocol that allows a user (or client) at a terminal to access a remote host (or server). TELNET operates with TCP transport using Port number 23, and allows the terminal and host to exchange 8-bit characters of information in a half-duplex manner. The primary standard for TELNET, RFC 864 [6-13], discusses the three objectives of the protocol; RFC 855 [6-14] considers the various TELNET options.

TELNET's first objective is to define the Network Virtual Terminal (NVT). The NVT is a hypothetical representation of a network-standard terminal, also called a canonical (or standard) form. When both ends of the connection convert their data representations into the canonical form, they can communicate regardless of whether one end is, say, a DEC VT-100 and the other an SNA Host. The defined NVT format is the 7-bit USASCII code, transmitted in 8-bit octets. Figure 6-6 illustrates the conversion process from the local terminal/host format to the NVT format. The conversion typically occurs inside the devices, although an ancillary device such as a terminal server may perform the conversion for a number of similar devices.

The second objective of TELNET is to allow clients and servers to negotiate various options. This feature allows you to use a number of different terminals (some intelligent and some not so intelligent) with equal facility. To begin the negotiation, either or both ends of the connection state their desire to negotiate a particular option. The other end of the connection can accept or reject the proposal. TELNET defines four negotiation options: WILL, WON'T, DO, and DON'T. WILL *XXX* indicates that party's desire (or offer) to begin performing option *XXX*. DO *XXX* or DON'T

XXX are the returned positive or negative acknowledgements, respectively. DO *XXX* indicates that party's desire (or request) that the other party begin performing option *XXX*. WILL *XXX* and WON'T *XXX* are the returned positive and negative acknowledgements, respectively. For example, suppose the terminal wanted to use binary transmission. It would send a DO Binary Transmission to the remote host. The host could then respond with either a WILL Binary Transmission (a positive acknowledgement), or a WON'T Binary Transmission (a negative acknowledgement). If that terminal does not want its characters echoed across the TELNET connection it would send WON'T Echo; if the remote host agrees that no characters will be echoed it would return DON'T Echo.

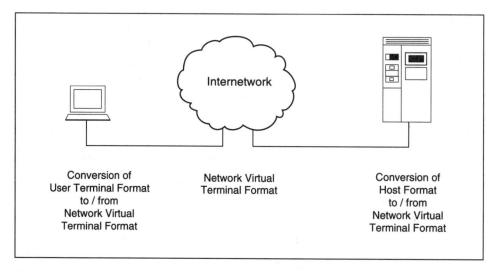

Figure 6-6. TELNET Network Virtual Terminal Operation

The third concept of TELNET is one of symmetry in the negotiation syntax. This symmetry allows either the client or server ends of the connection to request a particular option as required, thus optimizing the service provided by the other party.

TELNET commands consist of a mandatory two-octet sequence and an optional third octet. The first octet is always the Interpret as Command (IAC) character, Code 255. The second octet is the code for one of the commands listed below. The third octet is used when options are to be negotiated, and contains the option number of interest. For example, the command "IAC DO Terminal Type" would be represented by FF FD 18 (hexadecimal), corresponding to the Codes 255 253 24 (which are represented in decimal). RFC 854 defines the following TELNET commands:

Command	Code	Meaning
SE	240	End of subnegotiation parameters.
NOP	241	No operation.
Data Mark	242	The data stream portion of a Synch. This should always be accompanied by a TCP Urgent notification.
Break	243	NVT character BRK.
Interrupt Process	244	The function IP.
Abort output	245	The function AO.
Are You There	246	The function AYT.
Erase character	247	The function EC.
Erase Line	248	The function EL.
Go ahead	249	The GA signal.
SB	250	Indicates that what follows is subnegotiation of the indicated option.
WILL (option code)	251	Indicates the desire to begin performing, or confirmation that you are now performing, the indicated option.
WON'T (option code)	252	Indicates the refusal to perform, or continue performing, the indicated option.
DO (option code)	253	Indicates the request that the other party perform, or confirmation that you are expecting the other party to perform, the indicated option.
DON'T (option code)	254	Indicates the demand that the other party stop performing, or confirmation that you are no longer expecting the other party to perform, the indicated option.
IAC	255	Data Byte 255.

RFC 1060 lists the following TELNET options, along with the reference documents that provide further information:

Option	Name	Reference
0	Binary Transmission	RFC 856
1	Echo	RFC 857
2	Reconnection	NIC 50005
3	Suppress Go Ahead	RFC 858
4	Approx Message Size Negotiation	*See reference* [3-5]
5	Status	RFC 859
6	Timing Mark	RFC 860
7	Remote Controlled Trans and Echo	RFC 726
8	Output Line Width	NIC 50005
9	Output Page Size	NIC 50005
10	Output Carriage-Return Disposition	RFC 652
11	Output Horizontal Tab Stops	RFC 653
12	Output Horizontal Tab Disposition	RFC 654
13	Output Formfeed Disposition	RFC 655
14	Output Vertical Tabstops	RFC 656
15	Output Vertical Tab Disposition	RFC 657
16	Output Linefeed Disposition	RFC 658
17	Extended ASCII	RFC 698
18	Logout	RFC 727
19	Byte Macro	RFC 735
20	Data Entry Terminal	RFC 1043
22	SUPDUP	RFC 736
22	SUPDUP Output	RFC 749

Option	Name	Reference
23	Send Location	RFC 779
24	Terminal Type	RFC 1091
25	End of Record	RFC 885
26	TACACS User Identification	RFC 927
27	Output Marking	RFC 933
28	Terminal Location Number	RFC 946
29	Telnet 3270 Regime	RFC 1041
30	X.3 PAD	RFC 1053
31	Negotiate About Window Size	RFC 1073
32	Terminal Speed	RFC 1079
33	Remote Flow Control	RFC 1080
34	Linemode	RFC 1116
35	X Display Location	RFC 1096
255	Extended-Options-List	RFC 861

Note the large number of documents available to describe individual options. Shein's "The TELNET Protocol" [6-15] provides an excellent description of the negotiation processes. The case study in Section 6.9.3 will consider the operation of the Terminal Type option.

6.6 Simple Mail Transfer Protocol (SMTP)

The Simple Mail Transfer Protocol is based on a straightforward model of client/server computing. The model includes a sender and receiver, both of which have access to a file system for message storage. Some type of communication channel links sender and receiver, completing the model. SMTP is intended to be a dependable message delivery system, although it does not provide absolute end-to-end reliability. It is based upon TCP transport, however, which increases its effectiveness. The standard governing the SMTP system is specified in RFC 821 [6-16], while the message format is contained in "Standard for the Format of ARPA Internet Text Messages," RFC 822 [6-17]. Electronic mail is one of the most popular office automation functions today, and Reference [6-18] describes some of the many commercial gateways and packages that are available for electronic messaging on LANs.

6.6.1 Message Transfer

The transfer of an electronic message can be divided into several distinct stages, all supported by the SMTP model (see Figure 6-7). First, the user provides input to an interface system, known as the user agent, which facilitates the entry of the mail message. Then the message is sent to the Sender-SMTP, which assigns an arbitrary Port number to the process and establishes a TCP connection with Port number 25 on its peer (Receiver-SMTP). While establishing that connection, the receiver identifies itself to the sender. Next, the mail message is transferred, using the RFC 822 format (discussed in the following section). Finally, the sender signals its desire to terminate the connection, which is acknowledged by the receiver. After that acknowledgement, the TCP connection is closed.

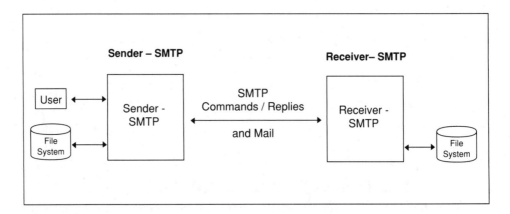

Figure 6-7. Simple Mail Transfer Protocol (SMTP) Model

6.6.2 Message Format

RFC 822 [6-17] defines the message format used with SMTP. The message consists of a header, which contains a number of fields and the message text. A blank line separates the header from the text. Many of the header fields are optional and depend on local implementation; however, some variation of the example below will be present in most systems. The following example of a mail format is taken from Appendix A of RFC 822 and is described as "about as complex as you're going to get."

```
Date        :  27 Aug 76 0932 PDT
From        :  Ken Davis <KDavis@This-Host.This-net>
Subject     :  Re: The Syntax in the RFC
Sender      :  KSecy@Other-Host
Reply-To :  Sam.Irving@Reg.Organization
To          :  George Jones <Group@Some-Reg.An-Org>,
               Al.Neuman@MAD.Publisher
cc          :  Important folk:
                  Tom Softwood <Balsa@Tree.Root>,
                  "Sam Irving"@Other-Host;,
               Standard Distribution:
                  /main/davis/people/standard@Other-Host,
                  "<Jones>standard.dist.3"@Tops-20-Host>;
Comment     :  Sam is away on business. He asked me to handle
               his mail for him.  He'll be able to provide  a
               more  accurate  explanation  when  he  returns
               next week.
In-Reply-To: <some.string@DBM.Group>, George's message
X-Special-action:  This is a sample of user-defined field-
               names.  There could also be a field-name
               "Special-action", but its name might later be
               preempted
Message-ID: <4231.629.XYzi-What@Other-Host>
```

Note that the header fields are separated from the field contents by a colon. This example shows 11 fields in use, which is certainly more than most host mail systems use.

6.6.3 SMTP Commands

SMTP commands are comprised of a command code and an argument. The command codes are four alphabetic characters in either upper or lower case. The command code is separated from the argument by one or more space characters. Reverse path and forward path arguments are case-sensitive since each host may have a particular convention for mail addresses. The character sequence carriage return-line feed (<CRLF>) ends the argument field. Optional arguments are enclosed within square brackets.

Command Code and Argument	Usage
HELO <SP> <domain> <CRLF>	Identifies Sender-SMTP to Receiver-SMTP
MAIL <SP> FROM:<reverse-path> <CRLF>	Deliver mail datato mailbox(es)
RCPT <SP> TO:<forward-path> <CRLF>	Identify mail data recipient
DATA <CRLF>	The mail data
RSET <CRLF>	Abort current mail transaction
SEND <SP> FROM:<reverse-path> <CRLF>	Deliver mail data to terminal(s)
SOML <SP> FROM:<reverse-path> <CRLF>	Send or Mail
SAML <SP> FROM:<reverse-path> <CRLF>	Send and Mail
VRFY <SP> <string> <CRLF>	Verify that the argument identifies a user
EXPN <SP> <string> <CRLF>	Verify that the argument identifies a mailing list
HELP [<SP> <string>] <CRLF>	Send information
NOOP <CRLF>	No operation
QUIT <CRLF>	Send OK reply, then close channel
TURN <CRLF>	Exchange Sender/Receiver roles

Note: <SP> represents a Space character
<CRLF> represents Carriage Return, Line Feed characters

6.6.4 SMTP Replies

The SMTP Reply messages are three digits long, and each digit has special significance. These replies are similar to the FTP codes in that the first digit is more general, whereas the third digit is more specific. The values for the first digit are:

    1yz ....Positive Preliminary reply
    2yz ....Positive Completion reply
    3yz ....Positive Intermediate reply
    4yz ....Transient Negative Completion reply
    5yz ....Permanent Negative Completion reply

The values for the second digit are:

    x0z ....Syntax
    x1z ....Information
    x2z ....Connections
    x3z ....Unspecified as yet
    x4z ....Unspecified as yet
    x5z ....Mail system

The third digit gives a finer definition for each of the function categories specified by the second digit. An example would be:

    500: Syntax error, command unrecognized
    501: Syntax error in parameters or arguments
    502: Command not implemented
    503: Bad sequence of commands
    504: Command parameter not implemented

If you require more information, turn to RFC 821 for specifics on command usage, state diagrams that detail the command implementation, and command/reply sequences. We will study an example of SMTP in Section 6.9.4.

6.7 NetBIOS

NetBIOS, the Network Basic Input Output System, was developed by IBM and Sytek, Inc. (now Hughes LAN Systems, Inc., Mountain View, CA) for use with the IBM PC Network program. Just as ROMBIOS enables a PC's operating system and application programs to access its local I/O devices, NetBIOS provides applications access to network devices. NetBIOS is considered an OSI Session Layer interface and has become a de facto standard. The expansion of LANs into internetworks and the popularity of TCP/IP as the primary internetworking protocol suite has created a need for the NetBIOS interface to operate over the Internet protocols. From an architectural perspective, combining NetBIOS support at the OSI Session Layer with the TCP or UDP protocols at the Transport Layer is a natural way to support the numerous existing LAN applications in a distributed internetwork environment.

Just as different vendors have written ROM BIOS routines specific to their PCs, LAN operating system vendors have also come up with their own implementations of NetBIOS. Haugdahl's *Inside NetBIOS* [6-19] describes some of these variants. RFC 1001 [6-20] and RFC 1002 [6-21] define a standard for NetBIOS support within the Internet community, and hopefully, the rigorous detail contained in these RFCs will eliminate the multiple-implementation (semi-proprietary) issue that has crept into LAN environments.

Before delving into the specifics of NetBIOS use within the context of the Internet protocols, you need some background in the operation of NetBIOS. NetBIOS provides four types of primitives: Name Service, Session Service, Datagram Service, and Miscellaneous functions. Application programs use these services to locate network resources, establish and terminate connections, and transfer data.

The Name Service permits you to refer to an application, representing a resource, by a name on the internetwork. The name consists of 16 alphanumeric characters, which may be either exclusive (unique to an application) or shared (used by a group). The application registers the name to ensure that no other applications raise any objections to its use. The Name Service primitives are Add Name, Add Group Name, and Delete Name.

The Session Service is used for the reliable exchange of data between two NetBIOS applications. Each data message may be from 0 to 131,071 octets in length. The Session Service primitives are somewhat analogous to the TCP primitives discussed in Chapter 5 and include: Call, Listen, Hang Up, Send, Receive, and Session Status.

The Datagram Service provides unreliable, non-sequenced, and connectionless data transfer. The data may be transferred in two ways. In one technique, the datagram sender registers a name under which the data will be sent and specifies the name to which it will be sent. The second technique broadcasts the datagram. The Datagram Service primitives are Send Datagram, Send Broadcast Datagram, Receive Datagram, and Receive Broadcast Datagram.

Miscellaneous Functions generally control the operation of the network interface and are implementation-dependent. These functions include Reset, Cancel, Adapter Status, Unlink, and Remote Program Load. IBM's token ring implementation added the Find Name primitive, which determines whether a particular name is registered on the network. (Four of the NetBIOS primitives listed above—Reset, Session Status, Unlink, and Remote Program Load—are considered local implementation issues that do not impact interoperability, and are therefore considered outside the scope of the Internet specification.)

RFC 1001 defines three types of NetBIOS end nodes and two NetBIOS support servers. The end nodes include the Broadcast (B), Point-to-Point (P), and Mixed Mode (M) types. Each of these types is specified by the operations it is allowed to perform. The NetBIOS support servers include the NetBIOS Name Server nodes (NBNS) and the NetBIOS Datagram Distribution nodes (NBDD). The NBNS manages and validates names used within the internetwork. NBNS formats the NetBIOS names to be valid Domain Name System (DNS) names and allows the NBNS to function in a fashion similar to the DNS Query service. The NBDD extends the NetBIOS datagram functions to the internet, which does not support multicast or broadcast transmissions. All of the nodes and servers are combined in various topologies of local and interconnected networks; RFC 1001 defines these details.

6.7.1 NetBIOS Name Service

NetBIOS's operation over UDP or TCP transport begins with the NetBIOS Name Service registering the name of the application to be used. The Name Query is the process by which the IP address associated with a NetBIOS name is discovered. Depending on the type of node in use (B, P, or M), the queries are either broadcast or directed to the NBNS. The exact procedures are described in RFC 1001.

NetBIOS Name Service messages use Port number 137 and are compatible with the DNS header format shown in Figure 6-8a. The structure includes a header followed by four entries — the Question section, Answer section, Authority section, and Additional Resource section. A typical Name Query message would include the NetBIOS name in the Question section, followed by a Response message that provides details about the name, including its IP address. When an IP address has been found for the target name, either the Session Service (using TCP) or the Datagram Service (using UDP) may be implemented.

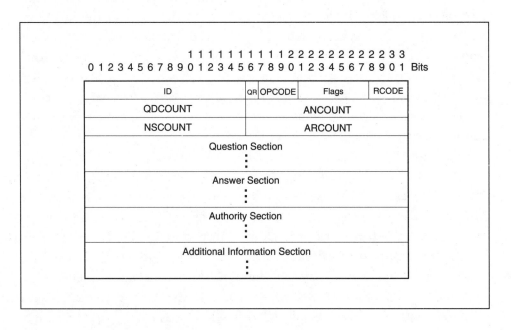

Figure 6-8a. NetBIOS Name Service Header

6.7.2 NetBIOS Session Service

The NetBIOS Session Service uses Port number 139 and is implemented in three phases: session establishment, steady state, and session close. Session establishment determines the IP address and the TCP port of the called name, and establishes a TCP connection with the remote device. Steady state provides data transfer and keep-alive functions. Session close terminates the session and triggers the close of the TCP session. Figure 6-9 illustrates these conditions; note the differences between the TCP and NetBIOS functions.

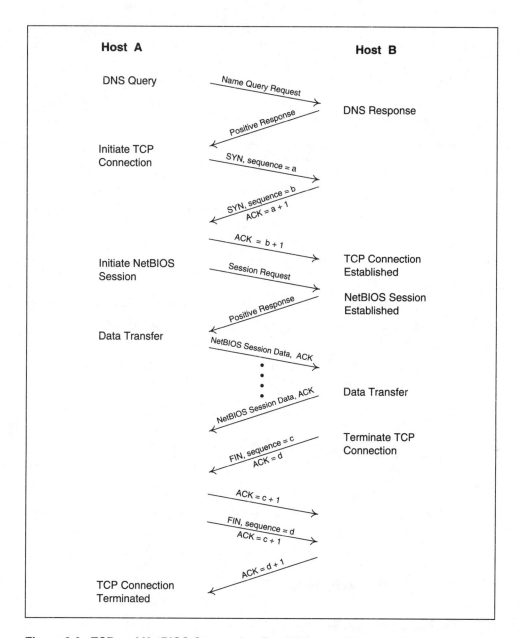

Figure 6-9. TCP and NetBIOS Connection Establishment/Disconnect Events

Figure 6-8b shows the format of the NetBIOS Session Service header. The Session Service header consists of a 4-octet header and a trailer that depends on the type of packet being transmitted. Three fields comprise the header: a Session Type field (1 octet), a Flags field (1 octet), and a Length field (2 octets). Values for the Session Type field are:

Value (hexadecimal)	Packet Type
00	Session message
81	Session request
82	Positive Session response
83	Negative Session response
84	Retarget Session response
85	Session Keep Alive

The Flags field (1 octet) uses only Bit 7, all others are set to ZERO. Bit 7 is used as an extension to the Length field (also 1 octet), which specifies the number of octets contained in the trailer (i.e., non-header) fields. When used in combination with the Flag Extension Bit, the cumulative length of the Trailer field(s) has a maximum value of 128K octets.

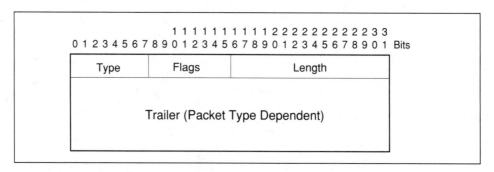

Figure 6-8b. NetBIOS Session Header

6.7.3 NetBIOS Datagram Service

NetBIOS datagrams utilize UDP transport with Port number 138. The complete Net-BIOS datagram includes the IP header (20 octets), UDP header (8 octets), the Net-BIOS datagram header (14 octets), and the NetBIOS data. The NetBIOS data consists of the Source and Destination NetBIOS names (255 octets each) and up to 512 octets of NetBIOS user data. The complete NetBIOS datagram can be up to 1,064 octets in length, but it may need fragmentation if the maximum IP datagram length is 576 octets.

NetBIOS datagrams require a Name Query operation to determine the IP address of the destination name. The NetBIOS datagram can then be transmitted within a UDP datagram or multiple UDP datagrams, as required. Three transmission modes are available: unicast, which transmits to a unique NetBIOS name; multicast, which transmits to a group NetBIOS name; and broadcast, which uses the Send Broadcast Datagram primitive.

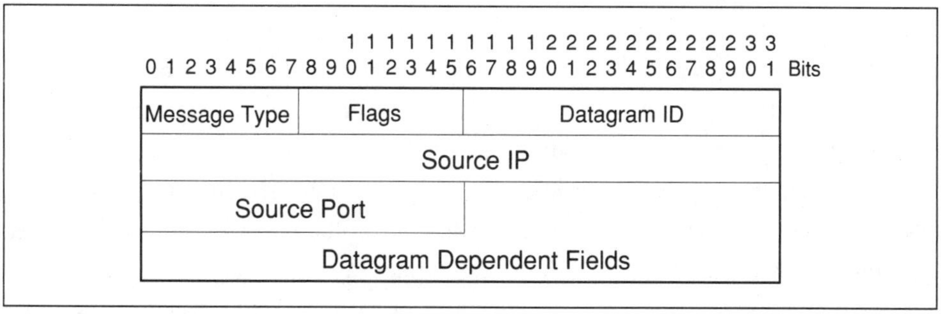

```
                    1 1 1 1 1 1 1 1 1 1 2 2 2 2 2 2 2 2 2 2 3 3
  0 1 2 3 4 5 6 7 8 9 0 1 2 3 4 5 6 7 8 9 0 1 2 3 4 5 6 7 8 9 0 1  Bits
 ┌─────────────┬───────────┬─────────────────────────────────────┐
 │Message Type │   Flags   │            Datagram ID              │
 ├─────────────┴───────────┴─────────────────────────────────────┤
 │                          Source IP                             │
 ├───────────────────────────────────┬────────────────────────────┤
 │            Source Port            │                            │
 ├───────────────────────────────────┴────────────────────────────┤
 │                   Datagram Dependent Fields                    │
 └────────────────────────────────────────────────────────────────┘
```

Figure 6-8c. NetBIOS Datagram Header

Figure 6-8c illustrates the NetBIOS Datagram header. The Msg Type field (1 octet) defines the datagram function:

Value (hexadecimal)	Msg_Type
10	Direct_Unique_Datagram
11	Direct_Group Datagram
12	Broadcast datagram
13	Datagram error
14	Datagram Query request
15	Datagram Positive Query response
16	Datagram Negative Query response

The flags (1 octet) define the first datagram fragment, whether more fragments will follow, and the type of source node (B, P, or M). The remaining fields support datagram service, with a Datagram ID (2 octets), the Source IP address (4 octets),

Source Port (2 octets), Datagram Length (2 octets), and a Packet Offset (2 octets). Datagram-specific user data fields complete each message. We'll see an example of NetBIOS packet operation in Section 6.9.5.

6.8 Troubleshooting the Process/Application Connection

Upper-layer protocol problems can be challenging to diagnose for several reasons. First, the Application/Process Layer interfaces with the end user. As we know, humans can cause well-ordered computer systems much consternation. Second, the Process/Application Layer must offer numerous options to meet the needs of its diverse clientele (humans). These options may use different file types (options for FTP) or data communication parameters (required to support a particular TELNET connection.)

To diagnose these problems, you should begin by determining whether the end-to-end connectivity functions are getting the data to the required destination. If they're not, use the techniques discussed in earlier chapters to determine where in the Network Interface, Internet, or Host-to-Host layers the problem resides, and troubleshoot the failure. If data is getting through, then an upper-layer problem may exist.

Keep in mind that just because data is being received doesn't mean that it is being interpreted properly—if my terminal is transmitting ASCII characters and your host is expecting EBCDIC, we'll exchange bits, but we won't communicate. A logical question to ask, then, is whether the application is being used properly. We've all experienced problems on our PCs that have turned out to be configuration errors. The Process/Application Layer applications are no exception. As long as there's a human element, the probability of error exists. Unfortunately, that probability is higher than any of us care to admit.

A second possibility is that the two application processes are unable to communicate with each other because of internal implementation differences. Even in this day of "open systems" (and the Internet protocols are about as open as you can get), interoperability difficulties should not be eliminated from consideration.

In addition to the protocol analyzer, a number of host-based utilities are available to monitor and diagnose Process/Application Layer problems. An excellent source of information on these utilities is RFC 1147, "FYI on a Network Management Tool Catalog: Tools for Monitoring and Debugging TCP/IP Internets and Interconnected Devices" [6-22]. Many of these tools are devised for UNIX platforms. Examples include:

- *etherfind*—a traffic monitor that runs under the Sun Operating System.
- *Internet Rover*—a network monitor for 4.x BSD UNIX systems that includes modules to test TELNET, FTP, and SMTP.
- *mconnect*—a utility available with 4.x BSD UNIX systems to test SMTP connections
- *netstat*—a utility available with 4.x BSD UNIX that will report routing table, TCP connections, and traffic statistics.
- *snmpwatch*—a network monitoring utility, compatible with a number of UNIX versions, that reports SNMP variables that have changed in value.

In summary, consult the management utilities included with your operating system and the tools listed in RFC 1147 for assistance with diagnosing upper-layer protocol problems.

6.9 Case Studies

Each of the case studies that follows illustrates the operation of a particular Process/Application Layer protocol. Admittedly, we could write volumes on each of the protocols that we've studied, but space does not permit full elaboration. Keep in mind, however, that the best references are the protocol-specific RFCs themselves, along with several supplements. These include RFC 1060, "Assigned Numbers," RFC 1122, "Requirements for Internet Hosts: Communication Layers" and RFC 1123, "Requirements for Internet Hosts-Application and Support," all of which provide details on specific parameters. Given these caveats, let's look at the operation of the upper-layer protocols.

6.9.1 Using TFTP

In our first case study, a Sun workstation (shown as Sun IPX in Trace 6.9.1a) and a PC running TCP/IP workstation software attempt to use TFTP to read and write small source files.

In Frame 1, the Sun IPX initiates a connection to Station XT with a Read Request (RRQ) for file "TFTP_test" in netascii mode. Details of that frame (Trace 6.9.1b) indicate that the Sun IPX has selected Source Transaction ID 1167 (Source port=1167) with Destination port=69, which is defined as the TFTP port. The connection is accepted in Frame 2. Station XT selects TID 1183 (Source port=1183) and returns the Sun IPX TID as the destination (Destination port=1167). The TFTP header indicates a DATA packet, Block number = 1, with 128 octets of data. Frame 3 acknowledges receipt of the data and terminates that connection.

Given that success, Sun IPX next attempts to write the same file, using the Write Request (WRQ) from TID=1167 in Frame 6. Station XT sends an ACK, selecting TID 1184 (Source port=1184) and designating Block number=0. The 128 octets of data is successfully written from Port 1167 (Sun IPX) to Port 1184 in Frame 8. An ACK from Station XT is sent in Frame 9, terminating the connection.

The next two operations are not so successful. In Frame 10, the Sun IPX sends an RRQ for file "\test" in netascii node. Unfortunately, this file does not exist on Station XT. An ERROR packet, indicating an access violation, is returned in frame 11. The Sun acknowledges its mistake and terminates the connection in Frame 12.

The Sun IPX makes one more attempt in Frame 16, this time a WRQ of the same file ("\test"), which still does not exist. The Sun IPX selects TID=1167 again, while Station XT assigns TID=1186 in Frame 17. Note that the ACK sent in response to the WRQ uses Block number=0 (Frame 17). The Sun IPX then attempts to write the file. But it is empty (nonexistent) and no data is transferred. Station XT acknowledges the previous frame and terminates the connection.

TFTP thus performs as advertised—it transfers files with simplicity. It cannot overcome the faulty memory of the user, however, who can't seem to remember which files do and do not exist!

Sniffer Network Analyzer data 10-Mar-92 at 13:08:44, TFTPTEST.TRC, Pg 1

SUMMARY	Delta T	Destination	Source	Summary
M 1		Station XT	Sun IPX	TFTP Read request
				File=TFTP_test
2	0.108	Sun IPX	Station XT	TFTP Data packet NS=1 (Last)
3	0.001	Station XT	Sun IPX	TFTP Ack NR=1
6	1.236	Station XT	Sun IPX	TFTP Write request
				File=TFTP_test
7	0.109	Sun IPX	Station XT	TFTP Ack NR=0
8	0.002	Station XT	Sun IPX	TFTP Data packet NS=1 (Last)
9	0.021	Sun IPX	Station XT	TFTP Ack NR=1
10	4.024	Station XT	Sun IPX	TFTP Read request File=\test
11	0.432	Sun IPX	Station XT	TFTP Error response
				(Access violation)

12	0.014	Station XT	Sun IPX	TFTP Ack NR=1
16	5.124	Station XT	Sun IPX	TFTP Write request File=\test
17	0.141	Sun IPX	Station XT	TFTP Ack NR=0
18	0.001	Station XT	Sun IPX	TFTP Data packet NS=1 (Last)
19	0.020	Sun IPX	Station XT	TFTP Ack NR=1

Trace 6.9.1a. TFTP Operation Summary

Sniffer Network Analyzer data 10-Mar-92 at 13:08:44, TFTPTEST.TRC, Pg 1

- - - - - - - - - - - - - - - - Frame 1 - - - - - - - - - - - - - - - - -
UDP: ——— UDP Header ———
UDP:
UDP: Source port = 1167 (TFTP)
UDP: Destination port = 69
UDP: Length = 29
UDP: No checksum
UDP:
TFTP: ——— Trivial file transfer ———
TFTP:
TFTP: Opcode = 1 (Read request)
TFTP: File name = "TFTP_test"
TFTP: Mode = "netascii"
TFTP:
TFTP: [Normal end of "Trivial file transfer".]
TFTP:

- - - - - - - - - - - - - - - Frame 2 - - - - - - - - - - - - - - - - -
UDP: ——— UDP Header ———
UDP:
UDP: Source port = 1183 (TFTP)
UDP: Destination port = 1167
UDP: Length = 140
UDP: Checksum = F0DC (correct)
UDP:
TFTP: ——— Trivial file transfer ———
TFTP:
TFTP: Opcode = 3 (Data packet)
TFTP: Block number = 1
TFTP: [128 bytes of data] (Last frame)
TFTP:
TFTP: [Normal end of "Trivial file transfer".]
TFTP:

```
- - - - - - - - - - - - - - - Frame 3 - - - - - - - - - - - - - - - - -
UDP: —— UDP Header ——
UDP:
UDP: Source port = 1167 (TFTP)
UDP: Destination port = 1183
UDP: Length = 12
UDP: No checksum
UDP:
TFTP: —— Trivial file transfer ——
TFTP:
TFTP: Opcode = 4 (Ack)
TFTP: Block number = 1
TFTP:
TFTP: [Normal end of "Trivial file transfer".]
TFTP:


- - - - - - - - - - - - - - - Frame 6 - - - - - - - - - - - - - - - - -
UDP: —— UDP Header ——
UDP:
UDP: Source port = 1167 (TFTP)
UDP: Destination port = 69
UDP: Length = 29
UDP: No checksum
UDP:
TFTP: —— Trivial file transfer ——
TFTP:
TFTP: Opcode = 2 (Write request)
TFTP: File name = "TFTP_test"
TFTP: Mode = "netascii"
TFTP:
TFTP: [Normal end of "Trivial file transfer".]
TFTP:


- - - - - - - - - - - - - - - Frame 7 - - - - - - - - - - - - - - - - -
UDP: —— UDP Header ——
UDP:
UDP: Source port = 1184 (TFTP)
UDP: Destination port = 1167
UDP: Length = 12
UDP: Checksum = B7CB (correct)
UDP:
TFTP: —— Trivial file transfer ——
TFTP:
```

TFTP: Opcode = 4 (Ack)
TFTP: Block number = 0
TFTP:
TFTP: [Normal end of "Trivial file transfer".]
TFTP:

- - - - - - - - - - - - - - - Frame 8 - - - - - - - - - - - - - - - - -
UDP: —— UDP Header ——-
UDP:
UDP: Source port = 1167 (TFTP)
UDP: Destination port = 1184
UDP: Length = 140
UDP: No checksum
UDP:
TFTP: —— Trivial file transfer ——-
TFTP:
TFTP: Opcode = 3 (Data packet)
TFTP: Block number = 1
TFTP: [128 bytes of data] (Last frame)
TFTP:
TFTP: [Normal end of "Trivial file transfer".]
TFTP:

- - - - - - - - - - - - - - Frame 9 - - - - - - - - - - - - - - - - -
UDP: —— UDP Header ——-
UDP:
UDP: Source port = 1184 (TFTP)
UDP: Destination port = 1167
UDP: Length = 12
UDP: Checksum = B7CA (correct)
UDP:
TFTP: —— Trivial file transfer ——-
TFTP:
TFTP: Opcode = 4 (Ack)
TFTP: Block number = 1
TFTP:
TFTP: [Normal end of "Trivial file transfer".]
TFTP:

- - - - - - - - - - - - - - Frame 10 - - - - - - - - - - - - - - -
UDP: —— UDP Header ——-
UDP:
UDP: Source port = 1167 (TFTP)

UDP: Destination port = 69
UDP: Length = 25
UDP: No checksum
UDP:
TFTP: ——— Trivial file transfer ———-
TFTP:
TFTP: Opcode = 1 (Read request)
TFTP: File name = "\test"
TFTP: Mode = "netascii"
TFTP:
TFTP: [Normal end of "Trivial file transfer".]
TFTP:

- - - - - - - - - - - - - - - Frame 11 - - - - - - - - - - - - - - - - -
UDP: ——— UDP Header ———
UDP:
UDP: Source port = 1185 (TFTP)
UDP: Destination port = 1167
UDP: Length = 41
UDP: Checksum = 7497 (correct)
UDP:
TFTP: ——— Trivial file transfer ———-
TFTP:
TFTP: Opcode = 5 (Error response)
TFTP: Error code = 2 (Access violation)
TFTP: Error message = "unable to open file for read"
TFTP:
TFTP: [Normal end of "Trivial file transfer".]
TFTP:

- - - - - - - - - - - - - - - Frame 12 - - - - - - - - - - - - - - - - -
UDP: ——— UDP Header ———
UDP:
UDP: Source port = 1167 (TFTP)
UDP: Destination port = 1185
UDP: Length = 12
UDP: No checksum
UDP:
TFTP: ——— Trivial file transfer ———-
TFTP:
TFTP: Opcode = 4 (Ack)
TFTP: Block number = 1
TFTP:

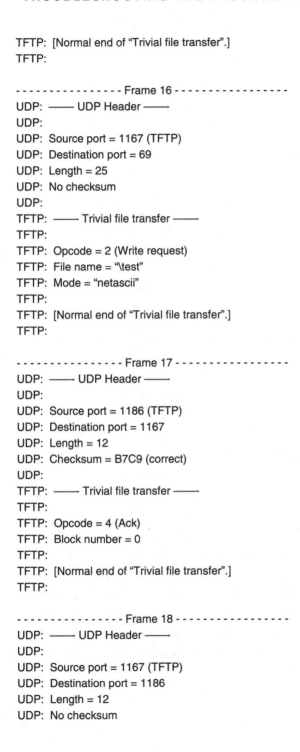

TFTP: [Normal end of "Trivial file transfer".]
TFTP:

- - - - - - - - - - - - - - - Frame 16 - - - - - - - - - - - - - - - -
UDP: —— UDP Header ——
UDP:
UDP: Source port = 1167 (TFTP)
UDP: Destination port = 69
UDP: Length = 25
UDP: No checksum
UDP:
TFTP: —— Trivial file transfer ——
TFTP:
TFTP: Opcode = 2 (Write request)
TFTP: File name = "\test"
TFTP: Mode = "netascii"
TFTP:
TFTP: [Normal end of "Trivial file transfer".]
TFTP:

- - - - - - - - - - - - - - - Frame 17 - - - - - - - - - - - - - - - -
UDP: —— UDP Header ——
UDP:
UDP: Source port = 1186 (TFTP)
UDP: Destination port = 1167
UDP: Length = 12
UDP: Checksum = B7C9 (correct)
UDP:
TFTP: —— Trivial file transfer ——
TFTP:
TFTP: Opcode = 4 (Ack)
TFTP: Block number = 0
TFTP:
TFTP: [Normal end of "Trivial file transfer".]
TFTP:

- - - - - - - - - - - - - - - Frame 18 - - - - - - - - - - - - - - - -
UDP: —— UDP Header ——
UDP:
UDP: Source port = 1167 (TFTP)
UDP: Destination port = 1186
UDP: Length = 12
UDP: No checksum

UDP:
TFTP: ─── Trivial file transfer ───
TFTP:
TFTP: Opcode = 3 (Data packet)
TFTP: Block number = 1
TFTP: [0 bytes of data] (Last frame)
TFTP:
TFTP: [Normal end of "Trivial file transfer".]
TFTP:

- - - - - - - - - - - - - - - Frame 19 - - - - - - - - - - - - - - - -
UDP: ─── UDP Header ───
UDP:
UDP: Source port = 1186 (TFTP)
UDP: Destination port = 1167
UDP: Length = 12
UDP: Checksum = B7C8 (correct)
UDP:
TFTP: ─── Trivial file transfer ───
TFTP:
TFTP: Opcode = 4 (Ack)
TFTP: Block number = 1
TFTP:
TFTP: [Normal end of "Trivial file transfer".]
TFTP:

Trace 6.9.1b. TFTP Operation Details

6.9.2 Collaborative Efforts of FTP, ARP, and TFTP

In the case study in Section 5.7.1, we examined the process by which a device can obtain its boot and configuration files (known as load and parameter images) from the internetwork. The following case study shows a similar process, using the ARP and TFTP protocols. ARP determines the device's (in this case, a bridge) Internet (IP) address, and TFTP transfers the load and parameter files to the bridge. We'll also use FTP to transfer a new version of the bridge's load image to the TFTP server prior to the start of the ARP/TFTP sequence. Let's see what happens when these three processes must interact.

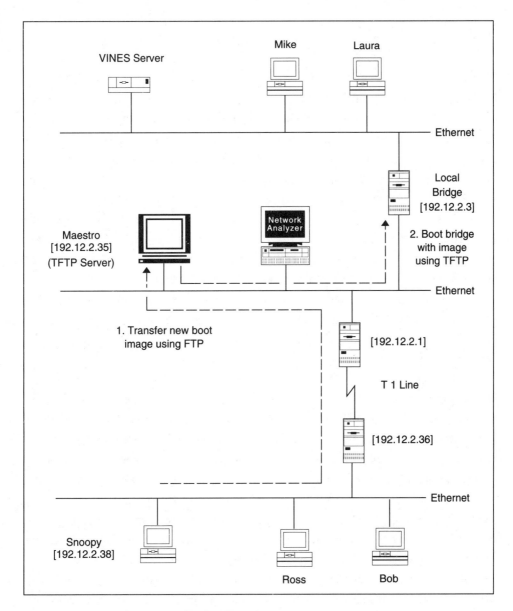

Figure 6-10. File Transfer of Bridge Boot Image

The topology of this internetwork consists of local and remote Ethernet segments connected via bridges (see Figure 6-10). The network manager, Ross, has received a new version of the bridge software from the manufacturer on an MS-DOS formatted floppy. Ross uses FTP Software's PC/TCP to transfer the new bridge software from a PC (known as Snoopy) to the TFTP Server, which is a Sun SPARCStation (known as Maestro). Ross establishes a TCP control connection to Port number 21 on Maestro (Frames 2 through 4 of Trace 6.9.2a) and logs in (Frames 5 through 12). Next, Ross stores the new bridge boot image (filename rb1w1.sys) on Maestro in subdirectory /home/tftpboot (Frame 13). Maestro initiates an FTP data connection to Snoopy's Port number 20 in Frames 15 through 17, and the ASCII file transfer begins in Frame 19. Since the file is rather large, it does not complete until Frame 305, at which time both the FTP and TCP connections are terminated (Frames 306 through 314 of Trace 6.9.2b).

Next, Ross resets the local bridge (known as MX-3510) so that it can obtain and boot from the new load image. The bridges Ross uses are designed to get their boot and configuration files from a number of different servers that might exist on a network. In Frame 315, the bridge broadcasts for a proprietary boot server; in Frame 316, the bridge broadcasts for a BOOTP server; in Frame 317, the bridge broadcasts for a DEC file server using DEC's Maintenance Operations Protocol (MOP); finally, in Frame 318, the bridge broadcasts an ARP message looking for its Internet address. This operation is successful and the bridge uses its IP address to broadcast a TFTP Read request (Frame 320). The SPARCstation (Maestro) responds, triggering the bridge to request a file transfer of the boot image using TFTP (Frame 327). Unfortunately, the file transfer is not successful (see Frame 1393). Details of the error response (Trace 6.9.2c) indicate a Transfer Size Error, with "22 bytes of additional data present." This error message prompts Ross to speculate that the boot image file should have been transferred in FTP Binary mode instead of ASCII mode.

Ross begins again, this time setting the FTP transfer mode to Binary when he loads the file from Snoopy to Maestro. A TCP connection between Snoopy and Maestro is established (Frames 1408 through 1410 of Trace 6.9.2d), and the FTP file transfer begins. But this time the File Type is set for Image (Type I in Frame 1417). The Binary (or Image) data connection is opened in Frame 1426 and completes in Frame 1692 (Trace 6.9.2e). The local bridge is again reset and its boot sequence started (Frames 1696 through 1707). The boot image (filename x004db3.img) is transferred from Maestro to the local bridge, using TFTP in Frames 1708 through 2774. A second file (x004db3.prm) is transferred in Frames 2787 through 2819. The bridge boot sequence is now complete. The lesson learned: check the data representation parameter, or file type, to avoid corrupting the transferred file.

Sniffer Network Analyzer data 30-Aug-89 at 14:07:42, BINARY.ENC, Pg 1

SUMMARY	Delta T	Destination	Source	Summary
M 1		AB0000020000	Local Bridge	MOP RC System ID Receipt=0
2	1.2376	Maestro	Snoopy	TCP D=21 S=20294 SYN SEQ=19468734 LEN=0 WIN=2048
3	0.0009	Snoopy	Maestro	TCP D=20294 S=21 SYN ACK=19468735 SEQ=716544001 LEN=0 WIN=4096
4	0.0016	Maestro	Snoopy	TCP D=21 S=20294 ACK=716544002 WIN=2048
5	0.1115	Snoopy	Maestro	FTP R PORT=20294 220 maestro FTP server (SunOS 4.1) ready.<0D><0A>
6	0.0374	Maestro	Snoopy	FTP C PORT=20294 USER root<0D><0A>
7	0.0073	Snoopy	Maestro	FTP R PORT=20294 331 Password required for root.<0D><0A>
8	0.0255	Maestro	Snoopy	FTP C PORT=20294 PASS bugoff<0D><0A>
9	0.0479	Snoopy	Maestro	FTP R PORT=20294 230 User root logged in.<0D><0A>
10	0.1621	Maestro	Snoopy	TCP D=21 S=20294 ACK=716544104 WIN=1946
11	21.4760	Maestro	Snoopy	FTP C PORT=20294 PORT 192,12,2, 38,79,71<0D><0A>
12	0.0127	Snoopy	Maestro	FTP R PORT=20294 200 PORT command successful <0D><0A>
13	0.0105	Maestro	Snoopy	FTP C PORT=20294 STOR /home/tftpboot /rb1w1.sys_v2.0<0D><0A>
14	0.0169	Snoopy	Maestro	TCP D=20294 S=21 ACK=19468819 WIN=4096
15	0.0601	Snoopy	Maestro	TCP D=20295 S=20 SYN SEQ=719936001 LEN=0 WIN=24576
16	0.0020	Maestro	Snoopy	TCP D=20 S=20295 SYN ACK=719936002 SEQ=19468825 LEN=0 WIN=2048

17	0.0006	Snoopy	Maestro	TCP	D=20295 S=20
					ACK=19468826 WIN=24576
18	0.0018	Snoopy	Maestro	FTP	R PORT=20294 150
					ASCII data connection for
					/home/tftpboot/rb1w1...
19	0.1108	Maestro	Snoopy	TCP	D=20 S=20295
					ACK=719936002 SEQ=19468826
					LEN=1189 WIN=2048
20	0.0065	Maestro	Snoopy	TCP	D=20 S=20295
					ACK=719936002 SEQ=19470015
					LEN=1460 WIN=2048
21	0.0058	Maestro	Snoopy	TCP	D=20 S=20295
					ACK=719936002 SEQ=19471475
					LEN=1460 WIN=2048
22	0.0024	Snoopy	Maestro	TCP	D=20295 S=20
.					ACK=19472935 WIN=24576
.					
.					

Trace 6.9.2a. Boot Image Transfer Using FTP ASCII Connection

Sniffer Network Analyzer data 30-Aug-89 at 14:07:42, BINARY.ENC, Pg 1

SUMMARY	Delta T	Destination	Source	Summary	
.					
.					
.					
301	0.0059	Maestro	Snoopy	TCP	D=20 S=20295
					ACK=719936002 SEQ=19739400
					LEN=1123 WIN=2048
302	0.0053	Maestro	Snoopy	TCP	D=20 S=20295
					ACK=719936002 SEQ=19740523
					LEN=1460 WIN=2048
303	0.0039	Maestro	Snoopy	TCP	D=20 S=20295 FIN
					ACK=719936002 SEQ=19741983
					LEN=627 WIN=2048
304	0.0007	Snoopy	Maestro	TCP	D=20295 S=20
					ACK=19742611 WIN=23949
305	0.0098	Snoopy	Maestro	FTP	R PORT=20294
					226 ASCII Transfer
					complete.<0D><0A>
306	0.0003	Snoopy	Maestro	TCP	D=20295 S=20 FIN

				ACK=19742611 SEQ=719936002
				LEN=0 WIN=24576
307	0.0020	Maestro	Snoopy	TCP D=21 S=20294
				ACK=716544246 WIN=1804
308	0.0015	Maestro	Snoopy	TCP D=20 S=20295
				ACK=719936003 WIN=2048
309	45.9027	Maestro	Snoopy	FTP C PORT=20294 QUIT<0D><0A>
310	0.0091	Snoopy	Maestro	FTP R PORT=20294
				221 Goodbye.<0D><0A>
311	0.0060	Maestro	Snoopy	TCP D=21 S=20294 FIN
				ACK=716544260 SEQ=19468825
				LEN=0 WIN=1790
312	0.0006	Snoopy	Maestro	TCP D=20294 S=21
				ACK=19468826 WIN=4096
313	0.0009	Snoopy	Maestro	TCP D=20294 S=21 FIN
				ACK=19468826 SEQ=716544260
				LEN=0 WIN=4096
314	0.0020	Maestro	Snoopy	TCP D=21 S=20294
				ACK=716544261 WIN=1790
315	9.3205	09008780FFFF	Local Bridge	Ethertype=0889 (Unknown)
316	4.0209	Broadcast	Local Bridge	BOOTP Request
317	4.0194	AB0000010000	Local Bridge	MOP DL Request Program
				Device Type=UNA
				Program Type=System
318	8.0203	Broadcast	Local Bridge	ARP C HA=080087004DB3 PRO=IP
319	3.0660	Local Bridge	Maestro	ARP R PA=[192.12.2.3]
				HA=080087004DB3 PRO=IP
320	0.9553	Broadcast	Local Bridge	TFTP Read request
				File=x004db3.img
321	0.0168	Local Bridge	Maestro	UDP D=2001 S=1416 LEN=524
322	0.0037	Maestro	Local Bridge	UDP D=1416 S=2001 LEN=70
323	3.9820	Broadcast	Local Bridge	ARP C PA=[192.12.2.35] PRO=IP
324	0.0004	Local Bridge	Maestro	ARP R PA=[192.12.2.35]
				HA=080020103553 PRO=IP
325	7.9964	Maestro	Local Bridge	ARP C PA=[192.12.2.35] PRO=IP
326	0.0004	Local Bridge	Maestro	ARP R PA=[192.12.2.35]
				HA=080020103553 PRO=IP
327	0.0010	Maestro	Local Bridge	TFTP Read request
				File=x004db3.img
328	0.0167	Local Bridge	Maestro	TFTP Data packet NS=1
329	0.1344	Maestro	Local Bridge	TFTP Ack NR=1
330	0.0015	Local Bridge	Maestro	TFTP Data packet NS=2
331	0.0021	Maestro	Local Bridge	TFTP Ack NR=2

.
.
.

1390	0.0013	Local Bridge	Maestro	TFTP Data packet NS=532
1391	0.0022	Maestro	Local Bridge	TFTP Ack NR=532
1392	0.0012	Local Bridge	Maestro	TFTP Data packet NS=533
1393	0.0012	Maestro	Local Bridge	TFTP Error response (Not defined)
1394	0.0018	Maestro	Local Bridge	TFTP Write request File=loaderr.dmp
1395	3.0193	Local Bridge	Maestro	TFTP Error response (File not found)
1396	0.0047	Broadcast	Local Bridge	TFTP Read request File=type57.img
1397	3.0045	Local Bridge	Maestro	UDP D=2002 S=1421 LEN=27
1398	0.9889	09008780FFFF	Local Bridge	Ethertype=0889 (Unknown)

Trace 6.9.2b. ASCII File Transfer Completion and Unsuccessful Bridge Boot

Sniffer Network Analyzer data 30-Aug-89 at 14:07:42, BINARY.ENC, Pg 1

```
- - - - - - - - - - - - - - - - Frame 1393 - - - - - - - - - - - - - - -
DLC: —— DLC Header ——
DLC:
DLC: Frame 1393 arrived at 14:09:49.7524; frame size is 88 (0058 hex) bytes.
DLC: Destination = Station Sun   103553, Maestro
DLC: Source     = Station Xyplex004DB3, Local Bridge
DLC: Ethertype  = 0800 (IP)
DLC:
IP:  —— IP Header ——
IP:
IP:  Version = 4, header length = 20 bytes
IP:  Type of service = 00
IP:        000. .... = routine
IP:        ...0 .... = normal delay
IP:        .... 0... = normal throughput
IP:        .... .0.. = normal reliability
IP:  Total length = 74 bytes
IP:  Identification = 539
IP:  Flags = 0X
IP:  .0.. .... = may fragment
IP:  ..0. .... = last fragment
```

IP: Fragment offset = 0 bytes
IP: Time to live = 100 seconds/hops
IP: Protocol = 17 (UDP)
IP: Header checksum = D049 (correct)
IP: Source address = [192.12.2.3]
IP: Destination address = [192.12.2.35]
IP: No options
IP:
UDP: —— UDP Header ——
UDP:
UDP: Source port = 2003 (TFTP)
UDP: Destination port = 1417
UDP: Length = 54
UDP: No checksum
UDP:
TFTP: —— Trivial file transfer ——
TFTP:
TFTP: Opcode = 5 (Error response)
TFTP: Error code = 0 (Not defined)
TFTP: Error message = "Transfer size error"
TFTP:
TFTP: *** 22 byte(s) of additional data present ***
TFTP:
TFTP: [Abnormal end of "Trivial file transfer".]
TFTP:

Trace 6.9.2c. TFTP Error Response Details

Sniffer Network Analyzer data 30-Aug-89 at 14:07:42, BINARY.ENC, Pg 1

SUMMARY	Delta T	Destination	Source	Summary
.				
.				
.				
1399	4.0200	Broadcast	Local Bridge	BOOTP Request
1400	4.0185	AB0000010000	Local Bridge	MOP DL Request Program
				Device Type=UNA
				Program Type=System
1401	8.0202	Broadcast	Local Bridge	ARP C HA=080087004DB3 PRO=IP
1402	3.0631	Local Bridge	Maestro	ARP R PA=[192.12.2.3]
				HA=080087004DB3 PRO=IP

1403	0.9579	Broadcast	Local Bridge	TFTP	Read request File=x004db3.img
1404	0.0180	Local Bridge	Maestro	UDP	D=2001 S=1423 LEN=524
1405	0.0037	Maestro	Local Bridge	UDP	D=1423 S=2001 LEN=70
1406	3.9809	Broadcast	Local Bridge	ARP	C PA=[192.12.2.35] PRO=IP
1407	0.0004	Local Bridge	Maestro	ARP	R PA=[192.12.2.35] HA=080020103553 PRO=IP
1408	25.2853	Maestro	Snoopy	TCP	D=21 S=20296 SYN SEQ=19468830 LEN=0 WIN=2048
1409	0.0010	Snoopy	Maestro	TCP	D=20296 S=21 SYN ACK=19468831 SEQ=739648001 LEN=0 WIN=4096
1410	0.0016	Maestro	Snoopy	TCP	D=21 S=20296 ACK=739648002 WIN=2048
1411	0.1149	Snoopy	Maestro	FTP	R PORT=20296 220 maestro FTP server (SunOS 4.1) ready.<0D><0A>
1412	0.0377	Maestro	Snoopy	FTP	C PORT=20296 USER root<0D><0A>
1413	0.0075	Snoopy	Maestro	FTP	R PORT=20296 331 Password required for root.<0D><0A>
1414	0.0249	Maestro	Snoopy	FTP	C PORT=20296 PASS bugoff<0D><0A>
1415	0.0480	Snoopy	Maestro	FTP	R PORT=20296 230 User root logged in.<0D><0A>
1416	0.1375	Maestro	Snoopy	TCP	D=21 S=20296 ACK=739648104 WIN=1946
1417	6.2568	Maestro	Snoopy	FTP	C PORT=20296 TYPE I<0D><0A>
1418	0.0015	Snoopy	Maestro	FTP	R PORT=20296 200 Type set to I.<0D><0A>
1419	0.1605	Maestro	Snoopy	TCP	D=21 S=20296 ACK=739648124 WIN=1926
1420	23.3762	Maestro	Snoopy	FTP	C PORT=20296 PORT 192,12,2,38, 79,73<0D><0A>
1421	0.0126	Snoopy	Maestro	FTP	R PORT=20296 200 PORT command successful <0D><0A>
1422	0.0118	Maestro	Snoopy	FTP	C PORT=20296 STOR /home/tftpboot

					/rb1w1.sys_v2.0<0D><0A>
1423	0.0919	Snoopy	Maestro	TCP	D=20297 S=20 SYN
					SEQ=744128001
					LEN=0 WIN=24576
1424	0.0015	Maestro	Snoopy	TCP	D=20 S=20297 SYN
					ACK=744128002 SEQ=19468841
					LEN=0 WIN=2048
1425	0.0006	Snoopy	Maestro	TCP	D=20297 S=20
					ACK=19468842 WIN=24576
1426	0.0018	Snoopy	Maestro	FTP	R PORT=20296
					150 Binary data connection
					for /home/tftpboot/rb1w...
1427	0.1065	Maestro	Snoopy	TCP	D=20 S=20297
					ACK=744128002 SEQ=19468842
					LEN=1460 WIN=2048
1428	0.0031	Maestro	Snoopy	TCP	D=20 S=20297
					ACK=744128002 SEQ=19470302
					LEN=1460 WIN=2048
1429	0.0013	Snoopy	Maestro	TCP	D=20297 S=20
					ACK=19471762 WIN=24576

.
.
.

Trace 6.9.2d. Boot Image Transfer Using FTP Binary Connection

Sniffer Network Analyzer data 30-Aug-89 at 14:07:42, BINARY.ENC, Pg 1

SUMMARY	Delta T	Destination	Source	Summary	
.					
.					
.					
1687	0.0087	Maestro	Snoopy	TCP	D=20 S=20297
					ACK=744128002 SEQ=19738450
					LEN=1460 WIN=2048
1688	0.0031	Maestro	Snoopy	TCP	D=20 S=20297
					ACK=744128002 SEQ=19739910
					LEN=1460 WIN=2048
1689	0.0002	Snoopy	Maestro	TCP	D=20297 S=20
					ACK=19739910 WIN=24576
1690	0.0026	Maestro	Snoopy	TCP	D=20 S=20297 FIN
					ACK=744128002 SEQ=19741370

				LEN=240 WIN=2048
1691	0.0005	Snoopy	Maestro	TCP D=20297 S=20
				ACK=19741611 WIN=22876
1692	0.0092	Snoopy	Maestro	FTP R PORT=20296
				226 Binary Transfer
				complete.<0D><0A>
1693	0.0003	Snoopy	Maestro	TCP D=20297 S=20 FIN
				ACK=19741611 SEQ=744128002
				LEN=0 WIN=24576
1694	0.0020	Maestro	Snoopy	TCP D=21 S=20296
				ACK=739648268 WIN=1782
1695	0.0008	Maestro	Snoopy	TCP D=20 S=20297
				ACK=744128003 WIN=2048
1696	31.6613	09008780FFFF	Local Bridge	Ethertype=0889 (Unknown)
1697	4.0209	Broadcast	Local Bridge	BOOTP Request
1698	4.0194	AB0000010000	Local Bridge	MOP DL Request Program
				Device Type=UNA
				Program Type=System
1699	8.0204	Broadcast	Local Bridge	ARP C HA=080087004DB3 PRO=IP
1700	3.0628	Local Bridge	Maestro	ARP R PA=[192.12.2.3]
				HA=080087004DB3 PRO=IP
1701	0.9584	Broadcast	Local Bridge	TFTP Read request
				File=x004db3.img
1702	0.0168	Local Bridge	Maestro	UDP D=2001 S=1426 LEN=524
1703	0.0037	Maestro	Local Bridge	UDP D=1426 S=2001 LEN=70
1704	3.9820	Broadcast	Local Bridge	ARP C PA=[192.12.2.35] PRO=IP
1705	0.0004	Local Bridge	Maestro	ARP R PA=[192.12.2.35]
				HA=080020103553 PRO=IP
1706	7.9964	Maestro	Local Bridge	ARP C PA=[192.12.2.35] PRO=IP
1707	0.0004	Local Bridge	Maestro	ARP R PA=[192.12.2.35]
				HA=080020103553 PRO=IP
1708	0.0010	Maestro	Local Bridge	TFTP Read request
				File=x004db3.img
1709	0.0168	Local Bridge	Maestro	TFTP Data packet NS=1
1710	0.1344	Maestro	Local Bridge	TFTP Ack NR=1
1711	0.0015	Local Bridge	Maestro	TFTP Data packet NS=2
1712	0.0021	Maestro	Local Bridge	TFTP Ack NR=2
.				
.				
.				
2771	0.0012	Local Bridge	Maestro	TFTP Data packet NS=532
2772	0.0022	Maestro	Local Bridge	TFTP Ack NR=532
2773	0.0011	Local Bridge	Maestro	TFTP Data packet NS=533 (Last)

2774	0.0019	Maestro	Local Bridge	TFTP Ack NR=533
2775	11.3936	09008780FFFF	Local Bridge	Ethertype=0889 (Unknown)
2776	4.0129	Broadcast	Local Bridge	BOOTP Request
2777	4.0195	AB0000010000	Local Bridge	MOP DL Request Program
				Device Type=UNA
				Program Type=System
2778	8.0205	Broadcast	Local Bridge	ARP C HA=080087004DB3 PRO=IP
2779	3.0610	Local Bridge	Maestro	ARP R PA=[192.12.2.3]
				HA=080087004DB3 PRO=IP
2780	0.9599	Broadcast	Local Bridge	TFTP Read request
				File=x004db3.prm
2781	0.0159	Local Bridge	Maestro	UDP D=2001 S=1440 LEN=524
2782	0.0016	Maestro	Local Bridge	UDP D=1440 S=2001 LEN=70
2783	3.9846	Broadcast	Local Bridge	ARP C PA=[192.12.2.35] PRO=IP
2784	0.0004	Local Bridge	Maestro	ARP R PA=[192.12.2.35]
				HA=080020103553 PRO=IP
2785	7.9971	Maestro	Local Bridge	ARP C PA=[192.12.2.35] PRO=IP
2786	0.0004	Local Bridge	Maestro	ARP R PA=[192.12.2.35]
				HA=080020103553 PRO=IP
2787	0.0010	Maestro	Local Bridge	TFTP Read request
				File=x004db3.prm
2788	0.0163	Local Bridge	Maestro	TFTP Data packet NS=1
2789	0.0147	Maestro	Local Bridge	TFTP Ack NR=1
2790	0.0015	Local Bridge	Maestro	TFTP Data packet NS=2
2791	0.0021	Maestro	Local Bridge	TFTP Ack NR=2
.				
.				
.				
2814	0.0012	Local Bridge	Maestro	TFTP Data packet NS=14
2815	0.0021	Maestro	Local Bridge	TFTP Ack NR=14
2816	0.0013	Local Bridge	Maestro	TFTP Data packet NS=15
2817	0.0022	Maestro	Local Bridge	TFTP Ack NR=15
2818	0.0012	Local Bridge	Maestro	TFTP Data packet NS=16 (Last)
2819	0.0021	Maestro	Local Bridge	TFTP Ack NR=16

Trace 6.9.2e. Binary File Transfer Completion and Successful Bridge Boot

6.9.3 Selecting the Proper Terminal Option for TELNET

In Section 6.5 we studied TELNET and discussed a number of options for converting the local terminal/host format into the Network Virtual Terminal format. These options are a common source of TELNET incompatibilities.

In this example, users attached to an Ethernet have two options for communicating with an SNA host (see Figure 6-11). The first option is to use DEC VT-100 terminals through a terminal server connected to the Ethernet. The second option is to use FTP Software Inc.'s popular package PC/TCP on a workstation to connect directly to the Ethernet. The users discover, however, that the terminal server option does not work while the PC/TCP option does. Let's explore why.

The first attempt to access the SNA host is via the terminal server, shown in Trace 6.9.3a. The terminal session begins with a TCP connection in Frames 32 through 34 and continues with the TELNET option negotiations. These include the Terminal Type (Frames 36 through 41), End of Record (Frames 42 through 44), Binary Transmission (Frames 45 through 47) and so on. Data transfer from the SNA host begins in Frame 53, but has little success. The terminal server is allowing a rather small window size, ranging from 0 to 256 octets. In Frame 112, the terminal server resets the TCP connection, terminating communication. At this point, the user sees the terminal server prompt on his VT-100 terminal and realizes that the host connection has failed.

To test the process, the network administrator, James, goes to a workstation that has the PC/TCP software package and attempts the same session with the SNA host (see Trace 6.9.3b). Frames 94 through 96 show the TCP connection being established, followed by the same TELNET option negotiation sequence. A significant difference is the window size that the Workstation allows (1707-2048 octets) and the orderly termination of the TCP connection in Frames 256 through 259. This time, James is able to log into the host, conduct his business, and properly terminate the connection. Since this session is successful but the one via the Terminal Server was not, James decides to check the options negotiated in each case.

Returning to Trace 6.9.3a, the only option open for negotiation is the Terminal Type, beginning in Frame 39, which we know from the Interpret as Command (IAC) Subnegotiation (SB). Trace 6.9.3c shows the details of that negotiation. The SNA host sends FF FA 18 H, meaning "Interpret as Command, Subnegotiation of option 18H (Terminal Type)." The terminal server responds in Frame 41 with FF FA 18...H, indicating that its terminal type is an IBM-3278-2 (shown in the ASCII decode of Frame 41).

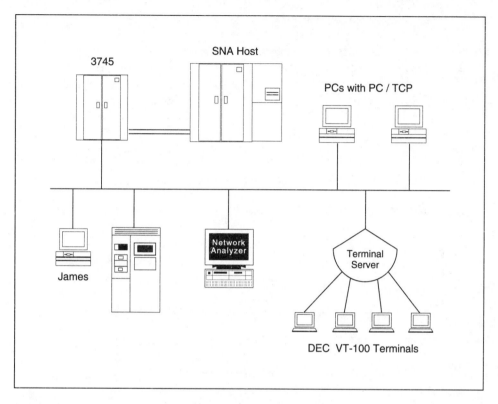

Figure 6-11. TELNET access to IBM using TN3270

James performs a similar analysis of the trace derived from the workstation's successful connection to the host. Reviewing Trace 6.9.3b, the terminal type negotiation is requested in Frame 97 and occurs in Frames 99 and 100. In Frame 99 of Trace 6.9.3d, the SNA host indicates the negotiation of the terminal type (FF FA 18H), but this time the response is different. The workstation responds with IBM-3278-2-E instead of the IBM-3278-2, which the Terminal Server sent. This difference suggests to James that the terminal server was not supporting the Extended (E) Attribute set, causing the connection to fail. A check of the defined TELNET terminal types in RFC 1060 and RFC 1091 [6-22] confirms that the two were indeed different. The workstation software supported the IBM-3278-2-E type, allowing the host connection to succeed. The Terminal Server did not provide support, so that connection failed. What appeared to be a small problem inhibited communication. Readers needing additional details on TN3270 should consult reference [6-24].

Sniffer Network Analyzer data 22-Nov-91 at 15:04:36, JK1.ENC, Pg 1

SUMMARY	Delta T	Destination	Source	Summary
32	38.6694	SNA Host	Term Server	TCP D=23 S=5029 SYN SEQ=159638 LEN=0 WIN=256
33	0.0016	Term Server	SNA Host	TCP D=5029 S=23 SYN ACK=159639 SEQ=849951745 LEN=0 WIN=4096
34	0.0021	SNA Host	Term Server	TCP D=23 S=5029 ACK=849951746 WIN=256
35	0.0020	SNA Host	Term Server	Telnet C PORT=5029 IAC Do Echo
36	0.0273	Term Server	SNA Host	Telnet R PORT=5029 IAC Do Terminal type
37	0.0032	SNA Host	Term Server	TCP D=23 S=5029 ACK=849951749 WIN=253
38	0.0022	SNA Host	Term Server	Telnet C PORT=5029 IAC Will Terminal type
39	0.0033	Term Server	SNA Host	Telnet R PORT=5029 IAC SB ...
40	0.0023	SNA Host	Term Server	TCP D=23 S=5029 ACK=849951755 WIN=250
41	0.0027	SNA Host	Term Server	Telnet C PORT=5029 IAC SB ...
42	0.0258	Term Server	SNA Host	Telnet R PORT=5029 IAC Do End of record
43	0.0023	SNA Host	Term Server	TCP D=23 S=5029 ACK=849951761 WIN=250
44	0.0033	SNA Host	Term Server	Telnet C PORT=5029 IAC Will End of record
45	0.0034	Term Server	SNA Host	Telnet R PORT=5029 IAC Do Binary transmission
46	0.0022	SNA Host	Term Server	TCP D=23 S=5029 ACK=849951767 WIN=250
47	0.0499	SNA Host	Term Server	Telnet C PORT=5029 IAC Will Binary transmission
48	0.0041	Term Server	SNA Host	Telnet R PORT=5029 IAC Do Echo
49	0.0027	SNA Host	Term Server	TCP D=23 S=5029 ACK=849951770 WIN=253
50	0.0014	Term Server	SNA Host	Telnet R PORT=5029 IAC Won't Echo

51	0.0017	SNA Host	Term Server	Telnet C PORT=5029
				IAC Won't Echo
52	0.0024	SNA Host	Term Server	TCP D=23 S=5029
				ACK=849951773 WIN=256
53	0.0029	Term Server	SNA Host	Telnet R PORT=5029 <05>...
54	0.0022	SNA Host	Term Server	TCP D=23 S=5029
				ACK=849951783 WIN=246
55	0.0602	Term Server	SNA Host	Telnet R PORT=5029 <05>...
56	0.0031	SNA Host	Term Server	TCP D=23 S=5029
				ACK=849952029 WIN=10
57	0.0018	Term Server	SNA Host	Telnet R PORT=5029 <11>...
58	0.0482	SNA Host	Term Server	TCP D=23 S=5029
				ACK=849952029 WIN=256
59	0.0146	SNA Host	Term Server	TCP D=23 S=5029
				ACK=849952037 WIN=256
60	3.5586	SNA Host	Term Server	Telnet C PORT=5029 }...
61	0.0662	Term Server	SNA Host	Telnet R PORT=5029 <05>...
62	0.0024	SNA Host	Term Server	TCP D=23 S=5029
				ACK=849952083 WIN=210
63	0.0348	SNA Host	Term Server	TCP D=23 S=5029
				ACK=849952083 WIN=256
64	0.0482	Term Server	SNA Host	Telnet R PORT=5029 <05>...
65	0.0025	SNA Host	Term Server	TCP D=23 S=5029
				ACK=849952093 WIN=246
66	0.0573	Term Server	SNA Host	Telnet R PORT=5029 <05>...
67	0.0031	SNA Host	Term Server	TCP D=23 S=5029
				ACK=849952339 WIN=10
68	0.0490	SNA Host	Term Server	TCP D=23 S=5029
				ACK=849952339 WIN=256
69	0.0016	Term Server	SNA Host	Telnet R PORT=5029 ...
70	0.0031	SNA Host	Term Server	TCP D=23 S=5029
				ACK=849952595 WIN=0
71	0.0275	SNA Host	Term Server	TCP D=23 S=5029
				ACK=849952595 WIN=256
72	0.0017	Term Server	SNA Host	Telnet R PORT=5029 ...
73	0.0031	SNA Host	Term Server	TCP D=23 S=5029
				ACK=849952851 WIN=0
74	0.0252	SNA Host	Term Server	TCP D=23 S=5029
				ACK=849952851 WIN=256
75	0.0019	Term Server	SNA Host	Telnet R PORT=5029 ...
76	0.0032	SNA Host	Term Server	TCP D=23 S=5029
				ACK=849953107 WIN=0

77	0.0240	SNA Host	Term Server	TCP	D=23 S=5029
					ACK=849953107 WIN=255
78	0.0017	Term Server	SNA Host	Telnet R PORT=5029 ...	
79	0.0044	SNA Host	Term Server	TCP	D=23 S=5029
					ACK=849953362 WIN=0
80	0.0244	SNA Host	Term Server	TCP	D=23 S=5029
					ACK=849953362 WIN=256
81	0.0014	Term Server	SNA Host	Telnet R PORT=5029	
					<00><00><11>[a<\...
82	0.0021	SNA Host	Term Server	TCP	D=23 S=5029
					ACK=849953377 WIN=241
83	8.5150	SNA Host	Term Server	Telnet C PORT=5029 }\}<11>...	
84	0.0670	Term Server	SNA Host	TCP	D=5029 S=23
					ACK=159718 WIN=4096
85	1.0446	Term Server	SNA Host	Telnet R PORT=5029 <05>...	
86	0.0031	SNA Host	Term Server	TCP	D=23 S=5029
					ACK=849953633 WIN=0
87	0.0505	SNA Host	Term Server	TCP	D=23 S=5029
					ACK=849953633 WIN=255
88	0.0020	Term Server	SNA Host	Telnet R PORT=5029 ...	
89	0.0038	SNA Host	Term Server	TCP	D=23 S=5029
					ACK=849953888 WIN=0
90	0.0250	SNA Host	Term Server	TCP	D=23 S=5029
					ACK=849953888 WIN=256
91	0.0016	Term Server	SNA Host	Telnet R PORT=5029 ...	
92	0.0031	SNA Host	Term Server	TCP	D=23 S=5029
					ACK=849954144 WIN=0
93	0.0260	SNA Host	Term Server	TCP	D=23 S=5029
					ACK=849954144 WIN=256
94	0.0016	Term Server	SNA Host	Telnet R PORT=5029 ...	
95	0.0031	SNA Host	Term Server	TCP	D=23 S=5029
					ACK=849954400 WIN=0
96	0.0259	SNA Host	Term Server	TCP	D=23 S=5029
					ACK=849954400 WIN=256
97	0.0016	Term Server	SNA Host	Telnet R PORT=5029 @...	
98	0.0031	SNA Host	Term Server	TCP	D=23 S=5029
					ACK=849954656 WIN=0
99	0.0258	SNA Host	Term Server	TCP	D=23 S=5029
					ACK=849954656 WIN=256
100	0.0015	Term Server	SNA Host	Telnet R PORT=5029 <1D>...	
101	0.0025	SNA Host	Term Server	TCP	D=23 S=5029
					ACK=849954776 WIN=136

102	0.0384	SNA Host	Term Server	TCP D=23 S=5029
				ACK=849954776 WIN=256
103	2.7735	SNA Host	Term Server	Telnet C PORT=5029
				}\~<11>\}...
104	0.0239	Term Server	SNA Host	Telnet R PORT=5029 <05>...
105	0.0022	SNA Host	Term Server	TCP D=23 S=5029
				ACK=849954780 WIN=252
106	1.9587	Term Server	SNA Host	Telnet R PORT=5029 <05>...
107	0.0022	SNA Host	Term Server	TCP D=23 S=5029
				ACK=849954790 WIN=246
108	2.2797	Term Server	SNA Host	Telnet R PORT=5029 <05>...
109	0.0021	SNA Host	Term Server	TCP D=23 S=5029
				ACK=849954800 WIN=246
110	3.2919	Term Server	SNA Host	Telnet R PORT=5029
				<11><00><06>@<00>...
111	0.0025	SNA Host	Term Server	TCP D=23 S=5029
				ACK=849954815 WIN=241
112	0.0116	SNA Host	Term Server	TCP D=23 S=5029 RST WIN=0

Trace 6.9.3a. Host Access via Terminal Server (Summary)

Sniffer Network Analyzer data 22-Nov-91 at 17:01:38, JK2.ENC, Page 1

SUMMARY	Delta T	Destination	Source	Summary
94	0.0003	SNA Host	Workstation	TCP D=23 S=28207 SYN
				SEQ=112068096 LEN=0
				WIN=2048
95	0.0015	Workstation	SNA Host	TCP D=28207 S=23 SYN
				ACK=112068097
				SEQ=1722719745
				00LEN=0 WIN=4096
96	0.0006	SNA Host	Workstation	TCP D=23 S=28207
				ACK=1722719746 WIN=2048
97	0.0283	Workstation	SNA Host	Telnet R PORT=28207
				IAC Do Terminal type
98	0.0126	SNA Host	Workstation	Telnet C PORT=28207
				IAC Will Terminal type
99	0.0045	Workstation	SNA Host	Telnet R PORT=28207 IAC SB ...
100	0.0013	SNA Host	Workstation	Telnet C PORT=28207 IAC SB ...
101	0.0262	Workstation	SNA Host	Telnet R PORT=28207
				IAC Do End of record

102	0.0015	SNA Host	Workstation	Telnet C PORT=28207
				IAC Will End of record
103	0.0034	Workstation	SNA Host	Telnet R PORT=28207
				IAC Do Binary transmission
104	0.0014	SNA Host	Workstation	Telnet C PORT=28207
				IAC Do End of record
105	0.0754	Workstation	SNA Host	TCP D=28207 S=23
				ACK=112068124 WIN=4096
106	0.0007	SNA Host	Workstation	Telnet C PORT=28207
				IAC Will Binary transmission
107	0.0100	Workstation	SNA Host	Telnet R PORT=28207 <05>...
108	0.2144	SNA Host	Workstation	TCP D=23 S=28207
				ACK=1722719777 WIN=2017
109	0.0017	Workstation	SNA Host	Telnet R PORT=28207 <05>...
110	0.2181	SNA Host	Workstation	TCP D=23 S=28207
				ACK=1722720031 WIN=1763
140	4.0319	SNA Host	Workstation	Telnet C PORT=28207 }...
141	0.0862	Workstation	SNA Host	Telnet R PORT=28207 <05>...
142	0.1659	SNA Host	Workstation	TCP D=23 S=28207
				ACK=1722720077 WIN=1717
143	0.6708	Workstation	SNA Host	Telnet R PORT=28207 <05>...
144	0.0008	SNA Host	Workstation	TCP D=23 S=28207
				ACK=1722720087 WIN=1707
145	0.0506	Workstation	SNA Host	Telnet R PORT=28207 <05>...
146	0.0016	SNA Host	Workstation	TCP D=23 S=28207
				ACK=1722721371 WIN=2048
202	17.0982	SNA Host	Workstation	Telnet C PORT=28207 }...
203	0.0559	Workstation	SNA Host	TCP D=28207 S=23
				ACK=112068172 WIN=4096
206	1.7954	Workstation	SNA Host	Telnet R PORT=28207 <05>...
207	0.0016	SNA Host	Workstation	TCP D=23 S=28207
				ACK=1722722830 WIN=2048
216	5.9596	SNA Host	Workstation	Telnet C PORT=28207
				}\~<11>\}...
217	0.0457	Workstation	SNA Host	TCP D=28207 S=23
				ACK=112068181 WIN=4096
218	0.5606	Workstation	SNA Host	Telnet R PORT=28207 <05>...
219	0.0008	SNA Host	Workstation	TCP D=23 S=28207
				ACK=1722722834 WIN=2044
220	1.5828	Workstation	SNA Host	Telnet R PORT=28207 <05>...
221	0.0008	SNA Host	Workstation	TCP D=23 S=28207
				ACK=1722722844 WIN=2034
222	1.3582	Workstation	SNA Host	Telnet R PORT=28207 <05>...

223	0.0007	SNA Host	Workstation	TCP	D=23 S=28207
					ACK=1722722854 WIN=2024
224	1.3963	Workstation	SNA Host	Telnet R PORT=28207
					<11><00><06>@<00>...
225	0.0007	SNA Host	Workstation	TCP	D=23 S=28207
					ACK=1722722869 WIN=2009
256	16.3941	SNA Host	Workstation	TCP	D=23 S=28207 FIN
					ACK=1722722869
					SEQ=112068181
					LEN=0 WIN=2009
257	0.0014	Workstation	SNA Host	TCP	D=28207 S=23
					ACK=112068182 WIN=4096
258	0.0058	Workstation	SNA Host	TCP	D=28207 S=23 FIN
					ACK=112068182
					SEQ=1722722869
					LEN=0 WIN=4096
259	0.0007	SNA Host	Workstation	TCP	D=23 S=28207
					ACK=1722722870 WIN=2009

Trace 6.9.3b. Host Access via PC (Summary)

Sniffer Network Analyzer data 22-Nov-91 at 15:04:36, JK1.ENC, Pg 1

- - - - - - - - - - - - - - - - Frame 39 - - - - - - - - - - - - - - - - -
Telnet:——— Telnet data ———
Telnet:
Telnet:IAC SB ...

ADDR	HEX		ASCII
0000	08 00 87 00 AA 61 02 60	8C 2E 21 56 08 00 45 00	.....a.`..!V..E.
0010	00 2E F9 11 00 00 1E 06	FE EA 90 48 04 0F 90 48	...........H...H
0020	80 2E 00 17 13 A5 32 A9	3C 05 00 02 6F 9D 50 18	......2.<...o.P.
0030	10 00 F1 01 00 00 FF FA	18 01 FF F0	....

- - - - - - - - - - - - - - - Frame 40 - - - - - - - - - - - - - - - - -
TCP: ——— TCP header ———
TCP:
TCP: Source port = 5029
TCP: Destination port = 23 (Telnet)
TCP: Sequence number = 159645
TCP: Acknowledgment number = 849951755
TCP: Data offset = 20 bytes

TCP: Flags = 10
TCP: ..0. .... = (No urgent pointer)
TCP: ...1 .... = Acknowledgment
TCP: .... 0... = (No push)
TCP: .... .0.. = (No reset)
TCP: .... ..0. = (No SYN)
TCP: ....0 = (No FIN)
TCP: Window = 250
TCP: Checksum = 17FD (correct)
TCP: No TCP options
TCP:

```
ADDR   HEX                                                      ASCII
0000   02 60 8C 2E 21 56 08 00    87 00 AA 61 08 00 45 00       .`..!V.....a..E.
0010   00 28 00 5D 00 00 40 06    D5 A5 90 48 80 2E 90 48       .(.]..@....H...H
0020   04 0F 13 A5 00 17 00 02    6F 9D 32 A9 3C 0B 50 10       ........o.2.<.P.
0030   00 FA 17 FD 00 00 00 00    00 00 00 00                   ............
```

- - - - - - - - - - - - - - - - Frame 41 - - - - - - - - - - - - - - - - -
Telnet:——- Telnet data ——-
Telnet:
Telnet:IAC SB ...

```
ADDR   HEX                                                      ASCII
0000   02 60 8C 2E 21 56 08 00    87 00 AA 61 08 00 45 00       .`..!V.....a..E.
0010   00 38 00 5E 00 00 40 06    D5 94 90 48 80 2E 90 48       .8.^..@....H...H
0020   04 0F 13 A5 00 17 00 02    6F 9D 32 A9 3C 0B 50 18       ........o.2.<.P.
0030   01 00 D1 E6 00 00 FF FA    18 00 49 42 4D 2D 33 32       ..........IBM-32
0040   37 38 2D 32 FF F0                                        78-2..
```

Trace 6.9.3c. TELNET Parameters from Terminal Server

Sniffer Network Analyzer data 22-Nov-91 at 17:01:38, JK2.ENC, Pg 1

- - - - - - - - - - - - - - - Frame 99 - - - - - - - - - - - - - - - - -
Telnet:——- Telnet data ——-
Telnet:
Telnet:IAC SB ...

ADDR	HEX		ASCII
0000	00 00 C0 A6 99 27 02 60	8C 2E 21 56 08 00 45 00	.....'.`..!V..E.
0010	00 2E FE 8B 00 00 1E 06	F9 89 90 48 04 0F 90 48	...........H...H
0020	80 15 00 17 6E 2F 66 AE	9E 05 06 AE 06 04 50 18	....n/f.......P.
0030	10 00 63 78 00 00 FF FA	18 01 FF F0	..cx........

- - - - - - - - - - - - - - - Frame 100 - - - - - - - - - - - - - - - -

Telnet:——- Telnet data ——-
Telnet:
Telnet:IAC SB ...

ADDR	HEX		ASCII
0000	02 60 8C 2E 21 56 00 00	C0 A6 99 27 08 00 45 10	.`..!V.....'..E.
0010	00 3A 00 05 00 00 40 06	D5 F4 90 48 80 15 90 48	.:....@....H...H
0020	04 0F 6E 2F 00 17 06 AE	06 04 66 AE 9E 0B 50 18	..n/......f...P.
0030	07 F7 10 1F 00 00 FF FA	18 00 49 42 4D 2D 33 32	..........IBM-32
0040	37 38 2D 32 2D 45 FF F0		78-2-E..

Trace 6.9.3d. TELNET Parameters from PC

6.9.4 SMTP Interoperability Problems

One of the premises of any mail system—be it the postal service, voice messaging, or an electronic text system—is that it must be a duplex, not a simplex, operation. Duplex means that if I send you a message, you should be able to reply to
me. Let's see what happens when this assumption is invalid.

The network in this case study is a single token ring to which a number of dissimilar workstations are attached (see Figure 6-12). The underlying operating systems are all variants of UNIX, running on IBM RS/6000 and Sun SPARCstation II
workstations. All of these workstations are implementing an SMTP package, and
theoretically should be interoperable. Unfortunately, this theory proves incorrect.

When the RS/6000 sends a message to the Sun SPARCstation II (SS2), the message is delivered properly. But when the SS2 replies to the message, the delivery fails. The process for each workstation is as follows:

1. The user invokes the workstation's native mail program (Sendmail) to send a message.
2. The Sendmail program invokes SMTP for delivery via the network.
3. The recipient workstation obtains the SMTP message from the network and sends it to its native mail program (also Sendmail in this case).
4. The Sendmail program deposits the message in the recipient user's mailbox.

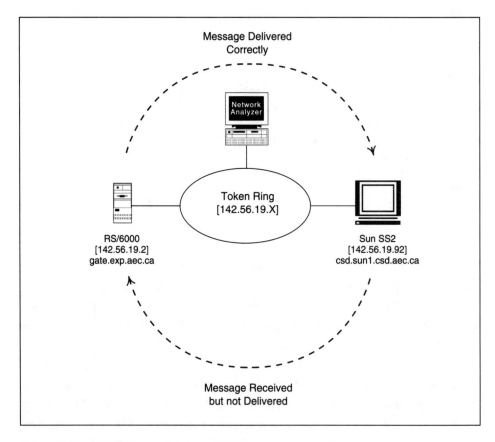

Figure 6-12. Mail Delivery Incompatibilities

The process thus involves two significant operations. One—Steps 1 and 4—is visible to the workstation but invisible to the network, while the other—Steps 2 and 3— is visible to the network but invisible to the workstation.

In Trace 6.9.4, we see the portion that is visible to the network and thus available for capture by the network analyzer (note that this trace was filtered to remove non-SMTP frames, so all frames are not necessarily in sequential order). The first scenario involves the RS/6000 sending a message to the SS2. The following steps are involved:

1. Establishing the SMTP connection:
   HELO <SP> <source mailbox> <CRLF>
   shown in Frames 535-537

2. Identifying the message originator:
   MAIL <SP> FROM: <source mailbox> <CRLF>
   shown in Frames 538-539

3. Identifying the message recipient:
   RCPT <SP> TO: <receiving mailbox> <CRLF>
   shown in Frames 540-541

4. Transferring the text of the message:
   DATA <CRLF>
   shown in Frames 542-548

5. Closing the SMTP connection:
   QUIT <CRLF>
   shown in Frames 549-550

To verify that the message was delivered, the recipient host (SS2) transmits a "delivering mail ..." message in Frame 550. The host process (invisible to the network) then takes over, delivering the mail to the recipient's mailbox. The message appears at the SS2, and all is well.

To verify the connectivity, the SS2 then attempts to reply to the message from the RS/6000. Unfortunately, this operation is unsuccessful, and the failure is not readily apparent from the network's point of view. Reviewing Trace 6.9.4, we see a similar mail scenario:

1. Establishing connection: Frames 580-582
2. Identifying originator: Frames 583-594
3. Identifying recipient: Frames 595-597
4. Transferring text: Frames 598-603
5. Closing connection: Frames 604-605

This message was never delivered from the SS2 to the RS/6000, although that isn't readily apparent from the trace file. The clue that a problem existed was found by comparing the acknowledgement messages from the recipients. Recall that the message from the RS/6000 to the SS2 was received and delivered to the end user. The SS2 returned the following message in Frame 548:

```
250 Mail accepted <0D><0A>
```

The message from the SS2 to the RS/6000 was received but not delivered to the end user. The RS/6000 returned the following message in Frame 603:

```
250 Ok <0D><0A>
```

The differences in the two host acknowledgements prompted the network manager, Chris, to check the error log on the RS/6000 host. This is what he found:

```
—- Transcript of session follows —-
>>> HELO gate.exp.aec.ca
<<< 553 Local configuration error, hostname not recognized as local
554 <cdutchyn@gate.exp.aec.ca.>... Service unavailable: Bad file number
```

```
    —- Unsent message follows —-
Received: from csd_sun1.csd.aec.ca by gate.exp.aec.ca (AIX 3.1/UCB
5.61/4.03)
          id AA28142; Thu, 16 Apr 92 11:30:44 -0600
Received: by csd_sun1.csd.aec.ca.csd.aec.ca
   id AA00372; Thu, 16 Apr 92 11:37:42 MDT
Date: Thu, 16 Apr 92 11:37:42 MDT
From: cdutchyn@csd.aec.ca (Christopher J. Dutchyn)
Message-Id: <9204161737.AA00372@csd_sun1.csd.aec.ca.csd.aec.ca>
To: cdutchyn@gate.exp.aec.ca.
Subject: This is a test.

This is a test response.  If it were a real response, it would contain
more information about what you should know.

Chris
```

The message indicates that the SS2 placed an extra period (.) at the end of the intended recipient's address. Therefore, the recipient was noted as <cdutchyn@gate.exp.aec.ca.> instead of <cdutchyn@gate.exp.aec.ca>. When the address was delivered to the RS/6000 (gate.exp.aec.ca), the RS/6000 was unable to recognize its own address because of the additional period. As a result, the connection failed at the HELO message and the following message was returned:

```
553 Local Configuration error,
   hostname not recognized as local
```

Since this error message occurred in the SMTP process within the RS/6000 host and was never transmitted via the network to the SS2, the message transfer appeared fine from a protocol point of view. Only when the error log of the RS/6000 host was examined did the actual source of the problem (the extraneous period after "ca") surface. Chris then studied the configuration of the SS2 host in greater detail, discovered a configuration error in the name server, and corrected the problem.

Sniffer Network Analyzer data 16-Apr-92 at 10:35:48, file SMTP.TRC, Pg 1

SUMMARY	Delta T	Destination	Source	Summary
535		RS/6000	SUN SS2	SMTP R PORT=2047
				220 csd_sun1.csd.aec.ca.
				csd.aec.ca
536	0.004	SUN SS2	RS/6000	SMTP C PORT=2047
				HELO gate.exp.aec.ca
				<0D><0A>
537	0.007	RS/6000	SUN SS2	SMTP R PORT=2047
				250 csd_sun1.csd.aec.ca.
				csd.aec.ca
				Hello gate.exp....
538	0.003	SUN SS2	RS/6000	SMTP C PORT=2047
				MAIL From:<cdutchyn
				@gate.exp.aec.ca><0D><0A>
539	0.143	RS/6000	SUN SS2	SMTP R PORT=2047
				250 postmaster
				... Sender ok<0D><0A>
540	0.012	SUN SS2	RS/6000	SMTP C PORT=2047
				RCPT To:<cdutchyn
				@csd_sun1.csd.aec.ca>
				<0D><0A>
541	0.111	RS/6000	SUN SS2	SMTP R PORT=2047
				250 <cdutchyn
				@csd_sun1.csd.aec.ca>
				... Recipient ok...
542	0.004	SUN SS2	RS/6000	SMTP C PORT=2047
				DATA<0D><0A>
543	0.055	RS/6000	SUN SS2	SMTP R PORT=2047
				354 Enter mail,
				end with "." on
				a line by itself<0D>...
545	0.026	SUN SS2	RS/6000	SMTP C PORT=2047
				Received: by
				gate.exp.aec.ca
547	0.200	SUN SS2	RS/6000	SMTP C PORT=2047 .<0D><0A>
548	0.008	RS/6000	SUN SS2	SMTP R PORT=2047
				250 Mail accepted
				<0D><0A>
549	0.004	SUN SS2	RS/6000	SMTP C PORT=2047 QUIT<0D><0A>

550	0.003	RS/6000	SUN SS2	SMTP R PORT=2047 221 csd_sun1.csd.aec.ca. csd.aec.ca delivering mail...
580	63.636	SUN SS2	RS/6000	SMTP R PORT=1041 220 gate.exp.aec.ca
581	0.006	RS/6000	SUN SS2	SMTP C PORT=1041 HELO csd_sun1.csd.aec.ca. csd.aec.ca<0D><0A>
582	0.007	SUN SS2	RS/6000	SMTP R PORT=1041 250 gate.exp.aec.ca Hello csd_sun1.csd.aec.ca. csd....
583	0.004	RS/6000	SUN SS2	SMTP C PORT=1041 MAIL From:<cdutchyn @csd.aec.ca><0D><0A>
594	1.229	SUN SS2	RS/6000	SMTP R PORT=1041 250 <cdutchyn @csd.aec.ca>... Sender ok<0D><0A>
595	0.006	RS/6000	SUN SS2	SMTP C PORT=1041 RCPT To:<cdutchyn @gate.exp.aec.ca.> <0D><0A>
597	1.029	SUN SS2	RS/6000	SMTP R PORT=1041 250 <cdutchyn @gate.exp.aec.ca.> Recipient ok<0D>...
598	0.004	RS/6000	SUN SS2	SMTP C PORT=1041 DATA<0D><0A>
599	0.018	SUN SS2	RS/6000	SMTP R PORT=1041 354 Enter mail, end with "." on a line by itself<0D>...
600	0.016	RS/6000	SUN SS2	SMTP C PORT=1041 Received: by csd_sun1.csd.aec.ca. csd.aec.ca.
602	0.035	RS/6000	SUN SS2	SMTP C PORT=1041 .<0D><0A>
603	0.117	SUN SS2	RS/6000	SMTP R PORT=1041 250 Ok<0D><0A>
604	0.006	RS/6000	SUN SS2	SMTP C PORT=1041 QUIT<0D><0A>

605   0.022   SUN SS2   RS/6000   SMTP R PORT=1041
                                          221 gate.exp.aec.ca
                                          closing connection<0D><0A>

Trace 6.9.4. SMTP Mail Service Summary

6.9.5 NetBIOS and TCP Interactions

The following example of NetBIOS service illustrates how all of the DARPA layers must cooperate in order to ensure proper protocol operation. The objective in this case study is for one workstation (shown as Art in Trace 6.9.5a) to use the resources on another workstation, known as Robert. The trace begins with Art broadcasting a NetBIOS Name Service (DNS) Query looking for Robert. Details of the query in Frame 1 of Trace 6.9.5b show a Source port of 275 assigned to NetBIOS service within the UDP header. The query consists of a single question, providing the name, type, and class of the object. The response returned in Frame 2 provides necessary details about Robert. These include the uniqueness of the name, and that Robert is a B-type (broadcast) node with an IP address of [XXX.YYY.200.85]. Now that Art knows more about Robert, he can use Robert's resources.

Frames 3-5 show a TCP connection initiated by Art and accepted by Robert. The NetBIOS Session Service begins in Frame 6 and is shown in detail in Trace 6.9.5c. Art begins with a NetBIOS Session Request message (Type=81) having a length of 74 octets. The data consists of the called and calling names, ROBERT and ARTL, respectively. Robert then responds with a Positive Response (or Session Confirm) message, Type=82. The logical session is now established.

Art must now negotiate the language he will use to communicate with Robert. To do so, he uses the Server Message Block (SMB) protocol. SMB was developed by Microsoft Corp. to enable a DOS-based client workstation to communicate with its server. SMB information is carried as data inside a NetBIOS message. Speaking in OSI terms, NetBIOS is providing the Session Layer (i.e., logical) connection while SMB information defines the format of the data to be transmitted and thus provides Presentation Layer functions. We see the protocol being negotiated in Frames 9 and 11.

The connection that Art is really after—access to Robert's disk drive—is shown in Frames 13 and 15 (see Trace 6.9.5d). This process is completed in Frame 19. Art may then search the specified directory on Robert's disk (Frame 22), finding one file in Frame 24. A subsequent search (Frame 26) returns ten additional filenames (Frame 28). No more files are noted in Frame 33, prompting Art to his next task: finding the disk attributes (Frames 35 and 38). Finished with his work, Art then issues a SMB Disconnection message (Frame 40), which is acknowledged in Frame 42. The TCP connection is then torn down, using the FIN messages from both Art and Robert in Frames 44 and 45, respectively.

Notice the pattern of protocol operation: first, TCP establishes the end-to-end connection before NetBIOS and SMB undertakes the logical session. When there is no longer a need for communication, the higher-layer protocol (SMB) terminates the logical connection, and TCP then terminates the end-to-end connection. We will use this process of multi-layer protocol interaction in our final case study, which investigates the operation of a Windows-based workstation.

Sniffer Network Analyzer data 6-Nov-87 at 11:04:32, TCPNETB.ENC, Pg 1

SUMMARY	Delta T	Destination	Source	Summary
M 1		Broadcast	Art	DNS C ID=41128
				OP=QUERY NAME=ROBERT
2	0.0018	Art	Robert	DNS R ID=41128 STAT=OK
3	0.0243	Robert	Art	TCP D=139 S=257 SYN
				SEQ=172249 LEN=0 WIN=1024
4	0.0028	Art	Robert	TCP D=257 S=139 SYN
				ACK=172250 SEQ=257461
				LEN=0 WIN=2152
5	0.0160	Robert	Art	TCP D=139 S=257
				ACK=257462 WIN=1024
6	0.0046	Robert	Art	NETB D=ROBERT S=ARTL<00>
				Session request
7	0.0041	Art	Robert	NETB Session confirm
8	0.0204	Robert	Art	TCP D=139 S=257
				ACK=257466 WIN=1020
9	0.0106	Robert	Art	SMB C PC NETWORK PROGRAM 1.0
10	0.0043	Art	Robert	TCP D=257 S=139
				ACK=172391 WIN=2011
11	0.0036	Art	Robert	SMB R Negotiated Protocol 0
12	0.0191	Robert	Art	TCP D=139 S=257
				ACK=257507 WIN=979
13	0.0096	Robert	Art	SMB C Connect A:\\ROBERT\DISK

14	0.0048	Art	Robert	TCP D=257 S=139
				ACK=172451 WIN=1951
15	0.0077	Art	Robert	SMB R T=8F15 Connected
16	0.0138	Robert	Art	TCP D=139 S=257
				ACK=257550 WIN=936
17	0.0347	Robert	Art	SMB C End of Process
18	0.0057	Art	Robert	TCP D=257 S=139
				ACK=172490 WIN=1912
19	0.0057	Art	Robert	SMB R OK
20	0.0163	Robert	Art	TCP D=139 S=257
				ACK=257589 WIN=897
21	0.1437	Art	Robert	TCP D=257 S=139
				ACK=172490 WIN=2152
22	19.4487	Robert	Art	SMB C Search \????????.???
23	0.0054	Art	Robert	TCP D=257 S=139
				ACK=172551 WIN=2091
24	0.0157	Art	Robert	SMB R 1 entry found (done)
25	0.0157	Robert	Art	TCP D=139 S=257
				ACK=257676 WIN=810
26	0.0676	Robert	Art	SMB C Search \????????.???
27	0.0054	Art	Robert	TCP D=257 S=139
				ACK=172612 WIN=2030
28	0.0276	Art	Robert	SMB R 10 entries found (done)
29	0.0188	Robert	Art	TCP D=139 S=257
				ACK=258150 WIN=1024
30	0.1490	Art	Robert	TCP D=257 S=139
				ACK=172612 WIN=2152
31	0.0852	Robert	Art	SMB C Continue Search
32	0.0052	Art	Robert	TCPD=257 S=139
				ACK=172681 WIN=2083
33	0.0098	Art	Robert	SMB R No more files
34	0.0135	Robert	Art	TCP D=139 S=257
				ACK=258194 WIN=980
35	0.0127	Robert	Art	SMB C Get Disk Attributes
36	0.0051	Art	Robert	TCP D=257 S=139
				ACK=172720 WIN=2044
37	0.2589	Art	Robert	TCP D=257 S=139
				ACK=172720 WIN=2152
38	0.9522	Art	Robert	SMB R Got Disk Attributes
39	0.0144	Robert	Art	TCP D=139 S=257
				ACK=258243 WIN=931
40	4.5501	Robert	Art	SMB C T=8F15 Disconnect

41	0.0059	Art	Robert	TCP D=257 S=139 ACK=172759 WIN=2113
42	0.0057	Art	Robert	SMB R OK
43	0.0173	Robert	Art	TCP D=139 S=257 ACK=258282 WIN=892
44	0.0146	Robert	Art	TCP D=139 S=257 FIN ACK=258282 SEQ=172759 LEN=0 WIN=892
45	0.0029	Art	Robert	TCP D=257 S=139 FIN ACK=172760 SEQ=258282 LEN=0 WIN=2113
46	0.0116	Robert	Art	TCP D=139 S=257 ACK=258283 WIN=892
47	2.5477	Robert	Art	TCP D=139 S=257 ACK=258283 WIN=892
48	0.0018	Art	Robert	TCP D=257 S=139 RST WIN=892

Trace 6.9.5a. NetBIOS over UDP and TCP (Summary)

Sniffer Network Analyzer data 6-Nov-87 at 11:04:32, TCPNETB.ENC, Pg 1

- - - - - - - - - - - - - - - - Frame 1 - - - - - - - - - - - - - - - - -
DLC: ——- DLC Header ——
DLC:
DLC: Frame 1 arrived at 11:04:51.3527; frame size is 92 (005C hex) bytes.
DLC: Destination = BROADCAST FFFFFFFFFFFF, Broadcast
DLC: Source   = Station Bridge011084, Art
DLC: Ethertype = 0800 (IP)
DLC:
IP: ——- IP Header ——
IP:
IP: Version = 4, header length = 20 bytes
IP: Type of service = 00
IP: 000. .... = routine
IP: ...0 .... = normal delay
IP: .... 0... = normal throughput
IP: .... .0.. = normal reliability
IP: Total length = 78 bytes
IP: Identification = 19
IP: Flags = 0X

IP: .0.. .... = may fragment
IP: ..0. .... = last fragment
IP: Fragment offset = 0 bytes
IP: Time to live = 30 seconds/hops
IP: Protocol = 17 (UDP)
IP: Header checksum = 1420 (correct)
IP: Source address = [XXX.YYY.200.99]
IP: Destination address = [255.255.255.255]
IP: No options
IP:
UDP: ——— UDP Header ———
UDP:
UDP: Source port = 275 (NetBIOS)
UDP: Destination port = 137
UDP: Length = 58
UDP: Checksum = 8153 (correct)
UDP:
DNS: ——— Internet Domain Name Service header ———
DNS:
DNS: ID = 41128
DNS: Flags = 01
DNS: 0... .... = Command
DNS: .000 0... = Query
DNS: .... ..0. = Not truncated
DNS: ....1 = Recursion desired
DNS: Flags = 1X
DNS: ...1 .... = Broadcast packet
DNS: Question count = 1, Answer count = 0
DNS: Authority count = 0, Additional record count = 0
DNS:
DNS: Question section:
DNS: Name = ROBERT
DNS: Type = NetBIOS name service (NetBIOS name,32)
DNS: Class = Internet (IN,1)
DNS:
DNS: [Normal end of "Internet Domain Name Service header".]
DNS:

- - - - - - - - - - - - - - - - Frame 2 - - - - - - - - - - - - - - - - -
DLC: ——— DLC Header ———
DLC:
DLC: Frame 2 arrived at 11:04:51.3545; frame size is 104 (0068 hex) bytes.
DLC: Destination = Station Bridge011084, Art

```
DLC: Source      = Station U-B   F5D800, Robert
DLC: Ethertype  = 0800 (IP)
DLC:
IP:  ——- IP Header ——-
IP:
IP:  Version = 4, header length = 20 bytes
IP:  Type of service = 00
IP:         000. .... = routine
IP:         ...0 .... = normal delay
IP:         .... 0... = normal throughput
IP:         .... .0.. = normal reliability
IP:  Total length = 90 bytes
IP:  Identification = 18756
IP:  Flags = 0X
IP:  .0.. .... = may fragment
IP:  ..0. .... = last fragment
IP:  Fragment offset = 0 bytes
IP:  Time to live = 60 seconds/hops
IP:  Protocol = 17 (UDP)
IP:  Header checksum = 2483 (correct)
IP:  Source address = [XXX.YYY.200.85]
IP:  Destination address = [XXX.YYY.200.99]
IP:  No options
IP:
UDP: ——- UDP Header ——-
UDP:
UDP: Source port = 137 (NetBIOS)
UDP: Destination port = 275
UDP: Length = 70
UDP: Checksum = EC85 (correct)
UDP:
DNS: ——- Internet Domain Name Service header ——-
DNS:
DNS: ID = 41128
DNS: Flags = 85
DNS: 1... .... = Response
DNS: .... .1.. = Authoritative answer
DNS: .000 0... = Query
DNS: .... ..0. = Not truncated
DNS: Flags = 0X
DNS: ...0 .... = Unicast packet
DNS: 0... .... = Recursion not available
DNS: Response code = OK (0)
```

DNS: Question count = 0, Answer count = 1
DNS: Authority count = 0, Additional record count = 0
DNS: Answer section:
DNS: Name = ROBERT
DNS: Type = NetBIOS name service (NetBIOS name,32)
DNS: Class = Internet (IN,1)
DNS: Time-to-live = 0 (seconds)
DNS: Node flags = 00
DNS: 0... .... = Unique NetBIOS name
DNS: .00. .... = B-type node
DNS: Node address = [XXX.YYY.200.85]
DNS:
DNS: [Normal end of "Internet Domain Name Service header".]
DNS:

Trace 6.9.5b. NetBIOS Name Service Query/Response

Sniffer Network Analyzer data 6-Nov-87 at 11:04:32, TCPNETB.ENC, Pg 1

- - - - - - - - - - - - - - - - Frame 6 - - - - - - - - - - - - - - - - -
DLC: —— DLC Header ——
DLC:
DLC: Frame 6 arrived at 11:04:51.4023; frame size is 132 (0084 hex) bytes.
DLC: Destination = Station U-B   F5D800, Robert
DLC: Source   = Station Bridge011084, Art
DLC: Ethertype = 0800 (IP)
DLC:
IP: —— IP Header ——
IP:
IP: Version = 4, header length = 20 bytes
IP: Type of service = 00
IP: 000. .... = routine
IP: ...0 .... = normal delay
IP: .... 0... = normal throughput
IP: .... .0.. = normal reliability
IP: Total length = 118 bytes
IP: Identification = 281
IP: Flags = 0X
IP: .0.. .... = may fragment
IP: ..0. .... = last fragment
IP: Fragment offset = 0 bytes

346

IP: Time to live = 30 seconds/hops
IP: Protocol = 6 (TCP)
IP: Header checksum = 8A9D (correct)
IP: Source address = [XXX.YYY.200.99]
IP: Destination address = [XXX.YYY.200.85]
IP: No options
IP:
TCP: —— TCP header ——
TCP:
TCP: Source port = 257
TCP: Destination port = 139
TCP: Sequence number = 172250
TCP: Acknowledgment number = 257462
TCP: Data offset = 20 bytes
TCP: Flags = 10
TCP: ..0. .... = (No urgent pointer)
TCP: ...1 .... = Acknowledgment
TCP: .... 0... = (No push)
TCP: .... .0.. = (No reset)
TCP: .... ..0. = (No SYN)
TCP: ....0 = (No FIN)
TCP: Window = 1024
TCP: Checksum = EFCD (correct)
TCP: No TCP options
TCP: [78 byte(s) of data]
TCP:
NETB: —— NetBIOS Session protocol ——
NETB:
NETB: Type = 81 (Session request)
NETB: Flags = 00
NETB: Total session packet length = 74
NETB: Called NetBIOS name = ROBERT
NETB: Calling NetBIOS name = ARTL<00>
NETB:

- - - - - - - - - - - - - - - Frame 7 - - - - - - - - - - - - - - - - -
DLC: —— DLC Header ——
DLC:
DLC: Frame 7 arrived at 11:04:51.4065; frame size is 60 (003C hex) bytes.
DLC: Destination = Station Bridge011084, Art
DLC: Source   = Station U-B F5D800, Robert
DLC: Ethertype = 0800 (IP)
DLC:

```
IP: ——— IP Header ———
IP:
IP:   Version = 4, header length = 20 bytes
IP:   Type of service = 00
IP:        000. .... = routine
IP:        ...0 .... = normal delay
IP:        .... 0... = normal throughput
IP:        .... .0.. = normal reliability
IP:   Total length = 44 bytes
IP:   Identification = 2
IP:   Flags = 0X
IP:   .0.. .... = may fragment
IP:   ..0. .... = last fragment
IP:   Fragment offset = 0 bytes
IP:   Time to live = 60 seconds/hops
IP:   Protocol = 6 (TCP)
IP:   Header checksum = 6DFE (correct)
IP:   Source address = [XXX.YYY.200.85]
IP:   Destination address = [XXX.YYY.200.99]
IP:   No options
IP:
TCP: ——— TCP header ———
TCP:
TCP:  Source port = 139
TCP:  Destination port = 257
TCP:  Sequence number = 257462
TCP:  Acknowledgment number = 172328
TCP:  Data offset = 20 bytes
TCP:  Flags = 18
TCP:  ..0. .... = (No urgent pointer)
TCP:  ...1 .... = Acknowledgment
TCP:  .... 1... = Push
TCP:  .... .0.. = (No reset)
TCP:  .... ..0. = (No SYN)
TCP:  .... ...0 = (No FIN)
TCP:  Window = 2074
TCP:  Checksum = 8471 (correct)
TCP:  No TCP options
TCP:  [4 byte(s) of data]
TCP:
NETB: ——— NetBIOS Session protocol ———
NETB:
NETB: Type = 82 (Positive response)
```

NETB: Flags = 00
NETB: Total session packet length = 0
NETB:

Trace 6.9.5c. NetBIOS Session Request/Confirm

Sniffer Network Analyzer data 6-Nov-87 at 11:04:32, TCPNETB.ENC, Pg 1

- - - - - - - - - - - - - - - Frame 13 - - - - - - - - - - - - - - - - -
DLC: —— DLC Header ——-
DLC:
DLC: Frame 13 arrived at 11:04:51.4744; frame size is 114 (0072 hex) bytes.
DLC: Destination = Station U-B   F5D800, Robert
DLC: Source   = Station Bridge011084, Art
DLC: Ethertype = 0800 (IP)
DLC:
IP: —— IP Header ——-
IP:
IP: Version = 4, header length = 20 bytes
IP: Type of service = 00
IP: 000. .... = routine
IP: ...0 .... = normal delay
IP: .... 0... = normal throughput
IP: .... .0.. = normal reliability
IP: Total length = 100 bytes
IP: Identification = 285
IP: Flags = 0X
IP: .0.. .... = may fragment
IP: ..0. .... = last fragment
IP: Fragment offset = 0 bytes
IP: Time to live = 30 seconds/hops
IP: Protocol = 6 (TCP)
IP: Header checksum = 8AAB (correct)
IP: Source address = [XXX.YYY.200.99]
IP: Destination address = [XXX.YYY.200.85]
IP: No options
IP:
TCP: —— TCP header ——-
TCP:
TCP: Source port = 257

TCP: Destination port = 139
TCP: Sequence number = 172391
TCP: Acknowledgment number = 257507
TCP: Data offset = 20 bytes
TCP: Flags = 10
TCP: ..0. .... = (No urgent pointer)
TCP: ...1 .... = Acknowledgment
TCP: .... 0... = (No push)
TCP: .... .0.. = (No reset)
TCP: .... ..0. = (No SYN)
TCP: ....0 = (No FIN)
TCP: Window = 979
TCP: Checksum = D716 (correct)
TCP: No TCP options
TCP: [60 byte(s) of data]
TCP:
NETB: ——- NetBIOS Session protocol ——
NETB:
NETB: Type = 00 (Session data)
NETB: Flags = 00
NETB: Total session packet length = 56
NETB:
SMB: ——- SMB Tree Connect Command ——-
SMB:
SMB: Function = 70 (Tree Connect)
SMB: Tree id   (TID) = 0000
SMB: Process id (PID) = 0000
SMB: File pathname = "\\ROBERT\DISK"
SMB: Password = ""
SMB: Device name = "A:"
SMB:

- - - - - - - - - - - - - - - - Frame 15 - - - - - - - - - - - - - - - - -
DLC: ——- DLC Header ——
DLC:
DLC: Frame 15 arrived at 11:04:51.4870; frame size is 97 (0061 hex) bytes.
DLC: Destination = Station Bridge011084, Art
DLC: Source   = Station U-B F5D800, Robert
DLC: Ethertype = 0800 (IP)
DLC:
IP: ——- IP Header ——
IP:
IP: Version = 4, header length = 20 bytes

```
IP:  Type of service = 00
IP:        000. .... = routine
IP:        ...0 .... = normal delay
IP:        .... 0... = normal throughput
IP:        .... .0.. = normal reliability
IP:  Total length = 83 bytes
IP:  Identification = 4
IP:  Flags = 0X
IP:  .0.. .... = may fragment
IP:  ..0. .... = last fragment
IP:  Fragment offset = 0 bytes
IP:  Time to live = 60 seconds/hops
IP:  Protocol = 6 (TCP)
IP:  Header checksum = 6DD5 (correct)
IP:  Source address = [XXX.YYY.200.85]
IP:  Destination address = [XXX.YYY.200.99]
IP:  No options
IP:
TCP: ——- TCP header ——-
TCP:
TCP: Source port = 139
TCP: Destination port = 257
TCP: Sequence number = 257507
TCP: Acknowledgment number = 172451
TCP: Data offset = 20 bytes
TCP: Flags = 10
TCP: ..0. .... = (No urgent pointer)
TCP: ...1 .... = Acknowledgment
TCP: .... 0... = (No push)
TCP: .... .0.. = (No reset)
TCP: .... ..0. = (No SYN)
TCP: .... ...0 = (No FIN)
TCP: Window = 1951
TCP: Checksum = 97A2 (correct)
TCP: No TCP options
TCP: [43 byte(s) of data]
TCP:
NETB: ——- NetBIOS Session protocol ——-
NETB:
NETB: Type = 00 (Session data)
NETB: Flags = 00
NETB: Total session packet length = 39
NETB:
```

SMB: ——— SMB Tree Connect Response ———
SMB:
SMB: Function = 70 (Tree Connect)
SMB: Tree id   (TID) = 0000
SMB: Process id   (PID) = 0000
SMB: Return code = 0,0 (OK)
SMB: Maximum transmit size = 8240
SMB: TID = 8F15
SMB:

Trace 6.9.5d. NetBIOS with Server Message Block Information

6.9.6 Implementing Multiple Protocol Stacks

Much has been said about workstation environments that allow the user to perform multiple operations simultaneously, such as printing while working on a spread-
sheet. Such environments include IBM's OS/2 and Microsoft's Windows and LAN
Manager. In any operating system, the user must be sure that the application is compatible with the environment. When multiple applications are involved, the scenario
gets more complex. Let's look at what can happen in an environment that mixes
DOS, OS/2, Windows, and a TCP/IP workstation package.

The internetwork in question contains two token rings in two separate locations.
One ring contains an OS/2 Server and a number of workstations, and the other ring
contains an SNA host. Routers connect the two rings (see Figure 6-13). The network
administrator decides to experiment and combine multiple protocol stacks and operating systems on his workstation. For his experiment, he plans to use a TCP/IP workstation package to access the SNA host via the router. His workstation is running Windows, and the DOS-based TCP/IP workstation package resides on an OS/2 Server.

Trace 6.9.6a begins with the Windows workstation (shown as Windows WS)
entering the token ring. Frames 1 through 7 show the workstation transmitting
two MAC Duplicate Address Test frames, reporting a change in its Stored Upstream
Address (SUA) to the Configuration Report Server (CRS), and obtaining its initialization parameters from the Ring Parameter Server (RPS). Beginning in Frame
8, the Windows workstation begins to log into the OS/2 Server, known as ISC-
SWEST. NetBIOS Name Service messages verify the various names that Windows WS requires. A NetBIOS session is initialized in Frame 35 and confirmed
in Frame 37. The protocol is then negotiated (Frames 39 and 43) and the SMB

connection established (Frames 47 and 51). Subsequent Frames 52 through 470 (not shown) complete the login and establish a session with a print server, PrtSrv S. Beginning in Frame 471, a connection is made to a second print server, PrtSrv N. This connection follows a similar sequence of events: find the name (Frame 471), initialize the session (Frame 477), negotiate the protocol (Frame 481), and establish the connection (Frame 489). The workstation is then idle for a few seconds while the administrator ponders his next move.

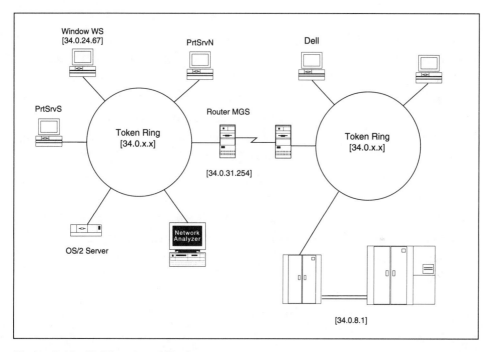

Figure 6-13. Multi-protocol Environment

The administrator starts Windows, shown in Frame 519. The TCP/IP workstation program that is required to access the remote SNA host is resident on the OS/2 Server. Since that program is DOS-based, the administrator opens a DOS Window and begins to load the file (shown as PFTP in Frame 582). The file opens properly (Frame 586), is read from the OS/2 Server (Frames 597 through 864, not shown in the trace), and closes (Frames 865 through 868). The Windows workstation is now ready to connect to the remote host using FTP. The workstation [34.0.24.67] broadcasts an ARP look-

353

ing for the router that can connect it to the host [34.0.31.254]. It finds the router (Frame 874) and establishes a TCP connection (Frames 875 through 877) to Port=5044. A second TCP connection to Port=5054 is established (Frames 913 through 917), but is terminated shortly thereafter (Frames 922 through 924). The last indication of TCP-related protocol activity is in Frame 926; subsequent frames are NetBIOS Keep Alives (Frame 927), LLC Polls (Frames 928 through 934) and MAC-layer transmissions (Frame 935). It appears that the TCP/IP application is no longer active.

An indication that a problem exists comes in Frame 1001, a Report Soft Error frame (see Trace 6.9.6b). This frame is sent from Windows workstation to the Ring Error Monitor (REM), indicating receiver congestion. In other words, the receiver of Windows workstation does not have sufficient buffer space for all the data that it is receiving. These MAC Report Soft Error frames continue to be transmitted, with no higher-layer processes active. Note that the remainder of the trace (Frames 1072 through 1093) shows no NetBIOS Session Alive messages and that the Windows workstation does not answer the polls from the OS/2 Server. The workstation has been reduced to its MAC-layer operation.

The problem was traced to an incompatibility between the DOS application, the DOS Window (under Microsoft Windows), and the OS/2 LAN Server. The problem was resolved by operating the TCP/IP workstation program from a DOS-based, rather than a Windows-based, workstation. Multi-layer incompatibilities can produce unusual behaviors!

Sniffer Network Analyzer data 30-May-91 at 10:53:14, TCPWIN.TRC, Pg 1

SUMMARY		Delta T	Destination	Source	Summary
M	1		Windows WS	Windows WS	MAC Duplicate Address Test
	2	0.002	Windows WS	Windows WS	MAC Duplicate Address Test
	3	0.490	Config Srv	Windows WS	MAC Report SUA Change
	4	0.012	Broadcast	Windows WS	MAC Standby Monitor Present
	5	0.000	Param Server	Windows WS	MAC Request Initialization
	6	0.005	Windows WS	Station RPS.	MAC Initialize Ring Station
	7	0.000	Station RPS.	Windows WS	MAC Response
	8	0.010	NetBIOS	Windows WS	NETB Check name ISCW7166<00>
	9	0.990	NetBIOS	Windows WS	NETB Check name ISCW7166<00>
	10	0.499	NetBIOS	Windows WS	NETB Check name ISCW7166<00>
	11	0.500	NetBIOS	Windows WS	NETB Check name ISCW7166<00>

12	0.499	NetBIOS	Windows WS	NETB Check name ISCW7166<00>
13	0.499	NetBIOS	Windows WS	NETB Check name ISCW7166<00>
14	0.500	NetBIOS	Windows WS	NETB Check group ISCDWEST<00>
15	0.999	NetBIOS	Windows WS	NETB Check group ISCDWEST<00>
16	0.499	NetBIOS	Windows WS	NETB Check group ISCDWEST<00>
17	0.499	NetBIOS	Windows WS	NETB Check group ISCDWEST<00>
18	0.499	NetBIOS	Windows WS	NETB Check group ISCDWEST<00>
19	0.499	NetBIOS	Windows WS	NETB Check group ISCDWEST<00>
20	0.486	Broadcast	Windows WS	MAC Standby Monitor Present
21	6.373	NetBIOS	Windows WS	NETB Check name DATZ343
22	0.624	Broadcast	Windows WS	MAC Standby Monitor Present
23	0.013	NetBIOS	Windows WS	NETB Check name DATZ343 ISCDWES
24	0.499	NetBIOS	Windows WS	NETB Check name DATZ343 ISCDWES
25	0.500	NetBIOS	Windows WS	NETB Check name DATZ343 ISCDWES
26	0.499	NetBIOS	Windows WS	NETB Check name DATZ343 ISCDWES
27	0.499	NetBIOS	Windows WS	NETB Check name DATZ343 ISCDWES
28	0.529	NetBIOS	Windows WS	SMB C Transaction \MAILSLOT\NET\NETLOGON
29	0.144	NetBIOS	Windows WS	NETB Find name ISCSWEST
30	0.002	Windows WS	OS/2 Server	NETB Name ISCSWEST recognized
31	0.001	OS/2 Server	Windows WS	LLC C D=F0 S=F0 SABME P
32	0.001	Windows WS	OS/2 Server	LLC R D=F0 S=F0 UA F
33	0.000	OS/2 Server	Windows WS	LLC C D=F0 S=F0 RR NR=0 P
34	0.000	Windows WS	OS/2 Server	LLC R D=F0 S=F0 RR NR=0 F
35	0.000	OS/2 Server	Windows WS	NETB D=21 S=01 Session init
36	0.001	Windows WS	OS/2 Server	LLC R D=F0 S=F0 RR NR=1
37	0.000	Windows WS	OS/2 Server	NETB D=01 S=21 Session conf
38	0.000	OS/2 Server	Windows WS	LLC R D=F0 S=F0 RR NR=1
39	0.002	OS/2 Server	Windows WS	SMB C PC NET PGM 1.0 (more)
40	0.001	Windows WS	OS/2 Server	LLC R D=F0 S=F0 RR NR=2
41	0.000	Windows WS	OS/2 Server	NETB D=01 S=21 Data ACK
42	0.000	OS/2 Server	Windows WS	LLC R D=F0 S=F0 RR NR=2
43	0.009	Windows WS	OS/2 Server	SMB R Negotiated Protocol 4
44	0.000	OS/2 Server	Windows WS	LLC R D=F0 S=F0 RR NR=3
45	0.001	OS/2 Server	Windows WS	NETB D=21 S=01 Data ACK
46	0.001	Windows WS	OS/2 Server	LLC R D=F0 S=F0 RR NR=3
47	0.002	OS/2 Server	Windows WS	SMB C Setup account DATZ343 SMB C Connect

				?????\\ISCSWEST\IPC$
48	0.001	Windows WS	OS/2 Server	LLC R D=F0 S=F0 RR NR=4
49	0.000	Windows WS	OS/2 Server	NETB D=01 S=21 Data ACK
50	0.000	OS/2 Server	Windows WS	LLC R D=F0 S=F0 RR NR=4
51	0.056	Windows WS	OS/2 Server	SMB R Setup
				SMB R IPC Connected
.				
.				
.				
471	0.004	NetBIOS	Windows WS	NETB Find name PRTSRVN
472	0.003	Windows WS	PrtSvrN	NETB Name PRTSRVN recognized
473	0.001	PrtSvrN	Windows WS	LLC C D=F0 S=F0 SABME P
474	0.001	Windows WS	PrtSvrN	LLC R D=F0 S=F0 UA F
475	0.000	PrtSvrN	Windows WS	LLC C D=F0 S=F0 RR NR=0 P
476	0.000	Windows WS	PrtSvrN	LLC R D=F0 S=F0 RR NR=0 F
477	0.000	PrtSvrN	Windows WS	NETB D=F6 S=04 Session init
478	0.001	Windows WS	PrtSvrN	LLC R D=F0 S=F0 RR NR=1
479	0.001	Windows WS	PrtSvrN	NETB D=04 S=F6 Session conf
480	0.000	PrtSvrN	Windows WS	LLC R D=F0 S=F0 RR NR=1
481	0.002	PrtSvrN	Windows WS	SMB C PC NET PGM 1.0 (more)
482	0.001	Windows WS	PrtSvrN	LLC R D=F0 S=F0 RR NR=2
483	0.001	Windows WS	PrtSvrN	NETB D=04 S=F6 Data ACK
484	0.000	PrtSvrN	Windows WS	LLC R D=F0 S=F0 RR NR=2
485	0.004	Windows WS	PrtSvrN	SMB R Negotiated Protocol 0
486	0.000	PrtSvrN	Windows WS	LLC R D=F0 S=F0 RR NR=3
487	0.001	PrtSvrN	Windows WS	NETB D=F6 S=04 Data ACK
488	0.001	Windows WS	PrtSvrN	LLC R D=F0 S=F0 RR NR=3
489	0.001	PrtSvrN	Windows WS	SMB C Connect
				LPT1:\\PRTSRVN\LASER3N
490	0.001	Windows WS	PrtSvrN	LLC R D=F0 S=F0 RR NR=4
491	0.001	Windows WS	PrtSvrN	NETB D=04 S=F6 Data ACK
492	0.000	PrtSvrN	Windows WS	LLC R D=F0 S=F0 RR NR=4
493	0.008	Windows WS	PrtSvrN	SMB R T=11D1 Connected
494	0.000	PrtSvrN	Windows WS	LLC R D=F0 S=F0 RR NR=5
495	0.001	PrtSvrN	Windows WS	NETB D=F6 S=04 Data ACK
.				
.				
.				
519	0.727	OS/2 Server	Windows WS	SMB C Open \BIN\WINSTART.BAT
520	0.001	Windows WS	OS/2 Server	LLC R D=F0 S=F0 RR NR=87
521	0.000	Windows WS	OS/2 Server	NETB D=02 S=22 Data ACK
522	0.001	OS/2 Server	Windows WS	LLC R D=F0 S=F0 RR NR=92

.
.
.

582	1.248	OS/2 Server	Windows WS	SMB C Open \BIN\PFTP.EXE
583	0.001	Windows WS	OS/2 Server	LLC R D=F0 S=F0 RR NR=90
584	0.000	Windows WS	OS/2 Server	NETB D=02 S=22 Data ACK
585	0.002	OS/2 Server	Windows WS	LLC R D=F0 S=F0 RR NR=95
586	0.043	Windows WS	OS/2 Server	SMB R F=0016 Opened
587	0.001	OS/2 Server	Windows WS	LLC R D=F0 S=F0 RR NR=96
588	0.004	OS/2 Server	Windows WS	NETB D=22 S=02 Data ACK
589	0.000	Windows WS	OS/2 Server	LLC R D=F0 S=F0 RR NR=91
590	0.014	OS/2 Server	Windows WS	SMB C F=0016 Rd Bk Raw 64 at 0
591	0.002	Windows WS	OS/2 Server	NETB D=02 S=22 Data ACK
592	0.000	Windows WS	OS/2 Server	LLC R D=F0 S=F0 RR NR=92
593	0.001	Windows WS	OS/2 Server	NETB D=02 S=22 Data, 64 bytes
594	0.000	OS/2 Server	Windows WS	LLC R D=F0 S=F0 RR NR=97
595	0.001	OS/2 Server	Windows WS	LLC R D=F0 S=F0 RR NR=98
596	0.003	OS/2 Server	Windows WS	NETB D=22 S=02 Data ACK

.
.
.

865	0.007	OS/2 Server	Windows WS	SMB C F=0016 Close
866	0.001	Windows WS	OS/2 Server	LLC R D=F0 S=F0 RR NR=118
867	0.000	Windows WS	OS/2 Server	NETB D=02 S=22 Data ACK
868	0.003	Windows WS	OS/2 Server	SMB R Closed
869	0.000	OS/2 Server	Windows WS	LLC R D=F0 S=F0 RR NR=77
870	0.002	OS/2 Server	Windows WS	LLC R D=F0 S=F0 RR NR=78
871	0.004	OS/2 Server	Windows WS	NETB D=22 S=02 Data ACK
872	0.001	Windows WS	OS/2 Server	LLC R D=F0 S=F0 RR NR=119
873	0.124	Broadcast	Windows WS	ARP C PA=[34.0.31.254] PRO=IP
874	0.001	Windows WS	Router MGS	ARP R PA=[34.0.31.254] HA=00003000EF30 PRO=IP
875	0.014	Router MGS	Windows WS	TCP D=21 S=5044 SYN SEQ=0 LEN=0 WIN=512
876	0.071	Windows WS	Router MGS	TCP D=5044 S=21 SYN ACK=1 SEQ=76544276 LEN=0 WIN=8192
877	0.009	Router MGS	Windows WS	TCP D=21 S=5044 ACK=76544277 WIN=512
878	0.066	Windows WS	Router MGS	FTP R PORT=5044 220-FTPSERVE at ISCH00ARNA, 11:01:08 on 05/30/91<0D>...
879	0.010	Router MGS	Windows WS	TCP D=21 S=5044 ACK=76544387 WIN=511

880	0.585	PrtSvrS	Windows WS	LLC C D=F0 S=F0 RR NR=5 P
881	0.000	Windows WS	PrtSvrS	LLC R D=F0 S=F0 RR NR=6 F
882	2.006	Broadcast	Windows WS	MAC Standby Monitor Present
883	0.689	Broadcast	Windows WS	MAC Standby Monitor Present
884	0.301	OS/2 Server	Windows WS	LLC C D=F0 S=F0 RR NR=78 P
885	0.000	PrtSvrN	Windows WS	LLC C D=F0 S=F0 RR NR=6 P
886	0.000	Windows WS	OS/2 Server	LLC R D=F0 S=F0 RR NR=119 F
887	0.000	Windows WS	PrtSvrN	LLC R D=F0 S=F0 RR NR=6 F
888	0.106	Router MGS	Windows WS	FTP C PORT=5044 USER datz343<0D><0A>
889	0.080	Windows WS	Router MGS	TCP D=5044 S=21 ACK=15 WIN=8178
890	0.015	Windows WS	Router MGS	FTP R PORT=5044 331 Send password please.<0D><0A>
891	0.008	Router MGS	Windows WS	TCP D=21 S=5044 ACK=76544414 WIN=511
892	0.520	Windows WS	PrtSvrS	LLC C D=F0 S=F0 RR NR=6 P
893	0.000	PrtSvrS	Windows WS	LLC R D=F0 S=F0 RR NR=5 F
894	2.305	Router MGS	Windows WS	FTP C PORT=5044 PASS puffer<0D><0A>
895	0.036	Windows WS	Router MGS	TCP D=5044 S=21 ACK=28 WIN=8165
896	0.377	Windows WS	Router MGS	FTP R PORT=5044 230 DATZ343 is logged on<0D><0A>
897	0.007	Router MGS	Windows WS	TCP D=21 S=5044 ACK=76544441 WIN=511
898	0.538	PrtSvrS	Windows WS	LLC C D=F0 S=F0 RR NR=5 P
899	0.000	PrtSvrN	Windows WS	LLC C D=F0 S=F0 RR NR=6 P
900	0.000	OS/2 Server	Windows WS	LLC C D=F0 S=F0 RR NR=78 P
901	0.000	Windows WS	PrtSvrS	LLC R D=F0 S=F0 RR NR=6 F
902	0.000	Windows WS	PrtSvrN	LLC R D=F0 S=F0 RR NR=6 F
903	0.000	Windows WS	OS/2 Server	LLC R D=F0 S=F0 RR NR=119 F
904	2.554	Router MGS	Windows WS	FTP C PORT=5044 port 34,0,24,67, 19,190<0D><0A>
905	0.093	Windows WS	Router MGS	TCP D=5044 S=21 ACK=52 WIN=8141
906	0.012	Windows WS	Router MGS	FTP R PORT=5044 200 Port request OK.<0D><0A>
907	0.004	Broadcast	Windows WS	MAC Standby Monitor Present
908	0.004	Router MGS	Windows WS	TCP D=21 S=5044 ACK=76544463 WIN=511
909	0.039	Router MGS	Windows WS	FTP C PORT=5044 LIST<0D><0A>

910	0.048	Windows WS	Router MGS	TCP D=5044 S=21
				ACK=58 WIN=8135
911	0.971	Windows WS	PrtSvrS	LLC C D=F0 S=F0 RR NR=6 P
912	0.000	PrtSvrS	Windows WS	LLC R D=F0 S=F0 RR NR=5 F
913	0.217	Windows WS	Router MGS	TCP D=5054 S=20 SYN
				SEQ=167535876
				LEN=0 WIN=8192
914	0.007	Router MGS	Windows WS	TCP D=20 S=5054 SYN
				ACK=167535877 SEQ=0
				LEN=0 WIN=512
915	0.004	Windows WS	Router MGS	FTP R PORT=5044 125
				List started OK.<0D><0A>
916	0.008	Router MGS	Windows WS	TCP D=21 S=5044
				ACK=76544485 WIN=511
917	0.025	Windows WS	Router MGS	TCP D=5054 S=20
				ACK=1 WIN=8192
918	0.004	OS/2 Server	Windows WS	LLC C D=F0 S=F0 RR NR=78 P
919	0.000	PrtSvrN	Windows WS	LLC C D=F0 S=F0 RR NR=6 P
920	0.000	Windows WS	OS/2 Server	LLC R D=F0 S=F0 RR NR=119 F
921	0.000	Windows WS	PrtSvrN	LLC R D=F0 S=F0 RR NR=6 F
922	0.055	Windows WS	Router MGS	TCP D=5054 S=20 FIN ACK=1
				SEQ=167535877
				LEN=187 WIN=8192
923	0.008	Router MGS	Windows WS	TCP D=20 S=5054 FIN
				ACK=167536065 SEQ=1
				LEN=0 WIN=511
924	0.044	Windows WS	Router MGS	TCP D=5054 S=20
				ACK=2 WIN=8191
925	0.014	Windows WS	Router MGS	FTP R PORT=5044 250
				List completed
				successfully.<0D><0A>
926	0.166	Router MGS	Windows WS	TCP D=21 S=5044
				ACK=76544519 WIN=511
927	1.447	Windows WS	PrtSvrS	NETB Session alive
928	0.001	PrtSvrS	Windows WS	LLC R D=F0 S=F0 RR NR=6
929	2.259	PrtSvrN	Windows WS	LLC C D=F0 S=F0 RR NR=6 P
930	0.000	OS/2 Server	Windows WS	LLC C D=F0 S=F0 RR NR=78 P
931	0.000	Windows WS	PrtSvrN	LLC R D=F0 S=F0 RR NR=6 F
932	0.000	Windows WS	OS/2 Server	LLC R D=F0 S=F0 RR NR=119 F
933	0.998	PrtSvrS	Windows WS	LLC C D=F0 S=F0 RR NR=6 P
934	0.000	Windows WS	PrtSvrS	LLC R D=F0 S=F0 RR NR=6 F
935	0.667	Broadcast	Windows WS	MAC Standby Monitor Present

.
.
.

996	0.215	Broadcast	Windows WS	MAC Standby Monitor Present
997	0.567	Windows WS	PrtSvrN	NETB Session alive
998	0.414	PrtSvrN	Windows WS	LLC C D=F0 S=F0 RR NR=6 P
999	0.000	Windows WS	PrtSvrN	LLC R D=F0 S−F0 RR NR=6 F
1000	0.670	Windows WS	PrtSvrN	LLC C D=F0 S=F0 RR NR=6 P
1001	0.328	Error Mon.	Windows WS	MAC Report Soft Error

.
.
.

1071	0.678	Error Mon.	Windows WS	MAC Report Soft Error
1072	0.046	Windows WS	PrtSvrS	LLC C D=F0 S=F0 RR NR=6 P
1073	0.273	PrtSvrS	Windows WS	LLC C D=F0 S=F0 RR NR=6 P
1074	0.000	OS/2 Server	Windows WS	LLC C D=F0 S=F0 RR NR=78 P
1075	0.000	Windows WS	PrtSvrS	LLC R D=F0 S=F0 RR NR=6 F
1076	0.000	Windows WS	OS/2 Server	LLC R D=F0 S=F0 RR NR=119 F
1077	0.053	Windows WS	OS/2 Server	LLC C D=F0 S=F0 RR NR=119 P
1078	0.675	Windows WS	PrtSvrS	LLC R D=F0 S=F0 DM
1079	1.189	Error Mon.	Windows WS	MAC Report Soft Error
1080	0.087	Broadcast	Windows WS	MAC Standby Monitor Present
1081	1.047	Windows WS	OS/2 Server	LLC C D=F0 S=F0 RR NR=119 P
1082	1.904	Error Mon.	Windows WS	MAC Report Soft Error
1083	1.095	Windows WS	OS/2 Server	LLC C D=F0 S=F0 RR NR=119 P
1084	2.184	Error Mon.	Windows WS	MAC Report Soft Error
1085	0.777	Broadcast	Windows WS	MAC Standby Monitor Present
1086	0.037	Windows WS	OS/2 Server	LLC C D=F0 S=F0 RR NR=119 P
1087	2.183	Error Mon.	Windows WS	MAC Report Soft Error
1088	0.815	Windows WS	OS/2 Server	LLC C D=F0 S=F0 RR NR=119 P
1089	2.183	Error Mon.	Windows WS	MAC Report Soft Error
1090	0.815	Windows WS	OS/2 Server	LLC C D=F0 S=F0 RR NR=119 P
1091	0.961	Broadcast	Windows WS	MAC Standby Monitor Present
1092	1.221	Error Mon.	Windows WS	MAC Report Soft Error
1093	0.815	Windows WS	OS/2 Server	LLC C D=F0 S=F0 RR NR=119 P

Trace 6.9.6a.   TCP/IP Protocols Under Windows (Summary)

Sniffer Network Analyzer data 30-May-91 at 10:53:14, TCPWIN.TRC, Pg 1

```
- - - - - - - - - - - - - - Frame 1001 - - - - - - - - - - - - - - - -
DLC: ——- DLC Header ——-
DLC:
DLC:  Frame 1001 arrived at  10:56:07.766; frame size is 48 (0030 hex) bytes.
DLC:  AC: Frame priority 0,  Reservation priority 0,  Monitor count 1
DLC:  FC: MAC frame,  PCF attention code: None
DLC:  FS: Addr recognized indicators: 00, Frame copied indicators: 00
DLC:  Destination = Functional address C00000000008, Error Mon.
DLC:  Source     = Station IBM  6B95E7, Windows WS
DLC:
MAC: ——- MAC data ——-
MAC:
MAC:  MAC Command: Report Soft Error
MAC:  Source: Ring station, Destination: Ring Error Monitor
MAC:  Subvector type: Isolating Error Counts
MAC:      0 line errors,    0 internal errors,    0 burst errors
MAC:        0 AC errors,      0 abort delimiters transmitted
MAC:  Subvector type: Non-Isolating Error Counts
MAC:      0 lost frame errors,  3 receiver congestion,  0 FC errors
MAC:        0 frequency errors,   0 token errors
MAC:  Subvector type: Physical Drop Number 00000000
MAC:  Subvector type: Upstream Neighbor Address 400006020014
MAC:
```

Trace 6.9.6b. Windows Workstation Report Soft Error Details

In this chapter, we have completed our tour of the DARPA protocol stack as far as user applications are concerned. We have one more higher-layer topic to consider: the management of TCP/IP-based internetworks. We will study the Simple Network Management Protocol (SNMP) and Common Management Information Protocol (CMIP) in Chapter 7.

6.10 References

[6-1]   Stallings, William. *Handbook of Computer-Communications Standards*, Vol. 3, second edition. McMillan Publishing Company, 1990.

[6-2]   Braden, R. "Requirements for Internet Hosts: Application and Support"
        RFC 1123, Internet Engineering Task Force, October 1989.

[6-3]   Reynolds, J. K., et. al. "Assigned Numbers." RFC 1340, ISI, July 1992.

[6-4]   Sollins, K. R. "The TFTP Protocol (Revision 2)." RFC 783, MIT, June
        1981.

[6-5]   Postel, J. "File Transfer Protocol." RFC 959, ISI, October 1985.

[6-6]   Romkey, John. "FTP's Tiresome Problems." *ConneXions* (September 1987):
        9-11.

[6-7]   Sun Microsystems, Inc. "RPC: Remote Procedure Call Protocol Specifi-
        cation, Version 2." RFC 1057, June 1988.

[6-8]   Sun Microsystems, Inc. "XDR: External Data Representation Standard."
        RFC 1014, June 1987.

[6-9]   Sun Microsystems, Inc. "NFS: Network File System Protocol Specifica-
        tion." RFC 1094, March 1989.

[6-10] Peacock, Jeffrey. "Two Sound Technologies." UNIX Review, (March 1991):
        18-22.

[6-11] Sanderson, Don. "Distributed File Systems: Stepping Stone to Distributed
        Computing." LAN Technology (May 1991): 41-52.

[6-12] Malamud, Carl. *Analyzing Sun Networks*. Van Nostrand Reinhold, 1992.

[6-13] Postel, J. et. al. "TELNET Protocol Specification." RFC 854, ISI, May 1983.

[6-14] Postel, J. et. al. "TELNET Option Specifications." RFC 855, ISI, May 1983.

[6-15]   Shein, Barry. "The TELNET Protocol." ConneXions (October 1989): 32-38.

[6-16]   Postel, J. "Simple Mail Transfer Protocol." RFC 821, ISI, August 1982.

[6-17]   Crocker, David H. "Standard for the Format of ARPA Internet Text Messages." RFC 822, University of Delaware, August 1982.

[6-18]   Blum, Daniel. "Crossing the enterprise with LAN E-mail messages." Network World (March 2, 1992):1-47.

[6-19]   Haugdahl, J. Scott. *Inside NetBIOS*, 3rd edition. Architecture Technology Corporation, 1992.

[6-20]   NetBIOS Working Group. "Protocol Standard for a NetBIOS Service on TCP/UDP Transport: Concepts and Methods." RFC 1001, March 1987.

[6-21]   NetBIOS Working Group. "Protocol Standard for a NetBIOS Service on a TCP/UDP Transport: Detailed Specifications." RFC 1002, March 1987.

[6-22]   Spine, R. editor. "FYI on a Network Management Tool Catalog: Tools for Monitoring and Debugging TCP/IP Internets and Interconnected Devices." RFC 1147, SPARTA, Inc., April 1990.

[6-23]   VanBokkelen, J. "TELNET Terminal-Type Option." RFC 1091, FTP Software, Inc., February 1989.

[6-24]   Nasr, Alex. "Tn3270: An Interoperability Option." *3TECH, The 3Com Technical Journal* (Winter 1992): 51-59.

CHAPTER 7

Managing the Internet

The term *network management* means different things to different people. A corporate executive might consider the value of his or her internetwork—such as the data and time savings that come from internetworking—and the costs associated with downtime. A vendor sees potential sales opportunities; any incompatibilities between the network management system and the devices to be managed mean a potential sales opportunity. Finally, the network manager—the person in the trenches, catching it from users, corporate managers, and vendors— sees "network management" as a dream; it's something he or she will be able to accomplish once all the fires are out and as long as no new fires erupt in the meantime.

So how can network managers find the time to design a plan to save time? And where does troubleshooting end and management begin? These issues have faced many managers of TCP/IP-related internetworks, and they undoubtedly gave rise to the development of the most popular protocol for internetwork management: the Simple Network Management Protocol (SNMP). In this chapter, we'll study the alternatives for managing TCP/IP-based internetworks, SNMP, and other options from ISO and IEEE. We'll begin by discussing the issue of network management in general.

7.1 Managing Internetworks

All major players in the computing marketplace offer some type of network management system. These vendors include IBM, DEC, Hewlett-Packard, Novell, Proteon, and a host of others. The requirement for network management systems undoubtedly grew out of the need to manage numerous terminals that were initially connected to mainframes and later to LANs. Today, network or internetwork management systems assist the human manager in understanding and dealing with the complexities of the internetwork.

Network management systems have many common threads, regardless of their size, shape, or manufacturer. ISO 7498-4, [7-1], which accompanies the Open Systems Interconnection Reference Model (OSI-RM), summarizes these similarities and offers a framework for network management. The standard divides the functions of network management into five Specific Management Functional Areas (SMFAs), shown in Figure 7-1. These include fault management, accounting management, configuration management, performance management, and security management. We'll look at each of these areas individually, although in practice there is some overlap between them.

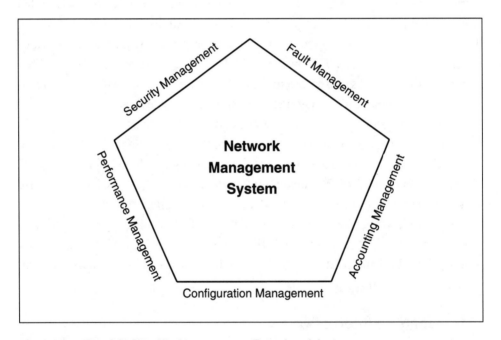

Figure 7-1. The OSI Specific Management Functional Areas

7.1.1 Fault Management

A fault within open systems is defined as something that causes those systems "to fail to meet their operational objectives." Three elements are involved in managing system faults: detection of the fault, isolation of the fault to a particular component, and correction of the fault. Fault management, therefore, may include the maintenance of error logs, error detection processes, and diagnostic testing procedures. For many managers, the term *network management* is synonymous with *fault management*.

7.1.2 Accounting Management

As businesses strive to more clearly identify their sources of revenue and expense, the practice of charging individual groups or organizations for their use of network resources is becoming more common. Accounting management provides mechanisms to identify costs, inform the users of costs incurred, and associate tariff information with resource use.

7.1.3 Configuration Management

Configuration management involves detailing parameters of network configuration, the current topology, and operational status of the network, as well as associating user names with devices. Also included is the ability to change the configuration of the system when necessary. Medium to large networks often find that the human resource costs necessary to move, add, and change network devices such as terminals (sometimes known as the MAC costs) can be very high.

7.1.4 Performance Management

Performance and fault management are difficult to separate. High performance usually implies a low incident of faults. Performance management, however, goes beyond minimizing faults; it is responsible for gathering statistics on the operation of the network, maintaining and analyzing logs of the state of the system, and optimizing network operation.

7.1.5 Security Management

With recent news about viruses, worms, and hackers into the Internet, network security has become a new sub-industry. The issue of security management includes the ability to create, delete, and control security services; distribute security-related information; or report security-related events. Other areas of responsibility include enforcing secure passwords for users; controlling access to subnets or hosts via bridges, routers, or gateways; and providing remote access to network elements for purposes of network diagnostics.

7.1.6 Managing TCP/IP-based Internetworks

After our discussion about managing open systems, it's logical to ask if there's any difference between managing generic open systems and TCP/IP-based internetworks. Theoretically, the answer is no, since all internetworks are based on some type of layered architecture, be it OSI, DARPA, or SNA. Practically, however, there are big differences. First, there's a difference in perspective: TCP/IP-based internetworks are designed to be multivendor systems; systems built upon SNA or DECnet are single-vendor systems. Managers of multi-vendor systems start with different assumptions than those who purchase all their equipment from one supplier. If you know it's your job (not the vendor's) to integrate all of the sub-systems, you'll look at management as an integral part of the internetwork, not an ancillary element.

A second difference lies in the implementation of network management systems and the protocols available for use. Within the Internet community, the Simple Network Management Protocol (SNMP) has gathered the most support from network management system vendors and from internetworking device manufacturers. A second standard, known as the Common Management Information Protocol (CMIP) has received international support from organizations such as the ISO, CCITT, and IEEE. A TCP/IP-based version of CMIP, known as CMOT (CMIP over TCP/IP), is also available as RFC 1189, but it has not gathered the widespread support of SNMP. Both SNMP and CMIP/CMOT are based on an Agent/Manager paradigm, which resembles the Client/Server paradigm with which we are all familiar. We'll study this model in the next section.

The Internet Activities Board (IAB) supports the use of both SNMP and CMIP/CMOT, as discussed in RFC 1052 [7-2]. Two papers in the August 1990 issue of *ConneXions, The Interoperability Report*, [7-3] and [7-4], provide practical information on the management of TCP/IP-based internetworks. References [7-5] through [7-7] discuss the various options available for managing TCP/IP-based internetworks. Marshall Rose's [7-8] and Uyless Black's [7-9] books are also valuable references in the network management arena.

7.2 The Agent/Manager Model

In the last few years, computing architectures have migrated from centralized, mainframe-based environments to distributed, minicomputer environments to today's popular client/server LAN environments. The architecture of network management systems has mirrored the migration path of computing architectures. They have moved from host-based systems to distributed systems to today's systems, which use a methodology called the Agent/Manager Model (shown in Figure 7-2), which resembles the Client/Server paradigm. (Agent/Manager is also called the Managed System/Managing System.)

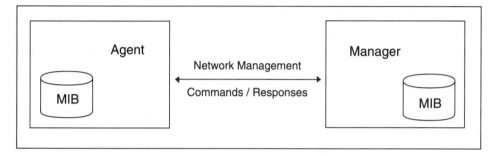

Figure 7-2. The Agent/Manager Model

To begin, the Agent/Manager system manages devices, which are called *objects*. ISO 7498-4 [7-1] defines four characteristics for each object: its attributes, its operations, the notifications it issues, and its relationships with other objects. Thus, the term *object* goes beyond a physical device to encompass the device's behaviors. The definition for each object is contained in the Management Information Base (MIB), which we will discuss in the next section.

The Agent resides in the object and reports the object's current status to the Manager. It is becoming more common for internetworking devices such as bridges and routers to come with Agent software preinstalled, rather than requiring additional software.

The Manager is a console that maintains global knowledge of the internetwork in question. The console includes three functions: a Graphical User Interface (GUI), a database, and communications facilities. The GUI enables the human manager to visualize the internetwork. With most systems, the GUI draws a topological map that indicates the location and status (normal, abnormal, alarm, and so on.) of each managed element and the links between elements. The console's database keeps track of the internetwork elements and the parameters for those elements. The console also includes a mechanism for communicating with the managed elements, using a protocol such as SNMP or CMIP. These three functions enable the Manager to see what is happening on the internetwork, communicate with the devices being managed to query or modify parameters, and dynamically oversee the internetwork's operation. Two excellent articles that describe the Agent/Manager paradigm are [7-10] and [7-11].

Two popular implementations of the Agent/Manager paradigm are SNMP and CMIP/CMOT. Over the past few years, a controversy has raged in the internetworking industry over whether the SNMP or the CMIP/CMOT protocol will emerge as the predominant choice for network management. Both have a number of advantages and disadvantages. For example, SNMP is a proven technology, CMIP is unproven. SNMP is relatively inexpensive in its implementation, CMIP is not. On the other hand, CMIP is much more powerful than SNMP, although many current internetwork applications are satisfied with SNMP. CMIP is also an international (ISO) standard, SNMP is a de facto (Internet) standard. CMIP is connection-oriented, hence more reliable, while SNMP is connectionless. References [7-12] and [7-13] provide further details on the underlying philosophies of these two protocols; we will look at them individually in Sections 7.4 and 7.5. By most indications, SNMP appears to be the industry leader, and for that reason we will concentrate our discussion on SNMP.

Once you've implemented the Agent/Manager paradigm and selected a way to communicate (i.e., SNMP or CMIP) between internetwork elements, you're almost ready to manage the internetwork. The final issue to consider is the type and amount of information you need to keep track of. We will discuss the nature of management information in the next section.

7.3 Network Management Information

In the previous section, we discussed how the Agent/Manager model carries network management information between devices on a distributed, managed internetwork. The type and amount of network management information transmitted over the internet determines the amount of processing and storage the Agent and the Manager will require, and it may also impact the choice of network management protocol—simple (SNMP) or more complex (CMIP/CMOT).

The information is contained within a management system, which, because of the complexity of the information being managed, consists of multiple components: the Structure of Management Information (SMI), the Management Information Base (MIB), and the protocol (such as SNMP). The SMI identifies the structures that describe the management information, the MIB details the objects to be managed, and the protocol communicates between Agent and Manager. Individual documents describe these three components. SMI is detailed in RFC 1155 [7-14]. MIBs are defined in RFC 1212 [7-15], with two different MIBs, designated MIB-I and MIB-II, detailed in RFC 1156 [7-16] and RFC 1213 [7-17], respectively. The two management protocols have separate documents: RFC 1157 [7-18] for SNMP, and RFC 1189 [7-19] for CMIP/CMOT.

7.3.1. The Structure of Management Information

Since internetworks can be quite large and can maintain voluminous amounts of information about each device, network managers need a way to organize and manage that information. The SMI provides a mechanism to name and organize objects. The MIB stores the information about each managed object.

The SMI uses a conceptual tree, with various objects representing the leaves, to help users visualize the structure of the Internet. The objects are represented using the concepts from an ISO protocol, known as Abstract Syntax Notation - 1 (ASN.1), [7-20]. The SMI assigns each object a sequence of integers, known as an Object Identifier, to locate its position on the tree (see Figure 7-3).

The root of the tree has no name, but it has three branches, called children. Different standards bodies administer different branches: the CCITT is in charge of Branch 0; ISO administers Branch 1; CCITT and ISO jointly administer Branch 2.

ISO designates its branch for several organizations. For example, it has given Subtree 3 to other international organizations. ISO gives Subtree 1 to the U.S. Department of Defense (DOD), which uses it for the Internet objects. So far in the Internet subtree, all Object Identifiers begin with 1.3.6.1, which means that they belong to the ISO, ORG, DOD, Internet subtree.

The Internet subtree has four branches: Directory (1), Mgmt (2), Experimental (3), and Private (4). Directory is planned for the OSI Directory; Mgmt is used for objects defined in the Internet Activities Board (IAB)-approved documents; Experimental is used for Internet experiments; and Private is defined unilaterally.

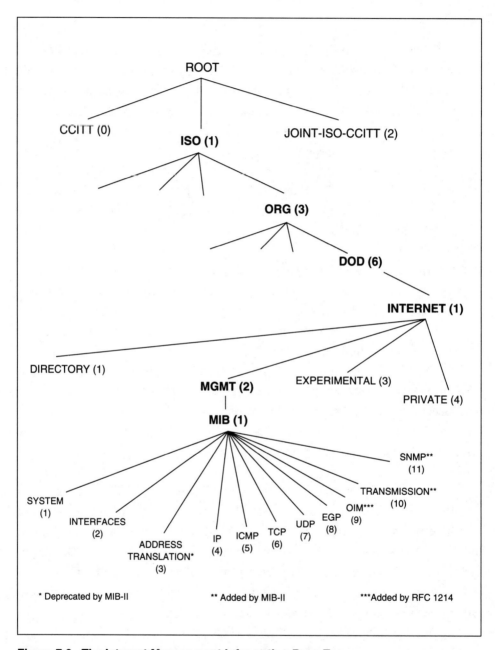

Figure 7-3. The Internet Management Information Base Tree

The Internet Assigned Numbers Authority (IANA), given in RFC 1060, administers the Experimental and Private branches. IANA designates Branch 1 under the Private subtree for Enterprises and assigns vendors an Enterprise subtree to identify their various devices. For example, an Object identifier associated with the ABC Company would be designated 1.3.6.1.4.1.a. The *1.3.6.1* designates the Internet subtree, *4.1* indicates a Private, Enterprise subtree and *a* is assigned to the ABC Company. The ABC Company could further assign identifiers for its bridges, routers, NICs, and so on; for example, 1.3.6.1.4.1.a.1.1.

This naming structure has been described as having the form *prefix.version.tail* [7-13]. In the example above, the prefix is *1.3.6.1.4* (the Private subtree), although a Mgmt subtree (1.3.6.1.2) used with the various MIBs is also common. The version designator indicates the version of the MIB being employed. Both MIB-I and MIB-II use Mgmt 1 as their version number. Thus, 1.3.6.1.2.1 becomes the prefix.version notation for any objects defined by either MIB-I or MIB-II. The MIB specifies the tail portion of the Object Identifier.

In addition to the Object Identifier, the SMI defines six object types. These include the NetWorkAddress, IpAddress, Counter, Gauge, TimeTicks, and Opaque. For example, the IpAddress type represents a 32-bit internet address. Further explanations about the syntax and usage of the types are given in RFC 1155.

7.3.2 Management Information Bases

While the SMI defines the tree structure for the Object Identifiers, the MIB defines information about the actual objects being managed and/or controlled. For example, the MIB might store an IP routing table and its table entries.

Two versions of the Internet MIB have been published: MIB-I (RFC 1156, [7-16]) and the enhanced MIB-II (RFC 1213, [7-17]). Within each MIB, the objects are divided into various groups. Grouping the objects accomplishes two objectives: it allows a more orderly assignment of Object Identifiers, and it defines the objects that the Agents must implement. The currently defined groups include:

Group	Object ID	Description
System	mib-2 1	Description of that entity.
Interfaces	mib-2 2	Number of network interfaces that can send/receive IP datagrams.
AT	mib-2 3	Tables of Network Address to Physical Address translations.
IP	mib-2 4	IP routing and datagram statistics.
ICMP	mib-2 5	ICMP I/O statistics.
TCP	mib-2 6	TCP connection parameters and statistics.
UDP	mib-2 7	UDP traffic statistics and datagram delivery problems.
EGP	mib-2 8	EGP traffic, neighbors, and states.
Transmission	mib-2 10	Transmission media information (future use).
SNMP	mib-2 11	SNMP-related objects.

MIB-II has rendered the Address Translation (AT) group obsolete and added the Transmission and SNMP groups. MIB-II has also added new values, variables, tables, columns, and so on to other groups. For example, the standard mentions a CMOT Object Identifier (mib-2 9), which is described in RFC 1214 on OSI Internet Management (OIM). Other sources of information on MIBs include VandenBerg's "MIB II Extends SNMP Interoperability" [7-21], Perkins' "How to Read and Use an SNMP MIB" [7-22], Stewart's "Development and Integration of a Management Information Base" [7-23], and 3Com Corporation's *Introduction to Simple Network Management Protocol: A Self-Study Guide* [7-24].

A number of MIBs, both standard and vendor-specific (private), are under development. One example is the RMON MIB, used for Remote Network Monitoring. Its functions include managing critical functions of remote networks, such as traffic thresholds, collisions on a particular segment, and alarms [7-25]. An example of a private MIB are DEC's extensions to support DECnet Phase IV, detailed in RFC 1289. This MIB complements the Internet MIB but provides additional support for specific DEC hardware and protocols, such as the Remote Bridge Management Software (RBMS) and the Digital Data Communications Message Protocol (DDCMP).

Below is a representative list of currently available MIBs:

RFC	Subject
1156	Management Information Base (MIB-I)
1212	Concise MIB Definitions
1213	Management Information Base (MIB-II)
1214	OSI Internet Management MIB
1227	SNMP MUX Protocol and MIB
1229	Extensions to the generic-interface MIB
1230	IEEE 802.4 Token Bus MIB
1231	IEEE 802.5 Token Ring MIB
1238	CLNS MIB
1253	OSPF Version 2 MIB
1284	Managed Objects for Ethernet
1285	FDDI MIB
1286	Managed Objects for Bridges
1289	DECnet Phase IV MIB Extensions
1304	Managed Objects for the SMDS SIP Interface

7.4 Simple Network Management Protocol (SNMP)

So far, we've discussed two of the three elements of a network management system: the Structure of Management Information (SMI) and the Management Information Base (MIB). These elements provide management information and the mechanism for accessing that information. The third element is the protocol used between the Agent and Manager.

The Internet Activities Board (IAB) determined the need for a network management protocol and reported it in RFC 1052 [7-2]. The IAB concluded that SNMP should be used in the short term, with OSI-based management strategies as the long-term solution. Network managers, however, needed solutions that could be implemented immediately. Since SNMP was available, it became the protocol of choice. Many analysts predict that it will be the favored long-term solution as well. SNMP, which we will study in this section, is used predominantly with TCP/IP-based internets. CMIP/CMOT is intended for OSI-based internetworks and IEEE 802 LANs. As TCP/IP-based internetworks migrate to OSI, their network management strategies should follow an SNMP-to-CMIP migration as well. We will discuss the OSI and IEEE strategies in Sections 7.5 and 7.6.

7.4.1 SNMP Architecture

The Simple Network Management Protocol was based upon the Simple Gateway Monitoring Protocol (SGMP), described in RFC 1028. It was developed to be an efficient means of sending network management information over a UDP transport, using Port numbers 161 (SNMP) and 162 (SNMPTRAP).

Although SNMP is an application, it is somewhat different from the other application protocols discussed in Chapter 6. As articulated by Case, et. al., "network management is an application fundamentally different in its requirements than any other application that makes use of the network" [7-26]. These differences include network management's need for ubiquity, supporting instrumentation, and robustness that may not be necessary for other upper-layer processes.

In the SNMP architecture (see Figure 7-4) are several elements that we explored earlier in this chapter. SNMP offers a management system that includes the SNMP Manager. The managed system includes an SNMP Agent, resources to be managed, and the SNMP messages (such as the Get and the GetResponse) that communicate the management information. Note that the protocol implements only five messages. Some excellent articles describing SNMP and its place in the network management arena are given in references [7-27] through [7-33].

7.4.2 SNMP Messages

SNMP is a "polling" protocol, in which the Manager asks a question (the poll), and the Agent responds. UDP transport transmits all SNMP messages, and all messages use Port number 161 except the Trap message, which uses Port number 162. The standard does not require SNMP implementations to accept messages that exceed 484 octets in length, although support for larger datagrams is recommended.

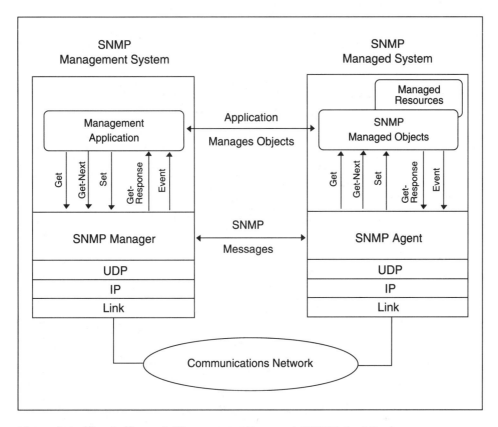

Figure 7-4. Simple Network Management Protocol (SNMP) Architecture
(©1990, IEEE)

The SNMP message follows the UDP header and is placed within a transmission frame (see Figure 7-5). The message consists of a Version Identifier, an SNMP Community name, and the SNMP Protocol Data Units (PDUs). The Version Identifier ensures that both SNMP endpoints use the same version of the protocol. The Community name is encoded as a string of octets and used for authentication; it ensures the proper relationship between the requesting SNMP Manager and the responding SNMP Agent. The combination of the Version Identifier and the Community name is sometimes called the Authentication header. This header is found in all SNMP messages.

Five PDUs are defined for SNMP. These include the GetRequest, GetResponse, GetNextRequest, SetRequest, and Trap. The GetRequest allows the SNMP Manager to access information stored in the Agent. The GetNextRequest is similar, but allows the Manager to obtain multiple values in the tree. SetRequest is used to change the value of a variable. GetResponse is a response to the GetRequest, Get-NextRequest, or SetRequest, and also contains error and status information. Finally, the Trap PDU reports on an event that has occurred.

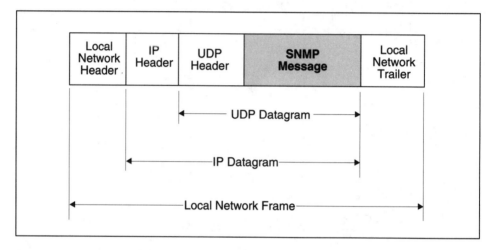

Figure 7-5. SNMP Message within a Transmission Frame

PDUs have two general structures, one for the Request/Response PDUs and another for the Trap (see Figures 7-6a and 7-6b, respectively.) The Request/Response PDUs contain five fields that identify and transfer the management information in question. The first subfield is a PDU Type, which specifies which of the five PDUs is in use. The values are:

Value	PDU Type
0	GetRequest
1	GetNextRequest
2	GetResponse
3	SetRequest
4	Trap

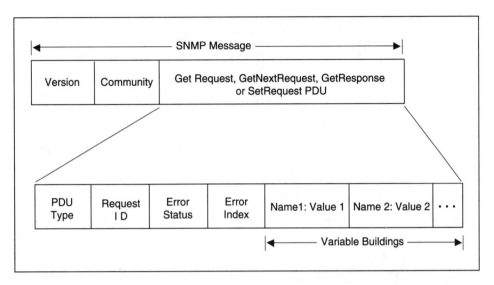

Figure 7-6a. SNMP GetRequest, GetNextRequest, GetResponse, and SetRequest PDU Structures

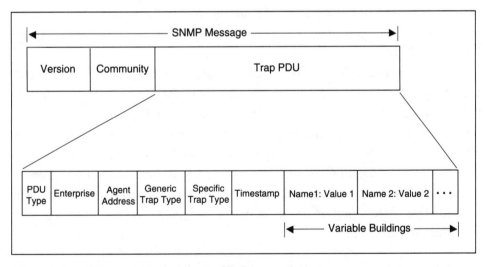

Figure 7-6b. SNMP Trap PDU Structure

The Request ID field correlates the request from the SNMP Manager with the response from the SNMP Agent. The Error Status field indicates that some exception occurred while processing the request. Values for that field are:

Value	Error	Description
0	noError	No error
1	tooBig	Operation results are too big for a single SNMP message
2	noSuchName	Unknown variable name
3	badValue	Incorrect value or variable when using SetRequest
4	readOnly	SetRequest not allowed for read-only variable
5	genErr	Other error

The Error Index field points to the variable in the Variable Bindings field that caused the error. The first variable is given Variable number 1, the second Variable number 2, and so on. The last field is the Variable Bindings (VarBind) field, which contains the management information being requested. A VarBind pairs an object name with its value. An example of a VarBind would be a sysDescr (System Description) for subtree 1.3.6.1.2.1.1.1 paired with a value that indicates the vendor-specified name for that system.

Because the Trap PDU reports on events rather than responding to the manager's query, it requires a different message structure. Seven fields follow the the Trap PDU's Version and Community fields (review Figure 7-6b.) The first field is the PDU Type, with the Trap assigned Type = 4. The second field is called Enterprise and contains the SNMP Agent's sysObjectID, which indicates the type of network management system located in that Agent. Next, the Agent Address field contains the IP address of the SNMP Agent that generated this trap. The Generic Trap Type specifies the exact type of message. There are seven possible values for this field:

Value	Trap	Description
0	coldStart	The sending protoco entity is reinitializing; the agent configuration or protocol entity implementation may be altered.

Value	Trap	Description
1	warmStart	The sending protocol entity is reinitializing; however, no alterations have been made.
2	linkDown	Communication link in the Agent has failed.
3	linkUp	Communication link in the Agent is now up.
4	Authentication Failure	The sending protocol entity has received an improperly authenticated message.
5	egpNeighborLoss	An EGP peer is down.
6	enterpriseSpecific	An enterprise-specific event has occurred, as defined in the Enterprise field that follows.

The Specific Trap Type elaborates on the type of trap indicated. The Timestamp field transmits the current value of the Agent's sysUpTime object, indicating when the indicated event occurred. As with the Request/Response PDUs, the Variable Bindings contain pairs of object names and values. Examples of the various SNMP PDUs will be explored in Section 7.9.

7.4.3 SNMP Directions

Despite its popularity, SNMP has some disadvantages. One obvious limitation is SNMP's use of a connectionless architecture based upon UDP transport. As discussed in Chapter 5, connectionless systems lack the reliability many applications may require. Second, it is cumbersome to retrieve SNMP information because the protocol offers no way to filter information. Thus, the SNMP Manager must obtain all the value(s) of the object(s), then determine whether they're of interest. (In contrast, CMIP allows conditional commands that query the value first, then determine whether the value should be transmitted.) Third, and associated with the information retrieval issue, polling of SNMP information (the GetRequest/GetResponse sequences) may consume precious internetwork bandwidth, especially if that polling is done over a WAN connection. References [7-11], [7-12], and [7-34] discuss the implications of these limitations in greater detail. Despite these limitations, SNMP has found widespread acceptance and is implemented by numerous vendors.

In addition to the benchmark standard, RFC 1157, a number of other documents describe the use and implementation of SNMP. These include:

RFC	Subject
1089	SNMP over Ethernet
1187	Bulk Table Retrieval with the SNMP
1215	Convention for Defining Traps
1227	SNMP MUX Protocol and MIB
1270	SNMP Communications Services
1283	SNMP over OSI
1298	SNMP over IPX
1303	Convention for Describing SNMP Agents

7.5 Common Management Information Protocol (CMIP/CMOT)

The ISO defined a framework for network management, ISO 7498-4 (discussed in Section 7.1) and the five Specific Management Functional Areas (SMFAs) shown in Figure 7-1. ISO further defines a Management Service interface that allows management applications to communicate within the OSI environment. This interface is the Common Management Information Service (CMIS) described in ISO/IEC 9595 [7-35]. The CMIS services provide for management operation, retrieval of information, and notification of network events. These services, along with the type of service, confirmed (C) or non-confirmed (NC), are listed below:

Service	Type	Description
M-GET	C	Information retrieval.
M-CANCEL-GET	C	Cancel outstanding M-GET.
M-SET	C/NC	Modify management information.
M-ACTION	C/NC	Perform an action.
M-CREATE	C	Create an instance of a managed object.
M-DELETE	C	Delete an instance of a managed object.
M-EVENT-REPORT	C/NC	Report of managed object event.

S. Mark Klerer's "The OSI Management Architecture: an Overview" [7-36] and Ian Sugarbroad's "An OSI-based Interoperability Architecture for Managing Hybrid Networks" [7-37] put the OSI network management architectural issues into perspective.

The second half of ISO's network management protocol story is the Common Management Information Protocol (CMIP), defined in ISO/IEC 9596-1 [7-38]. CMIP communicates network management information between systems. This protocol is much more rigorous than SNMP for several reasons. First, it was designed for open systems rather than for a single implementation such as the Internet, which necessarily increases the complexity of the operation. Second, CMIP is an association-oriented protocol, which means that the two CMIP processes must establish an association before sending any management messages. (Recall that SNMP is connectionless.) This association is governed by two ISO Application Layer standards: the Remote Operation Service Element (ROSE) and the Association Control Service Element (ACSE).

The benefits of CMIP's rigor are seen in the services it can perform beyond those available with SNMP. One example is filtering, which allows you to make an operation (such as an M-SET) conditional upon the value of an object's attribute. A second example is scoping, which allows you to apply the management operation to a portion of the object class. References [7-12] and [7-39] discuss these advantages in greater detail. These enhancements come with a price, however. The CMIP Agent consumes up to 400 Kbytes of memory, while its SNMP counterpart requires only 10 Kbytes [7-40].

As discussed earlier, the IAB (Internet Activities Board), as reported in RFC 1109, intended to provide a migration path from SNMP to CMIP, allowing TCP/IP-based internetworks to migrate to OSI protocols. RFC 1189 [7-19] defined the protocol portion of this migration—the CMOT (CMIP over TCP/IP) protocol suite. This protocol suite (see Figure 7-7) used the Internet protocols at the lower layers while incorporating the OSI management-related protocols, such as CMIP, at the higher layers. Either TCP or UDP may be used at the Transport Layer. Port numbers 163 (CMIP-Manager) and 164 (CMIP-Agent) are used for addressing at those layers. Lightweight Presentation Protocol (LPP), described in RFC 1085 [7-41], is defined for the Presentation Layer. LPP maps the ISO Management Service calls to or from TCP or UDP. References [7-42] and [7-43] provide further details on the design of CMOT.

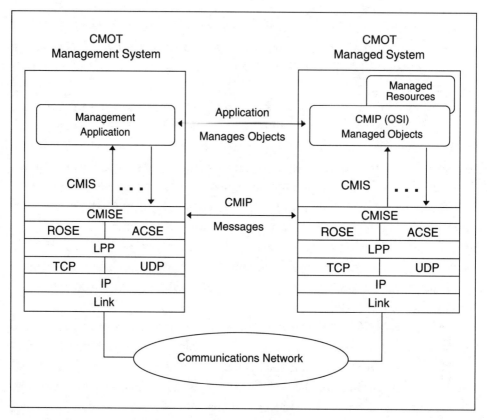

Figure 7-7. Common Management Information Protocol (CMOT) over TCP/IP Architecture *(©1990, IEEE)*

In addition to using the CMIP protocol, the OSI-based network management scheme required modifications to the MIB. In Section 7.3.2, we discussed the Internet standards and private MIBs that support the SNMP and/or CMIP protocols. At one time, the developers attempted to devise an SMI/MIB for use with both SNMP and CMIP. But as the development process got underway, the developers discovered that independent standards would best serve the industry. As a result, they wrote a MIB specifically for OSI Internetwork Management: RFC 1214 [7-44]. This MIB is a companion to the Internet MIB-II (RFC 1213) and makes the additions necessary to support CMIP.

One of the additions to MIB-II is a subtree for OSI Internet Management (OIM). Reviewing Figure 7-3, note that under MIB (1), group number 9 is defined for OIM.

This group number is reserved for OIM and has a subtree of its own, defined in RFC 1214. The structure of that subtree is:

Object	Identifier
cmotVersion:	oim 1
cmotACSEInfo:	oim 2
cmotSystemId:	oim 3
misc:	oim 4
objects:	oim 5
attributes:	oim 6
events:	oim 7
nameforms:	oim 8
actions:	oim 9

Other additions support ISO definitions, names, events, and name hierarchies as required by the OSI Structure of Management Information, designated ISO/IEC DIS 10165-1, 2, and 3. The OSI MIB itself is rather lengthy; readers contemplating a transition to OSI protocol stacks should study that document in its entirety.

7.6 IEEE LAN/MAN Management

The IEEE Project 802 LAN standards, such as 802.3 and 802.5, have been stable since the mid-1980s. With this basic architecture in place, the IEEE has been able to concentrate on the management of existing LANs and on emerging Metropolitan Area Network (MAN) architectures. The IEEE 802.1 standards, specifically 802.1B [7-45], are an outgrowth of those efforts.

The IEEE management structure is based on two other standards: the IEEE 802.2 Logical Link Control (LLC) and the ISO CMIP. It is sometimes referred to as CMOL (CMIP over LLC). The defined protocol uses the LLC connectionless service (called LLC Type 1), with the management information formatted according to the CMIP standard, ISO/IEC 9596-1 [7-38].

As a standards body, the IEEE has focused primarily on the Physical and Data Link Layers, with only a secondary interest in the rest of the OSI protocol stack. This focus extends to the functions it provides for LAN management. These functions are layered above the IEEE LAN/MAN Physical, Medium Access Control, and Logical Link Control Layers (see Figure 7-8).

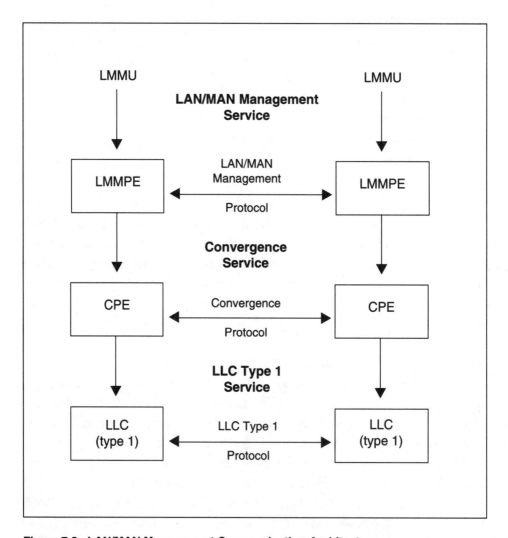

Figure 7-8. LAN/MAN Management Communication Architecture
(©1992, IEEE)

Three elements are necessary to communicate management information between hosts: the Convergence Protocol Entity (CPE), the LAN/MAN Management Protocol Entity (LMMPE), and the LAN/MAN Management Service (LMMS). The CPE, which uses the Convergence Protocol, is the lowest-layer element. The convergence function allows the two CPEs to be aware of the existence of their peers (detecting reboots, etc.) and to determine whether the information coming from their peers is in sequence and without loss or duplication. The LMMPE uses the LAN/MAN management protocol, derived from CMIP. The LMMS is the management service available to the LAN/MAN Management User (LMMU). LMMS uses the ISO CMIS to define its service offerings. The LMMUs are the Manager and Agent processes.

At this writing, the IEEE standards are still in draft form. Consult the IEEE standards office (see Appendix A) for current information regarding LAN/MAN management.

7.7 Network Management Systems

At the beginning of this chapter, we mentioned that the network management marketplace is a rapidly growing industry, comprised of a virtual "who's who" of internetworking vendors. The players in this market fall into two general categories: minicomputer and/or mainframe manufacturers, and internetworking device manufacturers. These two types of vendors come to internetwork management from two different perspectives. References [7-46] through [7-48] discuss implementations of network management systems that could be applied to TCP/IP-based internetworks.

The minicomputer/mainframe manufacturers use a host-centric approach to their internetwork management systems. As a result, their systems tend to use proprietary protocols to communicate network management information. For example, IBM's NetView is based on proprietary protocols and adds SNMP or CMIP/CMOT as required by the elements being managed. AT&T takes another approach, basing its system on the CMIP protocols but embellishing the standard when necessary. Other major players in this arena include DEC, Hewlett-Packard, and IBM. Their systems are described in references [7-49] through [7-52], respectively.

The second group of players in the network management market are vendors of internetworking devices such as bridges and routers, network operating systems, workstations, protocol analyzers, and other hardware devices. In many cases, the SNMP Manager software operates on a UNIX-based workstation. When considering one of these systems, determine the protocols and MIBs it supports. While most systems provide full support for SNMP, some do not support the TRAP PDU. If you must monitor vendor-specific MIBs, verify that the system supports these MIBs (and the specific objects and operations of those MIBs). References [7-53] through [7-56] are examples of recent articles describing network management systems from these vendors.

Within multivendor internetworks, it is not uncommon to have multiple network management systems as well. When this occurs, another, more global system must manage those separate management systems. This global manager would be called an Enterprise Manager. [7-57]. One example is the Open Software Foundation's (OSF) Distributed Management Environment (DME). Based on Hewlett-Packard's Open-View system, the DME integrates CMIP and SNMP into one cohesive system. With this system, the management protocol choice is dictated by the element management systems managing the end objects. The Enterprise Manager can communicate using either CMIP or SNMP and can integrate this information into one system.

7.8 Incorporating Agents into Internetworking Devices

The second half of the Manager/Agent paradigm is the Agent, and a number of manufacturers have begun to include Agent software in their internetworking devices. Vendors of subsystems that are physically remote from the central network location, such as bridges, routers, wiring hubs, and network interface cards, have expressed the greatest interest in Agents. *Network World* and AT&T Bell Laboratories recently conducted a series of tests of the compatibility between Agents and Managers (see References [7-58] through [7-60]). The tests identified areas of potential multi-vendor conflicts that can occur even when devices comply with the SNMP standard [7-58]. These reviews also scrutinized the vendors' documentation to discover limitations of a particular SNMP implementation. The case study in the next section will demonstrate the potential conflicts that can arise in this area.

Reference [7-61] discusses how SNMP Agents will be incorporated into the AppleTalk architecture. Network managers should become aware of the tremendous growth in this area, as other software architectures and operating systems will undoubtedly follow suit.

7.9 Case Study

Our final case study will consider the IEEE 802.3 network shown in Figure 7-9. The SNMP Manager is a PC-based application known as ExpressView from David Systems, Inc. (Sunnyvale, CA), running on a 386 PC. The SNMP Agent is a 10BASE-T hub card, model MX-3610, from Xyplex Inc. (Boxborough, MA). The David Systems and Xyplex products both claim to be compatible with MIB-I and MIB-II. Let's see if they are compatible with each other.

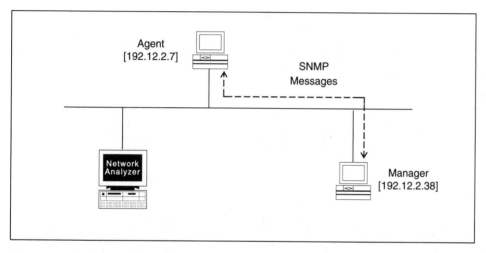

Figure 7-9. SNMP over Ethernet

To confirm compatibility, the network manager, Ross, instructs the SNMP Manager to query the System Group Objects (subtree 1.3.6.1.2.1.1 in Figure 7-10). There are seven objects to be queried. The Manager issues requests for these objects in the order in which they appear in the subtree (see Trace 7.9a.) The first request (Frame 31) asks for the sysDescr, the next for the sysObjectID and sysUpTime, and so on. Replies from the Agent begin in Frame 37. These identify the Xyplex system (MX-3610, 10-BASE-T Hub), the system up time, the system contact, and so on.

Trace 7.9b shows the details of these Request/Response pairs. Note that for every GetRequest from the SNMP Manager, a corresponding GetResponse is returned. Frames 31 and 37 show the details of all protocol layers, which include the IP and UDP headers. Within the UDP header, the Destination port = 161 specifies the SNMP protocol. Also note that the GetNextRequest in Frame 31 uses a Request ID of 227475461. The corresponding response (Frame 37) uses the same number for identification. The next GetNextRequest (Frame 32), uses a different Request ID (227541001), which is repeated in the corresponding GetResponse (Frame 38). This pattern of request/Response correlation continues through Frame 42.

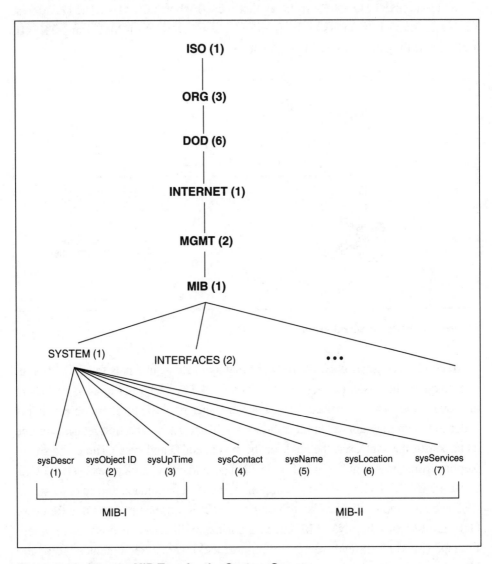

Figure 7-10. Internet MIB Tree for the System Group

Satisfied with these results, Ross decides to test the setRequest PDU in Frame 42. The object that he elects to change is the sysContact, object 1.3.6.1.2.1.1.4.0. The value of this object contains the name of the person responsible for the local network administration. Ross quickly realizes that he can accomplish two things with this one command: he can verify the compatibility of the two vendor's SNMP message set, and he can change his own personal job responsibilities by putting someone else's name in this field. To do this, Ross enters the Community name for security purposes, the Object ID (1.3.6.1.2.1.1.4.0), and the new value of that object (Bob Pjontek). The SNMP Agent on the hub responds in Frame 43 with the expected results. The SetRequest works, and Bob Pjontek is now the new network administrator. Ross wishes Bob well in his new responsibilities and moves on to the next test.

For his last compatibility check, Ross wishes to change the sysLocation object (1.3.6.1.2.1.1.6.0) using the SetRequest command in Frame 45. To Ross's surprise, the GetResponse returned by the Xyplex hub in Frame 46 contains an Error Status = 3, indicating that a bad value was included in the SetRequest command. The Error index shows that the bad value is the second variable (Ottawa Demo Lab). Ross is perplexed as to why this SetRequest failed, while the previous command (Frames 43 and 44) succeeded. The only clue is an error code on the console that reads Object: Unknown.

A close examination of the two vendors' product manuals reveals the incompatibility. The hub manual shows that it does not allow a SetRequest for the sysLocation object for reasons of security. Since SNMP offers limited security (via the Authentication header), the hub vendor elected to allow a GetRequest to all objects, a SetRequest to only some objects. This action does not violate the SNMP standard, but merely demonstrates the vendor's concern for internetwork security.

This experiment demonstrates another valuable lesson in today's "open systems" environments. The Internet protocols, being public domain standards, are about as open as you can get. Nevertheless, vendor-specific implementations must still be considered. This is another good example of why it's important to understand the vendor's implementation of the protocol as well as the protocol itself.

Sniffer Network Analyzer data 8-Sep-91 at 00:07:34, file SNMPTEST.ENC, Pg 1

SUMMARY	Delta T	Destination	Source	Summary
31	22.2384	Agent	Manager	SNMP Next sysDescr =
32	0.0031	Agent	Manager	SNMP Next sysObjectID, sysUpTime
33	0.0023	Agent	Manager	SNMP Next system.4 =
34	0.0019	Agent	Manager	SNMP Next system.5 =
35	0.0020	Agent	Manager	SNMP Next system.6 =
36	0.0020	Agent	Manager	SNMP Next system.7 = 0
37	0.0094	Manager	Agent	SNMP Got sysDescr = MX-3610 Xyplex 10BASE-T Hub<0A> Xyplex hardware MX-3610 00.00.00 Rom 440000<0A>Xypl...
38	0.0110	Manager	Agent	SNMP Got sysObjectID, sysUpTime
39	0.0086	Manager	Agent	SNMP Got system.4.0 = Ross Dunthorne, LAA Inc., Ottawa, Ontario.
40	0.0085	Manager	Agent	SNMP Got system.5.0 = MX-3610
41	0.0084	Manager	Agent	SNMP Got system.6.0 =
42	0.0085	Manager	Agent	SNMP Got system.7.0 = 78
43	16.3451	Agent	Manager	SNMP Set system.4.0 = Bob Pjontek, LAA Inc., Ottawa, Ontario.
44	0.0118	Manager	Agent	SNMP Got system.4.0 = Bob Pjontek, LAA Inc., Ottawa, Ontario.
45	49.9424	Agent	Manager	SNMP Set system.6.0 = Ottawa Demo Lab
46	0.0105	Manager	Agent	SNMP Got Bad value system.6.0 = Ottawa Demo Lab

Trace 7.9a. SNMP Message Summary

Sniffer Network Analyzer data 8-Sep-91 at 00:07:34, file SNMPTEST.ENC, Pg 1

- - - - - - - - - - - - - - - - Frame 31 - - - - - - - - - - - - - - - - -

```
DLC: ——— DLC Header ———
DLC:
DLC: Frame 31 arrived at  00:08:24.5855; frame size is 84 (0054 hex) bytes.
DLC: Destination = Station Xyplex004DB7, Agent
DLC: Source     = Station NwkGnl0813FE, Manager
DLC: Ethertype = 0800 (IP)
DLC:
IP:  ——— IP Header ———
IP:
IP:  Version = 4, header length = 20 bytes
IP:  Type of service = 00
IP:        000. .... = routine
IP:        ...0 .... = normal delay
IP:        .... 0... = normal throughput
IP:        .... .0.. = normal reliability
IP:  Total length = 70 bytes
IP:  Identification = 3658
IP:  Flags = 0X
IP:  .0.. .... = may fragment
IP:  ..0. .... = last fragment
IP:  Fragment offset = 0 bytes
IP:  Time to live = 255 seconds/hops
IP:  Protocol = 17 (UDP)
IP:  Header checksum = 2917 (correct)
IP:  Source address = [192.12.2.38]
IP:  Destination address = [192.12.2.7]
IP:  No options
IP:
UDP: ——— UDP Header ———
UDP:
UDP: Source port = 9669 (SNMP)
UDP: Destination port = 161
UDP: Length = 50
UDP: Checksum = F42C (correct)
UDP:
SNMP: ——— Simple Network Management Protocol ———
SNMP:
SNMP: Version = 0
SNMP: Community = public
```

SNMP: Command = Get next request
SNMP: Request ID = 227475461
SNMP: Error status = 0 (No error)
SNMP: Error index = 0
SNMP:
SNMP: Object = {1.3.6.1.2.1.1.1} (sysDescr)
SNMP: Value =
SNMP:

- - - - - - - - - - - - - - - Frame 32 - - - - - - - - - - - - - - - - -
UDP: —— UDP Header ——
UDP:
UDP: Source port = 9669 (SNMP)
UDP: Destination port = 161
UDP: Length = 64
UDP: Checksum = 69A2 (correct)
UDP:
SNMP: —— Simple Network Management Protocol ——
SNMP:
SNMP: Version = 0
SNMP: Community = public
SNMP: Command = Get next request
SNMP: Request ID = 227541001
SNMP: Error status = 0 (No error)
SNMP: Error index = 0
SNMP:
SNMP: Object = {1.3.6.1.2.1.1.2} (sysObjectID)
SNMP: Value = }
SNMP:
SNMP: Object = {1.3.6.1.2.1.1.3} (sysUpTime)
SNMP: Value = 0 hundredths of a second
SNMP:

- - - - - - - - - - - - - - - Frame 33 - - - - - - - - - - - - - - - - -
UDP: —— UDP Header ——
UDP:
UDP: Source port = 9669 (SNMP)
UDP: Destination port = 161
UDP: Length = 50
UDP: Checksum = DE29 (correct)
UDP:
SNMP: —— Simple Network Management Protocol ——
SNMP:

SNMP: Version = 0
SNMP: Community = public
SNMP: Command = Get next request
SNMP: Request ID = 227606553
SNMP: Error status = 0 (No error)
SNMP: Error index = 0
SNMP:
SNMP: Object = {1.3.6.1.2.1.1.4} (system.4)
SNMP: Value =
SNMP:

- - - - - - - - - - - - - - - Frame 34 - - - - - - - - - - - - - - - -
UDP: ——— UDP Header ———-
UDP:
UDP: Source port = 9669 (SNMP)
UDP: Destination port = 161
UDP: Length = 50
UDP: Checksum = D928 (correct)
UDP:
SNMP: ——— Simple Network Management Protocol ———-
SNMP:
SNMP: Version = 0
SNMP: Community = public
SNMP: Command = Get next request
SNMP: Request ID = 227672093
SNMP: Error status = 0 (No error)
SNMP: Error index = 0
SNMP:
SNMP: Object = {1.3.6.1.2.1.1.5} (system.5)
SNMP: Value =
SNMP:

- - - - - - - - - - - - - - - Frame 35 - - - - - - - - - - - - - - - -
UDP: ——— UDP Header ———-
UDP:
UDP: Source port = 9669 (SNMP)
UDP: Destination port = 161
UDP: Length = 50
UDP: Checksum = D427 (correct)
UDP:
SNMP: ——— Simple Network Management Protocol ———-
SNMP:
SNMP: Version = 0

SNMP: Community = public
SNMP: Command = Get next request
SNMP: Request ID = 227737633
SNMP: Error status = 0 (No error)
SNMP: Error index = 0
SNMP:
SNMP: Object = {1.3.6.1.2.1.1.6} (system.6)
SNMP: Value =
SNMP:

- - - - - - - - - - - - - - - Frame 36 - - - - - - - - - - - - - - - - -
UDP: —— UDP Header ——
UDP:
UDP: Source port = 9669 (SNMP)
UDP: Destination port = 161
UDP: Length = 51
UDP: Checksum = CE22 (correct)
UDP:
SNMP: —— Simple Network Management Protocol ——
SNMP:
SNMP: Version = 0
SNMP: Community = public
SNMP: Command = Get next request
SNMP: Request ID = 227803173
SNMP: Error status = 0 (No error)
SNMP: Error index = 0
SNMP:
SNMP: Object = {1.3.6.1.2.1.1.7} (system.7)
SNMP: Value = 0
SNMP:

- - - - - - - - - - - - - - - Frame 37 - - - - - - - - - - - - - - - - -
DLC: —— DLC Header ——
DLC:
DLC: Frame 37 arrived at 00:08:24.6065; frame size is 186 (00BA hex) bytes.
DLC: Destination = Station NwkGnl0813FE, Manager
DLC: Source   = Station Xyplex004DB7, Agent
DLC: Ethertype = 0800 (IP)
DLC:
IP: —— IP Header ——
IP:
IP: Version = 4, header length = 20 bytes
IP: Type of service = 00

```
IP:          000. .... = routine
IP:          ...0 .... = normal delay
IP:          .... 0... = normal throughput
IP:          .... .0.. = normal reliability
IP:   Total length = 172 bytes
IP:   Identification = 82
IP:   Flags = 0X
IP:   .0.. .... = may fragment
IP:   ..0. .... = last fragment
IP:   Fragment offset = 0 bytes
IP:   Time to live = 64 seconds/hops
IP:   Protocol = 17 (UDP)
IP:   Header checksum = F5A9 (correct)
IP:   Source address = [192.12.2.7]
IP:   Destination address = [192.12.2.38]
IP:   No options
IP:
UDP: —— UDP Header ——
UDP:
UDP: Source port = 161 (SNMP)
UDP: Destination port = 9669
UDP: Length = 152
UDP: No checksum
UDP:
SNMP: —— Simple Network Management Protocol ——
SNMP:
SNMP: Version = 0
SNMP: Community = public
SNMP: Command = Get response
SNMP: Request ID = 227475461
SNMP: Error status = 0 (No error)
SNMP: Error index = 0
SNMP:
SNMP: Object = {1.3.6.1.2.1.1.1.0} (sysDescr.0)
SNMP: Value  = MX-3610 - Xyplex 10BASE-T Hub<0A>Xyplex hardware MX-3610 00.00.00
Rom 440000<0A> ...
SNMP:


- - - - - - - - - - - - - - - - Frame 38 - - - - - - - - - - - - - - - - -
UDP: —— UDP Header ——
UDP:
UDP: Source port = 161 (SNMP)
UDP: Destination port = 9669
```

UDP: Length = 76
UDP: No checksum
UDP:
SNMP: —— Simple Network Management Protocol ——
SNMP:
SNMP: Version = 0
SNMP: Community = public
SNMP: Command = Get response
SNMP: Request ID = 227541001
SNMP: Error status = 0 (No error)
SNMP: Error index = 0
SNMP:
SNMP: Object = {1.3.6.1.2.1.1.2.0} (sysObjectID.0)
SNMP: Value = {1.3.6.1.4.1.33.1.4}
SNMP:
SNMP: Object = {1.3.6.1.2.1.1.3.0} (sysUpTime.0)
SNMP: Value = 1058882 hundredths of a second
SNMP:

- - - - - - - - - - - - - - - Frame 39 - - - - - - - - - - - - - - - -
UDP: —— UDP Header ——
UDP:
UDP: Source port = 161 (SNMP)
UDP: Destination port = 9669
UDP: Length = 93
UDP: No checksum
UDP:
SNMP: —— Simple Network Management Protocol ——
SNMP:
SNMP: Version = 0
SNMP: Community = public
SNMP: Command = Get response
SNMP: Request ID = 227606553
SNMP: Error status = 0 (No error)
SNMP: Error index = 0
SNMP:
SNMP: Object = {1.3.6.1.2.1.1.4.0} (system.4.0)
SNMP: Value = Ross Dunthorne, LAA Inc., Ottawa, Ontario.
SNMP:

- - - - - - - - - - - - - - - Frame 40 - - - - - - - - - - - - - - - -
UDP: —— UDP Header ——
UDP:

UDP: Source port = 161 (SNMP)
UDP: Destination port = 9669
UDP: Length = 58
UDP: No checksum
UDP:
SNMP: —— Simple Network Management Protocol ——
SNMP:
SNMP: Version = 0
SNMP: Community = public
SNMP: Command = Get response
SNMP: Request ID = 227672093
SNMP: Error status = 0 (No error)
SNMP: Error index = 0
SNMP:
SNMP: Object = {1.3.6.1.2.1.1.5.0} (system.5.0)
SNMP: Value = MX-3610
SNMP:
- - - - - - - - - - - - - - - - Frame 41 - - - - - - - - - - - - - - - - - -
UDP: —— UDP Header ——
UDP:
UDP: Source port = 161 (SNMP)
UDP: Destination port = 9669
UDP: Length = 51
UDP: No checksum
UDP:
SNMP: —— Simple Network Management Protocol ——
SNMP:
SNMP: Version = 0
SNMP: Community = public
SNMP: Command = Get response
SNMP: Request ID = 227737633
SNMP: Error status = 0 (No error)
SNMP: Error index = 0
SNMP:
SNMP: Object = {1.3.6.1.2.1.1.6.0} (system.6.0)
SNMP: Value =
SNMP:

- - - - - - - - - - - - - - - - Frame 42 - - - - - - - - - - - - - - - - - -
UDP: —— UDP Header ——
UDP:
UDP: Source port = 161 (SNMP)
UDP: Destination port = 9669

399

UDP: Length = 52
UDP: No checksum
UDP:
SNMP: —— Simple Network Management Protocol ——
SNMP:
SNMP: Version = 0
SNMP: Community = public
SNMP: Command = Get response
SNMP: Request ID = 227803173
SNMP: Error status = 0 (No error)
SNMP: Error index = 0
SNMP:
SNMP: Object = {1.3.6.1.2.1.1.7.0} (system.7.0)
SNMP: Value = 78
SNMP:

- - - - - - - - - - - - - - - Frame 43 - - - - - - - - - - - - - - - -
UDP: —— UDP Header ——
UDP:
UDP: Source port = 9669 (SNMP)
UDP: Destination port = 161
UDP: Length = 68
UDP: Checksum = 1198 (correct)
UDP:
SNMP: —— Simple Network Management Protocol ——
SNMP:
SNMP: Version = 0
SNMP: Community = xyplex
SNMP: Command = Set request
SNMP: Request ID = 227868677
SNMP: Error status = 0 (No error)
SNMP: Error index = 0
SNMP:
SNMP: Object = {1.3.6.1.2.1.1.4.0} (system.4.0)
SNMP: Value = Bob Pjontek, LAA Inc., Ottawa, Ontario.
SNMP:

- - - - - - - - - - - - - - - Frame 44 - - - - - - - - - - - - - - - -
UDP: —— UDP Header ——
UDP:
UDP: Source port = 161 (SNMP)
UDP: Destination port = 9669
UDP: Length = 68

UDP: No checksum
UDP:
SNMP: —— Simple Network Management Protocol ——
SNMP:
SNMP: Version = 0
SNMP: Community = xyplex
SNMP: Command = Get response
SNMP: Request ID = 227868677
SNMP: Error status = 0 (No error)
SNMP: Error index = 0
SNMP:
SNMP: Object = {1.3.6.1.2.1.1.4.0} (system.4.0)
SNMP: Value = Bob Pjontek, LAA Inc., Ottawa, Ontario.
SNMP:

- - - - - - - - - - - - - - - Frame 45 - - - - - - - - - - - - - - - - -
UDP: —— UDP Header ——
UDP:
UDP: Source port = 9669 (SNMP)
UDP: Destination port = 161
UDP: Length = 66
UDP: Checksum = 2C01 (correct)
UDP:
SNMP: —— Simple Network Management Protocol ——
SNMP:
SNMP: Version = 0
SNMP: Community = xyplex
SNMP: Command = Set request
SNMP: Request ID = 227999749
SNMP: Error status = 0 (No error)
SNMP: Error index = 0
SNMP:
SNMP: Object = {1.3.6.1.2.1.1.6.0} (system.6.0)
SNMP: Value = Ottawa Demo Lab
SNMP:

- - - - - - - - - - - - - - - Frame 46 - - - - - - - - - - - - - - - - -
UDP: —— UDP Header ——
UDP:
UDP: Source port = 161 (SNMP)
UDP: Destination port = 9669
UDP: Length = 66
UDP: No checksum

```
UDP:
SNMP: ——— Simple Network Management Protocol ———
SNMP:
SNMP: Version = 0
SNMP: Community = xyplex
SNMP: Command = Get response
SNMP: Request ID = 227999749
SNMP: Error status = 3 (Bad value)
SNMP: Error index = 2
SNMP:
SNMP: Object = {1.3.6.1.2.1.1.6.0} (system.6.0)
SNMP: Value  = Ottawa Demo Lab
SNMP:
```

Trace 7.9b. SNMP Message Details

In this chapter we looked at CMIP, the bridge between the Internet and OSI. In our concluding chapter, we'll study the ways in which a network manager can begin to make the transition from a TCP/IP-based internetwork to one that also includes OSI protocols and applications.

7.10 References

[7-1]   International Organization for Standardization, *Information Processing Systems — Open Systems Interconnection — Basic Reference Model-Part 4: Management framework*, ISO 7498-4-1989.

[7-2]   Cerf, V. "IAB Recommendations for the Development of Internet Network Management Standards." RFC 1052, NRI, April 1988.

[7-3]   Stine, Robert H., J. P. Holbrook, M. A. Patton, J. B. Van Bokkelen. "A Practical Introduction to Network Management." *ConneXions* (August 1990): 2-17.

[7-4]   Rose, Marshall T. "A Brief History of Network Management of TCP/IP Internets." *ConneXions* (August 1990):18-27.

[7-5]   Borsook, Paulina. "Meditations on TCP/IP Management." *Network World* (May 21, 1990): 61-66.

[7-6]   Jukovsky, Martin. "Managing A Network? TCP/IP Can Help You." *Digital News* (September 2, 1991): 29.

[7-7]   Fram, Bruce. "Net Management Protocols: A Good Place to Start, A Bad Place to Stop." *Data Communications* (November 1991): 158.

[7-8]   Rose, Marshall T. *The Simple Book: An Introduction to Management of TCP/IP-based Internets*. Englewood Cliffs, NJ: Prentice-Hall, 1991.

[7-9]   Black, Uyless. *Network Management Standards*. New York, NY: McGraw-Hill, 1992.

[7-10]   White, David W. "Internet Management — SNMP and CMOT: Two Ways to Do the Same Thing." *LAN Magazine* (July 1989):147-150.

[7-11]   Thomas, Larry J. "The Distributed Management Choice." *LAN Technology* (April 1992):53-70.

[7-12]   Ben-Artzi, Amatzia, et. al. "Network Management of TCP/IP Networks: Present and Future." *IEEE Network Magazine* (July 1990): 35-43.

[7-13]   McGloghrie, K. and Marshall T. Rose. "Network Management of TCP/IP-based internets." *ConneXions* (March 1989):3-9.

[7-14]   Rose, M. and K. McCloghrie. "Structure and Identification of Management Information for TCP/IP-based Internets." RFC 1155, Performance Systems International, May 1990.

[7-15]   Rose, M., et. al. "Concise MIB Definitions." RFC 1212, Performance Systems International, March 1991.

[7-16]   McCloghrie, K., et. al. "Management Information Base for Network Management of TCP/IP-based Internets." RFC 1156, Hughes LAN Systems, May 1990.

[7-17] McCloghrie, K. and M. Rose. "Management Information Base for Network Management of TCP/IP-based Internets: MIB-II." RFC 1213, Hughes LAN Systems, Inc. and Performance Systems International, March 1991.

[7-18] Case, J., et. al. "A Simple Network Management Protocol (SNMP)." RFC 1157, SNMP Research, May 1990.

[7-19] Warrier, U., et al. "The Common Management Information Services and Protocols for the Internet (CMOT and CMIP)." RFC 1189, Netlabs, October 1990.

[7-20] International Organization for Standardization. *Information Processing Systems: Open Systems Interconnection, Specification of Abstract Syntax Notation One (ASN.1)*, ISO 8824, December 1987.

[7-21] VandenBerg, Chris. "MIB II Extends SNMP Interoperability." *Data Communications* (October 1990): 119-124.

[7-22] Perkins, Dave. "How to Read and Use an SNMP MIB." *3TECH, The 3Com Technical Journal* (Spring 1991): 31-55.

[7-23] Stewart, Bob. "Development and Integration of a Management Information Base." *ConneXions* (June 1991): 2-11.

[7-24] 3Com Corporation. *Introduction to Simple Network Management Protocol Self Study Guide*. Document 8759-00, rev. A, August 1991.

[7-25] Hurwitz, Mike. "Manage From Kansas." *LAN Magazine* (February 1992): 113-126.

[7-26] Case, Jeffrey D., et. al. "Network Management and the Design of SNMP." *ConneXions* (March 1989): 22-26.

[7-27] Krall, Gary. "SNMP Opens New Lines of Sight." *Data Communications* (March 21, 1990): 45-50.

[7-28] Scott, Karyl. "SNMP Brings Order to Chaos." *Data Communications* (March 21, 1990): 25-27.

[7-29] Harrison, Bradford T. "SNMP Struts Its Stuff." *LAN Computing* (November 1990): 21-22.

[7-30] Simpson, David. "SNMP: Simple But Limited." *Systems Integration* (December 1990): 26-30.

[7-31] Knack, Kella. "Network Management Protocols." *LAN Computing* (May 7, 1991): 17-18.

[7-32] Ezerski, Michael B. "SNMP Completes the TCP/IP Solution." *Networking Management* (September 1991): 64-67.

[7-33] Jones, Katherine. "Network Management in the World of Standards: The Role of the SNMP Protocol in Managing Networks." *International Journal of Network Management* (September 4, 1991): 5-13.

[7-34] Smith, Tom. "User Survey Details SNMP Shortcomings". *Network World* (October 29, 1990): 19-59.

[7-35] International Organization for Standardization. *Information Processing Systems—Open Systems Interconnection—Common management information service definition*, ISO/IEC 9595, CCITT Recommendation X.710, IEEE 802.1-91/20, November 1990.

[7-36] Klerer, Mark. "The OSI Management Architecture: an Overview." *IEEE Network Magazine* (March 1988): 20-29.

[7-37]   Sugarbroad, Ian. "An OSI-Based Interoperability Architecture for Managing Hybrid Networks." *IEEE Communications Magazine* (March 1990): 61-69.

[7-38]   International Organization for Standardization. *Information Processing Systems—Open Systems Interconnection—Common management information protocol specification*, ISO/IEC 9596-1, CCITT X.711, IEEE 802.1-91/21, November 1990.

[7-39]   Presuhn, Randy. "Considering CMIP." *Data Communications* (March 21, 1990): 55-60.

[7-40]   Jander, Mary. "CMIP Gets a New Chance." *Data Communications* (September 1991): 51-56.

[7-41]   Rose, M.T. "ISO Presentation Services on top of TCP/IP based internets." RFC 1085, TWG, December 1988.

[7-42]   Lew, H. Kim and Jim Robertson. "TCP/IP network management with an eye toward OSI." *Data Communications* (August 1989): 123-130.

[7-43]   Ben-Artzi, Amatzia. "The CMOT Network Management Architecture." *ConneXions* (March 1989): 14-19.

[7-44]   Labarre, L. editor. "OSI Internet Management: Management Information Base." RFC 1214, MITRE, April 1991.

[7-45]   Institute of Electrical and Electronics Engineers. "LAN/MAN Management". Draft Standard P802.1B/D20, January 1992.

[7-46]   Fedor, Mark S. "Case Study: Using SNMP to Manage a Large Network." *ConneXions* (August 1990): 28-33.

[7-47] Herman, James. "Distributing the Wealth." *Network World* (July 15, 1991): 53-59.

[7-48] Pickens, John R. "Making Network Management Manageable." *3TECH, The 3Com Technical Journal* (Summer 1991): 23-30.

[7-49] Gilbert, William E. "Managing Networks In a Multi-Vendor Environment." *IEEE Communications Magazine* (March 1990): 41-60.

[7-50] Sylor, Mark W. "Managing Phase V DECnet Networks: the Entity Model." *IEEE Network* (March 1988): 30-36.

[7-51] Klemba, Keith S., et. al. "HP OpenView Network Management Architecture." *Hewlett-Packard Journal* (April 1990): 54-59.

[7-52] Campbell, Randall, et. al. "IBM's Network Management Approach." *IEEE Communications Magazine* (March 1990): 70-75.

[7-53] Scott, Karyl. "Taking Care of Business with SNMP." *Data Communications* (March 21, 1990): 31-41.

[7-54] Dolan, Tom. "SNMP Streamlines Multi-Vendor Network Management." *LAN Technology* (February 1991): 29-38.

[7-55] Mier, Edwin. "A Shopper's Bonanza." *Network World* (June 24, 1991): 41-59.

[7-56] Jander, Mary. "Users Rate SNMP Multivendor Network Management Systems." *Data Communications* (November 1991): 113-120.

[7-57] Thomas, Larry. *Personal Communication*, May 4, 1992.

[7-58] Mier, Edwin. "Network World, Bell Labs Evaluate SNMP on Bridges." *Network World* (April 22, 1991): 1-34.

[7-59]   Mier, Edwin. "Network World, Bell Labs Test Routers' SNMP Agents."
         Network World (July 1, 1991): 1-38.

[7-60]   Mier, Edwin. "NW/Bell Labs Tests Show SNMP Hub Standards Lag."
         Network World (August 19, 1991): 1-49.

[7-61]   Wylie, Margie. "SNMP Agents Infiltrating AppleTalk." *Macweek* (September 24, 1991): 1-100.

CHAPTER 8

Migrating TCP/IP Internets to OSI

In Chapter 1, we discovered that TCP/IP achieved widespread acceptance because of its ability to internetwork vastly different architectures. For example, even though IBM's SNA and DEC's DECnet were originally proprietary architectures, they have incorporated TCP/IP into their protocol suites in order to become more "open."

The concept of "open systems," as described by the familiar seven-layer Open Systems Interconnection Reference Model (OSI-RM), was developed to eliminate (or at least minimize) implementation incompatibilities between hosts. If your host and mine adhere to the same standard, we should be able to communicate. However, this doesn't always work because "open" is a relative term. You and I may both have the same protocols available on our hosts, yet differences in the implementation of those protocols may preclude true interoperability. (For two illustrations of this, review the TELNET example in Section 6.9.3 and the SNMP example in Section 7.9.)

The next issue we'll consider, then, is interoperability between the TCP/IP and OSI protocol suites. Although both are individually advertised as open, are they open when considered together? If not, how can we accomplish that interoperability?

8.1 TCP/IP and OSI: Coexistence or Controversy?

Every once in a while, the trade press publishes an article regarding transitions from TCP/IP to OSI-based internetworks designed to appeal to those who make their living in the networking trenches. Most such articles have eye-catching titles that use words like "conflict", "versus", and "mudslinging" to imply that there's a war going on between those who would encourage network managers to migrate to the OSI management protocols and those who prefer to stick with the proven, TCP/IP protocols they already use (see References [8-1] through [8-10]). Realizing the long term need for such a migration, the Internet community has issued RFC 1287, "Towards the Future Internet Architecture" [8-11], which discusses assumptions and strategies for that migration. Sensationalism aside, this issue generates strong emotions because any architectural transition of this magnitude is tremendously expensive.

Any TCP/IP to OSI transition must take into account three types of issues: protocol, political, and practical. The proper protocols are necessary to assure the interoperability of the end-user applications. Politics enter the decision regardless of whether your organization is in the public or private sector. If you're in government, you must consider the mandate to comply with the U.S. Government OSI Profile (GOSIP) and whether any loopholes exist that would exempt your organization from those regulations. If you're in the private sector, senior management will undoubtedly ask whether this is the strategically correct move and the impact it will have on corporate finances. Finally, you should consider the practical issues involved with the transition process, such as the time necessary to install the software and retrain users.

The rest of this chapter will consider the protocol, political, and practical issues that will impact your TCP/IP to OSI transition. We'll begin with the protocol issues.

8.2 Protocol Issues for Transition: Architectural Differences

The data communications industry has expended enormous resources on developing standards, whether they're for a single cable connector or an entire computer architecture. The purpose of these standards is to ensure interoperability. In other words, the standard theoretically ensures that my application can communicate with yours. When you compare the DARPA and OSI protocol architectures, their similarities and differences are immediately apparent (see Figure 8-1).

First, DARPA defined four layers, while OSI defined seven. The lower-layer functions of transmitting the actual bits are generic to both architectures. DARPA combines these functions into one layer (the Network Interface or Local Network Layer); while OSI makes two (Physical and Data Link). The next two layers provide parallel functions as well, though they use different names. The OSI Network and Transport Layers correspond to DARPA's Internet and Host-to-Host Layers. We see the greatest divergence at the upper layers. Recall from Chapter 2 that the DARPA architects were primarily interested in functionality, and therefore defined the upper-layer processes into one group, called the Process/Application Layer. OSI created a much finer delineation, defining the Session, Presentation, and Application Layers to cover these functions.

DARPA Layer	Example Internet Protocols				Example ISO Protocols				OSI Layer
Process / Application	FTP	SMTP	TFTP	SNMP	ISO 9040/9041 VT	ISO 8831/8832 JTM	ISO 8571/8572 FTAM	ISO 9595/9596 CMIP	Application
					ISO 8823/CCITT X.226 Connection-Oriented Presentation Protocol				Presentation
					ISO 8327/CCITT X.225 Connection-Oriented Session Protocol				Session
Host-to-Host	TCP		UDP		ISO 8073/CCITT X.224 Connection-Oriented Transport Protocol				Transport
Internet	IP				ISO 8473 Connectionless Network Service		ISO 8208/CCITT X.25 Packet Level Protocol		Network
Network Interface	LAN, MAN and WAN Options				ISO 8802-2				Data Link
					ISO 9314-2 FDDI	ISO 8802-3 CSMA/CD BUS	ISO 8802-4 TOKEN BUS	ISO 8802-5 TOKEN RING	ISO 7776 CCITT X.25 LAP/LAPB	ISO 7809 HDLC	
					Options from EIA, CCITT, IEEE, etc.				Physical

Figure 8-1. Comparing the Internet and ISO Protocol Suites

Thus, DARPA and OSI share the goals of inter-computer communication and interoperability. The way they implement these goals is similar at the lower layers. For example, you may use an IEEE 802.3 LAN in either architecture, but you'll see greater implementation differences at the higher layers.

One of these differences is the manner in which the two models address the inter-network entity. In Section 4.2, we examined the address structure used with the DARPA Internet Protocol. We discovered that there were five address classes (designated A, B, C, D, and E), all using a 32-bit wide address field. The equivalent ISO protocol, the Connectionless Network Layer Protocol (CLNP), ISO 8473, uses a much larger address space. Addressing, therefore, has a direct impact on the communication between network entities. The ISO addressing structure has the advantage of being able to support more devices on the internet. As RFC 1287 points out, there is some concern that some classes of IP addresses, e.g., Class B, will soon become exhausted.

Figure 8-2 shows an example of the ISO address structure used with GOSIP. These addresses are contained in a field that may be up to 20 octets long. The address is divided into two major sections: the Initial Domain Part (IDP) and the Domain Specific Part (DSP). The ISO standardizes the IDP and assigns it to a specific address-ing authority. Within the IDP are two subfields: the AFI and the IDI. The Authority and Format Indicator (AFI) defines the type of address being used within the DSP. The Initial Domain Indicator (IDI) determines the address domain to which the address belongs. For example, GOSIP uses an AFI of 47H and an IDI of 0005H, indicating the U.S. Government. The registration authority (the U.S. Government) then deter-mines the DSP, which uses a DSP Format Indicator (DFI) of 80H to specify GOSIP version 2. The remaining 16 octets of the DSP are assigned according to GOSIP ver-sion 2 [8-12]. RFC 1237 [8-13] and Michael Smith's article on TCP and OSI address-ing [8-14] provide additional insights into these addressing structures.

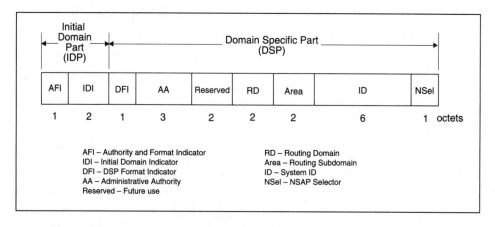

Figure 8-2. OSI Network Addressing Format

Another significant difference between the two models is in the applications that operate within the specific protocol stack. This is one area in which the interna-tional standards have built upon the lessons learned from their DARPA counter-parts. For example, the CCITT X.400 electronic messaging standard has a com-panion, X.500, to deal with directory-related issues. The X.400 standard also provides a richer set of functions, some of which are being considered as enhancements to SMTP. Other standards, such as Office Document Architecture (ODA), are not included in the DARPA architecture at all. You can see additional differences in network management philosophy and protocol implementation when you contrast the straightforward SNMP with the OSI's more complex CMIP.

In summary, lessons learned from the past are influencing protocol designs of the future. References [8-15] and [8-16] provide background information on the architectural issues surrounding application interoperability. Reference [8-17] discusses a proposed "skinny-stack," a subset of the OSI upper-layer protocols that would enable TCP/IP-based applications to operate over OSI transport.

8.3 Political Issues for Transition: GOSIP

In 1987, the U.S. Government's National Institute of Standards and Technology (NIST) began developing the standard that we now know as the Government Open System Interconnection Profile (GOSIP) [8-18]. GOSIP's intent was to define an OSI-based protocol suite that would ensure interoperability between OSI products. This protocol suite was a subset of the OSI protocols, focusing on specific end user requirements.

GOSIP became a Federal Information Processing Standard, FIPS 146, in February 1989, and a requirement for federal procurements in August 1990. Currently GOSIP is in its second version (FIPS 146-1), and plans for version 3 are underway. In addition to the U.S. Government, many state governments have adopted or considered GOSIP for their procurements as well. Other countries, including the United Kingdom, Canada, France, Belgium, Germany, Japan and Australia [8-19], have defined their own subsets of the OSI protocol suite.

GOSIP version 1 (FIPS 146) was intended to be the foundation upon which future GOSIP versions would be built. As such, it supported IEEE 802.3, 802.4, 802.5 (LANs), and CCITT X.25 (WANs) at the Physical and Data Link Layers. The Network Layer incorporated the Connectionless Network Protocol (ISO 8473), using the addressing scheme defined by OSI. At the Transport Layer, ISO Transport Protocol Class 4 (ISO 8073) provided guaranteed packet delivery. The upper layers concentrated on electronic mail and file transfer applications, reserving additional functionality for future releases.

GOSIP version 2 (FIPS 146-1) enhances those capabilities with support for additional protocols (see Figure 8-3). At the lower layers, it adds Integrated Services Digital Network (ISDN), plus RS-530 (the EIA RS-422 or RS-423 electrical interface using a 25-pin DB-25 connector) interfaces. The Network and Transport Layers add several options, including an optional connection-oriented network service; the End Station-Intermediate Station (ES-IS) protocol (ISO 9542); and an optional

Connectionless Transport protocol (ISO 8602). Two new upper-layer protocols increase the user's capabilities by adding a Virtual Terminal (ISO 9041) and Office Document Architecture (ISO 8613). Advanced requirements will include directory services, remote database access, and network management.

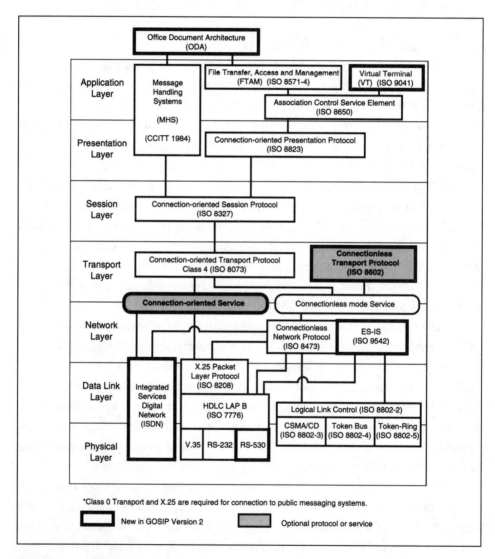

Figure 8-3. GOSIP Version 2 OSI Architecture
(Source: FIPS PUB 146-1, April 1991)

Given its support and mandate from various levels of government, a transition from TCP/IP-based internets to those based upon GOSIP or some other subset of the OSI protocols is sure to occur. In fact, issues regarding the transition have been the topic of discussions at conferences and in the trade press for several years. The burning question, therefore, becomes, when will the transition occur? The Internet community is preparing, and has issued a number of RFCs to support transition strategies. One in particular is RFC 1169, "Explaining the Role of GOSIP" [8-20]. Trade conferences (see References [8-21] through [8-23]) and magazines (see References [8-24] through [8-27]) have also expended a great deal of ink discussing the TCP/IP to OSI or TCP/IP to GOSIP transition.

Given that a transition will occur, let's discuss the technical issues of how it can be accomplished.

8.4 Practical Issues for Transition: Implementation Strategies

Now that we have discussed the theoretical aspects of a transition from a TCP/IP-based internetwork to one based upon the OSI protocols, you probably want to know how to accomplish such a feat. Fortunately, there are several approaches to this transition.

Returning to architectures shown in Figure 8-1, the first issue to address is the degree of incompatibility. In some cases, the lower-layer protocols may be consistent across the two environments. For example, both systems may be based upon an IEEE 802.3/Ethernet backbone, or both may use the X.25 protocol to access a Packet Switched Public Data Network (PSPDN). If this is the case, part of the problem is solved. If not, then an internetworking solution based upon LAN interconnect hardware such as a bridge or multiprotocol router may be required.

A number of alternatives have been proposed for making the higher-layer logical connection. The recognized reference for these alternatives is Marshall Rose's *The Open Book* [8-28]. Rose divides the alternatives into two general categories: protocol-based solutions (usually host-implemented), and service-based solutions (usually implemented in external hardware). References [8-29] and [8-30] provide summaries of the various approaches.

The first alternative is known as the Dual Stack, and it implements both the TCP/IP and OSI protocol stacks within one host. The best example is DEC's ADVANTAGE-NETWORKS, which we discussed in Section 2.3 and Figure 2-2. From a network management point of view, this approach is very appealing for its straightforward implementation with additional host software. One drawback is that the presence of two complete protocol stacks consumes large quantities of host memory and results in a topology that has two logical networks (TCP/IP and OSI) to manage.

Another protocol-based alternative is an Application Layer gateway. The gateway incorporates both the TCP/IP and OSI protocol stacks, allowing each host to operate in its native environment. Since the connectivity device is a gateway, protocol conversion at the Session through Application Layers is required. The gateway must also be application-dependent. In other words, it must be designed with a particular application, such as file transfer, in mind, and it must support the file transfer protocols, such as FTP or FTAM operating on the two hosts. The most popular application gateways support FTAM-FTP for file transfer and X.400-SMTP for electronic mail. Retix (Santa Monica, CA), SAIC (Campbell, CA), The Wollongong Group (Palo Alto, CA), and Worldtalk Corp. (Los Gatos, CA) are among the vendors that provide Application Layer gateways.

RFC 1006, "ISO Transport Service on top of the TCP" [8-31], describes a method for encapsulating OSI data into Transport Protocol Class 0 (TP0, from ISO 8073) packets and passing those packets on to TCP. This protocol is incorporated into a third alternative, the Transport Service Bridge (TS bridge) [8-32].

The TS bridge emulates the ISO Transport Service. This emulation allows an OSI application to communicate with an OSI peer, even if that peer resides on a TCP/IP-based host. The bridge function is implemented in software and provides a copy mechanism between the ISO TP4 (Transport Class 4, ISO 8073) primitives and the TCP primitives. For example, an OSI Connection Request primitive is copied to a TCP Connection Request primitive, which establishes a logical connection between the two hosts. Both environments see those primitives in their native semantics.

Both the RFC 1006 protocol and the TS bridge are incorporated into the ISO Development Environment (ISODE). This collection of software routines is available from a variety of sources. (See the ISODE subdirectory at NIC.DDN.MIL for further information.) ISODE is meant to provide publicly available OSI applications that will run over TCP/IP. Both SAIC and Wollongong offer TS bridge products.

The fourth alternative is also a service-based approach, known as a Network Tunnel. This approach is similar to tunneling in other environments, such as the

Banyan VINES and AppleTalk examples discussed in Chapter 3. With tunneling, a packet from one protocol stack is encapsulated within the format of another. For example, suppose an ISO application wishes to communicate with an ISO peer, but no physical network exists to connect those hosts. If a TCP/IP-based internetwork is available, the ISO CLNP packets could be encapsulated within IP datagrams for transport and unencapsulated at the receiving end, returning the data to its original ISO CLNP format. The addressing structures and techniques required for this approach are described in RFC 1069 [8-33] and RFC 1070 [8-34].

If the internet community is preparing for a transition, is the rest of the TCP/IP industry following suit? We'll conclude by looking at the results of a major study that may provide some interesting conclusions.

8.5 TCP/IP to OSI Transition: Will It Happen?

"If you build it, he will come." [8-35]

You've built a TCP/IP-based internet and now have one nagging question: "If I build an OSI-based internet, will I have anyone else to communicate with?" The proponents of OSI have asked us to build upon the ISO protocols for over a decade. Are their "if you implement it, they will come" theories correct, or are you merely building your own very expensive "field of dreams"?

There is no cookbook answer to such a dilemma. "Nothing ventured, nothing gained," the optimists would say. "If it's not broken, don't fix it," the more cautious would respond. Perhaps the truth can be found by considering the results of a study conducted by Infonetics Research, Inc. [8-36].

Infonetics' study focused on expected expenditures for TCP/IP and OSI-related products through 1994 (see Figure 8-4). The total worldwide expenditure for both hardware and software was $855 million in 1988 and is projected to grow to $2.471 billion by 1994. In 1989, the TCP/IP portion accounted for $575 million (67 percent) and the OSI portion $280 million (33 percent). By 1994, these figures are projected to be $1.920 billion for TCP/IP (78 percent) and $551 million (22 percent) for OSI. The conclusion is that predicted growth will not occur as rapidly as some OSI developers might have us think. In terms of expenditure ratios, OSI is projected to actually lose market share.

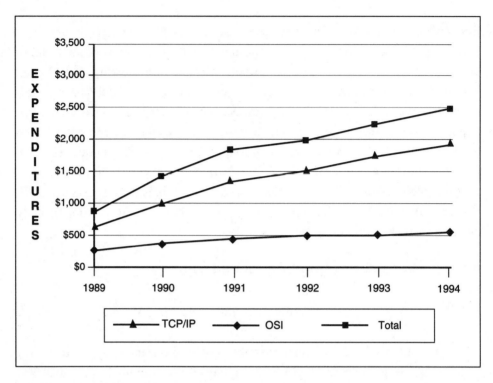

Figure 8-4. Worldwide TCP/IP and OSI Expenditure Forecast, 1988-94
(Millions of Dollars, both Hardware and Software OSI numbers include X.25)
(©1992 Infonetics Research, Inc. TCP/IP and OSI Market Forecast Update, March 1992)

Significant factors behind these results are the strength of the SNMP-based network management market and the challenge of testing the interoperability of new OSI-based products. OSI's strength appears to be in its application protocols, such as electronic mail and directory services. Access to Packet Switched Public Data Networks (PSPDNs) using the CCITT X.25 protocol is also expected to continue to be popular. This will not only support OSI growth, but will also maintain interest in TCP/IP-based protocols being sent via X.25 links. Infonetics concludes that TCP/IP-based internets will have a much longer life than many had anticipated, and that the growth in OSI internetworks will be slower.

Let's return to the question: Should you as an internetwork manager (or administrator or engineer) build your "field of dreams" using the OSI protocols? Or should you continue to use the well-known and well-understood TCP/IP protocols? The answer lies somewhere between these two extremes. It makes no sense to abandon the TCP/IP technologies that have served us so well for almost two decades. However, we will never realize truly open systems until consumers vote with their wallets and demand verification of the openness promised with the OSI protocols. A compromise position that allows the emerging OSI protocols to operate on top of TCP/IP transport may be a good posture to consider. In my case, however, I'll take the conservative approach — you can reach me on the Internet: mark@csn.org.

8.6 References

[8-1]   Cardozo, Mary. "OSI vs. TCP/IP: Mudslinging Isn't the Answer." *Network World* (March 20, 1989): 19-20.

[8-2]   DiDio, Laura. "Users Rely on TCP/IP, Wait for Interoperable OSI Wares." *Network World* (November 6, 1989): 25-28.

[8-3]   McClain, Gary. "What is OSI and What Can You Expect It to Do For You?" *Information Center* (June 1990): 12-17.

[8-4]   Korzeniowski, Paul. "OSI Obstacles Stall Movement's Momentum." *Software Magazine* (September 1990): 94-98.

[8-5]   Lynch, Daniel C. "The Transition from TCP/IP to OSI." *Journal of Information Systems Management* (Fall 1990): 48-52.

[8-6]   Phillips Publishing, Inc. "TCP vs. OSI: Conflict or Coexistence?" *Open Systems Report* (February 11, 1991): 1-8.

[8-7]   Roynan, James P. "OSI Versus TCP/IP." *LAN Computing* (April 9, 1991): 23-24.

[8-8]   Editorial. "TCP/IP Solves Problems for Users Waiting on OSI." *Network World* (July 22, 1991): 30.

[8-9] Mosher, Robyn E. "A Peaceful Coexistence for TCP/IP and OSI." *Networking Management* (August 1991): 36-40.

[8-10] Harrison, Bradford T. "TCP/IP Versus OSI: The Saga Continues." *LAN Computing* (August 1991): 17-20.

[8-11] Clark, D., et. al. "Towards the Future Internet Architecture." RFC 1287, MIT, December 1991.

[8-12] National Institute of Standards and Technology, National Computer Systems Laboratory. *Government Open Systems Interconnection Profile Users' Guide, Version 2*. NIST Special Publication 500-192, October 1991.

[8-13] Colella, Richard, et. al. "Guidelines for OSI NSAP Allocation in the Internet." RFC 1237, NIST, July 1991.

[8-14] Smith, Michael A. "TCP and OSI Network Addressing." *3TECH, The 3Com Technical Journal* (Winter 1991):74-82.

[8-15] Lew, H. Kim and Cyndi Jung. "Getting There From Here: Mapping From TCP/IP to OSI." *Data Communications* (August 1988): 1-8.

[8-16] Wallace, David. "How to Interwork Between TCP/IP and OSI." *Telecommunications* (April 1989): 46-54.

[8-17] Eckerson, Wayne. "COS Mulls Skinny Stack to Convert TCP/IP Users to OSI." *Network World* (December 23, 1991): 1-8.

[8-18] National Institute of Standards and Technology, National Computer Systems Laboratory. *U.S. Government Open Systems Interconnection Profile (GOSIP) Version 2.0*. FIPS PUB 146-1, April 3, 1991.

[8-19] Fisher, Sharon. "OSI Across the Water." *LAN Times* (July 1990):60.

[8-20] Cerf, V., et.al. "Explaining the Role of GOSIP." RFC 1169, IAB, August
        1990.

[8-21] Interop 90 Conference Notes. "OSI/GOSIP Transition", October 1990.

[8-22] Communication Networks-San Francisco Conference Notes. "TCP/IP to
        OSI: Are Users Ready to Make the Move?", July 1991.

[8-23] Sinkewicz, Ursula. "Issues for Open Networking," FOSE 92 Open Systems
        Networking Conference Notes, April 1992.

[8-24] Shaw, S. J. "TCP/IP Still Rules Federal Nets." *Network World* (March 14,
        1988): 44-46.

[8-25] Spencer, Lloyd T. "All GOSIP Is OSI, But Not Vice Versa." *LAN Times*
        (July 1990): 57.

[8-26] Shields, Jim. "Government Commits to Long-Term Goal of Interoperabil-
        ity." Government Computer News (May 14, 1990): 61-63.

[8-27] Malamud, Carl. "Where Systems Meet." *InfoWorld* (September 10, 1990):
        75-77.

[8-28] Rose, Marshall T. *The Open Book - A Practical Perspective on OSI*. Engle-
        wood Cliffs, NJ: Prentice Hall, 1990.

[8-29] Simpson, David. "TCP/IP-OSI: 5 Routes to Coexistence." *Systems Inte-
        gration* (April 1990): 81-88.

[8-30] Ladermann, Dan. "Integrating TCP/IP and OSI." *UNIX Review* (February
        1992): 29-36.

[8-31] Rose, Marshall, et. al. "ISO Transport Service on top of the TCP, Version
        3." RFC 1006, Northrop Research and Technology Center, May 1987.

[8-32] Rose, Marshall. "Transport-level 'Bridges' From TCP/IP to OSI/ISO." *ConneXions* (January 1988): 2-6.

[8-33] Callon, R., et. al., "Guidelines for the use of Internet-IP Addresses in the ISO Connectionless-Mode Network Protocol." RFC 1069, Digital Equipment Corporation, February 1989.

[8-34] Hagens, R., et. al., "Use of the Internet as a Subnetwork for Experimentation with the OSI Network Layer." RFC 1070, University of Wisconsin — Madison, February 1989.

[8-35] "Field of Dreams," Universal Pictures, 1989.

[8-36] Infonetics Research, Inc. "TCP/IP and OSI Market Forecast Update." March 1992.

Addresses of Standards Organizations

AT&T PUBLICATIONS
AT&T Technologies Commercial Sales
P.O. Box 19901
Indianapolis, IN 46219
Telephone (317) 322-6557
or (800) 432-6600

BELLCORE STANDARDS
Bell Communications Research
Information Management Services
60 New England Ave., DSC 1B-252
Piscataway, NJ 08854-4196
Telephone (908) 699-5800
or (800) 521-2673

**CCITT RECOMMENDATIONS
AND FEDERAL INFORMATION
PROCESSING STANDARDS (FIPS)**
U.S. Department of Commerce
National Technical Information Service
5285 Port Royal Road
Springfield, VA 22161
Telephone (703) 487-4650

CSA STANDARDS
Canadian Standards Association
178 Rexdale Boulevard
Rexdale, ONT M9W 1R3
Canada
Telephone (416) 747-4363

ECMA STANDARDS
European Computer Manufacturers
  Association
114, Rue de rhone CH-1204
Geneva, Switzerland
Telephone 41 22 35-36-34

ECSA STANDARDS
Exchange Carriers Standards Association
1200 G St. NW #500
Washington, DC 20005
(202) 628-6380

EIA STANDARDS
Electronic Industries Association
Standards Sales
2001 Pennsylvania Avenue
Washington, DC 20006
Telephone (202) 457-4966

FEDERAL STANDARD SALES
General Service Administration
GSA Specification Unit (WFSIS)
    Room 6039
7th & D Streets SW
Washington, DC 20407
Telephone (202) 472-2205

FIPS PUBLICATION SALES
National Technical Information Service
5285 Port Royal Road
Springfield, VA 22161
Telephone (703) 487-4650

IEEE STANDARDS
Institute of Electrical and Electronics
    Engineers
445 Hoes Lane
Piscataway, NJ 08855
Telephone (908) 981-0060
or (800) 678-4333

INTERNET STANDARDS
DDN Network Information Center
Government Systems, Inc.
14200 Park Meadow Drive
Suite 200
Chantilly, VA 22021
Telephone (703) 802-4535
or (800) 365-3642
(See Appendix D for further information)

ISO AND ANSI STANDARDS
American National Standards Institute
11 W. 42nd Street
New York, NY 10036
Telephone (212) 642-4900

ISO STANDARDS
International Organization for
    Standardization
1, Rue de Varembe
CH-1211
Geneva 20, Switzerland
Telephone 41 22 34 12 40

MILITARY STANDARDS SALES
Naval Publications and Forms Center
Commanding Officer
NPFC 43
5801 Tabor Avenue
Philadelphia, PA 19120
Telephone (215) 697-3321

NATIONAL INSTITUTE OF STANDARDS AND TECHNOLOGY
Technology Building 225
Gaithersburg, MD 20899
Telephone (301) 975-2816

Acronyms

A

A	Ampere
AARP	AppleTalk Address Resolution Protocol
ABP	Alternate Bipolar
ACK	Acknowledgement
ACS	Asynchronous Communication Server
ACTLU	Activate Logical Unit
ACTPU	Activate Physical Unit
ADSP	AppleTalk Data Stream Protocol
AEP	AppleTalk Echo Protocol
AFI	Authority and Format Indicator
AFP	AppleTalk Filing Protocol
AFRP	ARCNET Fragmentation Protocol
AGS	Asynchronous Gateway Server
AI	Artificial Intelligence
AM	Active Monitor
AMI	Alternate Mark Inversion
AMT	Address Mapping Table
ANSI	American National Standards Institute
API	Applications Program Interface
APPC	Advanced Program-to-Program Communication
ARE	All Routes Explorer
ARI	Address Recognized Indicator Bit
ARP	Address Resolution Protocol
ARPA	Advanced Research Projects Agency
ARPANET	Advanced Research Projects Agency Network
ASCII	American Standard Code for Information Interchange
ASI	Adapter Support Interface
ASN.1	Abstract Syntax Notation One

ASP......................AppleTalk Session Protocol
ATP......................AppleTalk Transaction Protocol

B

B8ZS....................Bipolar with 8 ZERO Substitution
BAPI....................Bridge Application Program Interface
BC........................Block Check
BIOS....................Basic Input/Output System
BITNET...............Because It's Time NETwork
BIU.....................Basic Information Unit
BOC.....................Bell Operating Company
BOOTP...............Bootstrap Protocol
BPDU..................Bridge Protocol Data Unit
bps.......................Bits Per Second
BPV.....................Bipolar Violations
BRI......................Basic Rate Interface
BSC.....................Binary Synchronous Communication
BSD.....................Berkeley Software Distribution
BTU.....................Basic Transmission Unit

C

CCIS....................Common Channel Interoffice Signaling
CCITT.................International Telegraph and Telephone Consultative
                       Committee
CCR.....................Commitment, Concurrency, and Recovery
CICS....................Customer Information Communication System
CLNP...................Connectionless Network Protocol
CLNS...................Connectionless-mode Network Services
CLTP...................Connectionless Transport Protocol
CMIP..................Common Management Information Protocol
CMIS...................Common Management Information Service
CMOL.................CMIP on IEEE 802.2 Logical Link Control
CMOT.................Common Management Information Protocol Over TCP/IP
CONS..................Connection-mode Network Services
COS.....................Corporation for Open Systems
CPE......................Convergence Protocol Entity
CPE......................Customer Premises Equipment

CRC ....Cyclic Redundancy Check
CREN ....The Corporation for Research and Educational Networking
CRS ....Configuration Report Server
CSMA/CD ....Carrier Sense Multiple Access with Collision Detection
CSNET ....Computer+Science Network
CSU ....Channel Service Unit
CTERM ....Command Terminal Protocol

D

DAP ....Data Access Protocol
DARPA ....Defense Advanced Research Projects Agency
DAT ....Duplicate Address Test
DCA.....................Defense Communications Agency
DCE ....Data Circuit-Terminating Equipment
DDCMP...............Digital Data Communications Message Protocol
DDN ....Defense Data Network
DDP ....Datagram Delivery Protocol
DECmcc ....DEC Management Control Center
DEMPR ....DEC Multiport Repeater
DIX ....DEC, Intel, and Xerox
DL........................Data Link
DLC ....Data Link Control
DLCI....................Data Link Connection Identifier
DMA....................Direct Memory Access
DNS ....Domain Name System
DOD ....Department of Defense
DQDB...................Distributed Queue Dual Bus
DPA ....Demand Protocol Architecture
DRP ....DECnet Routing Protocol
DSAP...................Destination Service Access Point
DSP......................Domain Specific Part
DSU ....Data Service Unit
DSU/CSU ....Data Service Unit/Channel Service Unit
DTE ....Data Terminal Equipment
DTR ....Data Terminal Ready

E

EBCDIC ....Extended Binary Coded Decimal Interchange Code
ECL ....End Communication Layer
ECSA...................Exchange Carriers Standards Association
EDI ....Electronic Data Interchange
EGA....................Enhanced Graphics Array
EGP ....Exterior Gateway Protocol
EIA ....Electronic Industries Association
ELAP...................EtherTalk Link Access Protocol
EOT ....End of Transmission
ESF......................Extended Superframe Format
ES-IS ....End System to Intermediate System Protocol

F

FAL.....................File Access Listener
FAT ....File Access Table
FCC ....Federal Communications Commission
FCI......................Frame Copied Indicator Bit
FCS ....Frame Check Sequence
FDDI...................Fiber Distributed Data Interface
FDM ....Frequency Division Multiplexing
FID......................Format Identifer
FIPS ....Federal Information Processing Standard
FM ....Function Management
FMD ....Function Management Data
FT1 ....Fractional T1
FTAM ....File Transfer Access and Management
FTP ....File Transfer Protocol

G

G ....Giga-
GB ....Gigabyte
GHz ....Gigahertz
GOSIP ....Government OSI Profile
GUI......................Graphical User Interface

H

H ....Hexadecimal
HDLC ....High Level Data Link Control
HLLAPI...............High Level Language API
Hz ....Hertz

I

IAB ....Internet Activities Board
IAC ....Interpret as Command
IANA ....Internet Assigned Numbers Authority
ICMP ....Internet Control Message Protocol
ICP......................Internet Control Protocol
IDI ....Initial Domain Indicator
IDP......................Initial Domain Part
IDP......................Internetwork Datagram Protocol
IEC......................International Electrotechnical Commission
IEEE ....Institute of Electrical and Electronics Engineers
IETF.....................Internet Engineering Task Force
I/G.......................Individual/Group
IGP......................Interior Gateway Protocol
IGRP...................Internet Gateway Routing Protocol
IMPS...................Interface Message Processors
I/O.......................Input/Output
IOC ....Inter-Office Channel
IP ....Internet Protocol
IPC......................Interprocess Communications Protocol
IPX......................Internetwork Packet Exchange
IR ....Internet Router
IRTF.....................Internet Research Task Force
ISDN...................Integrated Services Digital Network
IS-IS....................Intermediate System to Intermediate System Protocol
ISO.......................International Organization for Standardization
ISODE ....ISO Development Environment
ITU ....International Telecommunication Union
IXC ....Inter-Exchange Carrier

K

Kbps......................Kilo Bits per Second
KHz ....Kilohertz

L

LAA......................Locally-Administered Address
LAN......................Local Area Network
LAP ....Link Access Procedure
LAPB....................Link Access Procedure Balanced
LAPD....................Link Access Procedure D Channel
LAT......................Local Area Transport
LATA ....Local Access Transport Area
LAVC....................Local Area VAX Cluster
LEC ....Local Exchange Carrier
LF ....Largest Frame
LLAP....................LocalTalk Link Access Protocol
LLC ....Logical Link Control
LMMP ....LAN/MAN Management Protocol
LMMS ....LAN/MAN Management Service
LSL......................Link Support Layer

M

MAC....................Medium Access Control
MAN....................Metropolitan Area Network
Mbps....................Mega Bits per Second
MHS ....Message Handling Service
MHz......................Megahertz
MIB ....Management Information Base
MILNET...............MILitary NETwork
MIPS....................Millions Instructions Per Second
MIS ....Management Information Systems
MLID....................Multiple-Link Interface Driver
MNP ....Microcom Networking Protocol
MOP ....Maintenance Operations Protocol
MSAU ....Multistation Access Unit
MTA ....Message Transfer Agent

MTBF ....Mean Time Between Failure
MTTR ....Mean Time To Repair
MTU ....Maximum Transmission Unit
MUX....................Multiplex, Multiplexor

N

NACS ....NetWare Asynchronous Communications Server
NAK ....Negative Acknowledgement
NASI....................NetWare Asynchronous Service Interface
NAU ....Network Addressable Unit
NAUN ....Nearest Active Upstream Neighbor
NBP ....Name Binding Protocol
NCP ....Network Control Program
NCP ....NetWare Core Protocol
NCSI...................Network Communications Services Interface
NDIS...................Network Driver Interface Standard
NetBEUI ....NetBIOS Extended User Interface
NetBIOS ....Network Basic Input/Output System
NFS......................Network File System
NIC ....Network Information Center
NIC ....Network Interface Card
NICE...................Network Information and Control Exchange
NIS......................Names Information Socket
NIST ....National Institute of Standards and Technology
NLM ....NetWare Loadable Module
NMS ....Network Management Station
NOC....................Network Operations Center
NOS ....Network Operating System
NSF......................National Science Foundation
NSP......................Network Services Protocol
NT.......................Network Termination

O

OC1 ....Optical Carrier, level 1
ODA ....Office Document Architecture

ODI......................Open Data Link Interface
OIM ....OSI Internet Management
OSI......................Open Systems Interconnection
OSPF ....Open Shortest Path First

P

PABX...................Private Automatic Branch Exchange
PAD ....Packet Assembler and Disassembler
PAP......................Printer Access Protocol
PAR......................Positive Acknowledgement with Retransmission
PBX ....Private Branch Exchange
PCI......................Protocol Control Information
PCM.....................Pulse Code Modulation
PDN ....Public Data Network
PDU ....Protocol Data Unit
PEP ....Packet Exchange Protocol
POP......................Point of Presence
POP......................Post Office Protocol
POSIX ....Portable Operating System Interface - UNIX
POTS ....Plain Old Telephone System
PPP ....Point-to-Point Protocol
PSN......................Packet Switch Node
PSP ....Presentation Services Process
PSPDN.................Packet Switched Public Data Network
PTP ....Point-to-Point
PUC ....Public Utility Commission

R

RARP...................Reverse Address Resolution Protocol
RBOC ....Regional Bell Operating Company
RC.......................Routing Control
RD ....Route Descriptor
REM ....Ring Error Monitor
RFC ....Request for Comments
RFS......................Remote File System
RH ....Request/Response Header

RI ....Routing Information
RII ....Route Information Indicator
RIP ....Routing Information Protocol
RJE ....Remote Job Entry
ROSE ....Remote Operations Service Element
RPC ....Remote Procedure Call
RPS ....Ring Parameter Service
RSX ....Realtime resource-Sharing eXecutive
RT ....Routing Type
RU ....Request/Response Unit
RUIP ....Remote User Information Program

S

SABME ....Set Asynchronous Balanced Mode Extended
SAP.......................Service Access Point
SAP.......................Service Advertising Protocol
SCS ....System Communication Services
SDLC ....Synchronous Data Link Control
SGMP ....Simple Gateway Management Protocol
SIP ....SMDS Interface Protocol
SLIP......................Serial Line IP
SM ....Standby Monitor
SMB......................Server Message Block
SMDS ....Switched Multimegabit Data Service
SMI.......................Structure of Management Information
SMFA ....Specific Management Functional Area
SMTP....................Simple Mail Transfer Protocol
SNA ....System Network Architecture
SNADS ....Systems Network Architecture Distribution Services
SNAP....................Sub-Network Access Protocol
SNI........................Subscriber Network Interface
SNMP ....Simple Network Management Protocol
SOH ....Start of Header
SONET ....Synchronous Optical Network
SPP ....Sequenced Packet Protocol
SPX.......................Sequenced Packet Exchange

SR ....Source Routing
SRF......................Specifically Routed Frame
SRI.......................Stanford Research Institute
SRT......................Source Routing Transparent
SSAP ....Source Service Access Point
STE.......................Spanning Tree Explorer
SUA ....Stored Upstream Address
SVC ....Switched Virtual Circuit

T

TB ....Terabyte
TCB ....Transmission Control Block
TCP......................Transmission Control Protocol
TCP/IP ....Transmission Control Protocol/Internet Protocol
TDM ....Time Division Multiplexing
TELNET ....Telecommunications Network
TFTP....................Trivial File Transfer Protocol
TH........................Transmission Header
TLAP ....TokenTalk Link Access Protocol
TLI.......................Transport Layer Interface
TP ....Transport Protocol
TSR......................Terminate-and-Stay Resident
TTL......................Time-to-Live

U

UA ....Unnumbered Acknowledgement
UA ....User Agent
UDP.....................User Datagram Protocol
U/L.......................Universal/Local
ULP ....Upper Layer Protocols
UNMA.................Unified Network Management Architecture
UTP ....Unshielded Twisted Pair
UUCP ....UNIX to UNIX Copy Program

V

V ....Volt
VAN......................Value Added Network
VAP.......................Value-Added Process
VARP....................VINES Address Resolution Protocol
VFRP....................VINES Fragmentation Protocol
VGA ....Video Graphics Array
VICP.....................VINES Internet Control Protocol
VINES ....Virtual Networking System
VIP........................VINES Internet Protocol
VIPC.....................VINES Interprocess Communications
VLSI ....Very Large-Scale Integration
VMS ....Virtual Memory System
VRTP...................VINES Routing Update Protocol
VSPP ....VINES Sequenced Packet Protocol
VT.........................Virtual Terminal

W

WAN.....................Wide Area Network

X

XDR......................eXternal Data Representation
XID.......................Exchange Identification
XNS ....Xerox Network System

Z

ZIP ....Zone Information Protocol
ZIS ....Zone Information Socket
ZIT.......................Zone Information Table

Selected Manufacturers of TCP/IP-related Internetworking Products

Accton Technology Corp.
46750 Fremont Boulevard #104
Fremont, CA 94538
(510) 226-9800
(800) 926-9288
Fax: (510) 226-9833

ADAX, Inc.
630 Bancroft Way
Berkeley, CA 94710
(510) 548-7047
Fax: (510) 548-5526

ADC Kentrox
P.O. Box 10704
Portland, OR 97210
(503) 643-1681
(800) 733-5511
Fax: (503) 641-3341

ADI Systems
2115 Ringwood Avenue
San Jose, CA 95131
(408) 944-0100
(800) 228-0530
Fax (408) 944-0300

Advanced Computer Communications (ACC)
720 Santa Barbara Street
Santa Barbara, CA 93101
(805) 963-9431
(800) 444-7854
Fax: (805) 962-8499

Advanced Logic Research
9401 Jeronimo
Irvine, CA 92718
(714) 581-6770
(800) 444-4257
Fax: (714) 581-9240

The AG Group
2540 Camino Diablo #202
Walnut Creek, CA 94596
(510) 937-7900
Fax: (510) 937-24793

Alantec
47800 Westinghouse Drive
Fremont, CA 94539
(510) 770-1050
(800) 727-1050
Fax: (510) 770-1054

437

Alcatel Network Systems
2912 Wake Forest Road
Raleigh, NC 276095
(919) 850-6000
(Fax) (919) 850-6171

Alisa Systems, Inc.
221 E. Walnut, Suite 175
Pasadena, CA 91101
(818) 792-9474
(800) 992-5472
Fax: (818) 792-4068

Allen-Bradley
555 Briarwood Circle
Ann Arbor, MI 48108
(313) 998-2000
(800) 280-4362
Fax: (313) 668-2922

Alliant Computer Systems Corp.
One Monarch Drive
Littleton, MA 01460
(508) 486-4950

Allied Telesis, Inc.
575 E. Middlefield Road
Mountain View, CA 94070
(415) 964-2771
Fax: (415) 964-0944

Andrew Corporation
2771 Plaza Del Amo
Torrance, CA 90503
(213) 320-7126
(800) 733-0331
Fax: (213) 618-0386

Andyne Computing Ltd.
544 Princess Street, Suite 202
Kingston, ONT K7L 1C7
Canada

Anixter Brothers, Inc.
6602 Owens Drive, Suite 300
Pleasanton, CA 94588
(510) 463-1223
Fax: (510) 463-1255

Apple Computer, Inc.
20525 Mariani Avenue
Cupertino, CA 95014
(408) 996-1010
(800) 776-2333
Fax: (408) 974-6726

Applitek Corporation
100 Brickstone Square
Andover, MA 01810
(508) 475-4050
(800) 526-2489
Fax: (508) 475-0550

APT Communications, Inc.
9607 Dr. Perry Road
Ijamsville, MD 21754
(301) 831-1182
(800) 842-0626
Fax: (301) 874-5255

Asante Technologies
404 Tasman Drive
Sunnyvale, CA 94089
(408) 752-8388
(800) 662-9686
Fax: (408) 734-4864

ascom/IN-NET
15150 Avenue of Science #100
San Diego, CA 92128
(800) 283-3334
Fax: (619) 487-3697

ascom Timeplex Inc.
400 Chestnut Ridge Road
Woodcliff Lake, NJ 07675
(201) 391-1111
(800) 755-8526
Fax: (201) 573-6470

AT&T Computer Systems
Gatehall Drive
Parsippany, NJ 07054
(201) 397-4800
Fax: (201-397-4918

AT&T EasyLink Services
400 Interspace Parkway
Parsippany, NJ 07054
(800) 779-1111
Fax (201) 818-6534

Atlantix
4800 N. Federal Highway #301B
Boca Raton, FL 33431
(407) 362-9700
Fax: (407) 362-9772

Attachmate Corp.
13231 S.E. 36th Street
Bellevue, WA 98006
(206) 644-4010
(800) 426-6283
Fax: (206) 747-9924

Auspex Systems Inc.
2952 Bunker Hill Lane
Santa Clara, CA 95054
(408) 492-0900
Fax: (408) 492-0909

Autotrol Technology
12500 N. Washington
Denver, CO 80241
(303) 452-4919
Fax: (303) 252-2249

Avatar
65 South Street
Hopkinton, MA 01748
(508) 435-3000
(800) 282-3270
Fax: (508) 435-2470

Aydin Computer & Monitor Systems
700 Dresher Road
Horsham, PA 19044
(215) 657-7510
Fax: (215) 657-5470

Banyan Systems, Inc.
115 Flanders Road #5
Westboro, MA 01581
(508) 898-1000
(800) 828-2404
Fax: (508) 836-1810

BBN Communications Corp.
70 Fawcett Street
Cambridge, MA 02138
(617) 873-2000
Fax: (617) 491-0921

Beame & Whiteside Software
P.O. Box 8130
Dundas, ONT L9H 5E7
Canada
(416) 765-0822
Fax: (416) 765-0815

Bell Atlantic Software Systems
14 Washington Road Bldg. 2
Princeton Junction, NJ 08550
(609) 936-2900
Fax: (609) 936-2859

Bellcore
331 Newman Springs Road
Red Bank, NJ 07701-7030
(908) 758-2032

BGL Technology Corporation
451 Constitution Avenue
Camarillo, CA 93012
(805) 987-7305
Fax: (805) 987-7346

BICC Communications
103 Millbury Sreet
Auburn, MA 01501
(508) 832-8650
Fax: (508) 832-8689

Black Box Corporation
1000 Park Drive
P.O. Box 12800
Pittsburgh, PA 15241
(412) 746-5500
Fax: (412) 746-0746

BRIO Technology Inc.
444 Castro Street, Suite 810
Mountain View, CA 94041
(415) 961-4110
(800) 486-2746
Fax: (415) 961-4572

Brixton Systems
105 Montgomery Street
Cambridge, MA 02140
(617) 876-5359
Fax: (617) 868-8439

Bull HN Information Systems
Technology Park
2 Wall Street
Billerica, MA 01821
(508) 294-6000
Fax: (508) 294-6440

Bytex
120 Turnpike Road
Southborough, MA 01772
(508) 480-0840
(800) 227-1145
Fax: (508) 481-5111

C.ITOH Technology, Inc.
2515 McCabe Way
Irvine, CA 92714
(714) 660-0506
Fax: (714) 757-4423

Cabletron Systems, Inc.
P.O. Box 5005
Rochester, NH 03867-0505
(603) 332-9400
(800) 526-8378
Fax: (603) 332-4616

CACI Products
3344 N. Torey Pines Court
La Jolla, CA 92037
(619) 457-9681
Fax: (619) 457-1184

Cactus Computer, Inc.
1120 Metrocrest Drive, Suite 103
Carrollton, TX 75006
(214) 416-0525

California Microwave
985 Almanor Avenue
Sunnyvale, CA 94086
(408) 732-4000
(800) 772-5465
Fax: (408) 732-4244

Cayman Systems, Inc.
26 Landsdowne Street
Cambridge, MA 02139
(617) 494-1999
(800) 473-4776
Fax: (617) 494-9270

CBIS, Inc.
5875 Peachtree Industrial Boulevard
Bldg 100/170
Norcross, GA 30092
(404) 446-1332
Fax: (404) 446-9164

C.D., Ltd.
P.O. Box 907
Roslin, WA 98941
(206) 243-8700
Fax: (509) 649-3003

CE Software
1801 Industrial Circle
West Des Moines, IA 50565
(515) 224-1995
(800) 523-7638
Fax: (515) 224-4534

Chipcom Corporation
118 Turnpike Road
Southborough, MA 01772
(508) 460-8900
(800) 228-9930
Fax: (508) 460-8950

cisco Systems Inc.
1525 O'Brien Drive
Menlo Park, CA 94025
(415) 326-1941
(800) 553-6387
Fax: (415) 326-1989

Claflin & Clayton, Inc.
203 S.W. Cutoff
Northboro, MA 01532
(508) 393-7979
Fax (508) 393-8788

Clearpoint Research Corporation
35 Parkwood Drive
Hopkinton, MA 01848
(508) 435-2000
Fax: (508) 435-7530

CMC/Rockwell International
125 Cremona Drive
Santa Barbara, CA 93117
(805) 968-4262
(800) 262-8023
Fax: (805) 968-6478

Codenoll Technology
1086 N. Broadway
Yonkers, NY 10701
(914) 965-6300
Fax: (914) 965-9811

Codex/Motorola
20 Cabot Boulevard
Mansfield, MA 02048
(508) 261-4000
Fax: (508) 261-7105

Comdisco Systems, Inc.
919 E. Hillsdale Boulevard #300
Foster City, CA 94404
(415) 574-5800
Fax: (415) 358-3601

Comlink, Inc.
44790 S. Grimmer Boulevard, Suite 103
Fremont, CA 94538
(510) 490-4690
Fax: (510) 490-4664

Communication Machinery Corp.
125 Cremona Drive
Santa Barbara, CA 93117
(805) 968-4262
(800) 262-8023
Fax: (805) 968-6478

Communications Research Group
5615 Corporate Boulevard
Baton Rouge, LA 70808
(504) 923-0888
(800) 242-5278
Fax: (504) 926-2155

Compatible Systems Corporation
P.O. Drawer 17220
Boulder, CO 80308
(303) 444-9532
(800) 356-0283
Fax: (303) 444-9595

COMPAQ Computer Corporation
P.O. Box 692000
Houston, TX 77269
(713) 370-0670
(800) 345-1518
Fax: (713) 374-1740

Computer Logics
31200 Carter Street
Solon, OH 44139
(800) 828-0311
Fax: (216) 349-8620

Computer Network Technology
6500 Wedgwood Road
Maple Grove, MN 55369
(612) 550-8000
Fax: (612) 550-8800

Concord Communications Inc.
753 Forest Street
Marlborough, MA 01752
(508) 460-4646
Fax: (508) 481-9772

Concurrent Computer Corporation
One Technology Way
Westford, MA 01886
(508) 692-6200
Fax: (508) 692-7864

Control Data Corporation
4201 N. Lexington Avenue
Arden Hills, MN 55126
(612) 482-3030
Fax: (612) 482-3616

Coral Network Corporation
734 Forest Street
Marlborough, MA 01752
(508) 460-6010
Fax: (508) 481-6258

Corvus Systems
160 Great Oaks Boulevard
San Jose, CA 95119-1347
(408) 281-4100
Fax: (408) 578-4102

Cray Research, Inc.
655 Lone Oak Drive
Egan, MN 55121
(612) 683-7100
Fax: (612) 683-7199

Crescendo Communications, Inc.
710 Lakeway Drive, Suite 200
Sunnyvale, CA 94086
(408) 732-4400
Fax: (408) 732-4604

CrossComm Corporation
140 Locke Drive #C
Marlboro, MA 01752
(508) 481-4060
(800) 388-1200
Fax: (508) 481-4216

Cross Information Company
1881 Ninth Street, Suite 302
Boulder, CO 80302
(303) 444-7799
Fax: (303) 444-4687

Cryptall Communications Corp.
2 Thurber Boulevard
Smithfield, RI 02917
(401) 232-7600
Fax: (617) 255-5885

Crystal Point, Inc.
22122 20th Avenue S.E. #148
Bothell, WA 98021
(206) 487-3656
Fax: (206) 487-3773

CXR/Digilog
900 Business Center Drive #200
Horsham, PA 19044-3453
(215) 956-9570
(800) 344-4564
Fax: (215) 956-0108

Dalcon Computer Services
9720 Beechnut #406
Houston, TX 77036
(713) 771-8357
Fax: (713) 771-5164

Datability, Inc.
One Palmer Terrace
Carlstadt, NJ 07072
(201) 438-2400
Fax: (201) 438-2688

Data General Corporation
4400 Computer Drive
Westboro, MA 01580
(508) 366-8911
(800) 328-2436
Fax: (508) 366-1744

Data Interface Systems, Corp.
8701 N. MoPac Expressway #415
Austin, TX 78759
(512) 346-5641
(800) 351-4244
Fax: (512) 346-4035

Datapoint Corporation
8400 Datapoint Drive
San Antonio, TX 78229-8500
(512) 593-7900
(800) 733-1500
Fax: (512) 593-7472

David Systems Inc.
701 East Evelyn Avenue
Sunnyvale, CA 94088-3718
(408) 720-8000
(800) 762-7848
Fax: (408) 720-1337

Dayna Communications
50 S. Main Street, 5th Fl.
Salt Lake City, UT 84144
(801) 531-0203
Fax: (801) 359-9135

Daystar Digital, Inc.
5556 Atlanta Hwy.
Flowery Branch, GA 30542
(404) 967-2077
(800) 962-2077
Fax: (404) 967-3018

DCA 10Net Communications
7887 Washington Village Drive
Suite 200
Dayton, OH 45459
(513) 433-2238
(800) 782-1010
Fax: (513) 434-6305

Demax Software Inc.
999 Baker Way, Suite 500
San Mateo, CA 94404
(415) 341-9017
(800) 283-3629
Fax: (415) 341-5809

Dickens Data Systems
3850 Holcomb Bridge Road, Suite 230
Norcross, GA 30092
(404) 417-4622
Fax: (404) 242-6233

Digital Analysis Corporation
1889 Preston White Drive
Reston, VA 22091
(703) 476-5900
Fax: (703) 476-1918

**Digital Communications Associates
(DCA)**
1000 Alderman Drive
Alpharetta, GA 30201
(404) 442-4000
(800) 348-3221
Fax: (404) 442-4366

Digital Equipment Corporation (DEC)
146 Main Street
Maynard, MA 01754
(508) 493-5111
(800) 344-4825
Fax: (508) 493-8787

Digital Link
252 Humboldt Court
Sunnyvale, CA 94089
(408) 745-6200
(800) 441-1142
Fax: (408) 745-6250

Digital Research
70 Garden Court
Monterey, CA 93940
(408) 649-3896
(800) 274-4374
Fax: (408) 646-6248

Digital Technology
2300 Edwin C. Moses Boulevard
Dayton, OH 45408
(513) 443-0412
(800) 852-1252
Fax: (513) 226-0511

Digitech Industries
66 Grove Street
Ridgefield, CT 06877
(203) 438-3731
Fax: (203) 438-4184

Distinct Corporation
P.O. Box 3410
Saratoga, CA 95070
(408) 741-0781
Fax: (408) 741-0795

D-Link Systems
5 Musick
Irvine, CA 92718
(714) 455-1688
Fax: (714) 455-2521

DMA
1776 E. Jericho Tpke.
Huntington, NY 11743
(516) 462-0440
Fax: (516) 462-6652

Dove Computer
1200 N. 23rd Street
Wilmington, NC 28405
(919) 763-7918
(800) 788-3683
Fax: (919) 251-9441

Dowty Communications Inc.
9020 Junction Drive
Annapolis, MD 20701
(301) 317-7710
(800) 359-7710
Fax: (301) 317-7220

Eicon Technology Corporation
2196 32nd Avenue
Montreal, QUE Canada H8T 3H7
(514) 631-2592
Fax: (514) 631-3092

Emerging Technologies Inc.
900 Walt Whitman Road
Melville, NY 11747
(516) 271-4525
Fax: (516) 271-4814

Emulex Corporation
3545 Harbor Boulevard
Costa Mesa, CA 92626
(714) 662-5600
Fax: (714) 241-0792

Epilogue Technology Corporation
919 High Point Drive
Ventura, CA 93003-1414
(805) 650-7107
Fax:

Equinox Systems
14260 S.W. 119 Avenue
Miami, FL 33186
(305) 255-3500
(800) 275-3500
Fax: (305) 253-0003

Essex Systems Inc.
One Essex Green Drive
Peabody, MA 01960
(508) 532-5511
Fax: (508) 531-5541

Fairfield Software Inc.
200 W. Lowe Street
Fairfield, IA 52556
(515) 472-7077
Fax: (515) 472-7198

Falcon Microsystems, Inc
1801 McCormick Drive
Landover, MD 20785-5326
(301) 341-0146
Fax (301) 386-3583

Farallon Computing Inc.
2000 Powell Street, #600
Emeryville, CA 94608
(510) 596-9100
Fax: (510) 596-9020

FEL Computing
10 Main Street
P.O. Box 72
Williamsville, VT 05362
(802) 348-7171
(800) 639-4110
Fax: (802) 348-7124

FiberCom Inc.
3353 Orange Avenue N.E.
Roanoke, VA 24012
(703) 342-6700
(800) 423-1183
Fax: (703) 342-5961

Fibermux Corporation
9310 Topanga Canyon Boulevard
Chatsworth, CA 91311
(818) 709-6000
(800) 800-4624
Fax: (818) 709-1556

Fibronics International Inc.
1 Communications Way
Independence Park
Hyannis, MA 02601
(508) 778-0700
(800) 327-9526
Fax: (508) 778-0821

Forest Computer
1749 Hamilton Road
Okemos, MI 48864
(517)349-4700
Fax: (517)349-2947

Frederick Engineering Inc.
10200 Old Columbia Road
Columbia, MD 21046
(301) 290-9000
Fax: (301) 381-7180

Frontier Software Development Inc.
1501 Main Street, Suite 40
Tewksbury, MA 01876
(508) 851-8872
Fax: (508) 851-6956

Frontier Technologies Inc.
10201 N. Port Washington Rd. 13 West
Mequon, WI 53092
(414) 241-4555
Fax: (414) 241-7084

FTP Software, Inc.
2 High Street
North Andover, MA 01845
(508) 685-4000
Fax: (508) 794-4477

Gandalf Data Inc.
1020 S. Noel
Wheeling, IL 60090
(708) 541-6060
(800) 426-3253
Fax: (708) 541-6803

Gandalf Systems Corp.
Cherry Hill Industrial Center
Building #9
Cherry Hill, NJ 08003-1688
(609) 424-9400
Fax: (609) 751-4374

Gateway Communications, Inc.
2941 Alton Avenue
Irvine, CA 92714
(714) 553-1555
(800) 367-6555
Fax: (714) 553-1616

General DataCom, Inc.
1579 Straits Turnpike
Middlebury, CT 06762-1299
(203) 574-1118
Fax: (203) 758-8507

Gould Inc.
Computer Systems Division
6901 W. Sunrise Boulevard
Ft. Lauderdale, FL 33313-4499
(305) 587-2900

Glasgal Communications Inc.
151 Veterans Drive
Northvale, NJ 07647
(201) 768-8082
Fax: (201) 768-2947

Grafpoint Inc.
1485 Saratoga Avenue
San Jose, CA 95129
(408) 446-1919
(800) 426-2230
Fax: (408) 446-0666

Gupta Technologies
1040 Marsh Road
Menlo Park, CA 94025
(415) 321-9500
(800) 876-3267
Fax: (415) 321-5471

Halley Systems, Inc.
1590 Oakland Road
San Jose, CA 95131
(408) 441-2190
Fax: (408) 441-2199

Harris Computer Systems Division
2101 W. Cypress Creek Road
Fort Lauderdale, FL 33309
(305) 974-1700
(800) 666-4544
Fax (305) 977-5580

Hayes Microcomputer Products, Inc.
P.O. Box 105203
Atlanta, GA 30348
(404) 840-9200
Fax: (404) 447-0178

Helios Systems
1996 Lundy Avenue
San Jose, CA 95131
(408) 432-0292
Fax: (408) 432-7323

Hewlett-Packard Company
3000 Hanover Street
Palo Alto, CA 94304
(415) 857-1501
(800) 752-0900

Hewlett-Packard
Colorado Telecommunications Division
5070 Centennial Boulevard
Colorado Springs, CO 80919
(719) 531-4000
Fax: (719) 531-4505

Honeywell Information Systems
Federal Systems Divisions
7900 West Park Drive
McLean, VA 22102
(703) 827-3894
Fax (703) 827-3729

Hughes LAN Systems Inc.
1225 Charleston Road
Mountain View, CA 94043
(415) 966-7300
(800) 395-5267
Fax: (415) 960-3738

IBM
Old Orchard Road
Armouk, NY 10504
(914) 765-1900
(800) 426-2468
Fax: (800) 232-9426

IDEAssociates Inc.
29 Dunham Road
Billerica, MA 01821
(508) 663-6878
Fax: (508) 663-8851

IMAGEN Corporation
2650 San Tomas Expressway
Santa Clara, CA 95051
(408) 986-9400
Fax: (408) 727-3725

448

IMC Networks
16931 Milliken Avenue
Irvine, CA 92714
(714) 724-1070
(800) 624-1070
Fax: (714) 720-1020

Information Presentation Technologies
555 Chorro Street, Suite A
San Luis Obispo, CA 93405
(805) 541-3000
Fax: (805-541-3037

Informix Software, Inc.
16011 College Boulevard
Lenexa, KS 66219
(913) 599-7100
(800) 331-1763
Fax: (913) 599-8590

Infotron Systems Corp.
9 North Olney Avenue
Cherry Hill Industrial Center
Cherry Hill, NJ 08003
(609) 424-9400
(800) 937-1010
Fax: (609) 751-4370

IN-NET Corporation
15150 Avenue of Science #100
San Diego, CA 92128
(619) 487-3693
(800) 283-3334
Fax: (619) 487-3697

Intel Corporation
2402 W. Beardsley Road
Phoenix, AZ 85027
(602) 869-4647
(800) 538-3373
Fax: (800) 525-3019

INTERACTIVE Systems Corporation
2401 Colorado Avenue
Santa Monica, CA 90404
(213) 453-8649
Fax: (213) 829-3374

InterComputer Communication Corp.
8230 Montgomery Road
Cincinnati, OH 45236
(513) 745-0500
Fax: (513) 745-0327

InterCon Systems Corporation
950 Herndon Parkway, Suite 420
Herndon, VA 22070
(703) 709-9890
Fax: (703) 709-9896

InterConnections Incorporated
14711 N.E. 29th Place
Bellevue, WA 98007
(206) 881-5773
(800) 950-5774
Fax: (206) 867-5022

Interlan Inc.
155 Swanson Road.
Boxborough, MA 01719
(508) 263-9929
(800) 835-5526 or
(800) 526-8255
Fax: (508) 263-8655

449

Interlink Computer Sciences, Inc.
47370 Fremont Boulevard
Fremont, CA 94538
(510) 657-9800
(800) 422-3711
Fax: (510) 659-6381

International Data Sciences, Inc.
7 Wellington Road
Lincoln, RI 02865
(401) 333-6200
(800) 437-3282
Fax: (401) 333-3584

Internetix, Inc.
8903 Presidential Parkway #210
Upper Marlboro, MD 20772
(301) 420-7900
(800) 562-7292
Fax: (301) 420-4395

Interphase
13800 Senlac
Dallas, TX 75234
(214) 919-9000
Fax: (214) 919-9200

Ipswitch, Inc.
580 Main Street
Reading, MA 01867
(617) 942-0621
Fax: (617) 942-0823

J & L Information Systems
9238 Deering Avenue
Chatsworth, CA 91311
(818) 709-1778
Fax: (818) 882-1424

Jointer Software Inc.
P.O. Box 5630
Madison, WI 53705-0630
(608) 238-8637
Fax: (608) 238-8986

Lanera Corporation
720 North 9th Street
San Jose, CA 95112
(408) 286-8508
Fax: (408) 286-4206

Lanmaster
1401 North 14th Street
P.O. Box 845
Temple, TX 76503
(817) 771-2124
Fax: (817) 771-2379

Lannet Data Communications Inc.
7711 Center Avenue #600
Huntington Beach, CA 92647
(714) 891-1964
(800) 428-4723
Fax: (714) 891-7788

Lantronix
26072 Merit Circle, Suite 113
Laguna Hills, CA 92853
(714) 367-0050
Fax: (714) 367-0287

Lanwan Technologies
1566 La Pradera Drive
Campbell, CA 95008
(408) 374-8190
Fax: (408) 741-0152

Larse Corporation
4600 Patrick Henry Drive
P.O. Box 58138
Santa Clara, CA 95052
(408) 988-6600
Fax: (408) 986-8690

Legent Corporation
711 Powell Avenue SW
Renton, WA 98055-1291
(206) 228-8980
Fax: (206) 235-7560

LEXCEL
2600 E. Nutwood Avenue, Suite 800
Fullerton, CA 92631
(714) 680-0100
(800) 925-2623
Fax: (714) 680-0319

Livingston Enterprises, Inc.
6920 Knoll Center Pkwy, Suite 220
Pleasanton, CA 94566
(510) 426-0770
Fax: (510) 426-8951

Loral Command & Control
9970 Federal Drive
Colorado Springs, CO 80921
(719) 594-1000
Fax: (719) 594-1305

Luxcom Inc.
3249 Laurelview Court
Fremont, CA 94538
(510) 770-3300
Fax: (510) 770-3399

Madge Networks, Inc.
42 Airport Parkway
San Jose, CA 95110
(408) 441-1300
(800) 876-2343
Fax: (408) 441-1335

McData Corporation
310 Interlocken Parkway
Broomfield, CO 80021
(303) 460-9200
(800) 752-0388
Fax: (303) 465-4996

MCI Communications Corp.
8003 W. Park Drive
McLean, VA 22102
(800) 888-0800
Fax: (703) 260-7099

Mesa Graphics Inc.
P.O. Box 600
Los Alamos, NM 87544
(505) 672-1998

Micom Systems, Inc.
4100 Los Angeles Avenue
Simi Valley, CA 93063
(805) 583-8600
(800) 642-6687
Fax: (805) 583-1997

Microcom, Inc.
500 River Ridge Drive
Norwood, MA 02062-5028
(617) 551-1000
(800) 822-8224
Fax: (617) 551-1006

Micro Decisionware
2995 Wilderness Place
Boulder, CO 80301
(303) 443-2706
(800) 423-8737
Fax: (303) 443-2797

Micro Integration
215 Paca Street
Cumberland, MD 21502
(301) 777-3307
(800) 832-4526
Fax: (301) 777-3462

Microsoft Corporation
One Microsoft Way
Redmond, WA 98052-6399
(206) 882-8080
(800) 227-4679
Fax: (206) 883-8101

Micro Technology, Inc.
5065 E. Hunter Avenue
Anaheim, CA 92807
(714) 970-0300
(800) 999-9684
Fax: (714) 970-5413

Micro Tempus Corporation
800 South Street #295
Waltham, MA 02154
(617) 899-4046
Fax: (617) 899-2604

Microtest, Inc.
3519 E. Shea Boulevard, Suite 134
Phoenix, AZ 85028
(602) 971-6464
(800) 526-9675
Fax: (602) 971-6963

Miramar Systems
201 N. Salsipuedes Street #204
Santa Barbara, CA 93103
(805) 966-2432
Fax: (805) 965-1824

Mitsubishi
201 Broadway
Cambridge, MA 02139
(617) 621-7500
Fax (617) 621-7550

Momentum Software Corp.
401 S. Van Brunt Street
Englewood, NJ 07631
(800) 767-1462
(201) 871-0077
Fax: (201) 871-0807

Morning Star Technologies, Inc.
1760 Zollinger Road
Columbus, OH 43221
(614) 451-1883
Fax: (614) 459-5054

Motorola Codex
20 Cabot Boulevard
Mansfield, MA 02048
(508) 261-4000
(800) 544-0062
Fax: (508) 261-7118

Mt. Xinu, Inc.
2560 9th Street, Suite 312
Berkeley, CA 94710
(510) 644-0146
Fax: (510) 644-2680

MANUFACTURERS OF TCP/IP-RELATED PRODUCTS

Multi-Tech Systems
2205 Woodale Drive
Mounds View, MN 55112
(612) 785-3500
(800) 328-9717
Fax: (612) 785-9874

Mux Lab
165 Graveline Road
St. Laurent, QUE H4T 1R3
Canada
(514) 735-2741
(800) 361-1965
Fax: (514) 735-8057

National Semiconductor
2900 Semiconductor Drive
Santa Clara, CA 95052
(408) 721-5020
(800) 538-8510

NCR Corporation
1700 S. Patterson Boulevard
Dayton, OH 45479
(513) 445-5000
(800) 225-5627
Fax: (513) 445-1847

NCR Corporation
3245 Platte Spring Road
W. Columbia, SC 29170
(803) 796-9740
Fax: (803) 739-7745

NEC America
10 Rio Robles
San Jose, CA 95134
(408) 433-1250
(800) 222-4632
Fax: (408) 433-1239

Neon Software, Inc.
1009 Oak Hill Road, Suite 203
Lafayette, CA 94549
(510) 283-9771
Fax: (510) 283-6507

NetFrame Systems
1545 Barber Lane
Milpitas, CA 95035
(408) 944-0600
(800) 852-3726
Fax: (408) 434-4190

NetLabs Inc.
4920 El Camino Real
Los Altos, CA 94022
(415) 961-9500
(800) 447-9300
Fax: (415) 961-9300

Netlink
3214 Spring Forest Road
Raleigh, NC 27604
((919) 878-8612
(800) 638-5465
Fax: (919) 872-2132

NetManage, Inc.
20823 Stevens Creek Boulevard #100
Cupertino, CA 95014
(408) 973-7171
Fax: (408) 257-6405

Netronix
1372 N. McDowell Boulevard
Petaluma, CA 94954
(707) 769-3300
(800) 282-2535
Fax: (707) 763-6291

Netwise
2477 55th Street
Boulder, CO 80301
(303) 442-8280
(800) 733-7722
Fax: (303) 442-3798

Network Application Technology Inc.
1686 Dell Avenue
Campbell, CA 95008
(408) 370-4300
(800) 543-8887
Fax: (408) 370-4222

Network Equipment Technologies Inc.
800 Saginaw Drive
Redwood City, CA 94063
(415) 366-4400
(800) 234-4638
Fax: (415) 366-5675

Network General Corporation
4200 Bohannon Drive
Menlo Park, CA 94025
(415) 688-2700
(800) 395-3151
Fax: (415) 321-0855

Network Integrators
6007 Meridian Avenue
San Jose, CA 95120
(408) 927-0412
Fax: (408) 927-0412

Network Peripherals, Inc.
2880 Zanker Road
San Jose, CA 95134
(408) 954-7300
Fax: (408) 954-8031

Network Research Corp.
2380 N. Rose Avenue
Oxnard, CA 93030
(805) 485-2700
Fax: (805) 485-8204

Network Resources Corp. (NRC)
736 S. Hillview Drive
Milpitas, CA 95035
(408) 263-8100
Fax: (408) 263-8121

Network Solutions
8229 Boone Boulevard, 7th Fl.
Vienna, VA 22180
(703) 749-0150

Network Systems Corporation
7600 Boone Avenue N.
Minneapolis, MN 55428
(612) 424-4888
(800) 248-8777
Fax: (612) 424-1661

Networth, Inc.
8101 Ridgepoint Drive
Irving, TX 75063
(214) 869-1331
(800) 544-5255
Fax: (214) 556-0841

Newbridge Networks
593 Herndon Parkway
Herndon, VA 22070-5241
(703) 834-3600
(800) 332-1080
Fax: (703) 471-7080

454

Newport Systems Solutions, Inc.
4019 Westerly Place, Suite 103
Newport Beach, CA 92660
(714) 752-1511
(800) 368-6533
Fax: (714) 752-8389

Novell, Inc.
122 East 1700 South
Provo, UT 84606
(801) 429-7000
(800) 638-9273
Fax: (801) 429-5155

Novell, Inc.
2180 Fortune Drive
San Jose, CA 95131
(408) 473-8333
(800) 243-8526
Fax: (408) 435-1706

Nuvotech
2015 Bridgeway, Suite 204
Sausalito, CA 94965
(415) 331-7815
(800) 468-8683
Fax: (415) 331-6445

Nynex Information Solutions Group Inc.
Four W. Red Oak Lane
White Plains, NY 10604
(914) 644-7800

OpenConnect Systems Inc.
2033 Chennault Drive
Carrollton, TX 75006
(214) 490-4090
Fax: (214) 490-5052

Optical Data Systems (ODS)
1101 E. Arapaho Road
Richardson, TX 75081
(214) 234-6400
Fax: (214) 234-4059

Oracle Corp.
500 Oracle Parkway
Redwood Shores, CA 94065
(415) 506-7000
(800) 392-2999
Fax: (415) 506-7255

Pacer Software Inc.
7911 Herschel Avenue #402
La Jolla, CA 92037
(619) 454-0565
Fax: (619) 454-6267

Panda Programming
P.O. Box 2652
Seattle, WA 98111-2652
(206) 953-6769

Penril DataComm Networks
1300 Quince Orchard Boulevard
Gaithersburg, MD 20878
(301) 921-8600
(800) 473-6745
Fax: (301) 921-8376

Performance Technology
800 Lincoln Center
7800 IH-10 West, Suite 800
San Antonio, TX 78230
(512) 349-2000
(800) 327-8526
Fax: (512) 366-0123

Persoft Inc.
465 Science Drive
Madison, WI 53711
(608) 273-6000
(800) 368-5283
Fax: (608) 273-8227

Plexcom
65 Moreland Road
Simi Valley, CA 93065
(805) 522-3333
Fax (805) 583-4764

Prime Computer, Inc.
100 Crosby Drive
Prime Parkway
Natick, MA 01730
(508) 655-8000
Fax: (617) 275-1800

Process Software Corporation
959 Concord Street
Framingham, MA 01701
(508) 879-6994
Fax: (508) 879-0042

Proteon, Inc.
2 Technology Drive
Westborough, MA 01581
(508) 898-2800
(800) 545-7464
Fax: (508) 366-8901

ProTools Inc.
14976 N.W. Greenbrier Parkway
Beaverton, OR 97006
(503) 645-5400
(800) 743-4335
Fax: (503) 645-3577

PSI
165 Jordan Road
Troy, NY 12180
(518) 283-8860
Fax: (518) 283-8904

PureData
180 W. Beaver Creek Road
Richmond Hill, ONT L4B 1B4
Canada
(416) 731-6444
Fax: (416) 731-7017

Pyramid Technology Corporation
1295 Charleston Road
Mountain View, CA 94043
(415) 965-7200
Fax: (415) 967-4344

Rabbit Software Corp.
7 Great Valley Parkway E.
East Malvern, PA 19355
(215) 647-0440
(800) 722-2482
Fax: (215) 640-1379

Racal Data Communications
1601 N. Harrison Parkway
Sunrise, FL 33323-2899
(305) 846-1601
(800) 722-2555
Fax: (305) 846-5510

Racal-Interlan, Inc.
155 Swanson Road
Boxborough, MA 01719
(508) 263-9929
(800) 526-8255
Fax: (508) 263-8655

Racore Computer Products
170 Knowles Drive #204
Los Gatos, CA 95030
(408) 374-8290
(800) 635-1274
Fax: (408) 374-6653

RAD Data Communications Inc.
151 West Passaic Street
Rochelle Park, NJ 07662
(201) 587-8822
(800) 969-4723
Fax: (201) 587-8847

RAD Network Devices Inc.
7711 Center Avenue, Suite 600
Huntington Beach, CA 92647
(714) 891-1964
(800) 969-4723
Fax: (714) 891-7788

Republic Telcom Systems Corp.
6150 Lookout Road
Boulder, CO 80301
(303) 530-8600
(800) 621-0236
Fax: (303) 530-8625

Research Triangle Institute
3040 Cornwallis Road
P.O. Box 12194
Research Triangle Park, NC 27709-2194
(919) 541-6000
Fax: (919) 541-5985

Retix
2644 30th Street
Santa Monica, CA 90405
(310) 828-3400
(800) 255-2333
Fax: (310) 828-2255

RFI Communications & Security
360 Turtle Creek Court
San Jose, CA 95125-1389
(408) 298-5400
Fax: (408) 275-0156

RTMX-Uniflex
800 Eastowne Drive, Suite 111
Chapel Hill, NC 27514
(919) 493-1451
Fax: (919) 490) 2903

Samsung Software America
One Corporate Drive
Andover, MA 018104
(508) 685-7200
Fax: (508) 685-4940

SBE, Inc.
2400 Bisso Lane
Concord, CA 94520
(510) 680-7722
Fax: (800) 347-2666

SCI Systems
1300 S. Memorial Parkway
Huntsville, AL 35803
(205) 882-4304
Fax: (205) 882-4305 or 4871

457

**Science Applications International
  Corporation (SAIC)**
250 E. Hacienda Avenue
Campbell, CA 95008
(408) 374-2500
Fax: (408) 374-1680

SCOPE Incorporated
1860 Michael Faraday Drive
Reston, VA 22090
(703) 471-5600
Fax: (703) 471-1715

Shiva Corporation
One Cambridge Center
Cambridge, MA 02142
(617) 252-6300
(800) 458-3550
Fax: (617) 252-6852

Siemens Stromberg-Carlson
900 Broken Sound Parkway
Boca Raton, FL 33487
(407) 955-5000
Fax: (407) 955-6538

Silicon Graphics Inc
2011 N. Shoreline Boulevard
Mountain View, CA 94043
(415) 960-1980
(800) 326-1020
Fax: (415) 960-1284

Simpact Associates, Inc.
9210 Sky Park Court
San Diego, CA 92123
(619) 565-1865
(800) 275-1860
Fax: (619) 292-8015

Simware Inc.
20 Colonnade Road
Ottawa, ONT K2E 7M6
Canada
(613) 727-1779
(800) 267-7588 or 9991
Fax: (613) 727-8797

Sirius Systems, Inc.
Box 2202
Petersburg, VA 23804
(804) 733-7944
Fax (804) 861-0358

Sitka Corporations (TOPS)
950 Marina Village Parkway
Alameda, CA 94501
(510) 769-9669
(800) 445-8677
Fax: (510) 769-8773

SMC
35 Marcus Boulevard
Hauppauge, NY 11788
(516) 273-3100
(800) 992-4762
Fax: (516) 273-7935

SNMP Research
3001 Kimberlin Heights Road
Knoxville, TN 37920
(615) 573-1434
Fax: (615) 573-9197

Softronics
5085 List Drive
Colorado Springs, CO 80919
(719) 593-9540
(800) 225-8590
Fax: (719) 548-1878

SoftSwitch Inc.
640 Lee Road #200
Wayne, PA 19087
(215) 640-9600
Fax: (215) 640-7550

Software AG of North America, Inc.
11190 Sunrise Valley Drive
Reston, VA 22091
(703) 860-5050
Fax: (703) 391-6975

Software Kinetics Ltd.
65 Iber Road
Stittsville, ONT K2S 1E7
Canada
(613) 831-0888
Fax: (613) 831-1836

Solana Electronics
4907 Morena Boulevard, Suite 1404
San Diego, CA 92117
(619) 490-5050
Fax: (619) 490-5055

SONY Corporation
677 River Oaks Parkway
San Jose, CA 95134
(408) 432-1600AN
Fax: (408) 432-1874
Fax: 81-3-3448-7461

Spider Systems, Inc.
12 New England Executive Park
Burlington, MA 01803
(617) 270-3510
Fax: (617) 270-9818

StarNine Technologies
2126 Sixth Street
Berkeley, CA 94710
(510) 548-0391
Fax: (510) 548-0393

Star Tek Inc.
71 Lyman Street
Northborough, MA 01532
(508) 393-9393
(800) 225-8528
Fax: (508) 393-6934

SunConnect Inc.
2550 Garcia Avenue
Mountain View, CA 94043-1100
(415) 960-1300
(800) 872-4786
Fax: (415) 962-1952

Sun Microsystems, Inc.
2550 Garcia Avenue
Mountain View, CA 94043
(415) 960-1300
(800) 872-4786
Fax: (415) 336-3475

Sybase Inc.
6475 Christie Avenue
Emeryville, CA 94608
(510) 596-3500
Fax: (510) 658-9441

Synergy Software
2457 Perkiomen Avenue
Reading, PA 19606
(215) 779-0522
Fax: (215) 370-0548

Synernetics Inc.
85 Rangeway Road
North Billerica, MA 01862
(508) 670-9009
(800) 992-2446
Fax: (508) 670-9015

SynOptics Communications, Inc.
P.O. Box 58185
4401 Great America Parkway
Santa Clara, CA 95052-8185
(408) 988-2400
Fax: (408) 988-5525

Syntax, Inc.
1501 W. Valley Highway N
Auburn, WA 98001
(206) 833-2525
Fax: (206) 833-1368

Systems Center Inc.
1800 Alexander Bell Drive
Reston, VA 22091
(703) 264-8000
(800) 533-5128
Fax: (703) 260-0063

T3plus Networking Inc.
2840 San Tomas Expressway
Santa Clara, CA 95051
(408) 727-4545
(800) 477-7050
Fax: (408) 727-4545

Tandem Computers, Inc.
14231 Tandem Boulevard
Austin, TX 78728-6699
(512) 244-8359
Fax: (512) 244-8037

Tangent Computer Inc.
197 Airport Boulevard
Burlingame, CA 94010
(800) 223-6677
Fax: (415) 342-9380

Technically Elite Concepts Inc.
2615 Pacific Coast Highway #322
Hermosa Beach, CA 90254
(310) 379-2505
(800) 659-6975
Fax: (310) 379-5985

Tecmar
6225 Cochran Road
Solon, OH 44139-3377
(216) 349-0600
(800) 624-8560
Fax: (216) 349-0851

Technology Exchange Company
One Jacob Way
Reading, MA 01867
(800) 333-5177
Fax: (617) 944-7272

Tekelec
26580 W. Agoura Road
Calabasas, CA 91302
(818) 880-5656
(800) 835-3532
Fax: (818) 880-6993

TEKnique
911 N. Plum Grove Road
Schaumburg, IL 60173
(708) 706-9700
Fax: (708) 706-9735

Tektronix, Inc.
P.O. Box 1197
Redmond, OR 97756
(503) 923-0333
(800) 833-9200
Fax: (503) 923-4434

Telebit Corporation
1315 Chesapeake Terrace
Sunnyvale, CA 94089
(408) 745-3086
Fax: (408) 734-4333

Telecommunications Techniques Corp.
20410 Observation Drive
Germantown, MD 20876
(301) 353-1550
(800) 638-2049
Fax: (301) 353-0731

Telematics International, Inc.
1201 Cypress Creek Road
Ft. Lauderdale, FL 33309
(305) 772-3070
Fax: (305) 351-4405

Tenon Intersystems
1123 Chapala Street
Santa Barbara, CA 93101
(805) 963-6983
Fax: (805) 962-8202

TGV, Inc.
603 Mission Street
Santa Cruz, CA 95060
(408) 427-4366
(800) 848-3440
Fax: (408) 427-4365

Themis Computer
6681 Owens Drive
Pleasanton, CA 94588
(510) 734-0870
Fax: (510) 734-0873

The Mitre Corporation
7525 Colshire Drive
McLean, VA 22102
(703) 883-6728
Fax: (703) 883-3315

The Santa Cruz Operation (SCO)
400 Encinal Street P.O. Box 1900
Santa Cruz, CA 95061-1900
(408) 425-7222
Fax: (408) 458-4227

Thomas-Conrad Corporation
1908-R Kramer Lane
Austin, TX 78758
(512) 836-1935
(800) 332-8683
Fax: (512) 836-2840

3Com Corporation
5400 Bayfront Plaza
Santa Clara, CA 95052
(408) 764-5000
(800) 638-3266
Fax: (408) 764-5032

Tiara Computer Systems
1091 Shoreline Boulevard
Mountain View, CA 94043
(415) 965-1700
(800) 638-4272
Fax: (415) 965-2677

Trellis Software, Inc.
85 Main Street
Hopkinton, MA 01748
(508) 435-3066
Fax: (508) 435-0556

Tri-Data Systems, Inc.
3270 Scott Boulevard
Santa Clara, CA 94054
(408) 727-3270
(800) 874-3282
Fax: (408) 980-6565

Triticom
P.O. Box 444180
Eden Prairie, MN 55344
(612) 937-0772
Fax: (612) 937-1998

TRW Inc.
1760 Glenn Curtiss Street
Carson, CA 90746
(213) 764-9467
Fax: (213) 764-9491

UDS Motorola, Inc.
5000 Bradford Drive
Huntsville, AL 35805-1993
(205) 430-8000
(800) 451-2369
Fax: (205) 430-7265

Ultra Network Technologies
101 Daggett Drive
San Jose, CA 95134
(408) 922-0100
Fax: (408) 433-9287

Ungermann-Bass, Inc.
3900 Freedom Circle
Santa Clara, CA 95052-8030
(408) 496-0111
(800) 873-6381
Fax: (408) 970-7386

UniSoft Systems
6121 Hollis Street
Emeryville, CA 94608-2092
(510) 420-6400
Fax: (510) 420-6499

Unisys
P.O. Box 500
Blue Bell, PA 19424
(215) 986-4011
Fax: (215) 986-6850

Unisys Defense Systems
5151 Camino Ruiz
Camarillo, CA 93011-6004
(805) 987-6811

UNIX Systems Laboratories, Inc.
190 River Road
Summit, NJ 07901
(908) 522-5006
Fax: (908) 522-5463

U.S. Robotics Software
8100 N. McCormick Boulevard
Skokie, IL 60076-2920
(504) 923-0888
(800) 292-2988

UUNET Technologies/AlterNet
3110 Fairview Park Drive, #570
Falls Church, VA 22042
(703) 876-5050
Fax: (703) 876-5059

Verilink Corp.
145 Baytech Drive
San Jose, CA 95134
(408) 945-1199
(800) 543-1008
Fax: (408) 946-5124

VisiSoft
430 10th St. N.W., Suite 5008
Atlanta, GA 30318
(404) 874-0428
(800) 226-0428
Fax: (404) 874-6412

Vitalink Communications Corp.
6607 Kaiser Drive
Fremont, CA 94555
(510) 794-1100
(800) 443-5740
Fax: (510) 795-1085

Walker Richer & Quinn, Inc.
2815 Eastlake Avenue E.
Seattle, WA 98102
(206) 324-0350
(800) 872-2829
Fax: (206) 324-0407

Wall Data, Inc.
17769 NE 78th Place
Redmond, WA 98052-4992
(206) 883-4777
(800) 487-8622
Fax: (206) 885-9250

Wandel & Goltermann Technologies
2200 Gateway Centre Boulevard
Morrisville, NC 27560
(919) 460-3300
(800) 346-6332
Fax: (919) 481-4372

Wang Laboratories
1 Industrial Avenue
Lowell, MA 01851
(508) 459-5000
(800) 225-0654
Fax: (508) 967-7020

Webster Computer Corporation
2109 O'Toole Avenue, Suite J
San Jose, CA 95131
(408) 954-8054
(800) 457-0903
Fax: (408) 954-1832

WellFleet Communications Corp.
15 Crosby Drive
Bedford, MA 01730
(617) 275-2400
Fax: (617) 275-5001

Western Digital Corporation
8105 Irvine Center Drive
Irvine, CA 92718
(714) 932-5000
Fax: (714) 932-6098

White Pine Software, Inc.
40 Simon Street, Suite 201
Nashua, NH 03060
(603) 886-9050
Fax: (603) 886-9051

Wilcom Products
Rt. 3 Daniel Webster Hwy.
Laconia, NH 03246
(603) 524-2622
Fax: (603) 528-3804

The Wollongong Group, Inc.
1129 San Antonio Road
Palo Alto, CA 94303
(415) 962-7100
(800) 872-8649
Fax: (415) 969-5547

Worldtalk Corporation
475 Alberto Way
Suite 200
Los Gatos, CA 95032
(408) 374-5600
Fax: (408) 399-4013

Xerox Corporation
100 Clinton Avenue S., 5-B
Rochester, NY 14644
(716) 423-5090
Fax: (716) 423-5733

Xinetron Inc.
238A Walsh Avenue
Santa Clara, CA 95051
(408) 727-5509
(800) 345-4415
Fax: (408) 727-6499

Xircom
26025 Mureau Road
Calabasas, CA 91302
(800) 874-7875
(818) 878-7600
Fax: (818) 878-7630

Xyplex, Inc.
330 Codman Hill Road
Boxborough, MA 01719
(508) 264-9900
(800) 338-5316
Fax: (508) 264-9930

Zenith Electronics Corporation
Communication Products Division
1000 Milwaukee Avenue
Glenview, IL 60025
(708) 391-8000
(800) 788-7244
Fax: (708) 391-8919

Obtaining Internet Information

The Network Information Center (NIC) is the central repository of Internet information. Publications include the Request for Comments (RFC) documents, FYI documents, the *DDN Protocol Implementations and Vendors Guide*, the *DDN Protocol Handbook*, and others. The NIC is located at

DDN Network Information Center
Government Systems, Inc.
14200 Park Meadow Drive
Suite 200
Chantilly, VA 22021
Telephone: (703) 802-4535 or (800) 365-3642
Facsimile: (703) 802-8376
Internet: 192.112.36.5 (NIC.DDN.MIL)

RFCs may be obtained in hard copy from the NIC for a small fee, or online via the Internet. To obtain an RFC online, use FTP to log in to NIC.DDN.MIL, with name = anonymous and password = guest. The RFCs are located in subdirectory RFC, filename RFCnnnn.TXT or RFCnnnn.PS. The nnnn represents the RFC number, e.g. RFC1175. Both ASCII (TXT suffix) and PostScript (PS suffix) files are available. FYI documents may be obtained in a similar manner. The subdirectory is FYI, and the filenames are FYInn.TXT or FYInn.PS.

Other repositories of RFCs are also available. These include:

- FTP.NISC.SRI.COM (directory RFC, filename RFCnnnn.TXT or RFCnnnn.PS)

- NIS.NSF.NET (directory RFC, filename RFCnnnn.TXT-1)

- VENERA.ISI.EDU (directory in-notes, filename RFCnnnn.TXT or RFCnnnn.PS)

Note that some systems require leading zeros in the RFC number. In other words, if RFC868.TXT does not work, try RFC0868.TXT.

A second method of obtaining RFCs is to use electronic mail. The following is an excerpt from the HELP file, obtained via the Internet using this method.

This automated mail service is provided by the DDN Network Information Center. It allows access to NIC documents and information via ordinary electronic mail. This is especially useful for people who do not have access to the NIC via a direct Internet link, such as BITNET, CSNET, and UUCP sites.

To use the mail service, send a mail message to SERVICE@NIC.DDN.MIL. In the SUBJECT field, request the type of service you wish followed by any needed arguments. The message body is normally ignored; however, if the SUBJECT field is empty, the first line of the message body will be used as the request. Large files will be broken into smaller separate messages. However, a few files are too large to be sent through the mail system. Requests are processed automatically once a day.

The following services are currently available:

```
HELP .............................................This message; a list of current services
HOST xxx .....................................Returns information about host xxx
WHOIS xxx ..................................Used to get more details about a host
IEN nnn .......................................nnn is the IEN number or the word INDEX
IETF xxx ......................................xxx is a file name
INDEX .........................................Returns the master list of available index files
INTERNET-DRAFTS xxx...............xxx is a file name
NETINFO xxx .............................xxx is a file name or the word INDEX
```

RFC nnn ....nnn is the RFC number or the word INDEX

RFC nnn.PS ....To retrieve an available Postscript RFC. Check RFC INDEX for form of RFC.

FYI nnn ....nnn is the FYI number or the word INDEX

FYI nnn.PS ....To retrieve postscript versions of FYI files

SEND xxx ....xxx is a fully specified file name

WHOIS xxx ....Returns information about xxx from the WHOIS service. Use "WHOIS HELP" for information on how to use WHOIS.

Example SUBJECT lines:

```
HELP
RFC 82
RFC INDEX
RFC 1119.PS
FYI 1
IETF 1IETF-DESCRIPTION.TXT
INTERNET-DRAFTS 1ID-ABSTRACTS.TXT
NETINFO DOMAIN-TEMPLATE.TXT
SEND RFC: RFC-BY-AUTHOR.TXT
SEND IETF/1WG-SUMMARY.TXT
SEND INTERNET-DRAFTS/DRAFT-IETF-NETDATA-NETDATA-00.TXT
HOST DIIS
WHOIS KOSTERS, MARK
```

Send comments or suggestions to SUGGESTIONS@NIC.DDN.MIL. Send questions and bug reports to BUG-SERVICE@NIC.DDN.MIL.

Note that a space is required between the document type and the document number. In other words, RFC 1187 will work; RFC1187 will not.

467

A new service to assist users with Internet information was announced in the March 1992 issue of *ConneXions, the Interoperability Report*. Following is the text detailing the new service, which was obtained using "Help:Help", described below.

RFC-Info is an e-mail based service to help locate and retrieve RFCs and FYIs. Users can ask for "lists" of all RFCs and FYIs having certain attributes ("filters") such as their ID, keywords, title, author, issuing organization, and date. Once an RFC is uniquely identified (e.g., by its RFC number), it may also be retrieved.

To use the service, send e-mail to RFC-INFO@ISI.EDU with your requests in the body of the message. Feel free to put anything in the SUBJECT—the system ignores it. (All is case independent, obviously.)

To get started, you may send a message to RFC-INFO@ISI.EDU with requests such as in the following examples (without the bracketed explanations):

```
Help: Help                              [to get this information]
List: FYI                                 [list the FYI notes]
List: RFC                 [list RFCs with window as keyword or in title]
    Keywords: window
List: FYI                                [list FYIs about windows]
    Keywords: window
List: *                     [list both RFCs and FYIs about windows]
    Keywords: window
List: RFC              [list RFCs about ARPANET, ARPA NETWORK, etc.]
    title: ARPA*NET
List: RFC                    [list RFCs issued by MITRE, dated 7+8/1991]
    Organization: MITRE
    Dated-after:  Jul-01-1991
    Dated-before: Aug-31-1991
List: RFC                          [list RFCs obsoleting a given RFC]
    Obsoletes: RFC0010
List: RFC                    [list RFCs by authors starting with "Bracken"]
    Author: Bracken*             [* is a wild card that matches everything]
List: RFC                         [list RFCs by both Postel and Gillman]
    Authors: J. Postel                 [note, the "filters" are ANDed]
```

```
        Authors: R. Gillman
List: RFC                                    [list RFCs by any Crocker]
        Authors: Crocker
List: RFC                                    [list only RFCs by S.D. Crocker]
        Authors: S.D. Crocker
List: RFC                                    [list only RFCs by D. Crocker]
        Authors: D. Crocker
Retrieve: RFC                                [retrieve RFC-822]
        Doc-ID: RFC0822                      [note, always 4 digits in RFC#]

Help: Manual            [to retrieve the long user manual, 30+ pages]
Help: List                        [how to use the LIST request]
Help: Retrieve                [how to use the RETRIEVE request]
Help: Topics              [list topics for which help is available]
Help: Dates                       ["Dates" is such a topic]
List: keywords                    [list the keywords in use]
List: organizations       [list the organizations known to the system]
```

Please try using this service. Report problems to RFC-MANAGER@ISI.EDU

As a final note, announcements of new RFCs and other Internet-related technical issues are published in *ConneXions, the Interoperability Report*. Subscriptions to *ConneXions* may be obtained from:

Interop, Inc.
480 San Antonio Road
Suite 100
Mountain View, CA 94040
Telephone: (415) 941-3399 or (800) 468-3767
Facsimile: (415) 949-1779
Internet: connexions@interop.com

APPENDIX E

Ethernet Protocol Types

Hexadecimal	Description
0000-05DC	IEEE 802.3 Length Field (0-1500 decimal)
0101-01FF	Experimental (for development) — Conflicts with 802.3 length fields
0200	Xerox PUP — Conflicts with 802.3 length fields
0201	PUP Address Translation — Conflicts with 802.3 length fields
0600	Xerox XNS IDP
0800	DOD IP
0801	X.75 Internet
0802	NBS Internet
0803	ECMA Internet
0804	CHAOSnet
0805	X.25 Level 3
0806	ARP (for IP and for CHAOS)
0807	XNS Compatability
081C	Symbolics Private
0888-088A	Xyplex
0900	Ungermann-Bass network debugger
0A00	Xerox 802.3 PUP
0A01	PUP 802.3 Address Translation
0BAD	Banyan Systems Inc.
1000	Berkeley trailer negotiation
1001-100F	Berkeley Trailer encapsulation
1600	VALID
4242	PCS Basic Block Protocol
5208	BBN Simnet Private

```
6000 ..................... DEC Unassigned
6001 ..................... DEC MOP Dump/Load Assistance
6002 ..................... DEC MOP Remote Console
6003 ..................... DEC DECnet Phase IV
6004 ..................... DEC LAT
6005 ..................... DEC DECnet Diagnostics
6006 ..................... DEC DECnet Customer Use
6007 ..................... DEC DECnet SCA
6008 ..................... DEC unassigned
6009 ..................... DEC unassigned
6010-6014 ............. 3Com Corporation
7000 ..................... Ungermann-Bass download
7001 ..................... Ungermann-Bass NIU
7002 ..................... Ungermann-Bass NIU
7007 ..................... OS/9 Microware
7020-7029 ............. LRT (England)
7030 ..................... Proteon
7034 ..................... Cabletron
8003 ..................... Cronus VLN
8004 ..................... Cronus Direct
8005 ..................... HP Probe protocol
8006 ..................... Nestar
8008 ..................... AT&T
8010 ..................... Excelan
8013 ..................... SGI diagnostic type (obsolete)
8014 ..................... SGI network games (obsolete)
8015 ..................... SGI reserved type (obsolete)
8016 ..................... SGI "bounce server" (obsolete)
8019 ..................... Apollo
802E ..................... Tymshare
802F ..................... Tigan, Inc.
8035 ..................... Reverse ARP
8036 ..................... Aeonic Systems
8038 ..................... DEC LANBridge
```

8039 ....DEC Unassigned
803A ....DEC Unassigned
803B ....DEC Unassigned
803C ....DEC Unassigned
803D ....DEC Ethernet CSMA/CD Encryption Protocol
803E......................DEC Unassigned
803F......................DEC LAN Traffic Monitor
8040 ....DEC Unassigned
8041 ....DEC Unassigned
8042 ....DEC Unassigned
8044 ....Planning Research Corporation
8046 ....AT&T
8047 ....AT&T
8049 ....ExperData (France)
805B ....VMTP (Versatile Message Transaction Protocol,
                          RFC-1045, Stanford)
805C ....Stanford V Kernel production, Version 6.0
805D ....Evans & Sutherland
8060 ....Little Machines
8062 ....Counterpoint Computers
8065 ....University of Massachusetts, Amherst
8066 ....University of Massachusetts, Amherst
8067 ....Veeco Integrated Automation
8068 ....General Dynamics
8069 ....AT&T
806A ....Autophon (Switzerland)
806C ....ComDesign
806D ....Compugraphic Corporation
806E-8077 ....Landmark Graphics Corporation
807A ....Matra (France)
807B ....Dansk Data Elektronic A/S (Denmark)
807C ....Merit Internodal
807D ....VitaLink Communications
807E......................VitaLink Communications

807F.......................VitaLink Communications
8080.......................VitaLink Communications bridge
8081......................Counterpoint Computers
8082......................Counterpoint Computers
8083......................Counterpoint Computers
8088......................Xyplex
8089......................Xyplex
808A......................Xyplex
809B......................Kinetics EtherTalk - AppleTalk over Ethernet
809C......................Datability
809D......................Datability
809E......................Datability
809F......................Spider Systems, Ltd. (England)
80A3......................Nixdorf Computer (West Germany)
80A4-80B3...........Siemens Gammasonics Inc.
80C0......................Digital Communication Associates
80C1......................Digital Communication Associates
80C2......................Digital Communication Associates
80C3......................Digital Communication Associates
80C6......................Pacer Software
80C7......................Applitek Corporation
80C8-80CC...........Integraph Corporation
80CD......................Harris Corporation
80CE......................Harris Corporation
80CF-80D2...........Taylor Inst.
80D3......................Rosemount Corporation
80D4......................Rosemount Corporation
80D5......................IBM SNA Services over Ethernet
80DD......................Varian Associates
80DE......................Integrated Solutions TRFS
                        (Transparent Remote File System)
80DF......................Integrated Solutions
80E0-80E3............Allen-Bradley
80E4-80F0............Datability

80F2......................Retix
80F3......................Kinetics, AppleTalk ARP (AARP)
80F4......................Kinetics
80F5......................Kinetics
80F7......................Apollo Computer
80FF-8103 ....Wellfleet Communications
8107......................Symbolics Private
8108......................Symbolics Private
8109......................Symbolics Private
8130......................Waterloo Microsystems
8131......................VG Laboratory Systems
8137......................Novell (old) NetWare IPX (ECONFIG E option)
8138......................Novell
8139-813D............KTI
9000......................Loopback (Configuration Test Protocol)
9001......................Bridge Communications XNS Systems Management
9002......................Bridge Communications TCP/IP Systems Management
9003......................Bridge Communications
FF00......................BBN VITAL LANBridge cache wakeup

Used with permission from FTP Software, Inc.

Link Service Access Point (SAP) Addresses

Table F-1. IEEE-Administered LSAPs

Address (hexadecimal)	Assignment
00	Null LSAP
02	Individual LLC Sublayer Management Function
03	Group LLC Sublayer Management Function
06	ARPANET Internet Protocol (IP)
0E	PROWAY (IEC955) Network Management & Initialization
42	IEEE 802.1 Bridge Spanning Tree Protocol
4E	EIA RS-511 Manufacturing Message Service
7E	ISO 8208 (X.25 over IEEE 802.2 Type 2 LLC)
8E	PROWAY (IEC 955) Active Station List Maintenance
AA	Sub-Network Access Protocol (SNAP)
FE	ISO Network Layer Protocol
FF	Global LSAP

Table F-2. Manufacturer-Implemented LSAPs

Address (hexadecimal)	Assignment
04	IBM SNA Path Control (individual)
05	IBM SNA Path Control (group)
18	Texas Instruments
80	Xerox Network Systems (XNS)

86..........................Nestar
98..........................ARPANET Address Resolution Protocol (ARP)
BC..........................Banyan VINES
E0..........................Novell NetWare
F0..........................IBM NetBIOS
F4..........................IBM LAN Management (individual)
F5..........................IBM LAN Management (group)
F8..........................IBM Remote Program Load (RPL)
FA ....Ungermann-Bass

Internet Parameters

The following is an excerpt from RFC 1340, "Assigned Numbers," by J. Reynolds and J. Postel, July 1992. RFC 1340 is maintained by the Internet Assigned Numbers Authority (IANA) at USC-Information Sciences Institute (ISI). This excerpt shows addresses, port numbers, and parameters that assist in the troubleshooting and analysis of TCP/IP-based internetworks. For complete information, obtain RFC 1340, as shown in Appendix D. This excerpt includes the following topics:

- Data Notations
- Transmission Order of Bytes
- Significance of Bits
- Special Addresses
- Version Numbers
- Protocol Numbers
- Well-Known Port Numbers
- Internet Multicast Addresses
- IANA Ethernet Address Block
- IP TOS Parameters
- IP Time to Live Parameter
- Domain System Parameters
- BOOTP Parameters
- Network Management Parameters
- Ethernet Vendor Address Components
- Address Resolution Protocol Parameters
- Reverse Address Resolution Protocol Operation Codes
- Dynamic Reverse ARP
- Inverse Address Resolution Protocol
- X.25 Type Numbers

- Public Data Network Numbers
- TELNET Options
- Protocol and Service Names

You will find each of these topics discussed under a heading in this appendix.

Data Notations

The convention in the documentation of Internet Protocols is to express numbers in decimal order and to picture data in "big-endian" order. That is, fields are described left to right, with the most significant octet on the left and the least significant octet on the right.

The order of transmission of the header and data described in this document is resolved to the octet level. Whenever a diagram shows a group of octets, the order of transmission of those octets is the normal order in which they are read in English. For example, in the following diagram the octets are transmitted in the order they are numbered:

```
0                   1                   2                   3
0 1 2 3 4 5 6 7 8 9 0 1 2 3 4 5 6 7 8 9 0 1 2 3 4 5 6 7 8 9 0 1
+-+-+-+-+-+-+-+-+-+-+-+-+-+-+-+-+-+-+-+-+-+-+-+-+-+-+-+-+-+-+-+-+
|       1       |       2       |       3       |       4       |
+-+-+-+-+-+-+-+-+-+-+-+-+-+-+-+-+-+-+-+-+-+-+-+-+-+-+-+-+-+-+-+-+
|       5       |       6       |       7       |       8       |
+-+-+-+-+-+-+-+-+-+-+-+-+-+-+-+-+-+-+-+-+-+-+-+-+-+-+-+-+-+-+-+-+
|       9       |      10       |      11       |      12       |
+-+-+-+-+-+-+-+-+-+-+-+-+-+-+-+-+-+-+-+-+-+-+-+-+-+-+-+-+-+-+-+-+
```

Transmission Order of Bytes

Whenever an octet represents a numeric quantity, the leftmost bit in the diagram is the high-order, or most significant, bit. That is, the bit labeled 0 is the most significant bit. For example, the following diagram represents the value 170 (decimal) represented in binary:

```
0 1 2 3 4 5 6 7
+-+-+-+-+-+-+-+-+
|1 0 1 0 1 0 1 0|
+-+-+-+-+-+-+-+-+
```

Significance of Bits

Similarly, whenever a multi-octet field represents a numeric quantity, the leftmost bit of the whole field is the most significant bit. When a multi-octet quantity is transmitted, the most significant octet is transmitted first.

Special Addresses

There are five classes of IP addresses: Class A through Class E. Of these, Class D and Class E addresses are reserved for experimental use. A gateway not participating in these experiments must ignore all datagrams with a Class D or Class E destination IP address. "ICMP Destination Unreachable" or "ICMP Redirect" messages must not result from receiving such datagrams.

There are certain special cases for IP addresses. These special cases can be concisely summarized using the earlier notation for an IP address:

```
IP-address ::=   { <Network-number>, <Host-number> }
```

or

```
IP-address ::= {<Network-number>, <Subnet-number>, <Host-number> }
```

The notation -1 is used to mean the field contains all 1 bits. Some common special cases are as follows:

(a)　　{0, 0}

This host on this network. Can only be used as a source address (see note later).

(b)　　{0, *<Host-number>*}

Specified host on this network. Can only be used as a source address.

    (c)   { -1, -1}

Limited broadcast. Can only be used as a destination address, and a datagram with this address must never be forwarded outside the (sub-)net of the source.

    (d)   {<Network-number>, -1}

Directed broadcast to specified network. Can only be used as a destination address.

    (e)   {<Network-number>, <Subnet-number>, -1}

Directed broadcast to specified subnet. Can only be used as a destination address.

    (f)   {<Network-number>, -1, -1}

Directed broadcast to all subnets of specified subnetted network. Can only be used as a destination address.

    (g)   {127, <any>}

Internal host loopback address. Should never appear outside a host.

Version Numbers

In the Internet protocol (IP) there is a field to identify the version of the internetwork general protocol. This field is 4 bits in size. The assigned internet version numbers are:

Decimal	Keyword	Version
0		Reserved
1-3		Unassigned
4	IP	Internet protocol
5	ST	ST Datagram Mode
6-14		Unassigned
15		Reserved

Protocol Numbers

In the Internet protocol (IP) there is a field, called "Protocol," to identify the the next level protocol. This is an 8-bit field. The assigned Internet protocol numbers are shown in Table G-1.

Table G-1. Assigned Internet protocol numbers

Decimal	Keyword	Protocol
0		Reserved
1	ICMP	Internet Control Message
2	IGMP	Internet Group Management
3	GGP	Gateway-to-Gateway
4		Unassigned
5	ST	Stream
6	TCP	Transmission Control
7	UCL	UCL
8	EGP	Exterior Gateway Protocol
9	IGP	any private interior gateway
10	BBN-RCC-MON	BBN RCC Monitoring
11	NVP-II	Network Voice Protocol
12	PUP	PUP
13	ARGUS	ARGUS
14	EMCON	EMCON
15	XNET	Cross Net Debugger
16	CHAOS	Chaos
17	UDP	User Datagram
18	MUX	Multiplexing
19	DCN-MEASDCN	Measurement Subsystems
20	HMP	Host Monitoring
21	PRM	Packet Radio Measurement
22	XNS-IDP	XEROX NS IDP
23	TRUNK-1	Trunk-1
24	TRUNK-2	Trunk-2
25	LEAF-1	Leaf-1

Table G-1. Assigned Internet protocol numbers *(continued)*

Decimal	Keyword	Protocol
26	LEAF-2	Leaf-2
27	RDP	Reliable Data Protocol
28	IRTP	Internet Reliable Transaction
29	ISO-TP4	ISO Transport Protocol Class 4
30	NETBLT	Bulk Data Transfer Protocol
31	MFE-NSP	MFE Network Services Protocol
32	MERIT-INP	MERIT Internodal Protocol
33	SEP	Sequential Exchange Protocol
34	3PC	Third-Party Connect Protocol
35	IDPR	Inter-Domain Policy Routing Protocol
36	XTP	XTP
37	DDP	Datagram Delivery Protocol
38	IDPR-CMTP	IDPR Control Message Transport Proto
39	TP++	TP++ Transport Protocol
40	IL	IL Transport Protocol
41-60		Unassigned
61		any host internal protocol
62	CFT	CFTP
63		any local network
64	SAT-EXPAK	SATNET and Backroom EXPAK
65		Unassigned
66	RVD	MIT Remote Virtual Disk Protocol
67	IPPC	Internet Pluribus Packet Core
68		any distributed file system
69	SAT-MON	SATNET Monitoring
70	VISA	VISA Protocol
71	IPCV	Internet Packet Core Utility
72	CPNX	Computer Protocol Network Executive
73	CPHB	Computer Protocol Heart Beat
74	WSN	Wang Span Network
75	PVP	Packet Video Protocol
76	BR-SAT-MON	Backroom SATNET Monitoring
77	SUN-ND	SUN ND PROTOCOL-Temporary
78	WB-MON	WIDEBAND Monitoring
79	WB-EXPAK	WIDEBAND EXPAK
80	ISO-IPISO	Internet Protocol
81	VMTP	VMTP

Table G-1. Assigned Internet protocol numbers *(continued)*

Decimal	Keyword	Protocol
82	SECURE-VMTP	SECURE-VMTP
83	VINES	VINES
84	TTP	TTP
85	NSFNET-IGP	NSFNET-IGP
86	DGP	Dissimilar Gateway Protocol
87	TCF	TCF
88	IGRP	IGRP
89	OSPFIGP	OSPFIGP
90	Sprite-RPC	Sprite RPC Protocol
91	LARP	Locus Address Resolution Protocol
92	MTP	Multicast Transport Protocol
93	AX.25	AX.25 Frames
94	IPIP	IP-within-IP Encapsulation Protocol
95	MICP	Mobile Internetworking Control Pro.
96	AES-SP3-D	AES Security Protocol 3-D
97	ETHERIP	Ethernet-within-IP Encapsulation
98	ENCAP	Encapsulation Header
99-254		Unassigned
255		Reserved

Well-Known Port Numbers

The *well-known ports* are controlled and assigned by the IANA and on most systems can only be used by system (or root) processes or by programs executed by privileged users.

Ports are used in the TCP to name the ends of logical connections that carry long-term conversations. For the purpose of providing services to unknown callers, a service contact port is defined. The list in Table G-2 specifies the port used by the server process as its contact port. The contact port is sometimes called the "well-known port."

To the extent possible, these same port assignments are used with the UDP.

The assigned ports use a small portion of the possible port numbers. For many years the assigned ports were in the range 0-255. Recently, however, the range for assigned ports managed by the IANA has been expanded to the range 0-1023.

Table G-2. Port assignments

Decimal	Keyword	Description
0/tcp		Reserved
0/udp		Reserved
1/tcp	tcpmux	TCP Port Service Multiplexer
1/udp	tcpmux	TCP Port Service Multiplexer
2/tcp	compressnet	Management Utility
2/udp	compressnet	Management Utility
3/tcp	compressnet	Compression Process
3/udp	compressnet	Compression Process
4/tcp		Unassigned
4/udp		Unassigned
5/tcp	rje	Remote Job Entry
5/udp	rje	Remote Job Entry
6/tcp		Unassigned
6/udp		Unassigned
7/tcp	echo	Echo
7/udp	echo	Echo
8/tcp		Unassigned
8/udp		Unassigned
9/tcp	discard	Discard
9/udp	discard	Discard
10/tcp		Unassigned
10/udp		Unassigned
11/tcp	systat	Active Users
11/udp	systat	Active Users
12/tcp		Unassigned
12/udp		Unassigned
13/tcp	daytime	Daytime
13/udp	daytime	Daytime
14/tcp		Unassigned
14/udp		Unassigned
15/tcp		Unassigned [was netstat]
15/udp		Unassigned
16/tcp		Unassigned
16/udp		Unassigned
17/tcp	qotd	Quote of the Day
17/udp	qotd	Quote of the Day
18/tcp	msp	Message Send Protocol

Table G-2. Port assignments *(continued)*

Decimal	Keyword	Description
18/udp	msp	Message Send Protocol
19/tcp	chargen	Character Generator
19/udp	chargen	Character Generator
20/tcp	ftp-data	File Transfer [Default Data]
20/udp	ftp-data	File Transfer [Default Data]
21/tcp	ftp	File Transfer [Control]
21/udp	ftp	File Transfer [Control]
22/tcp		Unassigned
22/udp		Unassigned
23/tcp	telnet	Telnet
23/udp	telnet	Telnet
24/tcp		any private mail system
24/udp		any private mail system
25/tcp	smtp	Simple Mail Transfer
25/udp	smtp	Simple Mail Transfer
26/tcp		Unassigned
26/udp		Unassigned
27/tcp	nsw-fe	NSW User System FE
27/udp	nsw-fe	NSW User System FE
28/tcp		Unassigned
28/udp		Unassigned
29/tcp	msg-icp	MSG ICP
29/udp	msg-icp	MSG ICP
30/tcp		Unassigned
30/udp		Unassigned
31/tcp	msg-auth	MSG Authentication
31/udp	msg-auth	MSG Authentication
32/tcp		Unassigned
32/udp		Unassigned
33/tcp	dsp	Display Support Protocol
33/udp	dsp	Display Support Protocol
34/tcp		Unassigned
34/udp		Unassigned
35/tcp		any private printer server
35/udp		any private printer server
36/tcp		Unassigned
36/udp		Unassigned

Table G-2. Port assignments *(continued)*

Decimal	Keyword	Description
37/tcp	time	Time
37/udp	time	Time
38/tcp		Unassigned
38/udp		Unassigned
39/tcp	rlp	Resource Location Protocol
39/udp	rlp	Resource Location Protocol
40/tcp		Unassigned
40/udp		Unassigned
41/tcp	graphics	Graphics
41/udp	graphics	Graphics
42/tcp	nameserver	Host Name Server
42/udp	nameserver	Host Name Server
43/tcp	nicname	Who Is
43/udp	nicname	Who Is
44/tcp	mpm-flags	MPM FLAGS Protocol
44/udp	mpm-flags	MPM FLAGS Protocol
45/tcp	mpm	Message Processing Module [recv]
45/udp	mpm	Message Processing Module [recv]
46/tcp	mpm-snd	MPM [default send]
46/udp	mpm-snd	MPM [default send]
47/tcp	ni-ftp	NI FTP
47/udp	ni-ftp	NI FTP
48/tcp		Unassigned
48/udp		Unassigned
49/tcp	login	Login Host Protocol
49/udp	login	Login Host Protocol
50/tcp	re-mail-ck	Remote Mail Checking Protocol
50/udp	re-mail-ck	Remote Mail Checking Protocol
51/tcp	la-maint	IMP Logical Address Maintenance
51/udp	la-maint	IMP Logical Address Maintenance
52/tcp	xns-time	XNS Time Protocol
52/udp	xns-time	XNS Time Protocol
53/tcp	domain	Domain Name Server
53/udp	domain	Domain Name Server
54/tcp	xns-ch	XNS Clearinghouse
54/udp	xns-ch	XNS Clearinghouse
55/tcp	isi-gl	ISI Graphics Language

488

Table G-2. Port assignments *(continued)*

Decimal	Keyword	Description
55/udp	isi-gl	ISI Graphics Language
56/tcp	xns-auth	XNS Authentication
56/udp	xns-auth	XNS Authentication
57/tcp		any private terminal access
57/udp		any private terminal access
58/tcp	xns-mail	XNS Mail
58/udp	xns-mail	XNS Mail
59/tcp		any private file service
59/udp		any private file service
60/tcp		Unassigned
60/udp		Unassigned
61/tcp	ni-mail	NI MAIL
61/udp	ni-mail	NI MAIL
62/tcp	acas	ACA Services
62/udp	acas	ACA Services
63/tcp	via-ftp	VIA Systems—FTP
63/udp	via-ftp	VIA Systems—FTP
64/tcp	covia	Communications Integrator
64/udp	covia	Communications Integrator
65/tcp	tacacs-ds	TACACS-Database Service
65/udp	tacacs-ds	TACACS-Database Service
66/tcp	sql*net	Oracle SQL*NET
66/udp	sql*net	Oracle SQL*NET
67/tcp	bootps	Bootstrap Protocol Server
67/udp	bootps	Bootstrap Protocol Server
68/tcp	bootpc	Bootstrap Protocol Client
68/udp	bootpc	Bootstrap Protocol Client
69/tcp	tftp	Trivial File Transfer
69/udp	tftp	Trivial File Transfer
70/tcp	gopher	Gopher
70/udp	gopher	Gopher
71/tcp	netrjs-1	Remote Job Service
71/udp	netrjs-1	Remote Job Service
72/tcp	netrjs-2	Remote Job Service
72/udp	netrjs-2	Remote Job Service
73/tcp	netrjs-3	Remote Job Service
73/udp	netrjs-3	Remote Job Service

Table G-2. Port assignments *(continued)*

Decimal	Keyword	Description
74/tcp	netrjs-4	Remote Job Service
74/udp	netrjs-4	Remote Job Service
75/tcp		any private dial out service
75/udp		any private dial out service
76/tcp		Unassigned
76/udp		Unassigned
77/tcp		any private RJE service
77/udp		any private RJE service
78/tcp	vettcp	vettcp
78/udp	vettcp	vettcp
79/tcp	finger	Finger
79/udp	finger	Finger
80/tcp	www	World Wide Web HTTP
80/udp	www	World Wide Web HTTP
81/tcp	hosts2-ns	HOSTS2 Name Server
81/udp	hosts2-ns	HOSTS2 Name Server
82/tcp	xfer	XFER Utility
82/udp	xfer	XFER Utility
83/tcp	mit-ml-dev	MIT ML Device
83/udp	mit-ml-dev	MIT ML Device
84/tcp	ctf	Common Trace Facility
84/udp	ctf	Common Trace Facility
85/tcp	mit-ml-dev	MIT ML Device
85/udp	mit-ml-dev	MIT ML Device
86/tcp	mfcobol	Micro Focus Cobol
86/udp	mfcobol	Micro Focus Cobol
87/tcp		any private terminal link
87/udp		any private terminal link
88/tcp	kerberos	Kerberos
88/udp	kerberos	Kerberos
89/tcp	su-mit-tg	SU/MIT Telnet Gateway
89/udp	su-mit-tg	SU/MIT Telnet Gateway
90/tcp	dnsix	DNSIX Securit Attribute Token Map
90/udp	dnsix	DNSIX Securit Attribute Token Map
91/tcp	mit-dov	MIT Dover Spooler
91/udp	mit-dov	MIT Dover Spooler
92/tcp	npp	Network Printing Protocol

Table G-2. Port assignments *(continued)*

Decimal	Keyword	Description
92/udp	npp	Network Printing Protocol
93/tcp	dcp	Device Control Protocol
93/udp	dcp	Device Control Protocol
94/tcp	objcall	Tivoli Object Dispatche
94/udp	objcall	Tivoli Object Dispatcher
95/tcp	supdup	SUPDUP
95/udp	supdup	SUPDUP
96/tcp	dixie	DIXIE Protocol Specification
96/udp	dixie	DIXIE Protocol Specification
97/tcp	swift-rvf	Swift Remote Vitural File Protocol
97/udp	swift-rvf	Swift Remote Vitural File Protocol
98/tcp	tacnews	TAC News
98/udp	tacnews	TAC News
99/tcp	metagram	Metagram Relay
99/udp	metagram	Metagram Relay
100/tcp	newacct	[unauthorized use]
101/tcp	hostname	NIC Host Name Server
101/udp	hostname	NIC Host Name Server
102/tcp	iso-tsap	ISO-TSAP
102/udp	iso-tsap	ISO-TSAP
103/tcp	gppitnp	Genesis Point-to-Point Trans Net
103/udp	gppitnp	Genesis Point-to-Point Trans Net
104/tcp	acr-nema	ACR-NEMA Digital Imag. & Comm. 300
104/udp	acr-nema	ACR-NEMA Digital Imag. & Comm. 300
105/tcp	csnet-ns	Mailbox Name Nameserver
105/udp	csnet-ns	Mailbox Name Nameserver
106/tcp	3com-tsmux	3COM-TSMUX
106/udp	3com-tsmux	3COM-TSMUX
107/tcp	rtelnet	Remote Telnet Service
107/udp	rtelnet	Remote Telnet Service
108/tcp	snagas	SNA Gateway Access Server
108/udp	snagas	SNA Gateway Access Server
109/tcp	pop2	Post Office Protocol—Version 2
109/udp	pop2	Post Office Protocol—Version 2
110/tcp	pop3	Post Office Protocol—Version 3
110/udp	pop3	Post Office Protocol—Version 3
111/tcp	sunrpc	SUN Remote Procedure Call

Table G-2. Port assignments *(continued)*

Decimal	Keyword	Description
111/udp	sunrpc	SUN Remote Procedure Call
112/tcp	mcidas	McIDAS Data Transmission Protocol
112/udp	mcidas	McIDAS Data Transmission Protocol
113/tcp	auth	Authentication Service
113/udp	auth	Authentication Service
114/tcp	audionews	Audio News Multicast
114/udp	audionews	Audio News Multicast
115/tcp	sftp	Simple File Transfer Protocol
115/udp	sftp	Simple File Transfer Protocol
116/tcp	ansanotify	ANSA REX Notify
116/udp	ansanotify	ANSA REX Notify
117/tcp	uucp-path	UUCP Path Service
117/udp	uucp-path	UUCP Path Service
118/tcp	sqlserv	SQL Services
118/udp	sqlserv	SQL Services
119/tcp	nntp	Network News Transfer Protocol
119/udp	nntp	Network News Transfer Protocol
120/tcp	cfdptkt	CFDPTKT
120/udp	cfdptkt	CFDPTKT
121/tcp	erpc	Encore Expedited Remote Pro.Call
121/udp	erpc	Encore Expedited Remote Pro.Call
122/tcp	smakynet	SMAKYNET
122/udp	smakynet	SMAKYNET
123/tcp	ntp	Network Time Protocol
123/udp	ntp	Network Time Protocol
124/tcp	ansatrader	ANSA REX Trader
124/udp	ansatrader	ANSA REX Trader
125/tcp	locus-map	Locus PC-Interface Net Map Ser
125/udp	locus-map	Locus PC-Interface Net Map Ser
126/tcp	unitary	Unisys Unitary Login
126/udp	unitary	Unisys Unitary Login
127/tcp	locus-con	Locus PC-Interface Conn Server
127/udp	locus-con	Locus PC-Interface Conn Server
128/tcp	gss-xlicen	GSS X License Verification
128/udp	gss-xlicen	GSS X License Verification
129/tcp	pwdgen	Password Generator Protocol
129/udp	pwdgen	Password Generator Protocol

492

Table G-2. Port assignments *(continued)*

Decimal	Keyword	Description
130/tcp	cisco-fna	cisco FNATIVE
130/udp	cisco-fna	cisco FNATIVE
131/tcp	cisco-tna	cisco TNATIVE
131/udp	cisco-tna	cisco TNATIVE
132/tcp	cisco-sys	cisco SYSMAINT
132/udp	cisco-sys	cisco SYSMAINT
133/tcp	statsrv	Statistics Service
133/udp	statsrv	Statistics Service
134/tcp	ingres-net	INGRES-NET Service
134/udp	ingres-net	INGRES-NET Service
135/tcp	loc-srv	Location Service
135/udp	loc-srv	Location Service
136/tcp	profile	PROFILE Naming System
136/udp	profile	PROFILE Naming System
137/tcp	netbios-ns	NETBIOS Name Service
137/udp	netbios-ns	NETBIOS Name Service
138/tcp	netbios-dgm	NETBIOS Datagram Service
138/udp	netbios-dgm	NETBIOS Datagram Service
139/tcp	netbios-ssn	NETBIOS Session Service
139/udp	netbios-ssn	NETBIOS Session Service
140/tcp	emfis-data	EMFIS Data Service
140/udp	emfis-data	EMFIS Data Service
141/tcp	emfis-cntl	EMFIS Control Service
141/udp	emfis-cntl	EMFIS Control Service
142/tcp	bl-idm	Britton-Lee IDM
142/udp	bl-idm	Britton-Lee IDM
143/tcp	imap2	Interim Mail Access Protocol v2
143/udp	imap2	Interim Mail Access Protocol v2
144/tcp	news	NewS
144/udp	news	NewS
145/tcp	uaac	UAAC Protocol
145/udp	uaac	UAAC Protocol
146/tcp	iso-tp0	ISO-IP0
146/udp	iso-tp0	ISO-IP0
147/tcp	iso-ip	ISO-IP
147/udp	iso-ip	ISO-IP
148/tcp	cronus	CRONUS-SUPPORT

Table G-2. Port assignments *(continued)*

Decimal	Keyword	Description
148/udp	cronus	CRONUS-SUPPORT
149/tcp	aed-512	AED 512 Emulation Service
149/udp	aed-512	AED 512 Emulation Service
150/tcp	sql-net	SQL-NET
150/udp	sql-net	SQL-NET
151/tcp	hems	HEMS
151/udp	hems	HEMS
152/tcp	bftp	Background File Transfer Program
152/udp	bftp	Background File Transfer Program
153/tcp	sgmp	SGMP
153/udp	sgmp	SGMP
154/tcp	netsc-prod	NETSC
154/udp	netsc-prod	NETSC
155/tcp	netsc-dev	NETSC
155/udp	netsc-dev	NETSC
156/tcp	sqlsrv	SQL Service
156/udp	sqlsrv	SQL Service
157/tcp	knet-cmp	KNET/VM Command/Message Protocol
157/udp	knet-cmp	KNET/VM Command/Message Protocol
158/tcp	pcmail-srv	PCMail Server
158/udp	pcmail-srv	PCMail Server
159/tcp	nss-routing	NSS-Routing
159/udp	nss-routing	NSS-Routing
160/tcp	sgmp-traps	SGMP-TRAPS
160/udp	sgmp-traps	SGMP-TRAPS
161/tcp	snmp	SNMP
161/udp	snmp	SNMP
162/tcp	snmptrap	SNMPTRAP
162/udp	snmptrap	SNMPTRAP
163/tcp	cmip-man	CMIP/TCP Manager
163/udp	cmip-man	CMIP/TCP Manager
164/tcp	cmip-agent	CMIP/TCP Agent
164/udp	smip-agent	CMIP/TCP Agent
165/tcp	xns-courier	Xerox
165/udp	xns-courier	Xerox
166/tcp	s-net	Sirius Systems
166/udp	s-net	Sirius Systems

Table G-2. Port assignments *(continued)*

Decimal	Keyword	Description
167/tcp	namp	NAMP
167/udp	namp	NAMP
168/tcp	rsvd	RSVD
168/udp	rsvd	RSVD
169/tcp	send	SEND
169/udp	send	SEND
170/tcp	print-srv	Network PostScript
170/udp	print-srv	Network PostScript
171/tcp	multiplex	Network Innovations Multiplex
171/udp	multiplex	Network Innovations Multiplex
172/tcp	cl/1	Network Innovations CL/1
172/udp	cl/1	Network Innovations CL/
173/tcp	xyplex-mux	Xyplex
173/udp	xyplex-mux	Xyplex
174/tcp	mailq	MAILQ
174/udp	mailq	MAILQ
175/tcp	vmnet	VMNET
175/udp	vmnet	VMNET
176/tcp	genrad-mux	GENRAD-MUX
176/udp	genrad-mux	GENRAD-MUX
177/tcp	xdmcp	X Display Manager Control Protocol
177/udp	xdmcp	X Display Manager Control Protocol
178/tcp	Nextstep	NextStep Window Server
178/udp	NextStep	NextStep Window Server
179/tcp	bgp	Border Gateway Protocol
179/udp	bgp	Border Gateway Protocol
180/tcp	ris	Intergraph
180/udp	ris	Intergraph
181/tcp	unify	Unify
181/udp	unify	Unify
182/tcp	audit	Unisys Audit SITP
182/udp	audit	Unisys Audit SITP
183/tcp	ocbinder	OCBinder
183/udp	ocbinder	OCBinder
184/tcp	ocserver	OCServer
184/udp	ocserver	OCServer
185/tcp	remote-kis	Remote-KIS

Table G-2. Port assignments *(continued)*

Decimal	Keyword	Description
185/udp	remote-kis	Remote-KIS
186/tcp	kis	KIS Protocol
186/udp	kis	KIS Protocol
187/tcp	aci	Application Communication Interface
187/udp	aci	Application Communication Interface
188/tcp	mumps	Plus Five's MUMPS
188/udp	mumps	Plus Five's MUMPS
189/tcp	qft	Queued File Transport
189/udp	qft	Queued File Transport
190/tcp	gacp	Gateway Access Control Protocol
190/udp	cacp	Gateway Access Control Protocol
191/tcp	prospero	Prospero
191/udp	prospero	Prospero
192/tcp	osu-nms	OSU Network Monitoring System
192/udp	osu-nms	OSU Network Monitoring System
193/tcp	srmp	Spider Remote Monitoring Protocol
193/udp	srmp	Spider Remote Monitoring Protocol
194/tcp	irc	Internet Relay Chat Protocol
194/udp	irc	Internet Relay Chat Protocol
195/tcp	dn6-nlm-aud	DNSIX Network Level Module Audit
195/udp	dn6-nlm-aud	DNSIX Network Level Module Audit
196/tcp	dn6-smm-red	DNSIX Session Mgt Module Audit Redir
196/udp	dn6-smm-red	DNSIX Session Mgt Module Audit Redir
197/tcp	dls	Directory Location Service
197/udp	dls	Directory Location Service
198/tcp	dls-mon	Directory Location Service Monitor
198/udp	dls-mon	Directory Location Service Monitor
199/tcp	smux	SMUX
199/udp	smux	SMUX
200/tcp	src	IBM System Resource Controller
200/udp	src	IBM System Resource Controller
201/tcp	at-rtmp	AppleTalk Routing Maintenance
201/udp	at-rtmp	AppleTalk Routing Maintenance
202/tcp	at-nbp	AppleTalk Name Binding
202/udp	at-nbp	AppleTalk Name Binding
203/tcp	at-3	AppleTalk Unused
203/udp	at-3	AppleTalk Unused

Table G-2. Port assignments *(continued)*

Decimal	Keyword	Description
204/tcp	at-echo	AppleTalk Echo
204/udp	at-echo	AppleTalk Echo
205/tcp	at-5	AppleTalk Unused
205/udp	at-5	AppleTalk Unused
206/tcp	at-zis	AppleTalk Zone Information
206/udp	at-zis	AppleTalk Zone Information
207/tcp	at-7	AppleTalk Unused
207/udp	at-7	AppleTalk Unused
208/tcp	at-8	AppleTalk Unused
208/udp	at-8	AppleTalk Unused
209/tcp	tam	Trivial Authenticated Mail Protocol
209/udp	tam	Trivial Authenticated Mail Protocol
210/tcp	z39.50	ANSI Z39.50
210/udp	z39.50	ANSI Z39.50
211/tcp	914c/g	Texas Instruments 914C/G Terminal
211/udp	914c/g	Texas Instruments 914C/G Terminal
212/tcp	anet	ATEXSSTR
212/udp	anet	ATEXSSTR
213/tcp	ipx	IPX
213/udp	ipx	IPX
214/tcp	vmpwscs	VM PWSCS
214/udp	vmpwscs	VM PWSCS
215/tcp	softpc	Insignia Solutions
215/udp	softpc	Insignia Solutions
216/tcp	atls	Access Technology License Server
216/udp	atls	Access Technology License Server
217/tcp	dbase	dBASE Unix
217/udp	dbase	dBASE Unix
218/tcp	mpp	Netix Message Posting Protocol
218/udp	mpp	Netix Message Posting Protocol
219/tcp	uarps	Unisys ARPs
219/udp	uarps	Unisys ARPs
220/tcp	imap3	Interactive Mail Access Protocol v3
220/udp	imap3	Interactive Mail Access Protocol v3
221/tcp	fln-spx	Berkeley rlogind with SPX auth
221/udp	fln-spx	Berkeley rlogind with SPX auth
222/tcp	fsh-spx	Berkeley rshd with SPX auth

Table G-2. Port assignments *(continued)*

Decimal	Keyword	Description
222/udp	fsh-spx	Berkeley rshd with SPX auth
223/tcp	cdc	Certificate Distribution Center
223/udp	cdc	Certificate Distribution Center
224-241		Reserved
243/tcp	sur-meas	Survey Measurement
243/udp	sur-meas	Survey Measurement
245/tcp	link	LINK
245/udp	link	LINK
246/tcp	dsp3270	Display Systems Protocol
246/udp	dsp3270	Display Systems Protocol
247-255		Reserved
345/tcp	pawserv	Perf Analysis Workbench
345/udp	pawserv	Perf Analysis Workbench
346/tcp	zserv	Zebra server
346/udp	zserv	Zebra server
347/tcp	fatserv	Fatmen Server
347/udp	fatserv	Fatmen Server
371/tcp	clearcase	Clearcase
371/udp	clearcase	Clearcase
372/tcp	ulistserv	Unix Listserv
372/udp	ulistserv	Unix Listserv
373/tcp	legent-1	Legent Corporation
373/udp	legent-1	Legent Corporation
374/tcp	legent-2	Legent Corporation
374/udp	legent-2	Legent Corporation
512/tcp	exec	remote process execution; authentication performed using passwords and UNIX loppgin names
512/udp	biff	used by mail system to notify users of new mail received; currently receives messages only from processes on the same machine
513/tcp	login	remote login a la telnet; automatic authentication performed based on priviledged port numbers and distributed databases that identify "authentication domains"
513/udp	who	maintains databases showing who's logged in to machines on a local net and the load average of the machine

Table G-2. Port assignments *(continued)*

Decimal	Keyword	Description
514/tcp	cmd	like exec, but automatic authentication is performed as for login server
514/udp	syslog	
515/tcp	printer	spooler
515/udp	printer	spooler
517/tcp	talk	like tenex link, but across machine—unfortunately, doesn't use link protocol (this is actually just a rendezvous port from which a tcp connection is established)
517/udp	talk	like tenex link, but across machine—unfortunately, doesn't use link protocol (this is actually just a rendezvous port from which a tcp connection is established)
518/tcp	ntalk	
518/udp	ntalk	
519/tcp	utime	unixtime
519/udp	utime	unixtime
520/tcp	efs	extended file name server
520/udp	router	local routing process (on site); uses variant of Xerox NS routing information protocol
525/tcp	timed	timeserver
525/udp	timed	timeserver
526/tcp	tempo	newdate
526/udp	tempo	newdate
530/tcp	courier	rpc
530/udp	courier	rpc
531/tcp	conference	chat
531/udp	conference	chat
532/tcp	netnews	readnews
532/udp	netnews	readnews
533/tcp	netwall	for emergency broadcasts
533/udp	netwall	for emergency broadcasts
540/tcp	uucp	uucpd
540/udp	uucp	uucpd
543/tcp	klogin	
543/udp	klogin	
544/tcp	kshell	krcmd

Table G-2. Port assignments *(continued)*

Decimal	Keyword	Description
544/udp	kshell	krcmd
550/tcp	new-rwho	new-who
550/udp	new-rwho	new-who
555/tcp	dsf	
555/udp	dsf	
556/tcp	remotefs	rfs server
556/udp	remotefs	rfs server
560/tcp	rmonitor	rmonitord
560/udp	rmonitor	rmonitord
561/tcp	monitor	
561/udp	monitor	
562/tcp	chshell	chcmd
562/udp	chshell	chcmd
564/tcp	9pfs	plan 9 file service
564/udp	9pfs	plan 9 file service
565/tcp	whoami	whoami
565/udp	whoami	whoami
570/tcp	meter	demon
570/udp	meter	demon
571/tcp	meter	udemon
571/udp	meter	udemon
600/tcp	ipcserver	Sun IPC server
600/udp	ipcserver	Sun IPC server
607/tcp	nqs	nqs
607/udp	nqs	nqs
666/tcp	mdqs	
666/udp	mdqs	
704/tcp	elcsd	errlog copy/server daemon
704/udp	elcsd	errlog copy/server daemon
740/tcp	netcp	NETscout Control Protocol
740/udp	netcp	NETscout Control Protocol
741/tcp	netgw	netGW
741/udp	netgw	netGW
742/tcp	netrcs	Network based Rev. Cont. Sys.
742/udp	netrcs	Network based Rev. Cont. Sys.
744/tcp	flexlm	Flexible License Manager
744/udp	flexlm	Flexible License Manager

Table G-2. Port assignments *(continued)*

Decimal	Keyword	Description
747/tcp	fujitsu-dev	Fujitsu Device Control
747/udp	fujitsu-dev	Fujitsu Device Control
748/tcp	ris-cm	Russell Info Sci Calendar Manager
748/udp	ris-cm	Russell Info Sci Calendar Manager
749/tcp	kerberos-adm	kerberos administration
749/udp	kerberos-adm	kerberos administration
750/tcp	rfile	
750/udp	loadav	
751/tcp	pump	
751/udp	pump	
752/tcp	qrh	
752/udp	qrh	
753/tcp	rrh	
753/udp	rrh	
754/tcp	tell	send
754/udp	tell	send
758/tcp	nlogin	
758/udp	nlogin	
759/tcp	con	
759/udp	con	
760/tcp	ns	
760/udp	ns	
761/tcp	rxe	
761/udp	rxe	
762/tcp	quotad	
762/udp	quotad	
763/tcp	cycleserv	
763/udp	cycleserv	
764/tcp	omserv	
764/udp	omserv	
765/tcp	webster	
765/udp	webster	
767/tcp	phonebook	phone
767/udp	phonebook	phone
769/tcp	vid	
769/udp	vid	
770/tcp	cadlock	

Table G-2. Port assignments (continued)

Decimal	Keyword	Description
770/udp	cadlock	
771/tcp	rtip	
771/udp	rtip	
772/tcp	cycleserv2	
772/udp	cycleserv2	
773/tcp	submit	
773/udp	notify	
774/tcp	rpasswd	
774/udp	acmaint_dbd	
775/tcp	entomb	
775/udp	acmaint_transd	
776/tcp	wpages	
776/udp	wpages	
780/tcp	wpgs	
780/udp	wpgs	
781/tcp	hp-collector	hp performance data collector
781/udp	hp-collector	hp performance data collector
782/tcp	hp-managed-node	hp performance data managed node
782/udp	hp-managed-node	hp performance data managed node
783/tcp	hp-alarm-mgr	hp performance data alarm manager
783/udp	hp-alarm-mgr	hp performance data alarm manager
800/tcp	mdbs_daemon	
800/udp	mdbs_daemon	
801/tcp	device	
801/udp	device	
996/tcp	xtreelic	TREE License Server
996/udp	xtreelic	XTREE License Server
997/tcp	maitrd	
997/udp	maitrd	
998/tcp	busboy	
998/udp	puparp	
999/tcp	garcon	
999/udp	applix	Applix ac
999/tcp	puprouter	
999/udp	puprouter	
1000/tcp	cadlock	
1000/udp	ock	

Registered Port Numbers

The Registered ports are not controlled by the IANA and on most systems can be used by ordinary user processes or programs executed by ordinary users.

Ports are used in the TCP to name the ends of logical connections that carry long-term conversations. For the purpose of providing services to unknown callers, a service contact port is defined. The list in Table G-3 specifies the port used by the server process as its contact port. The IANA cannot control uses of these ports, but it does register or list uses of these ports as a convienence to the community.

To the extent possible, these same port assignments are used with the UDP.

The Registered ports are in the range 1024-65535.

Table G-3. Port assignments

Keyword	Decimal	Description
blackjack	1025/tcp	network blackjack
blackjack	1025/udp	network blackjack
hermes	1248/tcp	
hermes	1248/udp	
bbn-mmc	1347/tcp	multimedia conferencing
bbn-mmc	1347/udp	multimedia conferencing
bbn-mmx	1348/tcp	multimedia conferencing
bbn-mmx	1348/udp	multimedia conferencing
sbook	1349/tcp	Registration Network Protocol
sbook	1349/udp	Registration Network Protocol
editbench	1350/tcp	Registration Network Protocol
editbench	1350/udp	Registration Network Protocol
equationbuilder	1351/tcp	Digital Tool Works (MIT)
equationbuilder	1351/udp	Digital Tool Works (MIT)
lotusnote	1352/tcp	Lotus Note
lotusnote	1352/udp	Lotus Note
ingreslock	1524/tcp	ingres
ingreslock	1524/udp	ingres
orasrv	1525/tcp	oracle
orasrv	1525/udp	oracle
prospero-np	1525/tcp	prospero nonprivileged
prospero-np	1525/udp	prospero nonprivileged
tlisrv	1527/tcp	oracle
tlisrv	1527/udp	oracle

Table G-3. Port assignments *(continued)*

Keyword	Decimal	Description
coauthor	1529/tcp	oracle
coauthor	1529/udp	oracle
issd	1600/tcp	
issd	1600/udp	
nkd	1650/tcp	
nkd	1650/udp	
callbook	2000/tcp	
callbook	2000/udp	
dc	2001/tcp	
wizard	2001/udp	curry
globe	2002/tcp	
globe	2002/udp	
mailbox	2004/tcp	
emce	2004/udp	CCWS mm conf
berknet	2005/tcp	
oracle	2005/udp	
invokator	2006/tcp	
raid-cc	2006/udp	raid
dectalk	2007/tcp	
raid-am	2007/udp	
conf	2008/tcp	
terminaldb	2008/udp	
news	2009/tcp	
whosockami	2009/udp	
search	2010/tcp	
pipe_server	2010/udp	
raid-cc	2011/tcp	raid
servserv	2011/udp	
ttyinfo	2012/tcp	
raid-ac	2012/udp	
raid-am	2013/tcp	
raid-cd	2013/udp	
troff	2014/tcp	
raid-sf	2014/udp	
cypress	2015/tcp	
raid-cs	2015/udp	
bootserver	2016/tcp	

Table G-3. Port assignments *(continued)*

Keyword	Decimal	Description
bootserver	2016/udp	
cypress-stat	2017/tcp	
bootclient	2017/udp	
terminaldb	2018/tcp	
rellpack	2018/udp	
whosockami	2019/tcp	
about	2019/udp	
xinupageserver	2020/tcp	
xinupageserver	2020/udp	
servexec	2021/tcp	
xinuexpansion1	2021/udp	
down	2022/tcp	
xinuexpansion2	2022/udp	
xinuexpansion3	2023/tcp	
xinuexpansion3	2023/udp	
xinuexpansion4	2024/tcp	
xinuexpansion4	2024/udp	
ellpack	2025/tcp	
xribs	2025/udp	
scrabble	2026/tcp	
scrabble	2026/udp	
shadowserver	2027/tcp	
shadowserver	2027/udp	
submitserver	2028/tcp	
submitserver	2028/udp	
device2	2030/tcp	
device2	2030/udp	
blackboard	2032/tcp	
blackboard	2032/udp	
glogger	2033/tcp	
glogger	2033/udp	
scoremgr	2034/tcp	
scoremgr	2034/udp	
imsldoc	2035/tcp	
imsldoc	2035/udp	
objectmanager	2038/tcp	
objectmanager	2038/udp	

Table G-3. Port assignments *(continued)*

Keyword	Decimal	Description
lam	2040/tcp	
lam	2040/udp	
interbase	2041/tcp	
interbase	2041/udp	
isis	2042/tcp	
isis	2042/udp	
isis-bcast	2043/tcp	
isis-bcast	2043/udp	
rimsl	2044/tcp	
rimsl	2044/udp	
cdfunc	2045/tcp	
cdfunc	2045/udp	
sdfunc	2046/tcp	
sdfunc	2046/udp	
dls	2047/tcp	
dls	2047/udp	
dls-monitor	2048/tcp	
dls-monitor	2048/udp	
shilp	2049/tcp	
shilp	2049/udp	
www-dev	2784/tcp	worldwide web—development
www-dev	2784/udp	worldwide web—development
NSWS	3049/tcp	
NSWS	3049/ddddp	
rfa	4672/tcp	remote file access server
rfa	4672/udp	remote file access server
commplex-main	5000/tcp	
commplex-main	5000/udp	
commplex-link	5001/tcp	
commplex-link	5001/udp	
rfe	5002/tcp	radio free ethernet
rfe	5002/udp	radio free ethernet
rmonitor_secure	5145/tcp	
rmonitor_secure	5145/udp	
padl2sim	5236/tcp	
padl2sim	5236/udp	
sub-process	6111/tcp	HP SoftBench Sub-Process Control

Table G-3. Port assignments *(continued)*

Keyword	Decimal	Description
sub-process	6111/udp	HP SoftBench Sub-Process Control
xdsxdm	6558/udp	
xdsxdm	6558/tcp	
afs3-fileserver	7000/tcp	file server itself
afs3-fileserver	7000/udp	file server itself
afs3-callback	7001/tcp	callbacks to cache managers
afs3-callback	7001/udp	callbacks to cache managers
afs3-prserver	7002/tcp	users and groups database
afs3-prserver	7002/udp	users and groups database
afs3-vlserver	7003/tcp	volume location database
afs3-vlserver	7003/udp	volume location database
afs3-kaserver	7004/tcp	AFS/Kerberos authentication service
afs3-kaserver	7004/udp	AFS/Kerberos authentication service
afs3-volser	7005/tcp	volume managment server
afs3-volser	7005/udp	volume managment server
afs3-errors	7006/tcp	error interpretation service
afs3-errors	7006/udp	error interpretation service
afs3-bos	7007/tcp	basic overseer process
afs3-bos	7007/udp	basic overseer process
afs3-update	7008/tcp	server-to-server updater
afs3-update	7008/udp	server-to-server updater
afs3-rmtsys	7009/tcp	remote cache manager service
afs3-rmtsys	7009/udp	remote cache manager service
man	9535/tcp	
man	9535/udp	
isode-dua	17007/tcp	
isode-dua	17007/udp	

Internet Multicast Addresses

Host Extensions for IP Multicasting (RFC 1112) specifies the extensions required of a host implementation of the Internet Protocol (IP) to support multicasting. Current addresses are listed below.

Address	Description
224.0.0.0	Reserved
224.0.0.1	All Hosts on this Subn

507

224.0.0.2	All Gateways on this Subnet (proposed)
224.0.0.3	Unassigned
224.0.0.4	DVMRP Routers
224.0.0.5	OSPFIGP OSPFIGP All Routers
224.0.0.6	OSPFIGP OSPFIGP Designated Routers
244.0.0.7	ST Routers
224.0.0.8	ST Hosts
224.0.0.9	RIP2 Routers
224.0.0.10-244.0.0.255	Unassigned
224.0.1.0	VMTP Managers Group
224.0.1.1	NTP Network Time Protocol
224.0.1.2	SGI—Dogfight
224.0.1.3	Rwhod
224.0.1.4	VNP
244.0.1.5	Artificial Horizons—Avaiator
224.0.1.6	NSS—Name Service Server
224.0.1.7	AUDIONEWS—Audio News Multicast
224.0.1.8	SUN NIS+ Information Service
224.0.1.9	MTP Multicast Transport Protocol
224.0.1.10-244.0.1.255	Unassigned
224.0.2.1	"rwho" Group (BSD) (unofficial)
224.0.2.2	SUN RPC PMAPPROC_CALLIT
224.0.3.0-224.0.3.255	RFE Generic Service
224.0.4.0-224.0.4.255	RFE Individual Conferences
224.1.0.0-224.1.255.255	ST Multicast Groups
224.2.0.0-224.2.255.255	Multimedia Conference Calls
232.x.x.x	VMTP transient groups

These addresses are listed in the Domain Name Service under MCAST.NET and 224.IN-ADDR.ARPA.

Note that when used on an Ethernet or on IEEE 802 network, the 23 low-order bits of the IP Multicast address are placed in the low-order 23 bits of the Ethernet or IEEE 802 net multicast address 1.0.94.0.0.0. See "IANA Ethernet Address Block" below.

508

IANA Ethernet Address Block

The Internet Assigned Numbers Authority (IANA) owns an Ethernet address block that be used for multicast address asignments or other special purposes.

The address block in IEEE binary (which is in bit transmission order) is:

```
0000 0000 0000 0000 0111 1010
```

In the normal Internet dotted decimal notation, this is 0.0.94 because the bytes are transmitted higher-order first and bits within bytes are transmitted lower-order first (see "Data Notation").

IEEE CSMA/CD and Token Bus bit transmission order: 00 00 5E

IEEE Token-Ring bit transmission order: 00 00 7A

Appearance on the wire (bits transmitted from left to right):

```
0                              23                              47
|                              |                               |
1000 0000 0000 0000 0111 1010 xxxx xxx0 xxxx xxxx xxxx xxxx
      |                                   |
Multicast Bit                       0 = Internet Multicast
                                    1 = Assigned by IANA for
                                        other uses
```

Appearance in memory (bits transmitted right-to-left within octets, octets transmitted left-to-right):

```
0                              23                              47
|                              |                               |
0000 0001 0000 0000 0101 1110 0xxx xxxx xxxx xxxx xxxx xxxx
 |                             |
Multicast Bit                  0 = Internet Multicast
                               1 = Assigned by IANA for other uses
```

The latter representation corresponds to the Internet standard bit-order, and is the format that most programmers have to deal with. Using this representation, the range of Internet Multicast addresses is:

```
01-00-5E-00-00-00  to  01-00-5E-7F-FF-FF  in hex,
or
1.0.94.0.0.0  to  1.0.94.127.255.255  in dotted decimal
```

IP TOS Parameters

This documents the default Type-of-Service values that are currently recommended for the most important Internet protocols. There are four assigned TOS values: low delay, high throughput, high reliability, and low cost. In each case, the TOS value is used to indicate "better." Only one TOS value or property can be requested in any one IP datagram.

Generally, protocols that are involved in direct interaction with a human should select low delay, while data transfers that may involve large blocks of data need high throughput. Finally, high reliability is most important for datagram-based Internet management functions.

Application protocols not included in these tables should be able to make appropriate choice of low delay (8 decimal, 1000 binary) or high throughput (4 decimail, 0100 binary).

Table G-4 shows recommended values for TOS.

Table G-4. Recommended values for TOS

Protocol	TOS	Value
TELNET1	1000	(minimize delay)
FTP		
Control	1000	(minimize delay)
Data2	0100	(maximize throughput)
TFTP	1000	(minimize delay)
SMTP3		
Command phase	1000	(minimize delay)

Table G-4. Recommended values for TOS *(continued)*

Protocol	TOS	Value
DATA phase	0100	(maximize throughput)
Domain Name Service		
UDP Query	1000	(minimize delay)
TCP Query	0000	
Zone Transfer	0100	(maximize throughput)
NNTP	0001	(minimize monetary cost)
ICMP		
Errors	0000	
Requests	00004	
Responses	<same as request>4	
Any IGP	0010	(maximize reliability)
EGP	0000	
SNMP	0010	(maximize reliability)
BOOTP	0000	

Notes:

1. Includes all interactive user protocols (e.g., rlogin).
2. Includes all bulk data transfer protocols (e.g., rcp).
3. If the implementation does not support changing the TOS during the lifetime of the connection, then the recommended TOS on opening the connection is the default TOS (0000).
4. Although ICMP request messages are normally sent with the default TOS, there are sometimes good reasons why they would be sent with some other TOS value. An ICMP response always uses the same TOS value as was used in the corresponding ICMP request message.

An application may (at the request of the user) substitute 0001 (minimize monetary cost) for any of the above values.

IP Time to Live Parameter

The current recommended default Time to Live (TTL) parameter within the Internet Protocol (IP) header (see RFC 791) is 64.

Domain System Parameters

The Internet Domain Naming System (DOMAIN) includes several parameters. These are documented in RFC 1034 and RFC 1035. The CLASS parameter is listed here. The per CLASS parameters are defined in separate RFCs. The Domain System Parameters are:

Decimal	Name
0	Reserved
1	Internet (IN)
2	Unassigned
3	Chaos (CH)
4	Hessoid (HS)
5-65534	Unassigned
65535	Reserved

BOOTP Parameters

The bootstrap protocol (BOOTP) describes an IP/UDP bootstrap protocol (BOOTP) that allows a diskless client machine to discover its own IP address, the address of a server host, and the name of a file to be loaded into memory and executed (see RFC 951). The BOOTP Vendor Information Extensions (RFC 1084) proposes an addition to the bootstrap protocol (BOOTP). The Vendor Extensions are:

Tag	Name	Data Length	Meaning
0	Pad	0	None
1	Subnet Mask	4	Subnet Mask Value
2	Time Zone	4	Time offset in seconds from UTC
3	Gateways	N	N/4 Gateway addresses
4	Time Server	N	N/4 Timeserver addresses

5	Name Server	N	N/4 IEN-116 Server addresses
6	Domain Server	N	N/4 DNS Server addresses
7	Log Server	N	N/4 Logging Server addresses
8	Quotes Server	N	N/4 Quotes Server addresses
9	LPR Server	N	N/4 Printer Server addresses
10	Impress Server	N	N/4 Impress Server addresses
11	RLP Server	N	N/4 RLP Server addresses
12	Hostname	N	Hostname string
13	Boot File Size	2	Size of boot file in 512 byte checks
14	Merit Dump File		Client to dump and the name of the file to dump it to
15-127	Unassigned		
128-154	Reserved		
255	End	0	None

Network Management Parameters

For the management of hosts and gateways on the Internet, a data structure for the information has been defined. This data structure should be used with any of several possible management protocols, such as the simple network management protocol (SNMP) (see RFC 1157) or the common management information protocol over TCP (CMOT). See Table G-5.

The data structure is the structure and indentification of management information for TCP/IP-based internets (SMI) (see RFC 1155), and the management information base for network management of TCP/IP-based internets (MIB-II).

The SMI includes the provision for parameters or codes to indicate experimental or private data structures. These parameter assignments are listed in Tables G-6 and G-7.

The older simple gateway monitoring protocol (SGMP) (see RFC 1028) also defined a data structure. The parameter assignments used with SGMP are included here for historical completeness. See Table G-8.

The network management object identifiers are under the iso (1), org (3), dod (6), internet (1), or 1.3.6.1 branch of the name space.

The SMI Network Management Directory Codes (Prefix: 1.3.6.1.1) are all reserved for future use.

Table G-5. SMI network management MGMT codes

Prefix: 1.3.6.1.2

Decimal	Name	Description
0	Reserved	
1	MTB	

Prefix: 1.3.6.1.2.1 (mib-2)

Decimal	Name	Description
0	Reserved	Reserved
1	system	System
2	interfaces	Interfaces
3	at	Address Translation
4	ip	Internet Protocol
5	icmp	Internet Control Message
6	tcp	Transmission Control Protocol
7	udp	User Datagram Protocol
8	egp	Exter Gateway Protocol
9	cmot	CMIP over TCP
10	transmission	Transmission
11	snmp	Simple Network Management
12	GenericIF	Generic Interface Extensions
13	Appletalk	Appletalk Networking
14	ospf	Open Shortest Path First
15	bgp	Border Gateway Protocol
16	rmon	Remote Network Monitoring
17	bridge	Bridge Objects
18	DecnetP4	Decnet Phase 4
19	Character	Character Streams
20	snmpParties	SNMP Parties
21	snmpSecrets	SNMP Secrets

Prefix: 1.3.6.1.2.1.10 (transmission)

Decimal	Name	Description
7	IEEE802.3	CSMACD-like Objects
8	IEEE802.4	Token Bus-like Objects
9	IEEE802.5	Token-Ring-like Objects
15	FDDI	FDDI Objects
18	DS1	T1 Carrier Objects
30	DS3	DS3 Interface Objects

Table G-5. SMI network management MGMT codes *(continued)*

31	SIP	SMDS Interface Objects
32	FRAME-RELAY	Frame Relay Objects
33	RS-232	RS-232 Objects
34	Parallel	Parallel Printer Objects

Table G-6. SMI network management experimental codes

Prefix: 1.3.6.1.3.

Decimal	Name	Description
0	Reserved	
1	CLNS	ISO CLNS Objects
2*	T1-Carrier	T1 Carrier Objects
3*	IEEE802.3	Ethernet-like Objects
4*	IEEE802.5	Token-Ring-like Objects
5*	DECNet-PHIV	DECNet Phase IV
6*	Interface	Generic Interface Objects
7*	IEEE802.4	Token Bus-like Objects
8*	FDDI	FDDI Objects
9	LANMGR-1	LAN Manager V1 Objects
10	LANMGR-TRAPS	LAN Manager Trap Objects
11	Views	SNMP View Objects
12	SNMP-AUTH	SNMP Authentication Objects
13*	BGP	Border Gateway Protocol
14*	Bridge	Bridge MIB
15*	DS3	DS3 Interface Type
16*	SIP	SMDS Interface Protocol
17*	Appletalk	Appletalk Networking
18	PPP	PPP Objects
19*	Character MIB	Character MIB
20*	RS-232 MIB	RS-232 MIB
21*	Parallel MIB	Parallel MIB
22	atsign-proxy	Proxy via Community
23*	OSPF	OSPF MIB
24	Alert-Man	Alert-Man
25	FDDI-Synoptics	FDDI-Synoptics
26*	Frame Relay	Frame Relay MIB
27*	rmon	Remote Network Management
28	IDPR	IDPR MIB
29	HUBMIB	IEEE 802.3 Hub MIB

Table G-6. SMI network management experimental codes *(continued)*

30	IPFWDTBLMIB	IP Forwarding Table MIB
31	LATM MIB	
32	SONET MIB	
33	IDENT	
34	MIME-MHS	
*	obsoleted	

Table G-7. SMI network management private enterprise codes

Prefix: 1.3.6.1.4.1.

Decimal	Name
0	Reserved
1	Proteon
2	IBM
3	CMU
4	Unix
5	ACC
6	TWG
7	CAYMAN
8	PSI
9	cisco
10	NSC
11	HP
12	Epilogue
13	U of Tennessee
14	BBN
15	Xylogics, Inc.
16	Timeplex
17	Canstar
18	Wellfleet
19	TRW
20	MIT
21	EON
22	Spartacus
23	Excelan
24	Spider Systems
25	NSFNET
26	Hughes LAN Systems
27	Intergraph
28	Interlan

Table G-7. SMI network management private enterprise codes *(continued)*

Decimal	Name
29	Vitalink Communications
30	Ulana
31	NSWC
32	Santa Cruz Operation
33	Xyplex
34	Cray
35	Bell Northern Research
36	DEC
37	Touch
38	Network Research Corp.
39	Baylor College of Medicine
40	NMFECC-LLNL
41	SRI
42	Sun Microsystems
43	Com
44	CMC
45	SynOptics
46	Cheyenne Software
47	Prime Computer
48	MCNC/North Carolina Data Network
49	Chipcom
50	Optical Data Systems
51	gated
52	Cabletron Systems
53	Apollo Computers
54	DeskTalk Systems, Inc.
55	SSDS
56	Castle Rock Computing
57	MIPS Computer Systems
58	TGV, Inc.
59	Silicon Graphics, Inc.
60	University of British Columbia
61	Merit
62	FiberCom
63	Apple Computer Inc.
64	Gandalf
65	Dartmouth

Table G-7. SMI network management private enterprise codes *(continued)*

Decimal	Name
66	David Systems
67	Reuter
68	Cornell
69	LMS
70	Locus Computing Corp.
71	NASA
29	Vitalink Communications
72	Retix
73	Boeing
74	AT&T
75	Ungermann-Bass
76	Digital Analysis Corp.
77	LAN Manager
78	Netlabs
79	ICL
80	Auspex Systems
81	Lannet Company
82	Network Computing Devices
83	Raycom Systems
84	Pirelli Focom Ltd.
85	Datability Software Systems
86	Network Application Technology
87	LINK (Lokales Informatik-Netz Karlsruhe)
88	NYU
89	RND
90	InterCon Systems Corporation
91	LearningTree Systems
92	Webster Computer Corporation
93	Frontier Technologies Corporation
94	Nokia Data Communications
95	Allen-Bradely Company
96	CERN
97	Sigma Network Systems, Inc.
98	Emerging Technologies, Inc.
99	SNMP Research
100	Ohio State University
101	Ultra Network Technologies

Table G-7. SMI network management private enterprise codes *(continued)*

Decimal	Name
102	Microcom
103	Martin Marietta Astronautic Group
104	Micro Technology
105	Process Software Corporation
106	Data General Corporation
107	Bull Company
108	Emulex Corporation
109	Warwick University Computing Services
110	Network General Corporation
111	Oracle
112	Control Data Corporation
113	Hughes Aircraft Company
114	Synernetics, Inc.
115	Mitre
116	Hitachi, Ltd.
117	Telebit
118	Salomon Technology Services
119	NEC Corporation
120	Fibermux
121	FTP Software Inc.
122	Sony
123	Newbridge Networks Corporation
124	Racal-Milgo Information Systems
125	CR SYSTEMS
126	DSET Corporation
127	Computone
128	Tektronix, Inc.
129	Interactive Systems Corporation
130	Banyan Systems Inc.
131	Sintrom Datanet Limited
132	Bell Canada
133	Crosscomm Corporation
134	Rice University
135	T3Plus Networking, Inc.
136	Concurrent Computer Corporation
137	Basser
138	Luxcom

Table G-7. SMI network management private enterprise codes *(continued)*

Decimal	Name
139	Artel
140	Independence Technologies, Inc. (ITI)
141	Frontier Software Development
142	Digital Computer Limited
143	Eyring, Inc.
144	Case Communications
145	Penril DataComm, Inc.
146	American Airlines
147	Sequent Computer Systems
148	Bellcore
149	Konkord Communications
150	University of Washington
151	Develcon
152	Solarix Systems
153	Unifi Communications Corp.
154	Roadnet
155	Network Systems Corp.
156	ENE (European Network Engineering)
157	Dansk Data Elektronik A/S
158	Morning Star Technologies
159	Dupont EOP
160	Legato Systems, Inc.
161	Motorola SPS
162	European Space Agency (ESA)
163	BIM
164	Rad Data Communications Ltd.
165	Intellicom
166	Shiva Corporation
167	Fujikura America
168	Xlnt Designs INC (XDI)
169	Tandem Computers
170	BICC
171	D-Link Systems, Inc.
172	AMP, Inc.
173	Netlink
174	C. Itoh Electronics
175	Sumitomo Electric Industries (SEI)

Table G-7. SMI network management private enterprise codes *(continued)*

Decimal	Name
176	DHL Systems, Inc.
177	Network Equipment Technologies
178	APTEC Computer Systems
179	Schneider & Koch & Co., Datensysteme GmbH
180	Hill Air Force Base
181	ADC Kentrox
182	Japan Radio Co.
183	Versitron
184	Telecommunication Systems
185	Interphase
186	Toshiba Corporation
187	Clearpoint Research Corp.
188	Ascom Gfeller Ltd.
189	Fujitsu America
190	NetCom Solutions, Inc.
191	NCR
192	Dr. Materna GmbH
193	Ericsson Business Communications
194	Metaphor Computer Systems
195	Patriot Partners
196	The Software Group Limited (TSG)
197	Kalpana, Inc.
198	University of Waterloo
199	CCL/ITRI
200	Coeur Postel
201	Mitsubish Cable Industries, Ltd.
202	SMC
203	Crescendo Communication, Inc.
204	Goodall Software Engineering
205	Intecom
206	Victoria University of Wellington
207	Allied Telesis, Inc.
208	Dowty Network Systems A/S
209	Protools
210	Nippon Telegraph and Telephone Corp.
211	Fujitsu Limited
212	Network Peripherals Inc.

Table G-7. SMI network management private enterprise codes *(continued)*

Decimal	Name
213	Netronix, Inc.
214	University of Wisconsin (Madison)
215	NetWorth, Inc.
216	Tandberg Data A/S
217	Technically Elite Concepts, Inc.
218	Labtam Australia Pty. Ltd.
219	Republic Telcom Systems, Inc.
220	ADI Systems, Inc.
221	Microwave Bypass Systems, Inc.
222	Pyramid Technology Corp.
223	Unisys_Corp
224	LANOPTICS LTD. Israel
225	NKK Corporation
226	MTrade UK Ltd.
227	Acals
228	ASTEC, Inc.
229	Delmarva Power
230	Telematics International, Inc.
231	Siemens Nixdorf Informations Syteme AG
232	Compaq
233	NetManage, Inc.
234	NCSU Computing Center
235	Empirical Tools and Technologies
236	Samsung Group
237	Takaoka Electric Mfg. Co., Ltd.
238	Netrix Systems Corporation
239	WINDATA
240	RC International A/S
241	Netexp Research
242	Internode Systems Pty Ltd.
243	netCS Informationstechnik GmbH
244	Lantronix
245	Avatar Consultants
246	Furukawa Electoric Co. Ltd.
247	AEG Electrcom
248	Richard Hirschmann GmbH & Co.
249	G2R Inc.

Table G-7. SMI network management private enterprise codes *(continued)*

Decimal	Name
250	University of Michigan
251	Netcomm, Ltd.
252	Sable Technology Corporation
253	Xerox
254	Conware Computer Consulting GmbH
255	Compatible Systems Corp.
256	Scitec Communications Systems Ltd.
257	Transarc Corporation
258	Matsushita Electric Industrial Co., Ltd.
259	ACCTON Technology
260	Star-Tek, Inc.
261	Codenoll Tech. Corp.
262	Formation, Inc.
263	Seiko Instruments, Inc. (SII)
264	RCE (Reseaux de Communication d'Entreprise SA.)
265	Xenocom, Inc.
266	AEG KABEL
267	Systech Computer Corporation
268	Visual
269	SDD (Scandinavian Airlines Data Denmark A/S)
270	Zenith Electronics Corporation
271	TELECOM FINLAND
272	BinTec Computersystems
273	EUnet Germany
274	PictureTel Corporation
275	Michigan State University
276	GTE Telecom Incorporated
277	Cascade Communications Corp.
278	Hitachi Cable, Ltd.
279	Olivetti
280	Vitacom Corporation
281	INMOS
282	AIC Systems Laboratories Ltd.
283	Cameo Communications, !nc.
284	Diab Data AB
285	Olicom A/S
286	Digital-Kienzle Computersystems

Table G-7. SMI network management private enterprise codes *(continued)*

Decimal	Name
287	CSELT(Centro Studi E Laboratori Telecomunicazioni)
288	Electronic Data Systems
289	McData Corporation
290	Harris Computer Systems Division (HCSD)
291	Technology Dynamics, Inc.
292	DATAHOUSE Information Systems Ltd.
293	DSIR Network Group
294	Texas Instruments
295	PlainTree Systems Inc.
296	Hedemann Software Development
297	Fuji Xerox Co., Ltd.
298	Asante Technology
299	Stanford University
300	Digital Link
301	Raylan Corporation
302	Datacraft
303	Hughes
304	Farallon Computing, Inc.
305	GE Information Services
306	Gambit Computer Communications
307	Livingston Enterprises, Inc.
308	Star Technologies
309	Micronics Computers Inc.
310	Basis, Inc.
311	Microsoft
312	US West Advance Technologies
313	University College London
314	Eastman Kodak Company
315	Network Resources Corporation
316	Atlas Telecom
317	Bridgeway
318	American Power Conversion Corp.
319	DOE Atmospheric Radiation Measurement Project
320	VerSteeg CodeWorks
321	Verilink Corp
322	Sybus Corportation
323	Tekelec

Table G-7. SMI network management private enterprise codes *(continued)*

Decimal	Name
324	NASA Ames Research Center
325	Simon Fraser University
326	Fore Systems, Inc.
327	Centrum Communications, Inc.
328	NeXT Computer, Inc.
329	Netcore, Inc.
330	Northwest Digital Systems
331	Andrew Corporation
332	DigiBoard
333	Computer Network Technology Corp.
334	Lotus Development Corp.
335	MICOM Communication Corporation
336	ASCII Corporation
337	PUREDATA Research/USA
338	NTT DATA
339	Empros Systems International
340	Kendall Square Research (KSR)
341	Martin Marietta Energy Systems
342	Network Innovations
343	Intel Corporation
344	Proxar
345	Epson Research Center
346	Fibernet
347	Box Hill Systems Corporation
348	American Express Travel Related Services
349	Compu-Shack
350	Parallan Computer, Inc.
351	Stratacom
352	Open Networks Engineering, Inc.
353	ATM Forum
354	SSD Management, Inc.
355	Automated Network Management, Inc.
356	Magnalink Communications Corporation
357	TIL Systems, Ltd.
358	Skyline Technology, Inc.
359	Nu-Mega Technologies, Inc.
360	Morgan Stanley & Co. Inc.

Table G-7. SMI network management private enterprise codes *(continued)*

Decimal	Name
361	Integrated Business Network
362	L & N Technologies, Ltd.
363	Cincinnati Bell Information Systems, Inc.
364	OSCOM International
365	MICROGNOSIS
366	Datapoint Corporation
367	RICOH Co. Ltd.
368	Axis Communications AB
369	Pacer Software
370	Axon Networks Inc.
371	Brixton Systems, Inc.
372	GSI
373	Tatung Co., Ltd.
374	DIS Research LTD
375	Quotron Systems, Inc.
376	Dassault Electronique
377	Corollary, Inc.
378	SEEL, Ltd.
379	Lexcel
380	W.J. Parducci & Associates, Inc.
381	OST
382	Megadata Pty Ltd.
383	LLNL Livermore Computer Center
384	Dynatech Communications
385	Symplex Communications Corp.
386	Tribe Computer Works
387	Taligent, Inc.
388	Symbol Technology, Inc.
389	Lancert
390	Alantec
391	Ridgeback Solutions
392	Metrix, Inc.
393	Excutive Systems/XTree Company
394	NRL Communication Systems Branch
395	I.D.E. Corporation
396	Matsushita Electric Works, Ltd.
397	MegaPAC

Table G-7. SMI network management private enterprise codes *(continued)*

Decimal	Name
398	Pilkington Communication Systems
440	Amnet, Inc.
441	Chase Research
442	PEER Networks
443	Gateway Communications, Inc.
444	Peregrine Systems
445	Daewoo Telecom
446	Norwegian Telecom Research
447	WilTel
448	Ericsson-Camtec
449	Codex
450	Basis
451	AGE Logic
452	INDE Electronics
453	ISODE Consortium
454	J.I. Case
455	Trillium Digital Systems
456	Bacchus Inc.
457	MCC
458	Stratus Computer
459	Quotron
460	Beame & Whiteside
461	Cellular Technical Servuces

Table G-8. SGMP vendor-specific codes

Prefix: 1,255

Decimal	Name
0	Reserved
1	Proteon
2	IBM
3	CMU
4	Unix
5	ACC
6	TWG
7	CAYMAN
8	NYSERNET

Table G-8. SGMP vendor-specific codes *(continued)*

Decimal	Name
9	cisco
10	BBN
11	Unassigned
12	MIT
1-254	Unassigned
255	Reserved

Ethernet Vendor Address Components

Ethernet hardware addresses are 48 bits, expressed as 12 hexadecimal digits (0-9, plus A-F, capitalized). These 12 hex digits consist of the first/left 6 digits (which should match the vendor of the Ethernet interface within the station) and the last/right 6 digits, which specify the interface serial number for that interface vendor.

Ethernet addresses might be written unhyphenated (e.g., 123456789ABC), or with one hyphen (e.g., 123456-789ABC), but should be written hyphenated by octets (e.g., 12-34-56-78-9A-BC).

These addresses are physical station addresses, not multicast or broadcast, so the second hex digit (reading from the left) will be even, not odd.

At present, it is not clear how the IEEE assigns Ethernet block addresses. Whether in blocks of 2**24 or 2**25, and whether multicasts are assigned with that block or separately. A portion of the vendor block address is reportedly assigned serially, with the other portion intentionally assigned randomly. If there is a global algorithm for which addresses are designated to be physical (in a chipset) versus logical (assigned in software), or globally assigned versus locally assigned addresses, some of the known addresses do not follow the scheme (e.g., AA0003; 02xxxx).

Table G-9. Ethernet vendor addresses components

Address	Vendor
00000C	Cisco
00000F	NeXT
000010	Sytek
00001D	Cabletron
000020	DIAB (Data Intdustrier AB)
000022	Visual Technology
00002A	TRW

Table G-9. Ethernet vendor addresses components *(continued)*

Address	Vendor
00005A	S & Koch
00005E	IANA
000065	Network General
00006B	MIPS
000077	MIPS
00007A	Ardent
000089	Cayman Systems—Gatorbox
000093	Proteon
00009F	Ameristar Technology
0000A2	Wellfleet
0000A3	Network Application Technology
0000A6	Network General (internal assignment, not for products)
0000A7	NCD—X-terminals
0000A9	Network Systems
0000AA	Xerox—Xerox machines
0000B3	CIMLinc
0000B7	Dove—Fastnet
0000BC	Allen-Bradley
0000C0	Western Digital
0000C6	HP Intelligent Networks Operation (formerly Eon Systems)
0000C8	Altos
0000C9	Emulex—Terminal Servers
0000D7	Dartmouth College (NED Router)
0000DD	Gould
0000DE	Unigraph
0000E2	Acer Counterpoint
0000EF	Alantec
0000FD	High Level Hardvare (Orion, UK)
000102	BBN—BBN internal usage (not registered)
001700	Kabel
00802D	Xylogics, Inc.—Annex terminal servers
00808C	Frontier Software Development
0080C2	IEEE 802.1 Committee
0080D3	Shiva
00AA00	Intel
00DD00	Ungermann-Bass
00DD01	Ungermann-Bass

Table G-9. Ethernet vendor addresses components *(continued)*

Address	Vendor
020701	Racal/Interlan—UNIBUS or QBUS machines, Apollo
020406	BBN—BBN internal usage (not registered)
026086	Satelcom MegaPac (UK)
02608C	3Com—IBM PC; Imagen; Valid; Cisco
02CF1F	CMC—Masscomp; Silicon Graphics; Prime EXL
080002	3Com (Formerly Bridge)
080003	ACC (Advanced Computer Communications)
080005	Symbolics—Symbolics LISP machines
080008	BBN
080009	Hewlett-Packard
08000A	Nestar Systems
08000B	Unisys
080010	AT&T
080011	Tektronix, Inc.
080014	Excelan—BBN Butterfly, Masscomp, Silicon Graphics
080017	NSC
08001A	Data General
08001B	Data General
08001E	Apollo
080020	Sun—Sun machines
080022	NBI
080025	CDC
080026	Norsk Data (Nord)
080027	PCS Computer Systems GmbH
080028	TI—Explorer
08002B	DEC
08002E	Metaphor
08002F	Prime Computer—Prime 50-Series LHC300
080036	Intergraph—CAE stations
080037	Fujitsu-Xerox
080038	Bull
080039	Spider Systems
080041	DCA Digital Comm. Assoc.
080046	Sony
080047	Sequent
080049	Univation
08004C	Encore

Table G-9. Ethernet vendor addresses components *(continued)*

Address	Vendor
08004E	BICC
080056	Stanford University
08005A	IBM
080067	Comdesign
080068	Ridge
080069	Silicon Graphics
08006E	Excelan
080075	DDE (Danish Data Elektronik A/S)
08007C	Vitalink—TransLAN III
080080	XIOS
080086	Imagen/QMS
080087	Xyplex—terminal servers
080089	Kinetics—AppleTalk-Ethernet interface
08008B	Pyramid
08008D	XyVision—XyVision machines
080090	Retix Inc—Bridges
AA0000	DEC—obsolete
AA0001	DEC—obsolete
AA0002	DEC—obsolete
AA0003	DEC—Global physical address for some DEC machines
AA0004	DEC—Local logical address for systems running DECNET

Address Resolution Protocol Parameters

The address resolution protocol (ARP) specified in RFC 826 has several parameters. The assigned values for these parameters are listed here.

Assignments:
Operation Code (op)

1   REQUEST
2   REPLY
Hardware Type (hrd)

Type	Description
1	Ethernet (10Mb)

2	Experimental Ethernet (3Mb)
3	Amateur Radio AX.25
4	Proteon ProNET Token Ring
5	Chaos
6	IEEE 802 Networks
7	ARCNET
8	Hyperchannel
9	Lanstar
10	Autonet Short Address
11	LocalTalk
12	LocalNet (IBM PCNet or SYTEK LocalNET)
13	Ultra link
14	SMDS
15	Frame Relay
16	Asynchronous Transmission Mode (ATM)

Protocol Type (pro)

Use the same codes as listed in RFC 1340, the section called "Ethernet Numbers of Interest" (all hardware types use this code set for the protocol type) or Appendix E of this book.

Reverse Address Resolution Protocol Operation Codes

The reverse address resolution protocol (RARP) specified in RFC 903 has the following operation codes:

Assignments:

Operation Code (op)

3	request Reverse
4	reply Reverse

Dynamic Reverse ARP

Assignments:

Operation Code (op)

5	DRARP-Request
6	DRARP-Reply
7	DRARP-Error

Inverse Address Resolution Protocol

The inverse address resolution protocol (AIRP) specified in RFC 1293 has the following operation codes:

Assignments:

Operation Code (op)

8	InARP-Request
9	InARP-Reply

X.25 Type Numbers

CCITT defines the high-order two bits of the first octet of call user data as follows:

00	Used for other CCITT recomendations (such as X.29)
01	Reserved for use by "national" administrative authorities
10	Reserved for use by international administrative authorities
11	Reserved for arbitrary use between consenting DTEs

Call User Data (hex)	Protocol
01	PAD
C5	Blacker front-end descr dev
CC	IP
CD	ISO-IP
DD	Network Monitoring

NOTE: ISO SC6/WG2 approved assignment in ISO 9577 (January 1990).

Public Data Network Numbers

One of the Internet Class A Networks is the international system of Public Data Networks. This section lists the mapping between the Internet Addresses and the Public Data Network Addresses (X.121).

The numbers in Table G-10 are assigned for networks that are connected to the Internet, and for independent networks. These independent networks are marked with an asterisk in the table.

Table G-10. Numbers assigned for networks connected to the Internet

Internet	Public Data Net	Description
014.000.000.000		Reserved
014.000.000.001	3110-317-00035 00	PURDUE-TN
014.000.000.002	3110-608-00027 00	UWISC-TN
014.000.000.003	3110-302-00024 00	UDEL-TN
014.000.000.004	2342-192-00149 23	UCL-VTEST
014.000.000.005	2342-192-00300 23	UCL-TG
014.000.000.006	2342-192-00300 25	UK-SATNET
014.000.000.007	3110-608-00024 00	UWISC-IBM
014.000.000.008	3110-213-00045 00	RAND-TN
014.000.000.009	2342-192-00300 23	UCL-CS
014.000.000.010	3110-617-00025 00	BBN-VAN-GW
014.000.000.011	2405-015-50300 00	CHALMERS*
014.000.000.012	3110-713-00165 00	RICE
014.000.000.013	3110-415-00261 00	DECWRL
014.000.000.014	3110-408-00051 00	IBM-SJ
014.000.000.015	2041-117-01000 00	SHAPE
014.000.000.016	2628-153-90075 00	DFVLR4-X25
014.000.000.017	3110-213-00032 00	ISI-VAN-GW
014.000.000.018	2624-522-80900 52	FGAN-SIEMENS-X25
014.000.000.019	2041-170-10000 00	SHAPE-X25
014.000.000.020	5052-737-20000 50	UQNET
014.000.000.021	3020-801-00057 50	DMC-CRC1
014.000.000.022	2624-522-80329 02	FGAN-FGANFFMVAX-X25
014.000.000.023	2624-589-00908 01	ECRC-X25*
014.000.000.024	2342-905-24242 83	UK-MOD-RSRE
014.000.000.025	2342-905-24242 82	UK-VAN-RSRE
014.000.000.026	2624-522-80329 05	DFVLRSUN-X25
014.000.000.027	2624-457-11015 90	SELETFMSUN-X25

Table G-10. Numbers assigned for networks connected to the Internet *(continued)*

Internet	Public Data Net	Description
014.000.000.028	3110-408-00146 00	CDC-SVL
014.000.000.029	2222-551-04400 00	SUN-CNUCE
014.000.000.030	2222-551-04500 00	ICNUCEVM-CNUCE
014.000.000.031	2222-551-04600 00	SPARE-CNUCE
014.000.000.032	2222-551-04700 00	ICNUCEVX-CNUCE
014.000.000.033	2222-551-04524 00	CISCO-CNUCE
014.000.000.034	2342-313-00260 90	SPIDER-GW
014.000.000.035	2342-313-00260 91	SPIDER-EXP
014.000.000.036	2342-225-00101 22	PRAXIS-X25A
014.000.000.037	2342-225-00101 23	PRAXIS-X25B
014.000.000.038	2403-712-30250 00	DIAB-TABY-GW
014.000.000.039	2403-715-30100 00	DIAB-LKP-GW
014.000.000.040	2401-881-24038 00	DIAB-TABY1-GW
014.000.000.041	2041-170-10060 00	STC
014.000.000.042	2222-551-00652 60	CNUCE
014.000.000.043	2422-510-05900 00	Tollpost-Globe AS
014.000.000.044	2422-670-08900 00	Tollpost-Globe AS
014.000.000.045	2422-516-01000 00	Tollpost-Globe AS
014.000.000.046	2422-450-00800 00	Tollpost-Globe AS
014.000.000.047	2422-610-00200 00	Tollpost-Globe AS
014.000.000.048	2422-310-00300 00	Tollpost-Globe AS
014.000.000.049	2422-470-08800 00	Tollpost-Globe AS
014.000.000.050	2422-210-04600 00	Tollpost-Globe AS
014.000.000.051	2422-130-28900 00	Tollpost-Globe AS
014.000.000.052	2422-310-27200 00	Tollpost-Globe AS
014.000.000.053	2422-250-05800 00	Tollpost-Globe AS
014.000.000.054	2422-634-05900 00	Tollpost-Globe AS
014.000.000.055	2422-670-08800 00	Tollpost-Globe AS
014.000.000.056	2422-430-07400 00	Tollpost-Globe AS
014.000.000.057	2422-674-07800 00	Tollpost-Globe AS
014.000.000.058	2422-230-16900 00	Tollpost-Globe AS
014.000.000.059	2422-518-02900 00	Tollpost-Globe AS
014.000.000.060	2422-370-03100 00	Tollpost-Globe AS
014.000.000.061	2422-516-03400 00	Tollpost-Globe AS
014.000.000.062	2422-616-04400 00	Tollpost-Globe AS
014.000.000.063	2422-650-23500 00	Tollpost-Globe AS

Table G-10. Numbers assigned for networks connected to the Internet *(continued)*

Internet	Public Data Net	Description
014.000.000.064	2422-330-02500 00	Tollpost-Globe AS
014.000.000.065	2422-350-01900 00	Tollpost-Globe AS
014.000.000.066	2422-410-00700 00	Tollpost-Globe AS
014.000.000.067	2422-539-06200 00	Tollpost-Globe AS
014.000.000.068	2422-630-07200 00	Tollpost-Globe AS
014.000.000.069	2422-470-12300 00	Tollpost-Globe AS
014.000.000.070	2422-470-13000 00	Tollpost-Globe AS
014.000.000.071	2422-170-04600 00	Tollpost-Globe AS
014.000.000.072	2422-516-04300 00	Tollpost-Globe AS
014.000.000.073	2422-530-00700 00	Tollpost-Globe AS
014.000.000.074	2422-650-18800 00	Tollpost-Globe AS
014.000.000.075	2422-450-24500 00	Tollpost-Globe AS
014.000.000.076	2062-243-15631 00	DPT-BXL-DDC
014.000.000.077	2062-243-15651 00	DPT-BXL-DDC2
014.000.000.078	3110-312-00431 00	DPT-CHI
014.000.000.079	3110-512-00135 00	DPT-SAT-ENG
014.000.000.080	2080-941-90550 00	DPT-PAR
014.000.000.081	4545-511-30600 00	DPT-PBSC
014.000.000.082	4545-513-30900 00	DPT-HONGKONG
014.000.000.083	4872-203-55000 00	UECI-TAIPEI
014.000.000.084	2624-551-10400 20	DPT-HANOVR
014.000.000.085	2624-569-00401 99	DPT-FNKFRT
014.000.000.086	3110-512-00134 00	DPT-SAT-SUPT
014.000.000.087	4602-3010-0103 20	DU-X25A
014.000.000.088	4602-3010-0103 21	FDU-X25B
014.000.000.089	2422-150-33700 00	Tollpost-Globe AS
014.000.000.090	2422-271-07100 00	Tollpost-Globe AS
014.000.000.091	2422-516-00100 00	Tollpost-Globe AS
014.000.000.092	2422-650-18800 00	Norsk Informas.
014.000.000.093	2422-250-30400 00	Tollpost-Globe AS
014.000.000.018	2624-522-80900 52	FGAN-SIEMENS-X25
014.000.000.094-014.255.255.254		Unassigned
014.255.255.255		Reserved
* independent network		

The standard for transmission of IP datagrams over the Public Data Network is specified in RFC 877.

TELNET Options

The TELNET protocol has a number of options that may be negotiated. These options are listed in Table G-11. The IAB Official Protocol Standards document provides more detailed information.

Table G-11. TELNET options

Option	Name
0	Binary Transmission
1	Echo
2	Reconnection
3	Suppress Go Ahead
4	Approx Message Size Negotiation
5	Status
6	Timing Mark
7	Remote Controlled Trans and Echo
8	Output Line Width
9	Output Page Size
10	Output Carriage-Return Disposition
11	Output Horizontal Tab Stops
12	Output Horizontal Tab Disposition
13	Output Formfeed Disposition
14	Output Vertical Tabstops
15	Output Vertical Tab Disposition
16	Output Linefeed Disposition
17	Extended ASCII
18	Logout
19	Byte Macro
20	Data Entry Terminal
22	SUPDUP
22	SUPDUP Output
23	Send Location
24	Terminal Type
25	End of Record
26	TACACS User Identification
27	Output Marking
28	Terminal Location Number
29	Telnet 3270 Regime
30	X.3 PAD

Table G-11. TELNET options *(continued)*

Option	Name
31	Negotiate About Window Size
32	Terminal Speed
33	Remote Flow Control
34	Linemode
35	X Display Location
36	Environment Option
37	Authentication Option
38	Encryption Option
255	Extended-Options-List

Protocol and Service Name

Table G-12 lists the official protocol names as they appear in the Domain Name System WKS records and the NIC Host Table. Their use is described in RFC 952.

A protocol or service may be up to 40 characters long and must be composed of uppercase letters, digits, or a hyphen. It must start with a letter and end with a letter or digit.

Table G-12. Official protocol names

Acronym	Stands for
ARGUS	ARGUS Protocol
ARP	Address Resolution Protocol

Table G-12. Official protocol names *(continued)*

Acronym	Stands for
AUTH	Authentication Service
BBN-RCC-MON	BBN RCC Monitoring
BL-IDM	Britton Lee Intelligent Database Machine
BOOTP	Bootstrap Protocol
BOOTPC	Bootstrap Protocol Client
BOOTPS	Bootstrap Protocol Server
BR-SAT-MON	Backroom SATNET Monitoring
CFTP	CFTP
CHAOS	CHAOS Protocol
CHARGEN	Character Generator Protocol
CISCO-FNA	CISCO FNATIVE
CISCO-TNA	CISCO TNATIVE

Table G-12. Official protocol names *(continued)*

Acronym	Stands for
CISCO-SYS	CISCO SYSMAINT
CLOCK	DCNET Time Server Protocol
CMOT	Common Mgmnt Info Services and Protocol over TCP/IP
COOKIE-JAR	Authentication Scheme
CSNET-NS	CSNET Mailbox Nameserver Protocol
DAYTIME	Daytime Protocol
DCN-MEAS	DCN Measurement Subsystems Protocol
DCP	Device Control Protocol
DGP	Dissimilar Gateway Protocol
DISCARD	Discard Protocol
DMF-MAIL	Digest Message Format for Mail
DOMAIN	Domain Name System
ECHO	Echo Protocol
EGP	Exterior Gateway Protocol
EHF-MAIL	Encoding Header Field for Mail
EMCON	Emission Control Protocol
EMFIS-CNTL	EMFIS Control Service
EMFIS-DATA	EMFIS Data Service
FINGER	Finger Protocol
FTP	File Transfer Protocol
FTP-DATA	File Transfer Protocol Data
GGP	Gateway Gateway Protocol
GRAPHICS	Graphics Protocol
HMP	Host Monitoring Protocol
HOST2-NS	Host2 Name Server
HOSTNAME	Hostname Protocol
ICMP	Internet Control Message Protocol
IGMP	Internet Group Management Protocol
IGP	Interior Gateway Protocol
IMAP2	Interim Mail Access Protocol version 2
INGRES-NET	INGRES-NET Service
IP	Internet Protocol
IPCU	Internet Packet Core Utility
IPPC	Internet Pluribus Packet Core
IP-ARC	Internet Protocol on ARCNET
IP-ARPA	Internet Protocol on ARPANET
IP-CMPRS	Compressing TCP/IP Headers

Table G-12. Official protocol names (continued)

Acronym	Stands for
IP-DC	Internet Protocol on DC Networks
IP-DVMRP	Distance Vector Multicast Routing Protocol
IP-E	Internet Protocol on Ethernet Networks
IP-EE	Internet Protocol on Exp. Ethernet Nets
IP-FDDI	Transmission of IP over FDDI
IP-HC	Internet Protocol on Hyperchannnel
IP-IEEE	Internet Protocol on IEEE 802
IP-IPX	Transmission of 802.2 over IPX Networks
IP-MTU	IP MTU Discovery Options
IP-NETBIOS	Internet Protocol Datagrams over NetBIOS Networks
IP-SLIP	Transmission of IP over Serial Lines
IP-WB	Internet Protocol on Wideband Network
IP-X25	Internet Protocol on X.25 Networks
IRTP	Internet Reliable Transaction Protocol
ISI-GL	ISI Graphics Language Protocol
ISO-TP4	ISO Transport Protocol Class 4
ISO-TSAP	ISO TSAP
LA-MAINT	IMP Logical Address Maintenance
LARP	Locus Address Resolution Protocol
LDP	Loader Debugger Protocol
LEAF-1	Leaf-1 Protocol
LEAF-2	Leaf-2 Protocol
LINK	Link Protocol
LOC-SRV	Location Service
LOGIN	Login Host Protocol
MAIL	Format of Electronic Mail Messages
MERIT-INP	MERIT Internodal Protocol
METAGRAM	Metagram Relay
MIB	Management Information Base
MIT-ML-DEV	MIT ML Device
MFE-NSP	MFE Network Services Protocol
MIT-SUBNET	MIT Subnet Support
MIT-DOV	MIT Dover Spooler
MPM	Internet Message Protocol (Multimedia Mail)
MPM-FLAGS	MPM Flags Protocol
MPM-SND	MPM Send Protocol
MSG-AUTH	MSG Authentication Protocol

Table G-12. Official protocol names *(continued)*

Acronym	Stands for
MSG-ICP	MSG ICP Protocol
MUX	Multiplexing Protocol
NAMESERVER	Host Name Server
NETBIOS-DGM	NETBIOS Datagram Service
NETBIOS-NS	NETBIOS Name Service
NETBIOS-SSN	NETBIOS Session Service
NETBLT	Bulk Data Transfer Protocol
NETED	Network Standard Text Editor
NETRJS	Remote Job Service
NI-FTP	NI File Transfer Protocol
NI-MAIL	NI Mail Protocol
NICNAME	Who Is Protocol
NFILE	A File Access Protocol
NNTP	Network News Transfer Protocol
NSW-FE	NSW User System Front End
NTP	Network Time Protocol
NVP-II	Network Voice Protocol
OSPF	Open Shortest Path First Interior GW Protocol
PCMAIL	Pcmail Transport Protocol
POP2	Post Office Protocol—Version 2
POP3	Post Office Protocol—Version 3
PPP	Point-to-Point Protocol
PRM	Packet Radio Measurement
PUP	PUP Protocol
PWDGEN	Password Generator Protocol
QUOTE	Quote of the Day Protocol
RARP	A Reverse Address Resolution Protocol
RATP	Reliable Asynchronous Transfer Protocol
RE-MAIL-CK	Remote Mail Checking Protocol
RDP	Reliable Data Protocol
RIP	Routing Information Protocol
RJE	Remote Job Entry
RLP	Resource Location Protocol
RTELNET	Remote Telnet Service
RVD	Remote Virtual Disk Protocol
SAT-EXPAK	Satnet and Backroom EXPAK
SAT-MON	SATNET Monitoring

Table G-12. Official protocol names (continued)

Acronym	Stands for
SEP	Sequential Exchange Protocol
SFTP	Simple File Transfer Protocol
SGMP	Simple Gateway Monitoring Protocol
SNMP	Simple Network Management Protocol
SMI	Structure of Management Information
SMTP	Simple Mail Transfer Protocol
SQLSRV	SQL Service
ST	Stream Protocol
STATSRV	Statistics Service
SU-MIT-TG	SU/MIT Telnet Gateway Protocol
SUN-RPC	SUN Remote Procedure Call
SUPDUP	SUPDUP Protocol
SUR-MEAS	Survey Measurement
SWIFT-RVF	Remote Virtual File Protocol
TACACS-DS	TACACS-Database Service
TACNEWS	TAC News
TCP	Transmission Control Protocol
TCP-ACO	TCP Alternate Checksum Option
TELNET	Telnet Protocol
TFTP	Trivial File Transfer Protocol
THINWIRE	Thinwire Protocol
TIME	Time Server Protocol
TP-TCP	ISO Transport Service on top of the TCP
TRUNK-1	Trunk-1 Protocol
TRUNK-2	Trunk-2 Protocol
UCL	University College London Protocol
UDP	User Datagram Protocol
NNTP	Network News Transfer Protocol
USERS	Active Users Protocol
UUCP-PATH	UUCP Path Service
VIA-FTP	VIA Systems-File Transfer Protocol
VISA	VISA Protocol

Table G-12. Official protocol names *(continued)*

Acronym	Stands for
oVMTP	Versatile Message Transaction Protocol
WB-EXPAK	Wideband EXPAK
WB-MON	Wideband Monitoring
XNET	Cross Net Debugger
XNS-IDP	Xerox NS I+DP

997   Reynolds, J.K.; Postel, J.B. Internet numbers. 1987 March; 42 p. (Format: TXT=123919 bytes) (Obsoleted by RFC 1020, RFC 1117; Updates RFC 990)

998   Clark, D.D.; Lambert, M.L.; Zhang, L. NETBLT: A bulk data transfer protocol NETBLT a bulk data transfer protocol. 1987 March; 21 p. (Format: TXT=57147 bytes) (Obsoletes RFC 969)

999   Westine, A.; Postel, J.B. Requests For Comments summary notes: 900-999. 1987 April; 22 p. (Format: TXT=62877 bytes) (Obsoleted by RFC 1000)

1000   Reynolds, J.K.; Postel, J.B. Request For Comments reference guide. 1987 August; 149 p. (Format: TXT=323960 bytes) (Obsoletes RFC 999)

1001   Defense Advanced Research Projects Agency, Internet Activities Board, End-to-End Services Task Force, NetBIOS Working Group; DARPA IAB End to End Services Task Force NetBIOS Working Group Protocol standard for a NetBIOS service on a TCP/UDP transport: Concepts and methods. 1987 March; 68 p. (Format: TXT=158437 bytes)

1002   Defense Advanced Research Projects Agency, Internet Activities Board, End-to-End Services Task Force, NetBIOS Working Group; DARPA IAB End to End Services Task Force NetBIOS Working Group Protocol standard for a NetBIOS service on a TCP/UDP transport: Detailed specifications. 1987 March; 85 p. (Format: TXT=170262 bytes)

1003   Katz, A.R. Issues in defining an equations representation standard. 1987 March; 7 p. (Format: TXT=19816 bytes)

1004   Mills, D.L. Distributed-protocol authentication scheme. 1987 April; 8 p. (Format: TXT=21402 bytes)

1005   Khanna, A.; Malis, A.G. ARPANET AHIP-E Host Access Protocol (enhanced AHIP). 1987 May; 31 p. (Format: TXT=69957 bytes)

RFC Index

This Appendix is excerpted from the RFC-INDEX file available from the various repositories of RFCs (see Appendix D). The online version indexes the RFCs in reverse numerical order, but this Appendix provides a chronological listing, in order, of RFCs 760-1453, dated January 1980 to April 1993. Following each RFC are notes included in the RFC INDEX file.

RFC citations appear in this format:

> ####   Author 1, Author 2, Author 3. *Title of RFC*. Issue date; *XX* p. (Format: PS=*XXX* bytes, TXT=*XXX* bytes) (Also FYI ####) (Obsoletes ####; Obsoleted by ####; Updates ####).

Following is an explanation of this format:

- #### is the RFC number.
- Author 1, Author 2, etc. are the names of the author or authors of the RFC.
- The title of the RFC follows.
- The issue date follows the title.
- *XX* p. is the total number of pages.
- The format and byte information, in parentheses, is next. The format, which can be ASCII text (TXT), PostScript (PS), or both, is noted, followed by an equals sign and the number of bytes for that version. (PostScript is a registered trademark of Adobe Systems, Inc.)
- Also FYI ####, also in parentheses, gives the equivalent FYI number if the RFC was also issued as an FYI document.

- "Obsoletes" refers to other RFCs, if any, that this one replaces.
- "Obsoleted by" refers to RFCs, if any, that have replaced this one.
- "Updates" refers to other RFCs, if any, that this one updates but does not replace.

In the case of "Obsoletes," "Obsoleted by," and "Updates" RFCs, only immediately succeeding and/or preceding RFCs are listed, not the entire history of each related earlier or later RFC in a related series.

Paper copies of all RFCs are available from the NIC, either individually or on a subscription basis. (For more information, contact NIC@NIC.DDN.MIL.) Online copies are available via FTP or Kermit from NIC.DDN.MIL as RFC:RFC####.TXT or RFC:RFC####.PS, where #### is the RFC number without leading zeroes.

Additionally, you can request RFCs through electronic mail from the automated NIC mail server by sending a message to SERVICE@NIC.DDN.MIL with a subject line of RFC #### for text versions or a subject line of RFC ####.PS for PostScript versions. To obtain the RFC index, the subject line of your message should read "RFC index."

RFC Index

760   Postel, J.B. DoD standard Internet Protocol. 1980 January; 41 p. (Format: TXT=84214 bytes) (Obsoletes IEN 123; Obsoleted by RFC 791, RFC 777).

761   Postel, J.B. DoD standard Transmission Control Protocol. 1980 January; 84 p. (Format: TXT=172234 bytes).

762   Postel, J.B. Assigned numbers. 1980 January; 13 p. (Format: TXT=25421 bytes) (Obsoletes RFC 758; Obsoleted by RFC 770).

763   Abrams, M.D. Role mailboxes. 1980 May 7; 1 p. (Format: TXT=965 bytes).

764   Postel, J.B. Telnet Protocol specification. 1980 June; 15 p. (Format: TXT=40874 bytes) (Obsoleted by RFC 854).

765   Postel, J.B. File Transfer Protocol specification. 1980 June; 70 p. (Format: TXT=150771 bytes) (Obsoletes RFC 542; Obsoleted by RFC 959).

766   Postel, J.B. Internet Protocol Handbook: Table of contents. 1980 July; 1 p. (Format: TXT=3585 bytes) (Obsoleted by RFC 774).

767   Postel, J.B. Structured format for transmission of multi-media documents. 1980 August; 33 p. (Format: TXT=62316 bytes).

768   Postel, J.B. User Datagram Protocol. 1980 August 28; 3 p. (Format: TXT=6069 bytes).

769   Postel, J.B. Rapicom 450 facsimile file format. 1980 September 26; 2 p. (Format: TXT=4194 bytes).

770   Postel, J.B. Assigned numbers. 1980 September; 15 p. (Format: TXT=27117 bytes) (Obsoletes RFC 762; Obsoleted by RFC 776).

771   Cerf, V.G., Postel, J.B. Mail transition plan. 1980 September; 9 p. (Format: TXT=19154 bytes).

772   Sluizer, S., Postel, J.B. Mail Transfer Protocol. 1980 September; 31 p. (Format: TXT=62858 bytes) (Obsoleted by RFC 780).

773   Cerf, V.G. Comments on NCP/TCP mail service transition strategy. 1980 October; 11 p. (Format: TXT=22818 bytes).

774   Postel, J.B. Internet Protocol Handbook: Table of contents. 1980 October; 3 p. (Format: TXT=3625 bytes) (Obsoletes RFC 766).

775   Mankins, D., Franklin, D., Owen, A.D. Directory oriented FTP commands. 1980 December; 6 p. (Format: TXT=9822 bytes).

777   Postel, J.B. Assigned numbers. 1981 January; 13 p. (Format: TXT=31065 bytes) (Obsoletes RFC 770; Obsoleted by RFC 790).

777   Postel, J.B. Internet Control Message Protocol. 1981 April; 14 p. (Format: TXT=80232 bytes) (Obsoletes RFC 760; Obsoleted by RFC 792).

778   Mills, D.L. DCNET Internet Clock Service. 1981 April 18; 5 p. (Format: TXT=9689 bytes).

779   Killian, E. Telnet send-location option. 1981 April; 2 p. (Format: TXT=2680 bytes).

780   Sluizer, S., Postel, J.B. Mail Transfer Protocol. 1981 May; 43 p. (Format: TXT=82951 bytes) (Obsoletes RFC 772; Obsoleted by RFC 788).

781   Su, Z. Specification of the Internet Protocol (IP) timestamp option. 1981 May; 2 p. (Format: TXT=4100 bytes).

782   Nabielsky, J., Skelton, A.P. Virtual Terminal management model. 1981; 20 p. (Format: TXT=44887 bytes).

783   Sollins, K.R. TFTP Protocol (revision 2). 1981 June; 18 p. (Format: TXT=23522 bytes) (Obsoletes IEN 133).

784   Sluizer, S., Postel, J.B. Mail Transfer Protocol: ISI TOPS20 implementation. 1981 July; 3 p. (Format: TXT=6030 bytes).

785   Sluizer, S., Postel, J.B. Mail Transfer Protocol: ISI TOPS20 file definitions. 1981 July; 3 p. (Format: TXT=7206 bytes).

786   Sluizer, S., Postel, J.B. Mail Transfer Protocol: ISI TOPS20 MTP-NIMAIL interface. 1981 July; 2 p. (Format: TXT=3245 bytes).

787   Chapin, A.L. Connectionless data transmission survey/tutorial. 1981 July; 41 p. (Format: TXT=86362 bytes).

788   Postel, J.B. Simple Mail Transfer Protocol. 1981 November; 62 p. (Format: TXT=112698 bytes) (Obsoletes RFC 780; Obsoleted by RFC 821).

789   Rosen, E.C. Vulnerabilities of network control protocols: An example. 1981 July; 15 p. (Format: TXT=26440 bytes).

790   Postel, J.B. Assigned numbers. 1981 September; 15 p. (Format: TXT=36186 bytes) (Obsoletes RFC 776; Obsoleted by RFC 820).

791   Postel, J.B. Internet Protocol. 1981 September; 45 p. (Format: TXT=97779 bytes) (Obsoletes RFC 760).

792   Postel, J.B. Internet Control Message Protocol. 1981 September; 21 p. (Format: TXT=30404 bytes) (Obsoletes RFC 777).

793   Postel, J.B. Transmission Control Protocol. 1981 September; 85 p. (Format: TXT=177957 bytes).

794   Cerf, V.G. Pre-emption. 1981 September; 4 p. (Format: TXT=6022 bytes) (Updates IEN 125).

795   Postel, J.B. Service mappings. 1981 September; 7 p. (Format: TXT=5460 bytes).

796   Postel, J.B. Address mappings. 1981 September; 7 p. (Format: TXT=11645 bytes) (Obsoletes IEN 115).

797   Katz, A.R. Format for Bitmap files. 1981 September; 2 p. (Format: TXT=3183 bytes).

798   Katz, A.R. Decoding facsimile data from the Rapicom 450. 1981 September; 17 p. (Format: TXT=39853 bytes).

799   Mills, D.L. Internet name domains. 1981 September; 6 p. (Format: TXT=14189 bytes).

800   Postel, J.B., Vernon, J. Request For Comments summary notes: 700-799. 1982 November; 10 p. (Format: TXT=18354 bytes).

801   Postel, J.B. NCP/TCP transition plan. 1981 November; 21 p. (Format: TXT=42041 bytes).

802   Malis, A.G. ARPANET 1822L Host Access Protocol. 1981 November; 43 p. (Format: TXT=62470 bytes) (Obsoleted by RFC 851).

803   Agarwal, A., O'Connor, M.J., Mills, D.L. Dacom 450/500 facsimile data transcoding. 1981 November 2; 14 p. (Format: TXT=33826 bytes).

804   International Telecommunication Union, International Telegraph and Telephone Consultative Committee; ITU CCITT CCITT draft recommendation T.4 [Standardization of Group 3 facsimile apparatus for document transmission]. 1981; 12 p. (Format: TXT=17025 bytes).

805   Postel, J.B. Computer mail meeting notes. 1982 February 8; 6 p. (Format: TXT=12522 bytes).

806   National Bureau of Standards; NBS Proposed Federal Information Processing Standard: Specification for message format for computer based

message systems. 1981 September; 99 p. (Format: TXT=216377 bytes) (Obsoleted by RFC 841).

807   Postel, J.B. Multimedia mail meeting notes. 1982 February 9; 6 p. (Format: TXT=11633 bytes).

808   Postel, J.B. Summary of computer mail services meeting held at BBN on 10 January 1979. 1982 March 1; 8 p. (Format: TXT=15930 bytes).

809   Chang, T. UCL facsimile system. 1982 February; 96 p. (Format: TXT=171153 bytes).

810   Feinler, E.J., Harrenstien, K., Su, Z., White, V. DoD Internet host table specification. 1982 March 1; 9 p. (Format: TXT=14659 bytes) (Obsoletes RFC 608; Obsoleted by RFC 952).

811   Harrenstien, K., White, V., Feinler, E.J. Hostnames Server. 1982 March 1; 5 p. (Format: TXT=8007 bytes) (Obsoleted by RFC 953).

812   Harrenstien, K., White, V. NICNAME/WHOIS. 1982 March 1; 3 p. (Format: TXT=5562 bytes) (Obsoleted by RFC 954).

813   Clark, D.D. Window and acknowledgement strategy in TCP. 1982 July; 22 p. (Format: TXT=39277 bytes).

814   Clark, D.D. Name, addresses, ports, and routes. 1982 July; 14 p. (Format: TXT=25426 bytes).

815   Clark, D.D. IP datagram reassembly algorithms. 1982 July; 9 p. (Format: TXT=15028 bytes).

816   Clark, D.D. Fault isolation and recovery. 1982 July; 12 p. (Format: TXT=20754 bytes).

817   Clark, D.D. Modularity and efficiency in protocol implementation. 1982 July; 26 p. (Format: TXT=47319 bytes).

818   Postel, J.B. Remote User Telnet service. 1982 November; 2 p. (Format: TXT=3809 bytes).

819   Su, Z., Postel, J.B. Domain naming convention for Internet user applica-
        tions. 1982 August; 18 p. (Format: TXT=36358 bytes).

820   Postel, J.B. Assigned numbers. 1982 August 14; 1 p. (Format: TXT=54213
        bytes) (Obsoletes RFC 790; Obsoleted by RFC 870).

821   Postel, J.B. Simple Mail Transfer Protocol. 1982 August; 58 p. (Format:
        TXT=124482 bytes) (Obsoletes RFC 788).

822   Crocker, D. Standard for the format of ARPA Internet text messages. 1982
        August 13; 47 p. (Format: TXT=109200 bytes) (Obsoletes RFC 733).

823   Hinden, R.M., Sheltzer, A. DARPA Internet gateway. 1982 September; 33
        p. (Format: TXT=62620 bytes) (Updates IEN 109, IEN 30).

824   MacGregor, W.I., Tappan, D.C. CRONUS Virtual Local Network. 1982
        August 25; 41 p. (Format: TXT=58732 bytes).

825   Postel, J.B. Request for Comments on Requests For Comments. 1982
        November; 2 p. (Format: TXT=4255 bytes) (Obsoleted by RFC 1111).

826   Plummer, D.C. Ethernet Address Resolution Protocol: Or converting net-
        work protocol addresses to 48.bit Ethernet address for transmission on
        Ethernet hardware. 1982 November; 10 p. (Format: TXT=22026 bytes).

827   Rosen, E.C. Exterior Gateway Protocol (EGP). 1982 October; 44 p. (For-
        mat: TXT=68436 bytes).

828   Owen, K. Data communications: IFIP's international "network" of experts.
        1982 August; 11 p. (Format: TXT=29922 bytes).

829   Cerf, V.G. Packet satellite technology reference sources. 1982 November;
        5 p. (Format: TXT=10919 bytes).

830   Su, Z. Distributed system for Internet name service. 1982 October; 16 p.
        (Format: TXT=32585 bytes).

831   Braden, R.T. Backup access to the European side of SATNET. 1982 Decem-
        ber; 5 p. (Format: TXT=12090 bytes).

832   Smallberg, D. Who talks TCP?. 1982 December 7; 13 p. (Format: TXT=43518 bytes) (Obsoleted by RFC 833).

833   Smallberg, D. Who talks TCP?. 1982 December 14; 13 p. (Format: TXT=43728 bytes) (Obsoletes RFC 832; Obsoleted by RFC 834).

834   Smallberg, D. Who talks TCP?. 1982 December 22; 13 p. (Format: TXT=43512 bytes) (Obsoletes RFC 833; Obsoleted by RFC 835).

835   Smallberg, D. Who talks TCP?. 1982 December 29; 13 p. (Format: TXT=43713 bytes) (Obsoletes RFC 834; Obsoleted by RFC 836).

836   Smallberg, D. Who talks TCP?. 1983 January 5; 13 p. (Format: TXT=44397 bytes) (Obsoletes RFC 835; Obsoleted by RFC 837).

837   Smallberg, D. Who talks TCP?. 1983 January 12; 14 p. (Format: TXT=45627 bytes) (Obsoletes RFC 836; Obsoleted by RFC 838).

838   Smallberg, D. Who talks TCP?. 1983 January 20; 14 p. (Format: TXT=45844 bytes) (Obsoletes RFC 837; Obsoleted by RFC 839).

839   Smallberg, D. Who talks TCP?. 1983 January 26; 14 p. (Format: TXT=45987 bytes) (Obsoletes RFC 838; Obsoleted by RFC 842).

840   Postel, J.B. Official protocols. 1983 April 13; 23 p. (Format: TXT=34868 bytes) (Obsoleted by RFC 880).

841   National Bureau of Standards. NBS Specification for message format for Computer Based Message Systems. 1983 January 27; 110 p. (Format: TXT=238774 bytes) (Obsoletes RFC 806).

842   Smallberg, D. Who talks TCP?—survey of 1 February 83. 1983 February 3; 14 p. (Format: TXT=46784 bytes) (Obsoletes RFC 839; Obsoleted by RFC 843).

843   Smallberg, D. Who talks TCP?—survey of 8 February 83. 1983 February 9; 14 p. (Format: TXT=47023 bytes) (Obsoletes RFC 842; Obsoleted by RFC 845).

844   Clements, R. Who talks ICMP, too?—survey of 18 February 1983. 1983 February 18; 5 p. (Format: TXT=9323 bytes) (Updates RFC 843).

845   Smallberg, D. Who talks TCP?—survey of 15 February 1983. 1983 February 17; 14 p. (Format: TXT=46806 bytes) (Obsoletes RFC 843; Obsoleted by RFC 846).

846   Smallberg, D. Who talks TCP?—survey of 22 February 1983. 1983 February 23; 14 p. (Format: TXT=46421 bytes) (Obsoletes RFC 845; Obsoleted by RFC 847).

847   Smallberg, D., Westine, A., Postel, J.B. Summary of Smallberg surveys. 1983 February; 2 p. (Format: TXT=3906 bytes) (Obsoletes RFC 846).

848   Smallberg, D. Who provides the "little" TCP services?. 1983 March 14; 5 p. (Format: TXT=11280 bytes).

849   Crispin, M.R. Suggestions for improved host table distribution. 1983 May; 2 p. (Format: TXT=5290 bytes).

850   Horton, M.R. Standard for interchange of USENET messages. 1983 June; 18 p. (Format: TXT=43871 bytes) (Obsoleted by RFC 1036).

851   Malis, A.G. ARPANET 1822L Host Access Protocol. 1983 April 18; 44 p. (Format: TXT=72042 bytes) (Obsoletes RFC 802; Obsoleted by RFC 878).

852   Malis, A.G. ARPANET short blocking feature. 1983 April; 13 p. (Format: TXT=17151 bytes).

853   Not issued.

854   Postel, J.B., Reynolds, J.K. Telnet Protocol specification. 1983 May; 15 p. (Format: TXT=39371 bytes) (Obsoletes RFC 764, NIC 18639).

855   Postel, J.B., Reynolds, J.K. Telnet option specifications. 1983 May; 4 p. (Format: TXT=6218 bytes) (Obsoletes NIC 18640).

856   Postel, J.B., Reynolds, J.K. Telnet binary transmission. 1983 May; 4 p. (Format: TXT=9192 bytes) (Obsoletes NIC 15389).

857 Postel, J.B., Reynolds, J.K. Telnet echo option. 1983 May; 5 p. (Format: TXT=11143 bytes) (Obsoletes NIC 15390).

858 Postel, J.B., Reynolds, J.K. Telnet Suppress Go Ahead option. 1983 May; 3 p. (Format: TXT=3825 bytes) (Obsoletes NIC 15392).

859 Postel, J.B., Reynolds, J.K. Telnet status option. 1983 May; 3 p. (Format: TXT=4443 bytes) (Obsoletes RFC 651).

860 Postel, J.B., Reynolds, J.K. Telnet timing mark option. 1983 May; 4 p. (Format: TXT=8108 bytes) (Obsoletes NIC 16238).

861 Postel, J.B., Reynolds, J.K. Telnet extended options: List option. 1983 May; 1 p. (Format: TXT=3181 bytes) (Obsoletes NIC 16239).

862 Postel, J.B. Echo Protocol. 1983 May; 1 p. (Format: TXT=1294 bytes).

863 Postel, J.B. Discard Protocol. 1983 May; 1 p. (Format: TXT=1297 bytes).

864 Postel, J.B. Character Generator Protocol. 1983 May; 3 p. (Format: TXT=7016 bytes).

865 Postel, J.B. Quote of the Day Protocol. 1983 May; 1 p. (Format: TXT=1734 bytes).

866 Postel, J.B. Active users. 1983 May; 1 p. (Format: TXT=2087 bytes).

867 Postel, J.B. Daytime Protocol. 1983 May; 2 p. (Format: TXT=2405 bytes).

868 Postel, J.B., Harrenstien, K. Time Protocol. 1983 May; 2 p. (Format: TXT=3140 bytes).

869 Hinden, R.M. Host Monitoring Protocol. 1983 December; 70 p. (Format: TXT=98720 bytes).

870 Reynolds, J.K., Postel, J.B. Assigned numbers. 1983 October; 26 p. (Format: TXT=57563 bytes) (Obsoletes RFC 820; Obsoleted by RFC 900).

871 Padlipsky, M.A. Perspective on the ARPANET reference model. 1982 September; 25 p. (Format: TXT=76037 bytes).

872   Padlipsky, M.A. TCP-on-a-LAN. 1982 September; 8 p. (Format: TXT=22994 bytes).

873   Padlipsky, M.A. Illusion of vendor support. 1982 September; 8 p. (Format: TXT=23673 bytes).

874   Padlipsky, M.A. Critique of X.25 Critique of X 25 Critique of X25. 1982 September; 13 p. (Format: TXT=37259 bytes).

875   Padlipsky, M.A. Gateways, architectures, and heffalumps. 1982 September; 8 p. (Format: TXT=23380 bytes).

876   Smallberg, D. Survey of SMTP implementations. 1983 September; 13 p. (Format: TXT=38529 bytes).

877   Korb, J.T. Standard for the transmission of IP datagrams over public data networks. 1983 September; 2 p. (Format: TXT=3385 bytes).

878   Malis, A.G. ARPANET 1822L Host Access Protocol. 1983 December; 48 p. (Format: TXT=77784 bytes) (Obsoletes RFC 851).

879   Postel, J.B. TCP maximum segment size and related topics. 1983 November; 11 p. (Format: TXT=22662 bytes).

880   Reynolds, J.K., Postel, J.B. Official protocols. 1983 October; 26 p. (Format: TXT=38840 bytes) (Obsoletes RFC 840; Obsoleted by RFC 901).

881   Postel, J.B. Domain names plan and schedule. 1983 November; 10 p. (Format: TXT=24070 bytes).

882   Mockapetris, P.V. Domain names: Concepts and facilities. 1983 November; 31 p. (Format: TXT=81574 bytes) (Obsoleted by RFC 1034, RFC 1035).

883   Mockapetris, P.V. Domain names: Implementation specification. 1983 November; 73 p. (Format: TXT=179416 bytes) (Obsoleted by RFC 1034, RFC 1035).

884   Solomon, M., Wimmers, E. Telnet terminal type option. 1983 December; 5 p. (Format: TXT=8166 bytes) (Obsoleted by RFC 930).

885   Postel, J.B. Telnet end of record option. 1983 December; 2 p. (Format: TXT=3346 bytes).

886   Rose, M.T. Proposed standard for message header munging. 1983 December 15; 16 p. (Format: TXT=31546 bytes).

887   Accetta, M. Resource Location Protocol. 1983 December; 16 p. (Format: TXT=37683 bytes).

888   Seamonson, L., Rosen, E.C. "STUB Exterior Gateway Protocol STUB Exterior Gateway Protocol." 1984 January; 38 p. (Format: TXT=55585 bytes).

889   Mills, D.L. Internet delay experiments. 1983 December; 12 p. (Format: TXT=27812 bytes).

890   Postel, J.B. Exterior Gateway Protocol implementation schedule. 1984 February; 3 p. (Format: TXT=6070 bytes).

891   Mills, D.L. DCN local-network protocols. 1983 December; 26 p. (Format: TXT=66769 bytes).

892   International Organization for Standardization. ISO ISO Transport Protocol specification [Draft]. 1983 December; 82 p. (Format: TXT=162564 bytes) (Obsoleted by RFC 905).

893   Leffler, S., Karels, M.J. Trailer encapsulations. 1984 April; 3 p. (Format: TXT=13695 bytes).

894   Hornig, C. Standard for the transmission of IP datagrams over Ethernet networks. 1984 April; 3 p. (Format: TXT=5868 bytes).

895   Postel, J.B. Standard for the transmission of IP datagrams over experimental Ethernet networks. 1984 April; 3 p. (Format: TXT=5156 bytes).

896   Nagle, J. Congestion control in IP/TCP internetworks. 1984 January 6; 9 p. (Format: TXT=27294 bytes).

897   Postel, J.B. Domain name system implementation schedule. 1984 February; 8 p. (Format: TXT=16139 bytes) (Updates RFC 881).

898   Hinden, R.M., Postel, J.B., Muuss, M., Reynolds, J.K. Gateway special

interest group meeting notes. 1984 April; 24 p. (Format: TXT=43504 bytes).

899   Postel, J.B., Westine, A. Request for Comments summary notes: 800-899. 1984 May; 18 p. (Format: TXT=41028 bytes).

900   Reynolds, J.K., Postel, J.B. Assigned numbers. 1984 June; 43 p. (Format: TXT=84610 bytes) (Obsoletes RFC 870; Obsoleted by RFC 923).

901   Reynolds, J.K., Postel, J.B. Official ARPA-Internet protocols. 1984 June; 28 p. (Format: TXT=42682 bytes) (Obsoletes RFC 880; Obsoleted by RFC 924).

902   Reynolds, J.K., Postel, J.B. ARPA Internet Protocol policy. 1984 July; 5 p. (Format: TXT=11317 bytes).

903   Finlayson, R., Mann, T., Mogul, J.C., Theimer, M. Reverse Address Resolution Protocol. 1984 June; 4 p. (Format: TXT=9572 bytes).

904   Mills, D.L. Exterior Gateway Protocol formal specification. 1984 April; 30 p. (Format: TXT=65226 bytes) (Updates RFC 827, RFC 888).

905   McKenzie, A.M. ISO Transport Protocol specification ISO DP 8073. 1984 April; 154 p. (Format: TXT=258729 bytes) (Obsoletes RFC 892).

906   Finlayson, R. Bootstrap loading using TFTP. 1984 June; 4 p. (Format: TXT=10329 bytes).

907   Bolt Beranek and Newman, Inc. BBN Host Access Protocol specification. 1984 July; 75 p. (Format: TXT=134566 bytes).

908   Velten, D., Hinden, R.M., Sax, J. Reliable Data Protocol. 1984 July; 56 p. (Format: TXT=101185 bytes).

909   Welles, C., Milliken, W. Loader Debugger Protocol. 1984 July; 127 p. (Format: TXT=217583 bytes).

910   Forsdick, H.C. Multimedia mail meeting notes. 1984 August; 11 p. (Format: TXT=25553 bytes).

911   Kirton, P. EGP Gateway under Berkeley UNIX 4.2 EGP Gateway under

Berkeley UNIX 4 2. 1984 August 22; 22 p. (Format: TXT=57043 bytes).

912   St. Johns, M. Authentication service. 1984 September; 3 p. (Format: TXT=4715 bytes) (Obsoleted by RFC 931).

913   Lottor, M. Simple File Transfer Protocol. 1984 September; 15 p. (Format: TXT=21784 bytes).

914   Farber, D.J., Delp, G., Conte, T.M. Thinwire protocol for connecting personal computers to the Internet. 1984 September; 22 p. (Format: TXT=58586 bytes).

915   Elvy, M.A., Nedved, R. Network mail path service. 1984 December; 11 p. (Format: TXT=22262 bytes).

916   Finn, G.G. Reliable Asynchronous Transfer Protocol (RATP). 1984 October; 54 p. (Format: TXT=113815 bytes).

917   Mogul, J.C. Internet subnets. 1984 October; 22 p. (Format: TXT=48326 bytes).

918   Reynolds, J.K. Post Office Protocol. 1984 October; 5 p. (Format: TXT=10166 bytes) (Obsoleted by RFC 937).

919   Mogul, J.C. Broadcasting Internet datagrams. 1984 October; 8 p. (Format: TXT=16838 bytes).

920   Postel, J.B., Reynolds, J.K. Domain requirements. 1984 October; 14 p. (Format: TXT=28621 bytes).

921   Postel, J.B. Domain name system implementation schedule—revised. 1984 October; 13 p. (Format: TXT=24059 bytes) (Updates RFC 897).

922   Mogul, J.C. Broadcasting Internet datagrams in the presence of subnets. 1984 October; 12 p. (Format: TXT=24832 bytes).

923   Reynolds, J.K., Postel, J.B. Assigned numbers. 1984 October; 47 p. (Format: TXT=99193 bytes) (Obsoletes RFC 900; Obsoleted by RFC 943).

924   Reynolds, J.K., Postel, J.B. Official ARPA-Internet protocols for connect-

ing personal computers to the Internet. 1984 October; 35 p. (Format: TXT=50543 bytes) (Obsoletes RFC 901; Obsoleted by RFC 944).

925   Postel, J.B. Multi-LAN address resolution. 1984 October; 15 p. (Format: TXT=31992 bytes).

926   International Organization for Standardization. ISO Protocol for providing the connectionless mode network services. 1984 December; 101 p. (Format: TXT=172024 bytes) (Obsoleted by RFC 994).

927   Anderson, B.A. TACACS user identification Telnet option. 1984 December; 4 p. (Format: TXT=5702 bytes).

928   Padlipsky, M.A. Introduction to proposed DoD standard H-FP. 1984 December; 21 p. (Format: TXT=61658 bytes).

929   Lilienkamp, J., Mandell, R., Padlipsky, M.A. Proposed Host-Front End Protocol. 1984 December; 52 p. (Format: TXT=138234 bytes).

930   Solomon, M., Wimmers, E. Telnet terminal type option. 1985 January; 4 p. (Format: TXT=6805 bytes) (Obsoletes RFC 884; Obsoleted by RFC 1091).

931   St. Johns, M. Authentication server. 1985 January; 4 p. (Format: TXT=9259 bytes) (Obsoletes RFC 912).

932   Clark, D.D. Subnetwork addressing scheme. 1985 January; 4 p. (Format: TXT=9509 bytes).

933   Silverman, S. Output marking Telnet option. 1985 January; 4 p. (Format: TXT=6943 bytes).

934   Rose, M.T., Stefferud, E.A. Proposed standard for message encapsulation. 1985 January; 10 p. (Format: TXT=22340 bytes).

935   Robinson, J.G. Reliable link layer protocols. 1985 January; 13 p. (Format: TXT=32335 bytes).

936   Karels, M.J. Another Internet subnet addressing scheme. 1985 February; 4 p. (Format: TXT=10407 bytes).

937   Butler, M., Postel, J.B., Chase, D., Goldberger, J., Reynolds, J.K. Post Office
        Protocol: Version 2. 1985 February; 24 p. (Format: TXT=43762 bytes)
        (Obsoletes RFC 918).

938   Miller, T. Internet Reliable Transaction Protocol functional and interface
        specification. 1985 February; 16 p. (Format: TXT=40561 bytes).

939   National Research Council. NRC Executive summary of the NRC report
        on transport protocols for Department of Defense data networks. 1985 Feb-
        ruary; 20 p. (Format: TXT=43485 bytes).

940   Gateway Algorithms and Data Structures Task Force. GADS Toward an
        Internet standard scheme for subnetting. 1985 April; 3 p. (Format: TXT=7061
        bytes).

941   International Organization for Standardization. ISO Addendum to the net-
        work service definition covering network layer addressing. 1985 April; 34
        p. (Format: TXT=70706 bytes).

942   National Research Council. NRC Transport protocols for Department of
        Defense data networks. 1985 February; 68 p. (Format: TXT=222477 bytes).

943   Reynolds, J.K., Postel, J.B. Assigned numbers. 1985 April; 50 p. (Format:
        TXT=108133 bytes) (Obsoletes RFC 923; Obsoleted by RFC 960).

944   Reynolds, J.K., Postel, J.B. Official ARPA-Internet protocols. 1985 April;
        40 p. (Format: TXT=63693 bytes) (Obsoletes RFC 924; Obsoleted by RFC
        961).

945   Postel, J.B. DoD statement on the NRC report. 1985 May; 2 p. (Format:
        TXT=5131 bytes) (Obsoleted by RFC 1039).

946   Nedved, R. Telnet terminal location number option. 1985 May; 4 p. (For-
        mat: TXT=6513 bytes).

947   Lebowitz, K., Mankins, D. Multi-network broadcasting within the Inter-
        net. 1985 June; 5 p. (Format: TXT=12854 bytes).

948   Winston, I. Two methods for the transmission of IP datagrams over IEEE 802.3 networks. 1985 June; 5 p. (Format: TXT=11843 bytes) (Obsoleted by RFC 1042).

949   Padlipsky, M.A. FTP unique-named store command. 1985 July; 2 p. (Format: TXT=4130 bytes).

950   Mogul, J.C., Postel, J.B. Internet standard subnetting procedure. 1985 August; 18 p. (Format: TXT=39010 bytes) (Updates RFC 792).

951   Croft, W.J., Gilmore, J. Bootstrap Protocol. 1985 September; 12 p. (Format: TXT=29038 bytes).

952   Harrenstien, K., Stahl, M.K., Feinler, E.J. DoD Internet host table specification. 1985 October; 6 p. (Format: TXT=12728 bytes) (Obsoletes RFC 810).

953   Harrenstien, K., Stahl, M.K., Feinler, E.J. Hostname Server. 1985 October; 5 p. (Format: TXT=8588 bytes) (Obsoletes RFC 811).

954   Harrenstien, K., Stahl, M.K., Feinler, E.J. NICNAME/WHOIS. 1985 October; 4 p. (Format: TXT=7623 bytes) (Obsoletes RFC 812).

955   Braden, R.T. Towards a transport service for transaction processing applications. 1985 September; 10 p. (Format: TXT=23066 bytes).

956   Mills, D.L. Algorithms for synchronizing network clocks. 1985 September; 26 p. (Format: TXT=68868 bytes).

957   Mills, D.L. Experiments in network clock synchronization. 1985 September; 27 p. (Format: TXT=70490 bytes).

958   Mills, D.L. Network Time Protocol (NTP). 1985 September; 14 p. (Format: TXT=31520 bytes) (Obsoleted by RFC 1119).

959   Postel, J.B., Reynolds, J.K. File Transfer Protocol. 1985 October; 69 p. (Format: TXT=151249 bytes) (Obsoletes RFC 765 [IEN 149]).

960   Reynolds, J.K., Postel, J.B. Assigned numbers. 1985 December; 60 p. (Format: TXT=129292 bytes) (Obsoletes RFC 943; Obsoleted by RFC 990).

961   Reynolds, J.K., Postel, J.B. Official ARPA-Internet protocols. 1985 December; 38 p. (Format: TXT=54874 bytes) (Obsoletes RFC 944; Obsoleted by RFC 991).

962   Padlipsky, M.A. TCP-4 prime. 1985 November; 2 p. (Format: TXT=2885 bytes).

963   Sidhu, D.P. Some problems with the specification of the Military Standard Internet Protocol. 1985 November; 19 p. (Format: TXT=45102 bytes).

964   Sidhu, D.P. Some problems with the specification of the Military Standard Transmission Control Protocol. 1985 November; 10 p. (Format: TXT=21542 bytes).

965   Aguilar, L. Format for a graphical communication protocol. 1985 December; 51 p. (Format: TXT=108361 bytes).

966   Deering, S.E., Cheriton, D.R. Host groups: A multicast extension to the Internet Protocol Host groups a multicast extension to the Internet Protocol. 1985 December; 27 p. (Format: TXT=61006 bytes) (Obsoleted by RFC 988).

967   Padlipsky, M.A. All victims together. 1985 December; 2 p. (Format: TXT=4820 bytes).

968   Cerf, V.G. Twas the night before start-up. 1985 December; 2 p. (Format: TXT=2573 bytes).

969   Clark, D.D., Lambert, M.L., Zhang, L. NETBLT: A bulk data transfer protocol NETBLT a bulk data transfer protocol. 1985 December; 15 p. (Format: TXT=40894 bytes) (Obsoleted by RFC 998).

970   Nagle, J. On packet switches with infinite storage. 1985 December; 9 p. (Format: TXT=24970 bytes).

971   DeSchon, A.L. Survey of data representation standards. 1986 January; 9 p. (Format: TXT=22883 bytes).

972   Wancho, F.J. Password Generator Protocol. 1986 January; 2 p. (Format: TXT=3890 bytes).

973   Mockapetris, P.V. Domain system changes and observations. 1986 January; 10 p. (Format: TXT=22364 bytes) (Obsoleted by RFC 1034, RFC 1035; Updates RFC 882, RFC 883).

974   Partridge, C. Mail routing and the domain system. 1986 January; 7 p. (Format: TXT=18581 bytes).

975   Mills, D.L. Autonomous confederations. 1986 February; 10 p. (Format: TXT=28010 bytes).

976   Horton, M.R. UUCP mail interchange format standard. 1986 February; 12 p. (Format: TXT=26814 bytes).

977   Kantor, B., Lapsley, P. Network News Transfer Protocol. 1986 February; 27 p. (Format: TXT=55062 bytes).

978   Reynolds, J.K., Gillman, R., Brackenridge, W.A., Witkowski, A., Postel, J.B. Voice File Interchange Protocol (VFIP). 1986 February; 5 p. (Format: TXT=9223 bytes).

979   Malis, A.G. PSN End-to-End functional specification. 1986 March; 15 p. (Format: TXT=39472 bytes).

980   Jacobsen, O.J., Postel, J.B. Protocol document order information. 1986 March; 12 p. (Format: TXT=24416 bytes).

981   Mills, D.L. Experimental multiple path routing algorithm. 1986 March; 22 p. (Format: TXT=59069 bytes).

982   Braun, H.W. Guidelines for the specification of the structure of the Domain Specific Part (DSP) of the ISO standard NSAP address. 1986 April; 11 p. (Format: TXT=22595 bytes).

983   Cass, D.E., Rose, M.T. ISO transport arrives on top of the TCP. 1986 April; 27 p. (Format: TXT=59819 bytes) (Obsoleted by RFC 1006).

984   Clark, D.D., Lambert, M.L. PCMAIL: A distributed mail system for personal computers PCMAIL a distributed mail system for personal computers. 1986 May; 31 p. (Format: TXT=69333 bytes) (Obsoleted by RFC 993).

985 National Science Foundation, Network Technical Advisory Group. NSF NTAG Requirements for Internet gateways—draft Requirements for Internet gateways draft. 1986 May; 23 p. (Format: TXT=59221 bytes) (Obsoleted by RFC 1009).

986 Callon, R.W., Braun, H.W. Guidelines for the use of Internet-IP addresses in the ISO Connectionless-Mode Network Protocol [Working draft]. 1986 June; 7 p. (Format: TXT=13950 bytes) (Obsoleted by RFC 1069).

987 Kille, S.E. Mapping between X.400 and RFC 822. 1986 June; 69 p. (Format: TXT=127540 bytes).

988 Deering, S.E. Host extensions for IP multicasting. 1986 July; 20 p. (Format: TXT=45220 bytes) (Obsoletes RFC 966; Obsoleted by RFC 1054, RFC 1112).

989 Linn, J. Privacy enhancement for Internet electronic mail: Part I: Message encipherment and authentication procedures. 1987 February; 23 p. (Format: TXT=63934 bytes) (Obsoleted by RFC 1040, RFC 1113).

990 Reynolds, J.K., Postel, J.B. Assigned numbers. 1986 November; 75 p. (Format: TXT=174784 bytes) (Obsoletes RFC 960; Obsoleted by RFC 1010).

991 Reynolds, J.K., Postel, J.B. Official ARPA-Internet protocols. 1986 November; 46 p. (Format: TXT=65205 bytes) (Obsoletes RFC 961; Obsoleted by RFC 1011).

992 Birman, K.P., Joseph, T.A. On communication support for fault tolerant process groups. 1986 November; 18 p. (Format: TXT=52313 bytes).

993 Clark, D.D., Lambert, M.L. PCMAIL: A distributed mail system for personal computers PCMAIL a distributed mail system for personal computers. 1986 December; 28 p. (Format: TXT=71725 bytes) (Obsoletes RFC 984; Obsoleted by RFC 1056).

994 International Organization for Standardization. ISO Final text of DIS 8473, Protocol for Providing the Connectionless-mode Network Service. 1986 March; 52 p. (Format: TXT=129006 bytes) (Obsoletes RFC 926).

995   International Organization for Standardization. ISO End System to Inter-
       mediate System Routing Exchange Protocol for use in conjunction with
       ISO 8473. 1986 April; 41 p. (Format: TXT=94069 bytes).

996   Mills, D.L. Statistics server. 1987 February; 3 p. (Format: TXT=6127 bytes).

997   Reynolds, J.K., Postel, J.B. Internet numbers. 1987 March; 42 p. (Format:
       TXT=123919 bytes) (Obsoleted by RFC 1020, RFC 1117; Updates RFC
       990).

998   Clark, D.D., Lambert, M.L., Zhang, L. NETBLT: A bulk data transfer pro-
       tocol NETBLT a bulk data transfer protocol. 1987 March; 21 p. (Format:
       TXT=57147 bytes) (Obsoletes RFC 969).

999   Westine, A., Postel, J.B. Requests For Comments summary notes: 900-999.
       1987 April; 22 p. (Format: TXT=62877 bytes) (Obsoleted by RFC 1000).

1000   Reynolds, J.K., Postel, J.B. Request For Comments reference guide. 1987
       August; 149 p. (Format: TXT=323960 bytes) (Obsoletes RFC 999).

1001   Defense Advanced Research Projects Agency, Internet Activities Board,
       End-to-End Services Task Force, NetBIOS Working Group. DARPA IAB
       End to End Services Task Force NetBIOS Working Group Protocol stan-
       dard for a NetBIOS service on a TCP/UDP transport: Concepts and meth-
       ods. 1987 March; 68 p. (Format: TXT=158437 bytes).

1002   Defense Advanced Research Projects Agency, Internet Activities Board,
       End-to-End Services Task Force, NetBIOS Working Group. DARPA IAB
       End to End Services Task Force NetBIOS Working Group Protocol stan-
       dard for a NetBIOS service on a TCP/UDP transport: Detailed specifica-
       tions. 1987 March; 85 p. (Format: TXT=170262 bytes).

1003   Katz, A.R. Issues in defining an equations representation standard. 1987
       March; 7 p. (Format: TXT=19816 bytes).

1004   Mills, D.L. Distributed-protocol authentication scheme. 1987 April; 8 p.
       (Format: TXT=21402 bytes).

1005   Khanna, A., Malis, A.G. ARPANET AHIP-E Host Access Protocol (enhanced AHIP). 1987 May; 31 p. (Format: TXT=69957 bytes).

1006   Rose, M.T., Cass, D.E. ISO transport services on top of the TCP: Version 3. 1987 May; 17 p. (Format: TXT=31935 bytes) (Obsoletes RFC 983).

1007   McCoy, W. Military supplement to the ISO Transport Protocol. 1987 June; 23 p. (Format: TXT=51280 bytes).

1008   McCoy, W. Implementation guide for the ISO Transport Protocol. 1987 June; 73 p. (Format: TXT=204664 bytes).

1009   Braden, R.T., Postel, J.B. Requirements for Internet gateways. 1987 June; 55 p. (Format: TXT=128173 bytes) (Obsoletes RFC 985).

1010   Reynolds, J.K., Postel, J.B. Assigned numbers. 1987 May; 44 p. (Format: TXT=78179 bytes) (Obsoletes RFC 990; Obsoleted by RFC 1060).

1011   Reynolds, J.K., Postel, J.B. Official Internet protocols. 1987 May; 52 p. (Format: TXT=74593 bytes) (Obsoletes RFC 991).

1012   Reynolds, J.K., Postel, J.B. Bibliography of Request For Comments 1 through 999. 1987 June; 64 p. (Format: TXT=129194 bytes).

1013   Scheifler, R.W. X Window System Protocol, version 11: Alpha update April 1987. 1987 June; 101 p. (Format: TXT=244905 bytes).

1014   Sun Microsystems, Inc. XDR: External Data Representation standard. 1987 June; 20 p. (Format: TXT=39316 bytes).

1015   Leiner, B.M. Implementation plan for interagency research Internet. 1987 July; 24 p. (Format: TXT=63159 bytes).

1016   Prue, W., Postel, J.B. Something a host could do with source quench: The Source Quench Introduced Delay (SQuID). 1987 July; 18 p. (Format: TXT=47922 bytes).

1017   Leiner, B.M. Network requirements for scientific research: Internet task force on scientific computing. 1987 August; 19 p. (Format: TXT=49512 bytes).

1018   McKenzie, A.M. Some comments on SQuID. 1987 August; 3 p. (Format: TXT=7931 bytes).

1019   Arnon, D. Report of the Workshop on Environments for Computational Mathematics. 1987 September; 8 p. (Format: TXT=21151 bytes).

1020   Romano, S., Stahl, M.K. Internet numbers. 1987 November; 51 p. (Format: TXT=146864 bytes) (Obsoletes RFC 997; Obsoleted by RFC 1062, RFC 1117).

1021   Partridge, C., Trewitt, G. High-level Entity Management System (HEMS). 1987 October; 5 p. (Format: TXT=12993 bytes).

1022   Partridge, C., Trewitt, G. High-level Entity Management Protocol (HEMP). 1987 October; 12 p. (Format: TXT=25348 bytes).

1023   Trewitt, G., Partridge, C. HEMS monitoring and control language. 1987 October; 17 p. (Format: TXT=40992 bytes) (Obsoleted by RFC 1076).

1024   Partridge, C., Trewitt, G. HEMS variable definitions. 1987 October; 74 p. (Format: TXT=126536 bytes).

1025   Postel, J.B. TCP and IP bake off. 1987 September; 6 p. (Format: TXT=11648 bytes).

1026   Kille, S.E. Addendum to RFC 987: (Mapping between X.400 and RFC-822). 1987 September; 4 p. (Format: TXT=7117 bytes) (Updates RFC 987).

1027   Carl-Mitchell, S., Quarterman, J.S. Using ARP to implement transparent subnet gateways. 1987 October; 8 p. (Format: TXT=21297 bytes).

1028   Davin, J., Case, J.D., Fedor, M., Schoffstall, M.L. Simple Gateway Monitoring Protocol. 1987 November; 38 p. (Format: TXT=82440 bytes).

1029   Parr, G. More fault tolerant approach to address resolution for a Multi-LAN system of Ethernets. 1988 May; 17 p. (Format: TXT=44019 bytes).

1030   Lambert, M.L. On testing the NETBLT Protocol over divers networks. 1987 November; 16 p. (Format: TXT=40964 bytes).

1031   Lazear, W.D. MILNET name domain transition. 1987 November; 10 p. (Format: TXT=20137 bytes).

1032   Stahl, M.K. Domain administrators guide. 1987 November; 14 p. (Format: TXT=29454 bytes).

1033   Lottor, M. Domain administrators operations guide. 1987 November; 22 p. (Format: TXT=37263 bytes).

1034   Mockapetris, P.V. Domain names—concepts and facilities. 1987 November; 55 p. (Format: TXT=129180 bytes) (Obsoletes RFC 973, RFC 882, RFC 883).

1035   Mockapetris, P.V. Domain names-implementation and specification. 1987 November; 55 p. (Format: TXT=125626 bytes) (Obsoletes RFC 973, RFC 882, RFC 883).

1036   Horton, M.R., Adams, R. Standard for interchange of USENET messages. 1987 December; 19 p. (Format: TXT=46891 bytes) (Obsoletes RFC 850).

1037   Greenberg, B., Keene, S. NFILE—a file access protocol NFILE a file access protocol. 1987 December; 86 p. (Format: TXT=197312 bytes).

1038   St. Johns, M. Draft revised IP security option. 1988 January; 7 p. (Format: TXT=15879 bytes).

1039   Latham, D. DoD statement on Open Systems Interconnection protocols. 1988 January; 3 p. (Format: TXT=6194 bytes) (Obsoletes RFC 945).

1040   Linn, J. Privacy enhancement for Internet electronic mail: Part I: Message encipherment and authentication procedures. 1988 January; 29 p. (Format: TXT=76276 bytes) (Obsoletes RFC 989; Obsoleted by RFC 1113).

1041   Rekhter, Y. Telnet 3270 regime option. 1988 January; 6 p. (Format: TXT=11608 bytes).

1042   Postel, J.B., Reynolds, J.K. Standard for the transmission of IP datagrams over IEEE 802 networks. 1988 February; 15 p. (Format: TXT=35201 bytes) (Obsoletes RFC 948).

1043   Yasuda, A., Thompson, T. Telnet Data Entry Terminal option: DODIIS implementation. 1988 February; 26 p. (Format: TXT=59478 bytes) (Updates RFC 732).

1044   Hardwick, K., Lekashman, J. Internet Protocol on Network System's HYPERchannel: Protocol specification. 1988 February; 43 p. (Format: TXT=103241 bytes).

1045   Cheriton, D.R. VMTP: Versatile Message Transaction Protocol: Protocol specification. 1988 February; 123 p. (Format: TXT=272058 bytes).

1046   Prue, W., Postel, J.B. Queuing algorithm to provide type-of-service for IP links. 1988 February; 11 p. (Format: TXT=30106 bytes).

1047   Partridge, C. Duplicate messages and SMTP. 1988 February; 3 p. (Format: TXT=5888 bytes).

1048   Prindeville, P.A. BOOTP vendor information extensions. 1988 February; 7 p. (Format: TXT=15423 bytes) (Obsoleted by RFC 1084).

1049   Sirbu, M.A. Content-type header field for Internet messages. 1988 March; 8 p. (Format: TXT=18923 bytes).

1050   Sun Microsystems, Inc. RPC: Remote Procedure Call Protocol specification. 1988 April; 24 p. (Format: TXT=51540 bytes) (Obsoleted by RFC 1057).

1051   Prindeville, P.A. Standard for the transmission of IP datagrams and ARP packets over ARCNET networks. 1988 March; 4 p. (Format: TXT=7779 bytes) (Obsoleted by RFC 1201).

1052   Cerf, V.G. IAB recommendations for the development of Internet network management standards. 1988 April; 14 p. (Format: TXT=30569 bytes).

1053   Levy, S., Jacobson, T. Telnet X.3 PAD option Telnet X3 PAD option Telnet X 3 PAD option. 1988 April; 21 p. (Format: TXT=48952 bytes).

1054   Deering, S.E. Host extensions for IP multicasting. 1988 May; 19 p. (Format: TXT=45465 bytes) (Obsoletes RFC 988; Obsoleted by RFC 1112).

1055   Romkey, J.L. Nonstandard for transmission of IP datagrams over serial lines: SLIP. 1988 June; 6 p. (Format: TXT=12911 bytes).

1056   Lambert, M.L. PCMAIL: A distributed mail system for personal computers. 1988 June; 38 p. (Format: TXT=85368 bytes) (Obsoletes RFC 993).

1057   Sun Microsystems, Inc. RPC: Remote Procedure Call Protocol specification: Version 2. 1988 June; 25 p. (Format: TXT=52462 bytes) (Obsoletes RFC 1050).

1058   Hedrick, C.L. Routing Information Protocol. 1988 June; 33 p. (Format: TXT=93285 bytes).

1059   Mills, D.L. Network Time Protocol (version 1) specification and implementation. 1988 July; 58 p. (Format: TXT=140890 bytes) (Obsoleted by RFC 1119).

1060   Reynolds, J.K., Postel, J.B. Assigned numbers. 1990 March; 86 p. (Format: TXT=177923 bytes) (Obsoletes RFC 1010).

1061   Not yet issued.

1062   Romano, S., Stahl, M.K., Recker, M. Internet numbers. 1988 August; 65 p. (Format: TXT=198729 bytes) (Obsoletes RFC 1020; Obsoleted by RFC 1117).

1063   Mogul, J.C., Kent, C.A., Partridge, C., McCloghrie, K. IP MTU discovery options. 1988 July; 11 p. (Format: TXT=27121 bytes) (Obsoleted by RFC 1191).

1064   Crispin, M.R. Interactive Mail Access Protocol: Version 2. 1988 July; 26 p. (Format: TXT=57813 bytes) (Obsoleted by RFC 1176, RFC 1203).

1065   McCloghrie, K., Rose, M.T. Structure and identification of management information for TCP/IP-based internets. 1988 August; 21 p. (Format: TXT=38858 bytes) (Obsoleted by RFC 1155).

1066   McCloghrie, K., Rose, M.T. Management Information Base for network management of TCP/IP-based internets. 1988 August; 90 p. (Format: TXT=135177 bytes) (Obsoleted by RFC 1156).

1067   Case, J.D., Fedor, M., Schoffstall, M.L., Davin, J. Simple Network Management Protocol. 1988 August; 33 p. (Format: TXT=69592 bytes) (Obsoleted by RFC 1098).

1068   DeSchon, A.L., Braden, R.T. Background File Transfer Program (BFTP). 1988 August; 27 p. (Format: TXT=51004 bytes).

1069   Callon, R.W., Braun, H.W. Guidelines for the use of Internet-IP addresses in the ISO Connectionless-Mode Network Protocol. 1989 February; 10 p. (Format: TXT=24268 bytes) (Obsoletes RFC 986).

1070   Hagens, R.A., Hall, N.E., Rose, M.T. Use of the Internet as a subnetwork for experimentation with the OSI network layer. 1989 February; 17 p. (Format: TXT=37354 bytes).

1071   Braden, R.T., Borman, D.A., Partridge, C. Computing the Internet checksum. 1988 September; 24 p. (Format: TXT=54941 bytes).

1072   Jacobson, V., Braden, R.T. TCP extensions for long-delay paths. 1988 October; 16 p. (Format: TXT=36000 bytes).

1073   Waitzman, D. Telnet window size option. 1988 October; 4 p. (Format: TXT=7639 bytes).

1074   Rekhter, J. NSFNET backbone SPF based Interior Gateway Protocol. 1988 October; 5 p. (Format: TXT=10872 bytes).

1075   Waitzman, D., Partridge, C., Deering, S.E. Distance Vector Multicast Routing Protocol. 1988 November; 24 p. (Format: TXT=54731 bytes).

1076   Trewitt, G., Partridge, C. HEMS monitoring and control language. 1988 November; 42 p. (Format: TXT=98774 bytes) (Obsoletes RFC 1023).

1077   Leiner, B.M., ed. Critical issues in high bandwidth networking. 1988 November; 46 p. (Format: TXT=116464 bytes).

1078   Lottor, M. TCP port service Multiplexer (TCPMUX). 1988 November; 2 p. (Format: TXT=3248 bytes).

1079   Hedrick, C.L. Telnet terminal speed option. 1988 December; 3 p. (Format: TXT=4942 bytes).

1080   Hedrick, C.L. Telnet remote flow control option. 1988 November; 4 p. (Format: TXT=6688 bytes).

1081   Rose, M.T. Post Office Protocol: Version 3. 1988 November; 16 p. (Format: TXT=37009 bytes) (Obsoleted by RFC 1225).

1082   Rose, M.T. Post Office Protocol: Version 3: Extended service offerings. 1988 November; 11 p. (Format: TXT=25423 bytes).

1083   Defense Advanced Research Projects Agency, Internet Activities Board. DARPA IAB IAB official protocol standards. 1988 December; 12 p. (Format: TXT=27128 bytes) (Obsoleted by RFC 1100).

1084   Reynolds, J.K. BOOTP vendor information extensions. 1988 December; 8 p. (Format: TXT=16327 bytes) (Obsoletes RFC 1048).

1085   Rose, M.T. ISO presentation services on top of TCP/IP based internets. 1988 December; 32 p. (Format: TXT=64643 bytes).

1086   Onions, J.P., Rose, M.T. ISO-TP0 bridge between TCP and X.25. 1988 December; 9 p. (Format: TXT=19934 bytes).

1087   Defense Advanced Research Projects Agency, Internet Activities Board. DARPA IAB Ethics and the Internet. 1989 January; 2 p. (Format: TXT=4582 bytes).

1088   McLaughlin, L.J. Standard for the transmission of IP datagrams over Net-BIOS networks. 1989 February; 3 p. (Format: TXT=5749 bytes).

1089   Schoffstall, M.L., Davin, C., Fedor, M., Case, J.D. SNMP over Ethernet. 1989 February; 3 p. (Format: TXT=4458 bytes).

1090   Ullmann, R. SMTP on X.25 SMTP on X 25. 1989 February; 4 p. (Format: TXT=6141 bytes).

1091   VanBokkelen, J. Telnet terminal-type option. 1989 February; 7 p. (Format: TXT=13439 bytes) (Obsoletes RFC 930).

1092 Rekhter, J. EGP and policy based routing in the new NSFNET backbone. 1989 February; 5 p. (Format: TXT=11865 bytes).

1093 Braun, H.W. NSFNET routing architecture. 1989 February; 9 p. (Format: TXT=20629 bytes).

1094 Sun Microsystems, Inc. NFS: Network File System Protocol specification. 1989 March; 27 p. (Format: TXT=51454 bytes).

1095 Warrier, U.S., Besaw, L. Common Management Information Services and Protocol over TCP/IP (CMOT). 1989 April; 67 p. (Format: TXT=157506 bytes) (Obsoleted by RFC 1189).

1096 Marcy, G.A. Telnet X display location option. 1989 March; 3 p. (Format: TXT=4634 bytes).

1097 Miller, B. Telnet subliminal-message option. 1989 April 1; 3 p. (Format: TXT=5490 bytes).

1098 Case, J.D., Fedor, M., Schoffstall, M.L., Davin, C. Simple Network Management Protocol (SNMP). 1989 April; 34 p. (Format: TXT=71563 bytes) (Obsoletes RFC 1067; Obsoleted by RFC 1157).

1099 Renyolds, J. Request for Comments Summary RFC Numbers 1000-1099. 1991 December; 22 p. (Format: TXT=49108 bytes).

1100 Defense Advanced Research Projects Agency, Internet Activities Board. DARPA IAB IAB official protocol standards. 1989 April; 14 p. (Format: TXT=30101 bytes) (Obsoletes RFC 1083; Obsoleted by RFC 1130).

1101 Mockapetris, P.V. DNS encoding of network names and other types. 1989 April; 14 p. (Format: TXT=28677 bytes) (Updates RFC 1034, RFC 1035).

1102 Clark, D.D. Policy routing in Internet protocols. 1989 May; 22 p. (Format: TXT=59664 bytes).

1103 Katz, D. Proposed standard for the transmission of IP datagrams over FDDI Networks. 1989 June; 9 p. (Format: TXT=19439 bytes) (Obsoleted by RFC 1188).

1104   Braun, H.W. Models of policy based routing. 1989 June; 10 p. (Format: TXT=25468 bytes).

1105   Lougheed, K., Rekhter, Y. Border Gateway Protocol (BGP). 1989 June; 17 p. (Format: TXT=37644 bytes) (Obsoleted by RFC 1163).

1106   Fox, R. TCP big window and NAK options. 1989 June; 13 p. (Format: TXT=37105 bytes).

1107   Sollins, K.R. Plan for Internet directory services. 1989 July; 19 p. (Format: TXT=51773 bytes).

1108   Kent, S. Security Options for the Internet Protocol. 1991 November; 17 p. (Format: TXT=41791 bytes) (Obsoletes RFC 1038).

1109   Cerf, V.G. Report of the second Ad Hoc Network Management Review Group. 1989 August; 8 p. (Format: TXT=20642 bytes).

1110   McKenzie, A.M. Problem with the TCP big window option. 1989 August; 3 p. (Format: TXT=5778 bytes).

1111   Postel, J.B. Request for comments on Request for Comments: Instructions to RFC authors. 1989 August; 6 p. (Format: TXT=11793 bytes) (Obsoletes RFC 825).

1112   Deering, S.E. Host extensions for IP multicasting. 1989 August; 17 p. (Format: TXT=39904 bytes) (Obsoletes RFC 988, RFC 1054).

1113   Linn, J. Privacy enhancement for Internet electronic mail: Part I—message encipherment and authentication procedures [Draft]. 1989 August; 34 p. (Format: TXT=89293 bytes) (Obsoletes RFC 989, RFC 1040).

1114   Kent, S.T., Linn, J. Privacy enhancement for Internet electronic mail: Part II—certificate-based key management [Draft]. 1989 August; 25 p. (Format: TXT=69661 bytes).

1115   Linn, J. Privacy enhancement for Internet electronic mail: Part III—algorithms, modes, and identifiers [Draft]. 1989 August; 8 p. (Format: TXT=18226 bytes).

1116   Borman, D.A.,ed. Telnet Linemode option. 1989 August; 21 p. (Format: TXT=47473 bytes) (Obsoleted by RFC 1184).

1117   Romano, S., Stahl, M.K., Recker, M. Internet numbers. 1989 August; 109 p. (Format: TXT=324666 bytes) (Obsoletes RFC 1062, RFC 1020, RFC 997; Obsoleted by RFC 1166).

1118   Krol, E. Hitchhikers guide to the Internet. 1989 September; 24 p. (Format: TXT=62757 bytes).

1119   Mills, D.L. Network Time Protocol (version 2) specification and implementation. 1989 September; 64 p. (Format: PS=535202 bytes) (Obsoletes RFC 1059, RFC 958).

1120   Cerf, V. Internet Activities Board. 1989 September; 11 p. (Format: TXT=26123 bytes) (Obsoleted by RFC 1160).

1121   Postel, J.B., Kleinrock, L., Cerf, V.G., Boehm, B. Act one—the poems Act one the poems. 1989 September; 6 p. (Format: TXT=10644 bytes).

1122   Braden, R.T., ed. Requirements for Internet hosts—communication layers Rquirements for Internet hosts communication layers. 1989 October; 116 p. (Format: TXT=295992 bytes).

1123   Braden, R.T.,ed. Requirements for Internet hosts—application and support. 1989 October; 98 p. (Format: TXT=245503 bytes).

1124   Leiner, B.M. Policy issues in interconnecting networks. 1989 September; 54 p. (Format: PS=315692 bytes).

1125   Estrin, D. Policy requirements for inter Administrative Domain routing. 1989 November; 18 p. (Format: TXT=55248 PS=282123 bytes).

1126   Little, M. Goals and functional requirements for inter-autonomous system routing. 1989 October; 25 p. (Format: TXT=62725 bytes).

1127   Braden, R.T. Perspective on the Host Requirements RFCs. 1989 October; 20 p. (Format: TXT=41267 bytes).

1128   Mills, D.L. Measured performance of the Network Time Protocol in the Internet system. 1989 October; 20 p. (Format: PS=633742 bytes).

1129   Mills, D.L. Internet time synchronization: The Network Time Protocol. 1989 October; 29 p. (Format: PS=551697 bytes).

1130   Defense Advanced Research Projects Agency, Internet Activities Board. DARPA IAB IAB official protocol standards. 1989 October; 17 p. (Format: TXT=33858 bytes) (Obsoletes RFC 1100; Obsoleted by RFC 1140).

1131   Moy, J. OSPF specification. 1989 October; 107 p. (Format: PS=857280 bytes) (Obsoleted by RFC 1247).

1132   McLaughlin, L.J. Standard for the transmission of 802.2 packets over IPX networks. 1989 November; 4 p. (Format: TXT=8128 bytes).

1133   Yu, J.Y., Braun, H.W. Routing between the NSFNET and the DDN. 1989 November; 10 p. (Format: TXT=23169 bytes).

1134   Perkins, D. Point-to-Point Protocol: A proposal for multi-protocol transmission of datagrams over Point-to-Point links. 1989 November; 38 p. (Format: TXT=87352 bytes) (Obsoleted by RFC 1171).

1135   Reynolds, J.K. Helminthiasis of the Internet. 1989 December; 33 p. (Format: TXT=77033 bytes).

1136   Hares, S., Katz, D. Administrative Domains and Routing Domains: A model for routing in the Internet. 1989 December; 10 p. (Format: TXT=22158 bytes).

1137   Kille, S.E. Mapping between full RFC 822 and RFC 822 with restricted encoding. 1989 December; 3 p. (Format: TXT=6436 bytes) (Updates RFC 976).

1138   Kille, S.E. Mapping between X.400(1988) / ISO 10021 and RFC 822. 1989 December; 92 p. (Format: TXT=191029 bytes) (Updates RFC 822, RFC 987, RFC 1026).

1139   Hagens, R.A. Echo function for ISO 8473. 1990 January; 6 p. (Format: TXT=14229 bytes).

1140   Defense Advanced Research Projects Agency, Internet Activities Board. DARPA IAB IAB official protocol standards. 1990 May; 27 p. (Format: TXT=60501 bytes) (Obsoletes RFC 1130; Obsoleted by RFC 1200).

1141   Mallory, T., Kullberg, A. Incremental updating of the Internet checksum. 1990 January; 2 p. (Format: TXT=3587 bytes) (Updates RFC 1071).

1142   Oran, D., ed. OSI IS-IS Intra-domain Routing Protocol. 1990 February; 206 p. (Format: TXT=425379, PS=12042 bytes).

1143   Bernstein, D.J. Q method of implementing Telnet option negotiation. 1990 February; 10 p. (Format: TXT=23331 bytes).

1144   Jacobson, V. Compressing TCP/IP headers for low-speed serial links. 1990 February; 43 p. (Format: TXT=120959 PS=534729 bytes).

1145   Zweig, J., Partridge, C. TCP alternate checksum options. 1990 February; 5 p. (Format: TXT=11052 bytes) (Obsoleted by RFC 1146).

1146   Zweig, J., Partridge, C. TCP alternate checksum options. 1990 March; 5 p. (Format: TXT=10955 bytes) (Obsoletes RFC 1145).

1147   Stine, R.H., ed. FYI on a network management tool catalog: Tools for monitoring and debugging TCP/IP internets and interconnected devices. 1990 April; 126 p. (Format: TXT=336906 PS=555225 bytes) (Also FYI 2)

1148   Kille, S.E. Mapping between X.400(1988) / ISO 10021 and RFC 822 Mapping between X 400 1988 ISO 10021 and RFC 822. 1990 March; 94 p. (Format: TXT=194292 bytes) (Updates RFC 822, RFC 987, RFC 1026, RFC 1138).

1149   Waitzman, D. Standard for the transmission of IP datagrams on avian carriers. 1990 April 1; 2 p. (Format: TXT=3329 bytes).

1150   Malkin, G.S., Reynolds, J.K. F.Y.I. on F.Y.I.: Introduction to the F.Y.I. notes. 1990 March; 4 p. (Format: TXT=7867 bytes) (Also FYI 1)

1151   Partridge, C., Hinden, R.M. Version 2 of the Reliable Data Protocol (RDP). 1990 April; 4 p. (Format: TXT=8293 bytes) (Updates RFC 908).

1152   Partridge, C. Workshop report: Internet research steering group workshop on very-high-speed networks. 1990 April; 23 p. (Format: TXT=64003 bytes).

1153   Wancho, F.J. Digest message format. 1990 April; 4 p. (Format: TXT=6632 bytes).

1154   Robinson, D., Ullmann, R. Encoding header field for internet messages. 1990 April; 7 p. (Format: TXT=12214 bytes).

1155   Rose, M.T., McCloghrie, K. Structure and identification of management information for TCP/IP-based internets. 1990 May; 22 p. (Format: TXT=40927 bytes) (Obsoletes RFC 1065).

1156   McCloghrie, K., Rose, M.T. Management Information Base for network management of TCP/IP-based internets. 1990 May; 91 p. (Format: TXT=138781 bytes) (Obsoletes RFC 1066).

1157   Case, J.D., Fedor, M., Schoffstall, M.L., Davin, C. Simple Network Management Protocol (SNMP). 1990 May; 36 p. (Format: TXT=74894 bytes) (Obsoletes RFC 1098).

1158   Rose, M.T.,ed. Management Information Base for network management of TCP/IP-based internets: MIB-II. 1990 May; 133 p. (Format: TXT=212152 bytes) (Obsoleted by RFC 1213).

1159   Nelson, R. Message Send Protocol. 1990 June; 2 p. (Format: TXT=3957 bytes).

1160   Cerf, V. Internet Activities Board. 1990 May; 11 p. (Format: TXT=28182 bytes) (Obsoletes RFC 1120).

1161   Rose, M.T. SNMP over OSI. 1990 June; 8 p. (Format: TXT=16036 bytes).

1162   Satz, G. Connectionless Network Protocol (ISO 8473) and End System to Intermediate System (ISO 9542) Management Information Base. 1990 June; 70 p. (Format: TXT=109893 bytes) (Obsoleted by RFC 1238).

1163   Lougheed, K., Rekhter, Y. Border Gateway Protocol (BGP). 1990 June; 29 p. (Format: TXT=69404 bytes) (Obsoletes RFC 1105).

1164   Honig, J.C., Katz, D., Mathis, M., Rekhter, Y., Yu, J.Y. Application of the Border Gateway Protocol in the Internet. 1990 June; 23 p. (Format: TXT=56278 bytes).

1165   Crowcroft, J., Onions, J.P. Network Time Protocol (NTP) over the OSI Remote Operations Service. 1990 June; 10 p. (Format: TXT=18277 bytes).

1166   Kirkpatrick, S., Stahl, M.K., Recker, M. Internet numbers. 1990 July; 182 p. (Format: TXT=566778 bytes) (Obsoletes RFC 1117, RFC 1062, RFC 1020).

1167   Cerf, V.G. Thoughts on the National Research and Education Network. 1990 July; 8 p. (Format: TXT=20682 bytes).

1168   Westine, A., DeSchon, A.L., Postel, J.B., Ward, C.E. Intermail and Commercial Mail Relay services. 1990 July; 23 p. (Format: PS=149816 bytes).

1169   Cerf, V.G., Mills, K.L. Explaining the role of GOSIP. 1990 August; 15 p. (Format: TXT=30255 bytes).

1170   Fougner, R.B. Public key standards and licenses. 1991 January; 2 p. (Format: TXT=3144 bytes).

1171   Perkins, D. Point-to-Point Protocol for the transmission of multi-protocol datagrams over Point-to-Point links. 1990 July; 48 p. (Format: TXT=92321 bytes) (Obsoletes RFC 1134).

1172   Perkins, D., Hobby, R. Point-to-Point Protocol (PPP) initial configuration options. 1990 July; 38 p. (Format: TXT=76132 bytes).

1173   VanBokkelen, J. Responsibilities of host and network managers: A summary of the "oral tradition" of the Internet. 1990 August; 5 p. (Format: TXT=12527 bytes).

1174   Cerf, V.G. IAB recommended policy on distributing internet identifier assignment and IAB recommended policy change to internet "connected" status. 1990 August; 9 p. (Format: TXT=21321 bytes).

1175   Bowers, K.L., LaQuey, T.L., Reynolds, J.K., Roubicek, K., Stahl, M.K., Yuan, A. FYI on where to start: A bibliography of internetworking information. 1990 August; 42 p. (Format: TXT=67330 bytes) (Also FYI 3)

1176   Crispin, M.R. Interactive Mail Access Protocol: Version 2. 1990 August; 30 p. (Format: TXT=67330 bytes) (Obsoletes RFC 1064).

1177   Malkin, G.S., Marine, A.N., Reynolds, J.K. FYI on Questions and Answers: Answers to commonly asked "new internet user" questions. 1990 August; 24 p. (Format: TXT=52852 bytes) (Also FYI 4) (Obsoleted by RFC 1206).

1178   Libes, D. Choosing a name for your computer. 1990 August; 8 p. (Format: TXT=18472 bytes) (Also FYI 5)

1179   McLaughlin, L. Line printer daemon protocol. 1990 August; 14 p. (Format: TXT=24324 bytes).

1180   Socolofsky, T.J., Kale, C.J. TCP/IP tutorial. 1991 January; 28 p. (Format: TXT=65494 bytes).

1181   Blokzijl, R. RIPE terms of reference. 1990 September; 2 p. (Format: TXT=2523 bytes).

1182   Not yet issued.

1183   Everhart, C.F., Mamakos, L.A., Ullmann, R., Mockapetris, P.V. New DNS RR definitions. 1990 October; 11 p. (Format: TXT=23788 bytes) (Updates RFC 1034, RFC 1035).

1184   Borman, D.A.,ed. Telnet Linemode option. 1990 October; 23 p. (Format: TXT=53085 bytes) (Obsoletes RFC 1116).

1185   Jacobson, V., Braden, R.T., Zhang, L. TCP extension for high-speed paths. 1990 October; 21 p. (Format: TXT=49508 bytes).

1186   Rivest, R.L. MD4 message digest algorithm. 1990 October; 18 p. (Format: TXT=35391 bytes).

1187   Rose, M.T., McCloghrie, K., Davin, J.R. Bulk table retrieval with the SNMP. 1990 October; 12 p. (Format: TXT=27220 bytes).

1188   Katz, D. Proposed standard for the transmission of IP datagrams over FDDI networks. 1990 October; 11 p. (Format: TXT=22424 bytes) (Obsoletes RFC 1103).

1189   Warrier, U.S., Besaw, L., LaBarre, L., Handspicker, B.D. Common Management Information Services and Protocols for the Internet (CMOT and CMIP). 1990 October; 15 p. (Format: TXT=32928 bytes) (Obsoletes RFC 1095).

1190   Topolcic, C., ed. Experimental Internet Stream Protocol: Version 2 (ST-II). 1990 October; 148 p. (Format: TXT=386909 bytes) (Obsoletes IEN 119).

1191   Mogul, J.C., Deering, S.E. Path MTU discovery. 1990 November; 19 p. (Format: TXT=47936 bytes) (Obsoletes RFC 1063).

1192   Kahin, B., ed. Commercialization of the Internet summary report. 1990 November; 13 p. (Format: TXT=35253 bytes).

1193   Ferrari, D. Client requirements for real-time communication services. 1990 November; 24 p. (Format: TXT=61540 bytes).

1194   Zimmerman, D.P. Finger User Information Protocol. 1990 November; 12 p. (Format: TXT=24626 bytes) (Obsoletes RFC 742; Obsoleted by RFC 1196).

1195   Callon, R.W. Use of OSI IS-IS for routing in TCP/IP and dual environments. 1990 December; 65 p. (Format: PS=381799 TXT=192628 bytes).

1196   Zimmerman, D.P. Finger User Information Protocol. 1990 December; 12 p. (Format: TXT=24799 bytes) (Obsoletes RFC 1194).

1197   Sherman, M. Using ODA for translating multimedia information. 1990 December; 2 p. (Format: TXT=3620 bytes).

1198   Scheifler, R.W. FYI on the X window system. 1991 January; 3 p. (Format: TXT=3629 bytes) (Also FYI 6)

1199   Reynolds, J. RFC Numbers 1100-1199. 1991 December; 22 p. (Format: TXT=46443 bytes).

1200   Defense Advanced Research Projects Agency, Internet Activities Board. DARPA IAB IAB official protocol standards. 1991 April; 31 p. (Format: TXT=67069 bytes) (Obsoletes RFC 1140; Obsoleted by RFC 1250).

1201   Provan, D. Transmitting IP traffic over ARCNET networks. 1991 February; 7 p. (Format: TXT=16959 bytes) (Obsoletes RFC 1051).

1202   Rose, M.T. Directory Assistance service. 1991 February; 11 p. (Format: TXT=21645 bytes).

1203   Rice, J. Interactive Mail Access Protocol: Version 3. 1991 February; 49 p. (Format: TXT=123325 bytes) (Obsoletes RFC 1064).

1204   Yeh, S., Lee, D. Message Posting Protocol (MPP). 1991 February; 6 p. (Format: TXT=11371 bytes).

1205   Chmielewski, P. 5250 Telnet interface. 1991 February; 12 p. (Format: TXT=27179 bytes).

1206   Malkin, G.S., Marine, A.N. FYI on Questions and Answers: Answers to commonly asked "new Internet user" questions. 1991 February; 32 p. (Format: TXT=72479 bytes) (Also FYI 4) (Obsoletes RFC 1177).

1207   Malkin, G.S., Marine, A.N., Reynolds, J.K. FYI on Questions and Answers: Answers to commonly asked "experienced Internet user" questions. 1991 February; 15 p. (Format: TXT=33385 bytes) (Also FYI 7)

1208   Jacobsen, O.J., Lynch, D.C. Glossary of networking terms. 1991 March; 18 p. (Format: TXT=41156 bytes).

1209   Piscitello, D.M., Lawrence, J. Transmission of IP datagrams over the SMDS Service. 1991 March; 11 p. (Format: TXT=25280 bytes).

1210   Cerf, V.G., Kirstein, P.T., Randell, B., eds. Network and infrastructure user requirements for transatlantic research collaboration: Brussels, July 16-18, and Washington July 24-25, 1990. 1991 March; 36 p. (Format: TXT=79048 bytes).

1211   Westine, A., Postel, J.B. Problems with the maintenance of large mailing lists. 1991 March; 54 p. (Format: TXT=96167 bytes).

1212 Rose, M.T., McCloghrie, K., eds. Concise MIB definitions. 1991 March; 19 p. (Format: TXT=43579 bytes).

1213 McCloghrie, K., Rose, M.T.,eds. Management Information Base for network management of TCP/IP-based internets: MIB-II. 1991 March; 70 p. (Format: TXT=146080 bytes) (Obsoletes RFC 1158).

1214 LaBarre, L.,ed. OSI internet management: Management Information Base. 1991 April; 83 p. (Format: TXT=172564 bytes).

1215 Rose, M.T.,ed. Convention for defining traps for use with the SNMP. 1991 March; 9 p. (Format: TXT=19336 bytes).

1216 Richard, P., Kynikos, P. Gigabit network economics and paradigm shifts. 1991 April 1; 4 p

1217 Cerf, V. Memo from the Consortium for Slow Commotion Research (CSCR). 1991 April 1; 5 p. (Format: TXT=11079 bytes).

1218 North American Directory Forum. Naming scheme for c=US Naming scheme for c US. 1991 April; 23 p. (Format: TXT=42698 bytes) (Obsoleted by RFC 1417).

1219 Tsuchiya, P. On the assignment of subnet numbers. 1991 April; 13 p. (Format: TXT=30609 bytes).

1220 Baker, F., ed. Point-to-Point Protocol extensions for bridging. 1991 April; 18 p. (Format: TXT=38165 bytes).

1221 Edmond, W. Host Access Protocol (HAP) specification: Version 2. 1991 April; 68 p. (Format: TXT=156550 bytes) (Updates RFC 907).

1222 Braun, H., Rekhter, Y. Advancing the NSFNET routing architecture. 1991 May; 6 p. (Format: TXT=15067 bytes).

1223 Halpern, J. OSI CLNS and LLC1 protocols on Network Systems HYPER-channel. 1991 May; 12 p. (Format: TXT=29601 bytes).

1224 Steinberg, L. Techniques for managing asynchronously generated alerts. 1991 May; 22 p. (Format: TXT=54303 bytes).

1225   Rose, M. Post Office Protocol: Version 3. 1991 May; 16 p. (Format: TXT=37340 bytes) (Obsoletes RFC 1081).

1226   Kantor, B. Internet protocol encapsulation of AX.25 frames Internet protocol encapsulation of AX 25 frames. 1991 May; 2 p. (Format: TXT=2573 bytes).

1227   Rose, M. SNMP MUX protocol and MIB. 1991 May; 13 p. (Format: TXT=25868 bytes)

1228   Carpenter, G., Wijnen, B. SNMP-DPI: Simple Network Management Protocol Distributed Program Interface. 1991 May; 50 p. (Format: TXT=96972 bytes).

1229   McCloghrie, K., ed. Extensions to the generic-interface MIB. 1991 May; 16 p. (Format: TXT=36022 bytes).

1230   McCloghrie, K., Fox, R. IEEE 802.4 Token Bus MIB IEEE 802 4 Token Bus MIB. 1991 May; 23 p. (Format: TXT=53100 bytes).

1231   McCloghrie, K., Fox, R., Decker, E. IEEE 802.5 Token Ring MIB IEEE 802 5 Token Ring MIB. 1991 May; 23 p. (Format: TXT=53542 bytes).

1232   Baker, F., Kolb, C., eds. Definitions of managed objects for the DS1 Interface type. 1991 May; 28 p. (Format: TXT=60757 bytes) (Obsoleted by RFC 1406).

1233   Cox, T., Tesink, K., eds. Definitions of managed objects for the DS3 Interface type. 1991 May; 23 p. (Format: TXT=49559 bytes) (Obsoleted by RFC 1407).

1234   Provan, D. Tunneling IPX traffic through IP networks. 1991 June; 6 p. (Format: TXT=12333 bytes).

1235   Ioannidis, J., Maguire, G. Jr. Coherent File Distribution Protocol. 1991 June; 12 p. (Format: TXT=29345 bytes).

1236   Morales, L. Jr., Hasse, P. IP to X.121 address mapping for DDN IP to X 121 address mapping for DDN. 1991 June; 7 p. (Format: TXT=12626 bytes).

1237   Collela, R., Gardner, E., Callon, R. Guidelines for OSI NSAP allocation in the internet. 1991 July; 38 p. (Format: PS=162808 TXT=119962 bytes).

1238   Satz, G. CLNS MIB for use with Connectionless Network Protocol (ISO 8473) and End System to Intermediate System (ISO 9542). 1991 June; 32 p. (Format: TXT=65159 bytes) (Obsoletes RFC 1162).

1239   Reynolds, J. Reassignment of experimental MIBs to standard MIBs. 1991 June; 2 p. (Format: TXT=3656 bytes) (Updates RFC 1229, RFC 1230, RFC 1231, RFC 1232, RFC 1233).

1240   Shue, C., Haggerty, W., Dobbins, K. OSI connectionless transport services on top of UDP: Version 1. 1991 June; 8 p. (Format: TXT=18140 bytes).

1241   Woodburn, R., Mills, D. Scheme for an internet encapsulation protocol: Version 1. 1991 July; 17 p. (Format: TXT=42468 PS=128921 bytes).

1242   Bradner, S., ed. Benchmarking terminology for network interconnection devices. 1991 July; 12 p. (Format: TXT=22817 bytes).

1243   Waldbusser, S., ed. Appletalk Management Information Base. 1991 July; 29 p. (Format: TXT=61985 bytes).

1244   Holbrook, J., Reynolds, J.,eds. Site Security Handbook. 1991 July; 101 p. (Format: TXT=259129 bytes) (Also FYI 8).

1245   Moy, J., ed. OSPF protocol analysis. 1991 July; 12 p. (Format: PS=64094 TXT=27492 bytes).

1246   Moy, J., ed. Experience with the OSPF protocol. 1991 July; 31 p. (Format: PS=146913 TXT=72180 bytes).

1247   Moy, J. OSPF version 2. 1991 July; 189 p. (Format: PS=1063028 TXT=44391 bytes) (Obsoletes RFC 1131).

1248   Baker, F., Coltun, R. OSPF version 2: Management Information Base. 1991 July; 42 p. (Format: TXT=77126 bytes) (Obsoleted by RFC 1252).

1249   Howes, T., Smith, M., Beecher, B. DIXIE protocol specification. 1991 August; 10 p. (Format: TXT=20693 bytes).

1250   Postel, J., ed. IAB official protocol standards. 1991 August; 28 p. (Format: TXT=65279 bytes) (Obsoletes RFC 1200; Obsoleted by RFC 1360).

1251   Malkin, G. Who's who in the internet: Biographies of IAB, IESG and IRSG members. 1991 August; 26 p. (Format: TXT=72721 bytes) (Also FYI 9) (Obsoleted by RFC 1336).

1252   Baker, F., Coltun, R. OSPF version 2: Management Information Base. 1991 August; 42 p. (Format: TXT=77250 bytes) (Obsoletes RFC 1248; Obsoleted by RFC 1253).

1253   Baker, F., Coltun, R. OSPF version 2: Management Information Base. 1991 August; 42 p. (Format: TXT=77232 bytes) (Obsoletes RFC 1252).

1254   Mankin, A., Ramakrishnan, K., eds. Gateway congestion control survey. 1991 August; 25 p. (Format: TXT=69793 bytes).

1255   North American Directory Forum. Naming scheme for c=US. 1991 September; 25 p. (Format: TXT=53783 bytes) (Obsoletes RFC 1218; Obsoleted by RFC 1417).

1256   Deering, S., ed. ICMP router discovery messages. 1991 September; 19 p. (Format: TXT=44628 bytes).

1257   Partridge, C. Isochronous applications do not require jitter-controlled networks. 1991 September; 5 p. (Format: TXT=11075 bytes).

1258   Kantor, B. BSD Rlogin. 1991 September; 5 p. (Format: TXT=10763 bytes) (Obsoleted by RFC 1282).

1259   Kapor, M. Building the open road: The NREN as test-bed for the national public network. 1991 September; 23 p. (Format: TXT=62944 bytes).

1260   Not yet issued.

1261   Williamson, S., Nobile, L. Transiton of NIC services. 1991 September; 3 p. (Format: TXT=4488 bytes).

1262   Cerf, V., ed. Guidelines for Internet measurement activities. 1991 October; 3 p. (Format: TXT=6381 bytes).

1263   O'Malley, S., Peterson, L. TCP Extensions considered harmful. 1991 October; 19 p. (Format: TXT=54078 bytes).

1264   Hinden, R. Internet routing protocol standardization criteria. 1991 October; 8 p. (Format: TXT=17016 bytes).

1265   Rekhter, Y., ed. BGP protocol analysis. 1991 October; 8 p. (Format: TXT=20728 bytes).

1266   Rekhter, Y., ed. Experience with the BGP protocol. 1991 October; 9 p. (Format: TXT=21938 bytes).

1267   Lougheed, K., Rekhter, Y. A Border Gateway Protocol 3 (BGP-3). 1991 October; 35 p. (Format: TXT=80724 bytes) (Obsoletes RFC 1105, RFC 1163).

1268   Rekhter, Y., Gross, P., eds. Application of the Border Gateway Protocol in the Internet. 1991 October; 13 p. (Format: TXT=31102 bytes) (Obsoletes RFC 1164).

1269   Willis, S., Burruss, J. Definitions of Managed Objects for the Border Gateway Protocol (version 3). 1991 October; 13 p. (Format: TXT=25717 bytes).

1270   Kastenholz, F., ed. SNMP communications services. 1991 October; 11 p. (Format: TXT=26164 bytes)

1271   Waldbusser, S. Remote network monitoring management information base. 1991 November; 81 p. (Format: TXT=184111 bytes).

1272   Mills, C., Hirsh, D., Ruth, G. Internet accounting: background. 1991 November; 19 p. (Format: TXT=46563 bytes).

1273   Schwartz, M. A measurement study of changes in service-level reachability in the global TCP/IP Internet. 1991 November; 8 p. (Format: TXT=19949 bytes).

1274   Barker, P., Kille, S. The COSINE and Internet X.500 Schema. 1991 November; 60 p. (Format: TXT=92827 bytes).

1275   Hardcastle-Kille, S. Replication Requirements to provide an Internet Direc-
        tory using X.500. 1991 November; 3 p. (Format: TXT=4616 PS=83736
        bytes).

1276   Hardcastle-Kille, S. Replication and Distributed Operations extensions to
        provide an Internet Directory using X.500. 1991 November; 17 p. (Format:
        TXT=33731 PS=217170 bytes).

1277   Hardcastle-Kille, S. Encoding Network Addresses to support operation over
        non-OSI lower layers. 1991 November; 12 p. (Format: TXT=22254
        PS=176169 bytes).

1278   Hardcastle-Kille, S. A string encoding of Presentation Address. 1991 Novem-
        ber; 7 p. (Format: TXT=10256 PS=128696 bytes).

1279   Hardcastle-Kille, S. X.500 and Domains. 1991 November; 15 p. (Format:
        TXT=26669 PS=170029 bytes).

1280   Postel, J., ed. IAB OFFICIAL PROTOCOL STANDARDS. 1992 March;
        32 p. (Format: TXT=70459 bytes) (Obsoletes RFCs 1250, 1100, 1083, 1130,
        1140, 1200; Obsoleted by RFC 1360).

1281   Pethia, R., Crocker, S., Fraser, B. Guidelines for the Secure Operation of
        the Internet. 1991 November; 10 p. (Format: TXT=22618 bytes).

1282   Kantor, B. BSD Rlogin. 1991 December; 5 p. (Format: TXT=10704 bytes)
        (Obsoletes RFC 1258).

1283   Rose, M. SNMP over OSI. 1991 December; 8 p. (Format: TXT=16814
        bytes) (Obsoletes RFC 1161).

1284   Cook, J., ed. Definitions of Managed Objects for the Ethernet-like Inter-
        face Types. 1991 December; 21 p. (Format: TXT=43225 bytes) (Obsoleted
        by RFC 1398).

1285   Case, J. FDDI Management Information Base. 1992 January; 46 p. (For-
        mat: TXT=99747 bytes).

1286   Decker, E., Langille, P., Rijsinghani, A., McCloghrie, K. Definitions of Managed Objects for Bridges. 1991 December; 40 p. (Format: TXT=79104 bytes).

1287   Clark, D., Chapin, L., Cerf, V., Braden, R., Hobby, R. Towards the Future Internet Architecture. 1991 December; 29 p. (Format: TXT=59812 bytes).

1288   Zimmerman, D. The Finger User Information Protocol. 1991 December; 12 p. (Obsoletes RFC 1196, RFC 1194, RFC 742).

1289   Saperia, J. DECnet Phase IV MIB Extensions. 1991 December; 64 p.

1290   Martin, J. There's Gold in them thar Networks! or Searching for Treasure in all the Wrong Places. 1991 December; 27 p. (Format: TXT=46997 bytes) (Also FYI 10) (Obsoleted by RFC 1402).

1291   Aggarwal, V. Mid-Level Networks—Potential Technical Services. 1991 December; 10 p. (Format: TXT=24314 bytes).

1292   Lang, R., Wright, R., eds. A Catalog of Available X.500 Implementations. 1992 January; 103 p. (Format: TXT=24314 bytes) (Also FYI 11).

1293   Brown, C. Inverse Address Resolution Protocol. 1992 January; 6 p. (Format: TXT=11368 bytes).

1294   Bradley, T., Brown, C., Malis, A. Multiprotocol Interconnect over Frame Relay. 1992 January; 28 p. (Format: TXT=54993 bytes).

1295   The North American Directory Forum. User Bill of Rights for entries and listings in the Public Directory. 1992 January; 2 p. (Format: TXT=3502 bytes) (Obsoleted by RFC 1417).

1296   Lottor, M. Internet Growth (1981-1991). 1992 January; 9 p. (Format: TXT=20103 bytes).

1297   Johnson, D. NOC Internal Integrated Trouble Ticket System Functional Specification Wishlist ("NOC TT REQUIREMENTS"). 1992 January; 12 p. (Format: TXT=3294 bytes).

1298   Wormley, R., Bostock, S. SNMP over IPX. 1992 February; 5 p. (Format: TXT=7878 bytes).

1299   Not yet issued.

1300   Greenfield, S. Remembrances of Things Past. 1992 February; 4 p. (Format: TXT=4964 bytes).

1301   Armstrong, S., Freier, A., Marzullo, K. Multicast Transport Protocol. February 1992; 38 p. (Format: TXT=91977 bytes).

1302   Sitzler, D., Smith, P., Marine, A. Building a Network Information Services Infrastructure. 1992 February; 13 p. (Format: TXT=29136 bytes) (Also FYI 12).

1303   McCloghrie, K., Rose, M. A Convention for Describing SNMP-based Agents. 1992 February; 12 p. (Format: TXT=22915 bytes).

1304   Cox, T., Tesink, K., eds. Definitions of Managed Objects for the SIP Interface Type. 1992 February; 25 p. (Format: TXT=52491 bytes).

1305   Mills, D. Network Time Protocol (Version 3) Specification, Implementation and Analysis. 1992 March; 120. (Format: TXT=307085,PS=815759 bytes) (Obsoletes RFC 1119, RFC 1059, RFC 958).

1306   Nicholson, A., Young, J. Experiences Supporting By-Request Circuit-Switched T3 Networks. 1992 March; 10 p. (Format: TXT=25789 bytes).

1307   Young, J., Nicholson, A. Dynamically Switched Link Control Protocol. 1992 March; 13 p. (Format: TXT=24145 bytes).

1308   Weider, C., Reynolds, J. Executive Introduction to Directory Services Using the X.500 Protocol. 1992 March; 4 p. (Format: TXT=9392 bytes) (Also FYI 13).

1309   Weider, C., Reynolds, J., Heker, S. Technical Overview of Directory Services Using the X.500 Protocol. 1992 March; 16 p. (Format: TXT=35694 bytes) (Also FYI 14).

1310   Chapin, Lyman, ed. The Internet Standards Process. 1992 March; 23 p. (Format: TXT=54739 bytes).

1311   Postel, J., ed. Introduction to the STD Notes. 1992 March; 5 p. (Format: TXT=11309 bytes).

1312   Nelson, R., Arnold, G. Message Send Protocol 2. 1992 April; 8 p. (Format: TXT=18038 bytes) (Obsoletes RFC 1159).

1313   Partridge, C. Today's Programming for KRFC AM 1313 Internet Talk Radio. 1992 April; 3 p. (Format: TXT=5445 bytes).

1314   Katz, A., Cohen, D. A File Format for the Exchange of Images in the Internet. 1992 April; 23 p. (Format: TXT=54073 bytes).

1315   Brown, C., Baker, F., Carvalho, C . Management Information Base for Frame Relay DTEs. 1992 April; 19 p. (Format: TXT=33826 bytes).

1316   Stewart, B., ed. Definitions of Managed Objects for Character Stream Devices. 1992 April; 17 p. (Format: TXT=35144 bytes).

1317   Stewart, B., ed. Definitions of Managed Objects for RS-232-like Hardware Devices. 1992 April; 17 p. (Format: TXT=30443 bytes).

1318   Stewart, B., ed. Definitions of Managed Objects for Parallel-printer-like Hardware Devices. 1992 April; 11 p. (Format: TXT=19571 bytes).

1319   Kaliski, B. The MD2 Message-Digest Algorithm. 1992 April; 17 p. (Format: TXT=25662 bytes).

1320   Rivest, R. The MD4 Message-Digest Algorithm. 1992 April; 20 p. (Format: TXT=32408 bytes) (Obsoletes RFC 1186).

1321   Rivest, R. The MD5 Message-Digest Algorithm. 1992 April; 21 p. (Format: TXT=35223 bytes).

1322   Estrin, D., Rekhter, Y., Hotz, S. A Unified Approach to Inter-Domain Routing. 1992 May; 38 p. (Format: TXT=96935 bytes).

1323   Jacobson, V., Braden, R., Borman, D. TCP Extensions for High Perfor-
        mance. 1992 May; 37 p. (Format: TXT=84559 bytes) (Obsoletes RFC 1072,
        RFC 1185).

1324   Reed, D. A Discussion on Computer Network Conferencing. 1992 May;
        11 p. (Format: TXT=24989 bytes).

1325   Malkin, G., Marine, A. FYI on Questions and Answers—Answers to Com-
        monly asked "New Internet User" Questions. 1992 May; 42 p. (Format:
        TXT=91885 bytes) (Also FYI 4) (Obsoletes RFC 1206, FYI 4).

1326   Tsuchiya, P. Mutual Encapsulation Considered Dangerous. 1992 May; 5 p.
        (Format: TXT=11278 bytes).

1327   Hardcastle-Kille, S. Mapping between X.400(1988) / ISO 10021 and RFC
        822. 1992 May; 113 p. (Format: TXT=228599 bytes) (Obsoletes RFC 987,
        RFC 1026, RFC 1138, RFC 1148; Updates RFC 822).

1328   Hardcastle-Kille, S. X.400 1988 to 1984 downgrading. 1992 May; 5 p. (For-
        mat: TXT=10007 bytes).

1329   Kuehn, P. Thoughts on Address Resolution for Dual MAC FDDI Networks.
        1992 May; 28 p. (Format: TXT=58151 bytes).

1330   ESCC X.500/X.400 Task Force. Recommendations for the Phase I Deploy-
        ment of OSI Directory Services (X.500) and OSI Message Handling Ser-
        vices (X.400) within the ESnet Community. 1992 May; 87 p. (Format:
        TXT=192926 bytes).

1331   Simpson, W. The Point-to-Point Protocol (PPP) for the Transmission of
        Multi-protocol Datagrams over Point-to-Point Links. 1992 May; 66 p. (For-
        mat: TXT=129892 bytes) (Obsoletes RFC 1171, RFC 1172).

1332   McGregor, G. The PPP Internet Protocol Control Protocol (IPCP). 1992
        May; 12 p. (Format: TXT=17613 bytes) (Obsoletes RFC 1172).

1333   Simpson, W. PPP Link Quality Monitoring. 1992 May; 15 p. (Format:
        TXT=29965 bytes).

1334   Lloyd, B., Simpson, W. PPP Authentication Protocols. 1992 October; 16
        p. (Format: TXT=33249 bytes).

1335   Wang, Z., Crowcroft, J. A Two-Tier Address Structure for the Internet: A
        Solution to the Problem of Address Space Exhaustion. 1992 May; 7 p. (For-
        mat: TXT=15419 bytes).

1336   Malkin, G. Who's Who in the Internet—Biographies of IAB, IESG and
        IRSG Members. 1992 May; 33 p. (Format: TXT=92120 bytes) (Also FYI
        9) (Obsoletes RFC 1251, FYI 9).

1337   Braden, R. TIME-WAIT Assassination Hazards in TCP. 1992 May; 11 p.
        (Format: TXT=22888 bytes).

1338   Fuller, V., Li, T., Yu, J., Varadhan, K. Supernetting: an Address Assignment
        and Aggregation Strategy. 1992 June; 20 p. (Format: TXT=47976 bytes).

1339   Dorner, S., Resnick, P. Remote Mail Checking Protocol. 1992 June; 6 p.
        (Format: TXT=13116 bytes).

1340   Reynolds, J., Postel, J. ASSIGNED NUMBERS. 1992 July; 139 p. (For-
        mat: TXT=232975 bytes) (Obsoletes RFCs 1060, 1010, 990, 960, 943, 923,
        900, 870, 820, 790, 776, 770, 762, 758, 755, 750, 739, 604, 503, 433, 349—
        IENs 127).

1341   Borenstein, N., Freed, N. MIME (Multipurpose Internet Mail Extensions)
        Mechanisms for Specifying and Describing the Format of Internet Message
        Bodies. 1992 June; 80 p. (Format: TXT=211117 PS=347082 bytes).

1342   Moore, K. Representation of Non-ASCII Text in Internet Message Head-
        ers. 1992 June; 7 p. (Format: TXT=15846 bytes).

1343   Borenstein, N. A User Agent Configuration Mechanism For Multimedia
        Mail Format Information. 1992 June; 10 p. (Format: TXT=29296 PS=59978
        bytes).

1344   Borenstein, N. Implications of MIME for Internet Mail Gateways. 1992
        June; 9 p. (Format: TXT=25873 PS=51812 bytes).

1345   Simonsen, K. Character Mnemonics & Character Sets. 1992 June; 103 p. (Format: TXT=249738 bytes).

1346   Jones, P. Resource Allocation, Control, and Accounting for the Use of Network Resources. 1992 June; 6 p. (Format: TXT=13085 bytes).

1347   Callon, R. TCP and UDP with Bigger Addresses (TUBA), A Simple Proposal for Internet Addressing and Routing. 1992 June; 9 p. (Format: TXT=26563 bytes).

1348   Manning, B. DNS NSAP RRs. 1992 July; 4 p. (Format: TXT=6872 bytes) (Updates RFCs 1034, 1035).

1349   Almquist, P. Type of Service in the Internet Protocol Suite. 1992 July; 28 p. (Format: TXT=68949 bytes) (Updates RFCs 1248, 1247, 1195, 1123, 1122, 1060, 791).

1350   Sollins, K. THE TFTP PROTOCOL (REVISION 2). 1992 July; 11 p. (Format: TXT=24600 bytes) (Obsoletes RFC 783).

1351   Davin, J., Galvin, J., McCloghrie, K. SNMP Administrative Model. 1992 July; 35 p. (Format: TXT=80722 bytes).

1352   Galvin, J., McCloghrie, K., Davin, J. SNMP Security Protocols. 1992 July; 41 p. (Format: TXT=95733 bytes).

1353   McCloghrie, K., Davin, J., Galvin, J. Definitions of Managed Objects for Administration of SNMP Parties. 1992 July; 26 p. (Format: TXT=59557 bytes).

1354   Baker, F. IP Forwarding Table MIB. 1992 July; 12 p. (Format: TXT=24906 bytes).

1355   Curran, J., Marine, A. Privacy and Accuracy Issues in Network Information Center Databases. 1992 August; 4 p. (Format: TXT=8859 bytes) (Also FYI 15).

1356   Malis, A., Robinson, D., Ullmann, R. Multiprotocol Interconnect on X.25 and ISDN in the Packet Mode. 1992 August; p 14. (Format: TXT=32044 bytes) (Obsoletes RFC 877).

1357   Cohen, D., ed. A Format for E-mailing Bibliographic Records. 1992 July;
        13 p. (Format: TXT=25022 bytes).

1358   Chapin, L. Charter of the Internet Architecture Board (IAB). 1992 August;
        p 5. (Format: TXT=11329 bytes).

1359   ACM SIGUCCS Networking Taskforce. Connecting to the Internet: What
        Connecting Institutions Should Anticipate. 1992 August; p 25. (Format:
        TXT=53450 bytes) (Also FYI 16).

1360   Postel, J., ed. IAB OFFICIAL PROTOCOL STANDARDS. 1992 Septem-
        ber; 33 p. (Format: TXT=71861 bytes) (Obsoletes RFCs 1280, 1250, 1100,
        1083, 1130, 1140, 1200).

1361   Mills, D. Simple Network Time Protocol (SNTP). 1992 August; p 10. (For-
        mat: TXT=23813 bytes).

1362   Allen, M. Novell IPX Over Various WAN Media (IPXWAN). 1992 Sep-
        tember; 18 p. (Format: TXT=30220 bytes).

1363   Partridge, C. A Proposed Flow Specification. 1992 September; 20 p. (For-
        mat: TXT=50215 bytes).

1364   Varadhan, K. BGP OSPF Interaction. 1992 September; 14 p. (Format:
        TXT=32122 bytes) (Obsoleted by RFC 1403).

1365   Siyan, K. An IP Address Extension Proposal. 1992 September; 6 p. (For-
        mat: TXT=12791 bytes).

1366   Gerich, E. Guidelines for Management of IP Address Space. 1992 Octo-
        ber; 8 p. (Format: TXT=17794 bytes).

1367   Topolcic, C. Schedule for IP Address Space Management Guidelines. 1992
        October; 3 p. (Format: TXT=4781 bytes).

1368   McMaster, D., McCloghrie, K. Definitions of Managed Objects for IEEE
        802.3 Repeater Devices. 1992 October; 40 p. (Format: TXT=83906 bytes).

1369   Kastenholz, F. Implementation Notes and Experience for The Internet Ether-
        net MIB. 1992 October; 7 p. (Format: TXT=13969 bytes).

1370   Internet Architecture Board. Applicability Statement for OSPF. 1992 October; 2 p. (Format: TXT=4304 bytes).

1371   Gross, P., ed. Choosing a "Common IGP" for the IP Internet (The IESG's Recommendation to the IAB). 1992 October; 9 p. (Format: TXT=18169 bytes).

1372   Hedrick, C., Borman, D. Telnet Remote Flow Control Option. 1992 October; 6 p. (Format: TXT=11099 bytes) (Obsoletes RFC 1080).

1373   Tignor, R. PORTABLE DUAs. 1992 October; 12 p. (Format: TXT=19932 bytes).

1374   Renwick, J., Nicholson, A. IP and ARP on HIPPI. 1992 October; 43 p. (Format: TXT=100904 bytes).

1375   Robinson, P. Suggestion for New Classes of IP Addresses. 1992 November; 7 p. (Format: TXT=16991 bytes).

1376   Senum, S. The PPP DECnet Phase IV Control Protocol (DNCP). 1992 November; 6 p. (Format: TXT=12449 bytes).

1377   Katz, D. The PPP OSI Network Layer Control Protocol (OSINLCP). 1992 November; 10 p. (Format: TXT=22110 bytes).

1378   Parker, B. The PPP AppleTalk Control Protocol (ATCP). 1992 November; 16 p. (Format: TXT=28497 bytes).

1379   Braden, R. Extending TCP for Transactions—Concepts. 1992 November; 38 p. (Format: TXT=91354 bytes).

1380   Gross, P., Almquist, P. IESG Deliberations on Routing and Addressing. 1992 November; 22 p. (Format: TXT=49416 bytes).

1381   Throop, D., Baker, F. SNMP MIB Extension for X.25 LAPB. 1992 November; 33 p. (Format: TXT=71254 bytes).

1382   Throop, D., ed. SNMP MIB Extension for the X.25 Packet Layer. 1992 November; 69 p. (Format: TXT=153878 bytes).

1383   Huitema, C. An Experiment in DNS Based IP Routing. 1992 December; 13 p. (Format: TXT=32681 bytes).

1384   Barker, P., Hardcastle-Kille, S. Naming Guidelines for Directory Pilots. 1993 January; 12 p. (Format: TXT=25871 bytes).

1385   Wang, Z. EIP: The Extended Internet Protocol: A Framework for Maintaining Backward Compatibility. 1992 November; 17 p. (Format: TXT=39124 bytes).

1386   Cooper, A., Postel, J. The US Domain. 1992 December; 31 p. (Format: TXT=62311 bytes).

1387   Malkin, G. RIP Version 2 Protocol Analysis. 1993 January; 3 p. (Format: TXT=5599 bytes).

1388   Malkin, G. RIP Version 2—Carrying Additional Information. 1993 January; 7 p. (Format: TXT=16228 bytes) (Updates RFC 1058).

1389   Malkin, G. RIP Version 2 MIB Extension. 1993 January; 13 p. (Format: TXT=23570 bytes).

1390   Katz, D. Transmission of IP and ARP over FDDI Networks. 1993 January; 11 p. (Format: TXT=22078 bytes).

1391   Malkin, G. The Tao of IETF—A Guide for New Attendees of the Internet Engineering Task Force. 1993 January; 19 p. (Format: TXT=41893 bytes) (Also FYI 17).

1392   Malkin, G., Parker, B., LaQuey, T., eds. Internet Users' Glossary. 1993 January; 53 p. (Format: TXT=104625 bytes) (Also FYI 18).

1393   Malkin, G. Traceroute Using an IP Option. 1993 January; 7 p. (Format: TXT=13141 bytes).

1394   Robinson, P. Relationship of Telex Answerback Codes to Internet Domains. 1993 January; 15 p. (Format: TXT=43777 bytes).

1395   Reynolds, J. BOOTP Vendor Information Extensions. 1993 January; 8 p.
        (Format: TXT=16315 bytes) (Obsoletes RFC 1084, RFC 1048; Updates
        RFC 951).

1396   Crocker, S. The Process for Organization of Internet Standards—Working
        Group (POISED)—Steve Crocker, Chair. 1993 January; 10 p. (Format:
        TXT=22097 bytes).

1397   Haskin, D. Default Route Advertisement In BGP2 And BGP3 Versions Of
        The Border Gateway Protocol. 1993 January; 2 p. (Format: TXT=4125
        bytes).

1398   Kastenholz, F. Definitions of Managed Objects for the Ethernet-like Inter-
        face Types. 1993 January; 17 p. (Format: TXT=36686 bytes) (Obsoletes
        RFC 1284).

1399   Not yet issued.

1400   Williamson, S. Transition and Modernization of the Internet Registration
        Service. 1993 March; 7 p. (Format: TXT=13009 bytes).

1401   Internet Architecture Board. Correspondence between the IAB and DISA
        on the use of DNS throughout the Internet. 1993 January; 8 p. (Format:
        TXT=12529 bytes).

1402   Martin, J. There's Gold in them thar Networks! or Searching for Treasure
        in all the Wrong Places. 1993 January; 39 p. (Format: TXT=71177 bytes)
        (Also FYI 10) (Obsoletes RFC 1290).

1403   Varadhan, K. BGP OSPF Interaction. 1993 January; 17 p. (Format:
        TXT=36174 bytes) (Obsoletes RFC 1364).

1404   Stockman, B. Model for Common Operational Statistics. 1993 January; 27
        p. (Format: TXT=52815 bytes).

1405   Allocchio, C. Mapping between X.400(1984/1988) and Mail-11 (DECnet mail). 1993 January; 19 p. (Format: TXT=33886 bytes).

1406   Baker, F., Watt, J., eds. Definitions of Managed Objects for the DS1 and E1 Interface Types. 1993 January; 50 p. (Format: TXT=97560 bytes) (Obsoletes RFC 1232).

1407   Cox, T., Tesink, K., eds. Definitions of Managed Objects for the DS3/E3 Interface Type. 1993 January; 43 p. (Format: TXT=90683 bytes) (Obsoletes RFC 1233).

1408   Borman, D., ed. Telnet Environment Option. 1993 January; 7 p. (Format: TXT=13937 bytes).

1409   Borman, D., ed. Telnet Authentication Option. 1993 January; 7 p. (Format: TXT=13119 bytes) (Obsoleted by RFC 1416).

1410   Postel, J., ed. IAB OFFICIAL PROTOCOL STANDARDS. 1993 March; 35 p. (Format: TXT=76525 bytes) (Obsoletes RFC 1360, RFC 1280, RFC 1250, RFC 1200 RFC 1100, RFC 1083, RFC 1130, RFC 1140).

1411   Borman, D., ed. Telnet Authentication: Kerberos Version 4. 1993 January; 4 p. (Format: TXT=7968 bytes).

1412   Alagappan, K. Telnet Authentication: SPX. 1993 January; 4 p. (Format: TXT=6953 bytes).

1413   St. Johns, M. Identification Protocol. 1993 February; 8 p. (Format: TXT=16292 bytes) (Obsoletes RFC 931).

1414   St. Johns, M., Rose, M. Identification MIB. 1993 February; 7 p. (Format: TXT=14166 bytes).

1415   Mindel, J., Slaski, R. FTP-FTAM Gateway Specification. 1993 January; 58 p. (Format: TXT=128262 bytes).

1416   Borman, D., ed. Telnet Authentication Option. 1993 February; 7 p. (Format: TXT=13271 bytes) (Obsoletes RFC 1409).

1417   The North American Directory Forum. NADF Standing Documents: A Brief Overview. 1993 February; 4 p. (Format: TXT=7271 bytes) (Obsoletes RFC 1295, RFC 1255, RFC 1218).

1418   Rose, M. SNMP over OSI. 1993 March; 4 p. (Format: TXT=7722 bytes) (Obsoletes 1161, 1283).

1419   Minshall, G., Ritter, M. SNMP over AppleTalk. 1993 March; 7 p. (Format: TXT=16471 bytes).

1420   Bostock, S. SNMP over IPX. 1993 March; 4 p. (Format: TXT=6763 bytes) (Obsoletes 1298).

1421   Linn, J. Privacy Enhancement for Internet Electronic Mail: Part I: Message Encryption and Authentication Procedures. 1993 February; 42 p. (Format: TXT=103895 bytes) (Obsoletes RFC 1113).

1422   Kent, S. Privacy Enhancement for Internet Electronic Mail: Part II: Certificate-Based Key Management. 1993 February; 32 p. (Format: TXT=86086 bytes) (Obsoletes RFC 1114).

1423   Balenson, D. Privacy Enhancement for Internet Electronic Mail: Part III: Algorithms, Modes, and Identifiers. 1993 February; 14 p. (Format: TXT=33278 bytes) (Obsoletes RFC 1115).

1424   Kaliski, B. Privacy Enhancement for Internet Electronic Mail: Part IV: Key Certification and Related Services. 1993 February; 9 p. (Format: TXT=17538 bytes).

1425   Rose, M., Stefferud, E., Crocker, D. SMTP Service Extensions. 1993 February; 10 p. (Format: TXT=20933 bytes).

1426   Rose, M., Stefferud, E., Crocker, D. SMTP Service Extension for 8bit-MIMEtransport. 1993 February; 6 p. (Format: TXT=11662 bytes).

1427   Moore, K. SMTP Service Extension for Message Size Declaration. 1993 February; 8 p. (Format: TXT=17857 bytes).

1428   Vaudreuil, G. Transition of Internet Mail from Just-Send-8 to 8bit-SMTP/MIME. 1993 February; 6 p. (Format: TXT=12065 bytes).

1429   Thomas, E. Listserv Distribute Protocol. 1993 February; 8 p. (Format: TXT=17760 bytes).

1430   Hardcastle-Kille, S., Huizer, E., Cerf, V., Hobby, R., Kent, S. A Strategic Plan for Deploying an Internet X.500 Directory Service. 1993 February; 20 p. (Format: TXT=47588 bytes).

1431   Barker, P. DUA Metrics. 1993 February; 19 p. (Format: TXT=42241 bytes).

1432   Quarterman, J. Recent Internet Books. 1993 March; 15 p. (Format: TXT=27090 bytes).

1433   Garrett, J., Wong, J., Hagan, J. Directed ARP. 1993 March; 18 p. (Format: TXT=41029 bytes).

1434   Dixon, R., Kushi, D. Data Link Switching: Switch-to-Switch Protocol. 1993 March; 33 p. (Format: TXT=80183 bytes).

1435   Knowles, S. IESG Advice from Experience with Path MTU Discovery. 1993 March; 2 p. (Format: TXT=2709 bytes).

1436   Anklesaria, F., McCahill, M., Lindner, P., Johnson, D., Torrey, D., Alberti, B. The Internet Gopher Protocol (a distributed document search and retrieval protocol). 1993 March; 16 p. (Format: TXT=36494 bytes).

1437   Borenstein, N., Linimon, M. The Extension of MIME Content-Types to a New Medium. 1993 April 1; 6 p. (Format: TXT=13357 bytes).

1438   Chapin, L., Huitema, C. Internet Engineering Task Force Statements Of Boredom (SOBs). 1993 April 1; 2 p. (Format: TXT=3045 bytes).

1439   Finseth, C. The Uniqueness of Unique Identifiers. 1993 March; 11 p. (Format: TXT=20478 bytes).

1440   Not yet issued.

1441   Case, J., McCloghrie, K., Rose, M., Waldbusser, S. Introduction to version 2 of the Internet-standard Network Management Framework. 1993 April; 13 p. (Format: TXT=26240 bytes).

1442   Case, J., McCloghrie, K., Rose, M., Waldbusser, S. Structure of Management Information for version 2 of the Simple Network Management Protocol (SNMPv2). 1993 April; 54 p. (Format: TXT=99200 bytes).

1443   Case, J., McCloghrie, K., Rose, M., Waldbusser, S. Textual Conventions for version 2 of the Simple Network Management Protocol. 1993 April; 31 p. (SNMPv2) (Format: TXT=62848 bytes).

1444   Case, J., McCloghrie, K., Rose, M., Waldbusser, S. Conformance Statements for version 2 of the Simple Network Management Protocol (SNMPv2). 1993 April; 32 p. (Format: TXT=59776 bytes).

1445   Galvin, J., McCloghrie, K. Administrative Model for version 2 of the Simple Network Management Protocol (SNMPv2). 1993 April; 47 p. (Format: TXT=102400 bytes).

1446   Galvin, J., McCloghrie, K. Security Protocols for version 2 of the Simple Network Management Protocol (SNMPv2). 1993 April; 51 p. (Format: TXT=111872 bytes).

1447   McCloghrie, K., Galvin, J. Party MIB for version 2 of the Simple Network Management Protocol (SNMPv2). 1993 April; 50 p. (Format: TXT=83712 bytes).

1448   Case, J., McCloghrie, K., Rose, M., Waldbusser, S. Protocol Operations for version 2 of the Simple Network Management Protocol (SNMPv2). 1993 April; 35 p. (Format: TXT=76416 bytes).

Trademarks

- PostScript is a trademark of Adobe Systems.

- ACC is a registered trademark of Advanced Computer Communications.

- Apple, the Apple logo, AppleShare, AppleTalk, Apple IIGS, EtherTalk, Laser-Writer, LocalTalk, Macintosh, and TokenTalk are registered trademarks; and APDA, Finder, Image Writer, and Quickdraw are trademarks of Apple Computer, Inc.

- UNIX is a registered trademark of AT&T and STREAMS, Transport Layer Interface, and Unix System 4 Release 4 are trademarks of AT&T.

- Banyan, the Banyan logo, and VINES are registered trademarks of Banyan Systems Inc.; and StreetTalk, VANGuard and NetRPC are trademarks of Banyan Systems, Inc.

- ENP is a trademark of Communications Machinery Corporation.

- COMPAQ is a trademark of COMPAQ Computer Corporation.

- CompuServe is a trademark of CompuServe.

- CRAY is the registered trademark of Cray Research, Inc.

- DEC, DECnet, LanWORKS, LAT, LAVC, Mailbus, Message Router, Micro-VAX, MOP, Rdb, ThinWire, Ultrix, VAX, VAX Cluster, and VMS Mail are trademarks, and Ethernet is a registered trademark of Digital Equipment Corporation.

- PC/TCP, PC/BIND, InterDrive, and LANWatch are registered trademarks of FTP Software, Inc.

- Hayes is a trademark of Hayes Microcomputer Products, Inc.

- HP is a trademark of the Hewlett-Packard Company.

- Intel and Ethernet are registered trademarks of Intel Corporation.

- Dispatcher/SMTP and WatchTower are trademarks of Intercon Systems Corporation.

- AS/400, DISOSS, IBM PC LAN, PC/AT, PC/XT, PROFS, SNA, SNADS, System/370, System/38, 3270 Display Station, DB2, ESCON, MicroChannel, VMS/ESA, MVS/SP, MVS/XA, Netbios, SAA, System View, VM/ESA, VM/XA, VSE/ESA, and VTAM are trademarks of International Business Machines Corporation; and AIX, AT, IBM, NetView, OS/2, OS/400, and PS/2 are registered trademarks of International Business Machines Corporation.

- X and X Window System are trademarks of the Massachusetts Institute of Technology.

- Microsoft, MS-DOS, and LAN Manager are registered trademarks of Microsoft Corporation.

- Network General and Sniffer Analyzer are trademarks of Network General Corporation.

- Hyperchannel is a trademark of Network Systems Corporation.

- C Network Compiler, C Network Compiler/386, IPX, NACS, NetWare, NetWare C Interface for DOS, NetWare for VMS, NetWare MHS, NetWare RPC, NetWare SQL, NetWare System Call for DOS, NetWare 386, NLM, Novell, Portable NetWare, RX-Net, SFT, SPX, Transaction Tracking System, VAP, and Xtrieve Plus are trademarks and Novell, NetWire, Btrieve, and XQL are registered trademarks of Novell, Inc.

- Prime is a trademark of Prime Computer Inc.

- Proteon and proNET are registered trademarks of Proteon, Inc.

- 4.2BSD and 4.3BSD are trademarks of the Regents of the University of California.

- Retix is a trademark of Retix.

- MultiNet is a trademark of TGV, Inc.

- SMC is a registered trademark of Standard Microsystems Corporation.

- Network File System, NFS, Open Network Computing, ONC, SPARC, Sun, SunOS, TOPS, and PC-NIFS are trademarks of Sun Microsystems, Inc.

- Symbolics and CHAOSnet are trademarks of Symbolics, Inc.

- Lattisnet is a trademark of SynOptics Communications.

- Tandem is a trademark of Tandem Computers, Inc.

- 3COM is a registered trademark and 3+ is a trademark of 3Com Corporation.

- Ungerman Bass is a trademark of Ungerman-Bass, Inc.

- TransLAN and Vitalink are trademarks of Vitalink Communications Corporation.

- Xerox, PUP, Clearinghouse, Interpress, Interscript, NS, XNS, and Open Look are trademarks and Ethernet and Xerox are registered trademarks of Xerox Corporation.

All other trademarks are the property of their respective owners.

Index